Colorado

WITHDRAWN

**Rocky Mountain National Park
& Northern Colorado**
p136

Boulder & Around
p107

Denver & Around
p62

**Vail, Aspen &
Central Colorado**
p174

**Mesa Verde &
Southwest Colorado**
p250

**Southeast Colorado &
the San Luis Valley**
p307

Benedict Walker, Carolyn McCarthy, Christopher Pitts,
Greg Benchwick, Liza Prado

Contents

PLAN YOUR TRIP

Welcome to Colorado ... 4

Colorado Map 6

Colorado's Top 25....... 8

Need to Know 20

If You Like.... 22

Month by Month 25

Itineraries 27

Outdoors 30

Rocky Mountains Road
Trips & Scenic Drives.... 41

Eat & Drink Like a Local . 52

Travel with Children.... 56

Regions at a Glance.... 59

SAN JUAN MOUNTAINS
P250

NICO DEBARMORE/500PX ©

KIVA, MESA VERDE
NATIONAL PARK P251

BOB KUO/500PX ©

ON THE ROAD

DENVER & AROUND 62
Denver 63
Golden 102
Morrison 105

BOULDER & AROUND 107
Boulder............. 108
Nederland 132

ROCKY MOUNTAIN NATIONAL PARK & NORTHERN COLORADO 136
Rocky Mountain
National Park 138
Estes Park 144
Fort Collins 150
Sterling 156
Cache la Poudre River... 157
Red Feather Lakes 159
Walden 159
Grand Lake 159
Granby 161
Hot Sulphur Springs 162
Kremmling............ 162
Steamboat Springs 163
Oak Creek 169
Craig................. 170
Dinosaur National
Monument.............171
Dinosaur 173
Meeker 173

VAIL, ASPEN & CENTRAL COLORADO 174
Denver to Summit
County 175
Idaho Springs 175

Georgetown............ 178
Winter Park 179
Loveland Pass.......... 183
Summit County....... 183
Dillon 184
Frisco 185
Keystone Resort........ 188
Arapahoe Basin
Ski Area 189
Breckenridge.......... 190
Fairplay.............. 199
Copper Mountain 200
Vail & the Holy Cross
Wilderness........... 201
Vail 201
Minturn 212
Beaver Creek.......... 214
Aspen & the
Maroon Bells 216
Glenwood Springs 216
Carbondale 220
Basalt................ 221
Aspen................ 222
Redstone 236
Salida &
Collegiate Peaks...... 237
Salida 238
Buena Vista........... 241
Twin Lakes............245
Leadville.............246

MESA VERDE & SOUTHWEST COLORADO 250
Mesa Verde
National Park 251
Mancos............... 256
Cortez & the
Four Corners.......... 257
Dolores............... 260
Rico.................. 261
Telluride.............. 261
Ridgway 268

Contents

TRAIL RIDGE ROAD, ROCKY
MOUNTAIN NATIONAL PARK
P138

BOB POOL/SHUTTERSTOCK ©

Ouray & the Million
Dollar Hwy 269
Silverton 273
Durango 275
Pagosa Springs 281
South Fork 283
Creede 284
Lake City 287
Crested Butte 288
Black Canyon
of the Gunnison
National Park 292
Curecanti National
Recreation Area 293
Gunnison 294
Montrose 296
Delta 298
Paonia 299
Colorado National
Monument 300
Grand Junction 301
Fruita 303
Palisade 304

SOUTHEAST
COLORADO &
THE SAN LUIS
VALLEY 307
**Southern Front
Range 310**

Colorado Springs 310
Cañon City 317
Florence 320
Cripple Creek 320
Manitou Springs 321
The Santa Fe Trail 324
Pueblo 325
La Veta 328
Trinidad 329
**The San Luis
Valley 332**
Fort Garland 332
Great Sand Dunes
National Park 332
Alamosa 335
San Luis 337
Antonito 338
Conejos River &
the South San Juans 339
Penitente Canyon 340
Del Norte 340
**Sangre de Cristo
Mountains 341**
Westcliffe 341
Crestone 344

UNDERSTAND

Colorado
Today 346
History 348
The Arts 353
Wildlife & the Land . . . 356

SURVIVAL
GUIDE

Directory A–Z 362
Transportation 370
Index 377
Map Legend 382

SPECIAL
FEATURES

Outdoors 30

**Rocky Mountains
Road Trips &
Scenic Drives 41**

**Eat & Drink
Like a Local 52**

Wildlife & the Land . . .356

Welcome to Colorado

Spectacular vistas, endless powder runs and mountain towns with echoes of the Old West – Colorado is a place that has long beckoned people to adventure.

Rocky Mountain High

The best-known Rocky Mountain state, with the highest concentration of peaks above 14,000ft, Colorado owes its public adoration to the alpine behemoths that rise abruptly out of the Great Plains. Countless hiking and biking trails climb above the treeline to wildflower-strewn meadows, while a plethora of scenic drives wend their ways up hairpin turns to cross the Continental Divide. Even during the peak summer season, when millions of tourists flood the state, visitors can still find solitude by camping at a remote glacial lake, or peering down at the world from atop a craggy summit.

Ski Country, USA

The combination of light, soft powder and frequent blue skies has made Colorado winters the stuff of legend. Hares and mountain lions leave white tracks, boarders and skiers weave through pine forests and open bowls, and hearthfires roar in mountain lodges. With World Cup groomers and steep-and-deep terrain off-piste, Colorado certainly has some of the best downhill skiing experiences on earth. Remarkable cross-country and backcountry terrain bring a whole other dimension to winter. If you're among the hardcore, you can make turns from Halloween through July.

Deserts & Canyons

Colorado isn't all mountains, though. Mesas, canyons and high desert hills also make up much of the state, particularly in the south and west. Boaters paddle through the Arkansas and Colorado River gorges, mountain bikers cruise desert singletrack outside towns like Fruita and Salida, and rock climbers can get outside even in winter at Shelf Road and Boulder. Mesa Verde, Hovenweep and Chimney Rock provide a glimpse of what Ancestral Puebloan life was like hundreds of years ago on the Colorado Plateau, a monumental desert landscape that extends into New Mexico, Utah and Arizona.

Culture Dose

If your Colorado playlist doesn't go beyond John Denver or *U2 Live at Red Rocks,* it's time for a reboot. A vibrant cultural scene has emerged in tandem with the thriving urban centers along the Front Range. Groups like the Lumineers, Tennis, and Nathaniel Rateliff and the Night Sweats have brought national attention to Denver musicians, and Red Rocks and Boulder's Fox Theatre remain uniquely epic concert venues. Art museums and galleries in both Denver and Aspen continue to expand as well, providing a shot of urban street cred to pair with your outdoor adventure.

Why I Love Colorado

By Christopher Pitts, Writer

Colorado is one of those special places where I always want to get up with the sun. Maybe it's because 18in of snow fell overnight and I'm itching to launch myself downhill, or I'm out camping in the backcountry, waking up to birdsong at the start of a perfect summer day. Or perhaps it's simply getting up early to watch a high-altitude sunrise spill over the curve of the eastern plains. Whatever it is that you enjoy doing, you can be sure that Colorado will amplify that times ten. Carpe diem.

For more about our writers, see p384

Above: Maroon Bells, Aspen (p224)

Colorado

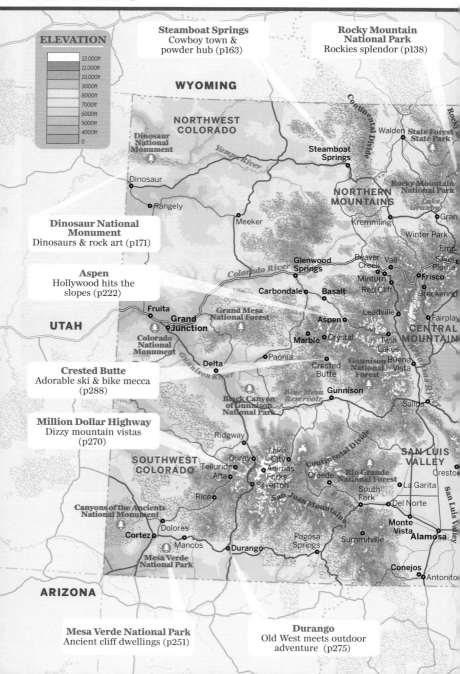

ELEVATION

| 12,000ft |
| 11,000ft |
| 10,000ft |
| 9000ft |
| 8000ft |
| 7000ft |
| 6000ft |
| 5000ft |
| 4000ft |
| 0 |

Steamboat Springs
Cowboy town &
powder hub (p163)

**Rocky Mountain
National Park**
Rockies splendor (p138)

**Dinosaur National
Monument**
Dinosaurs & rock art (p171)

Aspen
Hollywood hits the
slopes (p222)

Crested Butte
Adorable ski & bike mecca
(p288)

Million Dollar Highway
Dizzy mountain vistas
(p270)

Mesa Verde National Park
Ancient cliff dwellings (p251)

Durango
Old West meets outdoor
adventure (p275)

WYOMING

NORTHWEST
COLORADO

Dinosaur
National
Monument

Yampa River

Dinosaur

Rangely

Meeker

Steamboat
Springs

Walden

State Forest
State Park

Continental Divide

Rocky Mountain
National Park

Lake
Granby

NORTHERN
MOUNTAINS

Kremmling

Gran

Winter Park

Empi

Glenwood
Springs

Beaver
Creek

Vail

Silver
Plume

Colorado River

Minturn

Red Cliff

Frisco

Carbondale

Basalt

Breckenrid

UTAH

Fruita

Grand
Junction

Grand Mesa
National Forest

Leadville

Fairplay

Colorado
National
Monument

Aspen

CENTRAL
MOUNTAIN

Marble

Crystal

Twin
Lakes

Gunnison
River

Delta

Paonia

Crested
Butte

Gunnison
National
Forest

Buena
Vista

Black Canyon
of Gunnison
National Park

Blue Mesa
Reservoir

Gunnison

Salida

SOUTHWEST
COLORADO

Ridgway

Lake
City

Continental Divide

SAN LUIS
VALLEY

Crest

Telluride

Ouray

Alta

Animas
Forks

Creede

Rio Grande
National Forest

La Garita

San Luis Valley

Silverton

South
Fork

Del Norte

Rico

San Juan Mountains

Monte
Vista

Alamosa

Canyons of the Ancients
National Monument

Dolores

Pagosa
Springs

Summitville

Cortez

Mancos

Durango

Conejos

Antonito

Mesa Verde
National Park

ARIZONA

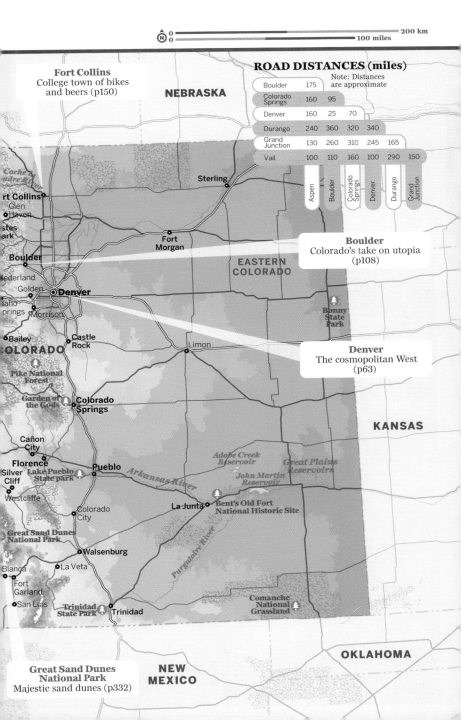

Colorado's
Top 25

Rocky Mountain National Park

1 With elk grazing under granite walls, alpine meadows rife with wildflowers and a winding road inching over the Continental Divide, the natural splendor of Rocky Mountain National Park (p138) packs a wallop. Don't get stuck behind a row of RVs on Trail Ridge Rd – lace up your hiking boots instead. Trails cater to every ability and ambition, from epic outings up Longs Peak to family-friendly romps in the Bear Lake area. And with a little effort, you can have the place all to yourself.

Denver

2 Home of the bearded and the buff, Denver's (p62) Mile High allure has never been greater. The secret is out: ample sunshine, a brewery on every corner and an endless supply of adrenaline-igniting fun are fueling the Rocky Mountain rush. Throw a vibrant economy into the mix, and you get artsy districts like RiNo (River North) and LoHi (Lower Highlands), where you can replenish your calories in slow-food market halls and gourmet restaurants, bookended by a day of gallery hopping and a night out with some rootsy, denim-clad rockers. Colorado State Capitol, p74

CRYSTAL BRINDLE/500PX ©

TERI VIRBICKIS/SHUTTERSTOCK ©

Boulder

3 Driving up Hwy 36 from Denver, you eventually reach the spot: an overlook that peers down upon Colorado's own Shangri-La, tucked up against the signature Flatirons and the sudden swell of the Front Range. If this first glimpse of Boulder (p108) takes your breath away, well, you wouldn't be the first. The lively epicenter is the pedestrian-only Pearl St Mall (pictured above), but it's the surrounding outdoors that really captivates Boulder's vibrant population of students, athletes, brainiacs and entrepreneurs.

Mesa Verde National Park

4 You don't just walk into the past at Mesa Verde (p251), the site of 600 ancient cliff dwellings. You scramble up 10ft ladders, scale rock faces and crawl through tunnels. Yes, it's interactive exploring at its most low-tech, but it also makes for one of the most exhilarating adventures in the West. It's also a place to puzzle out the archaeological and cultural clues left by its former inhabitants – Ancestral Puebloans who vacated the site in AD 1300 (for reasons still not fully understood).

Aspen

5 Here's a town (p222) unlike any other place in the American West. A cocktail of cowboy grit, Euro panache, Hollywood glam, Ivy League brains, fresh powder, live music and old money, where you can drop into an extreme double-black run or stomp to the crest of a Continental Divide pass. And did we mention the frothing hot tubs, fit baristas, multimillion-dollar estates and well-read barflies? Yet Aspen remains an eccentric and surprisingly friendly place, where a stranger's smile is still common currency.

Colorado National Monument

6 Witness the sinking sun set fire to otherworldly red-rock formations and hike stark and beautiful high desert trails. These canyon walls (p300) rise from the Uncompahgre Uplift of the Colorado Plateau, 2000ft above the Grand Valley of the Colorado River, to reveal the twinkling lights of Grand Junction, the shining green river and tree-lined fields of the Grand Valley – all of it a landscape that was once patrolled by dinosaurs.

Microbreweries

7 Colorado consistently ranks among the top three states for microbreweries per capita, and craft brewing has been elevated to a high art throughout. Each September Denver hosts the Great American Beer Festival (p79), luring in 780-odd brewers and over 60,000 enthusiastic drinkers. Best-of-show awards are judged across categories like Best Coffee Beer or Best Barrel-aged Strong Beer. But whatever town you're visiting, from tiny Del Norte to beer-centric Fort Collins, you won't go thirsty.

Dude Ranches

8 With wide-open ranges, wildflower meadows and snow-kissed peaks, seeing Colorado from the saddle is a whole other world. Experiences range from the real and rustic charm of herding cattle on a bona fide ranch in South Park to venturing out to a remote bison ranch with green credentials, or riding horses in the luxuriant Rocky Mountain retreat of Devil's Thumb (p179). Digs range from five-star refurbished log cabins with mod cons to starlit camps with an eye on the Milky Way.

JULIE GROPP/SHUTTERSTOCK ©

TOYOHIRO YAMADA/GETTY IMAGES ©

Vail

9 Darling of the rich and sometimes famous, Vail (p201) resembles an elaborate amusement park for grown-ups, where every activity has been designed to send a tingle down your spine – in maximum comfort, of course. Indeed, no serious skier would dispute its status as Colorado's best and most varied resort, with 5000-plus acres of powdery back bowls, chutes and wickedly fun terrain. Whether it's your first time on a snowboard or you're flashing perfect telemark turns in the Outer Mongolia Bowl, this might very well be the ski trip of your dreams.

Silverton & Old West Towns

10 A rediscovered vintage gem, Silverton (above, p273), much like the towns of Leadville, Cripple Creek and Old Colorado City, was launched by rugged pioneer types seeking mineral riches. Hollywood shot its share of Westerns here in the 1950s, but when the last mine closed in 1991 it seemed destined to become another atmospheric ghost town, abandoned like St Elmo and Ashcroft. Then came the Durango & Silverton Narrow Gauge Railroad and the experts-only Silverton Mountain Ski Area, and the town sprang back to life.

Dinosaur National Monument

11 One of the few places on earth where you can literally get your hands on a dinosaur skeleton, Dinosaur National Monument (p171) is tucked into the far northwest corner of Colorado, stretching across state lines to Utah. Among the largest dinosaur fossil beds in North America, it was discovered in 1909. Explore desert trails, examine ancient rock art (pictured above) or raft the Yampa River through the serene landscape of its twisting red-rock canyons. The visitor center overlooks thousands of bones in the Dinosaur Quarry.

SPORTSTOCK/GETTY IMAGES ©

Rafting the Arkansas River

12 Running from Leadville down the eastern flank of Buena Vista, through Browns Canyon National Monument, and then rocketing through the spectacular Royal Gorge at class V speeds, the Arkansas River (p239) is the longest and arguably the wildest river in the state. Brace yourself for yet another icy splash swamping the raft as you plunge into a roaring set of big waves, or surrender to the power of the current as your thoroughly drenched crew unintentionally spins backwards around a monster boulder. Is this fun? You bet!

Mountain Biking the Southwest

13 Although single-track enthusiasm is ubiquitous in Colorado, the trails zigzagging the red-rock landscape around Fruita (p303) are truly world class. Other hot spots for mountain biking are the sagebrush hills and aspens around Crested Butte (pictured above), the epic Monarch Crest Trail outside Salida and the lesser-known desert trails near Cortez. A spectrum of technical difficulty presents opportunities for all, and with a little goodwill, local bike shops are usually generous with fat-tire tips.

Riding Steam Trains

14 You don't have to be a train-spotter to appreciate a good belch of vintage coal-powered steam, the whine of steel on steel and the jolting grind of a narrow-gauge train rolling slowly through dynamite-cut tunnels and along ridges blessed with some of the most stunning mountain vistas imaginable. The best of the bunch is the impossibly scenic 45-mile Durango & Silverton Narrow Gauge Railroad (pictured far right, p275), but the Georgetown Loop and Cumbres & Toltec Scenic Railroad are other worthwhile rides.

Driving the Million Dollar Highway

15 This is one amazing stretch of road (p269). Driving this asphalt sliver south from Ouray towards Silverton positions drivers on the outside edge, a heartbeat from free fall. Much of it is cut into the mountains and gains elevation by switching back in tight hairpins and S-bends. The brooding mountains loom large and close, snow clinging to their lofty, mist-shrouded peaks even in high summer. In good weather the road is formidable; in drizzle, rain, fog or snow, it can be downright scary.

JAY KRISHNAN/SHUTTERSTOCK ©

Hiking Colorado's Fourteeners

16 Colorado is home to more than 50 peaks that are higher than 14,000ft. That's well over half the peaks of 14,000ft or more in the continental US. Two are accessible by road, one by rail; the rest you'll have to work for. Whether you decide to hike a short trail – just 3 miles to Quandary Peak (p192) near Breckenridge – tackle a multiday route to Longs Peak in Rocky Mountain National Park or make a run at Mt Elbert (below)– the tallest of them all – one adage holds true: no pain, no gain.

Breckenridge

17 Every mountain town in Colorado has its own distinct personality, but when it comes to the overall coolest? That might be historic Breckenridge (p190), where you'll find quirky museums alongside youth hostels, funky restaurants rubbing shoulders with kick-back breweries, and so many peaks outside of town they were numbered instead of named. A short spin from Denver, Breck offers the perfect introduction to the Colorado high country: gold-panning history, hiking, cycling, clear mountain streams and, of course, lots and lots of snow.

WORLDPICTURES/SHUTTERSTOCK ©

GALYNA ANDRUSHKO/SHUTTERSTOCK ©

Farm-to-Fork Dining

18 Colorado takes great pride in sustainable dining, and it's not uncommon here to sit down to grass-fed beef burgers at a local pub that also brews its own ale. The abundance is apparent at city farmers markets, immense natural-food stores and gourmet food trucks. From handcrafted ice cream sold from bike carts to the auteur restaurant with an amuse-bouche like a first kiss, Colorado dares to feature top-quality local ingredients as the new gold. Treat your taste buds at the Kitchen (p123), with locations in Boulder and Denver.

Durango

19 The cultural capital of southwest Colorado, Durango (p275) is a lovely town, rich in history yet elegantly modernized. The historic central precinct dates back to the 1880s, when the town was founded by the Denver & Rio Grande Railroad. Still tastefully authentic, it's a great base for exploring the San Juan mountain range and Mesa Verde National Park. Think of it as artsy, rootsy and even a bit quirky. The Durango & Silverton Narrow Gauge Railroad toots and puffs up to Silverton several times daily.

Great Sand Dunes National Park

20 Sculpted by wind and seemingly straight out of Arabia, these 55 sq miles of sand dunes appear out of nowhere. Ringed by mountain peaks and glassy wetlands, Great Sand Dunes National Park (p332) is both eerie and amazing. Distance is an elusive concept in this monochromatic, misplaced sea of sand. Watch as angles of sunlight form shifting shadows and the wind wipes clean your footprints. The most dramatic time is day's end, when sunset puts the dunes in high contrast.

GREG BOUCHILLON/SHUTTERSTOCK ©

Pikes Peak & Garden of the Gods

21 'Pikes Peak or bust!' The rallying cry of the Colorado gold rush put Pikes Peak (p321) on the map in 1859, and the *capitán* of Colorado Springs continues to lure adventurers with its cog railway, highway to the summit and even a lung-crushing marathon. The easternmost fourteener in Colorado, it's the de facto symbol of the southern Rockies for anyone making the long trip across the plains. Drive it, hike it or admire it from beneath the exquisitely thin red-rock spires of the Garden of the Gods (pictured above).

Telluride

22 Let Aspen and Vail grab the headlines. Telluride (p261) is Colorado's most remote ski destination, where tourism has developed at an easygoing pace. Unless you arrive by plane, it's no easy feat to get here, but you're also unlikely to want to leave. Situated in the heart of the rugged San Juans, the village is snuggled into an isolated box canyon and surrounded by peaks unspoiled by overdevelopment. Out of season, Telluride also throws some of Colorado's best festivals, with banner events celebrating film and bluegrass.

Black Canyon of the Gunnison National Park

23 A massive cleft in the landscape, the arresting Black Canyon of the Gunnison (p292) is a deep, narrow abyss that unexpectedly opens from the subdued undulations of the surrounding tablelands. The sheer walls of the Black Canyon – so called because daylight only briefly illuminates the narrow canyon floor – are dizzying in height, and veined with multicolored mineral deposits. It's one of the deepest, narrowest and longest canyons in North America – and the most off-the-beaten-track national park in the state. Adventurers, start here.

Steamboat Springs

24 No Colorado ski resort is more down-to-earth than this cow town that's turned out more Olympians than any other US city, and still greets visitors with a tip of the Stetson. Steamboat's (p163) magnetism holds true in all seasons: in summer visitors rumble down the hills on two wheels, raft white-water and soak off long hikes at the sweet Strawberry Park Hot Springs. In winter, its epic skiing is a bit too far for city day-trippers, leaving the delicious open-glade and aspen skiing all for you.

Fort Collins

25 Here's our idea of a perfect day. Check out a free fat-tire cruiser and roll through one of America's most bike-friendly cities. When you get warm, point it towards the shady river path along the Poudre and spend the afternoon tubing along the trickling water. Cap things off by spending the afternoon sampling craft beer from a handful of Colorado's finest breweries. Forget about Fort Collins (p150) as Colorado's underdog college town: this small city on the edge of the Front Range is a delightful destination in its own right.

Need to Know

For more information, see Survival Guide (p361)

Currency
US dollars ($)

Language
English

Visas
All foreign visitors must have a visa to enter the USA unless they are Canadian citizens or part of the Visa Waiver Program.

Money
ATMs are widely available. Credit and debit cards are accepted by most businesses.

Cell Phones
Coverage can be unreliable in mountain regions. SIM cards are readily available in large stores like Walmart or Target.

Time
Mountain Standard Time (MST) is seven hours behind GMT/UTC and observes daylight saving in summer.

When to Go

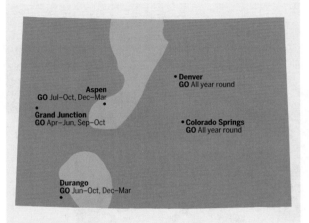

Denver
GO All year round

Aspen
GO Jul–Oct, Dec–Mar

Grand Junction
GO Apr–Jun, Sep–Oct

Colorado Springs
GO All year round

Durango
GO Jun–Oct, Dec–Mar

Warm to hot summers, mild to cool winters
Warm summers, cold winters

High Season
(Dec–Mar)

➡ Skiers and shredders arrive in droves.

➡ Vacancies are at a premium and ski resorts capitalize on this big time, charging three times more than their summer rates.

Shoulder
(Jun–Sep)

➡ Summer is a shoulder season because in some spots you can get great room rates, while others enjoy a second high season.

➡ Vacationers descend in droves on campsites, trails, rivers and crags throughout the mountains.

Low Season
(Apr–May & Oct–Nov)

➡ Many businesses close shop to get ready for the summer or winter crush.

➡ Early fall is brisk but lovely; spring means melting snow and very limited activities.

➡ Hotels (if open) slash room rates considerably.

Useful Websites

Colorado Tourism Board (www.colorado.com)

5280 (www.5280.com) Denver's best monthly magazine.

Opensnow (www.opensnow.com) Daily snow reports and powder forecasts.

Colorado Trail Explorer (http://cpw.state.co.us/CTS) Online map covering 39,000 miles of trails.

Lonely Planet (www.lonelyplanet.com/colorado) Destination info, hotel bookings, traveler forum and more.

Important Numbers

All phone numbers have a three-digit area code followed by a seven-digit local number. For long-distance and toll-free calls, dial 1 plus all 10 digits.

Country code	☑1
International dialing code	☑011
Operator	☑0
Emergency	☑911
Directory assistance (local)	☑411

Exchange Rates

Australia	A$1	$0.79
Canada	C$1	$0.79
Eurozone	€1	$1.18
Japan	¥100	$0.91
Mexico	MXN10	$0.57
New Zealand	NZ$1	$0.73
UK	£1	$1.29

For current exchange rates, see www.xe.com.

Daily Costs

Budget: Less than $100

➡ Campgrounds and summer hostels: $10–45

➡ Self-catering, food trucks, markets: $7–15

➡ Ski-town shuttles: free

➡ Backcountry hiking and skiing: free

Midrange: $100–250

➡ Winter hostels: $85–100

➡ Summer hotel rooms: $100–150

➡ Meals in local restaurants: $15–25

➡ Car rental: $30

Top End: More than $250

➡ Winter hotel rooms: $250–1200

➡ Meals in upscale restaurants: $25–100

➡ Ski-lift ticket: $100–190

➡ SUV rental: $60

Opening Hours

High-season hours follow. In rural areas, many businesses close on Sunday.

Businesses 9am–5pm Monday to Friday

Banks 8:30am–5pm Monday to Friday, 9am–noon on Saturday

Stores 10am–6pm Monday to Saturday, noon–5pm Sunday; shopping malls often extend to 8pm or 9pm

Supermarkets 7am–9pm; most cities have 24-hour supermarkets

Restaurants Breakfast 7am–10:30am (weekend brunch 9am–2pm); lunch 11:30am–2:30pm; and dinner 5–9:30pm, later on weekends

Bars & Pubs 4pm–midnight, to 2am on Friday and Saturday

Arriving in Colorado

Almost all visitors to Colorado come through **Denver International Airport** (DIA).

Train The University of Colorado A Line Train departs from the airport every 15 minutes (every 30 minutes off-peak) and goes to downtown's Union Station ($9, 37 minutes).

Taxi Queue outside Ground Transportation area (to downtown should cost about $60).

Uber & Lyft Drivers will meet you at passenger pickup.

Bus RTD (p370) operates SkyRide buses with frequent service between 3:30am and 1:10am to downtown Denver ($9, 55 minutes) and Boulder ($9, 70 minutes).

Shuttle SuperShuttle (p370) and others (rates from $33 per person) go to Denver, Boulder, Fort Collins, surrounding suburbs and parts of Wyoming. Some ski areas have shuttle services that are reasonably priced to and from Denver International Airport. Try **Colorado Mountain Express** (p370) for trips to mountains.

Getting Around

Car Essential for exploring the state, unless you stay on the Front Range or in a ski town. Rentals available in every town or city. Drive on the right.

Bus Limited service, but good in Boulder, Fort Collins and Denver.

Bicycle Bike-sharing programs in Denver, Boulder and Fort Collins. Bike paths in ski resort areas and cities help facilitate travel.

Train Amtrak's *California Zephyr* stops here between San Francisco and Chicago. There are a few steam-train routes.

Car Shares Uber and Lyft operate in most larger towns and all the resort areas. There are a few car-share programs in Denver, including Zipcar and Car2go.

For much more on **getting around**, see p370

If You Like...

Hiking

To try and pin down the best hikes in the Rocky Mountains is kind of like ranking the world's greatest sunsets. But in a mountain range this huge, there are some variations in what you can see.

Rocky Mountain National Park Longs Peak gets all the buzz, but for great backpacking head to Wild Basin. (p138)

San Juan Skyway Hikes here wander between classic alpine country, aspen meadows, red-rock escarpments and bubbling hot springs. (p45)

Maroon Bells Pristine wilderness with epic Continental Divide views from spectacular mountain passes. (p224)

Spanish Peaks Stark granite walls rising from mountain meadows, two looming peaks, ample wildlife and thin crowds. (p328)

Chautauqua Park For gorgeous Front Range views, tromp off through Boulder's open space, home to the Flatirons. (p109)

Old West Sites

Everyone from Harvard-educated blue bloods to pioneering entrepreneurs and desperate Southern families scorched by the Civil War came west, lured by gold and searching for a fresh start.

Bent's Old Fort National Historic Site This melting pot of Mexican, American, European and Native American culture sustained the Santa Fe Trail. (p325)

Leadville Colorado's highest incorporated city has plenty of boom-and-bust lore. (p246)

Ashcroft These mining-town ruins are 10 minutes from Aspen and accessible by cross-country trail in winter. (p223)

St Elmo Drive, bike or horse-trek to this atmospheric Collegiate Peaks ghost town. (p238)

Breckenridge This historic ski town sprouted in 1859 when the Colorado gold rush first took hold. (p190)

Snow Sports

Colorado has a ski town to fit every personality, ranging from chic to cheap, from resort to quick Front Range getaway. Check websites for package deals; better yet, get a season pass!

Vail Known for its spectacular back-bowl terrain, it's Colorado's largest resort and one of its glitziest. (p201)

Aspen The star-studded four mountains host celebs and the Winter X Games with epic terrain. (p222)

Winter Park Notable for Eagle Wind trees and SUV-sized moguls at Mary Jane. (p179)

Breckenridge Has Victorian charm and the highest chairlift in the US. (p190)

Copper Mountain Great back bowls and the awesome Woodward Barn, where shredders perfect their aerial acrobatics. (p200)

Telluride An old mining town reinvented as a top resort, and the slopes don't disappoint. (p261)

Steamboat Mountain Resort Excellent tree runs and an authentic Western small town; great for families. (p165)

Beer & Microbreweries

Although Colorado's long-established craft breweries have outgrown their 'micro' status, there's always another backyard hobbyist to challenge the status quo.

New Belgium Brewery Famous for Fat Tire, with a riotous tour that could end with you in costume. (p151)

Great Divide Brewery & Tap Room A Denver stalwart that's

never wavered from its mission: serving outstanding beer, plain and simple. (p91)

Ska Brewing Company Live music, top-notch brews and BBQs. (p280)

Black Shirt Brewing Specializing in red ales (in outstanding varieties), with live music and a casual air. (p89)

Avery Brewing Boulder's fave brewpub produces a beer list as eclectic as its clientele. (p125)

Odell Brewing Company Arguably the best craft brewer in the state. (p153)

Scenic Railways

These narrow-gauge railways provide views, thrills and a bit of oral history.

Durango & Silverton Narrow Gauge Railroad The longest and best of the bunch, and impossibly scenic. (p374)

Georgetown Loop Railroad A steep corkscrew track winds between the old mining towns of Georgetown and Silver Plume. (p179)

Pikes Peak Cog Railway Travels to the summit of Pikes Peak, whose vistas inspired the song 'America the Beautiful.' (p322)

Geology

From hidden 2000ft gorges to rock gardens and mind-bending arches, Colorado is home to some geologic masterworks.

Royal Gorge A deep, spectacular rift holding the Arkansas River, with a landmark bridge and scenic railway. (p318)

Garden of the Gods These odd boulders, fins and pinnacles are in a red-rock vein running through Colorado Springs. (p310)

Top: Stranahans Colorado Whiskey distillery (p78).

Bottom: Georgetown Loop Railroad (p179)

Great Dikes of the Spanish Peaks Sheer rock walls rising from mountain meadows like a primordial fence-line hemming the Spanish Peaks. (p328)

Black Canyon of the Gunnison National Park A deep, narrow abyss with sheer, multicolored walls scored with eerie crevices and pinnacles. (p292)

Distilleries

Colorado's microdistillery movement follows in the tracks of craft breweries. These artisanal tipples are no moonshine – many are award-winning.

Stranahans Colorado Whiskey This widely celebrated Denver craft whiskey is a staple of high-end cocktail menus. (p78)

Breckenridge Distillery Award-winning bourbon from the world's highest distillery. (p198)

Peach Street Distillers Palisade spirits producer whose brightest star is vodka infused with local peaches. (p306)

Montanya Distillery Award-winning rum spun into stunning cocktails, with production in Crested Butte and drinking in Silverton. (p291)

Deerhammer Single malt whiskey, gin and brandy from this Buena Vista brand. (p244)

Wildlife

Colorado is home to a wealth of wildlife, from moose, elk, deer and antelope to fox, wolf, black bear, mountain lion and the bald eagle.

Rocky Mountain National Park Moose wade through wetlands and elk graze by the entrance; sightings are frequent and satisfying. (p138)

San Juan Mountains On backcountry treks you can spot elk, black bears, mountain goats, beavers, otters and eagles. (p250)

Black Canyon of the Gunnison National Park The stomping ground of mule deer, bighorn sheep, black bears and mountain lions. (p292)

Alamosa National Wildlife Refuge Bald eagles, coyotes, elk and migrating cranes flank the Rio Grande at dawn and dusk. (p335)

Colorado Wolf & Wildlife Center Tour this wildlife sanctuary, where there are three subspecies of wolf, plus foxes and coyotes. (p322)

Hot Springs

From backcountry pools in the midst of nature to luxurious resorts, Colorado has a healing, natural hot spring with your name on it.

Mt Princeton Hot Springs A bit of everything: relaxation and swimming pools, a spa and a waterslide for the kiddos. (p241)

Glenwood Hot Springs The world's largest hot-springs pool has plenty of amenities and a perfect pit-stop location. (p217)

Strawberry Park Hot Springs Natural pools by the river outside Steamboat Springs, with lodging and spa packages. (p165)

Pagosa Hot Springs Overlooking the San Juan River are 22 pools; some get as hot as 111°F (44°C). (p282)

Valley View Hot Springs Little-known and off the grid, these clothing-optional pools are among the state's most tranquil. (p343)

Avalanche Ranch Get away from it all in a Rocky Mountain cabin, steps away from private pools. (p237)

Ouray Hot Springs Family-friendly pools along the Million Dollar Highway. (p270)

Museums

Colorado isn't just about outdoor fun. Stop by the following museums for a dose of local art and history.

Denver Art Museum Has one of the USA's largest Native American art collections, plus fabulous visiting exhibits. (p65)

Denver Museum of Nature & Science Dinosaur bones, outer space, Vikings, a planetarium and much more. (p69)

History Colorado Center Get up to speed on local history at this fabulous interactive museum. (p69)

Clyfford Still Museum The collected works of the little-known but powerful abstract expressionist. (p65)

Colorado Springs Fine Arts Center Home to some 23,000 pieces, with a great Latin American collection. (p310)

Aspen Art Museum Edgy, contemporary installations in Aspen. (p223)

Month by Month

TOP EVENTS

Boulder Creek Festival, May

Telluride Bluegrass Festival, June

Aspen Music Festival, July

Telluride Film Festival, September

Great American Beer Festival, October

January

Crowds are at their thickest around New Year and are present through to Martin Luther King Jr's birthday. In a good year, the snow is as abundant as après-ski parties.

☆ Winter X Games

ESPN's annual extreme winter sports competition takes place at Aspen's Buttermilk Mountain, with night and day events, including freestyle skiing, snowboarding and snowmobiling. (p228)

☆ National Western Stock Show

Saddle up for the state's biggest stock show (www.nationalwestern.com), a Denver tradition since 1906. We're talking rodeos, cattle, cowboys, Wild West shows, hundreds of vendors and more.

February

It's the height of the ski season. Mardi Gras is celebrated and resorts fill for Presidents' Day weekend. Advance reservations are crucial, with discounts available midweek.

✸ Carnival

Vail's jovial spin on Mardi Gras includes a parade and a king and queen. Breckenridge hosts a masquerade ball and a Fat Tuesday parade. (p195)

March

Coloradans swear the sun is always out – and it often is – but March is the beginning of the real sunshine, and spring break attracts families for the start of spring skiing.

✸ Frozen Dead Guy Days

Irreverent and a little creepy, this festival suits Nederland. The town welcomes spring by rallying around its cryogenically frozen mascot, 'Grandpa Bredo,' with a snowshoe race, dead guy look-alike contest and beer drinking. (p133)

April

Spring skiing and resort festivals! As room rates dip, midweek deals aren't hard to find (unless it's Easter). The Colorado Rockies baseball team starts knocking it out of the park at Coors Field.

☆ 5Point Film Festival

The Sundance of adventure cinema, with filmmakers celebrating the way the great outdoors transform our lives. Held in offbeat Carbondale, down valley from Aspen. (p220)

May

'Mud season' shuts down the high country, while Boulder and Denver start to warm up. Summer unofficially begins on Memorial Day weekend – time for paddling.

✸ Boulder Creek Festival

One of Colorado's biggest festivals comes to town. Boulder's traditional summer starter is all about food, drink, music and, above all, glorious sunshine. It all comes to a close with Bolder Boulder, a 10km race celebrated equally by wacky participants and spectators. (p115)

June

Summer festivals start, river runoffs peak and Arapahoe Basin finally closes for the season. All mountain passes are open and vacationing families start to hit the major parks and landmarks.

☆ Telluride Bluegrass Festival

Thousands of fans descend on Telluride for a weekend-long homage to bluegrass. Camping out is popular at this well-organized outdoor festival. (p264)

🏃 Pikes Peak International Hill Climb

When the first road to Pikes Peak was complete, this car race was born. Different classes of vehicle (pro trucks, motorbikes, stock cars etc) hammer up 12 miles of road and a climb of 4700ft. (p323)

🍻 Colorado Brewers' Festival

Taste the best of in-state suds in Fort Collins, with beers from the more than 40 Colorado breweries participating. Free music, too.

July

July ushers in 10 weeks of prime time for backcountry hikes and kayaking, now that the snow has melted.

☆ Aspen Music Festival

Classical musicians come from around the globe to play, teach and learn at this famous festival. Top-tier performers put on spectacular shows, while street corners burst into life with smaller groups. (p228)

August

A great time of year to get into the backcountry. Down mountain, bulls and bronco busters square off at dozens of country fairs.

🏃 Leadville Trail 100

One of the toughest mountain biking and foot races on earth, drawing trail runners – including the famed Tarahumara Indians – to race 100 miles at high altitude. Fewer than half of the competitors reach the finish line before the 30-hour limit is up. (p248)

September

With crisp fall air and golden aspens, the high country is paradise. It's still a great time for biking and hiking, with some off-season deals at resorts.

☆ Telluride Film Festival

Holding its own against the likes of Utah's Sundance, Telluride debuts plenty of celebrated films. It's helped launch the careers of Michael Moore and Robert Rodriguez, among others. (p264)

October

Mud season redux. Weather is turning, but at least the Denver Broncos are back in action. Discounts can be steep – even in Aspen – and you'll likely see snow fall before Halloween.

🏃 Emma Crawford Coffin Race

One of the state's kookier events (www.emmacrawfordfestival.com) sees custom-built wheeled coffins racing through Manitou Springs in the buildup to Halloween, in honor of the eponymous Crawford (d 1891), whose coffin was unearthed by erosion and slid down Red Mountain.

November

Ski season begins throughout the state. Early-season ski deals abound, though you won't find any bargains around Thanksgiving weekend, when the families return.

December

While snow cover is still hit or miss, once school lets out airports are jammed, rooms are booked and reservations become a must. Season rates peak during the holidays.

🍻 Snow Daze

Vail lets loose with one of the biggest early-season celebrations, a week-long festival with myriad competitions and activities, as well as plenty of live performances from big-name musical stars. (p207)

Itineraries

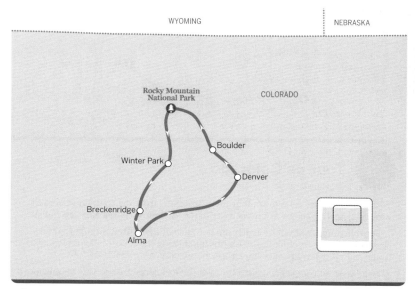

 Denver & the Northern Rockies

Combining urban cityscapes with alpine bliss, this is one unforgettable road trip. Crossing five mountain passes, it's only possible in summer or fall.

Start off in **Denver**, sampling the upstart restaurants and luminary bars of RiNo, museum-hopping and taking in a ball game or concert at Red Rocks. Head north through funky **Boulder**, pausing to take in some street theater before setting up camp in **Rocky Mountain National Park** to spend a day or two in the massive wilderness.

Drive Trail Ridge Rd across the Continental Divide (stopping for a selfie with a marmot) and then it's down to **Winter Park** and Devil's Thumb Ranch, where you can ride horses, mountain bike, fly-fish, hike and much, much more. Climb Berthoud Pass to reach I-70, then it's through the Eisenhower Tunnel or over Loveland Pass to Summit County and **Breckenridge**. Luxuriate in your last days here, exploring the quaint historical district and cycling, rafting, panning for gold and hiking during long summer days. From Breckenridge it's up over Hoosier Pass, down through the US's highest town – **Alma** (10,578ft) – to loop around back to Denver via South Park and gorgeous Hwy 285.

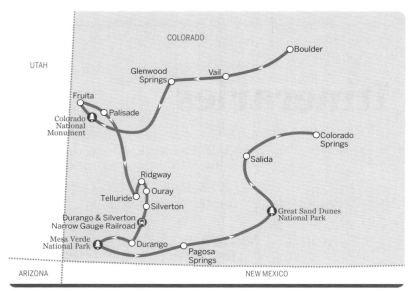

Tour de Colorado

2 WEEKS

With a couple of weeks you can tour the entire state, from the central peaks to the southwestern desert, from the Arkansas River to the sand dunes of the San Luis Valley.

For this summer or fall itinerary, start off in idyllic **Boulder**. Stretch your legs and prep your lungs by cycling the bike paths and hitting the trails of Chautauqua Park between sampling farm-to-table fare, coffeehouses and congenial brewpubs.

Head west on I-70, pausing for a break at Independence Pass or Vail Pass, before stopping in **Vail**, where you can run a river, cover thrilling terrain while downhill mountain biking and enjoy any number of fine dining options. Continue west, pausing in **Glenwood Springs** for a soak in the hot springs, to the stunning Wild West scenery of **Colorado National Monument**, with crumbling red-rock mesas and deep canyons. Camp overnight and hit **Fruita** for extraordinary desert singletrack, or **Palisade** for a day-long wine-tasting meander through the vineyards. Head south to the enchanted San Juan Mountains.

Climb back into the high country and dead-end in historic **Telluride**, in a stunning box canyon surrounded by steep peaks. Here you can take in a festival, ride the free gondola and enjoy the chic mountain vibe. Head out through scenic ranch country, hitting the hot springs outside **Ridgway**. If you're here in middle-to-late summer, consider a two-day backpacking trip in the nearby San Juan high country. Explore funky **Ouray** and link to **Silverton** via the wild Million Dollar Highway, a sinuous and steep journey through three mountain passes. If you need a break from being behind the wheel, drop into good-vibe **Durango** via the **Durango & Silverton Narrow Gauge Railroad**.

Detour to **Mesa Verde National Park** to explore stunning cliff dwellings. Camp here or enjoy a B&B in nearby Mancos. On your way east, take another soak in **Pagosa Springs**. Take Hwy 160 east to the **Great Sand Dunes National Park** on your way to **Salida** and the Collegiate Peaks Wilderness for world-class white-water rafting and hiking alongside grizzled mountain goats. Finish with Hwy 24 west to **Colorado Springs**, where you can indulge with a night at the Broadmoor.

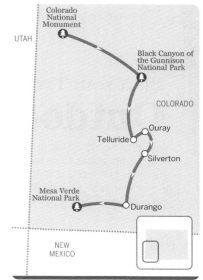

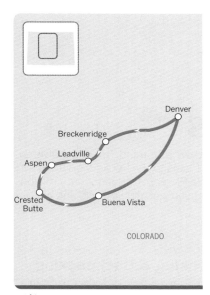

 Rocky Mountain High
1 WEEK

Fuel up with a great diner breakfast in **Denver** before jumping on I-70 to begin your summer high-country trip.

Veer off for **Breckenridge**, soaking up the Victorian ambience and summiting your first fourteener. Climb higher past the Climax Mine and spectacular peaks and then down to **Leadville**, and then scoot south on Hwy 82 towards Twin Lakes. From here, it's back to the heavens (with panoramas of the Continental Divide) on Independence Pass, which takes you right into idyllic **Aspen**.

In Aspen, spend two nights hiking in the Maroon Bells Wilderness, cycling to Ashcroft and eating at the Pine Creek Cookhouse. Continue to nearby but remote **Crested Butte** via the summer-only Kebler Pass. The wildflower capital of Colorado, charming 'CB' also boasts outstanding hiking, festivals and singletrack trails.

Next stop is the Arkansas River, the delight of anglers and rafters. Enjoy the cute Western atmosphere of **Buena Vista** or Salida. Take in ghost town St Elmo and soak in the healing waters of Mt Princeton Hot Springs. Meander back to Denver via the mountain route of Hwy 285.

5 DAYS **The Southwest**

From Grand Junction, explore the sublime scenery of the Colorado Plateau and San Juan Mountains.

Begin with the stunning **Colorado National Monument** – a high desert paradise. Camp overnight, then hit Black Ridge Canyons Wilderness and a hike beneath nine rock arches in Rattlesnake Canyon before heading south to the deep, eerie cleft of the **Black Canyon of the Gunnison**. Surrounded on three sides by towering 13,000ft peaks, **Telluride** is all strong coffee, historic buildings and big nature. You have more hiking to do here, whether it's to the top of Ajax Peak or Bridal Veil Falls, Colorado's highest waterfall at 365ft.

Circle around to **Ouray**, and then follow the white-knuckle Million Dollar Highway through **Silverton** to **Durango** – hop on the Durango & Silverton Narrow Gauge Railroad in either town. Explore the turquoise jewelry and art galleries of the town before driving deeper into the Four Corners and **Mesa Verde National Park**. These Ancestral Puebloan cliff dwellings are massive and transporting. Spend the night beneath the stars and you might feel your mind wander deep into dreamtime.

Plan Your Trip
Outdoors

Winter or summer, Colorado will blow your mind. Spanning diverse geographic zones from the Great Plains to the Rocky Mountains to the desert canyons of the Colorado Plateau, Colorado has a million-and-one adventure activities to get you wet, get you wild and get you pumped.

Top Ten Fourteeners

In Colorado 54 mountains top 14,000ft. Locals call them 'fourteeners' (often written as '14ers'), and many try to bag 'em all.

Rocky Mountain National Park
Longs Peak (p139)

Vail, Aspen & Central Colorado
Mt Elbert (p247)

Quandary Peak (p192)

Mount of the Holy Cross (p212)

Mt Princeton (p242)

Mt Massive (p247)

Uncompahgre Peak (p299)

Maroon Peak (p224)

Snowmass Mountain (p226)

Southeast Colorado
Pikes Peak (p321)

Hiking & Backpacking

Trails across the state beckon for day hikers and overnight backpackers between late May and early October. In the winter, with the right gear and right training, you can head out on snowshoe or backcountry ski to explore the wilderness as you've never seen it before. Many of these trails are accessible by county and forest service roads that are subject to closure; contact the local ranger district if you plan on hiking early or late in the season. Trails are accessible year-round in lower-elevation destinations, including most trails along the front range (outside Denver, Colorado Springs, Fort Collins and Boulder) and on the Western Slope in places like the Sand Dunes and Colorado National Monument.

Don't want to bring a backpack? Colorado has an incredible system of backcountry huts and yurts, where you can backpack in for a day, or link adventures over several 100 miles. Some of the top hut systems include 10th Mountain Division, San Juan Huts, Never Summer Yurts and Braun Huts.

Excellent long-distance trails for through-hiking include the Colorado Trail and the Continental Divide Trail.

Where to Hike
The Colorado Trail

The state's signature trail, also known as USFS Trail 1776, starts at Chatfield Reservoir near Denver before winding 500

SAFE HIKING

➡ Hikers should always have their own maps. Adequate trail maps can be found at park headquarters, ranger district offices or outdoor clothing and supply stores such as REI.

➡ Weather conditions can change in a blink, so bring layers and rain gear. Mid-to-late-summer afternoon monsoon rains are frequent and lightning is a real concern above the timberline. The catch-all rule is to stay off mountain peaks and passes after noon. It's also best to tell somebody where you are going and when you expect to be back.

➡ Always carry more than enough food and water (and water-purification equipment). Dehydration will sap your energy and can provoke altitude sickness.

➡ There are a few animals you may encounter, including cougar, rattlesnake, moose and bear. Generally speaking, it's best to make noise on the trail to avoid encounters, and keep clean campsites.

➡ If you get into trouble, try to call 911 from your cell phone, signal for help or send someone to find help. The Colorado Outdoor Search & Rescue Card (COR-SAR) helps fund search-and-rescue efforts throughout the state, and costs just $3 for one year and $12 for five years. You can buy it at outdoor retailers throughout the state.

miles to Durango through eight mountain ranges, seven national forests, six wilderness areas and five river systems. The **Colorado Trail Foundation** (www.coloradotrail.org) offers maps and books that describe the trail in detail.

Denver, Boulder & The Front Range

Denver From the Denver Metro Area, you can easily explore day hikes as far-away as Rocky Mountain National Park and Summit County, but there are plenty of hikes just outside the cities on the front range that are worthwhile. Front-range trails can be packed on weekends – consider weekday hikes to have more space to yourself.

While much of Denver's walking and biking centers on its kick-ass off-road bike trails, you can also find plenty of hiking in the mountains rising above the city. Most of these hikes fall within the Jefferson County Open Space.

Colorado Springs There are dozens of really cool hikes from Colorado Springs in places like Garden of the Gods and the wilderness surrounding Pikes Peak. With some fitness, you can ascend Pikes Peak in a day. Some drive to the top, others take the train, but the 13-mile Barr Trail leads from the Cog Railway station through Barr Camp at the halfway point and finally through the scree fields to the summit. You can make it a very doable day hike by taking the train halfway up to a spur that leads into Barr Camp, where you can join the Barr Trail to the summit, then ride the rails back down.

Boulder This visionary small city is surrounded by parkland paid for by a self-assessed tax that has been used to purchase vast swaths of city- and county-owned open space, including Chautauqua Park, which is where you'll find the best hiking in the area. In the mountains above the city, past the town of Nederland (only a 30-minute drive west of downtown) is the Indian Peaks Wilderness Area, where you'll find miles of hiking trails and backcountry campsites. The hike up to 12,000ft Arapaho Pass, accessed from the Fourth of July campground, is an especially nice day hike.

Fort Collins There are amazing hikes and bikes around Horsetooth Open Space and up the Cache la Poudre Canyon.

Rocky Mountain National Park

One of the top draws in all of Colorado, Rocky Mountain National Park is intersected by the Continental Divide and offers some of the best wildlife-viewing in the state. Its excellent hiking trails cross alpine meadows, skirt lakes and bring travelers into the wild and deeply beautiful backcountry.

NATIONAL PARKS & MONUMENTS

Bent's Old Fort National Historic Site (p32)	In southeastern Colorado, on the north bank of the Arkansas River, this small site was an early prairie trading post for settlers.
Black Canyon of the Gunnison National Park (p32)	The Gunnison River cuts this deep, narrow and scenic western Colorado gorge nearly 2500ft below the adjacent plateau. It also features forests of ancient piñon pines.
Colorado National Monument (p32)	Once dinosaur country, this 18,000-acre reserve near Grand Junction, in western Colorado, displays colorful and distinctive rock forms and spires, offering great hiking, climbing and biking.
Dinosaur National Monument (p32)	The Green and Yampa Rivers flow through this 298-sq-mile reserve in northeastern Utah and northwestern Colorado, where dinosaur fossils lie in impressive quarries. Native American petroglyphs embellish nearby scenic canyons.
Florissant Fossil Beds National Monument (p32)	Volcanic ash covering this former lake bed in the mountains west of Colorado Springs preserved 6000 acres of fossilized flora and fauna, including petrified sequoias.
Great Sand Dunes National Park (p32)	This spectacular dune field spreads for approximately 55 sq miles in the San Luis Valley, with the tallest dune rising – staggeringly – to almost 700ft.
Hovenweep National Monument (p32)	In southwestern Colorado and southeastern Utah, this 300-acre monument preserves the ruins of defensive fortifications that once protected a vital water supply for pre-Columbian inhabitants.
Mesa Verde National Park (p32)	In southwestern Colorado, covering 80 sq miles, this park is primarily an archaeological preserve. Its elaborate cliff dwellings are relics of Ancestral Puebloans.
Rocky Mountain National Park (p32)	Only a short hop from Denver, this park straddles the Continental Divide, offering 395 sq miles of alpine forests, lakes and tundra covered by summer wildflowers and grazed by bighorn sheep and elk.
Browns Canyon National Monument (p32)	The 21,586 acres of pristine canyons, wild river and remote forest are this national monument's hallmark. Top it off with amazing white-water rafting on the Arkansas for wild adventures in the heart of Colorado.
Yucca House National Monument	One of the largest archeological sites in southwest Colorado; you'll find large mounds of unexcavated Ancestral Puebloan ruins here.

Just know that in the peak season (July and August) you will have to make reservations for backcountry campsites, particularly if you plan on climbing Longs Peak and staying overnight on the mountain.

Central Mountains

Breckenridge, Vail and Aspen are all tremendous resort areas with more hiking trails than can be explored in an entire season. Most ski areas have a summer lift to a ski lodge with trail access. Views can be excellent, particularly in Vail and Snowmass; the groomed trails give you a taste of the high altitude with relatively smooth footing, but it ain't the wilderness.

One stunning hiking destination is the Maroon Bells. It's no secret, but if you start early and plan to hike all day, you can avoid the bused-in crowds and head up and over Buckskin Pass, where solitude can be yours and the views are breathtaking. Other options in the Aspen area include a hike to the famous Grottos and a trail to Conundrum Hot Springs. Outside Glenwood Springs, consider a trip to Hanging Lake.

The Collegiate Peaks Wilderness is a close second. Best accessed from Buena Vista on Hwy 24 or Leadville, it has eight peaks above 14,000ft. Vail or Minturn are the best departure points for Mount of the Holy Cross, while Quandary Peak holds the distinction of being the most accessible 14,000ft peak in the state, just outside Breckenridge.

If you want to sample the backcountry without having to rough it, look into the 10th Mountain Division Hut Association, which manages 29 backcountry huts between Vail and Aspen. They're stocked with firewood (some even have saunas) and connected by 350 miles of trails.

Northwest Colorado

Dominated by the Routt National Forest, there are three wilderness areas in this region: Flattops Wilderness, Sarvis Creek Wilderness and Mt Zirkel Wilderness. All are laced with excellent hiking trails, but the Mt Zirkel Wilderness is especially magical. Untamed and roadless, it's dotted with icy glacial lakes and granite faces, and is intersected by the Continental Divide and two major rivers, the Elk and the Encampment, both of which are being considered for protection under the Wild & Scenic Rivers Act. In the center of it all is the 12,180ft Mt Zirkel.

Fans of canyon country will want to check out Colorado National Monument. Most of the trails are relatively short, but the rewarding 6-mile Monument Canyon Trail skirts many of the park's most interesting natural features, including the Coke Ovens, the Kissing Couple and Independence Monument.

Southwest Colorado

Colorado's most diverse region features red-rock canyons, Mesa Verde National Park and spectacular high country – you may just want to head here directly. Black Canyon of the Gunnison National Park is a stunning place to stretch your legs. The easy 1.5-mile Oak Flat Trail offers good views of Black Canyon. At sunset take the 1.5-mile Warner Point Nature Trail to either High Point or Sunset View overlooks. Crested Butte has plenty of hiking in the wilderness surrounding town.

Telluride is a day hiker's dream town, with many trails accessible from downtown, including the 2.7-mile Jud Wiebe Trail. The Bear Creek Trail is slightly shorter – just over 2 miles – but includes

---

FIVE WAYS TO BE A GOOD BACKPACKER

➡ 'Leave only footprints; take only pictures.' There's no garbage collection in the backcountry, so make sure that whatever you pack in, you pack out.

➡ Water. Water. Water. You should have water sanitation or a water-filtration system to enjoy the backcountry. The best way to eliminate potential bacteria is to boil the lake, creek or river water, but filters work well, too.

➡ Have the essentials: a map and compass, extra layers of clothing, rain gear, extra food and water, flashlight, fire-starter kit (with waterproof matches and/or a lighter), camp stove, first-aid kit (with blister-care items), sunglasses, sunscreen, sleeping bag, tent and pocket knife.

➡ Only build fires where permitted, and only use dead and downed wood, rather than breaking dead limbs from standing trees. Make sure you put out your fire completely before breaking camp.

➡ Due to high-density backcountry traffic, Colorado authorities are now suggesting that campers actually pack out their own personal solid waste, and are even offering free bags with which to do the trick. It's no joke – human waste does impact the environment and the new guidelines are a response to that. At the very least, bury yours a minimum of 6in below the surface – at least 200ft from any watercourses – and pack out your toilet tissue.

a 1040ft climb to a waterfall. This trail also intersects the 12-mile Wasatch Trail. Backpackers should seek their solitude surrounded by the 14,000ft summits in the nearby Lizard Head and Mt Sneffels Wilderness Areas.

The region's jewel is the epic, craggy range of the San Juan Mountains. There are more than 25 peaks over 11,000ft here, including 14 of Colorado's fourteeners. Over the years the range has been explored by miners, skiers and mountaineers, but one look is enough to see that it's still untamed.

San Luis Valley & Southeast Colorado

While there is certainly something to be said for taking down a big-name mountain, backpackers seeking pristine nature, dramatic views and solitude will love the Spanish Peaks Wilderness. Extinct volcanoes that aren't part of the Continental Divide cordillera include East Spanish Peak at 12,683ft and West Spanish Peak at 13,625ft. There are trails to both summits and spectacular dikes that seem to erupt from the earth. All told there are three campgrounds and 65 miles of trails to explore.

Skiing & Snowboarding

Colorado's wealth of ski and snowboarding terrain is well known. There are bunny slopes and moguls, tree runs and back bowls, terrain parks and superpipes – plus the dry snow here is so light that it's often referred to as 'champagne powder.' Winter recreation built this state's tourism industry, transforming places such as Aspen and Vail and putting towns like Crested Butte, Steamboat, Breckenridge and Telluride on the map. These winter sports remain a central part of the Colorado lifestyle.

All major resorts have ski schools, with lessons running from bargain-basement $98 a day to over $600. There is also normally a Nordic ski center located close to major resorts for the cross-country set.

There has been a tremendous consolidation of ski-area ownership in Colorado, with Vail Resorts and Aspen being the largest companies in the state. This means that discounted season passes are often the best way to go if you ski for more than four days. Top season passes include the Vail Epic Pass (Vail, Beaver Creek,

Arapaho Basin, Keystone, Breckenridge, plus some out of state offerings) and the Rocky Mountain Superpass+ (Winter Park, Eldora, Copper, Steamboat and Crested Butte). Do some research to find lift ticket deals before you hit the mountains.

Lots of people seem to be taking to the backcountry these days. But use caution – the snowpack in Colorado is one of the most unstable in the entire world. Backcountry skiers should travel with avalanche beacon, shovel and probe and know how to use them. More importantly, they should know how to travel safely in avalanche country. The same applies to snowshoers and snowmobilers sharing this space.

Where to Ski
Northern Mountains

Although this section of the state does have tremendous hiking and mountain biking – normally indicators of a nearby ski resort – much of the best mountain terrain is protected in the Rocky Mountain National Park, where you can find good backcountry skiing and snowshoeing.

➡ **Steamboat Springs** One of the state's great all-around resorts, Steamboat Springs has 165 trails (3668ft vertical) and nearly 3000 acres with ample runs at every level. A great destination for multiday trips, it boasts a great town atmosphere alongside a whole lot of terrain. It's particularly renowned for tree skiing, and even intermediate skiers can weave through trees without the typical hazards. Serious skiers will also gravitate to a number of mogul runs on the hill. More than a few Olympic-caliber skiers and riders make their winter home here.

➡ **Eldora** More convenient than epic (although the 1400ft vertical drop in Corona Bowl will get your attention), Eldora Mountain Resort, 4 miles west of Nederland, has around 500 skiable acres and 25-plus miles of well-groomed Nordic trails. Its nearby location makes it an easy trip from Boulder or Denver.

➡ **Ski Grandby Ranch** While Grandby is mostly a summer destination, families interested in a cowboy-and-snowplow adventure might consider this small family-friendly resort.

Central Mountains

Summit County has one of the world's highest concentrations of ski, snowboard and winter-sports areas. If you're trying to decide where to base your winter vacation, here are the basics:

Ski Areas

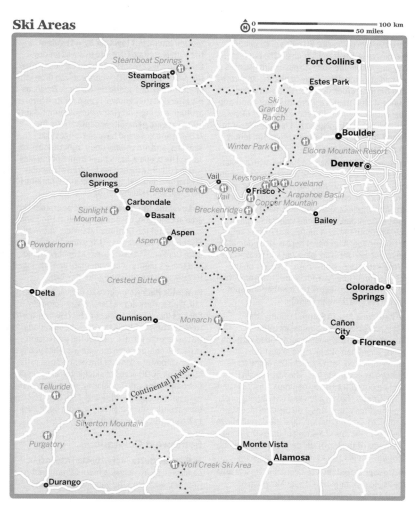

➡ **Vail & Beaver Creek** Vail is one of the largest ski resorts in the US, with 5289 skiable acres, 193 trails and three terrain parks. It lacks the downtown cohesion of Aspen or Telluride, as this is classic plaza-style resort development, but for sheer variety and thrills Vail is top-notch. What makes it really special are the back bowls – more than 4000 of the acres are on the back side of Vail Mountain with postcard views. The drawback has always been expense. Historically, Vail has angled to be the most expensive lift ticket in Colorado (often out-pricing Aspen by $1), and lodging doesn't come cheap either, but at least your ticket is also good at four other resorts, including nearby Beaver Creek. Beginners love Beaver Creek because the mountain is upside down, with easier runs at the top of the mountain plus great views. But there's plenty of expert terrain, including a World Cup downhill course.

➡ **Aspen & Around** With celebrity glitter, a historic downtown core and some of the best skiing in the state, Aspen is a terrific choice for those with a padded budget. One lift ticket grants access to the Four Mountains. Aspen and Aspen Highlands (the locals' under-the-radar choice) don't offer much for beginners, but there's plenty of upside-down-steep black terrain here. Snowmass is the biggest, and some say the best, of the bunch, with over 3000 acres, three terrain parks and 60 miles of groomed Nordic trails. Buttermilk is easily the best beginner hill in the state. Cross-country skiers should also make their way to historic Ashcroft and the Pine Creek Cookhouse. Down valley, Sunlight Mountain is a great little mom-and-pop resort that will save you some lift-ticket bucks, but still get you into some fun terrain. Closer to Grand Junction, Powderhorn offers fun family skiing at cheaper prices.

➡ **Breckenridge** Closer to Denver, with a jewel-box historic downtown and a ski resort spanning four luscious mountains covering 2900 acres, Breckenridge offers great atmosphere. Beginner and intermediate skiers have some of the best runs in Colorado. Advanced skiers have plenty to rave about too, and there's a state-of-the-art superpipe. A lift ticket here is also good at Keystone and A-Basin, plus Vail and Beaver Creek with a 3-day-plus pass. Also, it's on the free Summit County–wide public transportation system. Breckenridge is the number-one spot for partying in Summit County.

➡ **Keystone** Also in Summit County, the Keystone ski area encompasses three mountains of 3148 skiable acres laced with 135 trails, about half of which are expert runs. It's family-oriented, with almost 20% of the trails classed as beginner runs. The A51 Terrain Park is decked out with an array of jumps, jibs, rails and a superpipe. There's a fun and easy tubing area – perfect for young kids – on Dercum Mountain, and a CAT system that will take the daring above the lifts to the lips of a string of Black Diamond bowl runs at the top of the park. It's also the only Summit County resort to offer night skiing.

➡ **Copper Mountain** A self-contained resort area that's ideal for families, Copper Mountain has 2450 acres of skiable terrain accessed by 22 lifts and carved by 125 trails that are almost equally divided among beginners, intermediate, advanced and expert. There are 15-plus miles of groomed Nordic tracks, a tubing hill and free transportation to Keystone and Breckenridge. There's only a small village here, so eating and nightlife are somewhat limited – but it's made up for with consistently steep terrain that rides great.

➡ **Cooper** Cooper has one of the cheaper lift tickets in the state, plus a snowcat operation that takes you to some low-inclined hero-level powder. It's located just a few miles from the historic town of Leadville.

➡ **Arapahoe Basin** One of two day-use ski areas in the Central Mountains; locals dig

Arapahoe Basin because the lack of lodging and dining options keeps package tourists to a minimum. Put together by veterans of the 10th Mountain Division, this was among Colorado's first resorts. The top lift gets you to the summit (13,059ft), where you can drop into Montezuma Bowl on the back side. A-Basin, as it's affectionately known, is also for its irreverent attitude and big-partying ways. Summit County lift tickets are generally accepted here, too. A-Basin and Loveland have the longest ski seasons, and are usually open from October to June. The scene is at its peak from April to May – when other resorts have tapered off, people are barbecuing and suntanning in the parking lot here, between slushy spring ski runs.

➡ **Loveland Ski Area** The oldest operating ski area in Colorado, Loveland opened in 1943 and is set against the Continental Divide, above the Eisenhower Tunnel on I-70. It's only 56 miles from Denver, lift tickets are reasonably priced and there's plenty of intermediate and advanced terrain, with limited variety for newbies.

➡ **Winter Park** Connected to Denver by rail, Winter Park draws Denver and Colorado Springs locals, who flock here for down-to-earth weekend powder. It's a favorite of Coloradans, with awesome terrain without the pretension – expect to charge some mogul runs while you are here, as they are some of the best bumps in the state. The 3000 acres of skiable terrain occupy five mountains with some very steep chutes, but have limited open-bowl skiing. There are also six terrain parks serving all levels, from beginners to X Games–caliber talent.

Southwest Colorado

➡ **Crested Butte** Tucked behind Aspen (but separated by impassable mountains in winter), Crested Butte isn't the biggest resort in the state, but it is one of the best. Come here if you want a more casual, Western feel, because the town is downright adorable. It also boasts some of the best scenery: surrounded by forests and rugged mountain peaks in the West Elk and Maroon Bells Wilderness Areas, the landscape is mind-boggling. Way out of the way for day-trippers, it doesn't get heavy traffic. The mountain's 1167 acres are mostly geared toward expert skiers, with some of Colorado's sickest big-mountain terrain. Down low, intermediates will find something fun here.

➡ **Monarch** While there's no town attached, Monarch is a great little mountain, with good hike-to terrain up top. Locals love it because the lift still runs slow, the runs are still empty and the spirit of freedom still pervades this small resort with little pretension.

➡ **Telluride** Believe the stellar reviews – the quality of skiing at Telluride is truly world-class. The steep, fast, north-facing runs are the main reason it has an experts-only reputation, but there are some moderate trails, too, particularly in the Gorrono Basin. The best runs for non-experts are the aptly named See Forever and Lookout runs, both of which are graceful glides with panoramic views. For a bit more adrenaline, try the West Drain run. The Telluride Nordic Center can set up experienced cross-country skiers for a multiday backcountry trip between Telluride and Ouray along the San Juan Hut System.

➡ **Wolf Creek** Located 25 miles north of Pagosa Springs on US 160, this family-owned ski area is one of Colorado's last and best-kept secrets. It generally gets the biggest powder dumps in all the state. It's still mostly a locals' place that isn't overrun with the out-of-state crowd and covered with high-end boutiques, and it can be an awesome place to ride, with waist-high powder after a big storm. Seven lifts service 70 trails, from wide-open bowls to steep tree glades.

➡ **Silverton.** Only big-mountain skiers need apply at Colorado's most renegade ski area. There's just one lift here. In season, a guide takes you through the resort's massive uncharted runs, with requisite hikes about 12,000ft on most runs. A helicopter services the well-heeled set, but you can get into some serious fun on all the steeper-than-most-people-want-to-ski terrain. Skiers here travel with avalanche beacon, probe and shovel.

➡ **Purgatory**. This is popular with students from Durango, and gets plenty of deep snow.

Slope Grades

Ski and snowboard terrain is graded and signed with shapes and colors. Pay attention so you don't get in over your head.

➡ **Green (circle)** Beginner runs are called 'greenies' or 'bunny slopes.' This is where you learn and build your skills.

➡ **Blue (square)** Intermediate runs.

➡ **Blue/Black (blue square with a black diamond)** Intermediate to advanced. Must be confident and experienced.

➡ **Black Diamond** Advanced terrain.

➡ **Double Black Diamond** Expert skiers and riders only. Don't be a hero unless you are one.

➡ **Yellow (oval)** Freestyle. Used to designate terrain parks.

Cycling & Mountain Biking

There's a reason US Olympic cyclists train here. It would take a lifetime to ride every mile of Colorado's paved paths, fire roads and singletrack, not to mention the terrific road-riding that can be had on the state's numerous scenic byways and thin-air mountain passes. Ski resorts offer jumps, bermed-out mountain-bike trails and downhill riding with lift service.

Mountain cycling is so epic that you can ride on dedicated bike paths from Glenwood Springs to Aspen, and from Vail to Breckenridge. Gondolas, buses and even Lake Dillon ferries are all outfitted to tote bikes. These mountains have inspired grueling 100-mile bike races in Leadville and summer racing seasons throughout the state. They've also prompted many locals to ditch the car, shave their legs and go full-body spandex. The point is, in Colorado cycling is more than exercise – it's lifestyle.

In cities like Denver, Boulder and Fort Collins, you will find hundreds of miles of dedicated bike trails, plus a bike-friendly culture that includes shared bike programs, plenty of bike lanes and even the occasional cruiser ride.

In summer, annual bike tours such as Bicycle Tour of Colorado offer supported cycling through scenic routes for a week or more. It's ideal for cyclists who want a challenge but also the camaraderie of an enthusiastic group.

Rental rides are available in most big cities and major resort areas, with high-end road and mountain bikes generally on offer. Mountain-biking enthusiasts should pick up a copy of *The Mountain Biker's Guide to Colorado* (2012) by Dan Hickstein.

Where to Cycle

It would take too long to list every worthy path and route in this bike-friendly state. Summer sees many ski resorts wave goodbye to the snow set and say hello to the two-wheelers.

➡ **Around Grand Junction** The mix of flat roads and wineries is a tempting combination; some of the USA's best singletrack trails are near Fruita.

➡ **Crested Butte** Singletrack routes and amazing scenery in one of the birthplaces of mountain biking? Check and check.

ADVENTURE HIGHLIGHTS

ACTIVITY	LOCATION	DESCRIPTION	CONTACT
Ski touring & mountain biking	San Juan Mountain Range	Linked by trails in the gorgeous San Juans, these mountain huts between Telluride and Moab, Utah, are ideal for multiday adventures.	www.sanjuanhuts.com
Mountain biking	Buffalo Creek Mountain Bike Area	Some of the nation's best mountain-bike trails are just an hour from Denver, near great roadside camping.	www.frmbp.org
Rafting	Arkansas River	Colorado's top white-water river runs past Buena Vista, Salida and the Royal Gorge.	www.buffalojoe.com
Horseback riding	South Park	Platte Ranch offers guests a bona fide cowboy experience, with rides through open country on a working ranch.	719-836-1670
Rock & ice climbing	Ridgway	Elite women climbers teach renowned climbing courses for women of all abilities, climbing ice in winter and rocks in summer.	www.chickswithpicks.net
Hiking	Chautauqua Park	In Boulder, enjoy scenic foothill hikes or don climbing gear to get to the top of the third Flatiron.	http://bouldercolorado.gov/parks-rec/chautauqua-park
Backpacking	Mt Zirkel Wilderness	Trek peak to peak in this beautiful, lost wilderness area near Steamboat.	www.fs.usda.gov
Fishing	Fryingpan River	A fly-fishing paradise upstream from Basalt.	www.taylorcreek.com
Climbing	Rocky Mountain National Park	Break through the clouds on a guided alpine climbing adventure.	www.totalclimbing.com
Ski touring	State Forest State Park	Head to this remote park that sports its own supercool system of yurts and cabins.	www.neversummernordic.com
Rafting	Colorado River	The upper reaches of the state's namesake river outside Glenwood Springs provide plenty of excitement.	www.upthacreek.com

ACTIVITY	LOCATION	DESCRIPTION	CONTACT
Fishing	Arkansas River	Downstream from Salida you'll find up to 5000 trout per mile and plenty of public access.	www.arkanglers.com
Rafting	Cache la Poudre River	One of Colorado's most pristine river habitats also sports some kick-ass rapids.	www.coloradorafting.org

➡ **Salida** Epic rides year-round. Check out the Rainbow Trail, Monarch Crest Trail and 'S' mountain that bears down on town.

➡ **Central Mountains** This whole region is home to one of the state's best networks of paved bike paths. Great rides extend from Breckenridge, Keystone, Vail and Frisco. Everything you could want is here: road, tracks and gravel.

➡ **Denver** A cyclist's city, complete with bike-share program, bike-friendly public transportation and plenty of paths.

➡ **Boulder** Possibly more bike-crazed than Denver: paths and cycling lanes lead to virtually everywhere in town and beyond.

➡ **Fort Collins** A bike museum is spread across the whole town; jumping on a fixie is the way to get around here.

➡ **Buffalo Creek** This is one of the state's premier spots for mountain biking.

Rock Climbing & Mountaineering

Colorado climbing runs the gamut, from serious alpine-style mountain ascents to 14,000ft and gnarly traditional rock climbing up granite domes to sport-climbing adventures on pocketed limestone. In addition to a wealth of granite, sandstone and even limestone cliffs and outcrops, there are also many rock-climbing gyms, walls and outdoor bouldering parks – all the better to hone the skills for when you're ready to get serious. All the gyms offer instruction and plenty of outfitters offer intensive multiday clinics for newbies and those wishing to refine their skills, along with the equipment you need to stay safe on rock and ice.

Where to Climb
Around Boulder & Denver

Boulder's sticky Flatirons offer scores of classic routes. In fact there are 1145 rock-climbing routes in the Boulder area, with the majority found in the Flatirons (with walls up to 900ft high), Boulder Canyon and Eldorado Canyon, a spectacular site with dozens of 700ft climbs. There is decent climbing and bouldering outside of Denver by Morrison and in Clear Creek Canyon.

Northern Mountains

There are approximately dozens of climbing routes in Rocky Mountain National Park. Rock climbers won't want to miss Lumpy Ridge, while alpinists can take on serious ascents and leisurely walk-ups in the park's higher peaks, Horsetooth Reservoir near Fort Collins has some good bouldering.

Central Mountains

Camp Hale offers 22 climbing routes graded from 5.9 to 5.11c, and Independence Pass has 60 routes, including the intense bulge that is Bulldog Balcony. Buena Vista has great climbing at Elephant Rock and Bob's Rock off Tunnels Rd, and it has foam-core bouldering in its riverside park. There are thousands of climbs on the granite domes and spires in the South Platte area, between Conifer and 11 Mile Canyon, west of Colorado Springs. Rifle is one of the state's premier sport-climbing areas, with steep, pocketed climbs.

Southwest Colorado

Durango and Ouray are the stars of southwestern Colorado. Ouray Ice Park is a narrow slot canyon with 200ft walls and waterfalls frozen in thick sheets – perfect for ice-climbing. The mountains around here also offer tremendous alpine-style adventures. Colorado National Monument, near Grand Junction, has superb climbing in Unaweep Canyon and Monument Canyon, and you can climb in Black Canyon of the Gunnison National Park.

Southeast Colorado

All the best climbing in southern Colorado can be found on the limestone cliffs and pinnacles along Shelf Rd, near where the state's best early dinosaur finds were discovered. The Gallery, the Bank and the North End are the best sites.

Colorado Springs has a strict permit process for its top climbing destinations, Garden of the Gods and Red Rock Canyon. Penitente Canyon is a gorgeous canyon in the San Luis Valley with good sport climbs and even better camping.

Mountaineering

Unless you plan on tackling one of the estimated 161 technical high-altitude rock-climbing routes, mountaineering isn't necessary to bag peaks in Colorado. Intrepid mountaineers summit the fourteeners in the winter, a highly technical pursuit that requires training and proper gear (usually ice axe, crampons, snowshoes or backcountry skis, and avalanche gear), and cold-weather clothing. Cold climes can exacerbate the effects of altitude sickness and avalanches are a serious concern here. Most of the mountain areas have solid ice climbing.

Mt Elbert – Colorado's highest peak – is one of the least technical and avalanche-prone in winter. Longs Peak and Pikes Peak are also popular winter climbs that are reasonably low-risk (though that can change in a blink). The Maroon Bells, on the other hand, are as risky and technical as Colorado mountaineering gets. Bring a helmet for climbs with the risk of rock-fall (or person fall).

➡ **Summit Post** (www.summitpost.org) and **Mountain Project** (www.mountainproject.com) are solid online resources with basic climbing-route information, but getting proper maps and consulting with local ranger districts are a must, and guide services are always a good idea.

There are tons of backcountry skiing options in the state, including quick trips to mountain passes, or hut-to-hut skis. Climbers and skiers traveling in winter should take a beacon, shovel and probe; let people know where you are going and when you hope to be back; and consider the implications of solo travel.

Rafting, Paddling & Tubing

Colorado is one of the great paddling destinations, with a long white-water season lasting from late May until September. Everything from class I and II float trips to a raging class V can be yours on the state's rivers. The Arkansas River is the most-paddled body of water, with 150 miles of open water running from Leadville to the Royal Gorge. The run through Browns Canyon is arguably America's most iconic class-II run, while the Royal Gorge is one of the most scenic in the state, coming in at class III to V. The best Arkansas River paddling is in June and early July. July is a good time to move from group rafting trips into your own kayak.

You can take lessons just about anywhere in the state, including Fort Collins, Boulder or Denver, but the Rocky Mountain Outdoor Center in Salida has better scenery. The class III Blue River runs through Breckenridge in the heart of Summit County in the early season. Vail's Eagle River is a nice high-country early-season run, while the class V Gore Canyon on the Colorado offers up some of Colorado's biggest white water. Other classic Colorado River runs include Shoshone (class III), and easy, family-friendly float trips out of Kremmling. The Dolores River in southwest Colorado threads through the San Juan Mountains, past Anasazi ruins and petroglyphs, with a short, dam-controlled season; it makes a beautiful multiday trip. The Cache la Poudre River offers class II to V white water and is easily accessed from Fort Collins. Elk River Runs are a fun excursion from Steamboat.

White-water parks are found throughout the state, including parks in Boulder, Denver, Fort Collins, Buena Vista and Cañon City. Tubing is a popular summer pastime on Boulder Creek, on the Poudre River in Fort Collins, in Denver's Confluence Park, on the Yampa in Steamboat Springs and in Pagosa Springs. Think about using a helmet and life jacket when tubing – there are no lifeguards on duty.

Although Colorado isn't primarily a land of lakes, there are fun lakes and reservoirs throughout the state that will make canoeing, motor-boating or pontoon-boating a blast. Some top spots include Grand Lake, Steamboat Reservoir, 11 Mile Reservoir, Lake Dillon, Pueblo Reservoir, Boulder Reservoir and Rampart Reservoir.

People are also now running rivers and paddling lakes throughout Colorado on Stand-Up Paddleboards (SUPs). You can rent them at most kayak and rafting outfitters throughout the state.

Plan Your Trip

Rocky Mountains Road Trips & Scenic Drives

Colorado has 26 nationally designated Scenic & Historic Byways, as well as a number of mind-blowing drives that didn't make the official list, but should definitely make yours. Some will take all day and have you contemplating the passage of time; others are short hops to lonely mountain passes that are sure to leave you speechless but smiling. For road conditions consult www.codot.gov.

Cottonwood Pass

➡ 60 miles

Why Go?

Passing through spectacular country, Cottonwood Pass Rd alternates between asphalt and graded gravel (those sections are few and far between) as it winds its way for 60 miles to the fly-fishing mecca of Almont from the quaint and, dare we say, damn cute prison town (and paddler paradise) of Buena Vista.

For a fresh-air fix, it would be hard to beat this lesser-known nook of Colorado. The fly-fishing is paradisiacal and the high-country trails are shared with mountain goat herds.

The Route

In Buena Vista, W Main St becomes Cottonwood Pass Rd. It swerves past beaver ponds along Cottonwood Creek and skirts Cottonwood Hot Springs in the San Isabel National Forest. On the east side of the road is a turnoff to the Avalanche Trailhead, a spur of the Colorado Trail with

Drive Safely

Weather

➡ Go slower than posted speed limits in bad weather, particularly on I-70; multicar pileups are common.

➡ In winter, travel with snow tires or chains, ice scraper and emergency kit.

➡ Check for road closures and conditions at www.cotrip.org.

Wildlife & Cyclists

➡ Be careful driving at dawn and dusk, when wildlife is most active.

➡ To see wildlife, pull over – don't stop in the road.

➡ Always watch for cyclists, even on remote routes.

Colorado Driving Laws

➡ Cell phones can only be used by drivers with a hands-free device.

➡ Seat belts are mandatory for drivers and front-seat passengers.

➡ Helmets are not required for adults on motorcycles, but still recommended.

Rocky Mountain Driving Tours

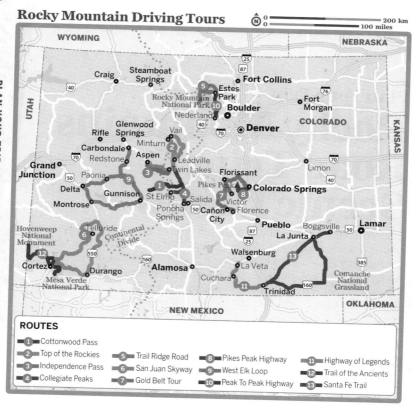

N 0 ⎯⎯⎯⎯ 200 km
0 ⎯⎯⎯⎯ 100 miles

ROUTES

1. Cottonwood Pass
2. Top of the Rockies
3. Independence Pass
4. Collegiate Peaks
5. Trail Ridge Road
6. San Juan Skyway
7. Gold Belt Tour
8. Pikes Peak Highway
9. West Elk Loop
10. Peak To Peak Highway
11. Highway of Legends
12. Trail of the Ancients
13. Santa Fe Trail

access to spectacular Collegiate Peaks Wilderness.

The road goes from moderately sinuous to downright jagged as you approach the edge of the timberline. To the east the Collegiate Peaks fan out against the blue sky as you drive through boulder-field moonscapes.

Bring a picnic and take a long lunch at the pass (p241) before dropping into the Gunnison National Forest and down through the Taylor River Canyon to Almont, where the Taylor and East Rivers form the mighty Gunnison. And if you've forgotten your rod and reel, check into the Almont Resort, which is located on Co 135 at the headwaters of the Gunnison River. They'll sort you out.

When to Go

The road is usually open from June to October.

Worth a Stop

Don't miss a soak in the creekside Cottonwood Hot Springs (p241) on the way up to the pass.

Top of the Rockies

➜ 115 miles

Why Go?

You'll cross three mountain passes, drop into four watersheds and glimpse Colorado's tallest peaks, as well as the headwaters of the Arkansas River. Not bad for a day's drive. Historic Leadville, the highest incorporated city in the US, made its name and plenty of cash in the silver boom. It is the hub of this drive, which can be done in two stages.

The Route

Start in Leadville. After a wander through the National Historic District (check out the Delaware Hotel), grab a slice at High Mountain Pies – the local favorite is usually packed. Head north from town on Hwy 91 over Fremont Pass before meeting up with I-70 near Copper Mountain.

Take the interstate west past Vail to Hwy 24, where if you time it right you can have a stroll through a terrific farmers market in downtown Minturn; drive through tiny Red Cliff, pay homage to the 10th Mountain Division, and perhaps get some rock climbing in at Camp Hale; before swerving up and over Tennessee Pass where Mt Massive looms supreme as you drive back through Leadville.

Further south, Mt Elbert dominates the horizon. Hang a right on Hwy 82 and head up to Twin Lakes, a historic mining town with some abandoned buildings on the lake shore, a couple of inns, spectacular mountain and lake views and countless stars. Bed down here or drive up and over Independence Pass (p224) and into Aspen (summer only).

When to Go

Roads are open year-round, with the least advantageous time being 'mud season' (April to June), when ski resorts and some of their infrastructure closes and weather hovers between winter and warmth.

Detour

If you've had fourteeners on the brain, why not top one of the state's two tallest peaks? Trailheads for both Mt Elbert (p247) and Mt Massive (p247) are easily accessible from this route.

Twin Lakes through Aspen's back gate will do just fine.

The Route

To call Twin Lakes a town is a bit of a stretch – this former mining camp was fed by steady stagecoach lines plying the trail between Leadville and Aspen – but it is a worthy destination in its own right. If you're here late in the season, you'll see camo-clad hunters, last-gasp family vacationers, Harley men and women and their hogs with bedrolls on the tailgate, and decked-out road cyclists with shaved legs and iPhones in their saddlebags.

Drive up a narrow ribbon of road above the tree line. Views are cinematic and spectacular – swatches of glacier are visible along the ridges of Twin Peaks. Tundra blooms at the top of the pass, where at 12,095ft you'll be on the edge of the Continental Divide. This, friends, is your own IMAX film.

As Hwy 82 continues over the pass, the views are just as marvelous, and multimillion-dollar properties begin to dot the landscape as you edge toward Aspen (one of them belongs to Kevin Costner).

When to Go

Although the pass is closed in winter (November to late May), you can still usually get up to the vast Twin Lakes, where the cross-country skiing and snowshoeing is magnificent.

Detour

If you have time, there's a terrific trail to the Interlaken, an old hotel, long since abandoned, that was fashionable in the 1890s. The trail leaves from the lower of the Twin Lakes.

Independence Pass

➡ 27.2 miles

Why Go?

You'll see plenty of old mining ruins and blow-your-mind views. If you don't have time to drive the entire Top of the Rockies route, this stretch of Hwy 82 from

Collegiate Peaks

➡ 57 miles

Why Go?

This is the essence of Colorado: stark and soaring granite cliffs, multiple 14,000ft peaks, geothermal hot springs, the powerful Arkansas River and a bit of ghost-town history, too.

The Route

The Collegiate Peaks Byway begins where the Top of the Rockies route ends, at Twin Lakes on Hwy 82, just below Independence Pass.

If you haven't yet explored the mining camp ruins at Twin Lakes, they're worth a look before you get on the road and head east on Hwy 82 to Hwy 24. Mt Yale will be the first of the Collegiate Peaks (part of the Sawatch Range) to reveal itself as you head into Buena Vista, a town that is absolutely worth your time. Ostensibly it's a prison town, but it's also recently become a magnet for groovy entrepreneurs who have opened restaurants, cafes, coffee roasters and even a distillery. Rock climbing and plenty of paddling are accessible from Main St and there are even some lovely campsites off Tunnels Rd.

From here the official byway advises you to stay on Hwy 24 out of town. We beg to differ: instead, drive west on County Rd 306 from the center of town for 0.7 miles. Turn left on County Rd 321 and continue south for 7.2 miles. Turn right onto County Rd 322, drive 0.8 miles to a fork in the road. Bear right and you'll be on Mt Princeton Rd, which will take you to the sprawling Mt Princeton Hot Springs Resort, at the base of magnificent Mt Princeton. Whether you choose to dip into the hot water by the river or scramble up into the mountains is a question only you can answer.

You could also continue from the gates of the resort up County Rd 162 to St Elmo, an old abandoned gold-mining town. The road narrows as it runs further up the canyon, with the river flowing by and towering mountains laid out on both sides. The remaining buildings were built in and around 1881.

From St Elmo make your way east again toward Hwy 285, and the historic districts of Poncha Springs and Salida, also the gateway to the wild and scenic Arkansas River. From there, there is 99 miles of Arkansas River paddling all the way to the Royal Gorge. Salida is also a great place to slip into a kayak for the first time.

When to Go

You can do most of the drive, except for St Elmo, year-round, though springtime is mud season and not the best time to explore the trails.

Worth a Stop

On the way back to the Mt Princeton resort from St Elmo, you'll pass Love Meadow (p241). Once a pioneer homestead belonging to an impressive woman widowed in her youth, it's now a small, beautiful wildlife sanctuary.

Trail Ridge Road

➡ 47 miles

Why Go?

This is the highest continuously paved through road in North America, so expect outrageous views. Few roads that get up this high are in such good condition, and exploring tundra trails spotted with wildflowers without having to hike up to this altitude is a treat.

The Route

The signature drive in Rocky Mountain National Park, Trail Ridge Road (p138) (Hwy 34) crosses over the Continental Divide in a series of switchbacks. On the drive from Estes Park to Grand Lake, you'll see snowcapped peaks, meandering streams, high-country meadows dotted with wildflowers in midsummer and, with luck, some wildlife too.

Archaeological evidence collected here suggests that humans transited this way for 6000 years. This former trade route was used by generations of Ute, Arapaho and Apache to traverse Milner Pass. Trail Ridge Road was originally surveyed in 1927 but not completed until 1932.

When to Go

Trail Ridge Road opens in late May and is closed at Many Parks Curve on the east

---

CURIOUS COLORADO

America's tallest sand dune is found in Great Sand Dunes National Park (p332), a bizarre desertscape of 700ft sand peaks.

TOP TUNES FOR COLORADO ROAD-TRIPPING

Colorado's highways and back roads mix asphalt and gravel, and hairpin turns with fast flats and deep canyons – a sensory journey enhanced with just the right tunes.

Colorado natives The state's indie acts are on the rise: listen to the Lumineers, Tennis, OneRepublic, and Nathaniel Rateliff and the Nightsweats, among other big groups.

Aspen-inspired Bounce between Rufus Wainwright, banjo legend Béla Fleck, Lake Street Dive and the Roots, all performers at the Aspen Music Festival and Jazz Aspen Snowmass.

Bluegrass The high-and-lonesome sound is a natural fit in the mountains. Local groups play at markets and brewpubs, and there are multiple bluegrass festivals in the state, including the biggie in Telluride. Yonder Mountain String Band, Paper Bird and Elephant Revival are among the best-known homegrown musicians.

Willie Nelson The country legend wrote the songs on *Red Headed Stranger*, arguably his greatest record, while on a road trip through Colorado in 1975. It's as native to this rugged country as the aspens themselves.

Jam Bands Get in the groove with Big Head Todd and the Monsters, the String Cheese Incident and the much-loved but now defunct Psychodelic Zombiez.

side by mid-October. You're more likely to see dramatic snowy scenery in May, when the pass first opens.

Worth a Stop

Before driving into the park, stop by the Stanley Hotel (p147) in Estes Park, the inspiration for Stephen King's *The Shining*.

Detour

Consider a 9-mile detour up the original Fall River Road (p138), where you're likely to spot elk outside the Alpine Visitor Center.

San Juan Skyway

➡ 236 miles

Why Go?

Among the USA's best drives, the San Juan Skyway is a 236-mile loop which includes the so-called Million Dollar Highway, a handful of the region's coolest mountain towns and Mesa Verde National Park.

It's undoubtedly the best way to experience the drama of the San Juan range without strapping on your boots. Drive the Skyway and the tension of the daily grind gets lost somewhere among the towering peaks, picturesque towns and old mines around each bend, or evaporates in the bright sun of an intensely blue Colorado sky.

The Route

The climb on Hwys 62 and 145 skirts the biggest of the San Juans before you enter Telluride, preferably in time for some morning thrills on the slopes of the ski resort. If you're traveling in summer, climb on a mountain bike instead of the skis – just as fun and way cheaper. Grab lunch at the Butcher & The Baker (p265) and enjoy a bit more of the hills before pointing the car south for Cortez, where you should follow with dinner at lively Southwestern restaurant Pepperhead (p259).

Take a ranger-guided tour of the Cliff Palace in Mesa Verde National Park (p251), before you hit the road for Durango. Depart on the Durango & Silverton Narrow Gauge Railroad (p374) for a fascinating trip into the mineral-rich heart of the mountains.

Now you choose your own adventure: either continue north along the Million Dollar Highway to Ouray to end the San Juan Skyway loop, or head east to catch a surreal sunset over at Great Sand Dunes National Park (p332).

When to Go

Aspen trees glow in late September or early October. The Million Dollar Highway section between Silverton and Ouray may close in winter; chains are required and RVs (recreational vehicles) are not permitted at any time.

Gold Belt Tour

➡ 131 miles

Why Go?

Explore old mining haunts, petrified tree stumps (they're cooler than you think), the Royal Gorge, dinosaur footprints and galleries. In between you'll glimpse a long and wide mountain plateau with all the country romance of a Willie Nelson tune.

The Route

From Colorado Springs, take Hwy 24 past Pikes Peak and Manitou Springs into the high country, where you'll find Florissant Fossil Beds National Monument (p320). The entire area was once buried beneath ancient volcanic ash. A nature trail leads past sequoia-sized petrified stumps, and the surrounding countryside is special, too. While you're here consider stopping by the Hornbeck House, a 1878 homestead.

Between 1891 and 2005 more than 23.5 million ounces of gold were pulled from this mountain corridor – more gold than was ever found during the California and Alaska gold rushes *combined*. Most of the gold was mined in the twin cities of Cripple Creek and Victor. Both have seen better days. Cripple Creek is now a low-rent gambling destination with a strip mine still active above town, but the Cripple Creek & Victor Narrow Gauge Railroad (p321) is a treat. This 45-minute tour leads to Victor and back and includes many an old mining yarn. The views are marvelous. Cripple Creek also offers tours through an actual underground mine and a unique jailhouse museum.

From here you can travel south through the high-country meadows ringed with mountains along High Park Rd, which leads to Hwy 50 and the stunning Royal Gorge. The Royal Gorge Bridge & Park (p318) has historic kitsch and incredibly impressive views. Or you could take the slow journey along the graded Shelf Road (p319), a one-time stagecoach route. There is some fantastic rock climbing in the area and it's also where you'll find the Garden Park Fossil Area (p318), which once gave the world five new dinosaur species. Cañon City has some charm in its own right, along with easily arranged train and raft tours of the gorge.

When to Go

Summer is the best time to explore the high country and take in a rafting trip.

Detour

Not far from Cañon City, Florence blossoms with vintage, antique and found-art galleries, and the fabulous Florence Rose B&B (p320) is here, too. You can take the scenic Phantom Canyon Road (p319) directly from Victor to Florence.

Pikes Peak Highway

➡ 38 miles

Why Go?

Climbing a fourteener is a Colorado rite of passage, and who knows? Driving it might give you inspiration to take on the next one on your own two feet. On clear days you can look down on four states.

The Route

From Colorado Springs take US 24 west to the Pikes Peak Hwy/Toll Rd. First you'll skirt knife-edge drops into the valley below as Manitou Springs and Old Colorado City become scattered specks in the distance, then you'll roll through thick stands of pine and cedar and finally scree fields. You can thank eccentric tycoon Spencer Penrose for this luscious ribbon of surprisingly sound asphalt that winds up and up and up to the tippy (flat) top of Pikes Peak (p321). After Penrose built the road, he christened it with the first ever Pikes Peak International Hill Climb, a car race that still runs each June.

Before you embark on your journey make sure your brakes and tires are sound and remember that at altitude your car will have about half the horsepower it usually does. When driving back down, do so in a low gear. The Pikes Peak Hwy/Toll Rd is accessed via Manitou Springs (a fine place to have lunch, stroll and shop afterwards); it costs $50 per car (up to five people).

When to Go

The road is open most of the year, though it's sometimes closed during the winter.

Detour

After you get back into the flats, stop for a drink at the Broadmoor (p314), where you can experience Penrose's game-changing resort and one of the earliest tourist draws to Colorado.

West Elk Loop

➡ 205 miles

Why Go?

This gorgeous, six- to eight-hour lasso loop is pinned down by the twin summits of Mt Sopris on one end and the spectacular Black Canyon of the Gunnison on the other. In between are historic gold-mining towns, two mountain passes, the mountain-bike mecca of Crested Butte and glamorous Aspen.

The Route

Redstone, on Hwy 133, is famous for its coke ovens used to process coal; the historic town is a pleasant stroll, too. From here you'll navigate McClure Pass through 35 miles of stunning mountain scenery before descending along the North Fork River into Paonia, a quirky town with the Grand Mesa on one side, Mt Lamborn on the other, a coal mine and a green streak. The Victorian buildings in downtown's 10-block historic district are as cool as the locals.

Head south on 92 West Hwy through Delta and you'll see the stark, spectacular Black Canyon of the Gunnison National Park (p292), a 2000ft-deep gorge with outstanding hiking trails and rock climbing. From here the route follows Hwy 50 east to Gunnison from where you'll loop around on Hwy 135 into Crested Butte, the wildflower capital of Colorado, with a re-

stored Victorian core and looming Crested Butte Mountain, an awesome bike and ski destination. Next, take Hwy 12 over Kebler Pass and then head north on Hwy 133 to funky, progressive Carbondale.

When to Go

In summer, exuberant wildflower patches around Crested Butte are second to none. Kebler Pass closes in winter.

Detour

If Crested Butte sucks you in, overnight at the Inn at Crested Butte (p290) and wake up early the next day for a hike into the nearby Maroon Bells-Snowmass Wilderness Area (p224), one of the most dramatically beautiful wilderness areas in all of Colorado.

Peak to Peak Highway

➡ 55 miles

Why Go?

The Peak to Peak Highway is one of Colorado's most scenic drives and an excellent option for the trip between Rocky Mountain National Park and Denver or Boulder. This north–south route takes you past a series of breathtaking mountains (including the 14,255ft Longs Peak), alpine valleys and open meadows, passing one-horse towns along the way.

The Route

You can start in Estes Park, near Rocky Mountain National Park, and head south to Nederland, just west of Boulder, or do the route in reverse. Along the way are little mountain hamlets. These include Ward, a former boom town and bohemian magnet that has settled into an artfully ramshackle state of disrepair; Peaceful Valley, notable for its little onion-domed church perched on a hillside; and several other tiny towns with expansive mountain vistas.

There are national forest campgrounds near Peaceful Valley and Allenspark, as well as the Longs Peak Campground (p143), part of Rocky Mountain National Park. There are also places to stay in

HAYESEEN/GETTY IMAGES ©

Top: Cottonwood Pass (p41)

Bottom: Trail Ridge Road (p44)

Peaceful Valley, Ferncliff, Allenspark and south of Estes Park, mostly in the form of lodges, cabins and B&Bs. Before arriving in Nederland there's access to excellent hiking in the Indian Peaks Wilderness (p134) via Brainard Lake.

At the southern end of the trip, the Peak to Peak Highway starts from Nederland, Boulder's hippie holdout with a few cool cafes. Although most of the route – everything north of Allenspark – follows Hwy 7, at Nederland it follows Hwy 72.

When to Go

Accessible year-round. In summer, watch big cumulus clouds rolling lazily over the green and granite peaks. In fall, the aspens turn the hillsides gold, while winter brings a stark white landscape.

Detour

To stretch your legs along the way, take the road opposite the turnoff for Ward that leads up to Brainard Lake. The lake itself is small but enjoys a gorgeous setting and there are several great trails up into the high country. Stop in at the Millsite Inn, just north of the turnoff to Ward. The food is nothing special, but it's an interesting place for a bite and a beer, with plenty of local color, like local rock bands that channel 1971.

Highway of Legends

➡ 110 miles

Why Go?

This brief but epic detour liberates you from the interstate and escorts you through some of Colorado's most glorious countryside. It's a welcome detour from I-25 if you are headed north to Pueblo, Colorado Springs or Denver. If you're already privy to the majesty of the Spanish Peaks Wilderness, welcome home.

The Route

Your trip begins in Trinidad, where present-day Main St was once an important limb of the Santa Fe Trail. The Trinidad History Museum offers a primer, and while you're in town drop into Danielson Dry

Goods for some road sustenance. Coal mining was also an important part of Trinidad's history. You'll see a 'canary in the coal mine' statue on Main St, which is where Mother Jones once marched with miners during the strike that led to the Ludlow Massacre, a turning point in US labor relations.

From Trinidad take Hwy 12 through Cokedale, where you'll see 350 coal ovens on the roadside (they look almost Roman), then head up and over majestic Cucharas Pass and into Cuchara.

Dominated by extinct volcanoes, the Spanish Peaks, and Great Dikes that jut from meadows to mountains, this place is magic. The rambling Cucharas River has terrific fishing, the Dog Bar & Grill serves tasty pizza and occasional live music, and the hiking in the Spanish Peaks Wilderness (p328) is some of the best in the state. You can extend the nature bliss by veering east on a recently added extension to the byway.

County Rd 46 weaves through the San Isabel National Forest for 35 miles to Aguilar on the I-25, but we suggest staying on Hwy 12, which continues down the valley and into exceptionally cute La Veta, where there are more churches than paved roads, and the Spanish Peaks make for a spectacular backdrop as you check in to La Veta Inn (p329).

When to Go

The route is open year-round but it's especially nice in spring; while winter still lingers in the high country it's warmer here.

Worth a Stop

On your way down Hwy 12 from La Veta toward the I-25, stop at the excellent mining museum (p328) in Walsenburg before heading north.

Trail of the Ancients

➡ 135 miles

Why Go?

Explore the canyons, mountains and plains once inhabited by Ancestral Puebloans, with all of their mystery intact. This road trip connects Mesa Verde with Canyon

COLORADO EXTREME

North America's highest paved road reaches 14,258ft at the summit of Mt Evans. It's open only in summer. Take exit 240 off I-70 from Idaho Springs.

of the Ancients and Hovenweep National Monuments, and also wanders down to the Four Corners state boundaries.

The Route

Start at Mesa Verde National Park (p251), the true highlight of the itinerary. There are over 5000 archaeological sites within the 52,073 protected acres, including 600 Ancestral Puebloan cliff dwellings.

From Mesa Verde, take Hwy 145 north to Dolores through a windswept high desert landscape of cracked red earth, coyotes and sagebrush. Stop at the Anasazi Heritage Center (p260), where you can peruse more ancient artifacts, including pottery from AD 400.

Leave Dolores via Hwy 184 West and take Hwy 491 south to Cortez, where County Road G takes you to McElmo Canyon (continue on the same county road for Hovenweep). In McElmo Canyon you can stay at Kelly Place (p258), with kivas and private trails to ruins, and visit nearby Guy Drew Vineyard (p257) for a taster. Next stop, Canyon of the Ancients and Hovenweep National Monuments (p258): both are Ancestral Puebloan treasures that have been largely left alone for hundreds of years. These trails are so solitary, you can almost hear spirit-guide whispers on the wind.

Another branch of the byway leads southwest from Mesa Verde on Hwy 491 and then Hwy 160 to the actual Four Corners state boundaries.

When to Go

These roads are open year-round, but if you plan on doing a lot of hiking, they're best avoided in July and August, the hottest months.

Detour

To explore something more rugged, detour from Mesa Verde and head southwest of Cortez to Ute Mountain Tribal Park (p260), which houses a number of lesser-known ruins. Access to the park is possible only with the accompaniment of a Ute guide. Half- and full-day tours can include visits to their adjacent reservation. In addition to the cliff dwellings, original pottery is prevalent; you may even see shards along the trails.

From the state line you can continue your journey on Utah's Trail of the Ancients Byway or head to other Ancestral Puebloan treasures such as Chaco Canyon in New Mexico or Canyon de Chelly in Arizona.

Santa Fe Trail

➜ 285 miles

Why Go?

History buffs will love this day-long spin through southeastern Colorado. Although the official byway follows the original trail for 188 miles from the Kansas border into Trinidad, you can cut the route down to its best bits and make it a fun four-hour journey.

The Route

An endless prairie unfurls on both sides of the open two-lane highway as you take Hwy 350 northeast of Trinidad to La Junta. The scenery is all grasslands and wheat fields, sugar-beet farms, horse corrals and railroad yards. One of the best parts of driving the Santa Fe Trail is this countryside.

The signature sight is Bent's Old Fort National Historic Site (p325). Set just north of the Arkansas River – the natural and official border between the US and Old Mexico until 1846 – the fort was once a cultural crossroads. From 1833 to 1849 Native Americans, Mexicans, Europeans and Americans met, mingled, traded, danced and clashed here. The well-restored adobe fort has a blacksmith's shop, wood shop and fully stocked general store. Knowledgeable staff in period clothing lead tours and a 1-mile trail runs around the fort to the edge of the Arkansas River and back to the parking lot.

Kit Carson frequented the fort, but his last base of operations and final resting

Hovenweep National Monument (p258)

place is about 16 miles east of here in Boggsville. If time is short, skip Boggsville, turn back at the fort, and head west again into more history.

You'll want to stop at Iron Spring, where you can see authentic Santa Fe Trail wagon ruts and, if daylight is on your side and you've made an advance reservation, you can drive to the famed Picketwire Dinosaur Tracksite (p325), where dinosaur footprints are frozen in time. Both sites are in the Comanche National Grassland (p330).

When the Santa Fe Trail brings you back to Main St in Trinidad, don't forget to stop at the fabulous Trinidad History Museum (p329) to round out the journey.

When to Go

You can take this trip year-round.

Detour

If you have time there are two sites further east of Bent's Old Fort that shed light on the USA's dark side. Westward expansion made the USA, but it meant misery for many. The Sand Creek Massacre National Historic Site (p325), just off the Santa Fe Trail north of Lamar, was a pivotal point in US–Native American relations – an estimated 163 of Chief Black Kettle's Cheyenne people were massacred here by Colorado Volunteers, after the Cheyenne encamped in this desolate land in compliance with a recently introduced American law. The event ended the Indian Wars and paved the way for further white settlement in Colorado and beyond.

South of Lamar are the ruins of Camp Amache (p326), a World War II Japanese internment camp.

Food trucks, Denve

Plan Your Trip

Eat & Drink Like a Local

Colorado dining is all grown up. The meat-and-potatoes of yesterday is being replaced by quaint bistros, world cuisine and other experimental endeavors. And lucky for you, a few Mom-and-Pop shops still stick around to offer up good old Americana. Some local delicacies include game dishes, Rocky Mountain Oysters (bull, pig or sheep testicles) and, of course, fresh-caught rainbow trout. Resort areas such as Vail and Aspen truly have some of the USA's best restaurants.

➡ **Mom-and-Pop Restaurants** In small-town Colorado, expect to find down-home family dining.

Where Cowboys Go For Steak

Jimmy's
A soulful tequila bar and steakhouse that draws an A-list crowd. (p233)

Elway's
Carve into pricey porterhouses at Denver's top steakhouse. (p89)

Juicy Lucy's Steakhouse
People love Lucy's for its well-cooked meat and small-town-cafe feel. (p219)

Sweet Basil
One of Vail's top restaurants, this eatery boasts eclectic American fare and fantastic ambience. (p209)

Blue Star
This landmark spot offers top-cut steaks, as well as fresh fish and inventive chicken dishes. (p316).

Briar Rose
On the site of Breckenridge's original saloon, this is the place to come for atmospheric fine dining. (p197)

The Lowdown

Some restaurants don't take reservations at all, while others will let you reserve for only large parties (a small minority allows for reservations for small groups). In general, Colorado dining is informal.

➡ **Fine Dining** Farm-to-table and sustainable eats are getting more play here, especially at upscale restaurants in Boulder, Denver and the mountain resort areas.

➡ **Food Trucks & Food Halls** Upstart chefs are taking it to the streets and trying out new recipes in Denver's thriving food halls; trucks are found statewide.

The Sustainable Table

The most interesting and tasty – and perhaps most overdue – movement in Colorado dining is the general drift toward high-end farm-to-table cuisine. It's been a grassroots movement inspired by a widening interest and dependency on fresh local produce. From May (at the latest) through early October there are terrific weekly farmers markets in towns such as Denver, Boulder, Aspen, Telluride, Vail and tiny Minturn – and that doesn't even scratch the surface. It was only a matter of time before restaurants embraced the local breadbasket, too. For the inside skinny on regional growers, markets and restaurants, check out www.ediblecommunities.com.

The 'eat local' ethos is grounded in the philosophy made famous in Michael Pollan's *The Omnivore's Dilemma:* that food loses both nutrients and flavor the further it has to travel. So, food is always healthiest and most delicious when mileage is limited. Plus, without huge distances to cover, it's (theoretically) cheaper and pollution linked to the freight process is mitigated.

The problem for food-producing states such as Colorado has long been that out-of-state demand has trumped local dollars – for years much of the best-quality beef, lamb, pork and vegetables left town. No more. Head to Denver's Root Down (p88), in the chic Highlands area, or sample worldwide market flavors at the Denver Central Market (p84). In Boulder you can dine at Salt (p123) or Kitchen (p123).

Colorado Wine Country

Though miners brought grapevines to the area in the 19th century, cultivation was small-scale and adversely affected by Prohibition. The practice was resurrected as recently as the 1960s, when a Denver dentist opened the first Colorado winery using California grapes.

Today there are approximately 100 commercial wineries in the state, with most on the Western Slope. Though the Grand Valley and West Elks, near Grand Junction, have the largest concentration of vineyards, the area around Cortez and the Front Range are other areas that are developing. Planted between 4000ft and 7000ft above sea level, these vineyards are among the highest in the world. Sunny days, cool nights and low humidity cultivate what locals call ideal conditions for grapes, though the growing season is markedly shorter than in California.

As a result, faster-ripening varietals – such as Bordeaux, Rhone Valley, Merlot, Syrah and Viognier – do well here. But you'll also find Cabernet Sauvignon, Chardonnay and many others.

A Fork in the Wilderness

One Colorado dining experience could never be replicated in New York or Paris: the wilderness restaurant. In the high country, there is many a hidden gourmet table accessed only by ski trail, a gondola trip, a sleigh ride or hike. Your reward goes far beyond an appetizing plate and a bottle of wine. Picture a summit panorama, a roaring log fire and the truly hearty appetite earned from being out in the fresh mountain air.

Some of our favorites:

➡ **The Tenth** (p209)

➡ **Allreds** (p266)

➡ **Game Creek Restaurant** (p209)

➡ **Beano's Cabin** (p216)

➡ **Pine Creek Cookhouse** (p233)

➡ **Tennessee Pass Cookhouse** (p249)

The Alt Diet

With the lowest rates of obesity of any state, Coloradans seem to know how to eat. Of course, another factor is their appetite for activity, though in research published in the *International Journal of Obesity,* some scientists now speculate that even just living at high altitude will make you thinner. Regardless, Colorado is at the cutting edge when it comes to alternative eating.

For visitors, this discerning tendency might make your wait in bakery or deli lines a game of patience. But if you're picky, this might be the place for you. First of all, no one will bat an eye at any food allergies or restrictions. It's de rigueur these days to find gluten-free, vegan and vegetarian items on menus in urban and tourist areas – even at the local steakhouse. Many restaurants also nod to the latest food fads, so Paleo diet followers and fans of kale will do just fine.

Flavors of Mexico

While Colorado's Mexican cuisine probably isn't as good as that in New Mexico, it does have its moments. The food here tends toward Tex-Mex stylings (and this is where burrito giant Chipotle was born).

Pueblo is the Hispanic heartland of the state, with half of the city on the south side of the Arkansas River (once the official Mexico–US border). Alamosa also has deep

---

CRUISING THE VINEYARDS

The main destination for Colorado wine country touring is the area around Grand Junction and Palisade. Surrounded by blue sky and red rock, this fledgling vineyard area has a homespun, desert feel that's a stark contrast to the green hills of Sonoma. Here's how to start:

➡ Visit www.coloradowine.com to find out about upcoming festivals or special events.

➡ Download the agrotourism brochure and map from the Palisade Chamber of Commerce (p306). It's a handy guide to keep with you in the car.

➡ Mix it up – because how much wine tasting can you actually do in a day? Visit lavender farms and alpaca refuges interspersed with vineyards on the dusty back roads of Palisade.

➡ Consider a do-it-yourself tour by bicycle.

➡ Dine at top-notch restaurants with Colorado wine lists and knowledgeable servers to research some favorites to visit in person. We like Boulder's Salt (p123), Grand Junction's 626 on Rood (p302) and Inari's A Palisade Bistro (p306).

Mexican roots, and some ski towns do a surprisingly good job at making a Mexican fix.

Our favorites statewide include Taqueria El Nopal (p219) in Glenwood Springs, the Minturn Saloon (p214), Calvillo's (p337) in Alamosa, and Telluride's La Cocina de Luz (p265). In Denver, the street taco scene is alive and well.

High Hops & Spirits

Colorado has only 2% of the US population, but 10% of its breweries – with more than 230 of them across the state. Many are medal winners and some of the first big-name craft brewers, like New Belgium Brewery, started here. The Front Range leads the way as the largest market for craft brewing in the US, and Colorado leads the nation in drinking draft beer. It would seem that nearly every Colorado town has its own signature microbrew; start at the source in Fort Collins, then head out from there. Most large breweries will offer tours, with paid tastings at the end. Other than that, order a flight at the local brewery.

Real beer aficionados shouldn't miss Denver's Great American Beer Festival (p79), a three-day event that draws 49,000 people. In October, the Colorado Convention Center hosts this mammoth festival and competition. Unfortunately, tickets sell out almost the instant they go on sale, but you can also check out a number of festivals and dedicated events held around the state at www.coloradobeer.org.

In a state hung up on local ingredients and artisan product, craft distilleries were the logical next step. From garage operations to big names, these businesses are popping up in cities and mountain towns, mixing up those handcrafted rums, vodkas, whiskeys, gins and liqueurs that keep cocktail hours interesting.

Bar menus highlight local spirits and many distilleries offer their own tour. Based in Denver, Stranahans (p78) is a small-batch distiller that makes its whiskey from only 12 barrels per week out of locally grown barley. Another one to watch is Montanya (p291), a Crested Butte–based rum distiller with a number of awards under its belt (and amazing craft cocktails post-tour). Check out Peach Street Distillers (p306) in Palisade if you want to taste amazing Palisade peaches in a bottle.

THE BREAKFAST BURRITO

Nobody would actually sell these hot missiles in Mexico, but no matter. The breakfast burrito is one Mexican-inspired food group mastered far and wide here. It's served in diners and Jewish delis in Denver, in ski-punk coffee shops and straight from a bus in Leadville. Packed with protein (eggs, cheese, beans), fresh veggies and hot salsa, rolled to go in paper and foil, it may be the perfect breakfast for those on the go. Smuggle it onto the gondola, grind it in the car or hell, store it in your purse (just not for too long).

Breckenridge Distillery (p198) is a Summit County top pick.

Happy-hour Dining

Those coming from out of state might not suspect how seriously Coloradans take their happy hour. Indeed, for those who want to beat the bluebirds the next morning to ride 50 miles before work, the only option for socializing is to do it early. The tradition is savored by students, professionals, ski bums hitting apres-ski and everyone in between.

Because happy hour is so popular here, restaurants compete fiercely and offer incredible deals. Nowhere is this more apparent than in Colorado's fine-dining establishments, which may be out of reach for many during dinner hour, but offer incredible small-plate deals during happy hour that are cheaper than the local pizzeria – and far more delectable.

Limited, discounted happy-hour menus are offered in pubs and restaurants between around 3:30pm and 6pm (sometimes until 7pm). Go on the early end to get a table. Check restaurant websites for details. Few offer weekend deals, though some spots offer late-night happy hours from 10pm until close during the week.

In Denver hit up happy hour at Steuben's (p87). Old Boulder stand-bys MED (p123) and Jax Fish House (p124) have competition from Salt (p123) (and, of course, all the college bars on the Hill). You will also find a thriving tradition in every ski town, pub and brewhouse in the state.

Plan Your Trip
Travel with Children

With amazing mountain trails, ghost towns, hands-on museum exhibits and interactive art spaces, river rafting and some of the country's best family-friendly skiing and cycling, traveling families are spoiled for options in Colorado. The endless blue skies, fresh air, archaeological ruins and wild country do wonders to detach kids from their tablets, cell phones and iPods.

Best Regions for Kids

Denver

The capital is chock-a-block full of kid-positive museums, galleries and activities, year-round.

Central Colorado

Winter skiing and snowboarding give way to outdoor adventure parks, bike trails and white-water rafting in the green season.

Northern Colorado

It's all about the great outdoors in Northern Colorado with moose and elk herds at Rocky Mountain National Park (p138) and T. rex bones at Dinosaur National Monument (p171).

Southwest Colorado

Check out the cliff dwellings in Mesa Verde National Park (p251) or go on a mountain-biking expedition in Fruita.

Southeast Colorado

Colorado Springs packs a punch for natural and cultural attractions that kids love. Further afield, the Great Sand Dunes National Park induces awe.

Colorado for Kids

In Colorado's main cities, junior travelers should head for the many hands-on science museums, playgrounds, theme parks and family-fun centers, as well as the main attraction of wide-open spaces.

Denver, despite being the state capital, sets the tone as a truly outdoorsy city, with miles of cycling and walking trails, riverside parks and gardens and outdoor events and theme parks. Beyond the capital there are historic railroads to ride, canyons and peaks to climb and old Western towns to explore.

Most national and state parks have some kid-oriented exhibits, trails and programs. Join organized wildlife-spotting tours in the parks and reserves, or hook a trout in a tumbling mountain river. Tubing and rafting on some of these rivers is as exhilarating for kids as it is for parents, and camping and hiking opportunities abound.

The family-friendly icon is used in our listings to denote places that cater to families.

Children's Highlights

Festivals & Events

Boulder Creek Hometown Festival (p117) (Boulder) Pie-eating contests, the Great Zucchini Race and a kid-friendly 5K race.

Cherry Creek Arts Festival (p80) (Denver) Three days of food, fun and arts.

Great Fruitcake Toss (p313) (Colorado Springs) The cake that flies the furthest wins!

Hot Air Balloon Festival & Art in the Park (p167) (Steamboat Springs) Dozens of colorful balloons fly high above as an arts-and-crafts show unfolds below.

International Snow Sculpture Championship (p195) (Breckenridge) Watch snow art being made and vote for the best in show.

Lights of December (☎303-449-3774; www.boulderdowntown.com; Pearl Street Mall; ◷1st Sat Dec; 🚍205, 206) **FREE** (Boulder) A classic Christmas parade.

Ouray Ice Festival (p271) (Ouray) Four days of climbing competitions, plus an awesome ice-climbing wall for kids to scramble on.

Strawberry Days (www.strawberrydays.com; ◷Jun) (Glenwood Springs) A fun, long-running, community festival.

Indoor Options

Buell Children's Museum (p325) (Pueblo) Classic cars, bridges, jellyfish, fairy lands and more...

Buffalo Bill Museum & Grave (p103) (Golden) For the young cowboys and cowgirls.

CU Wizards (p127) (Boulder) Monthly science shows at Boulder's university.

Children's Museum (p65) (Denver) Engaging exhibits and activities, including cooking classes.

Denver Art Museum (p65) (Denver) Hands-on exhibits highlight world-class art.

Denver Museum of Nature & Science (p69) (Denver) The IMAX Theater and Planetarium are always a hit.

Fiske Planetarium (p112) (Boulder) Spectacular shows on a 65ft-diameter dome ceiling.

Manitou Penny Arcade (p324) (Manitou Springs) Introduce the next generation to the last generation's games.

Morrison Natural History Museum (p106) (Morrison) Guided tours of spectacular dinosaur bones, most found nearby.

Overdrive Raceway (p313) (Colorado Springs) Two-story indoor race track delights kids (and big kids) alike.

Royal Gorge Dinosaur Experience (p318) (Cañon City) Handle Jurassic-period fossils and life-size fossil casts. Play on the multistory ropes course afterwards.

Woodward Barn (p200) (Copper Mountain) Practice snowboard, BMX and skate-park tricks.

Dude Ranches

Drowsy Water Ranch (p161) (Granby) Horseback riding and home cooking, with accommodations in Western-themed cabins.

Echo Basin Ranch (p256) (Mancos) Basic, affordable and offers the whole gamut of ranch experiences.

Beaver Meadows Resort Ranch (p159) (Red Feather Lakes) Horseback riding, rafting, fishing and hiking activities.

Vista Verde Guest Ranch (p167) (Steamboat Springs) The most luxurious dude-ranch experience in Colorado.

Yellow Pine Guest Ranch (p329) (Cuchara) Terrific accommodations in deluxe log cabins.

Kid-friendly Hikes

Burly mountains (and altitude!) can be a challenge to little legs. Families with smaller children might want to stick to hikes under 3 miles. Some of our favorites:

Chautauqua Park (p109) (Boulder) Lots of fun rock scrambling.

Eldorado Canyon State Park (p113) (Boulder) Combine hikes with visits to the public pool.

Fish Creek Falls (p163) (Steamboat Springs) An easy hike with views of a spectacular 283ft waterfall.

Maroon Bells (p224) (Aspen) An iconic mountain setting with trails for all levels of hikers.

Mesa Verde National Park (p251) Check out ancient rock carvings on the 2.8-mile Petroglyph Loop.

Quandary Peak (p192) (Breckenridge) Colorado's 'easiest' fourteener: the summit is 3 miles from the trailhead.

Rocky Mountain National Park (p138) Try Wild Basin to Calypso Falls, or Lumpy Ridge for good family-friendly hikes.

St Mary's Glacier (p175) (Idaho Springs) Bring a sled for some summertime play in the snow!

Planning

Perhaps the most difficult part of a family trip is avoiding the temptation to squeeze in too much. Distances are deceptive, and any single corner of Colorado could easily fill a two-week family vacation.

Choose a few primary destinations and connect them with a flexible driving plan with potential stops. Book rooms at the major destinations and make advance reservations for horseback rides, rafting trips, scenic train rides and educational programs or camps (particularly in peak season), but allow time between bookings to follow your fancy.

Don't forget about the small mountain towns. Their festivals, rodeos and state fairs can be excellent family entertainment.

For all-round information and advice, check out Lonely Planet's *Travel with Children*.

Discounts for Kids

Child concessions often apply for tours, admission fees and transportation, with discounts as high as 50% off the adult rate. The definition of 'child' ranges from under 12 to under 16 years. Most sights also give free admission to children under two.

Resources

Colorado Parent (www.coloradoparent.com)

Family Travel Colorado (www.familytravel colorado.com)

Mile High Mamas (www.milehighmamas.com)

T.rex skeleton, Denver Museum of Nature & Science (p69)

What to Pack

Temperatures can vary widely throughout the day, especially in the mountains. Remember to bring layers and a warm hat, even in the summer.

Infant- and toddler-specific items like disposable diapers (nappies), wipes and formula are easy to come by, even in the smallest of towns. Prices tend to be lower in bigger towns, though; if you're driving, consider stocking up in the first city you hit.

Regions at a Glance

With so many Rocky Mountain vistas, craggy canyons and homespun warmth, in addition to hip cities you can walk or ride around, Colorado may spoil you for all future road trips. The whole state moves outdoors in summer, when festivals and live music bring people together under the sun. The Front Range cities of Denver and Boulder offer all the urban pleasures, but you're still in Colorado, so they also satisfy outdoor ambitions. Vail, Aspen and central Colorado act as an adventure hub for the vast majority of those who want to hike, bike or ski the state's famed high country. To really get away from it all, head to the northern mountains or explore the back roads of southwestern Colorado.

Denver & Around

Dining & Drinking
Entertainment
Shopping

Culinary Capital

Home country cookin', a booming microbrew scene, a tradition of farm-to-fork suppliers and a dash of Denver's art-deco airs and graces combine to make epicurean adventuring here a delight.

Rocky Mountain High

Share the buzz of big city galleries, museums, cinemas, theaters, sporting arenas and a nightlife circuit that's cruisy and chilled, but driven by Colorado kids who know how to enjoy life.

Superstylin'

Nowhere else in the state will you find as diverse a selection of department stores, boutiques, markets, grocers, malls and megamalls than Denver, where shopping is a preferred indoor pastime, especially in winter.

p62

Boulder & Around

Outdoors
Food & Beer
Museums

Hit the Trail

From Chautauqua Park to Eldorado Canyon and the stunning alpine terrain of the Indian Peaks Wilderness Area, Boulder is a hoofer's haven.

Eat + Drink = Merry

Foodies should hit adventuresome dining districts like Denver's Highlands and Five Points, and Boulder's Pearl Street, for a spate of new restaurants and slow-food markets. And forget about Coors: Colorado's inspired brewers have made these cities a beer drinker's nirvana.

Cultural Cred

Though the Denver Art Museum and Denver Museum of Nature & Science please crowds, don't miss the lesser-known gems, including the History Colorado Center and the Clyfford Still Museum.

p107

Rocky Mountain National Park & Northern Colorado

National Parks
Western Towns
Dinosaurs

The Rockies

Grazing elk, jewel-like lakes and waterfalls – Rocky Mountain National Park captivates everyone. To skip the crowds, blaze your own trail into the backcountry wilderness.

Cowboy Cool

Stetsons and chaps worn as nonchalantly as business suits in Steamboat Springs. The Cache la Poudre River, sunset horse rides, prairies and skiing through the trees – this is the unadulterated West.

Bone Yard

Dinosaur National Monument allows armchair paleontologists to walk among nearly whole skeletons of the largest animals ever to walk on earth, eerily frozen in rock.

p136

Vail, Aspen & Central Colorado

Snow Sports
Hiking
Water Sports

Powder Days

From glamorous Aspen and Vail to historic Breckenridge, this region boasts more tree runs, terrain parks, back bowls, cornices, cross-country trails and après-ski parties than any one snow-seeker can handle.

Trail Blazing

A trail network of over 1000 miles will take you to secluded grottoes and waterfalls, fishing holes, fourteeners and high-mountain passes. You can even do some of these trails on a mountain bike, too.

Four Rivers

This region offers epic paddling and transcendent fly-fishing on several great rivers, including the Arkansas, Colorado, Clear Creek and Roaring Fork.

p174

Mesa Verde & Southwest Colorado

Native Culture
Historic Towns
Wine Tasting

Ancient Ruins

Where else can you climb steep ladders to ancient cliff dwellings or drop into dark ceremonial kivas? Mesa Verde National Park in the Four Corners brings you face-to-face with the region's original inhabitants.

Wild West

The silver mining era left the San Juans dotted with historic mountain villages. Quaff a microbrew in a saloon in chic Telluride or ride the scenic narrow-gauge rail from Durango to Silverton.

Local Vineyards

Still the home of Colorado's best peaches, Palisade's sunny, mild microclimate has served another purpose for locals: planting vineyards. Drive its back roads to compare upstart winemakers.

p250

Southeast Colorado & the San Luis Valley

Outdoors
Rafting
History

Desert Vibes

With massive sand dunes, snow-capped peaks and shimmering wetlands, the diverse Great Sand Dunes National Park is the best reason to visit the San Luis Valley.

Running the Rapids

The Arkansas River flows from the intense Numbers through family-friendly Browns Canyon, culminating beneath the country's highest bridge. This is the majestic Royal Gorge – the signature trip of America's most paddled river.

Old West

America's rich past lives on along the historic Santa Fe Trail, at the state's first resort in Colorado Springs and along the old stagecoach roads leading to Cripple Creek.

p307

On the Road

Rocky Mountain National Park & Northern Colorado
p136

Boulder & Around
p107

Denver & Around
p62

Vail, Aspen & Central Colorado
p174

Mesa Verde & Southwest Colorado
p250

Southeast Colorado & the San Luis Valley
p307

Denver & Around

Includes ➡

Denver 63
Golden 102
Morrison 105

Best Places to Eat

➡ Acorn (p88)
➡ Denver Central Market (p84)
➡ Hop Alley (p87)
➡ Root Down (p88)
➡ Tamales by La Casita (p84)

Best Places to Stay

➡ Crawford Hotel (p82)
➡ Queen Anne Bed & Breakfast Inn (p81)
➡ Hostel Fish (p81)
➡ Art – a Hotel (p82)
➡ Brown Palace Hotel (p83)

Why Go?

As an urban center, Denver has come a long way. Sure you'll still catch a Stetson or two walking down the 16th St Mall, but the Intermountain West's cosmopolitan capital now delights in a growing culinary and arts scene, plus plenty of brewpubs, great parks and cycling trails, and close proximity to spectacular hiking, skiing and camping in the Rocky Mountains.

Thanks to a re-urbanization of the city's central core, Denver now has name-worthy neighborhoods with flavors that are all their own – River North (RiNo) for hipster bars and eye-catching street art, Lower Highlands (LoHi) and South Broadway for great eateries and live music, Cherry Creek for glam, Lower Downtown (LoDo) for upscale restaurants and cocktail lounges as well as the Golden Triangle and Santa Fe for arts, theater and museums. In all, there's a neighborhood and a vibe for just about anybody.

When to Go
Denver

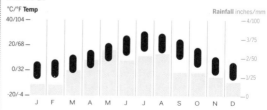

Jun–Aug Big crowds, higher prices. Hot days, balmy evenings, extended daylight.

Sep–Nov Cooler temperatures see parks and mountains at their prettiest.

Dec–Mar Short days and cold weather equal skiing weather. Crowds and prices drop.

Denver

📖 303, 720 / POP 693,100 / ELEV 5280FT

History

Between hell-raisin' gold rushers, US Army generals, warring Native American tribes and 'unsinkable' frontier women, Denver's past is colorful and chaotic, and people here relish and romanticize the Wild West history. It was rumors of gold that brought the human tide to the Front Range in the middle of the 19th century and established Denver as a major supply point at the foot of the Rocky Mountains, but Arapaho and Cheyenne buffalo hunters already occupied hundreds of camps in the area.

General William H Larimer was the city's white founder; in late 1859 he established a township at the confluence of Cherry Creek and the South Platte River and named it after the person who appointed the area to his control, Kansas Territorial Governor James W Denver. Without water or rail transportation, however, Denver's overnight rise soon stagnated, ending the first of many boom-and-bust cycles that have defined the city's growth.

Supplying gold and silver miners fostered the city's boom until 1893, when the Silver Panic destroyed the economy and sent the state into depression. The following year discovery of gold deposits in Cripple Creek rejuvenated Denver's stature as a center of finance and commerce. When this dried up it was coupled with the Great Depression.

In 1952, Denver's 12-story height limit was repealed and the skyline sprouted high-rises, but many of these suffered during the mid-1980s when an office-construction boom went – you guessed it – bust. The cycle reversed yet again in the 1990s, and by the millennium Denver was a hub for computer, telecommunication and tech firms. Colorado's important oil and gas industry went through similar cycles, riding the ups and downs of oil prices, conflicts overseas, and, most recently, the controversial spread of hydraulic fracturing, or fracking.

Denver gained a measure of national recognition in 2008, when it hosted the Democratic National Convention. But the attention was short lived, as the country careened into financial crisis. Denver weathered the Great Recession better than most cities, and has since emerged as a hot new destination – close to a thousand people relocate to Denver every week, and *US & World Report* named it the best American city to live in in 2016. The growth has brought fresh verve to Denver, bolstered by Colorado's first-in-the-nation vote to legalize recreational marijuana. To top it off, the Broncos were Superbowl champs in 2016. The city faces predictable challenges, from traffic to housing prices, but its evolution into a first-tier city seems well underway.

ℹ️ Resources

Lonely Planet (www.lonelyplanet.com) Destination information, hotel bookings, traveler forum and more.

Visit Denver (www.denver.org) Tourism office website with loads of information including an events calendar, day trips and activities.

Westword (www.westword.com) This free weekly is the best source for local events, opinion and alternative news.

5280 (www.5280.com) Good dining and arts listings in a glossy monthly.

ORIC (www.oriconline.org) Useful info and links for outdoor recreation.

Denver Post (www.denverpost.com) The mainstream newspaper in Denver.

◎ Sights

Most of Denver's sights are in the downtown and Golden Triangle districts.

Once you get outside the downtown area, getting around Denver's streets can be a bit of a challenge, with roads suddenly changing names, ending and running counter to the cardinal grid found in many older parts of town (save for downtown, which has a grid that sits diagonally to the cardinal points).

Keep in mind that Broadway (running north–south) and Ellsworth (running east–west) are considered '0' blocks. From these central starting points, addresses ascend by increments of 100 every block.

★**Union Station**   HISTORIC BUILDING
(Map p70; 📞 303-592-6712; www.unionstationin-denver.com; 1701 Wynkoop St; 🅿️; 🚇 55L, 72L, 120L, FF2, 🚆 A, B, C, E, W) Gorgeously restored, historic Union Station is Denver's main transportation hub, used by RTD (p101) light-rail lines, commuter buses and Amtrak (📞 800-872-7245; www.amtrak.com; 1701 Wynkoop St, Union Station; 🚇 55L, 72L, 120L, FF2, 🚆 A, B, C, E, W). But it's way more than that. Inside, the main hall doubles as a waiting area and lounge with leather couches and chairs, shuffleboard and free wi-fi. Swanky restaurants and coffee

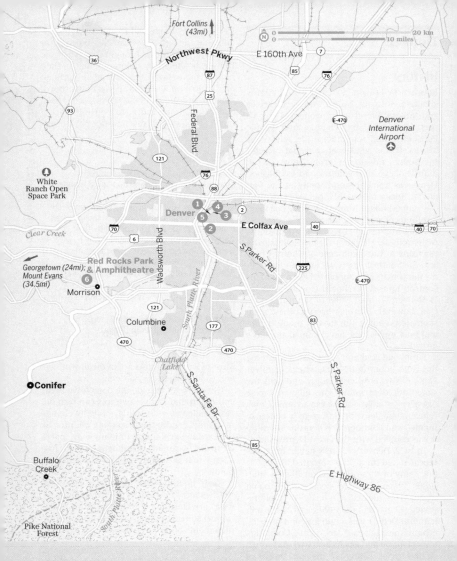

Denver & Around Highlights

1 Union Station (p63) Grabbing a drink or meal in the gorgeously renovated downtown train station.

2 Denver Art Museum (p65) Delving into one of the richest art collections in the state.

3 RiNo Nightlife (p89) Bar-hopping in Denver's hottest neighborhood, at happening spots like the Infinite Monkey Theorum.

4 Craft Breweries (p89) Sampling artisanal beers at some of the state's best breweries.

5 Confluence Park (p65) Playing in the sun and water where the Cherry Creek and South Platte River meet (and thousands of outdoorsy Denverites too).

6 Red Rocks Park & Amphitheatre (p103) Catching a concert (or taking a hike) at the most striking outdoor performance space you may ever see.

shops line the building along with boutiques and bars. Even one of Denver's best hotels – the Crawford (p82) – calls it home.

In summer, a **farmers market** (9am to 2pm Saturday) sets up outside, drawing a huge crowd. Just beyond it, a **pop-up fountain** comes to life, enticing kids (and kids at heart) to run and play through the urban sprinklers.

★**Denver Art Museum** MUSEUM

(Map p70; DAM; ☏ticket sales 720-865-5000; www.denverartmuseum.org; 100 W 14th Ave; adult/child $13/free, 1st Sat of month free; ⊙10am-5pm Tue-Thu, Sat & Sun, to 8pm Fri; P ♿; ☐0, 52) 🚶
DAM is home to one of the largest Native American art collections in the USA, and puts on special multimedia exhibits that vary from treasures of British art to *Star Wars* costumes. The Western American Art section of the permanent collection is justifiably famous. This isn't an old, stodgy art museum, and the best part is diving into the interactive exhibits, which kids love.

The landmark $110-million Frederic C Hamilton wing, designed by Daniel Libeskind, is quite simply awesome. Whether you see it as expanding crystals, juxtaposed mountains or just architectural indulgence, it's doubtless an angular modern masterpiece. If you think the place looks weird from the outside, look inside: shapes shift with each turn thanks to a combination of design and uncanny natural-light tricks.

★**Confluence Park** PARK

(Map p66; 2200 15th St; ♿; ☐10, 28, 32, 44) 🚶
Where Cherry Creek and South Platte River meet is the nexus and plexus of Denver's sunshine-loving culture. It's a good place for an afternoon picnic and there's a short white-water park for kayakers and tubers. Families also enjoy a small beach and shallow water areas for playing.

Head south from here along the **Cherry Creek Trail** and you can get all the way to Cherry Creek Shopping Center (p99) and beyond to Cherry Creek Reservoir. If you go southwest along the **Platte Trail**, you'll eventually ride all the way to Chatfield Reservoir. By heading north and connecting to the **Clear Creek Trail**, you can get to Golden.

★**Blair-Caldwell African American Museum** MUSEUM

(Map p66; ☏720-865-2401; https://history.denverlibrary.org/blair; 2401 Welton St, 3rd fl; ⊙noon-8pm Mon & Wed, 10am-6pm Tue, Thu & Fri, 9am-5pm Sat; P ♿; ☐43, ☐D) FREE Tucked into the 3rd floor of a public library, this multimedia museum provides an excellent overview of the history of African Americans in the Rocky Mountain region – from migration and settlement to discrimination and achievements. Exhibits on Wellington Webb, Denver's first African American mayor, as well as Five Points, Denver's historically black neighborhood, are particularly interesting.

Stop on the 2nd floor to peruse the Blair-Caldwell African American Research Library, an institution that provides much-needed resources on the rich cultural heritage of African Americans in the West.

★**Clyfford Still Museum** MUSEUM

(Map p70; ☏720-354-4880; www.clyffordstillmuseum.org; 1250 Bannock St; adult/child $10/free; ⊙10am-5pm Tue-Thu, Sat & Sun, to 8pm Fri; ☐0, 52) Dedicated exclusively to the work and legacy of 20th-century American abstract expressionist Clyfford Still, this fascinating museum's collection includes over 2400 pieces – 95% of his work – by the powerful and narcissistic master of bold. In his will, Still insisted that his body of work only be exhibited in a singular space, so Denver built him a museum. Free tours are offered throughout the week; check the website for dates and times.

For a slight discount on admission, purchase tickets online. Admission is free every Friday from 5pm to 8pm.

★**Children's Museum** MUSEUM

(Map p66; ☏303-433-7444; www.mychildsmuseum.org; 2121 Children's Museum Dr; $9; ⊙9am-4pm Mon, Tue, Thu & Fri, to 7:30pm Wed, 10am-5pm Sat & Sun; ♿; ☐10) A recent $16 million expansion has made the Children's Museum one of the hottest tickets in town...well, at least for kids. Highlights include an enclosed three-story climbing structure (helmets provided), a kids' kitchen with hands-on cooking classes, a 2300-sq-ft art studio, a maker space, a life-size marble run and a huge outdoor playground with lots of climbing, digging and splashing areas. Toddlers also enjoy a section with fun areas designed for crawlers and new walkers.

Free admission on the first Tuesday of the month, from 4pm to 8pm.

Mesteño MONUMENT

(Blue Mustang; Peña Blvd) Nicknamed 'Bluecifer,' this 32ft-high blue stallion with hellish, gleaming red eyes greets visitors to and

Denver

W 38th Ave

W 37th St

Bryant St
Zuni St
Wyandot St
Tejon St
Osage St

27

48

W 33rd Ave

43

35
87
W 32nd Ave
71
67

W 30th Ave

W 29th Ave

62
40
15

39th St

91

20

5

25
64
39

Union

Amtrak-
Union
Station

74

46

31

Broadway
24th St

50

16

22
88

3

i

**Confluence
Park**

12

Wazee St
Blake St
Market St
Larimer St
Lawrence St

22nd St
21st St
19th St

18

14

10

W 23rd Ave

South Platte River

**Children's
Museum 2**

11

Speer Blvd

Cherry Creek

16th St Mall
15th St
14th St

17th St

Broadway

Pepsi Center/
Elitch Gardens

79

Auraria Pkwy

Champa St

Welton St
Glenarm Pl
Court Pl

**Sports Authority Field
at Mile High**

80

**Auraria
West**

Colfax at
Auraria

Mile High Stadium Cir

W Colfax Ave

40

W Colfax Ave

Delaware St

Civic
Center
Park

State
Capitol

33

See Downtown
Area Map (p70)

W 13th Ave

Osage St

Lincoln
Park

S Platte River Trail

Federal Blvd

10th/Osage

73

W 10th Ave

51

61

Sunken
Gardens
Park

Cherry Creek Trail

21

13

W 8th Ave

6

36

Kalamath St

W 6th Ave

17

Santa Fe Dr

W 4th Ave

See Enlargement

Enlargement

54
65
85
82
75

76
E 1st Ave
86
47

W 1st Ave

Acoma St
Broadway
S Lincoln St

Golden (12mi)

W Ellsworth
Ave

E Ellsworth
Ave

89

19

W 2nd Ave

Yuma St

30

84

W Archer Pl

0   200 m
0   0.1 miles

Broadway
Lincoln St

W 1st Ave

Pho 95 (1.3mi)

W Bayaud Ave

West-Bar-Val
Wood Park

25

Chatfield
Reservoir (20mi)

South Platte Rv

W Bayaud Ave

Divino Wine &
Spirits (1.2mi)

24

See North Denver
Enlargement

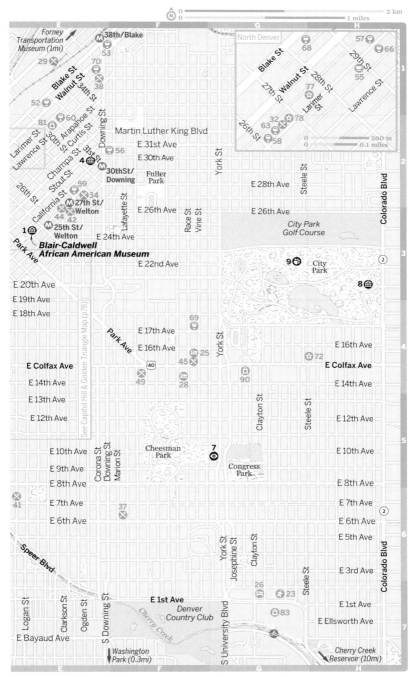

Denver

⊙ **Top Sights**
1 Blair-Caldwell African American
   Museum E3
2 Children's Museum B3
3 Confluence Park B3

⊙ **Sights**
4 Black American West Museum &
   Heritage Center E2
   Colorado Sports Hall of Fame ..... (see 80)
5 Commons Park C2
6 Denver Art Society C6
7 Denver Botanic Gardens G5
8 Denver Museum of Nature &
   Science H3
9 Denver Zoo G3
10 Downtown Aquarium B3
11 Elitch Gardens B3
12 Millennium Bridge C3
13 Museo de las Americas C5
14 Museum of Contemporary Art C3
15 National Velvet B2
16 RedLine D3
17 Rule Gallery C6

⊙ **Activities, Courses & Tours**
18 Confluence Kayaks B3
19 Denver Bouldering Club B6
20 Denver Skate Park C2
21 Evo D5
22 Platte Valley Trolley B3
23 Pura Vida Fitness & Spa G7
24 Stranahans Colorado Whiskey C7

⊙ **Sleeping**
25 Castle Marne Bed & Breakfast F4
26 JW Marriott Denver at Cherry
   Creek G7
27 Lumber Baron Inn Gardens B1
28 Mile High Guest House F4

⊙ **Eating**
29 Acorn E1
30 Beatrice & Woodsley A7
31 Biker Jim's Dogs D3
32 Denver Central Market G2
33 Domo Restaurant C4
34 Dunbar Kitchen & Tap House E2
35 Duo B2
36 El Taco De Mexico C6
37 Fruition Restaurant F6
38 Hop Alley E1
39 Just BE Kitchen B2
40 Little Man Ice Cream B2
41 Mizuna E6
42 Rolling Pin Bakeshop E3
43 Root Down C2

44 Rosenberg's Bagels & Delicatessan E3
45 SAME Café F4
46 Snooze D2
   Source .... (see 29)
47 Sweet Action Ice Cream A6
48 Tamales by La Casita B1
49 Voodoo Doughnut F4
50 Work & Class D2

⊙ **Drinking & Nightlife**
51 Bar Standard D5
52 Beryl's Beer Co E1
53 Black Shirt Brewing Co E1
54 BoyzTown A6
55 Crema Coffee House H1
56 Denver Wrangler F2
57 Finn's Manor H1
58 First Draft G2
59 Goed Zuur E2
60 Infinite Monkey Theorum E2
61 La Rumba D5
62 Linger B2
63 Matchbox G2
   Milk .... (see 51)
64 My Brother's Bar B2
65 Punch Bowl Social A6
66 Ratio Beerworks H1
67 Recess Beer Garden B2
   Sputnik .... (see 85)
68 Stem Ciders G1
69 Thin Man Tavern F4
70 Tracks E1
71 Williams & Graham B2

⊙ **Entertainment**
72 Bluebird Theater H4
73 Colorado Ballet C5
74 Coors Field D2
75 Hi-Dive A6
76 Landmark Mayan Theater A6
77 Larimer Lounge H1
78 Nocturne G2
79 Pepsi Center C3
80 Sports Authority Field at Mile High A4

⊙ **Shopping**
81 Botanico E2
82 Buffalo Exchange A6
83 Cherry Creek Shopping Center G7
84 Decade A7
85 Fancy Tiger Crafts A6
86 Hope Tank A6
87 Jewelius B2
88 REI B3
89 Sewn A6
90 Twist & Shout G4
91 Wilderness Exchange Unlimited B2

from Denver International Airport (p100), and is the subject of much controversy in Denver. Morbid factoid: during its creation, a piece of the 9000lb stallion fell on creator Luis Jiménez, severing an artery in his leg and leading to his death.

**Bronco Buster
& On the War Trail** MONUMENT
(Map p70; Civic Center Park; 🚻; 🚌 0, 9, 10, 52) In the early 1920s, Denver sculptor Alexander Phimister Proctor was commissioned to create two bronze sculptures for Civic Center Park (p72): *Bronco Buster* and *On the War Trail*. The works depict a cowboy and a Native American warrior, both paying homage to Colorado's Wild West roots. Fun fact: Proctor's model for the cowboy, Bill 'Slim' Ridings, was arrested for cattle rustling before the statue was done. Proctor bailed Ridings out so he could complete the statue.

Washington Park PARK
(Wash Park; www.washpark.com; cnr S Downing St & E Virginia Ave; P 🚻 🎿; 🚌 11, 12) People somehow just look better in Wash Park. They are fitter, trimmer, more tanned and even taller than your average Denverite. Must be the rec center found in the middle of the park ($5.50 for a day pass), which includes a pool, weights and more. Or maybe it's the bike path and lakes, nearby restaurants, volleyball games and tennis matches that mark this park as one of the city's best.

Denver Public Library LIBRARY
(Map p70; 📞 720-865-1111; www.denverlibrary.org; 10 W 14th Ave; ⏰ 10am-8pm Mon & Tue, to 6pm Wed-Fri, 9am-5pm Sat, 1-5pm Sun; P 🚻; 🚌 0, 9, 10, 52) Hardly a dusty bibliotheca, the Denver Public Library is an active and artsy place with whimsical postmodern architectural elements courtesy of renowned architect Michael Graves. In addition to its voluminous stacks, the library offers lectures, while shifting exhibits feature local historical and contemporary photography. On the 5th floor is the Western History & Genealogy Department.

RedLine ARTS CENTER
(Map p66; 📞 303-296-4448; www.redlineart.org; 2350 Arapahoe St; ⏰ 11am-5pm Tue-Sun; 🚻; 🚌 8, 38, 44, 48) FREE This remarkable contemporary arts center has a huge gallery space where work by emerging Coloradan artists is exhibited year-round. Fifteen artists in residence are hosted by RedLine each year, their studio space lining the gallery. Open to the public, it provides an opportunity for visitors to watch works of art being created. Various events promote similar community engagement, both inside and outside the center, with a focus on positive social change. Check the website for what's on.

I See What You Mean MONUMENT
(Map p70; Big Blue Bear; 700 14th St; 🚻; 🚌 1, 8, 19, 48, 🚈 D, F, H) Lawrence Argent's *I See What You Mean* is better known around town as the Big Blue Bear. This beloved 40ft-tall symbol of the city peers into the mammoth convention center with a friendly, playful spirit that has come to epitomize its city.

Scottish Angus Cow & Calf MONUMENT
(Map p78; cnr 12th Ave & Acoma St; 🚌 0, 52) Created by Dan Ostermiller, these bigger-than-life bronze sculptures of a cow and her calf pay homage to the historic cattle culture of Colorado. Originally commissioned by a local businessman for his ranch, it was gifted to the Denver Art Museum (p65) in 2006. Remarkable for their size and beauty, the pair are popular with kids for climbing and posing for photos.

**Denver Museum of
Nature & Science** MUSEUM
(Map p66; DMNS; 📞 303-370-6000; www.dmns.org; 2001 Colorado Blvd; museum adult/child $17/12, IMAX $10/8, Planetarium $5/4; ⏰ 9am-5pm; P 🚻; 🚌 20, 32, 40) The Denver Museum of Nature & Science is a classic natural-science museum with excellent temporary exhibits on topics like the biomechanics of bugs, Pompeii and mythical creatures. Permanent exhibits are equally engaging and include those cool panoramas we all loved as kids. The IMAX Theatre and Gates Planetarium are especially fun. Located on the eastern edge of City Park.

History Colorado Center MUSEUM
(Map p78; 📞 303-447-8679; www.historycoloradocenter.org; 1200 Broadway; adult/child $12/8; ⏰ 10am-5pm; P 🚻; 🚌 0, 10) Discover Colorado's frontier roots and high-tech modern triumphs at this sharp, smart and charming museum. There are plenty of interactive exhibits, including a Jules Verne–esque 'Time Machine' that you push across a giant map of Colorado to explore seminal moments in the Centennial State's history. Periodically, story times for toddlers and low-sensory morning sessions are offered before the museum opens.

Denver Botanic Gardens GARDENS
(Map p66; 📞 720-865-3500; www.botanicgardens.org; 1007 York St; adult/child $12.50/9; ⏰ 9am-5pm; P 🚻 🎿; 🚌 6, 10, 24) If you're hankering for greenery, this 23-acre Rocky Mountain garden is the perfect place to lose yourself. Local flora mixes with relatives from

Downtown Area

N

0 — 200 m
0 — 0.1 miles

Amtrak-Union Station

16
44
60
40
35
13
17
53
Market St

3 Union Station
Wynkoop St
24
Wazee St
36
Blake St
21st St
20th St
Larimer St
19th St
Lawrence St
Arapahoe St
22nd St
Curtis St

59
61
9
16th St Mall
29
Regional Transportation District
Market St
18th St
Denver Bus Center
27
19th St
Champa St
20th St

Tabor Center
17th St
Larimer St
Lawrence St
46
Arapahoe St
17th St
18th St
21
Stout St
California St
18th St/ California

43
57
32
31
34
38
39
49
25
15th St
14th St
16th St Mall
Curtis St
45
50
30
Champa St
56
16th St/ Stout
23
California St
Welton St

22
37
19
52
48
54
51
13th St
Champa St
14th St
Stout St
Downtown Tourist Information Center
62
16th St/ California
42
55
17th St
18th St

Speer Blvd
Cherry Creek Trail
8
Theatre District/ Convention Center
12
California St
Glenarm Pl
15th St
14th St
Tremont Pl
58
26
33
28
16th St Mall
Court Pl
Cleveland Pl

47
Colorado Convention Center
13th St
Welton St

W Colfax Ave
10
W Colfax Ave
Delaware St
Cherokee St
Denver City & County Building
7
5

Speer Blvd
Speer Blvd
Kalamath St
Santa Fe Dr
Fox St
Elati St
W 13th Ave
14
W 14th Ave
Bannock St
Denver Art Museum
2
15
11
6
Clyfford Still Museum
1
4
W 13th Ave

See Capitol Hill & Golden Triangle Area Map (p78)

Downtown Area

◉ Top Sights
1 Clyfford Still Museum............................D7
2 Denver Art Museum D7
3 Union Station..A1

◉ Sights
4 Big Sweep..D7
5 Bronco Buster & On the War Trail........D7
6 Byers-Evans House Museum...............D7
7 Civic Center Park..................................D6
8 Dancers..A5
9 David B Smith Gallery A2
10 Denver Firefighters Museum C6
11 Denver Public Library...........................D7
12 I See What You Mean B5
13 Robischon Gallery.................................B1
14 United States Mint................................C6
15 Yearling D7

◔ Activities, Courses & Tours
Civic Center Moves........................(see 7)
16 Colorado Cannabis Tours......................A1
17 Cook Street School of Culinary Arts C1

◉ Sleeping
18 Brown Palace Hotel..............................D4
Crawford Hotel................................(see 3)
19 Curtis..B4
20 Hostel Fish...C1
21 Hotel Monaco C3
22 Hotel Teatro...A4
23 Magnolia Hotel C3
24 Oxford Hotel A1

◉ Eating
25 Bistro Vendôme A3
Civic Center Eats ....(see 7)
26 Cooks Fresh Market D5
27 Elway's...C2
28 Food Court at Republic Plaza...............D5
29 Illegal Pete's..A2
Kitchen ....(see 29)
30 Little India B4

31 Market at Larimer Square......................A3
32 Osteria Marco A3
33 Pizza Colore Express D5
34 Rioja...A3

◉ Drinking & Nightlife
35 Beta Nightclub....................................... B1
36 Common Grounds...................................A1
37 Corner Office..B4
38 Crimson Room..A3
39 Crú...A3
40 Falling Rock Tap House B1
41 Great Divide Brewery & Tap Room....... D1
42 ink!...C4
43 Nallen's A3
44 Wynkoop Brewing Co A1

◉ Entertainment
45 Bovine Metropolis Theater....................B4
46 Clocktower Cabaret...............................B3
47 Colorado Convention Center................B5
48 Colorado Symphony Orchestra B4
49 Comedy Works A3
50 Dazzle..B4
51 Denver Center for the Performing
Arts..A4
52 Denver Performing Arts Complex.........A4
53 El Chapultepec.......................................C1
54 Ellie Caulkins Opera House...................B4
Opera Colorado ....(see 54)
55 Paramount Theatre................................D4

◉ Shopping
5 Green Boxes.................................(see 3)
56 Champa Fine Wine & Liquor C4
Cry Baby Ranch............................(see 25)
57 EVOO Marketplace..................................A3
Goorin Brothers............................(see 25)
58 I Heart Denver..D5
59 LoDo Wellness Center A2
60 MudHead Gallery.................................... B1
61 Tattered Cover Bookstore A2
62 Wild West Denver Store C4

faraway continents such as Australia and Africa to create a breathtaking landscape. Exhibits by well-known artists – think Alexander Calder and Dale Chihuly – are set among the flowers and fountains to complement the living art.

The **Mordecai Children's Garden** has excellent hands-on exhibits, including a water feature, Pipsqueak Pond, that's popular with the diaper set. Summer brings outdoor concerts to the gardens, while winter brings a holiday light show. Both are popular – be sure to buy tickets in advance.

Downtown Aquarium　　　　AQUARIUM
(Map p66; ☑303-561-4450; www.aquariumrestaurants.com; 700 Water St; adult/child $21/15; ⊙10am-9pm Sun-Thu, to 9:30pm Fri & Sat; P🚼; 🚌10) 🅿 Denver's old Ocean Journey Aquarium was sold in 2003 to a business that specializes in aquarium-themed restaurants. So it is that Downtown Aquarium is both a novelty restaurant and a public aquarium complete with a daily mermaid show. Tanks mostly have creatures from mountain rivers and coral reefs, though there's a desert exhibit with spiders and snakes and even a tiger den. Kids love it...plus it's a novel place to have a meal. Try the fish burger.

Robischon Gallery
GALLERY

(Map p70; ☑ 303-298-7788; www.robischongallery. com; 1740 Wazee St; ☉ 11am-6pm Tue-Fri, noon-5pm Sat; Ⓟ; ☒ A, B) FREE Robischon operates with a focus on emerging dialogues in art. Rotating exhibits take you to the cutting edge and you'll be able to dig art by some of the world's foremost contemporary artists such as Robert Motherwell and Christo.

Museum of Contemporary Art
GALLERY

(Map p66; ☑ 303-298-7554; www.mcadenver.org; 1485 Delgany St; adult/child/after 5pm $8/free/5; ☉ noon-7pm Tue-Thu, noon-10pm Fri, 10am-5pm Sat & Sun; Ⓟ; ☒ 6) This four-story museum was built with interaction and engagement in mind, and Denver's home for contemporary art can be provocative, confusing or delightful, depending on the show. Regardless, the work always makes you think. After your visit, head to the rooftop cafe for a drink and spectacular views of downtown Denver.

Commons Park
PARK

(Map p66; www.denvergov.org/parksandrecreation; cnr 15th & Little Raven Sts; 🚶 🚲; ☒ 10, 28, 32, 44) Affording views of downtown Denver and the Rockies, this spacious, hilly patch of green has bike paths, benches and plenty of people-watching. A lyrical curving stairway to nowhere known as Common Ground, by artist Barbara Grygutis, is an undeniable

centerpiece; it was commissioned by the Gates Family Foundation to commemorate the millennium. For more original art, head to the walkway along Little Raven St, where exhibits by international artists are often displayed.

Millennium Bridge
BRIDGE

(Map p66; extension of 16th St; 🚶 🚲) Allow us to be geeky for a second: this is the world's first cable-stayed bridge using a post-tensioned structural construction. If the technical jargon goes over your head, you'll be impressed by just looking up – the sweeping forms of the cables and white mast are a dramatic sight against Denver's consistently blue sky. The stunning bridge connects the LoDo neighborhood with Commons Park.

Yearling
MONUMENT

(Map p70; Horse on the Chair; 10 W 14th Ave; 🚶; ☒ 0, 9, 10, 52) This wonderful sculpture by Donald Lipski sits outside the Denver Public Library (p69), where it was installed in 1998 after spending a year in New York City's Central Park. The Horse on the Chair, as it's known, stands 21ft high and has a whimsy, humor and magic to it.

Civic Center Park
PARK

(Map p70; cnr Broadway & Colfax Ave; 🚶; ☒ 0, 9, 10, 52) In the shadow of the State Capitol's (p74) golden dome, this centrally located park

DENVER IN...

Two Days

Start your visit in LoDo, with its historic warehouses-turned-restaurants. Explore Union Station (p63) and brunch at Snooze (p85). Afterwards, window-shop on swanky Larimer Sq and head towards Civic Center Park, flanked by stately buildings. Spend the afternoon touring the State Capitol (p74) before dinner at artful Beatrice & Woodsley (p87).

On day two, visit the Denver Art Museum (p65), with its spectacular Native American art collection. History buffs will enjoy the History Colorado Center (p69) instead. Lunch at SAME Café (p84), leaving a little extra as a donation. Hop on a B-Cycle (p101) and enjoy the outdoors along the Cherry Creek Trail. Come nightfall, catch a show at the Denver Performing Arts Complex (p94).

Four Days

On day three, get yourself to the Denver Museum of Nature & Science (p69), then stroll through leafy City Park. Make your way to Confluence Park (p65) to cool off in the river. Follow the water to Elitch Gardens (p74) and ride the Mind Eraser roller coaster. In the evening, enjoy traditional Japanese fare at Domo (p87).

On your final day, drive to Red Rocks Park & Amphitheatre (p103) for a long hike. The setting, between 400ft-high red sandstone rocks, is spectacular. For a Latin-inspired dinner, try RiNo's Work & Class (p87). Afterwards, order a wine Popsicle at Infinite Monkey Theorum (p89).

hosts commuters waiting for their bus connections, politicos yammering into Bluetooth headsets, events of all sorts, and some of the most iconic public sculptures in the city.

Denver Art Society ARTS CENTER
(Map p66; DAS; ☑720-583-3728; www.denverartsociety.org; 734 Santa Fe Dr; ⊙10am-7pm Sun-Thu, to 10pm Fri & Sat; ⊡; ☐1) A co-op of local artists, DAS has ever-changing exhibits in its cavernous gallery. The basement houses dozens of open studios, where visitors can watch artists do their thing. Classes and workshops are offered for every level, including for kids, and most are quite affordable ($5 to $10).

Byers-Evans House Museum HISTORIC BUILDING
(Map p70; ☑303-620-4933; www.byersevanshousemuseum.org; 1310 Bannock St; adult/child $6/4; ⊙10am-4pm Mon-Sat, 1-4pm Sun; ⊡; ☐0, 52) It's a unique experience walking through this period house, painstakingly restored to the 1920s era with polished antiques, patterned wallpaper, thick drapes and period artwork; the rooms aren't roped off so you can wander into them. Guided tours run every hour starting 10:30am (Monday to Saturday) and 1:30pm (Sunday).

William Byers was the publisher of the *Rocky Mountains News* when he commissioned this grand house in 1883. Six years later, he sold it to William Gray Evans, head of the Denver Tramway Company and son of Governor John Evans.

Dancers MONUMENT
(Map p70; cnr Champa St & Speer Blvd; ⊡; ☐1, 48, ☒D, F, H) Frozen in joyful two-step, Jonathan Borofsky's whimsical *Dancers* invites rushing traffic to stop and play. The centerpiece of **Sculpture Park**, this 60ft sculpture supervises live music and lounging picnickers in summer and rises eerily from the snow in winter. Initially a controversial buy for conservative citizens, it's a symbol on scale with Denver's ambition to be the cultural capital of the West.

David B Smith Gallery GALLERY
(Map p70; ☑303-893-4234; www.davidbsmithgallery.com; 1543 Wazee St; ⊙noon-6pm Wed-Fri, to 5pm Sat; ☐20, 28, 32, 44) **FREE** David B Smith's taste for progressive American and international artists has made this space one of the most engaging small galleries in Denver.

Molly Brown House Museum HISTORIC BUILDING
(Map p78; ☑303-832-4092; www.mollybrown.org; 1340 Pennsylvania St; adult/child $11/5; ⊙tours 10am-3:30pm Tue-Sat, noon-3:30pm Sun; ⊡⊡; ☐6, 10, 15, 16) ⏶ This outstandingly preserved house, designed by the well-known architect William Lang, was built in 1889 and belonged to the most famous survivor of the *Titanic* disaster. You'll go through the house on a guided 45-minute tour, learning about this Colorado legend's unsinkable history.

Having survived the ill-fated voyage of 1912, Molly Brown became active in progressive politics and women's organizations, and was also a keen theater performer. She died in 1932, a woman ahead of her time.

Denver Zoo ZOO
(Map p66; ☑720-337-1400; www.denverzoo.org; 2300 Steele St; adult/child $17/12; ⊙9am-6pm, last admission 5pm; ⊡⊡; ☐20, 32, 40) Denver's world-class zoo has more than 700 animal species housed in considerate enclosures that do their best to mirror native habitats. There are native and exotic animals, including rhinos, gorillas and giant Komodo dragons. You won't want to miss the elephant passage and the tiger exhibit, which has bridges that pass 12ft above visitors' heads.

The zoo periodically offers free-admission days – check the website for info.

Forney Transportation Museum MUSEUM
(☑303-297-1113; www.forneymuseum.org; 4303 Brighton Blvd; adult/child $11/5; ⊙10am-4pm Mon-Sat, noon-4pm Sun; ⊡⊡; ☐48) This fascinating museum exhibits antique vehicles of all types – cars, motorbikes, bicycles, tricycles, railway engines and rolling stock, fire engines, airplanes and more. Even if you're not an automotive aficionado, the shifting industrial design over the years is interesting. Among many highlights is Amelia Earhart's 1923 Kissel Speedster in stunning canary yellow.

Rule Gallery GALLERY
(Map p66; ☑303-800-6776; www.rulegallery.com; 530 Santa Fe Dr; ⊙noon-6pm Tue-Fri, to 5pm Sat; ☐1, 9) **FREE** Robin Rule, whose name is lent to this clean space, has been a matron of Denver's experimental and contemporary art scene since the late 1980s. Usually hosting works by only one or two artists at a time, the Rule Gallery is a magnet for the city's artistic vanguard.

DENVER FOR KIDS

With loads of outdoor activities, there's plenty of space for the little ones to burn off their excess energy. Free activities in the fresh air include running like banshees in **Washington Park** (p69), playing in the pop-up fountains in front of **Union Station** (p63) and building sandcastles at **Confluence Park** (p65). For a few bucks you can check out the baby gorilla at the **Denver Zoo** (p73), paddle a kayak from **Confluence Kayaks** (p77) or rent bikes for the whole family from the city's **B-Cycle** (p101) program. If the kids are keen skaters, go to Denver's awesome **Skate Park** (p77) and watch them, uh, shred... dude.

The practical aspects of traveling with kids are also made easy in Denver. Sidewalks are wide and in good condition – perfect for strollers. There are elevators in most museums and hotels. Baby change facilities are prevalent and typically found in both women's and men's bathrooms. Grocery stores, small and large, sell baby and toddler supplies (think diapers, wipes, formula, baby food and more). And hotels typically have cribs and roll-out beds; they often allow kids 12 and under to stay for free too.

Big Sweep
MONUMENT

(Map p70; cnr 13th Ave & Acoma St; 🖩 0, 52) Large enough to whisk away a Volkswagen, this 31ft-tall dustpan's color was chosen by Claes Oldenburg and Coosje van Bruggen to complement Denver's clear blue skies. The scale was inspired by the vastness of Colorado's mountains and plains.

Colorado State Capitol
NOTABLE BUILDING

(Map p78; ☑ 303-866-2604; www.colorado.gov/capitoltour; 200 E Colfax Ave; ⊙ 7:30am-5pm Mon-Fri, tours 10am-3pm Mon-Fri; 👫; 🖩 0, 6, 9, 10, 15, 16, 52) **FREE** Sitting commandingly atop Capitol Hill, this stately neoclassical government building houses the Governor's Office, Senate and House of Representatives. Constructed using mostly Coloradan materials, the ornate interior befits the grand old building. Visitors can join free 45-minute tours – including 15 minutes in the dome – which depart hourly. A small museum on the 3rd floor gives a good historical overview of the building, including videos, placards and memorabilia.

Construction of the Capitol began in the 1890s from locally quarried rose onyx (Beulah red marble) and in 1908, to celebrate the Colorado gold rush, the superb dome was covered in 200oz of gold leaf. Down below facing Civic Center Park (p72), a popular photo op is the grand outer staircase, where the 13th step sits exactly 1 mile above sea level. (Previous attempts at marking the spot – in 1909 and 1969 – landed at the 15th and 18th steps.)

United States Mint
NOTABLE BUILDING

(Map p70; ☑ 303-405-4761; www.usmint.gov; 320 W Colfax Ave; ⊙ 8am-3:30pm Mon-Thu; 👫; 🖩 9, 16, 52) **FREE** The Denver Mint produces about 7.5 billion coins each year and offers free guided tours covering the history of the facility and detailed information about the minting process. Tickets are distributed same day only and they go quick! Arrive at 7am to be sure you get one (or five, which is the limit). Note: no bags, not even purses or fanny packs, are allowed on the tour, and no storage is provided; carry what you can in your pockets.

Black American West Museum & Heritage Center
MUSEUM

(Map p66; ☑ 720-242-7428; www.facebook.com/BAWMHC; 3091 California St; adult/child $10/6; ⊙ 10am-2pm Fri & Sat; 👫; 🖩 28, 34, 🚈 D) This small museum provides a window into the migration of African Americans to the West, including a look at their contributions during the pioneer era – according to museum statistics, one in three Colorado cowboys were African American. There is an eye-opening exhibit on the Dearfield Colony, an exclusively African American settlement in northern Colorado (now a ghost town).

The museum is set up in the former home of Dr Justina Ford, the first licensed African American female physician in Colorado. This 19th-century home was originally located 12 blocks away. Set to be demolished, it was moved to the current location and restored in order to house the museum.

Elitch Gardens
AMUSEMENT PARK

(Map p66; ☑ 303-595-4386; www.elitchgardens.com; 2000 Elitch Circle; adult/child $55/50; ⊙ 10:30am-9pm; 🅿 👫; 🖩 10) If you're finding all the museums a bit too serious, loosen up at this amusement park near downtown Denver – your

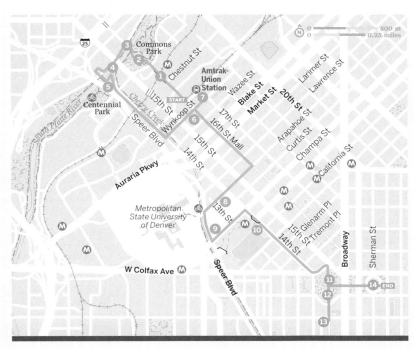

🏃 City Walk
Downtown Denver

START MILLENNIUM BRIDGE
END COLORADO STATE CAPITOL
LENGTH 3 MILES; FOUR HOURS

This tour ventures out of the tourist turkey shoot on the 16th St Mall and into the heart of the Mile High City.

Begin by strolling across ❶ **Millennium Bridge** (p72). This modernist footbridge is a bold symbol of contemporary Denver. Look ahead to the river: the city was born when gold was discovered in the currents below. Pass the rolling hills of ❷ **Commons Park** (p72), where you can soak up the Denver skyline before crossing another footbridge over the South Platte River. ❸ **National Velvet** (p76), a controversial sculpture of red...somethings (bean bags?) greets you on the other side. Descend to the far bank and take the paved path upstream. Soon you'll see kids across the river splashing in ❹ **Confluence Park** (p65), with its swimmable rapids where Platte River meets Cherry Creek.

If you're planning to head to the mountains, wander up to the enormous ❺ **REI** (p97) flagship store, where you can stock up on gadgets. Done shopping? Cross back over the water and take the footpath upstream beside Cherry Creek before taking the stairs up to Wynkoop St. At the corner you can hit ❻ **Tattered Cover Bookstore** (p97), our favorite Denver bookstore. But you're getting hungry, right? Head to ❼ **Union Station** (p63), where you can get a made-to-order deli sandwich or a sit-down meal.

Walk your meal off by heading a few blocks over to the ❽ **Denver Performing Arts Complex** (p94), where you can stand agape under ❾ **Dancers** (p73) and give a hug to ❿ **I See What You Mean** (p69). It's a straight shot up 14th St to ⓫ **Civic Center Park** (p72), where you can pose by ⓬ **Bronco Buster & On the War Trail** (p69), check out the remarkable architecture of the ⓭ **Denver Art Museum** (p65) and climb to the 13th step of the ⓮ **Colorado State Capitol** – exactly 1 mile above sea level.

DENVER FOR FREE

For cheapie fun, tour the **Colorado State Capitol** (p74) for free on weekdays, and almost all of the city's museums have free admission days at least once a month. The city's leafy parks provide tons of fresh entertainment and, if you're clever, you can use the **B-Cycle** (p101) program for *almost* free.

kids will love you for it. There's a water park, roller coasters, live entertainment and more. Go online to save on admission. If you're planning to go more than once, buy the season pass to save a bundle.

Kirkland Museum of Fine & Decorative Art   MUSEUM

(Map p78; ☑303-832-8576; www.kirklandmuseum.org; 1201 Bannock St; ☑0, 52) A fascinating museum, Kirkland showcases the beauty of decorative art – furnishings and decor – from every major design period from 1875 to 1990. It's displayed as if you'd walked into a home, with different rooms showcasing different design periods. Paintings by the namesake artist, Vance Kirkland, as well as other Colorado artists are also exhibited. The museum is set to open in a new space across from the Clyfford Still Museum (p65) in 2018. Check the website for opening hours and cost.

Museo de las Americas   MUSEUM

(Map p66; ☑303-571-4401; www.museo.org; 861 Santa Fe Dr; $5; ☑noon-5pm Tue-Sat; ☑; ☑1, 9) This small museum in the heart of the Santa Fe Arts District has innovative exhibits by Latin American and Latino artists. Shows range from rare collections of colonial artifacts to cutting-edge performance art. Programs celebrating the diversity of Latino culture are also regularly offered. The museum opens its doors for the city-wide First Friday (p80) event too.

Water World   AMUSEMENT PARK

(☑303-427-7873; www.waterworldcolorado.com; 8801 N Pecos St, Federal Heights; adult/child $42/37; ☑10am-6pm late May-early Sep; P☑; ☑19) Bust out the nacho cheese, sunscreen and water wings at this popular water park that has giant wave pools, plenty of slides and a handful of theme rides. Discounts on admission offered after 1:45pm.

Lakeside Amusement Park   AMUSEMENT PARK

(☑303-477-1621; www.lakesideamusementpark.com; 4601 Sheridan Blvd; entrance $3, unlimited rides $16-25; ☑hours vary; P☑; ☑44, 50, 51) This dilapidated fun park has old-school rides like wood roller coasters, the hammer, spinning swings as well as a kiddie area with mellow rides for tots. It's in a great lakeside location with mountain views. Ride coupons serve as tickets (one to six are needed, depending on the ride), though adrenaline junkies should opt for the unlimited ride bracelet.

Colorado Sports Hall of Fame   MUSEUM

(Map p66; ☑720-258-3888; www.coloradosports.org; 1701 Mile High Stadium Circle, Sports Authority Field at Mile High Stadium; ☑10am-3pm Mon-Sat Jun-Aug, 10am-3pm Thu-Sun Sep-May; P☑; ☑10, 20, 30, 31) **FREE** This small temple to Colorado's sporting prowess is in the Mile High Stadium (look for it near Gate #1). Beyond a gallery celebrating inductees to the Hall of Fame, there are exhibits on the Broncos, women in sports and athletes with disabilities. There's also a kids zone, where young visitors can play dress-up with professional jerseys and sports gear. A decent stop if you'll be at the stadium for a game (but not really worth a special visit).

Denver Firefighters Museum   MUSEUM

(Map p70; ☑303-892-1436; www.denverfirefightersmuseum.org; 1326 Tremont Pl; adult/child $7/5; ☑10am-4pm Mon-Sat; ☑; ☑9, 16, 52) Fire Station No 1 was built in 1909 and in 1978 it was turned into a museum exploring the history of firefighting in Denver. Mostly geared toward adults, there's lots of detail and signage. Kids, though, enjoy seeing the old steam equipment, sliding down a pole and getting kitted out in firefighting gear. The upstairs section is the old quarters where the firefighters slept.

The galleries include some interactive displays, mostly focused on fire-safety education for kids.

National Velvet   MONUMENT

(Map p66; 16th St pedestrian bridge; ☑☑) This much-maligned public pile of 'art' by John McEnroe appears to be a big red lingam-inspired mound of beans or sandbags. It lights up at night.

CELL   MUSEUM

(Map p78; Counterterrorism Education Learning Lab; ☑303-844-4000; www.thecell.org; 99 W 12th Ave; adult/student $8/5; ☑noon-7pm Tue, 10am-

5pm Wed-Sat, from noon Sun; 🚇0, 6, 10, 52) Indulge your fears and spy on your neighbors with the methods you learn at this over-the-top interactive learning center featuring plenty of footage from September 11, plus detailed exhibits on the life and work of the world's deadliest terrorists. You may ask yourself: with centers like this, has terrorism succeeded in making American society more paranoid?

🏃 Activities

There's a lot of talk about how Denver's people are among the slimmest in the USA, and it's easy to understand why. The city is checkered with lovely parks and green spaces, and the siren call of the rugged Front Range is ever-present. Plus, the sun is *always* shining: Denver is blessed with about 300 annual days of sunshine.

Denver's parks department (www.denver gov.org/dpr) manages 27 rec centers, dozens of outdoor and indoor pools, golf courses and more. All the rec centers are open to the public, with affordable day passes (adult/child $6/2).

Evo CYCLING, SNOW SPORTS
(Map p66; ☑303-831-7228; www.evo.com; 860 Broadway; ⊙10am-7pm Mon-Fri, to 6pm Sat, to 5pm Sun; 🚹; 🚇0, 6) The folks behind the counter at this outdoor gear shop might be the friendliest in town, and their rentals – bikes, snowboards and skis – are top-notch. Head to the back of the store for the bike mechanics.

Pura Vida Fitness & Spa SPA
(Map p66; ☑303-321-7872; www.puravidaclub. com; 2955 E 1st Ave, Suite 200; guest day pass $30; ⊙5am-10pm Mon-Thu, to 8pm Fri, 6am-7pm Sat, to 6pm Sun; 🚇1, 3, 46) Sleek as the *Starship Enterprise,* this modern spa is Denver's best. It isn't cheap, but it's a sure bet for modern workout facilities, yoga classes, group fitness sessions and a chance to sweat alongside Denver's business class.

Denver Skate Park SKATING
(Map p66; www.denvergov.org/parks; 2205 19th St; ⊙5am-11pm; 🚹; 🚇19, 52) **FREE** Possibly the best free skate park in the US, this 60,000 sq ft concrete park has various bowls and surfaces to suit all abilities. It's best for young skaters early on the weekends.

Kindness Yoga YOGA
(Map p78; ☑303-388-3000; www.kindnesscollec tive.com; 1280 Sherman St; 🚇0, 6, 10, 16) Denver's

top yoga studio offers a variety of classes for every-level yogi – from acro to nidra. Try the 'Kinda Hot' series for a moderately hot class with a mix of challenging and relaxing poses. Rental mats are available and the drop-in rate is recommended ('pay what you can' rules here). Sister studios located in LoDo, South Broadway and Golden.

Civic Center Moves HEALTH & FITNESS
(Map p70; ☑303-861-4633; www.facebook.com/ civiccentermoves; cnr Broadway & Colfax Ave, Civic Center Park; ⊙5:30am-7:15am, 11am-1pm & 6-7pm Mon-Thu; 🚇0, 9, 10, 52) **FREE** Join locals for free fitness classes in Civic Center Park (p72) – yoga, strength and conditioning, cardio workouts. Classes are geared for all levels, with modifications for those who need a little more, or less, intensity. In the winter, workouts move to the McNichols Building, on the northwest corner of the park. Check Facebook for class descriptions and times.

🍴 Courses

Cook Street School of Culinary Arts COOKING
(Map p70; ☑303-308-9300; www.cookstreet.com; 1937 Market St; classes from $75; ⊙9am-10pm; 🚹; 🚇52) Classes here are sharply focused, taking on ethnic flavors and cooking techniques from distant regions (such as North Africa, India or Spain), or an intense look at our favorite foods ('Steak & Spirits' class, anyone?). The instructors are well pedigreed and you'll leave stuffed.

Seasoned Chef COOKING
(☑303-377-3222; www.theseasonedchef.com; 999 Jasmine St, Suite 100; classes $75-160; 🚇10) This well-established cooking school offers three-hour classes on everything from knife skills and cooking basics to menu building and end-to-end sessions such as 'Tapas of the Southwest.'

Confluence Kayaks KAYAKING
(Map p66; ☑303-433-3676; www.confluenceka-aks.com; 2301 7th St; per day kayak packages from $55, tube rental $25, bike rental $45-65, classes $59-149; ⊙10am-8pm Mon-Fri, 10am-6pm Sat, noon-5pm Sun; 🚹; 🚇10) Located across from the Downtown Aquarium (p71), this kayak shop offers gear rental and lots of advice about the area's white water from laid-back, amiable staff. If you're a beginner, consider taking a lesson either in the shop's indoor pool or nearby Chatfield Reservoir. Inner tube and bike rentals also offered.

DENVER & AROUND DENVER

DENVER & AROUND DENVER

Denver
Bouldering Club CLIMBING

(Map p66; ☎ 303-351-5588; www.denverboulder-ingclub.com; 2485 W 2nd Ave, No 18/20; adult/child $16/8; ⊙ 11am-10pm Mon-Fri, 9am-7pm Sat & Sun; 🚇1) The instruction for serious climbers is better at the Colorado Mountain School (p145) in Estes Park, but this climbing gym in the heart of the city is a good way to get psyched for a trip into the mountains. It's also huge: a 7000-sq-ft facility with 15ft-tall bouldering walls, a workout area and free yoga on Monday nights.

☞ Tours

★ **Stranahans Colorado Whiskey** TOURS

(Map p66; ☎ 303-296-7440; www.stranahans.com; 200 S Kalamath St; regular/VIP tour $10/60; ⊙ tours 11am, 1pm, 3pm & 5pm Mon, Wed, Fri & Sat; 🚇3, 4) Only a dozen barrels of whiskey are produced at this family distillery each week, and they're damn good. Using award-winning water from the Rockies, Colorado barley and white-oak barrels, it's a rare taste of quality over quantity. Guided tours of the facility are available throughout the week, though limited space means it's best to sign up early and online.

Capitol Hill & Golden Triangle

⊙ Sights
1 CELL B5
2 Colorado State Capitol.......................... B4
3 History Colorado Center........................ B5
4 Kirkland Museum of Fine &
   Decorative Art A5
5 Molly Brown House Museum C4
6 Scottish Angus Cow & Calf................... A5

⊕ Activities, Courses & Tours
7 City Sessions... D3
8 Kindness Yoga.. B5

⊜ Sleeping
9 11th Avenue Hotel & Hostel.................. B5
10 Art – a Hotel B5
11 Capitol Hill Mansion B&B...................... C5
12 Denver International
    Hostel... D3
13 Patterson Historic Inn........................... C5
14 Queen Anne Bed &
    Breakfast Inn...................................... C1
15 Warwick.. C2

⊗ Eating
16 City O' City... B4
17 Cuba Cuba Café & Bar........................... A5
18 La Pasadita... D2
19 Steuben's Food Service......................... C3
20 WaterCourse Foods D3

⊙ Drinking & Nightlife
21 Ace.. C3
22 Charlie's.. D4
23 Church B5
24 Horseshoe Lounge C2
25 XBar D3

⊙ Entertainment
26 Curious Theatre...................................... B5
27 Fillmore Auditorium D3
28 Ogden Theatre.. D3
29 Quixote's True Blue................................ C3

⊙ Shopping
30 Capitol Hill Books C4
31 Wax Trax Records D4

City Sessions TOURS
(Map p78; ☑ 720-250-8828; www.citysessions-denver.com; 925 E 17th Ave, 3rd fl; tours from $129; ▢ 12, 20) City Sessions' small cadre of cannabis guides are all industry veterans and the owner leads many tours herself. Four-hour tours include stops at a grow operation, dispensary and glass-blowing demonstration, and a deep dive into cannabis production and trends. Private tours are also offered for a customized experience in medicinal marijuana, concentrates and more. Cannabis cooking classes in the works too.

Denver Microbrew Tours TOURS
(☑ 303-578-9548; www.denvermicrobrewtour.com; per person $40) This popular company offers tours and samples of local craft breweries in the LoDo and RiNo neighborhoods. Tours take two to three hours during the afternoon on Friday, Saturday or Sunday. The LoDo tour includes a $1 pint of the beer of your choice; the RiNo one can include a stop at a cider house.

Colorado Cannabis Tours TOURS
(Map p70; ☑ 303-420-8687; www.coloradocannabistours.com; tours $59-99; ▢ 55L, 72L, 120L, FF2, ▣ A, B, C, E, W) For a party-bus atmosphere (it's a pot tour, right?), Denver's original cannabis tour operator still delivers. Bus and limo tours range from 2½ to 4½ hours and include stops at a grow operation, up to

three different dispensaries, a glass-blowing demo and, of course, a grub-run at Cheba Hut, a cannabis-themed sandwich shop.

Tours leave from a designated spot near Union Station.

Platte Valley Trolley TOURS
(Map p66; ☑ 303-458-6255; www.denvertrolley.org; 1400 Platte St; adult/child $5/2; ⊙ departures every 30min 11am-5pm Thu-Mon; ▥; ▢ 10, 28, 32, 44) Ride the historic Platte Valley Trolley, which trundles along its tracks from the REI (p97) store south toward the football stadium. To be honest, the sights on the 25-minute trip aren't much – mostly the same stuff you see in a short walk around the area – but the stories from the history-buff staff are enlightening.

⭐ Festivals & Events

**Great American
Beer Festival** BEER
(☑ 303-447-0816; www.greatamericanbeerfestival.com; 700 14th St; $85; ⊙ Sep or Oct; ▢ 1, 8, 19, 48, ▣ D, F, H) Colorado has more microbreweries per capita than any other US state, and this hugely popular festival sells out in advance. More than 500 breweries are represented, from the big players to the home-brew enthusiasts. Only the Colorado Convention Center (p97) is big enough for these big brewers and their fat brews.

SPRINGING IN TO THE MILE HIGH CITY

Denver is smack in the middle of some of the United States' most stunning nature and, frankly, you'd be a fool to miss it. If you're flying, don't bring gear from home. The airlines' baggage fees will destroy your budget and there's tons of affordable, world-class gear to rent. The REI (p97) flagship store is a top option for camping and mountaineering supplies, kayaks, snowshoes and skis (*way* cheaper than renting at the slopes). The B-Cycle (p101) program doesn't cut it for serious cyclists, so rent road or mountain bikes at Evo (p77).

Most times of year, you can get a room without advance notice, but you'll always save money with the aggregators. The city has an international airport (p100), a decent public transit system and generally permissive liberal attitudes. The altitude may affect you. Drink lots of water and watch for sun exposure.

Denver Cruiser Ride   PARADE
(www.denvercruiserride.com; ☺May-Sep) **FREE**
Held monthly from May to September, Denver's Cruiser Ride is one of the biggest in the nation. Check the website for the starting point and the theme of the night – you'd hate to go dressed as 'Bible Belt and Panties' when it's actually 'Ski Bums & Bunnies' night. Folks typically meet up around 6pm; the ride starts around 8pm.

First Friday   CULTURAL
(www.rivernorthart.com) **FREE** On the first Friday of every month, Denverites come out for an art stroll, cruising galleries for free wine and fun conversations in the Santa Fe and RiNo Arts Districts. The event typically runs from 6pm to 10pm.

Five Points Jazz Festival   MUSIC
(www.artsandvenuesdenver.com; Welton St; ☺May; ♿; ☐12, 28, 43, ☐D) **FREE** This one-day jazz fest celebrates the historically African American neighborhood of Five Points, which was once home to several jazz clubs. Over 50 bands perform on stages set up on Welton St. Several kid-friendly activities – instrument making, drum circles, face painting – are offered, making it a fun event for all. Held the third Saturday of May.

PrideFest   LGBT
(www.facebook.com/pg/denverpridefest; ☺Jun; ☐0, 9, 10, 52) Denver's PrideFest is one of the nation's largest gay pride events, drawing tens of thousands of people for a joyful two-day celebration. Held in June, the festivities include a parade from Cheeseman Park to Civic Center Park (p72), plus events like the Dogs in Drag contest and the Big Gay 5K.

A Taste of Colorado   FOOD & DRINK
(☑303-295-6330; www.atasteofcolorado.com; cnr Broadway & Colfax Ave, Civic Center Park; ☺Sep; ♿; ☐0, 9, 10, 52) More than 50 restaurants cook up their specialties at food stalls; there's also booze, live music, and arts-and-crafts vendors at this Labor Day festival. Food and beverage tickets start at $10.

Cinco de Mayo   CULTURAL
(www.cincodemayodenver.com; cnr Broadway & Colfax Ave, Civic Center Park; ☺May; ♿; ☐0, 9, 10, 52) **FREE** Enjoy mariachis and margaritas at one of the country's biggest Cinco de Mayo celebrations, held over two days on the first weekend in May in Civic Center Park (p72). With three stages, over 350 exhibitors and food vendors, plus highlights like Chihuahua races and a parade, it's huge fun.

Cherry Creek Arts Festival   ART
(☑303-355-2787; www.cherryarts.org; cnr Clayton St & E 3rd Ave; ☺Jul; ♿; ☐24, 46) **FREE** During this sprawling celebration of visual, culinary and performing arts, Cherry Creek's streets are closed off and over 350,000 visitors browse the giant block party. The three-day event takes place around July 4.

420 Rally   MUSIC, FOOD & DRINK
(www.denver420rally.org; cnr Broadway & Colfax Ave, Civic Center Park; ☺Apr; ☐0, 9, 10, 52) **FREE** If 4:20pm is the best time to blaze a doobie, then 4/20 must be the best date to do it. That and rally for the legalization of cannabis nationwide. Denver's Civic Center Park (p72) hosts Colorado's original 420 Rally, which draws thousands of people and features music, vendors and an omnipresent blue haze (despite the fact that smoking pot in public is illegal).

Security is tight, so expect long lines to get in while bags are searched. No cannabis

– in any form – is sold at the event; head to a dispensary for that. Instead, you'll find paraphernalia, tees, hats, mementos...pretty much anything you can throw a marijuana leaf on. Lots of food trucks too. (You know, munchies and all.) City officials periodically threaten to cancel the event over littering or misconduct – check for the latest online before heading there.

Denver March Powwow   CULTURAL
(☑ 303-934-8045; www.denvermarchpowwow.org; 4600 Humboldt St, Denver Coliseum; adult/child $7/free; ◷ Mar; ♿; 🚌48) Since 1984, Denver has hosted an annual powwow, a time when tribes come together to celebrate and share their heritages through song and dance. This three-day event is one of the largest in the country, with almost 100 tribes represented in the festivities. Native American artwork and food are sold throughout. Open to the public, all are welcome.

🛏 Sleeping

Most of Denver's lodging is found in the greater downtown area, including the major international chains. Nightly rates have skyrocketed in recent years – book online to save big. For budget-conscious travelers, a few fancy (and not-so-fancy) hostels provide relief.

★ Hostel Fish   HOSTEL $
(Map p70; ☑ 303-954-0962; www.hostelfish. com; 1217 20th St; dm/r from $53/185; ❋🛜; 🚌38) This swanked-out hostel is an oasis for budget travelers. Stylish, modern and squeaky clean, dorms have themes – Aspen, Graffiti, Vintage Biker – and sleep five to 10 people in bunks. Mattresses are thick, duvets plush and each guest gets a locker and individual charging station. The common kitchen and frequent pub crawls make it easy to make new friends.

The only hiccup: a restaurant-bar with live music on the 1st floor. Great if you want to party. Bummer if you want to sleep. Bring earplugs. Better yet, request a room on the top floor.

Mile High Guest House   HOSTEL $
(Map p66; ☑ 720-531-2898; www.milehighguesthouse.com; 1445 High St; dm $38, r with shared bath $82; 🛜; 🚌15) A gorgeous old Denver mansion makes for a cool hostel and a welcome addition to Denver's budget lodging options. Large parlor rooms serve as dorms, outfitted with bunk beds (but no lockers,

oddly). Private rooms with shared bathrooms are also available and the friendly staff help organize group outings, like pub crawls, art walks and backyard BBQs. Convenient bus-friendly location.

Geared toward providing good budget accommodations; all guests must be age 33 and under and have student ID.

11th Avenue Hotel & Hostel   HOTEL $
(Map p78; ☑ 303-894-0529; www.11thavenuehotelandhostel.com; 1112 Broadway; dm $29, r with/ without bath $65/53; ♿❋@🛜; 🚌0, 6) This basic hotel/hostel is nowhere near fancy but new carpets, updated bathrooms and murals go a long way. The rooms are bare but clean plus dorm guests get huge lockers to store their belongings. On-site laundry facilities and common areas – both inside and out – are reminiscent of a freshman dorm. A safe and decent place for budget travelers.

Denver International Hostel   HOSTEL $
(Map p78; ☑ 303-832-9996; www.denverinternationalhostel.com; 630 E 16th Ave; dm $19; 🅿@🛜; 🚌15, 20) If every penny counts, then the Denver International Hostel might be your ticket. It's basic, a bit ramshackle and vaguely chaotic, but has a great downtown location. Dorms are single sex – with three bunks max – and have en-suite bathrooms. The common area in the basement has a large-screen TV, library and computers for guests to use.

★ Queen Anne Bed & Breakfast Inn   B&B $$
(Map p78; ☑ 303-296-6666; www.queenannebnb.com; 2147 Tremont Pl; r/ste from $160/230; 🅿♿❋🛜; 🚌28, 32) 🌿 Soft chamber music wafting through public areas, fresh flowers, manicured gardens and evening wine tastings create a romantic ambience at this eco-conscious B&B in two late-1800s Victorian homes. Featuring period antiques, private hot tubs and exquisite hand-painted murals, each room has its own personality.

Green features include mattresses made from recycled coils and infused with green-tea extracts to keep them smelling fresh, organic fabrics (just like the delicious full breakfast), and products and produce purchased from local merchants when possible. It even has free bikes.

Lumber Baron Inn Gardens   B&B $$
(Map p66; ☑ 303-477-8205; www.lumberbaron.com; 2555 W 37th Ave; r from $159; 🅿♿❋🛜; 🚌38) Built in 1890, this elegant B&B in the cooled-out Highlands neighborhood stands out from

the pack. Each of its five suites features ceiling murals, antique beds and Jacuzzi tubs; wi-fi and HD televisions keep guests connected. Continental breakfast included in the rate. Coffee service brought to your room for an extra fee.

Capitol Hill Mansion B&B   B&B $$

(Map p78; ☑ 303-839-5221; www.capitolhill-mansion.com; 1207 Pennsylvania St; r $164-249; P ⊖ ✳ 🎧; 🖾 10) Stained-glass windows, original 1890s woodwork and turrets make this delightful, gay- and family-friendly Romanesque mansion a special place to stay. Rooms are elegant, uniquely decorated and come with different special features (one has a solarium, another boasts Jacuzzi tubs). Breakfast is made using locally sourced and organic products; vegan and vegetarian options abound.

Hotel Monaco   BOUTIQUE HOTEL $$

(Map p70; ☑ 303-296-1717; www.monaco-denver.com; 1717 Champa St; r $209-269, ste $289-329; P ⊖ ✳ 🎧 ☲; 🖾 0, 6, 19, 10, 28, 32, 38, 52) This ultra-stylish hotel is a favorite with the celebrity set. Modern rooms blend art-deco and urban Western styles – think bold colors, bovine prints and fabulous feather beds. Don't miss the evening 'altitude adjustment hour,' when guests enjoy complimentary wine and snacks; mornings bring free coffee. The place is 100% pet friendly; staff will even deliver a goldfish to your room upon request.

Free bicycles are available for guest use. Rooms also come with yoga mats and access to a yoga channel.

Castle Marne Bed & Breakfast   B&B $$

(Map p66; ☑ 303-331-0621; www.castlemarne.com; 1572 Race St; r $174-314, ste $344; P ⊖ ✳ 🎧; 🖾 15, 20) Fall under the spell of Castle Marne, one of Denver's grandest old mansions. Located in the historic Wyman District, it dates from 1889 and is on the National Register of Landmarks. The feel is pre-1900 old-world elegance with modern-day convenience and comfort. Furnishings are authentic period antiques and family heirlooms, and offer a mood of quiet charm and romance.

Each of the nine rooms is a unique experience of taste and style, and they all come with indoor Jacuzzis or outside hot tubs. Bike rentals ($15 per day) available for exploring town on two wheels.

Patterson Historic Inn   HISTORIC HOTEL $$

(Map p78; ☑ 303-955-5142; www.pattersoninn.com; 420 E 11th Ave; r from $208; ✳ 🎧; 🖾 10) This 1891 grande dame was once a senator's home. It's now one of the best historic bed-and-breakfasts in town. The gardens are limited, but the Victorian charm, sumptuous breakfast and well-appointed chambers in the nine-room château will delight. Rooms come with modern touches such as silk robes, down comforters and flat-screen TVs.

Warwick   HOTEL $$

(Map p78; ☑ 303-861-2000; www.warwickhotels.com; 1776 Grant St; r from $180, ste from $330; P ⊖ ✳ 🎧 ☲; 🖾 20, 28, 32) Affordable luxury just east of downtown Denver is how the Warwick bills itself and, with some very cheap online specials, this can be true. Rooms here are larger than average and surprisingly modern. While the lackluster lobby leaves a bit to be desired, you are literally a jump from downtown, and the rooftop pool is a summertime perk.

★ Crawford Hotel   HOTEL $$$

(Map p70; ☑ 855-362-5098; www.thecrawfordhotel.com; 1701 Wynkoop St, Union Station; r $349-469, ste $589-709; ✳ 🎧 ☲; 🖾 55L, 72L,120L, FF2, 🅿 A, B, C, E, W) Set in the historic Union Station (p63), the Crawford Hotel is an example of Denver's amazing transformation. Rooms are luxurious and artful, with high ceilings and throwbacks like the art-deco headboards and claw-foot tubs. Service is impeccable and the station's bar, the Terminal, is a fun hangout. Steps away, there's light-rail service to Denver International Airport (p100).

The hotel shuttle – a Tesla – also provides door-to-door service for guests within a 2-mile radius.

★ Art – a Hotel   BOUTIQUE HOTEL $$$

(Map p78; ☑ 303-572-8000; www.thearthotel.com; 1201 Broadway; r $305-348, ste $382-518; P ✳ @ 🎧 ☲; 🖾 0, 6, 10, 52) As the name suggests, this hotel has intriguing artwork in the guest rooms and common areas, befitting its location, just around the corner from the Denver Art Museum (p65). Rooms are sizable and modern, and the large patio with fire pits and great views is perfect for happy-hour cocktails. The location close to downtown restaurants and attractions could hardly be better.

Omni Interlocken Resort & Golf Club   RESORT $$$

(☑ 303-438-6600; www.omniinterlocken.com; 500 Interlocken Blvd, Broomfield; d from $289; P ⊖ ✳ @ 🎧 ☲; 🖾 228) Have a glass of champagne

ST MARY'S GLACIER & JAMES PEAK

Wildflowers and windswept trails, boulders and snowfields – these are the disproportionately big rewards for the easy hike up to St Mary's Glacier area. It's a quick day escape from Denver, and the modest elevation gains, short distance (half-mile) and summer snow and ice make it ideal even for the littlest hikers. Although the area gets fairly busy on summer weekends, the views on a clear day are remarkable, and a scramble around the lake will bring you to the glacier itself.

If you want to make a day of it, the trail to James Peak (13,294ft) continues up another 3 miles past the base of the glacier to the summit. This gentle mountain on the Continental Divide was named after the botanist Edwin James, who made the first recorded summit of Pikes Peak in 1820 (Pike, of course, never made it to the top). It's a relatively moderate but beautiful climb.

To get here, take I-70 west from Denver, past Idaho Springs to Fall River Rd (exit 238). Turn right on Fall River Rd and continue for 10 miles until you reach the parking areas. There is a parking fee of $5 for these lots and it's best not to park elsewhere; the neighbors don't tolerate strangers parking on their turf. Get here early to secure a spot.

while checking into the impressive four-diamond Omni. Although the location isn't so hot – in the 'burbs between Denver and Boulder – rooms are spacious and well appointed, and the service is top-notch, with helpful and friendly staff. A big spa, two pools, 27 golf holes and shuttle add to the pluses list.

Oxford Hotel BOUTIQUE HOTEL **$$$**
(Map p70; ☑ 303-628-5400; www.theoxfordhotel. com; 1600 17th St; r from $466, ste from $580; ☺ ✳ ☎ ; ▦ 0, 15, 20) Marble walls, stained-glass windows, frescoes and sparkling chandeliers adorn the public spaces of this classy hotel built in 1891. Denver's first hotel has large rooms decked out with imported English and French antiques, claw-foot tubs and other nods to its past. Located just steps from Union Station (p63).

The extensive art collection on display includes several notable works and the art-deco Cruise Room Bar is one of Denver's swankiest cocktail lounges.

Curtis HOTEL **$$$**
(Map p70; ☑ 303-571-0300; www.thecurtis.com; 1405 Curtis St; r $269-449; ☺ ✳ @ ☎ ; ▦ 9, 10, 15, 20, 28, 32, 38, 43, 44) The Curtis is like stepping into a doo-bop Warhol wonderland: 13 themed floors, each devoted to a different genre of American pop culture. Rooms are spacious and very mod. Attention to detail – either through the service or the decor – is paramount at the Curtis, a one-of-a-kind hotel in the heart of downtown Denver.

The hotel's refreshingly different take on sleeping may seem too kitschy for some –

you can get a wake-up call from Elvis – but if you're tired of the same old international brands, this spot might just be your tonic.

Hotel Teatro BOUTIQUE HOTEL **$$$**
(Map p70; ☑ 303-228-1100; www.hotelteatro.com; 1100 14th St; r $254-356, ste $407; ☺ ✳ ☎ ; ▦ 9, 10, 15, 28, 32, 38, 43, 44) Elegant surroundings and impeccable service make this luxurious boutique hotel one of Denver's best. The 112 rooms and suites are gorgeous, done up with Indonesian sandstone foyers, art-deco and cherrywood furnishings and thick damask curtains. Across from the Denver Performing Arts Complex (p94), it's not surprising that Hotel Teatro would incorporate the theater into its name and decor.

JW Marriott Denver at Cherry Creek HOTEL **$$$**
(Map p66; ☑ 303-316-2700; www.jwmarriottdenver.com; 150 Clayton Lane; r $329-389, ste $699; ▣ ☺ ✳ ☎ ; ▦ 1, 3, 24, 46) Urban chic meets Western elegance at the JW. Spacious digs come with high-thread-count sheets, plump beds and marble bathrooms featuring top-class soaps and shampoos. The on-site bar is a popular place – you might even spot a Denver Bronco. Local artwork and colorful blown glass grace lobbies and rooms.

Brown Palace Hotel HISTORIC HOTEL **$$$**
(Map p70; ☑ 303-297-3111; www.brownpalace.com; 321 17th St; r $319-419; ▣ ☺ ✳ @ ☎ ; ▦ 10, 20, MALLRIDE) Standing agape under the stained-glass-crowned atrium, it's clear why this palace is shortlisted among the country's elite historic hotels. There's deco artwork, a four-star spa, imported marble and staff who

discreetly float down the halls. The smallish rooms, which have hosted presidents since Teddy Roosevelt's days, have a unique elegance – some modern, others hearkening to a distant era.

If it's out of budget, consider taking a guided tour ($15) or hang out for a while in the lobby and just pretend. The martinis are predictably perfect and served with a sterling bowl of warm pecans.

Magnolia Hotel HOTEL $$$
(Map p70; ☑888-915-1110; www.magnoliahoteldenver.com; 818 17th St; r/ste from $349/399; ❂✳@☎✹; 🚌0, 6, 19, 52, 🚇D, F, H) Housed in an old bank building, this 13-story European-style hotel offers old-world charm, modern amenities and good value in the heart of downtown. Its super-central location, good deals and bedtime milk and cookies are three major selling points.

Tasteful, stylish rooms and suites come in a variety of sizes, although some are a bit small, with a Western meets Euro flavor. Gym junkies will dig the on-site fitness center.

🍴 Eating

Denver's food scene is booming, with new restaurants, cafes and food trucks seemingly opening every month. Downtown offers the greatest depth and variety in Denver, though strollable neighborhoods like LoHi, RiNo, South Broadway, Uptown and Five Points hold some of Denver's best eateries. Check out www.5280.com for new eats.

⭐**Denver Central Market** FOOD HALL $
(Map p66; 2669 Larimer St; ⊙8am-9pm Sun-Thu, to 10pm Fri & Sat; 🚌44, 48) Set in a repurposed warehouse, this gourmet marketplace wows with its style and breadth of options. Eat a bowl of handmade pasta or an artisanal sandwich; consider a wood-fired pizza or street tacos. Or just grab a cocktail at the bar and wander between the fruit stand and chocolatier. Patrons eat at communal tables or on the street-side patio.

An easy date night or place to eat lunch. Any which way, there's something for everyone.

⭐**Civic Center Eats** FOOD TRUCK $
(Map p70; ☑303-861-4633; www.civiccenterconservancy.org; cnr Broadway & Colfax Ave, Civic Center Park; mains $5-10; ⊙11am-2pm Tue-Thu May-Oct; ⬇✹; 🚌0, 9, 10, 52) When the weather gets warm, head to Civic Center Park

(p72) for lunch. There, a huge number of food trucks – everything from BBQ and pizza to sushi and Indian – roll into the park and serve up hearty meals. Tables are set up, live bands play, office workers picnic on the grass. It's Denver at its best.

⭐**SAME Café** AMERICAN $
(Map p66; So All May Eat Café; ☑720-530-6853; www.soallmayeat.org; 2023 E Colfax Ave; by donation; ⊙11am-2pm Mon-Sat; ⬇; 🚌15) 🌿 This nonprofit cafe was founded by two former food-bank workers who wanted to provide organic and locally sourced meals for people struggling to make ends meet. The healthy and innovative fare changes daily (think tomato coconut soup and radish Parmesan pizza). Diners pay by donation. More, if they can afford it; less, if not. Walk-in volunteers very welcome.

Volunteering here or dropping in for lunch is one of the most rewarding experiences in Denver. The cafe demonstrates the most progressive thinking in the city's sustainable, local, community-oriented food movement.

⭐**Little Man Ice Cream** ICE CREAM $
(Map p66; ☑303-455-3811; www.littlemanicecream.com; 2620 16th St; ice cream $1.50-6.50; ⊙10am-1am; ⬇; 🚌32, 44) It's impossible to miss the 28ft-high dairy jug. From its window, cones of handcrafted ice cream – including several vegan options – are doled out from morning till night. Flavors change daily but expect everything from Chunky Chocolate to Earl Grey Tea & Cookies. A large plaza with plenty of seating and a swing set make it a popular meeting spot.

⭐**City O' City** VEGETARIAN $
(Map p78; ☑303-831-6443; www.cityocitydenver.com; 206 E 13th Ave; mains $9-14; ⊙7am-2am; ▨⬇; 🚌0, 6, 10, 16) 🌿 This popular vegan/vegetarian restaurant mixes retro decor with an innovative spin on greens, grains and seitan. The menu has a wide offering of items like kimchi pancakes, pumpkin curry pasta and fried cauliflower with waffles. More traditional palettes enjoy big salads and the best vegan pizza pie in D-Town. Reservations aren't accepted but a full bar makes waiting easy.

⭐**Tamales by La Casita** NEW MEXICAN $
(Map p66; ☑303-477-2899; www.tamalesbylacasita.net; 3561 Tejon St; dishes $3-10; ⊙7am-7pm Mon-Fri, from 9am Sat; ▨⬇; 🚌44) La Casita serves up the best tamales in Denver, hands down.

Two types are on deck: red chile and pork, and green chile and cheese (the latter is vegetarian and gluten-free). Order plain or make a plate of it with sides of beans and rice. Do like locals do and order extra chile to smother the plate in spicy goodness.

Snooze
BREAKFAST $

(Map p66; ☑ 303-297-0700; www.snoozeeatery.com; 2262 Larimer St; mains $7-12; ☺ 6:30am-2:30pm; ✿ ♿; ☐ 8, 38, 44, 48) *❂* This retro-styled cheery spot is one of the hottest post-party breakfast-and-brunch joints in town. It dishes up spectacularly crafted breakfast burritos and a smokin' salmon Benedict. The coffee's always good, but you have the option of an early-morning Bloody Mary. The wait can be up to an hour on weekends!

Other locations include Union Station (p63) in downtown Denver and Colorado Blvd near Cherry Creek.

WaterCourse Foods
VEGETARIAN $

(Map p78; ☑ 303-832-7313; www.watercourse-foods.com; 837 E 17th Ave; mains $11-15; ☺ 7am-10pm Sun-Wed, to 11pm Thu-Sat; ☑ ♿; ☐ 12, 20) The unrelentingly meaty menus of Denver can be a chore to navigate for vegetarians, so the smart, straightforward fare at Water-Course is a welcome reprieve. The breakfasts are cherished by locals, and dinner options – many of them with an Asian or Mexican influence – are uniformly well done.

Pho 95
VIETNAMESE $

(☑ 303-936-3322; www.pho95noodlehouse.com; 1401 S Federal Blvd; mains $6-12; ☺ 9am-9pm; ☑ ♿; ☐ 14, 30, 31) The best place for pho (noodle soup) in Denver is a bit out there, parked in the middle of a strip mall on a bleak stretch of Federal, but it's definitely worth the hike to slurp your way through a big, cheap bowl of noodles.

La Pasadita
MEXICAN $

(Map p78; ☑ 303-832-1785; 1959 Park Ave; mains $6-9; ☺ 11am-9:30pm Mon-Sat; ☑ ♿; ☐ 28, 32) This tiny, family-run Mexican joint is a favorite among locals. The food is authentic and cheap, and it's all handmade from whole ingredients. If you like heat, order the green chile plate – it's one of the best in town. The restaurant sits on a small triangular allotment surrounded by streets on all sides.

Voodoo Doughnut
DESSERTS $

(Map p66; ☑ 303-597-3666; www.voodoodoughnut.com; 1520 E Colfax Ave; doughnuts $1-3; ☺ 24hr; ♿; ☐ 15) People line Colfax to get their mitts on the delicious and sometimes far-out creations made at this Portland-based shop: doughnuts topped with strips of bacon, Froot Loops or bubble gum. Classic doughnuts – plain, glazed, powdered – are also sold but it's way more fun to order an Old Dirty Bastard (topped with chocolate frosting, Oreos and peanut butter). Cash only.

Rolling Pin Bakeshop
DESSERTS $

(Map p66; ☑ 720-708-3026; www.therollingpinbakeshop.com; 2716 Welton St; dishes $2-4; ☺ 6am-3pm Tue-Sun; ♿; ☐ 43, ☒ D) This European-style bakery is worth a stop if only for the spectacular 18-layer croissants, some stuffed with ham and Gruyère cheese, others filled with chocolate and dusted with powdered sugar. Consider, too, the apricot cheese danishes and French silk pies. All to die for. The bakery captures an old-world feel, with mosaic-tile floors, tin ceilings and a fabulous font.

Dunbar Kitchen & Tap House
PUB FOOD $

(☑ 720-630-7641; www.dunbarkitchenandtaphouse.com; 2844 Welton St; mains $9-15; ☺ 11am-10pm Mon-Thu, 11am-11pm Fri, 10am-11pm Sat, 10am-10pm Sun; ♿; ☐ 12, 28, 43, ☒ D) A barbershop turned pub, Dunbar is an unassuming place with high-end pub grub – burgers with homemade pimento bacon jam, Cajun mac 'n' cheese, hand-cut fries. Head to the sunny patio on warm days, where there are communal picnic tables and, occasionally, live music. Daily happy hour (2:30pm to 6:30pm) brings deals on Colorado craft beers – just $3.50 a pint!

Rosenberg's Bagels & Delicatessen
DELI $

(Map p66; ☑ 720-440-9880; www.rosenbergsbagels.com; 725 E 26th Ave; items $2-15; ☺ 6am-3pm Tue-Sun; ☎ ♿; ☐ 43, ☒ D) The bagels at this deli are the real deal, as close as you can get to a NYC bagel in Denver – the crust, a perfect thin shell, the inside warm and chewy. Traditional toppings – cream cheese, lox, white fish – are abundant and fresh. There's also a laundry list of made-to-order sandwiches. Want a starter? Consider the matzo-ball soup.

Source
MARKET $

(Map p66; ☑ 720-443-1135; www.thesourcedenver.com; 3350 Brighton Blvd; ☺ 8am-11pm; ☎ ♿; ☒ A) A repurposed iron foundry, this industrial-chic marketplace features shops specializing in artisanal breads, specialty cheeses and locally sourced produce. Crooked Stave, a sour-craft brewer, and Acorn (p88), one of the best restaurants in town, also call this home. A hot spot, especially on weekends and evenings.

Sweet Action Ice Cream ICE CREAM $

(Map p66; ☑ 303-282-4645; www.sweetactionicecream.com; 52 Broadway; cones $3.25-6.25; ⊙ 1-10pm Sun-Thu, to 11pm Fri & Sat; ⓜ; ☑ 0, 1, 52) Don't wander past this neighborhood icecream parlor expecting the same old chocolate chip: the seasonal, housemade flavors here include baklava, salted butterscotch and five spice. In the summer there are tons of fruit-based varieties such as ginger peach and blackberry lavender. Bonus: it also does vegan varieties.

Cooks Fresh Market SANDWICHES $

(Map p70; ☑ 303-893-2277; www.cooksfreshmarket.com; 1600 Glenarm Pl; sandwiches & salads $5-14; ⊙ 7am-8pm Mon-Fri, 9am-6pm Sat; ⓞ ☑ ⓜ; ☑ 8, 10, 19, 28, 32, MALLRIDE) Far and away the best deli in downtown, the attention to quality here is obvious in the take-out salads and sandwiches, selection of cheeses and expert pastries. Some gourmet cooking staples and bulk selection complete the picture, making this an ideal stop for supplies if you're picnicking in the park or heading out of town.

Manna from Heaven FOOD TRUCK $

(www.mannafoodtruck.com; mains $7-10) Specializing in Vietnamese fare, this food truck serves up one mean banh mi, with crunchy veggies, pork and a mayo-sriracha sauce on a fresh baguette. Plump pot stickers, perfectly grilled kebabs and even a naan wrap are close runners-up to top pick. Check the website for the truck's daily location and hours.

Illegal Pete's MEXICAN $

(Map p70; ☑ 303-623-2169; www.illegalpetes.com; 1530 16th St; mains $7-9; ⊙ 7am-midnight Mon-Wed, 7am-2:30am Thu & Fri, 9am-2:30am Sat, 9am-midnight Sun; ☑ ⓜ; ☑ MALLRIDE, 10, 19, 28, 32, 44) Around lunch, you'll queue to the door at Pete's, the best option for quick Mexican on the 16th St Mall. With rock posters plastering the window, a worn plank floor underfoot and inked-up staff behind the counter, the place has charm galore.

Market at Larimer Square CAFE $

(Map p70; ☑ 303-534-5140; www.themarketatlarimer.com; 1445 Larimer St, LoDo; pastries $3-7, sandwiches $9-13; ⊙ 6am-10pm Sun-Thu, to 11pm Fri & Sat; ⓞ ⓜ; ☑ 10, 28, 32, 38, 44) Situated in a historic building on Larimer Sq, the Market is an excellent coffee shop, deli and gourmet-food store. The place makes popular sandwiches and coffee drinks (like a Milky Way latte) and it can hardly keep up with demand for its cultishly popular cake, the Spring Fling, which layers zucchini bread, fresh fruit and cream-cheese icing.

Just BE Kitchen AMERICAN $

(Map p66; ☑ 303-284-6652; www.justbekitchen.com; 2364 15th St; mains $6-13; ⊙ 7am-3pm; ☑ ⓜ; ☑ 10, 28, 32, 44) Set in a simple, airy dining room, Just BE is an exclusively Paleo and gluten-free restaurant, and meals are also made without sugar, dairy or processed ingredients. Dishes sport names like 'wonder' (seasonal veggie hash), 'wholehearted' (pork green chile) and 'crave' (bacon cheeseburger). The setting is casual – order at the counter – and meals come out fast.

Food Court at Republic Plaza FAST FOOD $

(Map p70; ☑ 303-534-5128; 370 17th St; mains $5-12; ⊙ 7am-6pm Mon-Sat; ⓜ; ☑ MALLRIDE, 8, 19, 20, 28, 32) With chains big and small and fast-food prices, this 16th St Mall food court is easy for families and rushed office jockeys. The nosh isn't limited to the frightening thrill of Chick-fil-A patties, either; there are a few healthy options. On warm days, head outside to the sunny patio seating.

Biker Jim's Dogs FAST FOOD $

(Map p66; ☑ 720-746-9355; www.bikerjimsdogs.com; 2148 Larimer St; hot dogs $8-10; ⊙ 11am-10pm Sun-Thu, to 3am Fri & Sat; ⓜ; ☑ 8, 38) Biker Jim's passion for Harleys is only outpaced by his visionary zeal for encased meat. No kidding: the man is a revolutionary. The standard hits are an Elk Jalapeño Cheddar Brat and the Alaska Reindeer Sausage. Most folks opt for a topping too – everything from New Jersey–style chili to roasted cactus with curry jam.

Still Smokin FOOD TRUCK $

(☑ 720-300-4010; www.stillsmokinco.com; dishes $7-9; ⓜ) This popular food truck serves up barbecued dishes from different parts of the world – pulled-pork sandwiches, chicken 'n' waffles, lettuce wraps, tacos... All the meat is smoked in cherry and hickory wood and comes with handcrafted sauces ranging from whiskey to chipotle peach. It's worth tracking the truck down for the sweet-potato fries alone. Check the website for its location.

Pizza Colore Express ITALIAN $

(Map p70; ☑ 303-534-2111; www.pizzeriacolore.com; 1647 Court Pl; mains $7-10; ⊙ 8am-3pm Mon-Fri; ⓜ; ☑ 20, MALLRIDE) Big portions of inexpensive pasta and wood-oven pizzas are served at this casual Italian restaurant. The food is delicious (especially considering the price).

El Taco De Mexico
MEXICAN $

(Map p66; ☑303-623-3926; www.eltacodemexicodenver.com; 714 Santa Fe Dr; mains $6-9; ⊙7am-10pm Sun-Thu, to 11pm Fri & Sat; P🅿️; 🚌1, 9) Forget about ambience – this is a big yellow counter, fluorescent lights and a couple of slouching figures shoveling down tacos. But all will be forgiven when you rip into the chile relleno burrito, a glorious disaster of peppers, cheese, refried pinto beans and *salsa verde*.

Little India
INDIAN $

(Map p70; www.littleindiadenver.com; 1533 Champa St; mains $10-16; ⊙11am-10pm; 🚗🅿️; 🚌9, 15, 20, MALLRIDE) The lunch buffet ($11) attracts a load of office workers. After dark the atmosphere gets a bit more upscale, with couples snuggling into booths for a selection of curries and generously spiced rice dishes. One of three Denver locations, this place also has a full bar out the back.

★ Hop Alley
CHINESE $$

(Map p66; ☑720-379-8340; www.hopalleydenver.com; 3500 Larimer St; mains $10-25; ⊙5:30-10:30pm Mon-Sat; 🚗; 🚌12, 44) Hop Alley was a slur used for Denver's hardscrabble Chinatown in the 1880s, until a race riot and anti-Chinese legislation scattered the community. The moniker was reclaimed for this small bustling restaurant located in (what else?) a former soy-sauce plant. Come for authentic yet inventive Chinese dishes and equally creative cocktails, named after the signs of the Chinese zodiac.

Osteria Marco
ITALIAN $$

(Map p70; ☑303-534-5855; www.osteriamarco.com; 1453 Larimer St; panini & pizzas $12-18, mains $19-29; ⊙11am-10pm Sun-Thu, to 11pm Fri & Sat; 🚗🅿️; 🚌10, 28, 32, 38, 44) With housemade cheeses and house-cured deli meats, this isn't just another Italian pizza place. Grab a sun-drenched table outside or retreat to the brick-walled bistro downstairs to sample the delicious array of antipasti and *insalate* before tucking into gourmet pizza, panini or a more substantial main course like pork loin with prosciutto and Parmesan broccoli.

Work & Class
LATIN AMERICAN $$

(Map p66; ☑303-292-0700; www.workandclassdenver.com; 2500 Larimer St; mains $6-17; ⊙4-10pm Tue-Thu & Sun, to 11pm Fri & Sat; 🚌44) A small restaurant with a big punch, Work & Class serves

up a marriage of Latin and American cuisines: flaky empanadas, melt-in-your-mouth roasted lamb, shrimp ceviche and whole fried Idaho trout. Small plates mean you can try lots, plus meat is sold by the pound. Reservations aren't accepted but a $4 drinks-while-you-wait special helps the time pass quickly.

Beatrice & Woodsley
TAPAS $$

(Map p66; ☑303-777-3505; www.beatriceandwoodsley.com; 38 S Broadway; small plates $9-15; ⊙5-11pm Mon-Fri, 9:30am-2pm & 5-10pm Sat & Sun; 🚌0) Beatrice & Woodsley is the most artfully designed dining room in Denver. Chainsaws are buried into the wall to support shelves, there's an aspen growing through the back of the dining room and the feel is that of a mountain cabin being elegantly reclaimed by nature. The menu of mostly small plates is whimsical and European inspired.

Mix up two or three small plates with some hyper-kinetic elixirs.

Domo Restaurant
JAPANESE $$

(Map p66; ☑303-595-3666; www.domorestaurant.com; 1365 Osage St; mains $10-24; ⊙11am-2pm & 5-10pm; 🚌16, 33A) 'Japanese country food' doesn't really capture the refinement of dishes at Domo, which sports the best garden dining in all of Colorado – kind of like dining in Mr Miyagi's backyard. Inside, the traditional dining room has stone-slab tables and tree-trunk seating, with Japanese antiques on the walls. Dishes are explosively flavorful, each served with seven traditional Japanese sides.

Reservations not accepted. Come early or late on warm nights.

Bistro Vendôme
FRENCH $$

(Map p70; ☑303-825-3232; www.bistrovendome.com; 1420 Larimer Sq; mains $11-26; ⊙5-10pm Mon-Thu, to 11pm Fri, 10am-2:30pm & 5-11pm Sat, 10am-2:30pm & 5-9pm Sun; 🚌10, 28, 32, 38, 44) When you discover Vendôme, tucked behind the storefronts of historic Larimer Sq, it feels like your own little secret. Brunch is more casual than dinner, but both are done with scrupulous French technique: mussels in white wine and herb-roasted chicken are well-executed standards, while things get more adventurous with the grilled brioche with blueberry lavender compote and honey Boursin cheese.

Steuben's Food Service
AMERICAN $$

(Map p78; ☑303-803-1001; www.steubens.com; 523 E 17th Ave; mains $8-22; ⊙11am-11pm Mon-Thu, to midnight Fri, 10am-midnight Sat, to 11pm Sun; 🅿️;

DENVER'S FOOD ON WHEELS

Denver's foodie scene has taken to four wheels, two wheels, trolleys and more. Check out www.roaminghunger.com and www.denverstreetfood.com for daily locations. Top finds include:

Manna from Heaven (p86)

Still Smokin (p86)

Civic Center Eats (p84)

🚋20) 🚲 Although styled as a midcentury drive-in, the upscale treatment of comfort food (mac 'n' cheese, fried chicken, lobster rolls) and the solar-powered kitchen demonstrate Steuben's contemporary smarts. In summer, open garage doors lining the street create a breezy atmosphere and happy hour brings the most unbeatable deal around: a burger, hand-cut fries and beer for $7.

Sushi Den   SUSHI $$
(🛈303-777-0826; www.sushiden.net; 1487 S Pearl St; sushi $5-12, rolls $6-18; ⏰11:30am-2:30pm & 4:45pm-10:30pm Mon-Thu, to 11pm Fri, 4:30-11pm Sat, 5-10:30pm Sun; 🚋12) With fresh fish flown in from Japan's Nagahama Fish Market, this is – by far – the best sushi restaurant in Denver. Two brothers, Yasu and Toshi Kisaki, opened the restaurant in 1984, bringing creative and clever sushi to Denver. They haven't stopped since. Come hungry and make reservations!

Cuba Cuba Café & Bar   CUBAN $$
(Map p78; 🛈303-605-2822; www.cubacubacafe. com; 1173 Delaware St; mains $13-25; ⏰5-10pm Mon-Thu, to 10:30pm Fri & Sat; 🅿🍴; 🚋9, 52) Try the mango mojito at this swanky Cuban joint serving finger-lickin' BBQ spareribs, flavor-packed fried yucca, scrumptious sandwiches and sumptuous coconut shrimp. The back patio offers fantastic sunset city views; the bright blue-walled environs emit an island vibe. There's sometimes live music on Thursday nights.

Duo   MODERN AMERICAN $$
(Map p66; 🛈303-477-4141; www.duodenver.com; 2413 W 32nd Ave; mains $8-28; ⏰5-10pm Mon-Fri, 10am-2pm & 5-10pm Sat, 10am-2pm & 5-9pm Sun; 🚋32) 🚲 This cozy bistro-style eatery with exposed brick walls and well-worn stylings is poised, elegant, confident and, at times, simply remarkable. The seasonal menu focuses on locally sourced meats and greens.

Lamb shank makes it nearly year-round. Brunch here is a three-hour affair not to be missed.

⭐**Root Down**   MODERN AMERICAN $$$
(Map p66; 🛈303-993-4200; www.rootdowndenver. com; 1600 W 33rd Ave; small plates $8-19, mains $14-35; ⏰5-10pm Sun-Thu, 5-11pm Fri & Sat, 11am-2pm Fri, 10am-2:30pm Sat & Sun; 🍴; 🚋19, 52) 🚲 In a converted gas station, chef Justin Cucci has undertaken one of the city's most ambitious culinary concepts, marrying sustainable 'field-to-fork' practices, high-concept culinary fusions and a low-impact, energy-efficient ethos. The menu changes seasonally, but consider yourself lucky if it includes the sweet-potato falafel or Colorado lamb sliders. Vegetarian, vegan, raw and gluten-free diets very welcome.

Unlike the troupe of restaurants jumping on the sustainable bandwagon, Root Down is largely wind-powered, decorated with reused and reclaimed materials, and recycles everything. It's conceptually brilliant and one of Denver's most thrilling dining experiences. It also has a restaurant at Denver International Airport (p100).

⭐**Rioja**   MODERN AMERICAN $$$
(Map p70; 🛈303-820-2282; www.riojadenver.com; 1431 Larimer St; mains $19-39; ⏰11:30am-2:30pm Wed-Fri, 10am-2:30pm Sat & Sun, 5-10pm daily; 🍴; 🚋10, 28, 32, 38, 44) This is one of Denver's most innovative restaurants. Smart, busy and upscale, yet relaxed and casual – just like Colorado – Rioja features modern cuisine inspired by Italian and Spanish traditions and powered by modern culinary flavors.

People in the know mix a handful of starters such as foie gras mousse and a cheese plate tapas-style, before heading into regional favorites such as Colorado lamb or pan-roasted venison.

⭐**Acorn**   AMERICAN $$$
(Map p66; 🛈720-542-3721; www.denveracorn. com; 3350 Brighton Blvd, The Source; dishes $14-30; ⏰11:30am-10pm Mon-Sat, 5:30-10pm Sun; 🅿🍴🍸; 🚋12, 20, 48) The oak-fired oven and grill are the shining stars of this superb restaurant, where small plates of innovative and shareable eats make up meals. The menu changes seasonally but dishes like crispy fried pickles, oak-grilled broccolini and smoked-pork posole are hits. If dinner is too pricey, consider a midday meal (2:30pm to 5:30pm) – the menu is limited but more affordable.

Located in the Source, a renovated 19th-century foundry turned high-end urban marketplace.

Fruition Restaurant
MODERN AMERICAN $$$

(Map p66; ☑ 303-831-1962; www.fruitionrestaurant. com; 1313 E 6th Ave; mains $25-31; ☺ 5-10pm Mon-Sat, to 9pm Sun; ☑ 6, 12) ✎ Alex Seidel and Blake Edmunds are heavy hitters in Denver's fine-dining scene, pulling off their contemporary American plates (potato-wrapped oysters Rockefeller, duck with mascarpone crepe) with understated panache. The food is simply conceived, carefully executed and elegantly presented. Many of the greens, the chickens and the eggs come from Seidel's farm. A longtime favorite among locals.

Kitchen
MODERN AMERICAN $$$

(Map p70; ☑ 303-623-3127; www.thekitchenbistros. com; 1530 16th St; mains $11-40; ☺ 11am-9:30pm Mon & Tue, to 10:30pm Wed-Fri, 10am-10:30pm Sat, to 9:30pm Sun; ☎ ✎ ☻; ☑ 10, 19, 28, 32, 44, MALL-RIDE) ✎ Bringing a dash of Boulder sophistication to Denver's downtown, the Kitchen is renowned for its healthy, gourmet, farm-to-table creations. Expect everything from quiche du jour and beet salad with chèvre to lamb burgers with Fresno chilies and fries. Great cocktails too.

Elway's
STEAK $$$

(Map p70; ☑ 303-312-3107; www.elways.com; 1881 Curtis St; mains $27-50; ☺ 6:30am-11:30pm Mon-Wed, to 12:30am Thu & Fri, 9am-12:30am Sat, 9am-11:30pm Sun; ☎; ☑ 0, 1, 8, 48) Businesspeople and fat cats come to wax nostalgic about Denver's all-time top-performing quarterback and carve into pricey medium-rare porterhouses at Denver's top steakhouse, located inside the Ritz Carlton. If you're at Denver International Airport (p100) or in Cherry Creek, check out the sister restaurants.

Mizuna
FRENCH $$$

(Map p66; ☑ 303-832-4778; www.mizunadenver. com; 225 E 7th Ave; mains $28-43; ☺ 5-10pm Tue-Sat; ✎; ☑ 6) Mizuna is exclusive, expensive and exquisite. The small dining room only adds to the rarefied atmosphere and there's a certain pride knowing you're eating at one of the country's most renowned restaurants. The menu is eclectic and ever changing, with an emphasis on fresh seafood and locally sourced seasonal produce.

♉ Drinking & Nightlife

Denver's top nightlife districts include Uptown for gay bars and a young professional crowd, LoDo for loud sports bars and heavy drinking, RiNo for hipsters, LoHi for an eclectic mix, and South Broadway and Colfax for Old School wannabes.

If you consider yourself a beer snob, you might mistake Denver for a foamy, malty corner of heaven. Forget about that watery stuff made in Golden: the brewing culture around these parts is truly world class, with craft and seasonal brews by the gallon, restaurants that sideline as craft breweries and kegs that arrive from beer regions as near as Boulder and as far as Munich. Simply put, Denver adores beer.

★ Williams & Graham
COCKTAIL BAR

(Map 66; ☑ 303-997-8886; www.williamsandgraham.com; 3160 Tejon St; ☺ 5pm-1am; ☑ 32,44) Denver's top speakeasy looks like an old Western bookstore, but ask for a seat and the cashier pushes a wall of books and leads you deeper into the era. Polished wood, gleaming brass features, antique lamps, tin ceilings and mixologists in aprons await. Cocktails are creative and artfully prepared – almost too beautiful to drink. Almost.

This is a small place, so reservations are a must. If you're wait-listed, warm up with a drink next door at Occidental, a small bar with big views of downtown Denver.

★ Black Shirt Brewing Co
BREWERY

(Map p66; ☑ 303-993-2799; www.blackshirtbrewingco.com; 3719 Walnut St; ☺ 11am-10pm Sun-Thu, to midnight Fri & Sat; ☻; ☑ 12, 44, ☒ A) Artisanal brewers create the all-red-ale menu at the popular BSB; ales take anywhere from two months to three years to brew. So careful are they with the handcrafted beers, the brewers developed lopsided glasses to showcase the aromas. Live music is part of the culture here, as is good food. A kitchen offers brick-oven pizzas and gourmet salads.

★ Infinite Monkey Theorum
WINERY

(Map p66; ☑ 303-736-8376; www.theinfinitemonkeytheorem.com; 3200 Larimer St; ☺ 4-8pm Mon, to 10pm Tue-Thu, 2-8pm Fri-Sun; ☑ 44) Infinite Monkey surprises with its sophisticated wines, made on site, using mostly grapes from Colorado's western slope. It surprises again by serving them not only by the glass but also by the can, slushy machine and even Popsicle. Unorthodox yes, but oh-so-tasty. Seating is in a cool-cat lounge, reminiscent of a '60s rec room, and outdoors on a spacious patio.

Tours and barrel tastings offered.

★ **Crema Coffee House** CAFE
(Map p66; ☑720-284-9648; www.cremacoffee-house.net; 2862 Larimer St; ⏱7am-5pm; 🛜; 🚍44) Noah Price, a clothing designer turned coffee impresario, takes his job seriously, selecting, brewing and pouring Denver's absolute-best coffee. The espresso and French-pressed are complete perfection, but it's the oatmeal latte, delicately infused ice teas and spectacularly eclectic menu – Moroccan meatballs to peanut-butter and jelly sandwiches with goat's cheese – that put this place over the top.

Finn's Manor BAR
(Map p66; www.finnsmanor.co; 2927 Larimer St; ⏱5pm-midnight Tue-Thu, 2pm-midnight Fri, noon-midnight Sat, noon-9pm Sun; 🚍44) Finn's has got it right. Give folks strong drinks and good food fast and they'll come. The concept: a small bar with a huge patio that has a variety of food trucks so you can drink and eat till your belly is content. Whiskey drinks rule but all cocktails are artfully poured and Colorado brews are always on tap.

Tracks GAY
(Map p66; ☑303-863-7326; www.tracksdenver.com; 3500 Walnut St; cover $10; ⏱9pm-2am Fri & Sat, hours vary Sun-Thu; 🚍44, 🚊A) Denver's best gay dance club has an 18-and-up night on Thursday, and Friday drag shows. There's a definite pretty-boy focus, with good music and a scene to match. Saturday is the biggest dance night. No cover before 10pm.

La Rumba CLUB
(Map p66; ☑303-572-8006; www.larumba-denver.com; 99 E 9th Ave; cover free-$5; ⏱9pm-2am Thu-Sat, 7pm-12:30am Sun; 🚍0, 6) Denver's most popular Latin dance club gets its merengue (and salsa and reggaeton and bachata) on every weekend, with DJs Thursday and Friday and live music Saturday. Come dressed to impress. Dance lessons ($10) offered most nights at 8pm too.

Falling Rock Tap House BAR
(Map p70; ☑303-293-8338; www.fallingrock-taphouse.com; 1919 Blake St; ⏱11am-2am; 🚍0, 15, 20) High fives and hollers punctuate the scene when the Rockies triumph and beer drinkers file in to forget an afternoon of drinking Coors at the ball park. There are – count 'em – 80-plus beers on tap and the bottle list has almost 150. With all the local favorites, this is *the* place to drink beer downtown.

Stem Ciders BAR
(Map 66; ☑720-443-3007; www.stemciders.com; 2811 Walnut St; ⏱4-10pm Mon-Thu, 3-11pm Fri, noon-11pm Sat, to 10pm; 🚲; 🚍44) Stem Ciders is all about craft cider. Think dry, complex, nuanced, not the sugary stuff your cousin brings to BBQs. The barrel-lined walls, garage doors and food trucks capture its essence. Add live bluegrass, food pairings and public barrel tappings, and you've got a hit. New to cider? Try 'Malice' – Stem's firstborn – a smooth crisp introduction to this under-appreciated brew.

Recess Beer Garden BEER GARDEN
(Map 66; ☑720-638-0020; www.recessbeer-garden.com; 2715 17th St; ⏱11am-2am; 🚍32, 44) A huge patio with leafy trees, picnic tables and a community garden is the centerpiece of Recess. A locals hangout with a chilled-out vibe, this is where Denverites come to kick back a few with friends. Twenty-four beers are on tap, many Colorado craft brews, plus there's a full bar. A kitchen serves decent pub food too.

Goed Zuur CRAFT BEER
(Map p66; ☑720-749-2709; http://goedzuur.com; 2801 Welton St; ⏱3pm-midnight Mon-Wed, to 1am Thu & Fri, 1pm-1am Sat, 1pm-midnight Sun; 🚍43, 🚊D) This stylish but welcoming pub serves only sour beers and wild ales – possibly the only such taproom in the country. Grab a stool at the long copper-topped bar and enjoy small pours of craft sours from Colorado and around the world. Gorgeous cheese and charcuterie plates balance the sours perfectly. A bit pricey overall, but definitely worth the splurge.

Beryl's Beer Co BREWERY
(Map p66; ☑720-420-0826; www.berylsbeerco.com; 3120 Blake St; ⏱3-10pm Mon-Thu, noon-11pm Fri & Sat, noon-9pm Sun; 🚍44) The name will tip you off to the niche here: barrel-aged beers. A variety of brews are aged in used barrels, from brandy to red wine, making for a unique hybrid flavor. (It also does experimental blends like ales and chai or pilsner and limeade.) On a quiet stretch of Blake St, the scene here is mellower than most.

First Draft BAR
(Map p66; (☑303-736-8400; www.firstdraftden-ver.com; 1309 26th St; ⏱noon-10pm Mon-Thu, noon-midnight Fri, 11am-midnight Sat, 11am-9pm Sun; 🚍44, 48) Young and hopping, this is a great place to sample craft beers, wine, cider, kombucha and more. Instead of a bartender,

there's a line of 20-plus taps. Buy a refillable charge card, scan it and pull yourself a glass – you're charged by the ounce. Long communal tables and a nice patio make it easy to mingle. Kitchen service too.

Ratio Beerworks   BREWERY
(Map 66; ☑303-997-8288; www.ratiobeerworks. com; 2920 Larimer St; ☺noon-11pm Sun-Thu, to midnight Fri & Sat; ☑44) In a spacious warehouse with a peppy mid-mod feel, Ratio Beerworks has quality brews, an upbeat crowd and plenty of indoor and patio seating. It's a good place to begin or end a brewery-hopping tour of the neighborhood. Go-to brews include the Antidote IPA and Hold Steady chocolate rye. The brewery also hosts regular arts and music events.

Crimson Room   LOUNGE
(Map p70; ☑720-639-6987; www.thecrimsonroom. com; 1403 Larimer St; ☺5pm-midnight Tue-Thu, to 2am Fri & Sat; ☑10, 28, 32, 38, 44) A nondescript red door near the corner of Larimer and 14th Sts leads down to this hidden cocktail lounge with cozy couches and velvet booths you just sink into. Live jazz or acoustic guitar fills the room as guests sip on creative cocktails and nibble on fine cheeses or sweets. Reservations recommended. Be sure to dress up!

Thin Man Tavern   BAR
(Map 66; ☑303-320-7814; www.thinmantavern. com; 2015 E 17th Ave; ☺3pm-2am; ☑20, 24) The Thin Man is a damn sight more stylish than most neighborhood taverns. It's decked out in all kinds of Catholic art and crosses, red string lights casting the place in a warm, sentimental glow. Stiff drinks and a good beer selection seal the deal. For live music, check out the basement-level Ubisububi Room.

Great Divide Brewery Company   BREWERY
(Map p70; ☑303-296-9460; www.greatdivide. com; 2201 Arapahoe St; ☺noon-8pm Sun-Tue, to 10pm Wed-Sat; ☑8, 38, 44, 48) This excellent local brewery does well to skip the same old burger menu and fancy digs to keep its focus on what it does best: crafting exquisite beer. Bellying up to the bar, looking onto the copper kettles and sipping Great Divide's spectrum of seasonal brews is an experience that will make a beer drinker's eyes light up. Tours available.

A second taproom in Great Divide's packaging and storage facility is located just a mile away in RiNo.

Crú   WINE BAR
(Map p70; ☑303-893-9463; www.cruawine bar.com; 1442 Larimer St; glass of wine $10-27; ☺2pm-midnight Mon-Thu, noon-2am Fri & Sat, 10:30am-3pm Sun; ☑10, 28, 32, 38, 44) This classy Larimer Sq wine bar is decked out in wine labels and glassware, with dim lighting and gentle music. It looks so bespoke it's surprising to learn it's a chain (Dallas, Austin). Come for happy hour (4pm to 6:30pm Monday to Friday) when flights of wine are $3 off and light fare includes mussels and goat's cheese beignets.

Matchbox   BAR
(Map 66; ☑720-437-9100; www.matchboxdenver. com; 2625 Larimer St; ☺4pm-2am Mon-Fri, noon-2am Sat & Sun; ☑44) Located in the ever-hip RiNo art district, this hole-in-the-wall appeals to the thick-glasses and blue-jeans crowd. Daily drink specials always include a beer plus a

DENVER & AROUND DENVER

LGBT+ DENVER

Even though Colorado has some very socially conservative areas, Denver is as progressive and broad-minded as you get in the inner-mountain West, and gay and lesbian travelers should expect no particular trouble. The bohemian Capitol Hill district, especially the bars on Colfax, are the center of the gay and lesbian scene. Head to Cheeseman Park during the day. For the latest news, events and goings-on, check out the online edition of Out Front Colorado (www.outfrontonline.com) or the website of the Center (www. glbtcolorado.org), the largest LGBT community center in the Rocky Mountain region. Top gay bars and hangout spots include the following:

Charlie's (p93)

BoyzTown (p93)

Tracks (p90)

XBar (p92)

Denver Wrangler (p92)

shot for six bucks. And yep, that's a bocce ball court out back.

XBar
GAY & LESBIAN

(Map p78; ☑ 303-832-2687; www.xbardenver.com; 629 E Colfax Ave; ☉ 3pm-2am Mon-Sat, noon-2am Sun; ☐ 15) Two stories of madness, with your typical gay anthems and a patio. XBar brings in a younger crowd and is an LGBTQ 'it' spot.

Ace
BAR

(Map p78; ☑ 303-800-7705; www.acedenver.com; 501 E 17th Ave; per hour $15; ☉ 4-11pm Mon-Wed, 2-11pm Thu & Sun, 2pm-1am Fri & Sat; ☐ 20) The best ping-pong bar in Denver. Come here for fun tournaments, hipster sightings, decent food and a raucous indoor-outdoor party that takes you deep into the pong underground – street rules apply.

Linger
LOUNGE

(Map 66; ☑ 303-993-3120; www.lingerdenver.com; 2030 W 30th Ave; ☉ 11:30am-2:30pm & 4-10pm Tue-Thu, to 11pm Fri, 10am-2:30pm & 4-11pm Sat, 10am-2:30pm Sun; ☐ 28, 32, 44) This rambling LoHi complex sits in the former Olinger mortuary. Come nighttime, they black out the 'O' and it just becomes Linger. There's an interesting international menu, but most people come for the tony feel and light-up-the-night rooftop bar, which has great views of downtown Denver and even a replica of the RV made famous by the Bill Murray smash *Stripes*.

ink!
CAFE

(Map p70; ☑ 303-825-4422; www.inkcoffee.com; 618 16th St; ☉ 6am-6pm Mon-Fri, from 7am Sat & Sun; ☎ 🛉 ; ☐ 9, 15, 20, MALLRIDE, ☐ D, F, H) This Aspen-based roaster has a convenient location on 16th St between the Convention Center and State Capitol building. While it lacks the atmosphere of your average neighborhood coffee shop (and sorry, no pictures of Aspen's slopes on the walls either), it serves up a good cup o' joe plus is a good spot to work.

There are also ink! outposts near Confluence Park (p65) and in RiNo.

Common Grounds
CAFE

(Map p70; ☑ 303-296-9248; www.commongrounds coffeehouse.com; 1550 17th St; ☉ 6:30am-9pm Mon-Fri, 7:30am-6pm Sat & Sun; ☎ 🛉 ; ☐ 0, 15, 20, MALLRIDE) Hidden on the ground floor of an office tower on the corner of Wazee and 17th St, Common Grounds is hands down the most pleasant cafe in the downtown area. Plenty of seating, a good wi-fi connection and lots of caffeine on offer.

Beta Nightclub
CLUB

(Map p70; ☑ 303-383-1909; www.betanightclub. com; 1909 Blake St; cover from $15; ☉ 9pm-2am Thu-Sat, 7pm-midnight Sun; ☐ 0, 15, 20) This huge club changes musical flavors like fashionable boutique sneakers. The best parties go off in the interior Beatport lounge, sending au courant bass, hip-hop and electro through a sound system that will rattle your fillings loose.

Denver Wrangler
GAY

(Map p66; ☑ 303-837-1075; www.denverwrangler. com; 3090 Downing St; ☉ 11am-2am; ☐ 12, 34, 43) Though it attracts an amiable crowd of gay male professionals after work, it becomes Denver's premiere pick-up bear scene on weekends. Three levels and great patio space make it easy to see and be seen. Come for the Sunday Beer Bust, when for $10 it's drink-all-you-can-drink beer from 4pm to 8pm.

My Brother's Bar
BAR

(Map 66; ☑ 303-455-9991; 2376 15th St; ☉ 11am-2am Mon-Sat; ☐ 10, 28, 32, 44) Classic rock and roll, lacquered booths and tables made from old wood barrels greet you inside Denver's oldest bar. Grab a seat on the leafy patio if it's nice outside. The bar is on a popular cycle path and has been a local institution since it opened.

Nallen's
IRISH PUB

(Map p70; ☑ 303-572-0667; 1429 Market St; ☉ 2pm-2am; ☐ 1, 6, 10, 19, 20, 28, 32, 44) Nallen's is a venerable Irish pub, and since opening in 1992 it's been the go-to place for a perfectly poured pint of Guinness. Happy hour is from 2pm to 7pm.

Wynkoop Brewing Co
BREWERY

(Map p70; ☑ 303-297-2700; www.wynkoop.com; 1634 18th St; ☉ 11am-midnight Sun-Thu, to 2am Fri & Sat; 🛉 ; ☐ MALLRIDE, ☐ A, B) Wynkoop's Rail Yard is this brewery's most celebrated red ale, and beer fans file into the spacious brewpub to knock it back while tossing darts, shooting pool or taking in the breeze on the wide porch. The taps change with the season and the menu offers passable pub standards. Brewery tours available Tuesday through Saturday.

There's some local history here, too. Colorado Governor John Hickenlooper and a group of developers founded the brewpub in 1988, kicking off the urban renewal that took LoDo from sketchy warehouse district to the luminary upscale digs of today.

Horseshoe Lounge LOUNGE
(Map p78; ☑303-832-1180; www.thehorseshoe-lounge.com; 414 E 20th Ave; ⊙3pm-2am Mon-Thu, from 1pm Fri, from 3pm Sat, from 2pm Sun; ☒28, 32) This neighborhood lounge-bar is totally laid back with couches and cozy chairs, a couple of booths, a pool table and dartboards. There's a full bar including craft brews plus 'shitty cans of beer' too. The bar counter is made up of about 23,000 dice (they say). Pub fare – pizza, subs, nachos – is decent.

Bar Standard CLUB
(Map p66; ☑303-534-0222; www.coclubs.com; 1037 Broadway; ⊙8pm-2am Wed-Sun; ☒0) From the sleek deco interior to the DJ roster, Bar Standard is an inimitable gem in Denver's nightclub scene. It's ice cold without the attitude and when the right DJ is on the tables it can be some of the best dancing in town. In the summer, head straight for the rooftop bar.

Milk CLUB
(Map 66; ☑303-832-8628; www.coclubs.com/milk; 1037 N Broadway; cover $5; ⊙9pm-2am Thu-Sun; ☒0, 6) Dance floors get packed at Milk, where goth rules and industrial and '80s tie for second. Plenty of pleather booths give you a place to catch your breath between sets. Wear a cape or your neon shades and stick to beer – drinks are served in tiny plastic cups with loads of ice. Look for the entrance in the alley.

Corner Office LOUNGE
(Map p70; ☑303-825-6500; www.thecornerofficedenver.com; 1401 Curtis St; ⊙6:30am-11pm Sun-Thu, to midnight Fri & Sat; ☎; ☒9, 15, 28, 32, 38, 43, 44) The cheery sensibility of this excellent retro-style lounge is demonstrated in the wall of clocks frozen at 5pm and waggish menu of cocktails ('the Secretary' comes with a rim of grape Kool-Aid powder). It's perfect for a drink after a show at nearby Denver Performing Arts Complex (p94). Food is hit or miss, unfortunately – stick with the booze.

Sputnik BAR
(Map 66; ☑720-570-4503; www.sputnikdenver.com; 3 S Broadway; ⊙10:30am-2am Mon-Fri, 10am-2am Sat & Sun; ☎; ☒0) The Sputnik does it all – it's simultaneously a plucky brunch spot, a neighborhood dive bar and an excellent place for espresso. Still, it's never more fun than when there's a show next door at the Hi-Dive (p94) and the indie rockers spill over for strong pours and a seat in the old-school photo booth.

If spending a long night of drinks, snacks and rock and roll still isn't enough for you, the long-running 'Hangover Brunch' does it right, with spicy Bloody Marys and lots of ragged morning-after style.

Church CLUB
(Map p78; ☑303-832-2383; www.coclubs.com; 1160 Lincoln St; cover $20; ⊙9pm-2am Fri-Sun; ☒0, 6, 10) There's nothing like ordering a stiff drink inside a cathedral built in 1865. Yes, this club, which draws a young and diverse crowd, is in a former house of the Lord. Lit by hundreds of altar candles and flashing blue strobe lights, the Church has three dance floors, acrobats and a couple of patios.

Arrive before 10pm to avoid the cover charge.

Punch Bowl Social LOUNGE
(Map 66; ☑303-765-2695; www.punchbowlsocial.com; 65 Broadway; ⊙11am-1am Mon-Thu, to 2am Fri, 8am-2am Sat, 8am-midnight Sun; ☎; ☒0, 1) This adult mega-entertainment-plex has ping-pong, bowling, shuffleboard, foosball, darts, Galaga...even marbles (free if you bring your own), plus plenty of strong drinks. There's a full menu of upscale pub food too.

Charlie's GAY
(Map p78; ☑303-839-8890; www.charliesdenver.com; 900 E Colfax Ave; ⊙11am-2am; ☒15) The quintessential Denver gay cowboy bar gets Brokeback on two dance floors (there's a non-country room for you city fellows). The nightly line-dancing classes are worth it. The bar brings in a mixed LGBTQ crowd.

BoyzTown GAY
(Map p66; ☑303-722-7373; www.boyztowndenver.com; 117 Broadway; ⊙3pm-2am Mon-Thu, from noon Fri-Sun; ☒0, 1, 52) This gay strip club (down to their Marky Mark's) is kind of trashy, but fun for sure. Shows start at 10pm.

☆ Entertainment

Denver is bursting with entertainment options. There's live music and theater practically everywhere, from intimate jazz clubs to the amazing multitheater Denver Center for the Performing Arts (p94). Denver is a four-sport town (one of few in the country) and also has professional soccer and lacrosse. Add to that comedy, movies, dance and yearly festivals and there's truly something for everyone.

DENVER & AROUND DENVER

★ **Denver Performing Arts Complex** PERFORMING ARTS

(Map p70; ☏720-865-4220; www.artscomplex. com; cnr 14th & Champa Sts; ☐9, 15, 28, 32, 38, 43, 44) This massive complex – one of the largest of its kind – occupies four city blocks and houses 10 major venues, including the historic Ellie Caulkins Opera House and the Boettcher Concert Hall. It's also home to the Colorado Ballet, Denver Center for the Performing Arts, Opera Colorado and the Colorado Symphony Orchestra. Not sure what you want to do tonight? Come here.

★ **Curious Theatre** THEATER

(Map p78; ☏303-623-0524; www.curioustheatre. org; 1080 Acoma St; tickets from $18; ☺box office 2-7pm Tue-Sat; ☐0, 6, 52) 'No guts, no story' is the tagline of this award-winning theater company, set in a converted church. Plays pack a punch with thought-provoking stories that take on social justice issues. Think race, immigration, sexuality. Stay for talkbacks at the end of each show, when actors engage with the audience about everything from the plot to the set.

It's a small theater, so there's not a bad seat in the house.

★ **El Chapultepec** JAZZ

(Map p70; ☏303-295-9126; www.thepeclodo. com; 1962 Market St; ☺7am-1am, music from 9pm; ☐38) This smoky, old-school jazz joint attracts a diverse mix of people. Since it opened in 1951, Frank Sinatra, Tony Bennett and Ella Fitzgerald have played here, as have Jagger and Richards. Local jazz bands take the tiny stage nightly, but you never know who might drop by.

Landmark Mayan Theatre CINEMA

(Map 66; ☏303-744-6799; www.landmarktheatres. com; 110 Broadway; ☂; ☐0) Even without the fancy sound system and enormous screen, this is the best place in Denver to take in a film. The 1930s movie palace is a romantic, historic gem and – bonus! – it serves beer.

Hi-Dive LIVE MUSIC

(Map 66; ☏303-733-0230; www.hi-dive.com; 7 S Broadway; ☐0) Local rock heroes and touring indie bands light up the stage at the Hi-Dive, a venue at the heart of Denver's local music scene. During big shows it gets deafeningly loud, cheek-to-jowl with hipsters and humid as an armpit. In other words, perfection.

Colorado Symphony Orchestra CLASSICAL MUSIC

(Map p70; CSO; ☏303-623-7876; www.colorado-symphony.org; 1000 14th St, Boettcher Concert Hall; ☺box office 10am-6pm Mon-Fri, noon-6pm Sat; ☂; ☐9, 15, 28, 32, 38, 43, 44) The Boettcher Concert Hall in the Denver Performing Arts Complex is home to this renowned symphony orchestra. The orchestra performs an annual 21-week Masterworks season, as well as concerts aimed at a broader audience – think live performances of movie scores during the screening of films like *La La Land* or *Harry Potter and the Prisoner of Azkaban*.

Denver Center for the Performing Arts THEATER

(Map p70; ☏303-893-4100; www.denvercenter. org; 1101 13th St; ☺box office 10am-6pm Mon-Sat & 1hr before each show; ☂; ☐9, 15, 28, 32, 38, 43, 44) The Denver Center for the Performing Arts is the theater wing of the huge Denver Performing Arts Complex. It has eight theaters, making it the country's largest nonprofit theater organization (and an easy place to turn for highbrow entertainment!). Productions include everything from traveling Broadway musicals to locally produced plays and experimental theater.

Theater junkies will enjoy a behind-the-scenes tour of the different theaters, dressing rooms, design studios and costume shops. Held every Monday and Saturday at 10am, the tour lasts around 90 minutes ($12).

Ogden Theatre LIVE MUSIC

(Map p78; ☏303-832-1874; www.ogdentheatre. com; 935 E Colfax Ave; ☺box office 10am-2pm Sat, 1hr before doors open show days; ☐15) One of Denver's best live-music venues, the Ogden Theatre has a checkered past. Built in 1917, it was derelict for many years and might have been bulldozed in the early 1990s, but it's now listed on the National Register of Historic Places. Bands such as Edward Sharpe & the Magnetic Zeros and Lady Gaga have played here.

Harry Houdini performed at this theater in 1919 and it appeared in the movie *The Rocky Horror Picture Show*. Jack Nicholson drove his Winnebago past the Ogden pulling into Denver in *About Schmidt*. If the house is packed, make for the upstairs level, where the catwalk extends on the wings and you'll have a beautiful bird's-eye view and plenty of room to move.

Bluebird Theater · LIVE MUSIC

(Map 66; ☎303-377-1666; www.bluebirdtheater.net; 3317 E Colfax Ave; ⛾; ⛳15) This medium-sized theater is general admission standing room and has terrific sound and clear sight lines from the balcony. The venue often offers the last chance to catch bands – Denver faves the Lumineers and Devotchka both headlined here – on their way up to the big time.

Buy tickets online – the box office only opens on show nights, 30 minutes before doors open.

Nocturne · JAZZ

(Map 66; ☎303-295-3333; www.nocturnejazz.com; 1330 27th St; cover $5-10; ⏰7-10:30pm Tue-Thu, to 12:30pm Fri & Sat; ⛳44) Art deco meets industrial chic at this jazz club in the heart of RiNo. Though featuring local and national musicians, the stars here are the artists in residence who take the stage for eight-week runs to perform works by a musical icon, of a particular genre or to explore their own compositions. Gussy up to fit in with the crowd.

Classic cocktails and an eclectic dinner menu – including five-course tasting menus inspired by popular jazz albums – also offered.

Paramount Theatre · CONCERT VENUE

(Map p70; ☎303-623-0106; www.paramountdenver. com; 1621 Glenarm Pl; ⛳10, MALLRIDE) Lots of red velvet and gold trimming deck out the Paramount, one of the premier midsized theaters in the West. Listed on the National Register of Historic Places, its recent acts include Paula Poundstone, Alice Cooper and Bush.

Grizzly Rose · LIVE MUSIC

(☎303-295-1330; www.grizzlyrose.com; 5450 N Valley Hwy; ⏰from 6pm Tue-Sun; ⛾; ⛳8) This is one kick-ass honky-tonk – 40,000 sq ft of hot live music – attracting real cowboys from as far as Cheyenne. The Country Music Association called it the best country bar in America. If you've never experienced line dancing, then put on the boots, grab the Stetson and let loose. Free dance lessons offered.

Just north of downtown, off I-25 (you'll have to drive or cab it), the Grizzly is famous for bringing in huge industry stars – Willie Nelson, LeAnn Rimes – and only charging $15 per ticket.

Fillmore Auditorium · LIVE MUSIC

(Map p78; ☎303-837-1482; www.fillmoreauditorium. org; 1510 Clarkson St; ⛳15) One of the major music venues in town, this place has hosted classic acts such as Parliament Funkadelic, big indies such as Feist, and even roller derby. The acoustics are far from perfect, but it's certainly one of Denver's essential venues.

Pepsi Center · STADIUM

(Map 66; ☎303-405-1111; www.pepsicenter.com; 1000 Chopper Circle; ⏰box office 10am-5pm Mon-Fri; ⛳1, 20, ⛳C, E, W) The mammoth Pepsi Center hosts the Denver Nuggets basketball team, the Colorado Mammoth of the National Lacrosse League and the Colorado Avalanche hockey team. In off season it's a mega concert venue.

Coors Field · BASEBALL

(Map 66; ☎303-292-0200; www.mlb.com/col/ ballpark; 2001 Blake St; ⛾; ⛳8, 38) The Colorado Rockies play baseball at the highly rated Coors Field from April to September. Tickets for the outfield – the Rockpile – cost $5. Not a bad deal. Tours of the stadium are available year round and include access to the field and Press Club. Tickets run $10 adults, $7 kids; reservations not required.

Ellie Caulkins Opera House · THEATER

(Map p70; ☎720-865-4220; www.artscomplex. com; cnr 14th & Curtis Sts; ⛳9, 15, 28, 32, 38, 43, 44) A major overhaul of this historic performance house – affectionately know as 'the Ellie' – endowed it with luxurious acoustics, excellent sight lines and a very modern feel. It's also huge – more than 2200 seats – so if you buy cheap seats be sure to bring opera glasses. Opera Colorado and Colorado Ballet typically perform on this stage.

Colorado Ballet · DANCE

(Map 66; ☎303-837-8888; www.coloradoballet. org; 1075 Santa Fe Dr; ⏰box office 9am-5pm Mon-Fri; ⛾; ⛳1, 9) The Colorado Ballet company has 30 professional dancers who come from all over the world. Most performances are staged at the Ellie Caulkins Opera House within the Denver Performing Arts Complex. The company's Armstrong Center for Dance is also home to a 135-seat black-box theater where new works are occasionally performed.

Opera Colorado · OPERA

(Map p70; ☎303-468-2030; www.operacolorado. org; cnr 14th & Curtis Sts; ⏰box office 10am-5pm Mon-Fri; ⛾; ⛳9, 15, 28, 32, 38, 43, 44) Founded in 1983, Opera Colorado is based in the Denver Performing Arts Complex (p94). The company performs classics like Puccini's *La Bohème* but also produces new works every season.

GOLD IN THEM HILLS – GAMBLING AT COLORADO'S HISTORIC MINING TOWNS

Colorado re-legalized low-stakes gambling in 1991 in historic mining towns such as Black Hawk and Central City. The stakes have gone up, with voters raising maximum bet limits to $100 in 2008. The Wild West towns still have the cool storefronts, which now lead into modern large-scale hotels and casinos such as **Ameristar** (☏720-946-4000; www.ameristar.com; 111 Richman St, Black Hawk; ⊙24hr; ☎⬥).

Black Hawk Colorado's biggest gambling town has 18 casinos, plus hotels, spas, nearby hiking trails and all-you-can-eat buffets. Think Vegas, Wild West style. They have all the major games, and betting goes up to $100 on a single wager.

Central City Just a mile from Black Hawk, Central City has fewer big casinos and makes for better shopping and bopping around the historic town center. It even has an **opera company** (☏303-292-6700; www.centralcityopera.org; 124 Eureka St, Central City; tickets from $20; ⬥).

Shows are typically in the Ellie Caulkins Opera House (p95). Tickets start at $20.

Comedy Works   COMEDY
(Map p70; ☏303-595-3637; www.comedyworks.com; 1226 15th St; ⬚1, 6, 10, 28, 32, 38, 43, 44) Denver's best comedy club occupies a basement space in Larimer Sq (enter down a set of stairs near the corner of Larimer and 15th) and routinely brings in up-and-coming yucksters from around the country. It can feel a bit cramped if you're claustrophobic, but the seats are comfortable and the quality of acts is top shelf.

Performances also take place at the slightly bigger Comedy Works South location, south of town.

Clocktower Cabaret   CABARET
(Map p70; ☏303-293-0075; www.clocktowercabaret.com; 1601 Arapahoe St; tickets $30-45; ⊙box office 2pm-intermission of last show, 1-5pm non-show days; ⬚10, 28, 32, 38, 43, 44, MALLRIDE) Bawdy, naughty and strangely romantic, the Clocktower Cabaret is a wild-child standout among LoDo's rather straight-laced (or at least straight) night spots. A table right up near the front will get you in the sparkling heart of the action, and if you parse the schedule, you might get a glance at the sexiest drag queens in Denver.

Dazzle   JAZZ
(Map p70; ☏303-839-5100; www.dazzledenver.com; 1512 Curtis St; cover free-$40; ⊙3:30pm-midnight Tue & Wed, to 1am Thu-Sat, to 10pm Sun; ⬚9, 15, 20, MALLRIDE) For live jazz, Dazzle is the longtime go-to place in Denver. Featuring mostly Colorado-based musicians, the club has late-night shows, a great happy hour ($4

martinis!) and a solid restaurant. A $15 minimum purchase – drinks or eats – is required for all shows. Located in the historic Baur's building downtown.

Bovine Metropolis Theater   COMEDY
(Map p70; ☏303-758-4722; www.bovinemetropolis.com; 1527 Champa St; ⬥; ⬚9, 15, 20, MALLRIDE) This long-standing black-box theater hosts a clutch of fresh-faced improv comedy performers who take the stage most nights of the week. Tickets typically are under $15; discounts are offered for buying online. Improv workshops also available, lasting from two hours to eight weeks.

Sports Authority Field at Mile High   STADIUM
(Map 66; ☏720-258-3000; www.sportsauthorityfieldatmilehigh.com; 1701 S Bryant St; adult/child tours $20/15; ⬥; ⬚10, 20, 30, 31) The much-lauded Denver Broncos football team and the Denver Outlaws lacrosse team play at Sports Authority Field, 1 mile west of downtown. This 76,000-seat stadium also has an eclectic schedule of events, including major rock concerts for superstars such as U2. Behind-the-scenes tours are organized through the Colorado Sports Hall of Fame (p76) and run about 90 minutes.

Comedy Works South   COMEDY
(☏720-274-6800; www.comedyworks.com; 5345 Landmark Pl, Greenwood Village; ⬚E, F, R) Located 13 miles south of Denver, this place is only worth the drive if there's an act you've been dying to see. The theater is spacious enough but prepare to jump through hoops before getting seated (including turning over your

cell phone). For VIP treatment and front-row seating, eat at the adjoining restaurant, Lucy's, before the show.

For comedy in downtown Denver, try its sister venue, Comedy Works.

Larimer Lounge
LIVE MUSIC

(Map 66; ☏ 303-296-1003; www.larimerlounge.com; 2721 Larimer St; cover free-$25; ☺4pm-2am; ▣44) This dive is a proving ground for acts from across the indie rock spectrum – last time we checked in, metalheads in clown makeup were sound-checking. With shows seven nights a week, it's a reliable bet for upcoming locals and good touring indie acts. There's also a patio to escape from the noise.

Quixote's True Blue
LIVE MUSIC

(Map p78; ☏ 303-861-7070; www.quixotes.com; 1700 Logan St; ☺7pm-2am Mon-Wed, 4pm-2am Fri & Sat; ▣20) Fight some windmills at this geeky-meets-freaky space kitted out with a quality PA system and a good bar. Most nights it's free, but sometimes there's a modest cover charge.

Colorado Convention Center
LIVE PERFORMANCE

(Map p70; ☏ 303-228-8000; www.denverconvention.com; 700 14th St; ☏; ▣1, 8, 19, 48, ▣D, F, H) At 2.2 million sq ft, this is a city within the city of Denver, centrally located and just steps away from some of LoDo's finest restaurants. The Bellco Theatre, a 5000-seat venue within the complex, hosts top names in music and comedy.

Casa Bonita
LIVE PERFORMANCE

(☏ 303-232-5111; www.casabonitadenver.com; 6715 W Colfax Ave, Lakewood; mains, required for entrance, $15-18; ☺11am-9pm Sun-Thu, to 10pm Fri & Sat; ▣16) The food is horrible (think greasy processed cheese and stone-gray guacamole), but this classic piece of American (and Mexican) kitsch is so entrenched in Denver lore, you just have to visit. There's a 30ft waterfall and cliff divers. Random skits. A gorilla. And the landmark restaurant even made an appearance in Colorado's other top cultural export: *South Park*.

Dick's Sporting Goods Park
STADIUM

(☏ 303-727-3500; www.dickssportinggoodspark.com; 6000 Victory Way, Commerce City; ▣62) Located just north of the city, this 18,000-seat stadium hosts the state's Major League Soccer team, the Colorado Rapids, plus plenty of summertime concerts.

🛍 Shopping

Despite its many chain stores, Denver has some excellent independent boutiques scattered throughout its neighborhoods, posing a problem for serious shoppers without a car. If you're on foot, the best districts for browsing are Larimer Sq, Cherry Creek and South Broadway, all of which are walkable areas with lots of appealing shops, some featuring locally designed clothes, art and housewares.

★REI
SPORTS & OUTDOORS

(Map 66; Recreational Equipment Incorporated; ☏ 303-756-3100; www.rei.com; 1416 Platte St; ☺9am-9pm Mon-Sat, to 7pm Sun; ▣; ▣10, 28, 32, 44) The flagship store of this outdoor-equipment supersupplier is an essential stop if you are heading to the mountains or just cruising through Confluence. In addition to top gear for camping, cycling, climbing and skiing, it has a rental department, maps and the Pinnacle, a 47ft-high indoor structure of simulated red sandstone for climbing and rappelling.

There's also a desk of Colorado's Outdoor Recreation Information Center (p100), where you can get information on state and national parks, and an on-site Starbucks, in case you need some caffeine to accompany the adrenaline.

★Tattered Cover Bookstore
BOOKS

(Map p70; ☏ 303-436-1070; www.tatteredcover.com; 1628 16th St; ☺6:30am-9pm Mon-Fri, 9am-9pm Sat, 10am-6pm Sun; ☏▣; ▣10, 19, 28, 32, 44, MallRide) There are plenty of places to curl up with a book in Denver's beloved independent bookstore. Bursting with new and used books, it has a good stock of regional travel guides and nonfiction titles dedicated to the Western states and Western folklore. There's a second smaller location on Colfax near City Park.

The Tattered Cover also has an on-site cafe and hosts free film and literature events.

★I Heart Denver
GIFTS & SOUVENIRS

(Map p70; www.iheartdenverstore.com; 500 16th St, Denver Pavilions, 2nd fl; ☺10am-9pm Mon-Sat, 11am-6pm Sun; ▣10, 28, 32, MALLRIDE) This welcoming shop on the 16th Street Mall sells everything Colorado. Well-made, totally appealing, I-must-have tees, hats, postcards, baby clothes, jewelry, artwork... All items sold are created by local artists and designers and it shows with flair and quirk. A perfect place to pick up a memento.

★ **Decade**   GIFTS & SOUVENIRS
(Map 66; ☎ 303-733-2288; www.facebook.com/
pg/decadedenver; 56 S Broadway; ⊙10am-6pm
Mon-Fri, 11am-6pm Sat, to 5pm Sun; ☐0) It's easy
to lose yourself, poking around this eclectic shop. Selling everything from mid-mod
furniture and handbags to baby clothes and
jewelry, it's a perfect place to window-shop,
buy a gift or get that stuffed-cat pillow
you've always wanted. Colorado mementos
are sprinkled throughout the store.

★ **Fancy Tiger Crafts**   ARTS & CRAFTS
(Map 66; ☎ 303-733-3855; www.fancytigercrafts.
com; 59 Broadway; ⊙10am-7pm Mon & Wed-Sat,
to 9pm Tue, 11am-6pm Sun; ☀; ☐0) So you
dig crochet and quilting? You knit a mean
sweater and have a few too many tattoos?
Welcome to Fancy Tiger Crafts, a sophisticated remodel of granny's yarn barn that's
ground zero for Denver's crafty hipsters.
There are classes in the back (including ones
by Jessica, 'mistress of patchwork') and a rad
selection of fabric, yarn and books.

If you are a little bit more hands off with
your homemade clothes, try Fancy Tiger
Clothing next door, where local designers
hock their wares.

5 Green Boxes   GIFTS & SOUVENIRS
(Map p70; ☎ 720-460-3705; www.5greenboxes.
com; 1701 Wynkoop St, Union Station; ⊙10am-7pm
Mon-Thu, to 9pm Fri & Sat, 11am-5pm Sun; ☐55L,
72L,120L, FF2, ☐A, B, C, E, W) This boutique sells
one-of-a-kind gifts, quality souvenirs and
home goods plus cards and accessories. Regardless of the item, the aesthetic throughout is classy, vintage and whimsical.

Divino Wine & Spirits   DRINKS
(☎ 303-778-1800; www.divinowine.com; 1240 S
Broadway; ⊙10am-10pm Mon-Thu, to 11pm Sat,
11am-7pm Sun; ☀; ☐0, 11) Bottles are stacked
from floor to ceiling in this southwest shop
– a little out of the way, but worth it for serious wine drinkers. It hosts events and does
tastings on the weekend, and the staff know
their stuff. The budget-conscious will want
to keep an eye on the rotating selection on
the '10 under 10' rack.

Colorado Mills   MALL
(☎ 303-384-3000; www.coloradomills.com; 14500
W Colfax Ave; ⊙10am-11pm Mon-Sat, 11am-6pm
Sun; ☀☀; ☐16, GS) This is a shoppers' paradise: a huge shopping mall west of the
downtown area with more than 200 specialty stores and 1.1 million sq ft of retail fun. All
the big retailers are represented, some with
discounted factory outlets, and there are restaurants and food halls. Catch a movie at the
United Artists multiplex theater.

**Wilderness Exchange
Unlimited**   SPORTS & OUTDOORS
(Map 66; ☎ 303-964-0708; www.wildernessx.com;
2401 15th St; ⊙11am-8pm Mon-Fri, 10am-7pm Sat,
to 6pm Sun; ☀; ☐10, 28, 32, 44) In addition
to carefully selected outdoor equipment,
this shop has an impressive collection of
quality used gear (including good deals on
hiking boots, skis and down jackets) in the
basement.

Hope Tank   GIFTS & SOUVENIRS
(Map 66; ☎ 720-837-1565; www.hopetank.org; 64
S Broadway; ⊙11am-7pm; ☐0, 1) Hope Tank
sells quirky and fun gifts – cheeky magnets,
cool kids' clothes, handcrafted jewelry, tees –
many with a hooray Colorado bent. All items
are created by artists, near and far. Best of
all, a percentage of each sale goes to support
charity; the name and mission of each is
listed on all items. Shop and save the world!

Sewn   CLOTHING
(Map 66; ☎ 303-832-1493; www.sewndenver.
com; 18 S Broadway; ⊙11am-6pm Mon-Sat, to
5pm Sun; ☐0) A clothing-and-hat boutique,
Sewn specializes in one-of-a-kind handmade items. Most of the designers are local or Colorado-based, though it's the work
of four designers that forms the heart of
the shop, lending it a cohesive quirky feel.
Head to the back to check out the vintage
clothing and homewares.

Jewelius   FASHION & ACCESSORIES
(Map 66; ☎ 303-975-6745; www.jewelius.com;
2405 W 32nd Ave; ⊙10am-7pm Mon-Sat, to 6pm
Sun; ☐32) This narrow shop is packed with
the latest in Colorado fashion, including accessories and jewelry. The best thing about
the boutique is that it won't break the bank
– items are well priced so you can do more
than just window shop!

Outdoors Geek   SPORTS & OUTDOORS
(☎ 303-699-6944; www.outdoorsgeek.com; 4431
Glencoe St; ⊙9am-6pm Mon-Fri, to 4pm Sat,
noon-4pm Sun; ☀; ☐34) ✿ This mom-and-
pop gear outfitter puts together packages
of top gear for hiking and camping and
either ships it to you or arranges a time
for you to pick it up at its headquarters.
The website also has great camping and
backpacking lists, including ones geared to
travel with kids.

Buffalo Exchange
CLOTHING

(Map 66; 303-866-0165; www.buffaloexchangecolorado.com; 51 Broadway; ⏰11am-9pm Mon-Sat, to 8pm Sun; ♿; 🚇0, 1) Part of a growing nationwide chain, Buffalo Exchange on South Broadway is a huge space with new and used clothing: retro, futuristic, trad and garish. You want a hip 1950s shirt, or a little something for a costume party? This is the place. Garments, shoes and accessories are bought and sold.

A smaller sister shop is located in Cap Hill.

Cherry Creek Shopping Center
MALL

(Map 66; 303-388-3900; www.shopcherrycreek.com; 3000 E 1st Ave; ⏰10am-9pm Mon-Sat, 11am-6pm Sun; 📶♿; 🚇1, 3, 83L) A large collection of exclusive international brands (Louis Vuitton, Burberry, Ralph Lauren, Tiffany) decorate the corridors of Denver's high-end shopping facility, anchored by the large Neiman Marcus department store. There's a movie theater and indoor play area too. Food choices range from cheap-and-quick mall standards such as Panda Express to the Tuscan fare and elegant linen-draped dining room of Brio.

Twist & Shout
MUSIC

(Map 66; 303-722-1943; www.twistandshout.com; 2508 E Colfax Ave; ⏰10am-9pm Mon-Sat, to 6pm Sun; ♿; 🚇15) The selection of used CDs at this brightly lit store is extensive, but head to the little den of used vinyl in the back for rare goodies, original pressings and surprising foreign imports. It also brings a discerning roster of in-store performances that run the gamut of musical tastes.

Botanico
DISPENSARY

(Map 66; 303-297-2273; www.botanicommj.com; 3054 Larimer St; ⏰9am-9:50pm; 🚇44) In the heart of RiNo, this small dispensary has a big following, thanks to great service, selection and prices, especially the early-bird specials. An express counter gets you in and out in a flash, or you can request a private room to talk weed options with an expert budtender. Botanico's website includes handy potency pie charts for each strain.

LoDo Wellness Center
DISPENSARY

(Map p70; 303-534-5020; www.lodowellnesscenter.com; 1617 Wazee St; ⏰10am-7pm; 🚇10, 19, 28, 32, 44, MALLRIDE) While many downtown pot shops cater shamelessly to weed-giddy tourists, LoDo Wellness Center offers a more down-to-earth atmosphere just off the 16th Street Mall. The roomy retail area has a varied selection of buds, edibles, concentrates and paraphernalia, as well as knowledgeable budtenders.

MudHead Gallery
CERAMICS, JEWELRY

(Map p70; 303-293-0007; www.themudheadgallery.com; 1720 Wazee St; ⏰10am-6pm Wed-Sat; 🚇0, 15, 20) MudHead is a well-regarded boutique specializing in Native American art, mostly Hopi and Navajo. Walking through the doors is kind of like walking into a museum – you'll see high-end vases, sculpture and jewelry anywhere your eyes land. Whether you're a collector or just curious, this shop is worth a stop.

Cry Baby Ranch
HOMEWARES

(Map p70; 303-623-3979; www.crybabyranch.com; 1419 Larimer St; ⏰10am-7pm Mon-Fri, to 6pm Sat, noon-5pm Sun; 🚇10, 28, 32, 38, 44) Peeking at the price tags of boots hand-tooled with skull and crossbones, it's quickly evident that this store is not for your workaday cowpoke, but the Western-themed homewares and eclectic, bizarre goods (Loretta Lynn clutch, anyone?) are a blast to browse.

EVOO Marketplace
FOOD

(Map p70; 303-974-5784; www.evoomarketplace.com; 1338 15th St; 375mL bottles $15-19; ⏰11am-5pm Mon, to 6pm Tue-Sat, to 4pm Sun; 🚇10, 28, 32, 38, 44) This specialty shop sells to-die-for extra-virgin olive oils and balsamic vinegars from across the US and around the world.

Goorin Brothers
FASHION & ACCESSORIES

(Map p70; 303-534-4287; www.goorin.com; 1410 Larimer St; ⏰10am-7pm Mon-Wed, to 8pm Thu, to 9pm Fri & Sat, 11am-6pm Sun; ♿; 🚇10, 28, 32, 38, 44) A stylish fedora will put a little bounce in your step while strutting through the ritzy Latimer Sq district. This San Francisco–based source of hip, quality headwear has a great range for men and women.

Wax Trax Records
MUSIC

(Map p78; 303-831-7246; www.waxtraxrecords.com; 638 E 13th Ave; ⏰10am-7pm Mon-Thu, to 8pm Fri & Sat, 11am-6pm Sun; 🚇10, 12) For more than 38 years, Wax Trax Records has been trading at this Denver location, stocking a huge quantity of CDs, DVDs, vinyl and music paraphernalia. Indie, alternative, punk, goth, folk, rock, hip-hop, jazz, reggae – anything that's a bit edgy you'll either find in store or it'll be ordered for you.

There are two adjacent shopfronts – one selling CDs and DVDs, the other exclusively vinyl.

Capitol Hill Books   BOOKS
(Map p78; ✆303-837-0700; www.capitolhillbooks.
com; 300 E Colfax Ave; ⏲10am-6pm Mon-Sat, to
5pm Sun; 🚌6, 15, 16) It doesn't have the selection or élan of the Tattered Cover Bookstore
(p97), but over its 30-year life Capitol Hill
has retained the rare magic of a *real* bookshop. The rugs are threadbare. The floor
creaks. Best of all, the book-loving staff are
quick with helpful suggestions.

Wild West Denver Store   GIFTS & SOUVENIRS
(Map p70; ✆303-446-8640; 715 16th St; ⏲9am-
8pm Mon-Sat, 9:30am-6pm Sun; 🚌0, 6, 19, 52,
MALLRIDE, 🚇D, F, H) There's a mess of Western
trinket stores along the 16th Street Mall with
nearly identical stock, but this has the largest
inventory of kitsch. It's full of knickknacks
and all manner of stuff featuring wolves, buffaloes and stereotypical depictions of Native
Americans. Come here for cheap tees and
magnets, maybe a snow globe.

Champa Fine Wine & Liquor   DRINKS
(Map p70; ✆303-571-5547; www.champaliquor.
com; 1600 Champa St; ⏲11am-11:45pm Mon-Sat,
to 10:45pm Sun; 🚌0, 6, 19, 52, MALLRIDE, 🚇D, F,
H) This well-stocked bottle shop opens up a
heavenly find for discerning self-caterers, offering a top selection of wine (though most
is imported from California) and a mix-and-
match six-pack option for visitors who want
to take a Colorado beer tour on the cheap.

ⓘ Information

TOURIST INFORMATION
The Tourist Information Center website (www.
denver.org) has great information about events.

Downtown Tourist Information Center
(✆303-892-1505; www.denver.org; 1575
California St; ⏲9am-6pm Mon-Fri, 9am-5pm
Sat, 10am-2pm Sun May-Oct, 9am-5pm Mon-
Fri, 9am-2pm Sat, 10am-2pm Sun Nov-Apr;
🚌9, 15, 20, MallRide, 🚇D, F, H) When you get
to town, make for the largest and most central
information center, located just off the 16th
St Mall. You can load up on brochures, browse
online travel pages and get solid information
from knowledgeable staffers. A small gift shop
sells high-quality souvenirs too.

DIA Information Booth (✆303-317-0629;
www.visitdenver.com; Denver International
Airport; ⏲hours vary; 🤚♿; 🚇A) Tourist and
airport information is available at this booth on
the east end of Denver International Airport's
central hall.

ORIC (Outdoor Recreation Information Center;
✆REI main line 303-756-3100; www.oriconline.
org; 1415 Platte St; ⏲hours vary; 🤚; 🚌10,

28, 32, 44) Inside REI, this information desk
is a must for those looking to get out of town
for outdoor adventure. It has maps and expert
information on trip planning and safety. The
desk is staffed by volunteers, so hours vary
wildly, but arriving on a weekend afternoon is
a good bet.

MEDICAL SERVICES
Denver Health (✆303-436-4949; www.
denverhealth.org; 777 Bannock St; ⏲24hr; ♿;
🚌52)

Rose Medical Center (✆303-320-2121; www.
rosemed.com; 4567 E 9th Ave; ⏲24hr; 🚌10)

St Joseph Hospital (✆303-812-2000; www.
sclhealth.org; 1375 E 19th Ave; ⏲24hr; 🚌12,
32)

University of Colorado Hospital (✆720-848-
9111; www.uch.edu; 12605 E 16th Ave, Aurora;
⏲24hr; 🚌15, 20, 89)

ⓘ Getting There & Away

Served by the largest airport in the US, criss-
crossed by major highways and intersected by
one of the country's few Amtrak lines, it's easy
to get to and from Denver.

AIR
Denver International Airport (DIA; ✆303-
342-2000; www.flydenver.com; 8500 Peña
Blvd; ⏲24hr; 🤚♿; 🚇A) is a major air hub and
one of the country's busiest facilities. In all, DIA
has 53 sq miles of land, making it the biggest
airport in the country by area. The facility has
an automated subway that links the terminal
to three concourses (Concourse C is almost 1
mile from the terminal). All to say, give yourself
a little extra time to find your way around. If
you get to your gate early, there are always
interesting public-art exhibits to help you pass
the time.

DIA is 24 miles from downtown. Take the
I-70 and exit 238 (Peña Blvd). From there, it's
12 miles to the main terminal. You'll see the
Teflon-coated fiberglass roof that peaks out to
mirror the mountains in the distance.

Private jets and charters tend to be serviced
through Centennial Airport to the south and
Rocky Mountain Metropolitan Airport (between
Denver and Boulder).

Transport Options
A complete Ground Transportation Center is
centrally located on the 5th level of DIA's terminal, near the baggage claim. All transportation
companies have their booths here and passengers can catch vans, shuttles and taxis outside
the doors.

Complimentary hotel shuttles represent
the cheapest means of getting to or from the

airport. Courtesy phones for hotel shuttles are available in the Ground Transportation Center.

An **RTD** light-rail (Line A; $9, 45 minutes) transports people from DIA to downtown Denver, servicing Denver suburbs along the way.

Taxi service to downtown Denver costs around $60, excluding tip.

There are a number of airport shuttle vans, such as **SuperShuttle** (☑ 800-258-3826; www.supershuttle.com; ☺ 24hr; ⌂ A), and limousine services. Airport shuttles to the Front Range and mountain/ski areas are also not hard to come by.

BUS

Greyhound offers frequent buses on routes along the Front Range and on transcontinental routes. All buses stop at the **Denver Bus Center** (☑ 303-293-6555; 1055 19th St; ☺ 6am-midnight; ☎; ⌂ 8, 48).

The **Colorado Mountain Express** (CME; ☑ 800-525-6363; www.coloradomountainexpress.com; 8500 Peña Blvd, Denver International Airport; ☎ ⓘ; ⌂ A) has shuttle services from Denver International Airport (DIA), downtown Denver or Morrison to Summit County, including Breckenridge and Keystone (adult/child $66/35, 2½ hours) and Vail (adult/child $84/44, three hours).

The **Colorado Springs Shuttle** (☑ 877-587-3456; www.coloradoshuttle.com; 8500 Peña Blvd, Denver International Airport; ☎ ⓘ; ⌂ A) offers trips from DIA to Colorado Springs (adult/child $50/25, two hours).

Regional Transportation District (RTD; ☑ 303-299-6000; www.rtd-denver.com; 1600 Blake St; ⌂ 10, 19, 28, 32, 44, MallRide) buses to Boulder (Route FF1, $4.50) carry bicycles in the cargo compartment and offer frequent service from **Union Station** (p63). To reach Golden, take the 16L bus ($4.50) that stops at the corner of Colfax and Broadway.

TRAIN

Amtrak's (p63) *California Zephyr* train runs daily between Chicago ($121–325, 19 hours) and San Francisco ($144–446, 33 hours) stopping in Denver's gorgeously renovated **Union Station** (p63).

❶ Getting Around

Getting from place to place in the Mile High City is amazingly easy, especially if you are in the downtown area. The **RTD** public transportation system is extensive, though it's easy enough to get around on foot, bike (with the shared **B-Cycle** program) or by cab. If you plan to do day hikes or head up to the mountains, rent a car.

BICYCLE

Denver has lots of bike lanes on the city streets and an excellent network of trails to get out of

town. These include routes along the Platte River Pkwy, the Cherry Creek Bike Path and a network that heads all the way out to Golden (about a two-hour ride). You can get all the information you need from a pair of excellent websites: **Bike Denver** (www.bikedenver.org) and **City of Denver** (www.denvergov.org), both of which have downloadable bike maps for the city.

B-Cycle (☑ 303-825-3325; www.denverbcycle.com; 1-day membership $9; ☺ 5am-midnight; ⓕ) This bike-share company has more than 80 stations throughout Denver. The daily rate ($9) includes unlimited rides as long as they're under 30 minutes.

BUS

Regional Transportation District provides public transportation throughout the Denver and Boulder area (local/regional fares $2.60/4.50). The website has schedules, routes, fares and a trip planner.

CAR & MOTORCYCLE

Street parking can be a pain, but there is a slew of pay garages in downtown and LoDo. Nearly all the major car-rental agencies have counters at Denver International Airport, though only a few have offices in downtown Denver.

Enterprise Rent-A-Car (☑ 303-293-8644; www.enterprise.com; 2255 Broadway; ☺ 7am-7pm Mon-Fri, 8am-4pm Sat & Sun; ⌂ 44, 48) is an international car-rental agency with several offices in the Denver metro area.

LIGHT-RAIL

RTD's light-rail system currently has eight lines servicing the Denver metro area.

The A Line runs from **Union Station** (p63) to **Denver International Airport**, stopping in different suburbs along the way.

The W Line runs from Union Station, past the **Pepsi Center** (p95) and Mile High Stadium to the Jefferson County Government Center on the outskirts of Golden.

The C Line runs along the eastern edge of downtown, continuing south to Englewood and Littleton, ending on Santa Fe and Mineral Sts. The D Line starts at 30th and Downing in Five Points, going straight through the city to hook up with the southern run of the C Line to Littleton.

The E and F lines run from either Union Station or 18th and California south along I-25 to the Denver Tech Center, ending at Lincoln Ave. The H Line from 18th and California will take you to Nine Mile, where you could potentially walk or bike to Cherry Creek Reservoir.

The R Line connects the southern suburbs to the A Line and Denver International Airport.

At the time of research, a ninth line was in the works to provide service to the town of Arvada, just northwest of Denver.

Fares are $2.60 locally (one to two fare zones), $4.50 regionally (three fare zones) and $9 for the airport. Bikes may be taken on the train if there is space. You purchase tickets from automated kiosks before boarding. Occasional ticket checkers pass through the trains to validate your ticket.

TAXI

Two major taxi companies offer door-to-door service in Denver:

Metro Taxi (☑ 303-333-3333; www.metrotaxi denver.com; ☺ 24hr)

Yellow Cab (☑ 303-777-7777; www.denver yellowcab.com; ☺ 24hr)

Golden

☑ 303 / POP 18,900 / ELEV 5675FT

Snuggled beneath the foothills and Table Mountain, the historic district of Golden has a few interesting museums, the highly regarded Colorado School of Mines and the massive Coors Brewery. A trip here makes for an interesting day trip from Denver, though if you're hankering for some time in small-town Colorado, this is a pleasant place to spend a night.

◉ Sights

'First Friday' events bring a pleasant street carnival with music, street performers and free carriage rides on (you guessed it!) the first Friday of the month, June through September. The hubbub takes place along Washington St, with the epicenter at 12th St.

★ Colorado School of Mines' Geology Museum   MUSEUM

(☑ 303-273-3815; www.mines.edu/geology_mu seum; 1310 Maple St, General Research Laboratory Bldg; ☺ 9am-4pm Mon-Sat, 1-4pm Sun; ⊞) **FREE**
With a collection of 50,000 minerals, fossils and gemstones, the School of Mines' Geology Museum is worth a stop, even if rocks aren't really your thing. Two floors of exhibits take visitors through a veritable journey of the earth's treasures (and a couple of the moon's too). Don't miss the walk-thru mine with sounds of dripping water and low lights; inside ultraviolet minerals glow brightly – a spectacular sight.

The museum also maintains a short geology trail, where you'll see dinosaur tracks and fossilized imprints of leafs and logs.

There are educational placards along the way but the museum also has pamphlets with more detailed information. The trailhead is just 600ft west.

★ Clear Creek History Park   HISTORIC BUILDING

(☑ 303-278-3557; www.goldenhistory.org; 11th St, btwn Illinois & Arapahoe Sts; ☺ dawn-dusk; ⊞) **FREE** Explore the life of a homesteader by walking through this re-created pioneer settlement. Here, original and replica 19th-century buildings – a cabin, two-seat outhouse, root cellar, schoolhouse, blacksmith shop and smokehouse – take visitors back in time. Self-guided tours are easy and fun. Alternatively, come when experts in period dress work the homestead and teach about life back when Golden was the Wild West; check the website for these special event dates.

American Mountaineering Museum   MUSEUM

(Bradford Washburn American Mountaineering Museum; ☑ 303-996-2755; www.mountaineering museum.org; 710 10th St; adult/child $7/3; ☺ 10am-4pm Mon, Tue & Thu-Fri, to 6pm Wed, noon-5pm Sat; P ⊞) If you've come to Colorado to climb, this museum will give you tingles of inspiration. There's a pile of stunning photos, historic climbing gear (some of which, like Peter Schoening's ice axe, are from legendary expeditions) and a display on the 10th Mountain Division, which trained in Colorado before the fight in WWII – you can still use its huts in the Colorado backcountry.

Golden History Center   MUSEUM

(☑ 303-278-3557; www.goldenhistory.org; 923 10th St; adult/child $5/3; ☺ 10am-4:30pm Wed-Mon; P ⊞) Golden's History Center provides a timeline, albeit zigzagging, of the city's growth and citizens. Rotating exhibits showcase the 15,000 artifacts in the museum's collection, ranging from 19th-century instruments to Jolly Rancher memorabilia. An exhibit on Golden's entrepreneurial spirit is particularly interesting; it highlights Coors, Boppy and other household names. Videos and sound recordings bring exhibits to life.

Coors Brewery   BREWERY

(MillerCoors; ☑ 303-277-2337; www.millercoors. com; cnr 13th & Ford Sts; ☺ 10am-4pm Thu-Sat & Mon, noon-4pm Sun; P) **FREE** Coors Brewery is now officially called MillerCoors, but try telling the locals that. There's been brewing on this site since 1873. Coors survived the Prohibition years by producing malted

RED ROCKS PARK & AMPHITHEATRE

Set between 400ft-high red sandstone rocks, **Red Rocks Park & Amphitheatre** (☑303-697-4939; www.redrocksonline.com; 18300 W Alameda Pkwy; ⊙5am-11pm; 🖈) is found 15 miles southwest of Denver. Acoustics are so good many artists record live albums here. The 9000-seat theater offers stunning views and draws big-name bands all summer. To see your favorite singer go to work on the stage is to witness a performance in one of the most exceptional music venues in the world. For many, it's reason enough for a trip to Colorado.

When the setting sun brings out a rich, orange glow from the rock formations and the band on stage launches into the right tune, Red Rocks Amphitheatre is a captivating experience, wholly befitting the park's 19th-century name, 'Garden of Angels.'

The natural amphitheater, once a Ute camping spot, has been used for performances for decades, but it wasn't until 1936 that members of the Civilian Conservation Corps built a formal outdoor venue with seats and a stage. Though it originally hosted classical performances and military bands, it debuted as a rock venue with style; the first rock quartet on this stage was John, Paul, George and Ringo. Since then, the gamut of artists who have recorded live albums here – such as U2, Neil Young, Dave Matthews and new-age piano tinkler John Tesh – is a testament to the pristine natural acoustics.

You scored tickets? Great. Now for the nitty-gritty. Eat in Morrison beforehand as the junk food from the food vendors is predictably expensive and the restaurants are crowded. Alternatively, you can bring a small cooler into the show, as long as there's no booze and it'll fit under your seat. Climbing on the stunning formations is prohibited; however, 250-plus steps lead to the top of the theater, offering views of both the park and Denver, miles off to the east.

Amazingly, Red Rocks Park can be almost as entertaining when it's silent. The amphitheater is only a tiny part of the 600-acre space. There are miles of hiking trails, opportunities to lose the crowds and take in lovely rock formations. There's information about the entire area on the website.

milk and porcelain products, and went on to produce the world's first beer shipped in aluminum cans. Each year 250,000 people take the brewery's free audioguided tour, which includes three samples for the over-21 crowd.

A free shuttle transports people from the car park. Be sure to leave your bags and strollers in the car – none are allowed on the tour.

Colorado Railroad Museum   MUSEUM
(☑303-279-4591; www.coloradorailroadmuseum.org; 17155 W 44th Ave; adult/child $15/5; ⊙9am-5pm; 🅿🖈) With more than 100 railroad engines, a 500yd looping track, cabooses and rolling stock, as well as paraphernalia and regalia, this is a must-stop for train fanatics touring the region. The stars of the show are the well-restored Galloping Goose railcars (or motors, if you want to get technical). Admission includes unlimited rides on the museum's steam engine (Saturday only).

Built in Ridgeway, CO, the small Galloping Goose railcars were made from converted cars (three of the original seven are

now at the museum). They were used to transport small groups of people and cargo through the mountainous region and keep the Rio Grande Southern line profitable in remote Colorado. There's also a comprehensive library of all things locomotive, the **Restoration Roundhouse**, a working turntable and Colorado's coolest model train downstairs. Located about 2 miles east of Golden.

Foothills Art Center   MUSEUM
(☑303-279-3922; www.foothillsartcenter.org; 809 15th St; adult/child $8/free; ⊙10am-5pm Tue-Sat, from noon Sun; 🖈) Housed in three historic buildings, including a Gothic-style church, this small, carefully managed arts center hosts works by local artists as well as traveling exhibits. Classes and workshops occasionally offered too.

Buffalo Bill Museum & Grave   MUSEUM
(☑303-526-0744; www.buffalobill.org; 987 1/2 Lookout Mountain Rd; adult/child $5/1; ⊙9am-5pm; 🅿🖈) This museum celebrates the life and legend of William F 'Buffalo Bill' Cody, an icon of the American West. At his request

he was buried at this site overlooking both the Great Plains and the Rockies, and today it attracts a steady stream of RVs to snap pictures of his statue. Located about 6 miles west of town.

The museum and gift shop are pure kitsch and probably not recommended for those with a progressive view on Native American history. Still, Bill's biography is a fascinating one: when he began his show-business career at the age of 26 in Chicago in 1872, he had already spent more than a decade as a fur trapper, gold prospector, cattle herder, Pony Express rider and army scout, crossing the Great Plains many times in the West's pioneering years. His show became hugely popular and traveled to England in 1887 for Queen Victoria's Golden Jubilee celebrations.

🏃 Activities

Golden Bike Library   CYCLING
(☑ 303-597-3600;   www.goldenbikelibrary.com; 1010 Washington Ave; first 2hr free, per day $10; ☺ 10am-4pm Thu-Sun; 🚲) Check out a bike for free – or cheap – to explore Golden on two wheels. Bikes come in a variety of sizes, are in great condition and include helmet, lock and even a water bottle. Staffers hand out maps and advice about places to go too. Located in a shed behind the visitor center (p105).

Fossil Trace Golf Club   GOLF
(☑ 303-277-8750; www.fossiltrace.com; 3050 Illinois St; 18 holes nonresident $80-90; ☺ 6am-9pm) Even if you're not building your Colorado itinerary around golf, it might be worth knocking around a few holes at the Fossil Trace Golf Club. Routinely considered among America's best courses, this unique round of golf offers a glimpse of fossils, challenging play and sweeping views. The course isn't cheap, but it's certainly memorable.

This course might be the only place on earth where you can hit the ball off the fairway and into the shadow of triceratops' tracks. The course is built in the scarred terrain of old mines, giving a fascinating landscape where rock formations jut abruptly from the grass.

🛌 Sleeping

Not many people stay the night in Golden, but if you have an extra day, you might consider checking in for a night on the edge

of the Rockies. Options in town include a handful of hotels and B&Bs.

Dove Inn   B&B **$$**
(☑ 303-278-2209; www.doveinn.com; 711 14th St; r/ste from $135/145; ❄🐾) Built in 1868, this B&B gives a nod to the home's past – Victorian wallpaper, ironwork beds, quilt bedspreads – but doesn't go overboard (no porcelain dolls or mounted deer heads here). Instead, rooms feel homey and relaxed, all with modern amenities and good beds. Breakfast (included) is a hit, as are the freshly baked cookies, served at midday.

Located just one block from the main drag.

Table Mountain Inn   HOTEL **$$**
(☑ 303-277-9898;   www.tablemountaininn.com; 1310 Washington Ave; r from $179, ste from $239; 🅿❄🐾) Some of the best rooms in town are found in this adobe hotel smack in the downtown area. The large Southwest-styled rooms have heavy wood furnishings and patios looking out to Table Mesa. Some even have fireplaces and jetted tubs. Service is friendly and the cantina downstairs is worth checking out.

🍴 Eating & Drinking

Golden has a decent selection of eateries, considering its size; look for restaurants, cafes and more along or near the main drag, Washington Ave.

Golden doesn't exactly have a raucous nightlife but, like many Colorado towns, it has a handful of breweries. If you're up for a beer that's not Coors (p102), head to Cannonball Creek, an award-winning brewery that has an ever-changing selection of beers on tap (and in the hopper).

D'deli   DELI **$**
(☑ 303-279-8020; www.ddelisubs.com; 1207 Washington Ave; sandwiches $9-15; ☺ 11am-5pm Mon-Sat, from noon Sun; 🐾🚲) Crusty, fresh bread and stacks of ingredients make this cozy deli an excellent place for lunch. Sandwiches come in half and whole sizes. The 'Heater,' a massive pile of turkey, bacon, pepper jack cheese, jalapeños, banana peppers and chipotle ranch, is the choice for spice fiends. Eat in or take your sandwiches to the nearby Golden Creek for a picnic.

Golden Farmers Market   MARKET **$**
(http://goldenchamber.org/farmers-market; cnr 10th & Illinois Sts; ☺ 8am-1pm Sat Jun-Sep; 🚲🐕) On Saturdays between June and September,

the city hosts the Golden Farmers Market featuring local produce and prepared foods. If you're looking to stock up on veggies, head to the Miller Farms stand and buy a $10 bag to stuff with as much organic produce as you can fit! The market sets up just west of the library.

Woody's Wood Fired Pizza & Watering Hole
PIZZA $

(☑ 303-277-0443; www.woodysgolden.com; 1305 Washington Ave; pizza $10-13; ⊗ 11am-midnight; ⚡ 👪) ⚑ After you make it past the 'watering hole' part of Woody's, with its selection of some of the area's best brews, order up a crusty, wood-fired pie. Sandwiches, salads and wings on offer too. It's hard not to love the laid-back locals and sustainable-business focus.

★ Abejas
AMERICAN $$

(☑ 303-952-9745; www.abejasgolden.com; 807 13th St; mains $12-28; ⊗ 11am-2:30pm & 5-9:30pm Mon-Fri, 9:30am-2:30pm & 5-9:30pm Sat & Sun; ⚡) Abejas is a bustling bistro with a rustic-chic setting – reclaimed barn wood, corrugated metal, even bungee cords set the tone. The menu is farm to table with food sourced as locally as possible. Lunch brings delights like the braised-lamb sandwich, while dinner has dishes like caramel-lacquered duck. Brunch is a great option for those on a budget.

Ali Baba Grill
MEDITERRANEAN $$

(☑ 303-279-2228; www.alibabagrill.com; 109 N Rubey Dr; mains $6-20; ⊗ 11am-9pm; ⚡ 👪) Sure, it looks like another drab strip-mall joint from the parking lot, but the Lebanese and Mediterranean cuisine here is awesome and every bit as surprising as the elaborate interior, which is likely Golden's only harem-themed dining room.

Cannonball Creek Brewing Company
BREWERY

(☑ 303-278-0111; www.cannonballcreekbrewing. com; 393 N Washington Ave; ⊗ 3-10pm Mon-Wed, 3-11pm Thu, noon-11pm Fri & Sat, noon-10pm Sun) A young brewery, Cannonball Creek has already won several medals at the Great American Beer Festival (p79), including a gold for its Trump Hands (India Pale Ale) and Solid Gold (Belgian-style Pale Ale). Despite the accolades though, this place maintains a laid-back, neighborhood feel with new brews almost always on deck. Food trucks provide solids most days of the week.

ⓘ Tourist Information

Colorado Trail Foundation (CTF; ☑ 303-384-3729; www.coloradotrail.org; 710 10th St; ⊗ 9am-5pm Mon-Fri) The CTF is a great resource for anyone with questions about any part of the Colorado Trail, which runs 567 miles from Denver to Durango. Friendly staffers are on hand to answer questions, and there are guidebooks and topo maps of the trail for sale. The CTF also helps keep the trail in good shape by training and organizing crews of volunteers. All of CTF's work is done in coordination with the US Forest Service and Bureau of Land Management.

Golden Chamber of Commerce/Visitor Center (☑ 303-279-3113; www.goldenchamber.org; 1010 Washington Ave; ⊗ 8:30am-5pm Mon-Fri, 10am-4pm Sat; 👪) This is the tourism nerve center for Golden, and you can stock up on brochures, maps, hotel and local info here. You can also pick up a walking-tour guide to the historic district.

Jefferson County Open Space Office (☑ 303-271-5925; http://jeffco.us/open-space; 700 Jefferson County Pkwy; ⊗ 7:30am-5:30pm Mon-Fri) This office provides information and permits for camping in the county's park system. Camping permits for Reynolds Park can be obtained here or arranged through a phone call.

ⓘ Getting There & Away

Downtown Denver is about 16 miles, by bike, from Golden's historic district. Riding takes about 1½ hours; the **Clear Creek Bike Trail** will get you most of the way along a clearly marked route.

RTD (p101) connects Golden with downtown Denver on bus line 16L ($4.50); pick it up at the corner of Colfax and Broadway.

The easiest, and fastest, route from downtown Denver is to head west on US 6. Exit at 19th St in Golden's historic district. It's about 14 miles away.

The light-rail W line ($4.50) runs from Denver's **Union Station** (p63) to the Jefferson County Government Building about 5 miles south of Golden's historic district. The Community Call-n-Ride bus ($2.60) passes from downtown to the light-rail station every half-hour.

Morrison

☑ 303, 720 / POP 430 / ELEV 5764FT

Billing itself as 'the nearest faraway place,' tiny Morrison is a National Historic District 20 miles southwest of Denver, hidden from the city skyline by the Hogback rock formations. Made up of a main drag with a few side streets, it echoes the feel of some of Colorado's more remote mountain towns. While the upturned red rocks on the banks of the town's Bear Creek are an attractive escape from Denver, most people visit Morrison on the way to Red Rocks Park & Amphitheatre (p103) or to fuel up before hiking the big hills in the surrounding Jefferson County Open Space Parks (p105).

⊙ Sights

★ Morrison Natural History Museum
MUSEUM

(☑ 303-697-1873; www.mnhm.org; 501 Hwy 8; adult/child $8/6; ⊙10am-5pm, last entry 4pm; P 🚻) This small but excellent museum has displays on Morrison during the Jurassic and Cretaceous periods. There are huge dinosaur skulls as well as a full skeleton of a pteranodon, the flying reptile made popular on the kids' TV show *Dinosaur Train*. Deeply knowledgeable guides give daily one-hour tours (10:15am, 12:15pm and 2:15pm), though visitors are welcome to check out the exhibits on their own.

You can also observe – and sometimes help – staff members clean fossils in the Paleontology Lab. Outdoors, small children will enjoy a sandpit filled with fossils to 'find.'

Dinosaur Ridge
ARCHAEOLOGICAL SITE

(☑ 303-697-3466; www.dinoridge.org; 16831 W Alameda Pkwy; exhibit hall $2, bus tour incl exhibit hall $8; ⊙9am-5pm Mon-Sat, from 10am Sun May-Oct, 9am-4pm Mon-Sat, from 10am Sun Nov-Apr; P 🚻) FREE Two interpretive trails as well as a self-guided tour showcase the impressive footprints and sandstone-encased fossils that make up Dinosaur Ridge. If little legs make hiking tough, a 45-minute guided bus tour is also offered and includes three stops and touchable fossils. A small exhibit hall with loads of fossils and hands-on exhibits is a hit with kids.

Located about 2 miles north of Morrison.

🛏 Sleeping & Eating

Cliff House Lodge
B&B $$

(☑ 303-697-9732; www.cliffhouselodge.net; 121 Stone St; cottages from $170; ♋🛜) If you spend the night in Morrison, this historic brick B&B is by far the best choice. The decor might be a little overboard – think knickknacks and mounted animal heads – but all of the cottages have hot tubs and the garden is a peaceful place to relax. Best of all, it's a stone's throw from Red Rocks Park & Amphitheatre (p103).

Willy's Wings
BARBECUE $

(☑ 303-697-1232; www.willyswings.com; 109 Bear Creek Ave; mains $6-10; ⊙11am-8pm Mon-Sat, to 7pm Sun; P 🚻) Frills? Forget about it. Situated in what looks like the mobile home of a displaced Texan auntie, this place has some good wings. Stay away if you're watching your waistline – just about everything on the menu is deep-fried, except the potato salad, which is thick with mayo. Weekday lunch specials include 10 wings, fries and a drink ($10).

Flights Wine Cafe
CAFE $$

(☑ 303-697-0492; www.flightswinecafe.com; 116 Stone St; wine flights $16-20, meals $7-16; ⊙4-9pm Tue-Thu, 4-10pm Fri, 2-10pm Sat, 11am-5pm Sun) Flights serves up over 100 wines – by the glass or flight – in a cozy cottage setting. A menu of gourmet sandwiches and flatbreads, salads, and appetizers like smoked-trout dip and warmed Brie complement the wines well. The best seating is on the leafy patio with a water feature for warm evenings and fire pit for cool ones.

Fort
AMERICAN $$$

(☑ 303-697-4771; www.thefort.com; 19192 Hwy 8; mains $25-55; ⊙5-11pm) This Colorado institution – an adobe-style 'fort' perched in the foothills 2 miles south of Morrison – has been around since 1963. The ambience is totally old school, a meeting of the Old West and a 1980s country club. Known as a meat-eaters paradise, people come here for the Rocky Mountain oysters and wild game dishes.

Over the summer months, the Fort hosts several festivals celebrating Native American history and heritage, including an annual powwow.

ⓘ Tourist Information

USFS South Platte Ranger Station (☑ 303-275-5610, campsite reservations only 877-444-6777; www.fs.usda.gov; 19316 Goddard Ranch Ct; ⊙8am-4:30pm Mon-Fri; 🚻) This US Forest Service outpost has information about hiking, fishing and camping in the South Platte River District, which includes Pike and San Isabel National Forests. Permits are available here for camping.

ⓘ Getting There & Away

Morrison is 20 miles southwest of Denver and 8 miles due south of Golden. It is easily reached by car, either from Colorado Hwy 470, or by taking County Rd 93 from I-70. There is no regular bus service.

Boulder & Around

Includes ➡

Boulder 108
Nederland 132

Best Places to Eat

➡ Frasca (p124)

➡ Oak at Fourteenth (p122)

➡ Brasserie Ten Ten (p123)

➡ Rayback Collective (p120)

➡ T/ACO (p120)

Best Places to Stay

➡ Chautauqua Lodge & Cottages (p118)

➡ Boulder Adventure Lodge (p118)

➡ Briar Rose B&B (p118)

➡ St Julien Hotel & Spa (p119)

Why Go?

Twenty-five square miles surrounded by reality. That's the joke about Boulder that never goes away. The weather is perfect, the surroundings – stone Flatirons, gurgling creek, ponderosa trails and manicured college campus – beg idling. And the populace – fit do-gooders with the beta on the best fair-trade coffee and hoppiest home brew – seals the stereotype.

Boulder's mad love of the outdoors was officially legislated in 1967, when it became the first US city to tax itself specifically to preserve open space. Thanks to such vision, people (and dogs) enjoy a number of city parks and open spaces while packs of cyclists whip up and down the Boulder Creek corridor.

For travelers looking for an outdoorsy holiday with the cultural outlets of an urban oasis – gourmet restaurants, lively bars, concerts and theater – Boulder is where it's at.

When to Go
Boulder

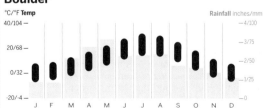

Jun–Aug Long sunny days, summer showers, farmers markets, hiking, biking and tubing.

Sep–Oct Students return, Indian summer, fall color, warm days, cool nights.

Jan–Feb Powder at Eldora, snowshoe or backcountry ski adventures in the Indian Peaks.

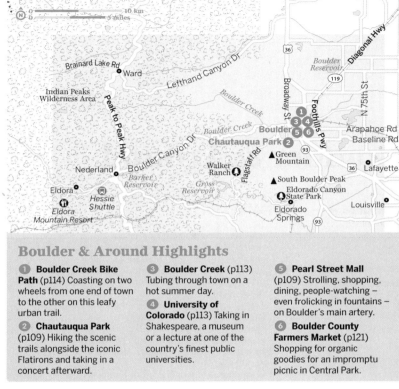

Boulder & Around Highlights

1 **Boulder Creek Bike Path** (p114) Coasting on two wheels from one end of town to the other on this leafy urban trail.

2 **Chautauqua Park** (p109) Hiking the scenic trails alongside the iconic Flatirons and taking in a concert afterward.

3 **Boulder Creek** (p113) Tubing through town on a hot summer day.

4 **University of Colorado** (p113) Taking in Shakespeare, a museum or a lecture at one of the country's finest public universities.

5 **Pearl Street Mall** (p109) Strolling, shopping, dining, people-watching – even frolicking in fountains – on Boulder's main artery.

6 **Boulder County Farmers Market** (p121) Shopping for organic goodies for an impromptu picnic in Central Park.

Boulder

📞 303, 720 / POP 97,385 / ELEV 5430FT

History

The Boulder foothills were a wintering spot for the nomadic Arapaho Nation in the early 19th century. Ute, Cheyenne, Comanche and Sioux were also documented in the Boulder valley before Europeans arrived. Later in the 19th century, American explorers Zebulon Pike and John Fremont were commissioned to explore the area. One of Fremont's men, William Gilpin, became the first governor of the Colorado Territory. His speculation on gold deposits in Boulder inspired Depression-saddled easterners to set out for Colorado.

The first European settlement in Boulder County was established at Red Rocks, on October 17, 1858. One of those early settlers, AA Brookfield, organized the Boulder City Town Company. In February 1859 he divided and sold land on either side of Boulder Creek, giving birth to the present-day city.

Boulder has always had strong educational roots. Colorado's first schoolhouse was erected at the southwest corner of Walnut and 15th St in 1860. In 1872 six of Boulder's most prominent citizens donated 44.9 acres of land in an area known as 'the Hill' for the establishment of a university. Two years later the first building, Old Main, was built with a combination of public and private dollars, and it is still standing. The University of Colorado (CU) opened its doors in September 1877 to 44 students, one professor and a president.

In 1898 Texas educators and local leaders conspired to bring a summer-long educational and cultural festival to Boulder. Part of the famed Chautauqua Movement, it drew orators, performers and educators, who traveled a national Chautauqua circuit of more than 12,000 sites. They brought lectures, performances, classes and exhibitions to small towns and cities. Boulder's Chautauqua was completed on July 4, 1898, and it had an incredible impact, not least of which was launching Boulder's parks and open-space preservation. The day after the grand opening, the city of Boulder purchased the eastern slope of Flagstaff Mountain from the United States government.

Purchasing land for preservation became and remains one of Boulder's top priorities. It now has over 54,000 acres dedicated to parks and open space.

In the 1950s, '60s and '70s, Boulder went through a major real-estate and business boom, with the arrival of megacompanies like IBM and Ball Aerospace and the meteoric rise of local enterprise Celestial Seasonings. Today, Boulder has more than 97,000 residents and nearly 33,000 students, yet its founding themes – nature, education, culture and progress – endure.

◉ Sights

Few towns have this combination of nature and culture. Whether you're climbing the Flatirons, cycling up Flagstaff (p113), roaming Pearl St or patrolling the campus at CU, there are plenty of sights and activities to keep you and the family smiling. Most sites are fairly centrally located, along W Pearl St or on the Hill, where you'll also find the university.

★**Chautauqua Park**　　　　PARK
(Map p110; ☑303-442-3282; www.chautauqua.com; 900 Baseline Rd; ▣HOP 2) This historic landmark park is the gateway to Boulder's most magnificent slab of open space adjoining the iconic Flatirons; its wide, lush lawn attracts picnicking families, sunbathers, Frisbee folk and students from nearby CU. It also gets lots of hikers, climbers and trail runners. It's a popular site so parking can be a hassle. During the summer of 2017 the City of Boulder piloted a free shuttle to several lots around the city to ease the congestion. Check the website for updates.

★**Pearl Street Mall**　　　　AREA
(Map p116; Pearl St, btwn 9th & 15th Sts; ⊞⊠; ▣205, 206, 208, HOP, SKIP) The highlight of downtown Boulder is the Pearl Street Mall, a vibrant pedestrian zone filled with kids' climbing boulders and splash fountains, bars, galleries and restaurants. Street performers often come out in force on weekends.

★**Dairy Arts Center**　　　ARTS CENTER
(Map p110; ☑303-440-7826; www.thedairy.org; 2590 Walnut St; prices vary; ⓟ⊞; ▣HOP) A historic milk-processing-factory-turned-arts-center, the Dairy is one of Boulder's top cultural hubs. Recently renovated, it's a state-of-the-art facility with three stages, four gallery spaces and a 60-seat cinema. There's always something going on – from lectures and plays to modern dance and art exhibits. There's a small cafe and bar on-site too.

Sunflower Farm　　　　FARM
(☑303-774-8001; www.sunflowerfarminfo.com; 11150 Prospect Rd, Longmont; $13, with pony rides $15; ⊙10am-2pm Wed-Sun Apr-May, 9am-1pm Wed-Sun Jun-Nov; ⓟ⊞) Set in the nearby city of Longmont, this 50-acre working farm with century-old barns welcomes families to Farmfest (its child-friendly program). Help feed baby animals, collect eggs, ride ponies and climb the giant tree house.

Butterfly Pavilion　　　　GARDENS
(☑303-469-5441; www.butterflies.org; 6252 W 104th Ave, Westminster; adult/child $11/7; ⊙9am-5pm; ⓟ⊞; ▣104) There are four indoor exhibit halls and acres of outdoor gardens here. Fluttering with over 1600 butterflies from all the rainforests of the world – not to mention furry tarantulas, armored scorpions and fuzzy millipedes – this spot is a whirl of color, excitement and joy for the kids (and big kids too). It's located in Westminster, 20 miles south on Hwy 36.

Boulder Reservoir　　　　LAKE
(☑303-441-3461; www.bouldercolorado.gov; 5565 N 51st St; adult/child Memorial Day to Labor Day $7/4, other times free; ⊙dawn-dusk; ⓟ⊞) When you're this far from the ocean, this is where folks come to suntan, swim and play in the water. There's a big sandy beach, lifeguards and a well-maintained visitor center and cafe. Kayak, paddleboard and sailboat rentals are offered ($15 to $30 per hour) along with SUP yoga classes ($35). Be sure to bring a hat and reapply sunscreen often – there's little shade here.

Dogs aren't allowed into the park between May 15 and Labor Day.

Museum of Boulder　　　MUSEUM
(Map p116; ☑303-449-3464; www.museumofboulder.org; 2205 Broadway; ⊞; ▣208, SKIP) The brand-new MOB is four times bigger than Boulder's original history museum, with plans for modern, interactive exhibits on all things Boulder-esque, from prehistoric

Boulder

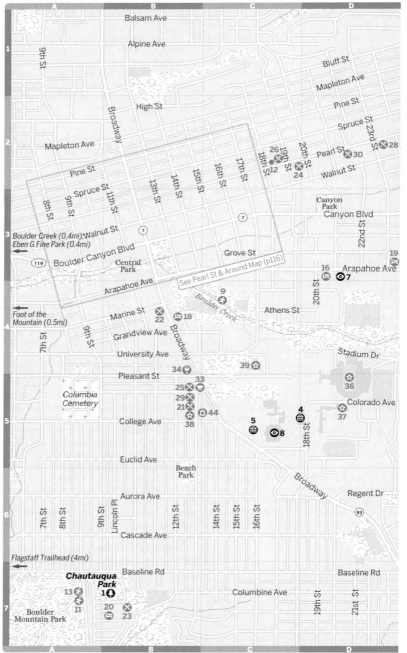

Boulder

◉ Top Sights
1 Chautauqua Park...............................B7
2 Dairy Arts Center.............................E2

◉ Sights
3 Carpenter Park & Pool.....................F4
4 CU Art Museum................................D5
5 CU Museum of Natural History..........C5
6 Fiske Planetarium.............................E6
7 Naropa University.............................D3
8 University of Colorado at Boulder.....C5

◉ Activities, Courses & Tours
9 Boulder Creek Bike Path...................C4
10 Boulder Rock Club............................F1
11 Flatirons..A7
12 Food Lab...C2
13 Royal Arch Trail...............................A7
14 White Water Tube.............................E1
15 Yoga Pod..F3

◉ Sleeping
16 Basecamp Boulder............................D3
17 Boulder Marriott...............................E3
18 Boulder University Inn.......................B4
19 Briar Rose B&B.................................D3
20 Chautauqua Lodge & Cottages..........B7

◉ Eating
21 Ado's Kitchen & Bar..........................B5
22 Alfalfa's..B4
23 Chautauqua Dining Hall....................B7
24 Dish Gourmet...................................C2
25 Half Fast Subs..................................B5
26 Mateo...C2
27 Rincón Argentino.............................E3
28 River & Woods..................................D2
29 Sink..B5
30 Snarf's..D2
31 Whole Foods Market..........................F1
32 Zolo Southwestern Grill....................E3

◉ Drinking & Nightlife
Boxcar Roasters.........................(see 12)
33 Innisfree Poetry Bookstore & Cafe.....B5
34 Owsley's Golden Road.......................B4

◉ Entertainment
35 CU Basketball...................................E6
36 CU Football......................................D5
37 CU Wizards.......................................D5
38 Fox Theatre......................................B5
39 Macky Auditorium Concert Hall........C4

◉ Shopping
40 Boulder Running Company.................E2
41 Boulder Ski Deals.............................E3
42 Common Threads..............................E1
CU Bookstore................................(see 8)
43 Fresh Baked......................................E2
44 Meow Meow.......................................C5
45 Outdoor Divas...................................F1
46 REI..E2

geology and early Native Americans, to marijuana legalization and space travel. There's a cool kids' area in the works plus a 'makers space' for aspiring inventors and a great rooftop deck too. Check the website for updates on admission costs and opening hours.

Central Park
PARK

(Map p116; Canyon Blvd; P ⊞; ⊟206, JUMP) A long blade of lush lawn spanning from the Museum of Contemporary Art at 13th St, and encompassing the Public Library (☑303-441-3100; www.boulderlibrary.org; 1001 Arapahoe Ave; ⊙9am-8pm Mon-Thu, 10am-6pm Fri & Sat, noon-6pm Sun; ☎⊞; ⊟JUMP), a twice-weekly seasonal farmers market (p121), the concert band shell and a large swath of the Boulder Creek Bike Path (p114), it's hard to avoid this park. A ramp leads to the Boulder Creek trail and the creek itself for tubing and kayaking.

Boulder Museum of Contemporary Art
MUSEUM

(Map p116; BMOCA; ☑303-443-2122; www.bmoca.org; 1750 13th St; adult/child $1/free; ⊙11am-5pm Tue-Sun; ⊞; ⊟203, 204, 205, 206, 208, 225, DASH, JUMP, SKIP) A historic brick house with three galleries of evocative modern art. Mixed-media exhibits can include such whimsy as neon installations and life-sized cards, while strange fashion concepts are displayed in the costume and wardrobe gallery upstairs. All exhibitions are temporary and rotate every three months. On Wednesdays when the farmers market blooms out front, the museum stays open till 8pm.

Eben G Fine Park
PARK

(Boulder Canyon Dr; P ⊞ ☺; ⊟205, N) A pleasant park along the south banks of Boulder Creek with plenty of grassy areas for picnicking and playing. It's a popular starting point for tubers too, with lots of entry points and small rapids. In May and June, the park's high water and sculpted ledges can get rocking, and you may even get flipped.

Fiske Planetarium
PLANETARIUM

(Map p110; ☑303-492-5002; www.colorado.edu/fiske; 2414 Regent Dr, University of Colorado; adult/child $10/7; ⊙hours vary; P ⊞; ⊟204, 209, DASH, SKIP) Don't be fooled by the tired lobby with its '80s-era displays: Fiske has one of the hottest projection and sound systems around, making for spectacular shows on its 65ft-diameter dome ceiling. Add to that seats that recline completely, and you're pulled into the scene all around you. Programming ranges from educational films –

black holes, volcanoes, Colorado skies – to laser shows set to the music of Lady Gaga, Beyoncé and Prince.

Celestial Seasonings
FACTORY

(☑303-581-1266; www.celestialseasonings.com; 4600 Sleepytime Dr; ⊙10am-4pm Mon-Sat, 11am-3pm Sun; P ⊞; ⊟205T, J) FREE If you like tea, you'll dig visiting Celestial Seasonings, one of the world's largest herbal tea producers. Visitors are treated to a 45-minute tour, including a campy historical video and a walk through the milling, mixing and packaging areas. The Mint Room – packed with mint and peppermint bundles – leaves you feeling like you're inside a lozenge. Be sure to check out the tasting room before your tour, where you can try any of Celestial Seasonings' 105 teas.

Tours leave every 30 to 60 minutes, first-come, first-served. Children five and over only.

CU Museum of Natural History
MUSEUM

(Map p110; ☑303-492-6892; www.colorado.edu/cumuseum; cnr Broadway & 15th St, Henderson Bldg; suggested donation $3; ⊙9am-5pm Mon-Fri, 9am-4pm Sat, 10am-4pm Sun; ⊞; ⊟204, 225, DASH, HOP, SKIP) Tucked into a nondescript university building, CU's natural history museum is far from forgettable. Two floors of multimedia exhibits showcase the geological evolution of Boulder – including impressive dinosaur skeletons and fossils – as well as anthropological discoveries of the southwest. A 'Discovery Corner' aimed at small children has fossils and bones to touch, and activity boxes. For teens and parents, there's also a 'Biolounge' – a quiet room with couches, free coffee, wi-fi and rotating exhibits on biodiversity.

National Center for Atmospheric Research
SCIENCE CENTER

(NCAR; ☑303-497-1000; www.scied.ucar.edu; 1850 Table Mesa Dr; ⊙8am-5pm Mon-Fri, 9am-5pm Sat & Sun; P ⊞) FREE Set near the Flatirons in a Tetris-like structure designed by IM Pei, NCAR is a research facility dedicated to the study of the earth's atmosphere and weather. Open to the public, it has two floors of multimedia exhibits, many interactive and quite interesting, to teach about its work. Free guided tours are offered at noon every Monday, Wednesday and Friday.

NCAR also maintains a short hiking trail with spectacular views and educational placards. The trail leads to more challenging hikes in the Boulder Open Space and Mountain Parks system.

Flagstaff Trailhead   VIEWPOINT
(☏303-441-3440; www.bouldercolorado.gov; Flagstaff Summit Rd; P🐾) This trailhead and parking area is just below the summit of Flagstaff Mountain (7283ft) and a short drive from downtown Boulder. The views over Boulder and Denver to the east are great, and the Continental Divide views to the west, spectacular. From here, a handful of fun hikes leads to even better vistas. The super-steep climb is also popular with hard-core cyclists.

Carpenter Park & Pool   PARK
(Map p110; ☏303-441-3427; www.bouldercolorado.gov; 1505 30th St; pool adult/child $7/4; ⊙park dawn-dusk, pool 6am-7:30pm Mon-Fri, 10am-6pm Sat & Sun; 🐾; 🚍J, BOUND, JUMP) Carpenter Park is named after Scott Carpenter, one of the original 'Mercury Seven' astronauts and a Boulder son. Families love the playground's rocket-shaped climbing structure and the outdoor pool and waterslide, while athletes come for Boulder's only 50m lanes. In winter the contoured hills (once the city dump!) are popular for sledding. Catch the Boulder Creek Bike Path (p114) here too.

CU Art Museum   MUSEUM
(Map p110; ☏303-492-8300; www.colorado.edu/cuartmuseum; 1085 18th St, Visual Arts Complex; ⊙11am-5pm Tue-Sat, during school yr to 7pm Tue & Thu; 🐾; 🚍204, 225, DASH, HOP, SKIP) FREE CU's art museum has three cavernous rooms, each featuring exhibits that change every few months. Works of art from the university's private collection, traveling exhibits and student/faculty works are typically showcased. Works purposely aren't labelled; get a free iPad from the information desk – or download the app – to learn more about each.

University of Colorado
at Boulder   UNIVERSITY
(Map p110; CU; ☏303-492-6301; www.colorado.edu; 1669 Euclid Ave; parking per hr $2-4; ⊙tours 9:30am & 1:30pm Mon-Fri, 10:30am Sat; P🐾; 🚍203, 204, 209, 225, AB, B, DASH, DD, DM, GS, J, SKIP, STAMPEDE) Prospective students and curious visitors can tour one of America's finest public universities, with a beautiful campus set above downtown, on what is known as the Hill. Free tours begin with a 45-minute information session followed by a 90-minute walking tour.

Naropa University   UNIVERSITY
(Map p110; ☏303-546-3572; www.naropa.edu; 2130 Arapahoe Ave; ⊙tours 1pm Mon-Fri during school year; P🐾; 🚍JUMP) FREE Naropa was founded by Tibetan Buddhist master Chögyam Trungpa Rinpoche, who escaped Tibet and climbed over the Himalayas into India as a young man. In 1970, at just 30, he began presenting teachings in the US and founded the Naropa Institute (now Naropa University) in 1974. It offers a contemplative education in psychology, environmental studies, music and more. The university periodically hosts public talks and events.

🏃 Activities
Boulder's much-deserved reputation as an ecotopia is rooted in the collective call for outdoor adventure with hundreds of miles of hiking, biking and running trails. But it's also a place to go inside and tune in with your inner 'om.' Whether that means yoga, a morning at a day spa or a food tour is up to you.

The main vein is the Boulder Creek Bike Path, shooting directly through town to the mountains, with north–south branches. Valmont Bike Park rewards well-padded riders with jumps and a half pipe. A number of shops offer rentals and route advice. B-Cycle has stations around town with hourly rentals.

★ Boulder Creek   WATER SPORTS
(🐾) An all-time favorite Boulder summer ritual is to tube down Boulder Creek. Most people put in at Eben G Fine Park and float as far as 30th St, or even 55th St. Be sure to check the water volume, especially early in the season; anything over 200 cu ft per second can be a real rodeo. Rent tubes at White Water Tube (p115) or Lolita's Market (p122).

★ Royal Arch Trail   HIKING
(Map p110; 900 Baseline Rd, Chautauqua Park; 🐾🐕; 🚍HOP 2) Challenging but not excruciating, this roughly 2½-hour, 3.6-mile, well-signed trail leads you up along the Flatirons. Hike through a vaguely red-rock canyon, then through a keyhole and up to a wonderful natural rock arch where you'll perch on boulders, gaze at the Boulder basin and, on clear days, glimpse the Denver skyline. Grab a trail map at the Chautauqua Park (p109) office.

Eldorado Canyon State Park   OUTDOORS
(☏303-494-3943; www.cpw.state.co.us; 9 Kneale Rd, Eldorado Springs; $8; ⊙dawn-dusk, visitor center 9am-5pm) Among the country's best

BOULDER IN...

Two Days

No matter the month, your first stop should be **Chautauqua Park** (p109). On your way, pick up lunch at **Dish Gourmet** (p121) to enjoy at the park. A great leg burner is the 4-mile **Royal Arch** (p113) hike. Afterward, head to **Pearl Street Mall** (p109) and explore Boulder's historic downtown, then join locals for brews and burgers at **Mountain Sun** (p125).

Wake up to Boulder's best brunch at **Tangerine** (p121). Grab two wheels – either bike-share or rental – and explore **Boulder Creek Bike Path** (p114), or join the Lycra-clad maniacs pedaling up **Flagstaff Mountain** (p113). Cap your day with a locavore dinner at **Oak at Fourteenth** (p122).

Four Days

On the third day, work up an appetite with a class at **Yoga Pod** (p114), then head to **Sanitas** (p125) for tacos and craft beer (and maybe some lawn games). Afterward, head to **Dairy Arts Center** (p109) for fine art and an indie film. For dinner, walk to **River & Woods** (p123) for comfort food with a twist.

On the last day, grab an early breakfast at **Lucile's** (p121), then drive up to **Nederland** (p132) for a hike. Get back in time for happy hour and tapas at the **MED** (p123). Then stroll down to the patio of **St Julien** (p119) for a taste of Boulder's Latin dance scene.

rock-climbing areas, Eldorado has Class 5.5 to 5.12 climbs. Suitable for all visitors, a dozen miles of hiking trails also link up to Chautauqua Park. A public pool (summer only) offers chilly swims in the canyon's famous spring water. Located 5 miles southwest of town.

For the park entrance, take Hwy 93 south from Boulder, then head west on Hwy 170 to the park gates. For climbing tips, visit the Boulder Rock Club beforehand.

Valmont Bike Park   CYCLING
(☑ 303-413-7219; www.valmontbikepark.org; 3160 Airport Rd; ☉ dawn-dusk; 📷; 📵 208) **FREE** With dirt trails, a slope-style terrain park and some massive jumps, this 40-acre public bike park is the pride and joy of Boulder. You don't have to be an adolescent to enjoy it, but do come as padded as possible – helmet goes without saying.

Flatirons   CLIMBING
(Map p110; 900 Baseline Rd, Chautauqua Park; 📵 HOP 2) The iconic Flatirons, three pointed rock faces that provide the backdrop to Boulder, aren't necessarily the most challenging climbs in the area, but they must be climbed. The most popular route is the Class 5.6, 10-pitch First Flatiron 'direct climb.' It's a slab crawl up 1000ft to amazing views in all directions, but it gets crowded on weekends.

Boulder Rock Club   CLIMBING
(Map p110; ☑ 303-447-2804; www.boulderrock-club.com; 2829 Mapleton Ave; day pass adult/child $19/12; ☉ 6am-11pm Mon-Fri, 8am-8pm Sat & Sun; 📷; 📵 205, BOUND) An incredible indoor climbing gym popular with local rock rats. This massive warehouse – 40ft high in places – is full of artificial rock faces cragged with ledges and routes, and the auto-belay system allows solo climbers an anchor. Lessons and courses available, with a special kids' program. Staff are a great resource for local climbing routes.

Boulder Creek Bike Path   CYCLING
(Map p110; 📷) The most utilized commuter bike path in town, this smooth and mostly straight creekside concrete path follows Boulder Creek (p113) from Foothills Pkwy all the way uphill to the split of Boulder Canyon and Four Mile Canyon Rd west of downtown – a total distance of over 5 miles one-way. It also feeds urban bike lanes that lead all over town.

Yoga Pod   YOGA
(Map p110; ☑ 303-444-4232; https://boulder.yoga pod.com; 1750 29th St, Shop 2020; drop-in class $18; ☉ 6:30am-9pm Mon-Thu, 6:30am-7:15pm Fri, 7:15am-7:45pm Sat, 8:30am-7:45pm Sun; 📵 BOUND) One of the best, if most oddly located, studios in Boulder. But don't let the 29th St Mall location throw you off. There's plenty of free parking, the place isn't corporate and the instruction is first rate.

Wonderland Lake Trailhead HIKING

(☑ 303-441-3440; www.bouldercolorado.gov; 4201 N Broadway; 👤 🐾; ☐ SKIP) This easily accessed North Boulder trailhead links to 2.4 miles of trails within the City of Boulder's terrific Open Space and Mountain Parks program. Fairly flat trails skirt a lovely artificial lake, surrounded by knee-high grasses and tucked up against the foothills. Dogs must be leashed.

University Bicycles CYCLING

(Map p116; ☑ 303-444-4196; www.ubikes.com; 839 Pearl St; per day rental from $25; ⊙ 10am-7pm Mon-Fri, to 6pm Sat, to 5pm Sun; 👤; ☐ HOP) There are plenty of bike rental shops in this town, but this cavernous place has the widest range of rides and the most helpful staff. For $25 you can get a townie bike for the day. All rentals include helmet, lock and flat repair kit.

White Water Tube WATER SPORTS

(Map p110; ☑ 720-239-2179; www.whitewater tubing.com; 2709 Spruce St; rental per day tube $16-21, paddleboard $35, kayak $45-50; ⊙ 10am-6pm May-Sep; 👤; ☐ 205, BOLT, HOP) For tube, kayak and paddleboard rentals, head to this little shop on the east side of town. For tubing on Boulder Creek, staffers provide drop-off at Eben G Fine Park and pickup, about two hours later, near 30th St (it takes that long to float down). Helmets and life jackets included. Look for the store tucked behind a dress shop.

🎓 Courses

Food Lab COOKING

(Map p110; ☑ 303-953-8364; www.foodlabboulder. com; 1825 Pearl St; $75-85; 👤; ☐ HOP) A huge stylish kitchen serves as the classroom in this community cooking school geared toward everyday folks who just plain love to cook. Classes are relaxed but informative and themes run the gamut from Backyard Cookouts to Argentina in a Night. Classes typically last three hours and are taught by local chefs.

👉 Tours

★ Local Table Tours FOOD & DRINK

(☑ 303-909-5747; www.localtabletours.com; tours $35-70; ⊙ hours vary) Go behind the scenes with one of these fun downtown walking tours presenting a smattering of great local cuisine and inside knowledge on food and wine or coffee and chocolate. The tours also highlight locally owned businesses with regional or sustainable food sources. The cocktail crawl is a hit.

Banjo Billy Tour BUS

(Map p116; ☑ 720-938-8885; www.banjobilly.com; adult/child $24/17; ⊙ hours vary; 👤) These acclaimed and entertaining 90-minute bus tours, some undertaken by the garrulous tour founder himself, mine city history for quirky tidbits and little-known incidents. Ghost tours are also offered in October. Tours depart from downtown in front of the Hotel Boulderado (p120) – look for a school bus that looks like a log cabin (well, kinda). Tickets available online.

★🎉 Festivals & Events

Conference on World Affairs CULTURAL

(☑ 303-492-2525; www.colorado.edu/cwa; 1669 Euclid Ave, University of Colorado; ⊙ early Apr; ☐ 204, 225, DASH, HOP, SKIP) **FREE** This fantastic week-long event brings the campus and town together with excellent public lectures, films, music, panel discussions and debates. Presentations are given by top thinkers, artists, politicos and economists – everyone from Annie Leibovitz to Henry Kissinger. It's a thought-provoking and inspiring event. It was started in 1948 as a forum for international affairs; topics change yearly.

Bolder Boulder SPORTS

(☑ 303-444-7223; www.bolderboulder.com; adult/child from $70/55; ⊙ Memorial Day; 👤; ☐ 209, STAMPEDE) With over 50,000 runners and pros mingling with costumed racers, live bands and sideline merrymakers, this may be the most fun 10km run in the US, ending at Folsom Field, CU's football stadium.

Boulder Creek Festival MUSIC, FOOD

(☑ 303-449-3137; www.bceproductions.com; Canyon Blvd, Central Park; ⊙ May; 👤; ☐ 203, 204, 225, AB, B, DASH, DD, DM, GS, SKIP) **FREE** Billed as the kick-off to summer and capped with the Bolder Boulder (p115), this summer festival is massive. Over 10 event areas feature more than 30 live entertainers and 500 vendors plus a whole carnival ride zone. There's food and drink, entertainment and sunshine. What's not to love?

Colorado Shakespeare Festival THEATER

(☑ 303-492-8008; www.coloradoshakes.org; 1030 Broadway, Mary Rippon Outdoor Theatre; adult/child from $20/10; ⊙ mid-Jun–mid-Aug; 👤; ☐ 204, 225, DASH, HOP, SKIP) 🎭 For over half a century, summer has seen professional actors putting on the Bard's tragedies and comedies in the lovely outdoor amphitheater at CU.

Pearl St & Around

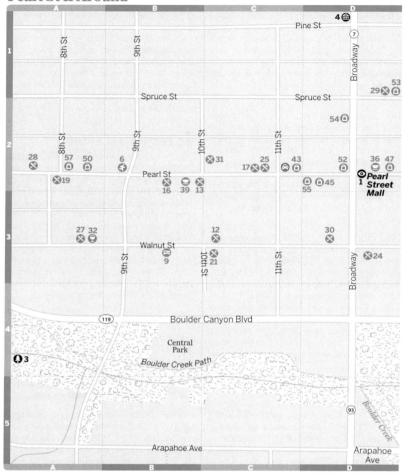

Free pre-show talks are often offered by the producing artistic director, to give historical background and context for the plays. The acclaimed series is a Boulder highlight.

Boulder Craft Beer Fest   BEER
(☎303-449-3774; www.boulderdowntown.com/craft-beer-festival; cnr 9th St & Dellwood Ave, North Boulder Park; tickets from $35; ⊙Aug; 🚍208, SKIP) Held in August, the Boulder Craft Beer Fest is a good old-fashioned afternoon lawn party. Over 30 local breweries participate, and tickets start at just $35 for unlimited 2oz pours. (By comparison Denver's Great

American Beer Festival can cost over a hundred bucks.) Between samples, you can play ping-pong and cornhole and catch some great live music.

Boulder Pride Fest   LGBT
(☎303-499-5777; www.outboulder.org; Canyon Blvd, Central Park; ⊙mid-Sep; ➐; 🚍203, 204, 225, AB, B, DASH, DD, DM, GS, SKIP) **FREE** A diverse, joyful party celebrating the LGBT community. Boulder Pride Fest hosts poetry performances and live music, speeches from community leaders, and a fair amount of

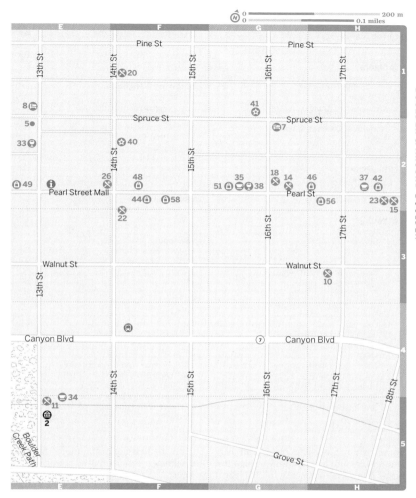

wellness and health-care information, all in Central Park.

Boulder Creek Hometown Festival FAIR
(☎303-449-3137; www.bceproductions.com; Canyon Blvd, Central Park; ☺Labor Day weekend; 🖟; 🚌203, 204, 225, AB, B, DASH, DD, DM, GS, SKIP) FREE This Labor Day fest caps summer with laughs including a pie-eating contest, the Great Zucchini Race (yes, zucchinis are outfitted with wheels) and live music. There's also a classic car and motorcycle show and a kid-friendly race.

Boulder Adventure Film Festival FILM
(www.adventurefilm.org; 2032 14th St, Boulder Theater; tickets from $15; ☺Oct; 🖟; 🚌208) Held in early October at the Boulder Theater (p127), this high-caliber outdoor-adventure film fest celebrates the great outdoors and the crazy things we do in it.

🛌 Sleeping

Boulder's lodging is made up of luxurious hotels and homey B&Bs with a few revamped motels and small inns filling in the middle. There's not much for those on a tight budget as lodging is pricey (and generally

Pearl St & Around

◎ Top Sights
1 Pearl Street Mall D2

◎ Sights
2 Boulder Museum of
   Contemporary Art E5
3 Central Park.. A4
4 Museum of Boulder D1

◎ Activities, Courses & Tours
5 Banjo Billy Tour E2
6 University Bicycles B2

◎ Sleeping
7 Bradley Boulder Inn...............................G2
8 Hotel Boulderado.................................... E1
9 St Julien Hotel & Spa.............................. B3

◎ Eating
10 Arabesque H3
11 Boulder County Farmers
   Market E5
12 Brasserie Ten Ten.................................... C3
13 Centro Mexican Kitchen B2
14 Foolish Craig's..G2
15 Frasca H2
16 Jax Fish House B2
17 Kitchen C2
18 Leaf G2
19 Lolita's Market & Deli A2
20 Lucile's F1
21 MED C3
22 Oak at Fourteenth....................................F3
23 Pizzeria Locale H2
24 Ruebens Burger Bistro D3
25 Salt...C2
26 Salvaggio's Italian Deli E2
27 Sherpa's A3

28 Spruce Confections A2
29 Sushi Zanmai D1
30 T/ACO...D3
31 Zoe Ma Ma C2

◎ Drinking & Nightlife
32 Bitter Bar A3
33 Bohemian Biergarten..............................E2
34 Boulder Dushanbe Teahouse...............E5
35 Cup G2
36 Ku Cha House of Tea D2
37 Laughing Goat...H2
   License No 1 .... (see 8)
38 Mountain Sun...G2
39 Trident Cafe B2

◎ Entertainment
40 Boulder Theater....................................... F2
41 eTown Hall G1

◎ Shopping
42 Beat Book Shop..H2
43 Boulder Book Store.................................C2
44 Into the Wind.. F2
45 Jackalope & Co D2
46 Momentum..H2
47 Nature's Own D2
48 Pedestrian Shops F2
49 Peppercorn E2
50 Piece, Love & Chocolate........................A2
51 Posterscene G2
52 Prana...D2
53 Rebecca's Herbal Apothecary D1
54 Savory Spice Shop D2
55 Smith Klein Gallery..................................D2
56 Starr's Clothing Co..................................H2
57 Two Hands Paperie..................................A2
58 Zuni F2

overpriced) but booking online can help. Many places also have special packages that range from spa treatments to champagne and chocolates.

★**Chautauqua Lodge
& Cottages**   HISTORIC HOTEL **$$**
(Map p110; ☎303-952-1611; www.chautauqua.com; 900 Baseline Rd; r from $103, cottages $196-303; [P][⊘][❄][🕏][🐾]; [🚌]HOP 2) Adjoining beautiful hiking trails to the Flatirons and in a leafy neighborhood inside Chautauqua Park, this is our top Boulder pick. It has contemporary rooms and one- to three-bedroom cottages with porches and patchwork-quilt beds. It's perfect for families and pets. All have full kitchens, though the wraparound porch of the Chautauqua Dining Hall is a local favorite for breakfast.

Two- to four-night minimum stay during summer. Discounted rates available in winter.

★**Boulder Adventure Lodge**   HOTEL **$$**
(A-Lodge; ☎303-444-0882; www.a-lodge.com; 91 Fourmile Canyon Dr; r from $159; [P][⊘][❄][🕏][🐾]; [🚌]N) You've come to Boulder to get outdoors, so why not stay nearer the action? Located a short distance from town, the A-Lodge has hiking, biking, climbing and fishing right from the property. Rooms are simple but well appointed, ranging from dorms to suites. There's a pool and fire pit, generating a warm esprit de corps among guests and staff alike.

★**Briar Rose B&B**   B&B **$$**
(Map p110; ☎303-442-3007; www.briarrosebb.com; 2151 Arapahoe Ave; r from $184; [❄][🕏]; [🚌]JUMP)

Gorgeous and comfy, this tranquil home is a stone's throw from Naropa University. A tall fence and landscaped garden insulate it from busy Arapahoe Ave. Inside there are cozy rooms with a Buddhist influence, reflecting the Zen monk practice of one of the owners. The organic vegetarian breakfast features a wide tea selection and there's one loaner bike.

Boulder Twin Lakes Inn   HOTEL $$
([phone] 303-530-2939; www.twinlakesinnboulder.com; 6485 Twin Lakes Rd; r from $148; [P][*][wifi][pet]; [bus]205W) Owned by a former Olympian, this midranger is both far from fancy and the center of town. Still, rooms are large and clean, and there's a communal kitchen, year-round Jacuzzi and laundry facilities. Plus it's within walking distance of the Twin Lakes along a gravel trail. Some rooms have kitchenettes and others, which sleep up to six, have sofa beds.

Foot of the Mountain   MOTEL $$
([phone] 303-442-5688; www.footofthemountainmotel.com; 200 Arapahoe Ave; r/ste from $139/199; [P][*][wifi][pet]; [bus]205, N) Nothing fancy here, but plenty of family-owned, wood-paneled charm. The motel itself looks like a cabin has been stretched out and bent around a parking lot, then tucked into a wooded glen at the foot of Flagstaff Mountain. Rooms are more quirky than comfy but therein lies its charm, and considering the competition, it's good value.

Boulder University Inn   MOTEL $$
(Map p110; [phone] 303-417-1700; www.boulderuniversity inn.com; 1632 Broadway; r from $144; [P][@][wifi][pet]; [bus]AB, B, JUMP, SKIP) While a Boulder motel room seems like robbery compared to its Kansan counterparts, keep in mind *it is Boulder*. Perks from this long-running business include the central location, friendly staff and updated rooms. There's even a heated outdoor pool. Located just off the Boulder Creek Bike Path.

★St Julien Hotel & Spa   HOTEL $$$
(Map p116; [phone] 720-406-9696, reservations 877-303-0900; www.stjulien.com; 900 Walnut St; r/ste from $400/650; [P][*][@][wifi][pet]; [bus]205, HOP, SKIP) In the heart of downtown, Boulder's finest four-star option is modern and refined, with photographs of local scenery and cork walls that warm the ambience. With fabulous views of the Flatirons, the back patio hosts

---

OPEN SPACE IS NO ACCIDENT

There aren't many towns like Boulder. Even in Colorado it's an anomaly. We're not just referencing its ability to simultaneously nurture the adventurous and athletic, the intellectual and spiritual, the beer-drinking masses and the culinary-snob set. We're talking about Boulder, the place. You know, that town so close to Denver it could easily have become a mere suburb or satellite town. Just look at the Hwy 36 corridor. From the I-25 north this highway roars through one suburb after another, but as it approaches Boulder the development stops and all you spy are those gorgeous Flatirons looming to the west. Why? Because long ago the city and county of Boulder got into the land-acquisition business.

It all started back in 1898 when the city helped purchase and set aside land that was marked for gold exploration and became Chautauqua Park (p109). In 1907 the government floated a public bond to buy Flagstaff Mountain, and in 1912 purchased and preserved 1200 more pristine mountain acres. Then, in 1967, Boulder voters legislated their love of the land by approving a sales tax specifically to buy, manage and maintain open space. This was historic. No other US city had ever voted to tax themselves specifically for open space. The sales-tax measure passed with 57% of the vote and Boulder's Open Space and Mountain Parks (www.osmp.org) office was launched. In 1989 76% of voters increased the tax by nearly 100%.

Still, even with an income stream, these days the government usually can't afford to buy whole parcels, and instead purchases 'conservation easements,' a legal agreement between the city and a landowner to protect their land's conservation value. Often they're used to purchase and protect wetlands and streams, keep agricultural land from being developed, and protect forests. While a good deal of Boulder's open space has been developed with trails, mapped and opened to the public, some parcels remain closed to visitors. But residents still feel the benefits: they live in a town buffered on all sides by vast open spaces that give Boulder its serenity.

BOULDER FOR KIDS

It's easy to keep the kids happy and busy here: most of what makes adults so giddy about a Boulder holiday – nature and adventure – ignites kids too. And there are also plenty of options for rainy days: a CU's **Wizards** (p127) show, a tour of the **National Center for Atmospheric Research** (p112) (sounds painful but kids really like it!) and the **Fiske Planetarium** (p112) are hits.

Boulder is very accommodating in practical terms too. Most restaurants have baby-change facilities (often in both the women's and men's bathrooms) and kids' menus; hotels have cribs, and museums and other sights offer reduced prices for children. The pavements, too, are wide and well kept, making it easy to explore town with a stroller.

live world music, jazz concerts and popular Latin dance parties. Rooms are spacious and plush. The on-site spa is considered one of the best around.

Hotel Boulderado　　　BOUTIQUE HOTEL **$$$**
(Map p116; ☑ 303-442-4344; www.boulderado.com; 2115 13th St; r from $313; P ✳ 🛜; 🚌 HOP, SKIP) With over a century of service, the charming Boulderado, full of Victorian elegance and wonderful public spaces, is a National Register landmark and a romantic getaway. Most rooms are modern, though some feature antiques and ornate wallpaper. Many have views of the Flatirons and Rocky Mountain foothills too. The stained-glass atrium and glacial water fountain accent the jazz-washed lobby.

Bradley Boulder Inn　　　INN **$$$**
(Map p116; ☑ 303-545-5200; www.thebradleyboulder.com; 2040 16th St; d $290; ➡ ✳ 🛜; 🚌 HOP) An elegant downtown Boulder mansion with polished wood, local art and stained glass salvaged from a nearby church, this is a great upscale option. More regal than cozy, it still does the job with great service, complimentary tea and baked goods, and an afternoon wine-and-cheese hour. Rooms are unique, some with fireplaces, Jacuzzis or balconies. Adults only.

Basecamp Boulder　　　HOTEL **$$$**
(Map p110; ☑ 303-449-7550; www.basecampboulder.com; 2020 Arapahoe Ave; r from $259; P ✳ @ 🛜 ✳ ✳; 🚌 JUMP) Great concept, less-than-perfect execution, but still a worthwhile option, especially for its central location. The mountaineering theme includes coolers as coffee tables and a climbing wall in the dining area. Rooms are comfortable, but a bit shabby for the rate. It's a glorified motel, after all, something clever decor can't entirely erase.

Boulder Marriott　　　HOTEL **$$$**
(Map p110; ☑ 303-440-8877; www.marriott.com; 2660 Canyon Blvd; r from $319; P ✳ 🛜; 🚌 205, 206, BOLT) This peach-tinted chain opens up

to the west, which means top-floor rooms get beautiful Flatirons views. Rooms are far from fashionable but they are comfortable and spacious with a desk, sofa and queen bed. Well run, it's less a resort and more of a business hotel with free wi-fi.

🍴 Eating

Farm to table is today's buzz phrase, and local food graces Boulder's stylish restaurants. There's a nod to health – restaurants cater to everything from gluten-free to paleo diets. But beyond that, there is a marked upswing in quality, with sophistication to rival the big US cities. No wonder *Bon Appétit* magazine rated Boulder the foodiest town in America.

★ T/ACO　　　MEXICAN **$**
(Map p116; ☑ 303-443-9468; www.tacocolorado.com; 1175 Walnut St; dishes $4-8; ⊙ 11am-10pm; 🍴 ✳; 🚌 208, SKIP) Super-fresh ingredients and inventive recipes mean T/ACO's tacos are little gems on a corn tortilla: braised pork belly, mango Caesar chicken, even a killer veggie taco with spaghetti squash and roasted poblano chili. Service is quick and friendly, and the margaritas are to die for. Come for Taco Tuesday when tacos start at $2 apiece.

★ Rayback Collective　　　FOOD TRUCK **$**
(☑ 303-214-2127; www.therayback.com; 2775 Valmont Rd; mains $6-12; ⊙ 11am-10pm Mon-Fri, to 11pm Sat, to 9pm Sun; 🍴 ✳ ✳; 🚌 205, BOLT) A plumbing-supplies warehouse turned urban oasis, Rayback is a snapshot of Boulder. A place to feel community. A huge outdoor space with fire pit and lawn games. A lounge with cozy chairs and live music. A bar serving up Colorado brews. A food-truck park with loads of good eats. Young, old, or even furry friends, are welcome here.

★ Rincón Argentino　　　ARGENTINE **$**
(Map p110; ☑ 303-442-4133; www.rinconargentinoboulder.com; 2525 Arapahoe Ave; mains $4-13;

11am-8pm Mon-Thu, to 9pm Fri & Sat; ✈️📶; 🚌 JUMP) Don't be turned off by the shopping plaza setting: Rincón packs a wallop of authentic Argentina. It bakes fresh empanadas – savory, small turnovers filled with spiced meat, or mozzarella and basil – which are perfect with a glass of Malbec. It also offers *milanesas (*breaded-beef-cutlet sandwiches); and gourds of yerba maté, a high-octane coffee alternative.

Boulder County Farmers Market MARKET $
(Map p116; ☎ 303-910-2236; www.boulderfarmers. org; 13th St, btwn Canyon Blvd & Arapahoe Ave; ⏰8am-2pm Apr-Nov plus 4-8pm Wed May-Oct; ✈️📶👶; 🚌203, 204, 205, 206, 208, 225, DASH, JUMP, SKIP) A massive spring and summer sprawl of colorful, mostly organic local food. Find flowers and herbs, as well as brain-sized mushrooms, delicate squash blossoms, crusty pretzels, vegan dips, grass-fed beef, raw granola and yogurt. Prepared food booths offer all sorts of international tasty treats. Live music is as standard as the family picnics in the park along Boulder Creek.

Zoe Ma Ma CHINESE $
(Map p116; ☎ 303-545-6262; www.zoemama.com; 2010 10th St; mains $6-15; ⏰11am-10pm Sun-Thu, to 11pm Fri & Sat; ✈️📶; 🚌206, SKIP, HOP) ✈️ At Boulder's hippest noodle bar you can find fresh street food at a long outdoor counter. Mama, the Taiwanese matriarch, is on hand, cooking and chatting up customers in her Crocs. Organic noodles are made from scratch, as are the garlicky melt-in-your-mouth pot stickers. A 15% tip is folded into the price of each dish.

Spruce Confections BAKERY $
(Map p116; ☎ 303-449-6773; www.spruceconfect ions.com; 767 Pearl St; cookies from $3.25; ⏰6:30am-5:15pm Mon-Fri, from 7am Sat & Sun; 📶; 🚌206) This is Boulder's go-to bakehouse, where the favorites are the Ol' B Cookie (chocolate, oats, cinnamon and coconut) and the Black Bottom Cupcake (chocolate with cheesecake filling). Pair either with the Spruce Juice, possibly the world's greatest iced vanilla latte. It has sinful scones, good homemade soups and salads too. There's another branch at 4684 Broadway.

Gurkhas INDIAN, NEPALESE $
(☎ 303-530-1551; www.gurkhasrestaurant.com; 6565 Gunpark Dr; mains $8-16; ⏰11am-2:30pm & 5-9pm; 📶; 🚌205, 205C, 205W) Gurkhas serves up authentic home-style Indian fare, some of the best in town. Think buttered and honeyed naan, creamy tikka masala, ten-

der, fresh coconut fish, and special veggie curries. The bummer is that it's way out in the Gunbarrel neighborhood, in the bowels of the tech parks and warehouses. Bottom line: if you've got a car, it's worth a trip.

Near Avery Brewing Company and Celestial Seasonings, this makes for a good post-tour lunch spot.

Snarf's DELI $
(Map p110; ☎ 303-444-7766; www.eatsnarfs.com; 2128 Pearl St; sandwiches $6-12; ⏰11am-10pm Mon-Sat, to 9pm Sun; 📶; 🚌204) Its claim to have the 'world's finest toasted sandwiches' is certainly a stretch, but we're happy to hand Snarf's the Boulder title. It does meatball subs and French dips, and piles prime rib and corned beef onto French rolls. There are salads and foot-long Italian subs too. The long line out the door says it all.

Dish Gourmet SANDWICHES $
(Map p110; ☎ 720-565-5933; www.dishgourmet.com; 1918 Pearl St; sandwiches $7-11; ⏰9am-6pm Mon-Fri, 11am-4pm Sat; 📶; 🚌204, HOP) Bank-length lines flank this gourmet deli at lunchtime. At $10 the sandwiches are hardly cheap but they are supremely satisfying. Think locally sourced meats roasted in-house, top-tier cheeses and fresh baguettes. Order a boxed lunch and take it on a trail for a mid-hike treat.

Half Fast Subs SANDWICHES $
(Map p110; ☎ 303-449-0404; www.halffastsubs. com; 1215 13th St; subs $7-12; ⏰10:30am-11pm Mon-Wed, 10:30am-12:30am Thu & Fri, 11am-12:30am Sat, 11am-10pm Sun; ✈️📶; 🚌203, 204, 225, DASH, SKIP) Deal with the line at lunch, or come for the daily happy hour (4pm to 7pm) that's 'guaranteed to kick your butt' (the 32oz pitcher of Long Island Ice Tea suggests they're serious). The endless sandwich board has tons of stuff for vegetarians, including baked tofu. Meat eaters should go for a gooey cheesesteak.

Tangerine BREAKFAST $
(☎ 303-443-2333; www.tangerineboulder.com; 2777 Iris Ave; mains $9-16; ⏰7am-2:30pm; ✈️📶; 🚌208) ✈️ It's worth leaving the downtown bubble for this true treat of a breakfast spot in a nondescript shopping plaza. Think polenta with poached eggs, spinach and romesco sauce; impeccable Benedicts; smoothies; and ricotta lemon pancakes with blueberry sauce. The combinations are original and very well done. Sweet servers pour bottomless cups of organic coffee at tables with bright orange booths.

Lucile's
CAJUN $

(Map p116; ☏ 303-442-4743; www.luciles.com; 2124 14th St; mains $8-15; ⊗ 7am-2pm Mon-Fri, from 8am Sat & Sun; 🅿 🌢 ; 🚇 208, HOP, SKIP) 🍴 This New Orleans–style diner has perfected breakfast, and the Creole egg dishes (served over creamy spinach alongside cheesy grits or perfectly blackened trout) are the thing to order. Start with a steaming mug of chicory coffee and an order of the powder-sugar-drenched beignets, the house specialty. Go early or be prepared to wait.

Sink
PUB FOOD $

(Map p110; ☏ 303-444-7465; www.thesink.com; 1165 13th St; mains $8-15; ⊗ 11am-2am, kitchen to 10pm; 🌢 ; 🚇 203, 204, 225, DASH, SKIP) A Hill landmark since 1923, the low-slung, graffiti-scrawled Sink has fed former president Obama, been featured on Food Network and even employed Robert Redford during his CU years – while he dropped out, it clearly hasn't. The dimly lit, cavernous dive still churns out legendary Sink burgers and slugs of local microbrews to the latest generation of students.

Lolita's Market & Deli
DELI $

(Map p116; ☏ 303-443-8329; www.facebook.com/ lolitasmarket; 800 Pearl St; sandwiches $5-9; ⊗ market 24hr, deli 7am-6pm; 🌢 ; 🚇 HOP) Whether you're on a run for late-night munchies, on an early morning hunt for trail snacks or, you know, Sunday morning bacon, this joint should be your de facto supply line. Think deli food and wasabi peas juxtaposed with bars of dark chocolate. Oh, and it also rents inner tubes ($10) for would-be Boulder Creek sailors during summer.

Salvaggio's Italian Deli
SANDWICHES $

(Map p116; ☏ 303-938-1981; kiosk cnr 14th & Pearl Sts; sandwiches $7-12; ⊗ 8am-4pm Mon-Fri; 🌢 ; 🚇 205) Serving excellent East Coast–style subs with a side of attitude, this busy kiosk and shop offers classic goodies such as slow-roasted prime rib subs, served on a fresh, crusty roll and dressed with horseradish and veggies. Use the nearby public benches for a simple picnic. There's a second location on Broadway, across from CU.

Arabesque
MIDDLE EASTERN $

(Map p116; ☏ 720-242-8623; www.arabesqueboulder .com; 1634 Walnut St; mains $9-12; ⊗ 9am-3pm Mon-Sat; 🅿 🌢 ; 🚇 204, 205, BOLT) This authentic family-run enterprise hits the sweet spot with excellent, slightly smoky baba ghanoush, fresh tabbouleh and *shawarma* wraps made with fresh bread and plenty of greens. Cold tea

comes with fresh mint and chunks of summer fruit. The setting is a brick cafe with shady patio seating – perfect on a summer day.

Ruebens Burger Bistro
BISTRO $

(Map p116; ☏ 303-443-5000; www.ruebensburger bistro.com; 1800 Broadway St; mains $7-14; ⊗ 11:30am-10pm Sun-Wed, to 2am Thu-Sat; 🌢 ; 🚇 208, SKIP) An owner-operated temple to the all-natural, hormone-free gourmet burger, all christened with cycling-themed names. The Mountain Biker comes with avocado, arugula and Swiss cheese, while the Paris Roubaix is topped with whole roasted green chilis and Swiss and cream cheeses. Ruebens also offers intriguing dishes like a build-your-own mac 'n' cheese and *moules frites* (mussels with fries).

Sherpa's
NEPALI $

(Map p116; ☏ 303-440-7151; www.sherpasrestau rant.com; 825 Walnut St; mains $7-15; ⊗ 11am-3pm & 5-9:30pm Sun-Wed, 11am-3pm & 5-10pm Thu-Sat; 🅿 🌢 ; 🚇 206) A friendly, fun Nepalese cafe set in a converted home at the edge of downtown. Dishes are simple, with home-style choices such as tofu *aloo* and a hearty Sherpa stew. Lunch specials are cheap, and the vine-shaded patio is a great spot for a mango lassi on a summer afternoon. The chef has summited Mt Everest 10 times!

Foolish Craig's
AMERICAN $

(Map p116; ☏ 303-247-9383; www.foolishcraigs. com; 1611 Pearl St; mains $6-14; ⊗ 8am-9:30pm Mon-Sat, to 9pm Sun; 🌢 ; 🚇 204, HOP) A longtime, much-loved breakfast joint famous for its build-your-own omelets and crepes. The more upscale dinner menu is worth trying, with options such as pulled pork, crab cakes and roasted brussels sprouts with fried leaves and sweet soy.

Alfalfa's
MARKET $

(Map p110; ☏ 720-420-8400; www.alfalfas.com; 1651 Broadway St; ⊗ 7am-10pm; 🌢 ; 🚇 204, 225, DASH, JUMP, SKIP) A small, community-oriented natural market with a wonderful selection of prepared food and an inviting indoor-outdoor dining area to enjoy it in.

★ Oak at Fourteenth
MODERN AMERICAN $$

(Map p116; ☏ 303-444-3622; www.oakatfourteenth. com; 1400 Pearl St; mains $13-30; ⊗ 11:30am-10pm Mon-Sat, 5:30-10pm Sun; 🚇 205, 206) Zesty and innovative, locally owned Oak manufactures top-notch cocktails and tasty small plates for stylish diners. Standouts include the grilled bacon-wrapped pork tenderloin and cucumber sashimi drizzled with passion fruit. Portions at this farm-to-table eatery are minimal – when it's this scrumptious, you notice. Waiters advise well. The only downside: it tends to be noisy, so save your intimate confessions.

★ Brasserie Ten Ten
BISTRO $$

(Map p116; ☑ 303-998-1010; www.brasserietenten.com; 1011 Walnut St; mains $15-27; ☺ 11am-10pm Mon-Thu, 11am-11pm Fri, 9am-11pm Sat, 9am-9pm Sun; ☑ 203, 204, 225, AB, B) A go-to place for both students and professors, this sunny French bistro has a refined menu and an elegant atmosphere – think fresh flowers, marble high tops and polished brass. Sure, it's fancy, but not too uppity to offer killer happy-hour deals on crepes, sliders, mussels and beer. Don't miss the truffle fries.

Reservations for parties of seven or more only.

Pizzeria Locale
PIZZA $$

(Map p116; ☑ 303-442-3003; www.localeboulder.com; 1730 Pearl St; pizzas $9-20; ☺ 11:30am-10pm Mon-Thu, to 10:30pm Fri & Sat, to 9pm Sun; ☑ ☝; ☑ 204, HOP) The obvious choice for a slice with style. Beloved stepchild of upscale Frasca (p124) (they share a kitchen), this southern Italian–style pizzeria fills with locals at the bar sipping *aperol* spritzers and house wine on barrel tap. Starters like *arancini* (risotto balls with a hint of orange) show off street cred. For deals, come between 4pm and 5:30pm.

The double-zero crust and a fast, super-hot firing produces pies that are crispy and chewy. While the Margherita is a well-done classic, combinations like corn and crème fraîche offer a happy surprise.

River & Woods
AMERICAN $$

(Map p110; ☑ 303-993-6301; www.riverandwoodsboulder.com; 2328 Pearl St; mains $13-29; ☺ 4-10pm Mon-Fri, 10am-2pm & 5-11pm Sat, 10am-2pm & 5-10pm Sun; ☑; ☑ HOP) Upscale comfort food is probably the best way to describe the menu at River & Woods, with forays into classical and avant garde. The ever-changing menu has covered everything from scallops, short ribs and gnocchi, to burgers, mac 'n' cheese and elk corn dogs; the duck wings are a perennial favorite. Somewhat pricey but memorable; the outdoor dining area is especially pleasant.

Mateo
FRENCH $$

(Map p110; ☑ 303-443-7766; www.mateorestaurant.com; 1837 Pearl St; mains $11-26; ☺ 11:30am-10pm Mon-Fri, 9am-2pm & 5-10pm Sat; ☑ 204) A casual dining hall with minimalist panache, an upscale but not fancy-pants crowd, and a damn fine kitchen specializing in French comfort cuisine – think braised lamb shoulder served over pasta, pork belly over organic rice, and *moules frites* (mussels with fries). Cheeses are artisanal, ingredients mostly local and the wine is quite fine. Half-priced *moules frites* ($7) during happy hour.

Salt
MODERN AMERICAN $$

(Map p116; ☑ 303-444-7258; www.saltthebistro.com; 1047 Pearl St; mains $15-30; ☺ 11am-9pm Mon-Thu, 11am-11pm Fri & Sat, 10am-9pm Sun; ☝; ☑ 208, HOP, SKIP) While farm-to-table is ubiquitous in Boulder, this is one spot that delivers and surpasses expectations. The handmade fettuccine with snap peas, radicchio and herb cream is a feverish delight. But Salt also knows meat: local and grass-fed, basted, braised and slow roasted to utter perfection. When in doubt, ask – the waiters really know their stuff.

Consider starting with a cocktail: the house mixologist has repeatedly won the competition for Boulder's best.

Kitchen
MODERN AMERICAN $$

(Map p116; ☑ 303-544-5973; www.thekitchenbistros.com; 1039 Pearl St; mains $12-39; ☺ 11am-9pm Mon, to 10pm Tue-Fri, 9am-2pm & 5-10pm Sat, to 9pm Sun; ☎ ☑; ☑ 206, HOP) ☝ The pioneer of farm-to-table cuisine in Boulder, Kitchen features clean lines, stacks of crusty bread and a daily menu. Super-fresh ingredients are crafted into rustic and gorgeous dishes: roasted acorn squash, grilled lamb burger, steamed mussels in cream. Be sure to save room for sticky toffee pudding. Visitors shouldn't miss community night, with family-style eating at a communal table.

Head upstairs for a more casual atmosphere and menu.

MED
MEDITERRANEAN $$

(Map p116; The Mediterranean; ☑ 303-444-5335; www.themedboulder.com; 1002 Walnut St; mains $9-27; ☺ 11am-10pm Mon-Wed, to 11pm Thu-Sat, to 9pm Sun; ☑ 206, HOP) A Boulder classic, this friendly, festive joint brings all the many flavors of the Mediterranean under one roof (and patio). Best of all, it's consistently good. Think wood-fired pizza, gyros and terrific tapas from gambas to bacon-wrapped dates to bruschetta. It has a full bar and worthwhile desserts, and is known for its happy-hour deals. Draws a fun crowd.

BOULDER & AROUND BOULDER

Leaf
VEGETARIAN **$$**

(Map p116; ☏303-442-1485; www.leafvegetarian restaurant.com; 2010 16th St; mains $13-18; ⏰11:30am-9pm Mon-Thu, 11:30am-10pm Fri, 10am-10pm Sat, 10am-9pm Sun; ☏; ☐204) ✎ This ethical and elegant kitchen serves meatless gems (Jamaican jerk tempeh, jackfruit enchiladas, spaghetti squash peanut noodles, 'sushi' salad made with seaweed) amid exposed brick walls and tiled ceilings dangling with striking wire lanterns. A perfect spot for a date night. Much of the produce used is grown at the restaurant's organic farm in nearby Lafayette.

Zolo Southwestern Grill
MEXICAN **$$**

(Map p110; ☏303-449-0444; www.zologrill.com; 2525 Arapahoe Ave; mains $7-26; ⏰11am-9:30pm Mon-Wed, to 10pm Thu & Fri, 10am-10pm Sat, to 9pm Sun; ☏ 👶; ☐205, HOP, BOLT) Zolo has been delighting residents with award-winning Southwestern fare and easy parking (it has its own lot) for years. The menu is a Colorado take on classic Mexican. Perennial favorites include *fundido* (warm goat Oaxaca cheese fondue), chicken enchiladas and the tortilla-crusted ahi tuna. And don't skip the tequila: with more than 150 choices, it's tough to go wrong.

Ado's Kitchen & Bar
AMERICAN **$$**

(Map p110; ☏720-465-9063; 1143 13th St; mains $9-25; ⏰9am-9pm Mon-Sat, to 3pm Sun; ☏ 👶; ☐204, 205, DASH, SKIP) Chef Ado serves up a mostly American menu – pork loin, spinach salad, salmon – with a few internationals like pad thai and chicken piccata, in this pleasant restaurant on the Hill. Reliably tasty dishes and affordable prices make up for a somewhat lackluster ambience and plating. It's a good option in an area that's better known for quick cheap eats.

Sushi Zanmai
SUSHI **$$**

(Map p116; ☏303-440-0733; www.sushizanmai. com; 1221 Spruce St; mains $6-21; ⏰11:30am-2pm & 5-10pm Sun-Fri, to midnight Sat; 👶; ☐208, HOP, SKIP) Fresh, good and kind of goofy. The chefs shout with delight as customers fill the space, which they do early and often. Kimono-clad waitstaff serve platters of sushi, grilled and brushed eel, toro hand rolls and specialty house rolls like the Colorado, with raw filet mignon. Trout, a common sushi in the mountains of Japan, is worth trying here.

Ramen is served on weekends.

Whole Foods Market
SUPERMARKET **$$**

(Map p110; ☏303-545-6611; www.wholefoods market.com; 2905 Pearl St; ⏰7am-10pm; 📶 👶; ☐205, BOLT, BOUND, HOP) The largest Whole Foods in the Rocky Mountain region – 77,000 sq ft – this supermarket is something to behold. The organic offerings are wide and varied and the never-ending prepared-food section has lots of seating inside and out. There's also a juice bar, an artisanal bakery and even a liquor store specializing in Colorado brews and booze.

Chautauqua Dining Hall
AMERICAN **$$**

(Map p110; ☏303-440-3776; www.chautauqua dininghall.com; Chautauqua Park; mains $9-27; ⏰8am-9pm; ☏ 👶; ☐HOP 2) On prime real estate in Chautauqua Park, this big farmhouse with wraparound porch is a favorite of hikers, especially for breakfast. Service isn't speedy, nor is the food a standout compared to the local offerings – it's all about the ambience. The menu is farm-to-table, supplied with produce and cured meats from a local farm.

Centro Mexican Kitchen
MEXICAN **$$**

(Map p116; ☏303-442-7771; www.centrolatinkitchen. com; 950 Pearl St; mains $8-26; ⏰11am-10pm Mon-Wed, 11am-1am Thu & Fri, 9:30am-1am Sat, 9:30am-10pm Sun; 👶; ☐HOP) This lively Mexican restaurant has a menu deep in classics like tacos, enchiladas and *tortas* (sandwiches) and some surprising dishes too, like stuffed peppers and *poc chuc* (Yucatecan-style pork). Happy hour brings great deals on margs and mojitos. Bring your dancing shoes on Sunday afternoon, when live Latin music turns the bar area into a dance floor.

★ Frasca
ITALIAN **$$$**

(Map p116; ☏303-442-6966; www.frascafoodand wine.com; 1738 Pearl St; mains $35, tasting menus $50-115; ⏰5:30-9:30pm Mon-Thu, to 10:30pm Fri, 5-10:30pm Sat; ☏; ☐HOP, 204) Deemed Boulder's finest by many (the wine service earned a James Beard award), Frasca has an impeccable kitchen and only the freshest farm-to-table ingredients. Rotating dishes range from earthy braised pork to housemade gnocchi and grilled quail served with leeks and wilted pea shoots. Reserve days, even weeks, in advance. Mondays offer 'bargain' $50 tasting menus with suggested wine pairings.

Jax Fish House
SEAFOOD **$$$**

(Map p116; ☏310-444-1811; www.jaxboulder.com; 928 Pearl St; mains $10-33; ⏰4-10pm Sun-Thu, to 11pm Fri & Sat; ☐206, HOP, SKIP) ✎ Running for two decades, this lively seafood shack is still an exquisite treat. Belly up to the circle bar for oysters and martinis, then splurge on fresh seafood flown in daily – think wild salmon or chilled lobster. Happy hour resembles a rush-hour subway car, but it's way more fun. Produce is locally sourced and the restaurant supports sustainable fisheries.

Drinking & Nightlife

Drinking here begins with absurd happy-hour deals. Must be a student thing. You'll find the student population rules the Hill (the neighborhood next to CU) and often spills over into downtown, making Pearl St a pedestrian party scene. Many restaurants double as bars or turn into all-out dance clubs come 10pm. And we haven't even mentioned the coffeehouses and breweries!

★ **Mountain Sun**   BREWERY
(Map p116; ☑ 303-546-0886; www.mountainsun pub.com; 1535 Pearl St; ⏰ 11am-1am; 🚸; 🚌 HOP, 205, 206) Boulder's favorite brewery cheerfully serves a smorgasbord of fine brews and packs in everyone from yuppies to hippies. Best of all is its community atmosphere. The pub grub, especially the burgers and chili, is delicious and it's fully family friendly, with board games and kids' meals. There's often live bluegrass and reggae on Sunday, Monday and Wednesday nights. Cash only.

★ **Sanitas Brewing**   BREWERY
(☑ 303-442-4130; www.sanitasbrewing.com; 3550 Frontier Ave; ⏰ 11:30am-10pm Sun-Thu, to 11pm Fri & Sat; 🚌 BOLT) The warehouse complex where Sanitas is located doesn't exactly scream charm, but wait till you get inside. The low-key tap room has an urban hipster feel with cement floors and high, family style tables, while patio seats have partial views of the Flatirons and great afternoon sun. A food shack serves mouthwatering tacos, but the line can be painfully slow.

Ask about the $1 train beer!

Bitter Bar   COCKTAIL BAR
(Map p116; ☑ 303-442-3050; www.thebitterbar. com; 835 Walnut St; ⏰ 5pm-midnight Mon-Thu, to 2am Fri & Sat; 🚌 HOP) A chic Boulder bar where killer cocktails, such as the lavender-infused Kiss the Sky or the elderflower tonic ice cubes in Guns n' Roses, make the evening slip happily out of focus. Happy hours that run till 8pm don't hurt either. The patio is great for conversation.

Avery Brewing Company   BREWERY
(☑ 303-440-4324; www.averybrewing.com; 4910 Nautilus Ct; ⏰ 3-11pm Mon, 11am-11pm Tue-Sun; 🚌 205) For craft breweries, how big is too big? Avery pushes the limit, with its imposing two-story building, complete with gift shop selling hats and tees. But the 1st-floor patio and tap room are lively and fun, while upstairs has a quieter restaurant feel. One thing's for sure: the beer's outstanding, from Apricot Sour to a devilish Mephistopheles Stout. Guided tours available.

Located about 6 miles northeast of downtown.

Fate Brewing Company   BREWERY
(☑ 303-449-3283; http://fatebrewingcompany. com; 1600 38th St; ⏰ 11am-10pm Mon-Fri, from 10am Sat & Sun; 🚌 J, JUMP, STAMPEDE) Man, that's some good beer. Fate has served award-winning brews, including effervescent Gose's and Kolsh's, and a to-die-for IPA. Bartenders are knowledgeable, and many guests enjoy their beer and food at the long U-shaped bar. A full kitchen serves inspired meals that make even a hamburger and fries look gourmet. Guided tours available.

Bohemian Biergarten   BEER HALL
(Map p116; ☑ 720-328-8328; www.bohemian biergarten.com; 2017 13th St; ⏰ 11:30am-2am; 🚌 208, HOP) This popular gastropub specializes in European brews and German and central European eats (think lots of brats and pretzels). Happy patrons drink steins of beer at worn communal tables that fill the small brick pub and patio. The scene gets younger – and rowdier – as the hours march on, but it draws a pretty diverse crowd.

Boulder Beer Company   BREWERY
(☑ 303-444-8448; https://boulderbeer.com; 2880 Wilderness Pl; ⏰ 11am-10pm; 🚌 208) Boulder Beer is Boulder's first craft brewery, though you'd never guess from the church-like building and spacious well-kept digs. A huge patio out back is kid- and dog-friendly, while a handful of indoor rooms have thick wood tables and a warm vibe. The beer is first-rate, and has inventive names like Hazed and Confused and Sweaty Betty. Guided tours available.

If you get the munchies, there's a full menu of tasty pub food.

License No 1   LOUNGE
(Map p116; ☑ 303-443-0486; www.license1 boulderado.com; 2115 13th St, Hotel Boulderado; ⏰ 5pm-midnight; 🚌 HOP, SKIP) Hidden in the basement of Hotel Boulderado (p120), License No 1 is a throwback to Prohibition times. It's a maze of dimly lit rooms, unfinished stone walls, deep leather chairs,

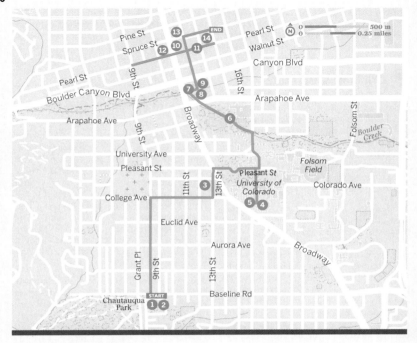

🚶 City Walk
Strolling Boulder

START CHAUTAUQUA PARK
END BOULDER THEATER
LENGTH 4.8 MILES; 4½ HOURS

Boulder isn't huge, but it's big enough to have pockets with different personalities, which you'll be able to absorb on this tour. Begin at **1 Chautauqua Park** (p109), which marked the city's initial foray into open-space preservation, a notion that now defines the city. The **2 Chautauqua Dining Hall** (p124) serves a hearty breakfast on the wraparound porch. From here, walk downhill along Baseline Rd and turn right along 9th St through one of Boulder's oldest residential neighborhoods. Turn right onto College Ave and keep walking until you hit 13th St.

This is the Hill, a tumbledown student district with hipster-slacker appeal. Imbibe college life by stepping into the graffiti-clad **3 Sink** (p122), where a young Robert Redford once toiled before stardom. Continue to Broadway. Make a right onto Pleasant St, and head onto the **4 University of Colorado** (p113) campus. Cut right until you hit 15th

St and pop into **5 CU Museum of Natural History** (p112), with exhibits on remarkable paleontology and archaeology discoveries in the region. Afterward head toward Varsity Lake and follow the walking path straight through to 17th St. Exit the campus here and descend the short hill to join the **6 Boulder Creek Bike Path** (p114).

Walk along the creek until you hit **7 Central Park** (p112) and the **8 Boulder Museum of Contemporary Art** (p112). On Wednesday or Saturday you can enjoy the Boulder County Farmers Market. Stop to see the striking **9 Dushanbe Teahouse** (p128).

Continue west on 13th St to Boulder's historic downtown center. If it's happy hour, stop in at **10 Bohemian Biergarten** (p125), just past Pearl St. Double back a block to enjoy the **11 Pearl Street Mall** (p109) and its renowned street performers. Browse the three-story **12 Boulder Book Store** (p128) before strolling Spruce St. Check out the historic **13 Hotel Boulderado** (p120) before finishing your tour with a show at the **14 Boulder Theater** (p127).

antique lighting and bartenders mixing strong drinks. Come here for live music on weekends, starting at 9pm. Ladies enjoy good drinks specials on Tuesdays.

Owsley's Golden Road   BAR
(Map p110; ☑303-440-1446; www.owsleysgoldenroad.com; 1301 Broadway St; ☉noon-2am; ☐204, 225, DASH, SKIP) A total dive bar with a Dead Head theme, Owsley's has a huge patio where live bands play (cover $5 to $20) and a back room with a pool table and a couple of pinball machines. Stick to beer and you'll be good. The bar is named after Owsley Stanley III, the Grateful Dead's original sound man and financial backer.

☆ Entertainment

For a small city, Boulder has a surprisingly rich array of entertainment options. There are beer and music festivals, movies and theater, and more. Having the university nearby helps; you can catch a CU football or basketball game or performances of all kinds at Macky Auditorium.

eTown Hall   LIVE MUSIC
(Map p116; ☑303-443-8696; www.etown.org; 1535 Spruce St; from $25; ☉hours vary; ☐HOP) Beautiful, brand-new and solar-powered, this repurposed church is the home of the eTown radio show (heard on National Public Radio). The show features rising and well-known artists and you can get in on it by attending a live taping in its 200-seat theater. Tapings run for two hours starting at 7pm, and are typically held on weeknights.

CU Football   FOOTBALL
(Map p110; ☑303-492-8337; www.cubuffs.com; 2400 Colorado Ave, Folsom Field; prices vary; ☉Sep-Nov; ☎☝; ☐209, STAMPEDE) Boulder sports fans may have allegiances to Denver's pro teams, but they have several teams of their own too, and they are all called the CU Buffaloes. Still, while college volleyball, gymnastics and baseball have their place, it's the football team that rules campus.

CU Wizards   LIVE PERFORMANCE
(Map p110; ☑303-492-5011; www.colorado.edu/cuwizards; Colorado Ave, Duane Physics Bldg G1B30; ☉shows 9:30am Sat; ☝; ☐209, STAMPEDE) FREE Science can be cool, and kids dig the free shows put on by CU's Wizards program. The science-based shows such as 'The Physics of the Game of Thrones' or 'The Chemistry of Cooking' are free, and held on one Satur-day per month. Shows last one hour and are geared toward fifth- to 10th-graders.

Macky Auditorium
Concert Hall   PERFORMING ARTS
(Map p110; ☑303-492-8423; www.colorado.edu/macky; 1595 Pleasant St #104, University of Colorado; prices vary; ☎; ☐204, 225, DASH, HOP, SKIP) With over 2000 seats, Macky is CU's main theater, hosting a wide range of events year-round – from TEDx talks to performances by award-winning musicians, singers and dancers. Check the website for upcoming shows; tickets can be purchased online or at the box office one hour before each performance.

Fox Theatre   LIVE MUSIC
(Map p110; ☑box office 720-645-2467; www.foxtheatre.com; 1135 13th St; cover varies; ☐203, 204, 225, AB, B, DASH, SKIP) You'll be elbowing your way through students to get near the stage of this excellent midsized venue, so head upstairs for a perch near the sound board for better views and acoustics. Bands on stage here are national touring acts, popular jam bands and indie rock. The box office opens on show nights only, starting at 6pm.

Boulder Theater   CINEMA, LIVE MUSIC
(Map p116; ☑303-786-7030; www.bouldertheater.com; 2032 14th St; ticket prices vary; ☉box office noon-6pm Mon-Fri, to 5pm Sat; ☐HOP) This opera-house-turned-movie-theater-turned-historic-venue brings in slightly under-the-radar acts like jazz great Charlie Hunter, the madmen rockers of Gogol Bordello, and West African divas Les Nubians. But it also screens classic films like *The Big Lebowski* and short-film festivals that can be enjoyed with a glass of beer.

CU Basketball   BASKETBALL
(Map p110; ☑303-492-8337; www.cubuffs.com; 950 Regent Dr, Coors Event Center; prices vary; ☉games Nov-Mar; ☎☝; ☐209, STAMPEDE) Seldom a pushover, rarely great, CU's basketball team is always fun to watch because the competition is usually stiff. And like most great schools, it has a transcendent baller from the not-too-distant past. Chauncey 'Mr Big Shot' Billups starred here before he became an NBA champ and finals MVP.

🔒 Shopping

Given the hipster student vibe, the yuppie cash flow and Boulder's status as a go-to green hot spot, it's not all that shocking to find a bit of shopping here. Along with some high-end vintage consignment houses, there are a few boutiques with designer labels and plenty of eco and athletic gear on offer too.

★ **Boulder Book Store** BOOKS
(Map p116; ☎303-447-2074; www.boulderbook store.net; 1107 Pearl St; ☺10am-10pm Mon-Sat, to 9pm Sun; 🛜 🦽; 🚌 208, HOP, SKIP) Boulder's favorite indie bookstore has a huge travel section downstairs, along with all the hottest new fiction and nonfiction. Check the

visiting-authors lineup posted at the entry and on its website.

★ **Common Threads** CLOTHING
(Map p110; ☎303-449-5431; www.shopcommon threads.com; 2707 Spruce St; ☺10am-6pm Mon, Tue & Thu-Sat, to 7pm Wed; 🚌205, BOLT, HOP) Vintage shopping at its most haute couture: this fun place is where to go for secondhand Choos and Prada purses. Prices are higher

---

CAFFEINE EXPLOSION!

Boulder literally explodes with cafes, with its diverse options tailored toward Lycra-clad cyclists, university students or bohemian life. These are our favorites.

Laughing Goat (Map p116; ☎303-440-4628; www.thelaughinggoat.com; 1709 Pearl St; ☺6am-11pm Mon-Fri, from 7am Sat & Sun; 🛜; 🚌203, 204, 205, 206, 208, 225, DASH, JUMP) Sure, the ambience might be diminished by the glow of two-dozen laptops, but the coffee is good (served in pint glasses too!) and locally roasted. The scene revolves around eyeballing college co-eds and tapping away at term papers – at least until the singer-songwriters start up. It hosts many up-and-coming musicians plus spoken-word artists.

Innisfree Poetry Bookstore & Cafe (Map p110; ☎303-495-3303; www.innisfreepoetry. com; 1301 Pennsylvania Ave; ☺7am-9pm Mon-Fri, to 6pm Sat & Sun; 🚌204, 225, DASH, SKIP) A cool, quiet spot on the Hill, Innis serves up a mean cup of fair-trade coffee along with a menu of innovative sandwiches, breakfast burritos and bagels (the Garden Pita is a must). The cafe also doubles as a poetry shop, selling all sorts of books – new and used, local and international – and hosting readings in the evenings.

Cup (Map p116; ☎303-449-5173; www.thecupboulder.com; 1521 Pearl St; ☺7am-10pm; 🛜; 🚌204, HOP) This welcoming loftlike space opens onto Pearl St, pouring forth the scent of damn good coffee and handpicked organic loose-leaf teas. It also does fresh quiche, wonderful cakes in cups, burly sandwiches and swift wi-fi (the last making it especially popular with students). Only bummer – service can be slow.

Boxcar Roasters (Map p110; www.boxcarcoffeeroasters.com; 1825 Pearl St; ☺7am-6pm Mon-Fri, 7:30am-6pm Sat, 8am-5pm Sun; 🛜; 🚌HOP) Asserting a PhD approach, this roaster offers single-pour beaker coffee that purists swear by, set in minimalist-hipster ambience. Bags of beans are reasonably priced. There's also a European-style deli on site serving up charcuterie, craft cheeses and lovely, thick-crust bread.

Trident Cafe (Map p116; ☎303-443-3133; www.tridentcafe.com; 940 Pearl St; ☺6:30am-11pm Mon-Fri, 7am-11pm Sat & Sun; 🛜 🦽; 🚌208, HOP) Brick walls, worn wood floors and red-vinyl booths are steeped in the aromatic uplift of damn good espresso. The attached bookstore sells used and collectible titles. Add in the shady back-garden patio and fine tea selection and you'll understand why this is the longtime favorite of Boulder's literary set. A thousand secrets and plot lines have been shared and hatched here.

Boulder Dushanbe Teahouse (Map p116; ☎303-442-4993; www.boulderteahouse.com; 1770 13th St; mains $8-24; ☺8am-9pm; 🦽; 🚌203, 204, 205, 206, 208, 225, DASH, JUMP, SKIP) It's impossible to find better ambience than this incredible Tajik teahouse, a gift from Dushanbe, Boulder's sister city. The elaborate carvings and paintings were reassembled over an eight-year period on Central Park's edge. It's too bad the fusion fare is so lackluster, but it's very much worth coming for a pot of tea.

Ku Cha House of Tea (Map p116; ☎303-443-3612; www.kuchatea.com; 1211 Pearl St; ☺10am-9pm Mon-Sat, 11am-8pm Sun; 🚌208) This traditional Chinese teahouse has an enormous selection of imported loose-leaf tea, including rare finds. In the back, patrons snuggle over steaming cups at low-slung tables, a huge skylight overhead. Snacks like mochi rice cake fuel the mood.

than at your run-of-the-mill vintage shop, but clothes, shoes and bags are always in good condition, and the designer clothing is guaranteed authentic. Offers fun classes on clothes altering and innovating.

⭐ Two Hands Paperie   STATIONERY

(Map p116; ☑ 303-444-0124; www.twohands paperie.com; 803 Pearl St; ⊘ 10am-6pm Mon-Sat, 11am-5pm Sun; 🚌 HOP) A paper lover's fantasy, this sunny shop specializes in writing supplies from around the world. Leather-bound journals, high-end stationery, sketchbooks, writing instruments, artful greeting cards, even a kids' section, keep the place hopping. Workshops are also offered in bookbinding, calligraphy, origami and more.

⭐ Peppercorn   FOOD, HOMEWARES

(Map p116; ☑ 303-449-5847; www.peppercorn. com; 1235 Pearl St; ⊘ 10am-6pm Mon-Thu & Sat, to 7pm Fri, 11am-5pm Sun; 🚌 208, SKIP) One of the coolest stores on Pearl, this kitchen, bed and bath supplier stocks upscale goods, locally produced foods, scores of specialized cookbooks and enough gizmos to delight a cooking geek. It's a fun place to spend too much time and money. See the website for classes and events.

⭐ Into the Wind   TOYS

(Map p116; ☑ 303-449-5906; www.intothewind. com; 1408 Pearl St; ⊘ 10am-9pm Mon-Sat, to 6pm Sun; ♿; 🚌 206) Your inner child will want to spend hours in this store. Not only does it sell the most beautiful kites, but there are games, puppets and toys to intrigue all ages and budgets.

Momentum   ARTS & CRAFTS

(Map p116; ☑ 303-440-7744; www.ourmomentum. com; 1625 Pearl St; ⊘ 10am-7pm Mon-Fri, 9am-7pm Sat, to 6pm Sun; 🚌 204, HOP) ✈ Committed to socially responsible and environmentally friendly business practices, Momentum makes you feel good about shopping. It sells the kitchen sink of unique global gifts – Zulu wire baskets, fabulous scarves from India, Nepal and Ecuador – all handcrafted and purchased at fair value from disadvantaged artisans. Every item purchased provides a direct economic lifeline to the artists.

Fresh Baked   DISPENSARY

(Map p110; ☑ 303-440-9393; www.freshbakedcolo rado.com; 2539 Pearl St; ⊘ 9am-9:50pm; 🚌 HOP) A longtime favorite among locals and visitors alike, Fresh Baked prides itself on expert service and top-notch cannabis, and

has won several awards since its founding in 2010. If there's a line, a couple of Pac-Man game tables make the wait seem shorter.

Piece, Love & Chocolate   CHOCOLATE

(Map p116; ☑ 303-449-4804; www.pieceloveand chocolate.com; 805 Pearl St; ⊘ 9am-6pm, closed Sun & Mon Jun-Aug; 🚌 206, JUMP) This tiny shop is a chocolate emporium, with a glass case of handmade chocolates, dipped snacks whipped up on-site and shelves of imports from milk to dark and every gradation in-between, many fair-trade and organic. A highlight is the velvety melted cup – a hot chocolate to remember. Chocolate-making workshops are offered too.

Absolute Vinyl Records & Stereo   MUSIC

(☑ 303-955-1519; 5360 Arapahoe Ave; ⊘ 11am-6:30pm; 🚌 206F, JUMP) Every town needs a temple to vinyl, a place where chilled-out clerks wipe down wax on Sunday afternoons while listening to classic Memphis blues. Young men come here when hunting for Smiths records, baby boomers for classic Dylan. There's also a paradise of jazz, blues and classical gems.

Rebecca's Herbal Apothecary   COSMETICS

(Map p116; ☑ 303-443-8878; www.rebeccasherbs .com; 1227 Spruce St; classes $25-70; ⊘ 10am-6pm Mon-Fri, from 11am Sat; ♿; 🚌 208, SKIP) A popular herbal apothecary where herbs are sold loose, in lotions and in oils. There are aromatherapy cases of tinctures and expert herbalists to guide you through it all. The Western school of herbal thought dominates the thinkspace here. Classes offer the basics about herbs, infusions and salves as well as instruction in DIY mineral makeup and baby body care.

Savory Spice Shop   FOOD

(Map p116; ☑ 303-444-0668; www.savoryspice shop.com; 2041 Broadway St; ⊘ 10am-6pm Mon-Sat, 11am-5pm Sun; ♿; 🚌 208, SKIP) Extremely popular, this growing regional chain is the place to search for a small-batch habanero hot sauce or to alchemize your own spice rub for your self-catering kit. In all there are 160 spices hand-blended from mostly organic sources. Plus, it just smells good.

Boulder Running Company   SHOES

(Map p110; ☑ 303-786-9255; www.boulderrunning company.com; 2775 Pearl St; ⊘ 10am-8pm Mon-Fri, 9am-8pm Sat, 10am-6pm Sun; ♿; 🚌 205, 205C, BOLT) Boulder's prime center for all the gear and specialty shoes you'll need for running track, street and trail. It even offers video analysis of your running stride on a treadmill before the fitting, which helps make sure you aren't injury prone in your new shoes (and probably doesn't hurt the insole sales either).

Also has info on upcoming regional races and triathlons.

Boulder Ski Deals SPORTS & OUTDOORS
(Map p110; ☑ 303-938-8799; www.boulderskideals. com; 2525 Arapahoe Ave; ☺ 10am-7pm Mon-Fri, 10am-6pm Sat, 11am-5pm Sun; ⊕; ☐ JUMP) Arguably the best deals on skis, snowboards, glasses, goggles and snow gear can be found at this laid-back but professional temple to all things extreme and powdery. It sells, it rents and the staff bro out – even with the ladies. Exceptional deals on season passes to Vail, Breckenridge, Beaver Creek and A-Basin.

Beat Book Shop BOOKS
(Map p116; ☑ 303-444-7111; www.beatbookshop. com; 1717 Pearl St; ☺ hours vary; ☐ 204) Tom Peters is the poet proprietor of this funky pile of consistently brainy, soulful books. We're talking more than 30 Kerouac titles, as well as classics from Ginsberg, Burroughs and (Beat-esque) Bukowski, among others. His opening hours vary but Peters claims to be here from afternoon into the night daily. Well worth a browse.

Pedestrian Shops SHOES
(Map p116; ☑ 303-449-5260; www.comfortable shoes.com; 1425 Pearl St; ☺ 10am-7pm Mon-Thu, 10am-8pm Fri & Sat, 11am-7pm Sun; ☐ 208, HOP, JUMP, SKIP) Set smack dab in the middle of the Pearl Street Mall, this is where to head for the comfortable kinds of footwear that are staples in earthy Bouldertown. Think Ecco, Dansko, Keen and Born. Find the last-pair rack for the best deals, and if you buy two you'll get a third pair free.

Starr's Clothing Co CLOTHING
(Map p116; ☑ 303-442-3056; www.starrsclothing co.com; 1630 Pearl St; ☺ 10am-7pm Mon-Sat, 11am-6pm Sun; ☐ 204) Established in 1914 and still Boulder's leading denim resource, this store is damn near warehouse-sized, with all manner of stressed, smooth and relaxed denim. It also carries the odd top-end designer label such as Southern California fave Free People.

The Farm DISPENSARY
(☑ 303-440-1323; www.thefarmco.com; 2801 Iris Ave; ☺ 8am-9:45pm Mon-Fri, from 9am Sat, from 11am Sun; ☐ BOLT, BOUND) Though it's a bit removed from the center, first-timers to pot will appreciate the Farm's spacious waiting area and large supply of paraphernalia and memorabilia – the cow tees are awesome – while regular users return for the huge selection and quality product. Budtenders are helpful and informative, and there's even an app for express service.

Nature's Own GIFTS & SOUVENIRS
(Map p116; ☑ 303-443-7625; www.naturesown. com; 1215 Pearl St; ☺ 10am-7pm; ☐ 208, HOP, SKIP) You'll be greeted by a roaring T-Rex as you walk in the door, a perfect introduction to a shop that's all about rocks and minerals. Polished stones are sold individually from bins, or check out the glass cases for items handcrafted out of gorgeous geodes and fossils. Jewelry is also sold. There's a kids' section, too, with science-y games and stuffed animals.

Zuni ART, JEWELRY
(Map p116; ☑ 303-443-9575; www.zuniboulder. com; 1424 Pearl St; ☺ 10am-8pm Mon-Sat, to 7pm Sun; ☐ 204, HOP, JUMP) Opened in 1992, this family-owned business specializes in Native American jewelry and collectibles (think pottery and fetishes) from Colorado and the Southwest. Navajo, Zuni Pueblo and Hopi items are mostly featured, all high-end, and many are created by some of the most talented artists from each tribe.

Jackalope & Co GIFTS & SOUVENIRS
(Map p116; ☑ 303-939-8434; 1126 Pearl St; ☺ 10am-8pm Mon-Fri, to 9pm Sat & Sun; ⊕; ☐ 208, HOP, SKIP) No question, Pearl St has its fair share of kitschy souvenir shops but Jackalope has the best variety – you'll find everything from T-shirts and hats to locally made candy and treats. Best of all, the love is spread evenly among Colorado, Boulder and CU items.

REI SPORTS & OUTDOORS
(Map p110; ☑ 303-583-9970; www.rei.com; 1789 28th St; ☺ 9am-9pm Mon-Sat, to 7pm Sun; ⊕; ☐ 205, 206, BOLT) The Denver flagship it is not, but the Boulder branch of America's largest and best outdoor outfitter rents sleeping bags, pads and tents, as well as anything else you might need for your stint in the Rocky Mountains. Free classes on the basics of camping, backpacking and climbing a Fourteener are also offered.

Outdoor Divas SPORTS & OUTDOORS
(Map p110; ☑ 303-449-3482; www.outdoordivas. com; 2317 30th St; ☺ 11am-6pm Mon-Sat, noon-5pm Sun; ⊕; ☐ 208, SKIP) This specialized

outdoor store for women knows its audience – the gear is top quality, the prices are competitive and the staff's knowledge on women-specific skiing, hiking and running gear is expert.

Meow Meow GIFTS & SOUVENIRS

(Map p110; ☑ 303-442-8602; 1118 13th St; ⊙ 10am-7pm Mon-Sat, 11am-5pm Sun; ⊕; ☐ 203, 204, 225, DASH, SKIP) Having pioneered the concept of 'upcycling,' this is the place for unique gifts, art, jewelry and clothes made from reused materials. It has a great local feel and lots of one-of-a-kind accessories for women. The card selection is hilarious.

Posterscene ART

(Map p116; ☑ 303-443-3102; www.posterscene. com; 1505 Pearl St; ⊙ 11am-6pm Mon-Thu, 11am-7pm Fri, 10am-8pm Sat, 10am-6pm Sun; ☐ 203, 204, 205, 206, DASH, SKIP, JUMP) Iconic images and original show posters from Janis Joplin, Dylan and the Dead make this a rock memorabilia paradise. But it isn't limited to high-end collectors items: it has a clutch of cool, inexpensive reproductions too.

Smith Klein Gallery ART

(Map p116; ☑ 303-444-7200; www.smithklein.com; 1116 Pearl Street Mall; ⊙ 10am-5pm Mon, to 6pm Tue-Thu, to 7pm Fri & Sat, noon-5pm Sun; ☐ 208, HOP, SKIP) Locally owned since 1984, this conservative-to-quirky gallery is worth a peek for some interesting paintings and the glass, bronze and wood sculptures (we like the ones crafted from vintage car doors). There's handblown glass and jewelry too.

Prana CLOTHING

(Map p116; ☑ 303-449-2199; www.prana.com; 1147 Pearl St; ⊙ 10am-9pm Mon-Sat, 11am-6pm Sun; ☐ 208, SKIP) ☑ Monks chant to the patter of beats overhead as shoppers consider organic-dyed yoga outfits. All the clothes are organized by size – a nice touch – and the signs encourage an awareness of 'cosmic order.' Aside from all this New Age excitement, Prana is wind-powered, hosts art events and offers free yoga.

CU Bookstore BOOKS

(Map p110; ☑ 303-492-6411; www.cubookstore. com; 1669 Euclid Ave; ⊙ 8am-6pm Mon-Thu, 8am-5pm Fri, 10am-5pm Sat; ☎; ☐ 203, 204, 209, 225, AB, B, DASH, SKIP, STAMPEDE) There are scads of CU merchandise outlets along the busy stretch of 13th St, but this is the school's official outfitter. In addition to textbooks and supplies it has the largest selection of gold-and-black goods of any store in Boulder. Located in the University Memorial Center.

ⓘ Information

RESOURCES

Lonely Planet (www.lonelyplanet.com) Destination information, hotel bookings, traveler forum and more.

Boulder Visitor Bureau (www.bouldercolorado usa.com) General visitor information, including searchable events, lodging and more.

Boulder Weekly (www.boulderweekly.com) Weekly arts, news and culture magazine.

Open Space and Mountain Parks (www.osmp. org) Boulder County government website focused on open space and parks info.

303 Cycling (www.303cycling.com) Info and discussion about mountain biking and road cycling in Boulder and the Front Range.

Get Boulder (www.getboulder.com) Visitor-friendly magazine with tips and info on Boulder events and attractions.

TOURIST INFORMATION

Boulder Visitor Center (☑ 303-442-2911; www.bouldercoloradousa.com; 2440 Pearl St; ⊙ 8:30am-5pm Mon-Fri; ☐ HOP) Set in the Boulder Chamber of Commerce, this visitor center offers basic information, maps and tips on nearby hiking trails and other activities. There's a more accessible **tourist information kiosk** (☑ 303-417-1365; cnr Pearl & 13th Sts; ⊙ 10am-8pm; ☐ 208, HOP, SKIP) on the Pearl Street Mall in front of the courthouse.

Boulder Ranger District (☑ 303-541-2500; 2140 Yarmouth Ave; ⊙ 8:30am-4:30pm Mon-Fri; ☐ 204) This US Forest Service outpost provides information on the national forests that surround the Rocky Mountain National Park, including campgrounds and trails that cross between the two.

Downtown Boulder (www.boulderdowntown. com) This alliance of downtown businesses offers comprehensive dining and event listings in the downtown area, including the Pearl Street Mall.

Get Boulder (www.getboulder.com) A local print and online magazine with helpful information on things to do in Boulder.

MEDICAL SERVICES

Boulder Community Health at Foothills Hospital (☑ 303-415-7000; www.bch.org; 4747 Arapahoe Ave; ⊙ 24hr; ☐ JUMP)

ⓘ Getting There & Away

Boulder sits about 30 miles northwest of Denver off Hwy 36, accessible from the I-25N from downtown Denver. Hwy 36 runs through Boulder on the way to Estes Park and the Rocky

Mountain National Park. Most of the major car-rental companies (Hertz, Avis, Enterprise) have shingles in Boulder, and if you rent here, you can avoid some of the hefty taxes that airport branches charge.

Denver International Airport (p371) Located just 45 miles from Boulder, this is the main entry point for travelers arriving by air.

Green Ride (☑ 303-997-0238; http://green-rideboulder.com; 4800 Baseline Rd, D110; 1-way $28-38) Serving Boulder and its satellite suburbs, this Denver International Airport shuttle is cheap and convenient ($28 to $38), working on an hourly schedule (3:25am to 11:25pm). The cheapest service leaves from the depot. Additional travelers in groups are discounted.

SuperShuttle (☑ 303-444-0808; www.supershuttle.com; 1-way from $84) This shuttle provides a private van service to the airport. The base fare includes up to three people; each additional person costs $25. Unless you have loads of luggage, parties of four or more are better served by a taxi.

Buses are run by **RTD** (☑ 303-299-6000; www.rtd-denver.com; per ride $2.60-4.50, day pass $5.20-9; ♿). Route FF1 buses travel between **Boulder Transit Center** (☑ 303-299-6000; www.rtd-denver.com; 1800 14th St; ☐204, 205, 208, N, DASH, HOP, JUMP, SKIP), aka Boulder Station, and Denver's Union Station ($4.50, 55 minutes). Route AB1 runs between the Table Mesa Park-n-Ride on Hwy 36 in Boulder and Denver International Airport ($9, one hour), with easy connections to downtown Boulder and the Hill.

ⓘ Getting Around

Renting a car can be useful to get into the high country, but Boulder itself is perfectly manageable by bicycle or public transportation.

RTD (p132) buses travel to Denver, Denver International Airport, Nederland and within Boulder. Dedicated bike lanes and paths make the city ideal for two-wheel traffic, and the downtown area is pleasantly walkable.

BICYCLE

Owning a bicycle is almost a Boulder prerequisite. Most streets have dedicated bike lanes and the Boulder Creek Bike Path is a must-ride commuter corridor. There are plenty of places to get your hands on a rental. With rental cruisers stationed all over the city, **Boulder B-Cycle** (☑ 303-532-4412; www.boulder.bcycle.com; 24hr rental $8; ⏱ office 9am-5pm Mon-Fri, 10am-3pm Sat) is a popular citywide program of hourly or daily bike rentals, but riders must sign up online first.

Full Cycle (☑ 303-440-7771; www.fullcyclebikes.com; 1211 13th St; daily rental $25-95;

⏱10am-7pm Mon-Fri, to 6pm Sat, to 5pm Sun; ♿; ☐203, 204, 225, AB, B, DASH, DD, GS, SKIP) This terrific bike shop rents cruisers on the cheap, and higher-end road and full-suspension mountain bikes. Ask staff about the best cycling routes (from easy Boulder Creek Trail to the searing pain of the 4-mile ride up Flagstaff). There's another branch on E Pearl.

University Bicycles (p115) There are plenty of rental shops in this town, but this cavernous place has the widest range of rides and the most helpful staff.

BUS

Boulder has superb public transportation, with several RTD bus routes lacing the city and connecting the Hill with downtown and North Boulder. Though some buses have numbers associated with their routes, many have names like BOUND, SKIP, JUMP and DASH. All buses have bike racks.

Boulder Transit Center, Boulder's public transportation hub, is a good place to pick up maps of the area's bus system. Offers free public parking on weekends too.

CAR & MOTORCYCLE

If staying downtown you won't need a vehicle, as countless diversions are just steps away. But if you are anchored to a car, most downtown parking is paid. Weekends bring a respite: downtown parking garages are free.

And a word of warning to all drivers: Boulder's traffic cameras levy speeding fines, starting from $40 – a downer when one of these beauties lands in your mailbox.

TAXI

Boulder Yellow Cab (☑ 303-699-8747; www.boulderyellowcab.com; ⏱24hr) This Boulder's biggest and best cab company – actually a subsidiary of Colorado's largest taxi conglomerate. There's a taxi stand on 11th St at the Pearl Street Mall. Meter rates run $2.50 for the first 1/9 mile (or fraction thereof), $2.25 each additional mile. This basically means most pay a minimum of $4.75 to use a cab. The flat rate to Denver International Airport is $84.

Nederland

☑303 / POP 1450 / ELEV 8230FT

From Boulder, the devastatingly scenic 17-mile route through Boulder Canyon emerges in the lively, ramshackle little berg of Nederland, a mountain-town magnet for hippies looking to get off the grid. These days, Nederland has a sagging, happenstantial quality to its weather-beaten buildings, which are not without a certain rugged charm. Several worthwhile restaurants and bars feed the hungry skiers and hikers heading to or from Eldora Mountain Resort and the Indian Peaks Wilderness Area, as well as motorists coming down the Peak to Peak Hwy, a 55-mile scenic byway that runs from Estes Park to the I-70.

◉ Sights

Wild Bear Mountain Ecology Center   NATURE CENTER
(☑ 303-258-0495; www.wildbear.org; 20 Lakeview Dr, Caribou Shopping Center, Unit 106; ⊘ noon-5:30pm Mon-Sat; ▥) This small nature center provides information about local trails as well as flora and fauna, mostly geared toward families. Workshops are offered year-round – think 'High Altitude Herb Walk' (identifying edible and medicinal plants in the forest), as well as some artsy ones (e.g. spinning wheel classes).

Carousel of Happiness   CAROUSEL
(☑ 303-258-3457; www.carouselofhappiness.org; 20 Lakeview Dr, Caribou Shopping Center; ride $1; ⊘ 10am-6pm Mon-Fri, to 7pm Sat & Sun May-Sep, 11am-6pm Thu-Mon Oct-Apr; ▥) In the center of town, this 1910 carousel is a highlight for kids (and some grown-ups too!). A labor of love (and 26 years), the vintage frame and mechanism were refurbished and the 56 whimsical animals hand-carved by a local, Scott Harrison, for the public to enjoy. Proceeds from the nonprofit go to children with special needs.

Nederland Mining Museum   MUSEUM
(www.bouldercounty.org; 200 N Bridge St; ⊘ 11am-5pm Fri-Sun May-Oct; ▥) **FREE** This small museum gives a peek into the 19th-century mining industry history in Nederland, the reason why the town exists. Heavy machinery, rusting tools and photos are displayed inside and out. At 2pm a staffer gives a talk about hard-rock mining, including real-life stories, which provides interesting context. Worth a quick stop.

⚡ Activities

The nearby Indian Peaks Wilderness Area provides ample recreation in summer and winter. Road cyclists often pedal the route between Boulder and Nederland and some charge on to the scenic Peak to Peak Hwy, making Nederland a logical stop. Tin Shed (p135) bike shop has good information about road and mountain-bike routes.

Eldora Mountain Resort   SNOW SPORTS
(☑ 303-440-8700; www.eldora.com; 2861 Eldora Ski Rd 140; lift ticket adult/child $94/54; ▥; ▥N) Aside from the Corona Bowl, which boasts a thrilling 1400ft vertical drop, this 680-acre ski area is mostly famous for its convenience – just 21 miles from Boulder. It's no Telluride, but there is some interesting terrain, plus a few expert trails and 11 lifts to help you explore it all. A highlight is the 40km-plus of well-groomed Nordic trails.

During winter, RTD buses (bus line N, round-trip $9) leave from the corner of Boulder's 14th and Walnut Sts for Eldora Mountain Resort.

✦✦ Festivals & Events

Frozen Dead Guy Days   PARADE
(☑ 303-506-1048; http://frozendeadguydays.org; ⊘ early Mar; ▥) This macabre, bizarre and wonderful festival brings life – about 15,000 souls – to Nederland in the early spring. A three-day blowout event, it celebrates Grandpa Bredo Morstoel, a Norwegian transplant who is cryogenically frozen, surrounded by dry ice in a local tuff shed, awaiting reanimation. Dozens of live bands, coffin races, polar plunging, salmon tossing and beer make this a must-do.

NedFest   MUSIC
(www.nedfest.org; 151 E St; adult/child day ticket from $45/free; ⊘ late Aug; ▥) An annual three-day gathering of area folkies and jam bands, this music fest is perfectly suited to the ex-hippie, mountain-town vibe. Campsites are set up along the reservoir and vendors do brisk business in food, drink and tie-dye all weekend. A family-friendly event; kids get in free.

⌷ Sleeping

Rainbow Lakes Campground   CAMPGROUND $
(☑ 303-541-2500; www.fs.usda.gov; off County Rd 116; campsite from $15; ℗) Surrounded by lodgepole pines, this campground sits at 10,000ft with access to brilliant hikes on the eastern side of Rocky Mountain National Park. Though an excellent option in the off-season, it receives lots of traffic in the summer. Bring your own water, or filter from the lakes, half a mile away. Campsites are first-come, first-served.

Boulder Creek Lodge   HOTEL $$
(☑ 303-258-9463; www.thebouldercreeklodge.com; 55 Lakeview Drive; r from $178; @ ⚡ ▥) Decent value for the Boulder area, this

lodge has a true mountain feel with high A-frame ceilings, big windows and log furniture everywhere. Rooms are simple and comfortable enough, each with an updated bathroom as well as mini-refrigerator and microwave. Located in town, it's within easy walking distance of all the restaurants and reservoir – a plus!

Eating

★ **Crosscut Pizzeria & Taphouse** PIZZA $
(☏ 303-258-3519; www.crosscutpizza.com; 4 E 1st St; pizzas $6-15; ⊙ 3-9pm Mon-Thu, 11:30am-9pm Fri-Sun May-Sep, 3-8pm Mon-Thu, 11:30am-9pm Fri & Sat, 11:30am-8pm Sun Oct-Apr; ☒ 🐾) Crosscut serves up some of the best Italian-style pizza in the Rockies – wood-fired, thin crust, topped with gourmet treats like pancetta and crimini mushrooms. There's craft beer and cider on tap. Wine too. And did we mention the homemade ice cream? Dine in the old-school building with three modern dining rooms, or on the patio alongside the creek.

Service is as friendly as it comes.

Deli at 8236 DELI $
(☏ 303-258-1113; 34 E 1st St; mains $6-10; ⊙ 9am-6pm; 🐾) There's nothing fancy about this place: it's a deli with old chairs and fluorescent lights. Here, it's all about the subs – hot, cold, pressed or not, the ingredients are quality and the combos perfection. The soups, too, keep customers coming on cold days; the clam chowder and lobster bisque are especially popular.

Salto Coffee Works CAFE $
(☏ 303-258-3537; www.saltocoffeeworks.com; 112 E 2nd St; mains $5-12; ⊙ 7am-9pm; 🛜 ☒ 🐾) This welcoming cafe, with roaring fires in winter and a stone patio in summer, adds some ambience to Ned. Skiers can start their day with egg sandwiches on brioche and great Ozo coffee. In the evenings, the après-ski and bike crowd can chomp on hefty salads and sandwiches, with gluten-free options; there's beer and wine too.

Tuesday typically brings live music – check the website for the calendar of events.

INDIAN PEAKS WILDERNESS AREA

Forming the impressive backdrop to Nederland, the Indian Peaks area is the most-used wilderness area in the country, thanks to super-active Boulderites. With grand scenery on the scale of a national park, Indian Peaks offers many fine hiking and camping opportunities, though reservations, even for backcountry sites, are required. Dogs are allowed on almost all trails, but must be on a leash. In winter the area is frequented by backcountry skiers and snowshoers. Equipment is easily rented in Boulder. Visitors should still go out with someone knowledgeable about avalanche safety, or get recommendations for low-risk areas.

There are two main access points: one south of Nederland past the village of Eldora and the other north of Nederland along the Peak to Peak Hwy. South of Nederland are the **Hessie** and **Fourth of July** trailheads. For Hessie, take the **Hessie Shuttle** (p135). From there you can reach **Lost Lake**, a good 2.7-mile round-trip, or head further for more lakes access. Fourth of July trail is among the most scenic, with access to **Arapaho Glacier** (7.9-mile round-trip). Another recommended option from this point is the hike up to the 12,000ft **Arapaho Pass** (6.4-mile round-trip). It's a gentle ascent but be prepared to spend the entire day – if the altitude doesn't slow you down, the scenery will. Note: the unpaved road to Fourth of July is best left to high-clearance or 4WD vehicles.

North of Nederland, the **Brainard Lake Recreation Area** has ample parking ($10) and campsites ($19), which always fill up. Brainard Lake itself is ringed by the paved entrance road. Highlights include the beautiful **Lake Isabelle** (4.9-mile round-trip) and the absolutely stunning (but mildly arduous) **Pawnee Pass** (9.1-mile round-trip), an all-day hike or a good overnighter.

For more information on Indian Peaks check out the **Nederland Visitors Center** (☏ 303-258-3936; 4 W 1st St; ⊙ 10am-4pm Thu-Mon; 🐾), which has maps and guidebooks. In the mall, **Ace Hardware** (p135) also sells topographic and USGS maps for the Indian Peaks area. It issues camping permits (required June to September 15), as well as hunting and fishing licenses. Camping permits are also available through the **Boulder Ranger District** (p131).

New Moon Bakery & Cafe CAFE $
(☑303-258-3569; www.newmoonbakery.com; 1 W 1st St; mains $3-10; ⊗6:30am-5pm Mon-Fri, 7am-6pm Sat & Sun; 🛜🚗🦽) Doubling as the town gossip hub, this busy cafe caters to Boulder tastes. Get your latte made with rice milk and your chocolate cookie free of gluten. Flavorful sandwiches and wraps hit the spot after a day of hiking – the bacon wrap is particularly tasty. A sunny patio seals the deal.

Kathmandu NEPALI, INDIAN $
(☑303-258-1169; www.kathmandurestaurant.us; 110 N Jefferson St; mains $12-16; ⊗11am-9:30pm; 🦽) A huge restaurant decked out in red, Kathmandu is a longtime visual staple offering solid Indian and Nepalese fare. The lunch buffet is a good deal but the offerings can sometimes fall short – stick to the menu instead. A kids' menu with American fare makes it easy to come with picky eaters. For a sweet treat, try the chai.

☆ Entertainment

Beyond a couple of brewpubs and occasional live music, there's no regular nightlife scene in Ned. Head to Boulder for more action.

Caribou Room LIVE MUSIC
(www.thecaribouroom.com; 55 Indian Peaks Dr; tickets from $10) This warehouse-turned-music-hall is one of the best unexpected places to go to a concert. The facility has a state-of-the-art sound system, a huge dance floor and balcony seating. A full kitchen serves solid eats and Colorado brews are always on tap. Recent lineups include Peter Rowan, Gasoline Lollipops and the Flatirons Jazz Orchestra. Incredibly, the facility is zero-waste and solar-powered.

🛍 Shopping

Crafted in Colorado GIFTS & SOUVENIRS
(☑303-258-3188; www.craftedincolorado.com; 35 E 1st St; ⊗10am-6pm Mon-Sat, 11am-5pm Sun) This boutique sells local artisan goods, from edgy sweatshirts to organic soap. Items are pricey but the quality is all there. For a bigger selection, check out the shop's online offerings.

Silver Stem DISPENSARY
(☑303-258-3552; www.silverstemcannabis.com; 1 W 1st St, Suite 1; ⊗10am-6:45pm Mon-Sat, to 5:45pm Sun) Right in the middle of town, Silver Stem is a tiny but popular dispensary – some customers even drive up from Boulder for the quality weed and chill service. Flower, edibles and concentrates all available.

Augustina's Winery WINE
(☑303-520-4871; www.augustinaswinery.com; 20 East Lakeview Dr #103; ⊗1-5pm Thu & Sun, 1-6pm Fri & Sat) Augustina's is a one-woman show. The owner-winemaker, Gussie Walter, drives a 1979 U-Haul to Palisades and Grand Junction every autumn to fetch her grapes then goes about the happy, messy business of crushing, fermenting and aging the wine all on her own. If you're looking for a bottle with a story, grab one here. Wine tastings on Saturday.

The wine is also sold at the Boulder County Farmers Market (p121).

ℹ Tourist Information

Indian Peaks Ace Hardware (☑303-258-3132; www.indianpeaksace.com; 74 Hwy 119 S; ⊗8am-7pm Mon-Sat, 8am-5pm Sun) Across from the Boulder Creek Lodge, this store sells topographic and USGS maps for the Indian Peaks area, and issues camping permits (required June to September 15), as well as hunting and fishing licenses.

Nederland Visitors Center (p134) Staffed by friendly locals, this visitor center has lots of information about where to eat, sleep and play in the area; located on the main drag in the center of town.

ℹ Getting There & Around

Nederland is about 17 miles west of Boulder, the road winding through the scenic Boulder Canyon. Denver is 45 miles away. You can get to Nederland either via Boulder, or take Hwy 72 via Golden, through the foothills. There's regular bus service from Boulder ($4.50, 30 minutes, every one to two hours).

Hessie Shuttle (☑303-678-6200; www.bouldercounty.org; 300 S Jackson St; ⊗8am-8pm Sat, 8am-6pm Sun Jun-Oct; 🦽) Since parking is severely limited for the Hessie hikes (including the Fourth of July trailhead and Arapaho Glacier), visitors are asked to take this shuttle (free, 20 minutes, every 15 minutes) from the RTD Park 'n' Ride in downtown Ned. Dogs on leashes are allowed. The shuttle drops passengers off at the Hessie trailhead; it runs on weekends only from June to October.

Tin Shed (☑303-258-3509; www.tinshed-sports.com; 112 E 2nd St; per day from $35; ⊗9am-6pm) Adjacent to Salto cafe, this full-service bike shop offers plenty of trail maps and advice, as well as ski-tuning in winter. Mountain-bike rentals, including helmet and tool kit, are available.

Rocky Mountain National Park & Northern Colorado

Includes →

Rocky Mountain
National Park 138
Estes Park 144
Fort Collins 150
Sterling 156
Cache la
Poudre River. 157
Red Feather Lakes . . .159
Walden 159
Grand Lake 159
Granby 161
Kremmling. 162
Steamboat Springs . .163
Oak Creek 169
Craig. 170
Dinosaur National
Monument. 171
Meeker 173

Best Places to Eat

→ Big Horn Restaurant (p148)
→ O-A Bistro (p160)
→ Laundry (p168)

Best Places to Stay

→ Stanley Hotel (p147)
→ Vista Verde Guest Ranch (p167)
→ Shadowcliff Lodge & Retreat Center (p160)

Why Go?

The wind whips wild and free through the northern reaches of Colorado. In the east you will find vast stretches of grasslands, and playful nights in the foothills college town of Fort Collins. Continue west through vertiginous canyons to the snow-capped peaks, wildflower-choked meadows and towering mountainscapes of Rocky Mountain National Park, world-class skiing in Steamboat, and more laid-back adventures in the open spaces and protected areas that keep this isolated corner of the Rockies pristine. After you pass the Continental Divide, the landscape turns from green to red, with slickrock biking excursions, river trips and dinosaur digging awaiting on the western edge.

Wherever you go in Northern Colorado, hiking, biking, skiing and rafting adventures await. Head down forgotten roads to visit mining ghost towns, or hike out into the wilderness for backcountry adventures that can stretch as far as your imagination.

When to Go
Estes Park

Jun–Sep Sunshine, perfect hiking and cool weather in the high country attract visitors.

Sep–Oct Temperatures drop and the tourists vacate. The aspens turn golden.

Nov–Apr Crisp air and tons of snowfall bring skiers to low-key resorts.

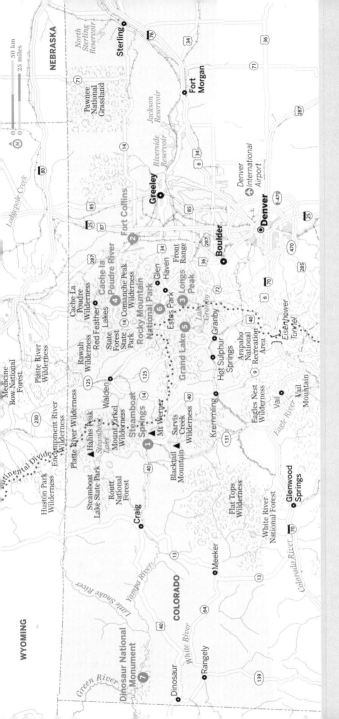

Rocky Mountain National Park & Northern Colorado Highlights

1 Steamboat Springs
(p163) Lazein hot springs, and hike and bike until your lungs hurt.

2 Fort Collins (p150)
Hop from brewery to brewery

before a day of exploration in the nearby foothills.

3 Longs Peak (p139)
Summit one of Colorado's most iconic 14,000ft peaks.

4 Cache la Poudre River

(p157) Try fly-fishing or a white-water raft adventure.

5 Shadowcliff Lodge & Retreat Center (p160)
Spend the day hiking and boating around Grand Lake.

6 Rocky Mountain National Park (p138)
Explore the wild corners and hard-to-summit peaks of this vast national park.

7 Dinosaur National Monument (p171) Marvel at them old bones before heading out on a five-day desert rafting trip.

Rocky Mountain National Park

📍970 / ELEV 8000–14,000FT

This is a place of natural spectacle on every scale: from hulking granite formations, many taller than 12,000ft, some over 130 million years old, to the delicate yellow burst of the glacier lily, one of the dozen alpine wildflowers that explode in short, colorful life at the edge of receding snowfields for a few days every spring.

And though it tops many travelers' itineraries and can get maddeningly crowded, the park has miles of less-beaten paths and the backcountry is a little-explored nature-lovers' wonderland. Excellent hiking trails crisscross alpine fields, skirt the edge of isolated high-altitude lakes and bring travelers to the wild, untamed heart of the Rockies.

⊙ Sights

Wonders of the natural world are the main attractions here: huge herds of elk and scattered bighorn sheep, pine-dotted granite slopes and blindingly white alpine tundra. However, there are a few museums and historic sites within the park's borders that are worthy of a glance and good for families.

Rocky Mountain National Park is surrounded by some of the most pristine wild area in the west: Comanche Peak and Neota Wilderness Areas in the Roosevelt National Forest to the north and Indian Peaks Wilderness to the south. The jagged spine of the Continental Divide intersects the park through its middle.

A severe flood washed through Rocky Mountain National Park in September 2013, and several campgrounds and trails were damaged or closed. While some of the damage still remains, almost everything is back up and running.

★**Moraine Park Museum**　　　MUSEUM
(📍970-586-1206; Bear Lake Rd; ⊙9am-4:30pm Jun-Oct; 👪) FREE Built by the Civilian Conservation Corps in 1923 and once the park's proud visitors lodge, this building has been renovated in recent years to host exhibits on geology, glaciers and wildlife. Kids will like the interactive exhibits and half-mile nature trail out the door.

Rocky Mountain National Park　　　NATIONAL PARK
(www.nps.gov/romo; vehicle 1/7 days $20/30, motorcycle, foot & bicycle days $10/15, annual passes $60) On top of the world, this mighty national park is home to loads of wild animals, plenty of great backwoods hiking and top scenic drives that are choked with RVs in summertime. As in most of America's national parks, the key is leaving the road system and getting into the backcountry.

Holzwarth Historic Site　　　HISTORIC SITE
(Never Summer Ranch; 📍park headquarters 970-586-1206; Trail Ridge Rd/US 34; ⊙10am-4pm Jun-Oct; P👪) When Prohibition was enacted in 1916, John Holzwarth Sr, a Denver saloon-keeper, started a new life as a subsistence rancher. This site houses several buildings kept in their original condition, and hosts historical reenactments and ranger-led programs. The Heritage Days celebration happens in late July.

The site lies at the end of a graded half-mile path, easily accessible with strollers.

Enos Mills Cabin Museum & Gallery　　　MUSEUM
(📍970-586-4706; www.enosmills.com; 6760 Hwy 7; $20; ⊙11am-4pm Tue & Wed summer, by appointment only; 👪) Naturalist Enos Mills (1870–1922) led the struggle to establish Rocky Mountain National Park. His infectious enthusiasm and passion for nature lived on with his daughter Enda Mills Kiley (who sadly passed away in 2009). Her father's incredible history is documented in his tiny cabin, built in 1885. The Mills family maintains an interpretive nature trail leading from the parking lot to the cabin, where news clippings and photographs recount Enos Mills' advocacy for the protection of the wild.

🏃 Activities

★**Trail Ridge Road**　　　SCENIC DRIVE
(www.nps.gov/romo; ⊙summer only) FREE Travel through the sky on this remarkable 48-mile road between Estes Park and Grand Lake. The road is only open summers, and can be jam-packed. But it is really worth it – by car, RV or bicycle. About 11 miles of the road sit above tree line.

Old Fall River Road　　　SCENIC DRIVE
With a maximum speed limit of 15mph, Old Fall River Rd offers motorists a graveled, slow-paced drive into the park's high country. Narrow, one-way (up) and without guardrails, it's also a bit hair-raising at times, and certainly not recommended for RVs.

Hiking & Backpacking

With over 300 miles of trail, traversing all aspects of its diverse terrain, the park is suited to every hiking ability. Those with the kids in tow might consider the easy hikes in the Wild Basin to Calypso Falls, or to Gem Lake in the Lumpy Ridge area, while those with unlimited ambition, strong legs and enough trail mix will be lured by the challenge of summiting Longs Peak. Regardless, it's best to spend at least one night at 7000ft to 8000ft prior to setting out to allow your body to adjust to the elevation. Before July many trails are snowbound and high water runoff makes passage difficult. In the winter avalanches are a hazard. Dogs and other pets are not allowed on the trails. All overnight stays in the backcountry require permits.

The golden rule in Colorado mountaineering: if you haven't made the summit by noon, return (no matter how close you are). It's the best way to avoid getting hit by lightning.

Longs Peak   HIKING
You need not worry about getting lonesome on the 15-mile (full-day) round-trip to Longs Peak (14,259ft) summit, as it's the centerpiece of many a hiker's itinerary. During summer, you're likely to find a line of more than 100 parked cars snaking down the road from the Longs Peak trailhead.

Lumpy Ridge   HIKING
Easily accessed from the north side of Estes Park, Lumpy Ridge offers some great hikes to places like Bridal Veil Falls and Gem Lake, plus some of the best rock climbing in the area. The Lumpy Ridge Loop circles around the granite crag in an 11-mile loop. Check in about raptor nesting before going here.

Lily Mountain   HIKING
(🚶) One of the easiest climbs in the area, Lily Mountain's 1.5-mile trail ascends almost 1000ft to the hike's namesake summit, offering an outstanding panorama that includes the Mummy Range, Continental Divide, Longs Peak, Estes Park and Estes Cone. The trailhead sits on the park border, 6 miles south of Estes Park on Hwy 7.

Twin Sisters Peak   HIKING
This up-and-back hike provides an excellent warm-up to climbing Longs Peak. In addition, the 11,428ft summit of Twin Sisters Peak offers unequaled views of Longs Peak. It's an arduous walk, gaining 2300ft in just 3.7 miles.

Milner Pass   HIKING
The Trail Ridge Rd crosses the Divide at Milner Pass (elevation 10,759ft), where trails head southeast to Mt Ida, the most accessible peak on the west side of the park. The trail climbs 2000ft in 4 miles, steeply at first through dense forest before emerging onto an exhilaratingly open tundra zone with fabulous views of the valleys below.

Glacier Gorge Junction   HIKING
Accessed from the Bear Lake trailhead, this busy network of trails threads through pine forest and over rushing streams, offering a spectrum of difficulty. The easy stroll to Alberta Falls is good for families.

Flattop Mountain Trail   HIKING
Surprisingly, this is the only hiking trail in the park to link the east and west sides. Reaching the Divide on Flattop Mountain from the Bear Lake trailhead entails a strenuous 4.5-mile climb, gaining 2800ft in elevation. From the summit, you have two equidistant options for continuing to Grand Lake: Tonahutu Creek Trail or the North Inlet Trail. Both offer plenty of backcountry campsites on the east side.

Lawn Lake Trailhead   HIKING
This 13.3-mile out and back hike takes you north of Estes Park to a gorgeous alpine lake. It's less traveled than the major park trails. Access this spot from Fall River Rd outside Estes.

Bear Lake Trailhead   HIKING
(🚶) This is a short and easy hike that's perfect for families or people with mobility challenges. There are 30 marked spots along the route – hike counterclockwise to follow the curated route. Get here on the Glacier Basin–Bear Lake shuttle.

Wild Basin   HIKING
In the park's southeast corner, Wild Basin offers several easy day hikes to cascading waterfalls, alpine lakes and swaths of wildflowers; all beneath some of the parks most stunning peaks. Set out from the Wild Basin Trailhead and you'll soon reach Copeland Falls.

Rock Climbing

Many of the park's alpine climbs are long one-day climbs or require an overnight stay on the rock face. Often the only way to accomplish a long climb and avoid afternoon thundershowers is to begin climbing at dawn – this can mean an approach hike

Rocky Mountain National Park

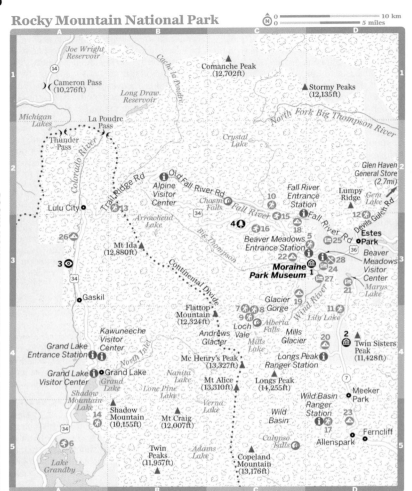

beginning at midnight! An alternative is to bivouac (temporary open-air encampment – no tents) at the base of the climb. Free bivouac permits are issued only to technical climbers and are mandatory for all overnight stays in the backcountry.

To minimize the environmental impact of backcountry use, the Rocky Mountain National Park Wilderness Office allows only a limited number of people to bivouac at four popular climbing areas. Phone reservations may be made from March to May 20 for the following restricted zones: Longs Peak area, including Broadway

below Diamond, Chasm View, Mills Glacier and Meeker Cirque; Black Lake area (Glacier Gorge), encompassing McHenry's Peak, Arrowhead, Spearhead and Chiefshead/Pagoda; the base of Notchtop Peak; and the Skypond/Andrews Glacier Area, including the Taylor/Powell Peaks and Sharkstooth Peak. Reservations are not needed nor accepted for other bivouacs.

Good bouldering and traditional rock climbing can be found at Lumpy Ridge (p139), accessed less than 2 miles north of Estes Park on Devils Gulch Rd.

Rocky Mountain National Park

◎ **Top Sights**
1 Moraine Park Museum..........................D3

◎ **Sights**
2 Enos Mills Cabin Museum & Gallery D4
3 Holzwarth Historic Site........................A3
4 Rocky Mountain National Park............C3

◉ **Activities, Courses & Tours**
5 Backcountry Hiking................................D3
6 Beacon Landing Marina.........................A5
7 Bear Lake Trailhead...............................C4
8 Flattop Mountain Trail..........................C4
9 Glacier Gorge Junction..........................C4
10 Lawn Lake Trailhead.............................C2
11 Lily Mountain..D4
Longs Peak...................................(see 20)
12 Lumpy Ridge..D3
13 Milner Pass..B2
14 Monarch Lake..A5

15 Old Fall River Road.................................C3
16 Trail Ridge Road.....................................C3
Twin Sisters Peak...........................(see 11)
17 Wild Basin..D5

🛌 **Sleeping**
18 Aspenglen Campground........................C3
19 Glacier Basin Campground....................C3
20 Longs Peak Campground.......................D4
21 Mary's Lake Lodge.................................D3
22 Moraine Park Campground....................C3
23 Olive Ridge Campground.......................D5
24 Riversong...D3
25 StoneBrook Resort on Fall River...........D3
26 Timber Creek Campground....................A3
27 YMCA of the Rockies – Estes Park
Center...D3

🍴 **Eating**
28 Rock Inn Mountain Tavern....................D3

For climbing gear try **Estes Park Mountain Shop** (970-586-6548; www.estesparkmountainshop.com; 2050 Big Thompson Ave; 2-person tents $12-16, bear boxes per night $3; ⊙8am-9pm). A small stock of climbing gear is also available from the Colorado Mountain School (p145).

Cycling & Mountain Biking

Mountain biking and cycling have continued to gain popularity despite the park's heavy traffic. It's a splendid way to see the park and wildlife, though bicycle travel is restricted to paved roads and to one dirt road, Fall River Rd. Those looking to ride technical routes on a mountain bike should go to Roosevelt National Forest.

On either a road bike or a mountain bike, climbing the paved Trail Ridge Rd (p138) has one big advantage over Fall River Rd (a 9-mile one-way climb of more than 3000ft): you can turn around should problems arise.

Less daunting climbs and climes are available on the park's lower paved roads. A popular 16-mile circuit is the Horseshoe Park/Estes Park Loop. For a bit more of a climbing challenge you can continue to Bear Lake Rd, an 8-mile-long route that rises 1500ft to the high mountain basin with a decent shoulder.

To avoid hypothermia and dehydration bring a set of dry, long-sleeved clothes, plus plenty of water.

New Venture Cycling CYCLING
(970-231-2736; www.newventurecycling.com; 2050 Big Thompson Ave, Estes Park;) Guided bike tours take you downhill through Rocky Mountain National Park on Trail Ridge Rd ($85). It takes about five hours over 29 miles, but lucky for you it's almost all downhill. Another easier ride ($50) takes you through the North Fork Canyon over 10 miles, taking about two hours – a better fit for families with tag-alongs.

Snowshoeing & Cross-country Skiing

From December into May, the high valleys and alpine tundra offer cross-country skiers unique opportunities to view wildlife and the winter scenery undisturbed by crowds. January and February are the best months for dry, powdery snowpack; spring snows tend to be heavy and wet. Most routes follow summer hiking trails, but valley bottoms and frozen streambeds typically have more snow cover and are less challenging. Ask about avalanche hazards before heading out – Colorado has one of the most dangerous snowpacks in the world with people dying in slides most years – and avoid steep open slopes.

Novices should consider hiring a guide or traveling with experienced leaders. Rangers lead weekend snowshoe hikes in the east side of the park from January to April, depending on snow conditions. Trailhead locations and times are available from the park visitor centers.

ROCKY MOUNTAIN NATIONAL PARK & NORTHERN COLORADO

ℹ FEES & PERMITS

For private vehicles, the park entrance fee is $20 for one day and $30 for seven. Annual passes are $60. Individuals entering the park on foot, bicycle, motorcycle or bus pay $10 each for one day and $15 for seven. All visitors receive a free copy of the park's information brochure, which contains a good orientation map and is available in English, German, French, Spanish and Japanese. A good option if you plan to visit any other national parks is to buy an annual National Parks and Federal Recreational Lands Annual Pass for $80.

Backcounty permits ($26 for a group of up to seven people for seven days) are required for overnight stays in the 260 designated backcountry camping sites in the park. They are free between November 1 and April 30. Phone reservations can be made only from March 1 to May 15. Reservations for sites and permits, by snail mail or in person, are accepted via the Wilderness Offices. (☑970-586-1242; www.nps.gov/romo; 1000 W Hwy 36, Estes Park, CO 80517)

A bear box to store your food in is required if you are staying overnight in the backcountry between May and October (established campsites already have them). These can be rented for around $3 to $5 per day from REI (p97) in Denver, the Estes Park Mountain Shop (p141) and Never Summer Mountain Products (☑970-672-3642; www.neversummermtn.com; 919 Grand Ave; ⊙9am-7pm) in Grand Lake. You need to practice bear-safe camping no matter where you camp in the park.

Permits can be obtained in person at Beaver Meadows Visitor Center (p144), Kawuneeche Visitor Center (p144), and (in summer only) at the Longs Peak (p144) and Wild Basin (p144) ranger stations. Generally speaking, there are always backcountry sites available.

Overnight trips require permits, and the USFS and NPS will have a list of closed trails.

You can gear up at the Estes Park Mountain Shop (p141).

Mountaineering

Rocky Mountain National Park has a total 124 named peaks. While Longs is the only one over 14,000ft, another 20 sit above 13,000ft, making this a top mountaineering spot. Before departing check in at wilderness offices (p142) for raptor closings as well as beta on climbing and bivouac permits.

Routes range from easy hikes up to daylong affairs on vertical cliffs, plus steep snow, ice and rock routes. Get classes at the Colorado Mountain School (p145).

🛏 Sleeping

The only overnight accommodations in the park are at campgrounds; the majority of motel or hotel accommodations are around Estes Park or Grand Lake. The closest thing the park has to the typical Civilian Conservation Corps–era lodges built by public works at parks like Yosemite and Yellowstone during the Great Depression is the YMCA of the Rockies (p147), which is on the park's border.

The park's formal campgrounds provide campfire programs, have public telephones and a seven-day limit during summer months; all except Longs Peak (p143) take RVs (no hookups). The water supply is turned off during winter.

You will need a backcountry permit (www.nps.gov/romo/planyourvisit/wilderness-camping.htm; permit for up to 7 people $26) to stay outside developed park campgrounds. None of the campgrounds have showers, but they do have flush toilets in summer and outhouse facilities in winter. Sites include a fire ring, a picnic table and one parking spot. Most have bear boxes for food storage.

Aspenglen Campground   CAMPGROUND $

(☑877-444-6777; www.recreation.gov; State Hwy 34; summer tent & RV sites $26) With only 54 sites, this is the smallest of the park's reservable camping grounds. There are many tent-only sites, including some walk-ins, and a limited number of trailers are allowed. This is the quietest campground in the park while still being highly accessible (5 miles west of Estes Park on US 34). Make reservations through the website.

Glacier Basin Campground   CAMPGROUND $

(☑877-444-6777; www.recreation.gov; off Bear Lake Rd; RV & tent sites summer $26) This developed campground is surrounded by evergreens, offering plenty of sun and shade. It also sports a large area for group camping and accommodates RVs. It is served by the shuttle buses on Bear Lake Rd throughout the summer. Make reservations through the website.

Moraine Park Campground CAMPGROUND $ (☑877-444-6777; www.recreation.gov; off Bear Lake Rd; summer tent & RV sites $26, winter $18) In the middle of a stand of ponderosa pine forest off Bear Lake Rd, this is the biggest of the park's campgrounds, approximately 2.5 miles south of the Beaver Meadows Visitor Center (p144) and with 245 sites. The walk-in, tent-only sites in the D Loop are recommended if you want some quiet. Make reservations through the website.

Reservations are accepted and recommended from the end of May through to the end of September; at other times of the year the campground is first-come, first-served. At night in the summer, there are numerous ranger-led programs in the amphitheater.

The campground is served by the shuttle buses on Bear Lake Rd through the summer.

Olive Ridge Campground CAMPGROUND $ (☑303-541-2500; www.recreation.gov; State Hwy 7; tent sites $26; ☺mid-May–Nov) This well-kept USFS campground has access to four trailheads: St Vrain Mountain, Wild Basin, Longs Peak and Twin Sisters. In the summer it can get full, though sites are mostly first-come, first-served.

Longs Peak Campground CAMPGROUND $ (☑970-586-1206; Longs Peak Rd, off State Hwy 7; tent sites $26; ☺closed winter; ℗) This is the base camp of choice for the early-morning ascent of Longs Peak (p139), one of Colorado's most easily accessible 14ers. The scenery is striking and its 26 spaces are for tents only, but don't expect much solitude in the peak of the summer.

There are no reservations: if you're planning to bag Longs Peak after sleeping here, get here early one day before the climb – according to rangers the only way to ensure a site during peak season is to show up before noon.

Timber Creek Campground CAMPGROUND $ (Trail Ridge Rd, US Hwy 34; tent & RV sites $26) This campground has 100 sites and remains open through the winter. No reservations accepted. The only established campground on the west side of the park, it's 7 miles north of Grand Lake. Unfortunately beetles ate all of the trees here, so there is no shade. Bring the sunblock or head elsewhere in the park.

🍴 Eating & Drinking

Rocky Mountain is a self-catered affair. Stop in Estes Park at the **Safeway** (☑970-586-4447; 451 E Wonderview Ave; ☺9am-7pm Mon-Fri, to 6pm Sat, 10am-4pm Sun; ℗ ❋) for picnic lunches and campfire dinners, or the cafeteria at the Alpine Visitor Center (p144).

The nightlife centers on the fire for ranger-led talks or ghost stories with your family and friends.

ℹ Information

CLIMATE

Weather in the park, as in all mountainous areas, is highly variable. Summer days often reach 70°F to 80°F (21°C to 27°C), yet a sudden shift in the weather can bring snow to the peaks in July. Nevertheless, the climate follows broadly predictable patterns based on season, elevation, exposure and location east or west of the Continental Divide. Strong winds are common above the treeline. July thundershowers typically dump 2in of rain on the park, while January is the driest month. Bear Lake (9400ft) normally has a January snow base of 25in. The Continental Divide causes a pronounced rain-shadow effect: Grand Lake (west of the Divide) annually averages 20in of moisture, while Estes Park receives only about 13in.

DANGERS & ANNOYANCES

If you're in easily accessible areas during high season, the biggest annoyance in Rocky Mountain National Park will likely be the other visitors. Roads clog with RVs, garbage fills every can to the brim and screaming children seem to multiply endlessly. Brace yourself, camper: it can be irritating.

But it might be more than fellow travelers giving you a headache: it could also be the altitude. High elevation can play all kinds of nasty tricks here, from relatively mild problems such as a pounding head and winded breathing to fairly serious symptoms of nausea, dehydration and fatigue. Stay hydrated, protect yourself from the sun, and if symptoms get really bad, head down to a lower elevation.

If you intend to get off the heavily beaten trail, take precautions in the spring and summer to avoid bites from wood ticks, which can transmit Colorado tick fever. Also be mindful of your food, which can attract wildlife. The park is home to black bears, moose and mountain lions. Although none of these poses a serious threat to visitors, you'll need to store your food in a bear bin and keep your campsite bear safe.

MAPS

Even though you'll get a driving map when you enter the park and some basic, nontechnical photocopied maps are available at some of the most popular trailheads, it's surprising that none of the visitor centers stocks high-quality topographic maps for hikers. You'll want to pick them up beforehand in Estes Park at **MacDonald Book Shop** (☑970-586-3450; www.macdonaldbookshop.com; 152 E Elkhorn Ave; ☺8am-8pm Mon-Sun, shorter hours in winter; ☎).

MEDICAL SERVICES

There are no care facilities in the park, but most rangers are trained to give emergency treatment. Emergency telephones are at **Longs Peak** (p144) and **Wild Basin ranger stations** (p144), as well as certain trailheads, including **Bear Lake** (p139) and **Lawn Lake** (p139).

TOURIST INFORMATION

The park has three full-service visitor centers – one on the east side, one on the west and one in the middle. Though they all have different displays and programs, this is where you can study maps and speak with rangers about permits and weather conditions.

Alpine Visitor Center (www.nps.gov/romo; Fall River Pass; ☺10:30am-4:30pm late May–mid-Jun, 9am-5pm late Jun-early Sep, 10:30am-4:30pm early Sep–mid-Oct; ⚿) The views from this popular visitor center and souvenir store at 11,796ft, and right in the middle of the park, are extraordinary. You can see elk, deer and sometimes moose grazing on the hillside on the drive up Old Fall River Rd. Much of the traffic that clogs Trail Ridge Rd all summer pulls into Alpine Visitor Center, so the place is a zoo. Rangers here give programs and advice about trails. You can also shop for knickknacks or eat in the cafeteria-style dining room.

Beaver Meadows Visitor Center (☑970-586-1206; www.nps.gov/romo; US Hwy 36; ☺8am-9pm late Jun–late Aug, to 4:30pm or 5pm rest of year; ⚿) The primary visitor center and best stop for park information if you're approaching from Estes Park. You can see a film about the park, browse a small gift shop and reserve backcountry camping sites.

Kawuneeche Visitor Center (☑970-627-3471; 16018 US Hwy 34; ☺8am-6pm last week May–Labor Day, 5pm Labor Day–Sep, to 4:30pm Oct-May; ⚿) This visitor center is on the west side of the park, and offers a film about the park, ranger-led walks and discussions, backcountry permits and family activities.

Longs Peak Ranger Station (Longs Peak Rd, off State Hwy 7; ☺8:30am-4:30pm summer) Eleven miles south of Estes Park.

Wild Basin Ranger Station (off County Hwy 115; ☺hours vary) Ranger services for the southeast corner of the park.

❶ Getting There & Away

Trail Ridge Rd (US 34) is the only east–west route through the park; the US 34 eastern approach from I-25 and Loveland follows the Big Thompson River Canyon. The most direct route from Boulder follows US 36 through Lyons to the east entrances. Another approach from the south, mountainous Hwy 7, passes by **Enos Mills Cabin** (p138) and provides access to campsites and trailheads on the east side of the divide. Winter closure of US 34 through the park makes access to the park's west side dependent on US 40 at Granby.

There are two entrance stations on the east side: **Fall River** (US 34) and **Beaver Meadows** (US 36). The **Grand Lake Entrance Station** (US 34) is the only entry on the west side. Year-round access is available through Kawuneeche Valley along the Colorado River headwaters to **Timber Creek Campground** (p143). The main centers of visitor activity on the park's east side are the **Alpine Visitor Center** (p144), on Trail Ridge Rd, and Bear Lake Rd, which leads to campgrounds, trailheads and the **Moraine Park Museum** (p138).

North of Estes Park, Devils Gulch Rd leads to several hiking trails. Further out on Devils Gulch Rd, you pass through the village of Glen Haven to reach the trailhead entry to the park along the North Fork of the Big Thompson River.

❶ Getting Around

A majority of visitors enter the park in their own cars, using the long and winding Trail Ridge Rd (US 34) to cross the Continental Divide. There are options for those without wheels, however. In summer a free shuttle bus operates from the **Estes Park Visitor Center** (p149) multiple times daily, bringing hikers to a park-and-ride location where you can pick up other shuttles. The year-round option leaves the Glacier Basin parking area and heads to Bear Lake, in the park's lower elevations. During the summer peak, a second shuttle operates between Moraine Park campground and the Glacier Basin parking area. The second shuttle runs on weekends only from mid-August through September.

Estes Park

☑970 / POP 6402 / ELEV 7522FT

Estes Park is just seconds from one of the US's most popular national parks. The town itself is a hotchpotch of T-shirt shops and ice-cream parlors, sidewalks jammed with tourists and streets plugged with RVs. But when the sun reflects just right off Lake Estes, or you spend an afternoon with a lazy coffee on the riverwalk, you might just find a little piece of zen.

Those expecting immediate views of the pristine beauty of Rocky Mountain National Park may be disappointed to find themselves watching brake lights on E Elkhorn Ave, the town's artery to both park entrances. But it's not all bad. Although the strip malls can be unsightly, Estes Park promises every convenience to the traveler, and in the off-season the place has a certain charm, as the streets quieten down, elk wander through town, and the prices of creekside cabins drop.

◉ Sights

Estes Park Museum   MUSEUM
(☑970-586-6256; www.estesnet.com/museum; 200 4th St; ⊙10am-5pm Mon-Sat, 1-5pm Sun; ⊕) **FREE** This community museum has a commendable rotation of exhibits on local culture. It's not only corny Ice Age mannequins either – you can also sit under the stars and listen to recorded histories in the main gallery, or learn more about the long history of floods that have ripped through town.

MacGregor Ranch Museum   RANCH
(☑970-586-3749; www.macgregorranch.org; 180 MacGregor Lane; adult/child $5/free; ⊙10am-4pm Tue-Sat Jun-Aug) In 1872 Alexander and Clara MacGregor arrived in Estes Park and settled beside Black Canyon Creek near Lumpy Ridge. Their granddaughter Muriel MacGregor bequeathed the ranch as an educational trust upon her death. It's a living museum featuring original living and working quarters; the ranch still raises Black Angus cattle. The main attraction is a cruise through the museum to check out the historic clothes, photographs and more.

The ranch is 1 mile north of Estes Park off Devils Gulch Rd. An NPS scenic and conservation easement helps fund the operation, and provides trail access to Lumpy Ridge.

Ariel Tramway   CABLE CAR
(☑970-586-3675; www.estestram.com; 420 E Riverside Dr; adult/child/senior $14/10/12; ⊙9am-6pm Memorial Day–Labor Day; ⓟ⊕) In the time you wait to be herded aboard a tram to the top of Prospect Mountain, you could have climbed Lily Mountain on your own two feet, but the tram is a good option for those with modest ambitions or special needs who still want the view.

🏃 Activities & Tours

★**Colorado Mountain School**   CLIMBING
(☑800-836-4008; https://coloradomountain-school.com; 341 Moraine Ave; half-day guided

GLEN HAVEN

Blink and you might just miss Glen Haven, a tiny outpost on the North Fork of the Big Thompson River, 7 miles east of Estes Park on Devils Gulch Rd. There isn't much here except a post office and general store, but the scenic approach makes it a worthwhile afternoon. Follow the narrow canyon road for 8 miles northwest from US 34 at Drake, site of the North Fork's confluence with the main channel in Big Thompson Canyon. The flood did some serious damage here, so don't expect a whole lot of services. Along the way there are handsome picnic spots; our favorite is right in Glen Haven on the narrow banks of the tumbling North Fork. Grab lunch at the **Glen Haven General Store** (☑970-586-2560; www.glenhavengeneralstore.com; 7499 Country Rd 43; ⊙9am-6pm May-Oct, shorter hours in winter; ⓟ), and delight in the gooey cinnamon rolls, cherry cobbler and deli items.

climbs per person from $125) Simply put, there's no better resource for climbers in Colorado – this outfit is the largest climbing operator in the region, has the most expert guides and is the only organization allowed to operate within Rocky Mountain National Park. It has a clutch of classes taught by world-class instructors.

Estes Lake Trail   WALKING
(Estes Lake) From the visitor center (p149), head out on this paved trail that circumnavigates Estes Lake. It's perfect for families, with about 3.5 miles around the lake. The north side is prettier, if you plan to just go one way.

Lake Estes Marina   BOATING
(☑970-586-2011; www.evrpd.com; 1770 Big Thompson Ave; ⊕) The marina on the north side of Lake Estes rents kayaks, stand-up paddleboards and canoes ($12), as well as pontoon boats and more. You can also get a pedal cart for the fam here.

Sombrero Ranch   HORSEBACK RIDING
(☑970-586-4577; www.sombrero.com; 1895 Big Thompson Ave; horseback rides from $48) With affordable guided trips into the national park or through a huge private ranch in the foothills, this quality outfitter has a variety

ROCKY MOUNTAIN NATIONAL PARK & NORTHERN COLORADO ESTES PARK

Estes Park

0 — 400 m
0 — 0.2 miles

Estes Park Mountain Shop (1mi);
Lake Estes Marina (1mi);
New Venture Cycling (1mi);
Sombrero Ranch (1mi)

Hillside La

Panorama Cir

Big Thompson Ave

Steamer Dr

Stanley Village

Steamer Pkwy

MacGregor Ave

Chiquita La

W Wonderview Ave

E Wonderview Ave

Black Canyon (0.3mi);
MacGregor Ranch Museum (1mi)

Deer Crest Resort (0.7mi)

Black Canyon Creek

Estes Valley Library

Virginia Dr

Big Horn Dr

Spruce Dr

Cleave St

Weist Dr

Park La

W Elkhorn Ave

E Elkhorn Ave

Fall River

Rock Ridge Rd

Moon Ridge

Courtney La

Davis St

Lott St

Moraine Ave

Prospect Village Dr

W Riverside Dr

E Riverside Dr

Riverside Dr

Moccasin St

Big Thompson River

Smokin' Dave's BBQ & Tap House (0.6mi)

Lake Estes Golf Course

Lake Estes

Lake Estes Trail

Estes Lake Trail

Estes Lake Trail

Stanley Park Fairgrounds

Manford Ave

N St Vrain Ave

S St Vrain Ave

USFS Estes Park Visitors Center

North Ct

4th St

5th St

3rd St

2nd St

1st St

South Ct

Comanche St

Aspen Ave

Columbine Ave

Prospect Ave

Estes Park Medical Center

Estes Park Conference Center

Stanley Ave

Stanley Circle Dr

Stanley Circle Dr

Highland La

St Vrain Ave

Estes Park Visitor Center

Estes Park

◉ **Sights**
1 Ariel Tramway C4
2 Estes Park Museum................................. G3

◔ **Activities, Courses & Tours**
3 Colorado Mountain School.................... B4
4 Estes Lake Trail... F2
5 Green Jeep Tours B3
6 Kirks Flyshop.. C3

◉ **Sleeping**
7 Silver Moon Inn B2
8 Stanley Hotel...D1

◉ **Eating**
9 Big Horn Restaurant.............................. A3

10 Claire's on the Park C2
11 Cousin Pat's Pub and Grill..................... F4
12 Ed's Cantina & Grill................................. D2
13 Lonigans B3
14 Molly B Restaurant.................................. C3
15 Nepal's Cafe.. C3
16 Safeway D1

◉ **Drinking & Nightlife**
17 Estes Park Brewery................................. B4
18 Wheel Bar C3

◉ **Shopping**
19 MacDonald Book Shop C3

of options. The evening 'steak fry' is a popular ride. Sombrero Ranch operates stables throughout the region.

Kirks Flyshop FISHING
(☑877-669-1859; www.kirksflyshop.com; 230 E Elkhorn Ave; tours from $99; ⊙7am-7pm) This full-service fly-fishing shop offers a number of guided packages in Rocky Mountain National Park and the surrounding waterways of the Front Range. It also rents out equipment, guides overnight hikes and offers float fishing and group excursions. Get your feet wet with the introductory two-hour evening hatch ($99). Trips include all the gear you need.

Green Jeep Tours DRIVING
(☑970-577-0034; www.epgjt.com; 157 Moraine Ave; tours from $65; ⊛) Offerings start with 3½-hour guided 4WD tours to waterfalls in Rocky Mountain National Park and move up to all-day affairs. Note that green is the color of the car, and is not representative of an environmentally friendly ethos.

🛌 Sleeping

Be warned: lodgings fill up very fast during the peak July and August period, when prices are sky high. You're likely to be out of luck if you travel west of Greeley without a reservation during summer. Off-season rates may be down to half that of summer prices, and many accommodations simply close for the winter.

★**YMCA of the Rockies –
Estes Park Center** RESORT $$
(☑888-613-9622; www.ymcarockies.org; 2515 Tunnel Rd; r & d from $109, cabins from $129;

P ⊕ ❄ � ⌂) Estes Park Center is not your typical YMCA boarding house. Instead it's a favorite vacation spot with families, boasting upmarket motel-style accommodations and cabins set on hundreds of acres of high alpine terrain. Choose from roomy cabins that sleep up to 10 or motel-style rooms for singles or doubles. Both are simple and practical.

Stanley Hotel HOTEL $$
(☑970-577-4000; www.stanleyhotel.com; 333 Wonderview Ave; r from $200; P ⌂ ⌂ ⌂) The white Georgian Colonial Revival hotel stands in brilliant contrast to the towering peaks of Rocky Mountain National Park that frame the skyline. A favorite local retreat, this best-in-class hotel served as the inspiration for Stephen King's cult novel *The Shining*. Rooms are decorated to retain some of the Old West feel while still ensuring all the creature comforts.

Mary's Lake Lodge LODGE $$
(☑970-586-5958; www.maryslakelodge.com; 2625 Marys Lake Rd; r & d from $134, cabins from $179; P ⊕ ❄ ⌂) This atmospheric old wooden lodge, perched on a ridge looking over its namesake lake, is an utterly romantic place to slumber. Built from polished pine logs, it reeks of Wild West ambience and has an amazing covered front porch with panoramic Rocky Mountain views.

**StoneBrook Resort
on Fall River** RESORT $$
(☑970-586-4629; www.stonebrookresort.com; 1710 Fall River Rd; d $180-270; P ⊕ ⌂) This adults-only collection of cabins looks out over Fall River and offers romantic retreats

with in-room Jacuzzis, fireplaces, kitchenettes and ample room to spread out. Some select cottages come with patios that overlook the bubbling river. The appointments are straight out of a cabin brochure, and are direct, honest and homey.

Deer Crest Resort
HOTEL $$

(☑970-586-2324; www.deercrestresort.com; 1200 Fall River Rd; d $119-129, ste from $149; P ⊖ ❀ 🤝 ⊠) There is a ton of options along the road out to Rocky Mountain National Park, but Deer Creek bests its neighbors with gas grills, lots of green space for the kids to run around in and the sound of the creek shushing guests to sleep. The on-site restaurant is also excellent.

Riversong
BOUTIQUE HOTEL $$

(☑970-586-4666; www.romanticriversong.com; 1766 Lower Broadview Dr; d from $199; P ⊖) Tucked down a dead-end dirt road overlooking the Big Thompson River, Riversong offers 10 romantic rooms with private bath in an arts-and-crafts-style mansion. The minimum stay is two nights, and prices vary by amenities. West of town take Moraine Ave, turn onto Mary's Lake Rd and take the first right.

Silver Moon Inn
HOTEL $$

(☑800-818-6006; www.silvermooninn.com; 175 Spruce Dr; d $225-265, ste from $350; P ⊖ ❀ @ 🤝 ⊠) The rooms here look over the creek, and offer plenty of thoughtful touches like fireplaces and private balconies in the deluxe rooms, restoration-style furniture and thick mattresses. There are creekside fire pits and wheelchair access to most rooms on the 1st floor. It's tucked between a rock outcropping and a stream on the western edge of town.

Black Canyon
LODGE $$$

(☑800-897-3730; www.blackcanyoninn.com; 800 MacGregor Ave; 1-/2-/3-bed r from $150/199/399; P ⊖ ❀ 🤝) A fine place to splurge, this lovely, secluded 14-acre property offers luxury suites and a 'rustic' log cabin (which comes with a Jacuzzi). The rooms are dressed out with stone fireplaces, dark wood and woven tapestries in rich dark colors, just like you imagined.

🍴 Eating

Ed's Cantina & Grill
MEXICAN $

(☑970-586-2919; www.edscantina.com; 390 E Elkhorn Ave; mains $9-12; ⊗11am-late Mon-Fri, 8am-10pm Sat & Sun; 🍴) With an outdoor patio right on the river, Ed's is a great place to kick back with a margarita. Serving Mexican and American staples, the restaurant is in a retro woodsy space with leather booth seating and bold primary colors.

Nepal's Cafe
NEPALI $

(☑970-577-7035; 184 E Elkhorn Ave, Unit H; buffet $9, mains $9-13; ⊗11am-9pm; 🍴) Lamp-heated lunch buffets are usually a no-no, but this place might make you reconsider. The curries are spiced just right and the *momo* (dumplings) are a filling option before or after a big hike. Come early for dinner, as the tiny place gets packed.

Lonigans
PUB FOOD $

(☑970-586-4346; www.lonigans.com; 110 W Elkhorn Ave; mains $9-12; ⊗11am-2am; 🍴) This pub and grill is a place to soak up Estes Park local flavor, mostly through the sidelong glances of the good ol' boys at the bar and boozy karaoke crooners. The menu – mostly burgers and American pub basics – includes Rocky Mountain Oysters, otherwise known as bull balls.

The kitchen closes at 10pm.

Molly B Restaurant
AMERICAN $

(☑970-586-2766; 200 Moraine Ave; breakfast $5-8; ⊗7am-4pm Thu-Tue; 🍴) This classic American breakfast place in town is easy to find and has a burly omelet and other greasy-spoon delights served among wood paneling and vinyl seats. Even the healthy food is delivered jumbo size, making the 'outrageous granola' no joke.

Smokin' Dave's BBQ & Tap House
BARBECUE $$

(☑866-674-2793; www.smokindavesbbqandtaphouse.com; 820 Moraine Ave; mains $8-20; ⊗11am-9pm Sun-Thu, to 10pm Fri & Sat; 🍴) Half-assed BBQ joints are all too common in Colorado's mountain towns, but Dave's, situated in a spare dining room, fully delivers. The buffalo ribs and pulled pork come dressed in a slightly sweet, smoky, tangy sauce and the sweet potato fries are crisply fried. Also excellent? The long, well-selected beer list.

Big Horn Restaurant
AMERICAN $$

(☑970-586-2792; www.estesparkbighorn.com; 401 W Elkhorn Ave; mains $10-22; ⊗6am-9pm, hours vary seasonally; 🍴) This local breakfast institution offers a side of grits along with the local gossip and the best huevos rancheros in town. If you get here on the way into the park, order a packed lunch with your breakfast, or come for a big salad and rib-eye dinner.

Claire's on the Park　　　AMERICAN $$
(☑970-586-9564; www.clairesonthepark.com; 225 Park Lane; mains $10-18; ☺7:30am-9pm summer, winter hours vary) Looking over the park with a broad wraparound porch, this is a great lunch spot. The copper-topped booths inside offer quiet retreats, and the salads are some of the freshest in town. The rest of the menu moves from tried-and-true Americana like burgers and pastrami sandwiches to a few interesting options like Rocky Mountain trout meunière and wild game meatloaf.

Cousin Pat's Pub and Grill　　AMERICAN $$
(☑970-586-7287; 451 S St Vrain Ave; mains $10-18; ☺11am-2pm; ﹢) This family-friendly burger and pizza pub has a cozy dining room and plenty to choose from on the extensive menu. The large fireplace in the dining room adds to the hometown warmth. The service is incredibly friendly, and it's a popular bar with locals, with a games room upstairs.

Rock Inn Mountain Tavern　　　STEAK $$$
(☑970-586-4116; www.rockinnestes.com; 1675 Hwy 66; mains $11-33; ☺11am-2am; ﹢) After a few days in the wilds of Rocky Mountain National Park, the rare porterhouse here seems heaven sent (even if the country band on stage can't pass as the accompanying choir of angels). Excellent stick-to-the-ribs fare and a crackling fire make it ideal for hikers looking to indulge.

Drinking & Nightlife

Wheel Bar　　　　　　　　　BAR
(www.thewheelbar.com; 132 E Elkhorn Ave; ☺10am-2am) Estes Park's favorite dive bar offers a rip-roaring good time, a killer porch out on the riverwalk, plus a mysterious wheel that truly reveals the difference between six drinks and more. Expect lots of flannel, free-wheeling locals and foot-long beards.

Estes Park Brewery　　　　BREWERY
(www.epbrewery.com; 470 Prospect Village Dr; ☺11am-2am) The town's brewpub serves pizza, burgers and wings, and at least eight different house beers, in a big, boxy room resembling a cross between a classroom and a country kitchen. Pool tables and outdoor seating keep the place rocking late into the night.

ℹ Tourist Information

Estes Park Visitor Center (☑970-577-9900; www.visitestespark.com; 500 Big Thompson Ave; ☺9am-8pm daily Jun-Aug, 8am-5pm Mon-Fri, 9am-5pm Sat & 10am-4pm Sun Sep-May) For help with lodging come here, just east of the US 36 junction.

Estes Valley Library (☑970-586-8116; www.estesvalleylibrary.org; 335 E Elkhorn Ave; ☺9am-9pm Mon-Thu, to 5pm Fri & Sat, 1-5pm Sun; ☏) With free wi-fi, large open spaces and tons of literature on the local area, Estes Park's central library is a good resource for travelers researching on the go.

USFS Estes Park Visitors Center (☑970-586-3440; 161 2nd St; ☺9am-5pm Mon-Fri) This center sells books and maps for the Arapaho and Roosevelt National Forests and has camping and trail information for hikers and mountain bikers. Camping permits for the heavily used Indian Peaks Wilderness Area, south of Rocky Mountain National Park, are required from June to September 15 and cost $5 per person.

ℹ Getting There & Away

The massive floods of September 2013 pummeled the town, with most of Main St flooding. Nearly every road leading to town was damaged and it took three weeks to get US 36 open again. Most businesses were able to open shortly after the flood, but the road on Big Thompson Canyon (US 34) still occasionally closes for repairs.

Estes Park is 34 miles west of Loveland via US 34, which you can access from I-25 (exit 257). Many visitors also come up by way of Boulder along US 36, passing through Lyons. Both are spectacular drives through rugged foothills, red rock formations and lush forest. A slower but more scenic route is the scenic Peak to Peak Hwy to Nederland. In summer you can get here on Trail Ridge Road from Grand Lake to the west.

The **Estes Park Shuttle** (☑970-586-5151; www.estesparkshuttle.com; one-way/round-trip $45/85) shuttle service connects Denver's airport to Estes Park about four times a day. The trip takes two hours.

ℹ Getting Around

Given the traffic, getting around Estes Park's compact downtown is easiest on foot. Estes Park has started a free shuttle service in the summer along the town's main arteries. The routes seem to change every year, but the service operates daily from about July to August, and then weekends only through September.

If you're traveling into Rocky Mountain National Park, there is a free 'Hiker Shuttle,' which leaves from the **Estes Park Visitors Center** (p149), making stops at Beaver Meadows

PEAK TO PEAK HIGHWAY

The Peak to Peak Hwy (Hwy 72) is one of the state's most scenic drives. If you're driving between Denver and Rocky Mountain National Park, definitely consider this route.

Rainbow Lakes Stop at the Mile 40 marker to head up to Rainbow Lakes and the Arapahoe Glacier Trails.

Brainard Lake The lake is beautiful, and there are good trails from here into the Indian Peaks backcountry.

Saint Malo Center On Hwy 7, just before the true start of the Peak to Peak, this wonderfully crafted church was visited by the pope in 1993.

Visitor Center and the park's Park & Ride lot, where you can transfer to other national park shuttles.

Cycling is a great way to get around the area, though few visitors seem to use this mode of transport (of course the altitude does make for some huffing and puffing). In summer, bike rentals spring up in the tourist area along E Elkhorn Ave.

Fort Collins

[☎]970 / POP 138,736 / ELEV 5003FT

Fort Collins is unassuming, direct, free-loving and gorgeous. The core downtown areas feature a world-class university campus, raucous nightlife, playful Victorian houses and tree-bordered avenues, a restaurant pedestrian zone, more brewpubs than you can possibly visit in a week, and a delightfully chilled air that feels unpretentious, honest and just about as open as you can get.

Just outside of town, you'll find mountain adventures in the Horsetooth Mountain Open Space (p151), Lory State Park (p150) and along the Cache la Poudre River (p157).

People often compare Fort Collins with Colorado's other favorite college town, Boulder. This former farming community doesn't have all the glitz of Boulder, but it's probably got more heart and soul...and that's just about right.

◉ Sights

Swetsville Zoo ZOO
([☎]970-484-9509; 4801 E Harmony Rd; entry by donation; ☉daylight hours; [♿]) Bill Swets, a former farmer, volunteer firefighter and insomniac, created a scrap-metal menagerie during his restless nights, a whimsical roadside curiosity. Swets' creations are a coy lesson in creative recycling – everything from the

grinning spider made from a VW bug to the heavy metal caricature of Monica Lewinsky.

Lory State Park STATE PARK
Sitting next to Horsetooth Reservoir, Lory State Park has 26 miles of trails perfect for mountain biking, hiking and strolling. From the east side you can paddle out on a canoe or kayak to explore the reservoir. Check about backcountry camping here, too.

The Farm at Lee Martinez Park ZOO
([☎]970-221-6665; www.fcgov.com; 600 N Sherwood St; $3.35; ☉10am-5pm Wed-Sat, noon-5pm Sun; [♿]) Pony rides and a barnyard of cows, turkeys and chickens make this shady riverside park a draw for families. In the summer there are storytellers and special events.

Avery House Museum HISTORIC BUILDING
(www.poudrelandmarks.com; 328 W Mountain Ave; ☉1-4pm Sat & Sun) [FREE] This 1879 home belonged to Franklin Avery, the city surveyor of Fort Collins. Avery's foresight is evident in the tree-lined, wide boulevards that grace the city center. The Avery House is a stop along the self-guided historical walking tour available from the Fort Collins Convention & Visitors Bureau (p156), with free guided tours that take you through the historic building.

**Fort Collins Museum
& Discovery Science Center** MUSEUM
([☎]970-221-6738; http://fcmod.org; 200 Mathews St; adult/senior over 60yr & child 3-12yr $9.50/6; ☉10am-5pm Tue-Sun; [P][♿]) The hands-on science exhibits focusing on electricity, physics and dinosaurs are designed for children, leaving adults some space to soak up the historical artifacts. The coolest thing on the grounds is an 1860s log cabin from the founding days of Fort Collins.

🏃 Activities & Tours

Horsetooth Mountain
Open Space   HIKING
(📞970-679-5470; www.larimer.org; 4200 W County
Rd 38E; parking permits $6; 🚻) This large hik-
ing, biking and boating area is just west of
Horsetooth Reservoir, 4 miles from Fort Collins. There are three backcountry camping
spots here, good rock climbing and plenty of
trails. Longer hikes can be had by connecting to the Blue Sky Trail or Lory State Park
(p150) trails.

Fort Collins Bike Share   CYCLING
(📞970-419-1050; http://bikefortcollins.org; Old
Town Sq; daily/weekly/annually $7/15/60, plus per
hour for rides over 30min $2, max hourly $18; 🚻)
🚲 **FREE** With locations popping up all over
town, this bike share program promises to
be a solid way to get around downtown and
have fun. The central office is located at the
old Bike Library in the Old Town Square.
Alas, the bikes aren't free anymore. But they
are nice rides, and it's a fun way to spend an
afternoon.

⭐ **New Belgium Brewery**   BREWERY
(📞970-221-0524; www.newbelgium.com; 500 Linden St; ⊙tasting room 10am-6pm Tue-Sat) **FREE**
Touring New Belgium's brewery brings you
face-to-face with the freewheeling essence of
Fort Collins' character: a tripartite passion
for beer, bicycles and sustainability. It's an
unforgettable few hours. The tour guides are
knowledgeable, smart and playful, and the
special selection of beers is among the nation's best. Reserve in advance online; tours
run daily on the half-hour.

🛏 Sleeping

⭐ **Armstrong Hotel**   BOUTIQUE HOTEL **$$**
(📞970-484-3883; www.thearmstronghotel.com;
259 S College Ave; d $129-159, studios $149-169,
q $159-179, ste $169-199; 🅿🌀❄@🛜) You'll
want to extend your stay at this elegantly
renovated boutique hotel in the heart of Old
Town. The amenities make it: a fleet of free
loaner bikes, large showers, feather duvets
and gratis wi-fi. The unique rooms have a
modern feel and it's one of the few spots
right in the action of Old Town.

Hilton Fort Collins   HOTEL **$$**
(📞970-482-2626; www.hiltonfortcollins.com; 425
W Prospect Rd; d from $200; 🅿🌀❄🛜) Right
at the edge of the university campus, this is
a pleasant and centrally located option. The
rooms are comfortably furnished, though

just a bit bland. The fitness center and indoor pool are nice touches.

🍴 Eating

⭐ **Lucile's Restaurant**   CAJUN **$**
(📞970-224-5464; www.luciles.com; 400 S Mel-
drum St; mains $7-12; ⊙7am-2pm) 🚲 Snuggled
in an old house, this restaurant is a cozy
dream - replete with creaking floors, win-
some waiters and fluffy, made-from-scratch
buttermilk biscuits. The Cajun home cookin' is fantastic; try the eggs Pontchartrain,
with pan-fried local trout, or the eggs New
Orleans, which comes smothered in spicy
sauce. Simply put: it's Fort Collins' best
breakfast.

Restaurant 415   AMERICAN **$**
(📞970-407-0415; www.thefourfifteen.com; 415 S
Mason St; mains $9-13; ⊙11am-2pm & 5-11pm Tue-
Thu, 11am-11pm Fri-Sun; 🍴) This large art-de-
co-inspired diner offers remarkable value.
The delicious sandwiches all come with
salad or soup, plus the drink of your choice.
Small and large plates such as mozzarella
fritti and steak and veggie skewers are great
for sharing, as are the pizzas. Check out the
special menu for vegan and gluten-free options.

Choice City Butcher & Deli   SANDWICHES **$**
(📞970-490-2489; www.choicecitybutcher.com;
104 W Olive St; sandwiches $7-15; ⊙7am-6pm Sun-
Wed, to 9pm Thu-Sat; 🚻) The butchers here are
straight from central casting - all forearms
and white aprons - and all of the five varieties of Reuben sandwiches win raves. They
serve dinner on the weekend, a predictably
meaty selection of American small plates
and mains.

Stuft   BURGERS **$**
(📞970-484-6377; www.stuftburgerbar.com; 210 S
College Ave; burgers $7-10; ⊙11am-10pm Sun-Thu,
to 2am Fri & Sat; 🚻) Grab a pencil and start
scribbling your dream order: the build-your-
own-burger concept succeeds through a list
of high-grade options like chipotle ketchup,
apple-cider bacon and fire-roasted chilies.
Add fresh-cut, skin-on french fries and a
good list of beer specials and lunch takes on
unlimited possibilities.

Tasty Harmony   VEGETARIAN **$**
(📞970-689-3234; www.tastyharmony.com; 160 W
Oak St; mains $7-14; ⊙11am-9pm Tue-Thu & Sun,
to 10pm Fri & Sat; 🍴) 🚲 Organic, vegetarian
dishes at this bright lunch spot are delicious,
with a menu focused on hearty sandwiches,

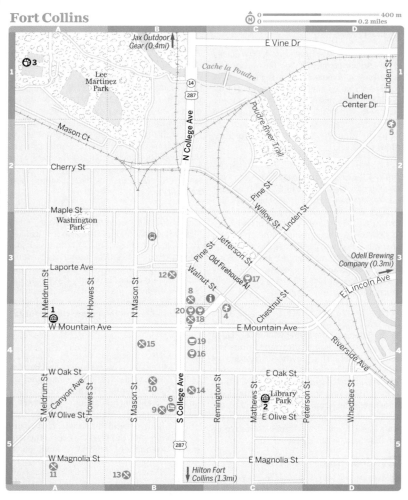

baked tofu dishes and soups. Tacos, with tempeh and Mexican jackfruit, are the highlight of the mix-and-match daily plate. End things right with the raw key lime pie.

Backcountry Delicatessen   SANDWICHES **$**
(☑970-482-6913; www.backcountry-deli.com; 140 N College Ave; sandwiches $7-10; ⊙7am-5pm; 👪) This brilliant little deli opens early so that outdoors-bound patrons can get out and on the trail with box lunches in their pack. The Pilgrim – a pile of turkey with cranberry sauce – was named one of the best sandwiches in America by *Esquire* magazine.

Austin's American Grill   AMERICAN **$$**
(☑970-224-9691; http://austinsamericangrill. com; 100 W Mountain Ave; mains $13-20; ⊙11am-9pm Mon-Thu, 11am-10pm Fri & Sat, 10am-9pm Sun) The appeal of this American grill is its simplicity. Simple ingredients, simple presentation, simple elegance...no frills, just good food and good service done right. The rotisserie chicken is the undisputed star, though going with the combo, which adds in a nicely sized order of slow-roasted ribs, is an excellent choice.

The booths by the window and patio offer great people-watching.

Fort Collins

Sights
1 Avery House Museum............................ A4
2 Fort Collins Museum & Discovery
    Science Center.................................... C5
3 The Farm at Lee Martinez Park A1

Activities, Courses & Tours
4 Fort Collins Bike Share.......................... C4
5 New Belgium Brewery........................... D2

Sleeping
6 Armstrong Hotel................................... B5

Eating
7 Austin's American Grill.......................... B4
8 Backcountry Delicatessen..................... B3

9 Choice City Butcher & Deli.................... B5
10 Jay's Bistro... B4
11 Lucile's Restaurant A5
12 Pueblo Viejo B3
13 Restaurant 415 .... B5
14 Stuft B4
15 Tasty Harmony.................................... B4

Drinking & Nightlife
16 Crown Pub.. B4
17 Elliot's Martini Bar C3
18 Lucky Joe's B4
    Mug's Coffee Lounge.....................(see 6)
19 Starry Night... B4
20 Town Pump B4

Pueblo Viejo MEXICAN $$
(☎970-221-1170; http://puebloviejocolorado.com; 185 N College Ave; mains $9-18; ⊙10am-10pm Sun-Thu, to 11pm Fri & Sat; ⊕) Something of a Fort Collins institution, Pueblo Viejo serves a sizable chile relleno that's better-than-average Colorado Mexican, but the place goes one step better with rich mole dishes, big margaritas and bottomless chips and salsa. It's a bit uneven, but always full. In the summer there's a breezy patio out back.

Jay's Bistro MODERN AMERICAN $$$
(☎970-482-1876; www.jaysbistro.net; 135 W Oak St; mains $19-35; ⊙11:30am-8:30pm Sun-Wed, to 10:30pm Thu-Sat; ⊛) Though the soft light, Frenchy paintings and jazz quartet give off a whiff of pretension, Jay's is the most sophisticated dining room in town. The menu is straight as an arrow (calamari, lamb shank, duck breast) but well executed and paired with a big wine list.

🍷 Drinking & Nightlife

Crown Pub PUB
(☎970-484-5929; www.crownpub.net; 134 S College Ave; ⊙11am-late; ☎⊕) All the dark-wood paneling, friendly barkeeps and a dead-center location make this no-nonsense watering hole a good place to cool your heels after walking around downtown. If you're too pressed for time to hit all the local breweries, this pub has a lot of local beer on tap.

Odell Brewing Company BREWERY
(☎970-498-9070; www.odellbrewing.com; 800 E Lincoln Ave; ⊙11am-6pm Mon, Tue & Thu, to 7pm Wed, Fri & Sat) New Belgium (p151) has the best tour, but Odell makes the best brew – not just in Fort Collins but in all of Colorado.

The bar is small and comfortable, and the brewers take pride in their work. If you taste but one Colorado beer, make it the subtle and perfectly round 90 Shilling Ale.

They offer free daily tours at noon, 1pm, 2pm and 3pm, with limited walk-in spaces.

Elliot's Martini Bar COCKTAIL BAR
(☎970-472-9802; http://elliotsmartini.com; 234 Linden St; ⊙4:30pm-2am Mon-Sat, 8pm-2am Sun) Tired of beer? Hit up Elliot's for an exhaustive list of high-octane cocktails. The 'Elliot's' martini is for classicists, but staff also entertain with way-out drinks – all served up in a martini glass, of course – including a tequila-based Smoke Monster, and Death in the Afternoon, a homage to Hemingway.

Mug's Coffee Lounge CAFE
(☎970-472-6847; www.mugscoffeelounge.com; 261 S College Ave; ⊙6am-9pm; ☎) Free wi-fi, strong coffee and good sandwiches keep this central, classy little place bustling throughout the day. Flat-bread sandwiches and other savory snacks are available.

Starry Night CAFE
(☎970-493-3039; www.cafestarrynight.com; 112 S College Ave; ⊙7am-10pm Mon-Thu, to 11pm Fri & Sat, 7:30am-9pm Sun; ☎) Free wi-fi and comfortable seats make this an ideal spot near downtown to take a load off, caffeinate and catch up on email. The baked goods hit the mark as well, especially the delightfully messy whipped-cream layered chocolate almond cake. For a bit more sustenance, order simple pasta salads or toast and jam.

Lucky Joe's IRISH PUB
(☎970-493-2213; www.luckyjoes.com; 25 Old Town Sq; ⊙noon-2am) Lots of wood and brick and

DAN LUCHS/SHUTTERSTOCK ©

GEORGIA EVANS/SHUTTERSTOCK ©

DAVID C STEPHENS/GETTY IMAGES ©

3

1. Black Bear (p358)
The largest populations of black bears live in areas where aspen trees propagate.

2. Elk (p359)
Some 2000 elk winter in the Rocky Mountain National Park's lower elevations.

3. Coyote (p359)
Howling coyotes commonly serenade winter campfires in the state.

4. Bighorn Sheep (p358)
An estimated 300 to 400 of these animals live permanently in the Mummy Range of the Rocky Mountain National Park.

a nightly singer-songwriter jam make this a warm and welcoming spot in the heart of Old Town. When it snows, warm up with an Irish coffee and enjoy the tunes; in summer, hit the big patio and take in foot traffic on the square.

Town Pump BAR
(☑970-493-4404; 124 N College Ave; ⊙11am-2am) A bona fide dive bar with a century of boozing under its belt, this is a comfortable place to knock back a couple of cold ones while rubbing elbows with the locals. If you go for the Cherry Bombs, beware: they're soaked in Everclear grain alcohol.

❶ Tourist Information

Colorado State Parks (☑ 970-491-1168; www.parks.state.co.us; 3745 E Prospect Rd; ⊙8am-6pm Memorial Day–Labor Day, to 5pm winter) Sharing a building with the Colorado Welcome Center, this office can arrange permits and reservations for camping in Colorado's state parks.

Colorado Welcome Center (☑970-491-4775; www.colorado.com; 3745 E Prospect Rd; ⊙8am-6pm Memorial Day–Labor Day, to 5pm winter; 🛜 ♿) Just off the highway, this office provides information about the Colorado Front Range.

Fort Collins Convention & Visitors Bureau (☑800-274-3678; www.visitftcollins.com; 19 Old Town Sq; ⊙8:30am-5pm Mon-Fri, 11am-5pm Sat & Sun; 🛜 ♿) Under the green awning in Old Town Sq, this brochure-packed information center has a helpful staff who take plenty of time with their guests. History buffs will want to get a copy of the center's walking tour, which passes buildings of historical import downtown.

USFS Canyon Lakes District Office & Visitor Center (☑970-295-6710; 2150 Centre Ave, Bldg E; ⊙9am-5pm Mon-Fri) Offers year-round information, and permits for firewood gathering and grazing. It is the hub for information on four wilderness areas, three national recreation trails, two historic districts and the Cache la Poudre, Colorado's only Wild and Scenic River.

❶ Getting There & Away

Fort Collins is 65 miles north of Denver, to the west of the I-25 corridor. Those arriving by car should take the Prospect Rd exit to reach downtown. From Boulder, take US 36 east and follow signs for the Northwest Hwy.

Fort Collins/Loveland Airport is serviced by **Allegiant Airlines** (☑702-505-8888; www.allegiantair.com) with connections through Denver, Las Vegas and Phoenix. This is the closest airport to Rocky Mountain National Park.

You can also get here via Greyhound, which has an unstaffed stop at the **Downtown Transit Center** (☑970-221-6620; www.ridetransfort.com; 250 N Mason St; ⊙7:30am-5:30pm Mon-Fri).

❶ Getting Around

This town ranks among America's most bicycle-friendly cities. There are bike lanes (and cyclists!) everywhere. To leave Fort Collins without cruising between breweries or along the Poudre River Trail would be a shame. Bikes to rent are everywhere.

Downtown Transit Center (250 N Mason St) With a customer information counter, lockers and bicycle racks, this central bus terminal also serves as Fort Collins' Greyhound stop. There is a train line from here to the South Transit Center.

Transfort Bus System (☑970-221-6620; www.ridetransfort.com) This is the town's public transportation network.

Sterling
☑970 / POP 14,777 / ELEV 3935FT

North of the I-76, Old Sterling sits in a cozy six-block grid. Edged by an active rail yard, it still has a dated brick-house charm, although new natural-gas money is injecting fresh life into the once depressed burg. When the sweet old ladies at the *Visitors Information Center* (☑970-522-8962; www.sterlingcolo.com; 12510 County Rd 370; ⊙9am-5pm Mon-Sat; ♿) in the rest area are asked what there is to see around here, and they reply with a shrug and 'Not much,' you get the feeling that this once major stop on the Overland Trail, a covered wagon superhighway that brought settlers west to the gold country, has seen its best and most historic days.

In reality, unless you are passing through town, there's no reason to visit Sterling. However, once you are here you will be rewarded with some quaint portraits of heartland America. Be sure to check out Pawnee National Grassland on your way to Fort Collins.

◉ Sights & Activities

Pawnee National Grassland PARK
(☑Crow Valley Recreation Area, Briggsdale 970-353-5004, Greeley Ranger District Office 970-346-5000, camping reservations 877-444-6777; www.fs.usda.gov; ♿) Get a glimpse of what the Great Plains may have looked like before the westward expansion in the 190,000-acre Pawnee

SOUTH PLATTE RIVER SCENIC BYWAY

If you're heading into Colorado from the northeast on I-76, one of the first spots you'll see is the Colorado Welcome Center (☑970-474-2054; www.colorado.com/JulesburgWelcomeCenter.aspx; 20934 County Rd 28; ◷8am-6pm Memorial Day–Labor Day, to 5pm Labor Day–Memorial Day). Part rest area, part information center, it's bordered by corral fencing around waist-high grass dotted with a tipi-like shade structure and a buffalo sculpture. Other than resting your weary dogs, there's no real other reason to visit Julesberg. But if you are curious about Overland Trail history, take the South Platte River Scenic Byway (www.byways.org; 20934 County Rd 28; 🚗), a 19-mile loop that circuits Ovid, the original Julesburg site and Fort Sedgewick, with pull-outs and interpretive panels installed throughout. From here, you can find dusty-bottomed back roads into the Pawnee National Grassland.

National Grassland, just 35 miles east of Fort Collins. Surrounding this semiprotected area, you'll find a patchwork of country roads, used more by frickin' frackers today than by ranchers, along with abandoned homesteads, rickety windmills and views that go on for miles in every direction.

Sterling Overland Trail Museum
MUSEUM

(☑970-522-3895; www.facebook.com/OverlandTrailMuseum; 21053 County Rd 370; adult/child $3/1.50; ◷9am-5pm Mon-Sat; 🅿🚗) You should definitely visit this museum, which sports a great collection handed down from the town's founding families. Out the front in the gravel beds are vintage plows and tractors, and inside are rooms packed with exhibits ranging from minerals to an insane collection of authentic arrowheads, plus 19th-century firearms, bear- and buffalo-skin coats, and vintage pianos, dolls and radios. It even has dinosaur fossils.

Overland Trail Recreation Area
HIKING

(☑970-522-9700; www.sterlingcolo.com; Overland Trail; ◷4:30am-11pm; 🚗) Across the road from the visitors center (p156) this concrete path follows the Overland Trail along the river for just over half a mile. According to signs you can fish small- and largemouth bass here.

🛏 Sleeping & Eating

Crow Valley Recreation Area
CAMPGROUND $

(☑970-346-5000; www.fs.usda.gov; Weld County Rd 77; RV & tent sites $13-18; 🅿) If you wish to camp in the Pawnee Grasslands, head to this campground off Hwy 14 near Briggsdale. It's not the most stunning camping ground of your life, but it is elm- and cottonwood-shaded, with potable water, restrooms

and fire pits. It even has a volleyball court and baseball diamond.

Old Town Bistro
AMERICAN $

(☑970-526-5402; www.oldtownbistro-sterling.com; 402 W Main St; mains $10-15; ◷6am-9pm Mon-Sat, 7am-3pm Sun) Arguably the best dining spot in Sterling, this little corner bistro offers up an endless list of salads, good views onto the downtown square from the large picture windows and a throwback nod to the charms of small-town America.

J & L Cafe
DINER $

(☑970-522-3625; 423 N 3rd St; mains $6-11; ◷5:15am-8pm; 🚗) A local joint steeped in country music where the men wear cowboy hats and the women talk with a hint of Western twang. It serves breakfast all day, burgers, chili and chicken-fried steak. And pie. Always pie. And strong coffee. Diner coffee. This is real Americana as you live and breathe.

❶ Getting There & Away

Sterling is 125 miles northeast of Denver off I-76. For a pretty drive, get back through **Pawnee National Grassland** to Fort Collins.

Cache la Poudre River

☑970 / ELEV 5000–10,200FT

To cruise along Hwy 14 – from the mouth of the Cache la Poudre (rhymes with 'neuter') River Canyon at Laporte to Walden 92 miles west – is a stunning venture. The ribbon of pavement winds through the foothills along the aspen- and pine-edged river in some of Colorado's most scenic country.

For those who want to camp without the intense backcountry commitment, the sites along the Cache la Poudre are the best highly accessible campsites in the west. The area

WORTH A TRIP

WILD ANIMAL SANCTUARY

This large 720-acre wildlife sanctuary (☑303-536-0118; www.wildanimalsanctuary.org; 1946 County Rd 53, Keenesburg; adult/child $30-15, guided tours per person $100; ☺9am-sunset) is about 30 minutes east of Denver by car on your way to Fort Morgan. It has over 400 large predators – including lions, tigers, bears, mountain lions, wolves and more – that have been rescued from zoos, circuses and abusive roadside attractions. The highlight of the visit is a cruise along the 1.5-mile elevated walkway (a Guinness record holder). At the end, the tiger round house gives you a pretty close view of these massive cats.

Even people who don't love zoos may like a visit here, because the animals are in very large enclosures of five to 25 acres; the elevated walkway means that humans come into less contact with the animals. There are a number of heart-rending stories and pictures along the way, documenting the path of these 'retired' animals. The new visitor center includes snack and gift shops.

Insider tip: come either right when they open or three hours before close, when the animals are most active. Yes... bears sleep in the winter.

offers stunning wilderness, a place where mule deer, elk and wild trout often outnumber human visitors. One of Colorado's biggest wildfires ever ran through here in 2012, and much of the area south of the river has been scorched.

The area is largely designated as a National Heritage Area, and the Wild & Scenic Rivers Act protects 76 miles of the Cache la Poudre River for conservation and recreation.

🏃 Activities

Thirty miles of the Cache la Poudre River are designated as 'wild' for being free of dams and diversions and having undisturbed shorelines; the remaining 46-mile protected section is designated 'recreational' – meaning it can be accessed by roads. White-water enthusiasts should check with experienced guide services or the USFS before putting into the river and finding unrunnable rapids, like the frothing Narrows.

State Forest State Park PARK
(☑303-470-1144; www.parks.state.co.us; Hwy 12 Mile 56; day passes $7, RV & tent sites $16-20) This lost piece of Colorado backcountry has mountains and alpine lakes galore, a cool backcountry huts system and even some sand dunes up north.

🛏 Sleeping

Most people camp here, but there are a few homegrown cabins. The tiny burg of Rustic, 32 miles west of the US 287–Hwy 14 junction, offers services and decent cabin lodging, but the USFS camping along Hwy 14 is the best lodging in the area by far.

You can get information at the USFS Visitor Center (☑970-881-2152; 34500 Poudre Canyon Hwy/Hwy 14) just west of Idylwilde, which occupies the handsome Arrowhead Lodge, built in 1935 and listed on the National Register of Historic Places. Of the campgrounds under its jurisdiction, Big Bend Campground is a favorite, with shady sites within earshot of the rushing water.

Never Summer Nordic CABIN $
(☑970-723-4070; www.neversummernordic.com; 247 County Rd 41, Walden; yurts $85-120) Never Summer maintains seven yurts (canvas-walled portable structures equipped with wood-burning stoves, beds and kitchens) and one cabin in State Forest State Park. They are open during the summer and winter. Connect your winter backcountry ski trip by traveling from yurt to yurt, but make sure you are safe in avalanche country.

Big Bend Campground CAMPGROUND $
(☑office 970-498-2770; Poudre Canyon Hwy; tent sites $12; ℗) Of the many quality campgrounds along the river this is a winner for its simple, shady, grassy sites and a memorable view. There are only nine sites, which fill up fast in the summer. No reservations are accepted.

☆ Entertainment

★Mishawaka Amphitheatre LIVE MUSIC
(☑970-481-9466; www.themishawaka.com; 13714 Poudre Canyon Hwy/Hwy 14; ☺summer only) Reggae and bluegrass, jam bands and folkies – this place knows how to book acts that fit the natural surroundings of the canyon environment. It holds 900 but somehow manages to feel cozy. All told, one of our favorite venues in Colorado.

❶ Getting There & Away

Your best bet is going by car. From Fort Collins, follow Hwy 14 west up through the canyon and on to Cameron Pass. After Cameron Pass you enter North Park, and can continue to Granby and Steamboat Springs.

Red Feather Lakes

Red Feather Lakes is a remote, scrappy little town in the pine-dotted hills around the Lone Pine Creek drainage, about 50 miles northwest of Fort Collins. It's far more rustic than other mountain areas and the scenery is less dramatic, but the seclusion can more than make up for it.

Nordic ski trails for all abilities offer one-hour to full-day loops at Beaver Meadows Resort Ranch (☑970-881-2450; www.beaver-meadows.com; 100 Marmot Dr 1; d $79-89, condos $139-169, cabins $109-169; ℗), which is open daily year-round.

The Great Stupa of Dharmakaya (☑888-788-7221; www.shambhalamountain.org; 151 Shambhala Way, Shambhala Mountain Center; donation recommended; ☉9am-7pm) has an electrifying energy and is one of the most significant examples of Buddhist architecture in North America. It's really powerful coming here, and worth the extra miles to get down to the Shambhala Mountain Center (☑970-881-2184; tent/dm/r/ste per person incl all meals $79/109/147/263) Buddhist retreat, which supported the creation of the 108ft tall structure. The stupa is located a short walk up from the center of Shambhala village, taking you over little bridges and past prayer flags to an arching meadow.

Fishing and lakeside USFS campsites are available at Dowdy Lake Campground (☑877-444-6777; www.recreation.gov; Dowdy Lake Rd; RV & tent sites $22-29; ☉May-Sep) and West Lake Campground (☑877-444-6777; www.recreation.gov; off County Rd 74E; RV & tent sites $22-29; ☉May-Sep). Both campgrounds are overseen by the Canyon Lakes Ranger District. About 9 miles west along 74E/Deadman Rd, there are sites at the North Fork Poudre Campground (☑970-295-6700; www.recreation.gov; 74E/Deadman Rd; RV & tent sites $14; ☉Jun-Nov). The Shambhala Mountain Center is about 30 minutes away, but is a top pick.

❶ Getting There & Away

From Fort Collins take US 287 north for 21 miles and turn left (west) at Livermore on Larimer County Rd 74E; follow it for 24 miles to **Red Feather Lakes Ranger Station** (☑970-881-2937; 274 Dowdy Lake Rd; ☉9am-5pm Mon-Fri Memorial Day–Labor Day), operated by the Roosevelt National Forest.

Walden

☑970 / POP 734 / ELEV 8099FT

Little Walden lies under the shadow of the rough Medicine Bow, Summer, Rabbit Ears and Park Ranges, at the center of an expansive 1600-sq-mile valley in a region locals refer to as North Park. There isn't much to the self-proclaimed 'moose-watching capital of Colorado,' but the north–south Main St is scattered with motels, restaurants and a creaky old movie theater. The only incorporated town in Jackson County, Walden is a modest supply point for outdoor enthusiasts and hunters looking to grab a burger and get out of the elements for the night.

Most people come to Walden and its surrounding wilderness on Hwy 14 from Fort Collins to the east, or Steamboat Springs to the west. Head north on Hwy 125 to Wyoming, or south to Granby.

Grand Lake

☑970 / POP 450 / ELEV 8437FT

As the western gateway to Rocky Mountain National Park, Grand Lake is a foil to the bustling hub of Estes Park. The charming downtown historic district has a number of friendly local cafes and art galleries. The namesake lake – with a yacht club founded in 1901 – is deep-blue glorious, and offers a different suite of recreational thrills in the summer. An amble along the boardwalk lining Grand Ave is pleasant, with a hodgepodge of corny souvenir shops, decent restaurants, T-shirt stores and a few character-filled bars.

◉ Sights & Activites

Kauffman House Museum   MUSEUM
(☑Grand Lake Historical Society 970-627-3351; www.kauffmanhouse.org; 407 Pitkin St; $5; ☉11am-5pm Jun-Aug; ⊕) The Ezra Kauffman House is an 1892 log building that operated as a hotel until 1946. Now on the National Register of Historic Places, it contains period furniture, old skis, quilts and other dusty artifacts. Hardly hair-raising, but a nice stop for history buffs.

Monarch Lake   HIKING
(www.coloradoswildareas.com/wilderness_area/
indian-peaks-wilderness; Indian Peaks Wilderness
West) A fun hike from the southern end of
Granby Lake (accessed from Hwy 6 on the
road between Granby and Grand Lakes),
takes you up to Monarch Lake, where you
can loop around a scenic alpine lake for a
4.1-mile round-trip. Routes continue up
from here into the Indian Peaks Wilderness
West.

**Grand Lake Metro Recreation
District**   CYCLING, HIKING
(☑970-627-8328; www.grandlakerecreation.com;
928 Grand Ave, Suite 204; ☉8am-5pm Mon-Fri;
📶) With good maps and information about
biking and hiking in the Arapaho National
Forest, Nordic skiing and golf, this government office serves all-season outdoor recreation information. It can also offer dog
owners guidance about getting Fido on the
trail.

Beacon Landing Marina   BOATING
(☑970-627-3671; www.beaconlanding.us; 1026
County Rd 64; 2hr pontoon rental $75; ☉10am-
6pm Mon-Sat, noon-6pm Sun) This marina on
Lake Granby, just south of Shadow Mountain Lake, can arrange pontoons, speedboats, Jet Skis and other waterborne machines for rent, and hosts guided fishing
expeditions on the lakes.

Sombrero Ranch   HORSEBACK RIDING
(☑970-627-3514; www.sombrero.com; 304 W
Portal Rd; rides $50; ☉rides depart on the hour
8am-4pm Jun-Aug; 📶) Check out this top
operation for rides in Rocky Mountain
National Park and beyond. They have trail
rides, sleigh rides, breakfast rides, dinner
rides, and stables throughout Northern
Colorado.

🛏 Sleeping & Eating

★**Shadowcliff Lodge & Retreat
Center**   LODGE $
(☑970-627-9220; www.shadowcliff.org; 405 Sum-
merland Park Rd; dm/d/cabins $25/75/120; ☉May
25-Sep 30; ➾@🤶) 🍃 Overlooking Grand
Lake, this ecofriendly mountain resort,
perched in a beautiful setting with gorgeous
views of both the lake and the mountains,
is among the best-value accommodations
in Colorado. Rooms and dorms are simple
and clean, and guests gather around the fire
or grand piano in the book-lined common
room downstairs.

Gateway Inn   INN $$
(☑877-627-1352; www.gatewayinn.com; 200 W
Portal Rd; d $100-200; P➾❄🤶) Right at the
entrance to town, this pine lodge has grand
views from its restaurant terrace. The
rooms are quite large with pine log fur-
nishings, softish beds and plenty of room
to spread out with the family. A fire pit
and hot tub outside add to the list of
amenities.

Fat Cat Cafe   BREAKFAST $
(☑970-627-0900; 916 Grand Ave; mains $5-10;
☉7am-1pm; 📶) Consider yourself lucky if
you find yourself rolling into Grand Lake
half-starving on a Sunday morning. The
Fat Cat does its breakfast buffet ($12) and
brunch with hearty expertise: biscuits and
gravy, bottomless drinks, scrambled 'Scotch
eggs' and omelets that come drooping off
the plate.

Bluewater Bakery   BAKERY $
(☑970-627-5416; www.bluewaterbakery.com; 928
Grand Ave; mains $5-12; ☉7:30am-6pm Sat-Mon,
winter hours vary; 🤶) This friendly bakery,
cafe and breakfast-slash-lunch spot offers
water views from its sidewalk tables. The
large breakfasts include savory salsa and
crisp home potatoes and are a great filling
start to a long day on the lake or up in the
park. Of course, the baked goods are another
highlight.

★**O-A Bistro**   MODERN AMERICAN $$
(☑970-627-5080; www.o-abistro.com; 200 W Por-
tal Rd, Lower Level of Gateway Inn; prix fixe $25-30;
☉7am-2pm & 5-10pm; 📶) Located on the low-
er level of the Gateway Inn, this is a favorite
of Grand Lake's dining scene. Highlights
are made-from-scratch soups and a long,
thoughtful wine list. A five- or six-course
prix fixe is the best dining experience in the
area.

☆ Entertainment

Rocky Mountain Repertory   THEATER
(☑970-627-3421; www.rockymountainrep.com;
800 Grand Ave; tickets from $35) The best of
Broadway in Colorado, this hometown
theater focuses largely on musicals. The acting isn't what you see on 42nd St, but it's
just as fun.

ℹ Tourist Information

Grand Lake Visitor Center (☑970-627-3402;
www.grandlakechamber.com; cnr West Portal
Rd & Hwy 34; ☉9am-5pm Mon-Sat, 10am-4pm

ARAPAHO NATIONAL WILDLIFE REFUGE

For bird-watchers, the Arapaho National Wildlife Refuge (www.fws.gov/refuge/arapaho) is one of the best destinations in Colorado: nearly 200 species of birds frequent the summer sagebrush and wetlands of the Arapaho National Wildlife Refuge, 105 (long, if lovely) miles west of Fort Collins by the Cache la Poudre–North Park Scenic Byway (Hwy 14). The star of the show is the sage grouse and its spring mating ritual – the lek – an elaborate, territorial display of spiked tail feathers, puffy chests and nearly comical braggadocio.

To find the Refuge Headquarters (970-723-8202; http://arapaho.fws.gov; 953 Jackson County Rd 32; 7am-3:30pm Mon-Fri) FREE head 8 miles south of Hwy 14 via Hwy 125, then 1 mile east on Jackson County Rd 32.

If you are visiting the refuge or its surrounding backcountry, the dusty hamlet of Walden is the nearest place for a hot shower and decent shelter.

Sun Jun-Aug) Has another office downtown at 928 Grand Ave (enter from the Garfield Ave side).

Kawuneeche Visitor Center (p144) For information and permits for Rocky Mountain National Park; a bit north of town on US 34.

Getting There & Away

By car, Grand Lake is 102 miles northwest of Denver. Take I-70 west to the I-40 exit and continue west over the Berthound Pass, which can be a white-knuckle experience in inclement weather. In summer get here from Estes Park on Trail Ridge Rd through Rocky Mountain National Park.

Home James Transportation Services (800-359-7503; www.homejamestransportation.com; DIA to Grand Lake $97) runs door-to-door shuttles to Denver International Airport (2½ hours). Reservations are required.

Granby

970 / POP 1200 / ELEV 7939FT

At the junction of US 40 and US 34, Granby is a convenient and authentic home-grown stop for those heading into Rocky Mountain National Park or several other nearby recreation and ski areas. The USFS Sulphur District Ranger Office (970-887-4100; 62429 US 40; 8am-5pm Mon-Fri year-round, 8am-5pm Sat & Sun summer) for the Arapaho National Recreation Area is at the east end of town and has useful hiking brochures for the Continental Divide National Scenic Trail, the Never Summer Wilderness Area and the Winter Park–Fraser–Tabernash area. It is also the place to get permits for backcountry camping in the Indian Peaks Wilderness.

Activities

Sky Granby Ranch SKIING (www.granbyranch.com; lift tickets $58) This small family-friendly ski area has night skiing, tons of beginner terrain and mountain biking in the summer.

Sleeping & Eating

Drowsy Water Ranch RANCH $$$ (970-725-3456; www.drowsywater.com; 1454 County Hwy 219; weekly rates from $2300; P) As an all-inclusive experience, home cookin', daily guided horseback rides and evening programs are all part of the weekly price here. Even though it ain't fancy, the Fosha family offers the most genuine 'dude ranch' experience in Colorado. The cabin accommodations are decked out in Western-themed coziness and it's an ideal space for families looking to escape the urban grind.

Midtown Cafe AMERICAN $ (http://granbycafe.com; cnr 4th St & Agate Ave; mains $7-9; 7am-5pm; P) For a look at the local arts scene, stop by this bookstore-art-gallery-cafe. The large open dining room fills with locals who enjoy the big breakfasts and excellent sandwiches.

Ian's Mountain Bakery AMERICAN $ (970-887-1176; www.iansmountainbakery.com; 358 E Agate Ave; mains $5-9; 6:30am-7pm Mon-Fri, to 2pm Sat) If you're just stopping in town for a bite, your best bet is Ian's, where Ian covers the breakfast burrito in a tangy sauce, turns out killer biscuits and gravy, and chats with patrons over strong coffee.

Getting There & Away

Granby is located on Hwy 40. You can get to Rocky Mountain National Park from here in summer on

Hwy 34. Hwy 40 takes you to Steamboat Springs and Winter Park.

Hot Sulphur Springs

📶 970 / POP 663 / ELEV 7680FT

When you roll through the sleepy little village of Hot Sulphur Springs, it's hard to imagine its glory days as a happening tourist destination. In the late 1860s William Byers, founder of the *Rocky Mountain News,* acquired most of the land in the area from itinerant Utes with a combination of legal maneuvering and the aid of the US Army, and he immediately began promoting it to tourists. At one time its rivalry with Grand Lake was so serious that a struggle over which town would be the Grand County seat led to a fatal shoot-out between elected officials. Hot Sulphur Springs prevailed politically, but never suffered the tourist invasion of Grand Lake – a blessing and curse, as these days it seems to be wilting in a slow economic decline.

◉ Sights & Activities

Pioneer Village Museum   MUSEUM
(📶 970-725-3939;   www.grandcountymuseum.com; 110 E Byers Ave; adult/senior/child $5/4/3; ⊙10am-5pm Wed-Sat; 🚻) This small community museum has exhibits on early settlers (both native and white), skiing and artifacts from the nearby Windy Gap archaeology area.

Hot Sulphur Springs
Resort & Spa   HOT SPRINGS
(📶 970-725-3306;   www.hotsulphursprings.com; 5609 County Rd 20; pool adult/child $18.50/11.50) Unlike the hot pools in Glenwood Springs, this spa doesn't chlorinate the water, allowing the heady mix of sulfates, chlorides, magnesium and other minerals to soothe bathers just as it has done for generations. The 24 pools have been enclosed by cement and tile and are separated by temperature, ranging from 95°F (35°C) to a deeply satisfying, if challenging, 112°F (44.4°C).

Dave Perri's Guide Service   FISHING, HUNTING
(📶 970-725-3531; www.traditionalelkhunt.com; 8hr guided fishing for 2 adults $395) A local guide operating on the Colorado River, Perri is one of the few licensed to work the excellent waters in the area. Early spring and summer are the busiest time for wading trips. In winter he leads week-long hunting trips in the Troublesome Basin Area for elk and mule deer, reached via a 7- to 10-mile horseback ride.

🛏 Sleeping & Eating

Canyon Motel   MOTEL **$**
(📶 888-489-3719; www.canyonmotelcolorado.com; 221 Byers Ave; d $64-99; 🅿🐾) If you aren't staying at the hot springs, try this roadside motel for a clean stopover. The rooms are simple, paneled with pine and extremely clean. Some have kitchens and there's a grill for guests to use.

Glory Hole Cafe   BREAKFAST **$**
(📶 970-725-3237; 512 W Byers Ave; breakfast $5-10; ⊙6am-2pm Wed-Mon; 🚻) Most of the menu is standard diner fare in lumberjack portions, but the French toast – fluffy, expertly golden slices smothered in homemade blueberry syrup – is worth a stop. It gets absolutely slammed for breakfast on the weekends, so come off-hours or be prepared to wait.

ℹ Information

Hot Sulphur Springs has no formal tourist office, but the **Pioneer Village Museum** (p162) is a good source of information.

ℹ Getting There & Away

At the foot of 12,804ft Byers Peak, Hot Sulphur Springs is midway between Granby and Kremmling on US 40.

Greyhound will make a flag stop in Hot Sulphur Springs if it's arranged in advance.

Kremmling

📶 970 / POP 1444 / ELEV 7313FT

Sometimes overlooked on the way from Denver to Steamboat Springs, the little cowboy town of Kremmling merits a quick stop to check out local restaurants, and maybe take a rafting trip. There are a couple of decent lunch spots and some antique shopping in the tiny downtown area. The town has long been known as a popular base for hunters and snowmobilers and a lot of effort has recently been made to encourage mountain bikers and rafting expeditions.

🏃 Activities

Mad Adventures Whitewater
Rafting   RAFTING
(📶 800-451-4844; www.madadventures.com; Hwy 40, Mile 185; 🚻) Making runs on the Upper Colorado and Clear Creek, this is a solid operator. The Upper Colorado has class I–III

waters and is good for families. Clear Creek kicks it up with class II–IV.

🛏 Sleeping

Hotel Eastin HOTEL, HOSTEL **$**
(📞 866-546-0815; www.hoteleastincolorado.com; 105 S 2nd St; dm $25-60, d $68-175; ☻📶) Built in 1906, this former sarsaparilla plant has cozy Western-themed rooms (Zane Grey stayed in Number 120), cowhide headboards and creaky floors. It has back-to-basic rooms (with a shared bathroom in the basement) that are highly passable.

Allington Inn & Suites HOTEL **$$**
(📞 800-981-4091; www.allingtoninn.com; 215 W Central Ave; d $117-135; 🅿❄📶🐾) The nicest place to stay in Kremmling happens to be one of the best-value places around. The rooms are modern and comfortable, there's an indoor swimming pool and breakfast is included. Book a room on the north side of the building for cliff views.

❶ Information

BLM Kremmling Field Office (📞 970-724-9004; 210 S 6th St; ⊙ 8:30am-4pm Mon-Fri) This office has information about multi-use federal land, issues permits and has maps of the area.

Kremmling Chamber & Visitor Center (📞 970-724-3472; 203 Park Ave; ⊙ 8:30am-5pm Mon-Fri, to 3pm Sat) The women at this centrally located visitor center could hardly be nicer; after chatting with them for 10 minutes you'll consider moving here. You can get information about local activities and suggestions about where to eat and sleep.

❶ Getting There & Away

This is a layover. Head north on Hwy 40, and you cross Rabbit Ears Pass to Steamboat Springs. Head east on 40 for side journeys to Hot Sulphur Springs and Granby. Head south and you'll hit Silverthorne.

Steamboat Springs

📞 970 / POP 12,100 / ELEV 6695FT

Sitting on the edge of the Western Slope, Steamboat Springs is an idyllic ski town that's unpretentious, direct, laid-back and just about as Colorado-friendly as you can get.

The ski area here is one of the best in the West, offering terrific skiing for the whole family. Summer is almost as popular as winter, with hiking, backpacking, white-water rafting, mountain biking and a host of other outdoor activities.

The action centers on the historic Old Town, where cowboys and ski bums, millionaires and dirtbags connect in the bistros, bars and old-time Western haberdasheries of this former railroad town. There's also a few choice hot springs to heal your bones after a day exploring the mountains.

The main ski area on Mt Werner is located about five miles up from town in an area called Steamboat Village. Here you will find a little resort village with hotels and T-shirt, ski and bike shops.

⊙ Sights

Fish Creek Falls WATERFALL
(🚻) Just 5 miles out of town, Fish Creek Falls is a wonderful hike for families. The 0.8-mile loop takes you to a scenic overlook with views across to the 283ft waterfall. From there, you can cut down past picnic areas, and hook up to a bridge that sits below the falls. The overlook section is wheelchair accessible.

To get here from Hwy 40, go north on 3rd St then take a right on Fish Creek Falls Rd. It's 4 miles to the parking lot and trailhead.

Pearl Lake State Park STATE PARK
(http://cpw.state.co.us; $7) A glorious spot for camping and canoeing, this small alpine lake backs up to aspen and evergreen forests, and has some excellent lake-front campsites ($20). Try to get a lower campsite bordering the lake; numbers 24 to 32 are best. They have two yurts ($80) here too, plus a short trail to Coulton Creek.

Mount Zirkel Wilderness PARK
One of the five original wilderness areas in Colorado, Mount Zirkel Wilderness is an untamed, roadless expanse dotted with icy glacial lakes and granite faces, and is rife with opportunities for isolated backcountry hiking and camping. It's intersected by the Continental Divide and two major rivers, the Elk and the Encampment. Locals swear by the Zircle Circle hike, which connects Gilpin and Gold Creek Lakes in a glorious alpine trek over roughly 10 miles.

Top hikes accessed easily from Steamboat include the Mad Creek and Red Dirt Trails, both easily accessed by following Elk River Rd north from Steamboat. Boldly rising from the center of the area is the 12,180ft Mount Zirkel, named by famed mountaineer Clarence King to honor the

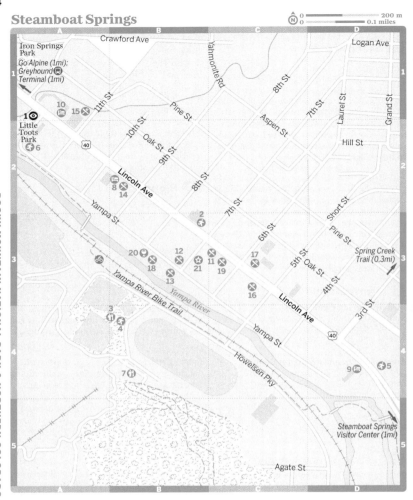

Steamboat Springs

ROCKY MOUNTAIN NATIONAL PARK & NORTHERN COLORADO STEAMBOAT SPRINGS

German petrologist with whom he reconnoitered the country in 1874. The area is *huge* and can provide a place to get off the grid, even during Colorado's busiest seasons.

The most popular entry points are in the vicinity of Steamboat Springs, though it's also approachable from Walden or Clark. Detailed maps and information on hiking, mountain biking, fishing and other activities in this beautiful area are available at the USFS Hahns Peak Ranger Office (p169).

Trails Illustrated publishes Hahns Peak/ Steamboat Lake and Clark/Buffalo Pass maps, while Jay and Therese Thompson describe the walks in *The Hiker's Guide to the Mount Zirkel Wilderness*.

Bud Werner Memorial Library   LIBRARY
(1289 Lincoln Ave; ⊘ 9am-8pm Mon-Thu, to 6pm Fri, to 5pm Sat, 10am-5pm Sun; ⊕) A perfect indoor break for families, this library has awesome interactive games in the kids' area, a sweet fish tank, free wi-fi and story time. Oh yeah, it has books, too.

Steamboat Lake State Park   STATE PARK
(☑ 970-879-7019; http://cpw.state.co.us; $7) If you like boating, fishing and bird-watching,

Steamboat Springs

⊚ Sights
1 Bud Werner Memorial Library A1

⊙ Activities, Courses & Tours
2 Bucking Rainbow Outfitters B3
  Hosted Tours Adventures
    & Lodging Center .... (see 11)
3 Howelsen Hill Ski Area B4
4 Howler Alpine Slide B4
5 Old Town Hot Springs D4
6 Orange Peel Bikes A2
7 Steamboat Springs Winter
  Sports Club B4

⊜ Sleeping
8 Hotel Bristol B2
9 Rabbit Ears Motel D4
10 Western Lodge A1

⊗ Eating
11 Backcountry
  Delicatessen C3
12 Carl's Tavern B3
13 E3 Chophouse B3
14 Harwigs B2
15 Laundry A1
16 Mambo Italiano C3
17 Steamboat Springs
  Farmers Market C3
18 Sweet Pea Market B3
19 Winona's C3

⊙ Drinking & Nightlife
20 Sunpies Bistro B3

⊙ Entertainment
21 Ghost Ranch Saloon B3

this is an incredible place to stay. The campsites ($20 to $26) on the water are pretty good, but could be a little shadier. A grouping of 10 small cabins ($90), with mattresses and mini fridges, offer some creature comforts. There are 7 miles of trails around the park, open to hiking and mountain biking.

Hahns Peak   MOUNTAIN
On the windswept plain at the base of a picturesque peak lies this quasi–ghost town, 27 miles north of Steamboat Springs via Elk River Rd (Routt County Rd 129). It was once the terminus of the railroad from Wyoming, and has a rich history as a secluded harbor for outlaws. (Rumor has it that Butch Cassidy was jailed here in a bear cage.)

Stagecoach State Park   STATE PARK
(http://cpw.state.co.us; daily passes $7) Sixteen miles south of Steamboat Springs via US 40, Hwy 131 and Routt County Rd 14, Stagecoach State Park is the nearest inexpensive camping (RV and tent campsites $10 to $24) to Steamboat Springs. The park is on the edge of a large reservoir in a good location for trips into the Flat Tops Wilderness, Sarvis Creek Wilderness and Blacktail Mountain.

In summer campers entertain themselves with fishing and a modest, 8-mile network of hiking trails, while speedboats zoom along the water. In winter camping is limited (rangers clear snow from four sites) and activities in the park include snowmobiling, Nordic skiing and ice fishing. Every year developers say they are going to reopen a ski area near here.

🏃 Activities & Tours

The nicest spring around is 3 miles from Old Town at Strawberry Park. It's open until midnight on Friday and Saturday with natural pools overlooking a stream. Most of the other spas are in the area around 13th St on both sides of the river; look for the map and brochure *A Walking Tour of the Springs of Steamboat* for more information.

★ Strawberry Park
Hot Springs   HOT SPRINGS
(⌨ 970-879-0342; www.strawberryhotsprings.com; 44200 County Rd; per day adult/child $15/8; ⊙ 10am-10:30pm Sun-Thu, to midnight Fri & Sat; ⊛) 🚗 Steamboat's favorite hot springs are actually outside the city limits, and offer great back-to-basics relaxation. The natural pools sit lovingly beside a river. After dark it is adults only and clothing optional (though most people wear swimsuits these days); you'll want a headlamp if you are visiting at this time. On weekends, expect a 15- to 45-minute wait to park.

Steamboat Mountain Resort   SNOW SPORTS
(⌨ ticket office 970-871-5252; www.steamboat.com; lift tickets adult/child $120/75; ⊙ ticket office 8am-5pm) The stats of the Steamboat Ski Area speak volumes for the town's claim as 'Ski Town, USA' – 165 trails, 3668ft vertical and nearly 3000 acres. With excellent powder and trails for all levels, this is the main draw for winter visitors and some of the best skiing in the US. In summer check out the Steamboat Bike Park.

Steamboat Bike Park
MOUNTAIN BIKING

(www.steamboat.com; Steamboat Mountain Resort; $25; ⊙gondola rides 8:30am-4:30pm Jun 10-Aug 28) Come summertime, Steamboat Mountain Resort turns the mountain into a theme park of sorts. There are plans for a mountain coaster and putt-putt golf course nearby. The real highlight is the 50 miles of bermed-out trails that extend across the whole mountain. You can pay for a gondola ride and lay waste to the trails from the top.

Wild West Balloon Adventures
BALLOONING

(☑ 800-748-2487; www.wildwestballooning.com; 42415 Deerfoot Lane; adult/child $245/175) Floating silently over the mountains is a breathtaking experience, and this 45-minute ride includes a snack and a Champagne toast. The scenery is perhaps most stunning on clear winter mornings.

Bucking Rainbow Outfitters
RAFTING, FISHING

(☑ 970-879-8747; www.buckingrainbow.com; 730 Lincoln Ave; inner tubes $18, rafting $50-100, fishing $150-500) This excellent outfitter has fly-fishing, rafting, outdoor apparel and the area's best fly shop, but it's most renowned for its rafting trips on the Yampa and beyond. Rafting trips run from half-day to full-day excursions. Two-hour in-town fly-fishing trips start at $155 per person. It has a tube shack that runs shuttles from Sunpies Bistro on Yampa St.

Old Town Hot Springs
HOT SPRINGS

(☑ 970-879-1828; www.oldtownhotsprings.org; 136 Lincoln Ave; adult/child $18/11, waterslide $7; ⊙ 5:30am-10pm Mon-Fri, 7am-9pm Sat, 8am-9pm Sun; ♠) Smack dab in the center of town, the water here is warmer than most other springs in the area. Known by the Utes as the 'medicine springs,' the mineral waters here are said to have special healing powers. Because there's a 230ft waterslide, a climbing wall and plenty of shallow areas, this is your best family-friendly hot springs in town.

Orange Peel Bikes
CYCLING

(☑ 970-879-2957; www.orangepeelbikes.com; 1136 Yampa St; bike rental per day $20-65; ⊙10am-6pm Mon-Fri, to 5pm Sat; ♠) In a funky old building at the end of Yampa, this is perfectly situated for renting a bike to ride the trails crisscrossing Howelsen Hill. A staff of serious riders and mechanics can offer tons of information about local trails, including maps. This is the coolest bike shop in town, hands down.

Devil's Causeway
HIKING

One of the most spine-tingling hikes in the area is found south of Steamboat near the town of Yampa in the Flat Tops Wilderness. The hike itself takes you over 6 miles (there and back) along a thin spine that gets as skinny as 3ft across, with precipitous 50ft drops on either side (rad!).

Howelsen Hill Ski Area
SNOW SPORTS

(☑ 970-879-8499; http://steamboatsprings.net; Howelsen Pkwy; lift tickets adult/child $25/15; ⊙1-8pm Tue-Fri, 10am-4pm Sat & Sun; ♠) Among the country's oldest ski areas in continuous use and on the Colorado State Register of Historic Places, this is a relatively modest hill by current standards – only 14 runs, one double chair, a Poma lift, a magic carpet and a boardwalk area. It's the place to go if you're minding your budget. There are 13 miles (21km) of Nordic trails here.

Howler Alpine Slide
AMUSEMENT PARK

(www.steamboatalpineslide.com; 645 Howelsen Pkwy; rides $12) Head up the lift at the Howelsen Hill Ski Area in summer for an adrenaline-pumped rip down the 2400ft alpine slide (think of it as a bobsled track but with wheels). It's a blast! You can get discounts with multiple rides. It's also fun just to ride to the top of the lift and head out on a hike.

Steamboat Ski Touring Center
SNOW SPORTS

(☑ 970-879-8180; www.nordicski.net; Steamboat Blvd; day passes adult/child $20/13) Near the base of Mt Werner, this Nordic ski center has excellent cross-country trails: some on a golf course, others through the forest. The facility also has good food – home-cooked soups and chili served with homemade bread and baked goods.

Hosted Tours Adventures & Lodging Center
OUTDOORS

(☑ 970-870-7901; www.hostedtours.com; 635 Lincoln Ave; ⊙10am-7pm) This small shack sits right on the main drag and is operated by its ultra-friendly owner, Brad. His information about accommodations, activities and the local scene is excellent.

Steamboat Springs Winter Sports Club
SNOW SPORTS

(☑ 970-879-0695; www.sswsc.org; 845 Howelsen Pkwy; ⊙10am-7pm Mon-Sat, noon-6pm Sun with seasonal variations) This century-old winter-sports club has scores of former and current Olympians as members. In winter it has programs and classes for all ages and ability levels.

Steamboat Ski
& Snowboard School   SNOW SPORTS
(☑ 877-783-2628; www.steamboat.com; Mt Werner Circle; 3-day beginner adult courses $499) There are a variety of classes for learning or sharpening skills at the Steamboat Ski Area. The beginner package lasts three days and is for absolute novices, including several hours of daily instruction and lift tickets. Serious skiers can take classes from Olympic champion Billy Kidd here too.

Steamboat Powdercats   SKIING
(☑ 970-879-5188; www.steamboatpowdercats. com; tours $600) Want to nail some untracked lines? This tried-and-true cat-skiing operator offers guided backcountry tours on Buffalo Pass. Your guide will provide you with beacon, shovel and probe to keep you safe... and the cats are heated!

★ Festivals & Events

Hot Air Balloon Festival
& Art in the Park   ARTS, BALLOONING
(☑ 877-754-2269; www.steamboatchamber.com; West Lincoln Park; ⊙ mid-Jul; ⊕) This festival sends over 40 colorful balloons into the clear skies above town, while a large arts-and-crafts show unfolds in West Lincoln Park. Call Steamboat's Chamber of Commerce for more information.

Strings Music Festival   MUSIC
(☑ 970-879-5056; www.stringsmusicfestival.com; 900 Strings Rd; ⊙ Jun-Sep; ⊕) This long-running summer music festival hosts some 70 performances through the summer across a range of genres, including rock, blues, bluegrass, jazz and chamber music. When the weather is nice you can snag cheap seats on the lawn.

First Friday Art Walk   ART
(Lincoln Ave; ⊙ 5-9pm 1st Fri of each month; ⊕) Steamboat Springs' monthly Art Walk transforms local shops into galleries and sends wine-sipping visitors along the Lincoln Ave promenade between 4th and 12th Streets.

🛏 Sleeping

Strawberry Hot Springs Lodging   CABIN $
(☑ 970-879-0342; http://strawberryhotsprings. com; 44200 County Rd 36; cabins $60-70, camping $50) Right beside the pools at Strawberry Hot Springs, you'll find rustic cabins

– including a gypsy wagon – and camping. Despite early-morning rights to the hot tubs, you are probably better off staying back in Steamboat. It has no electricity (you get gas lanterns) and you'll need your own linens. Be sure to reserve ahead. Weekend reservations require a two-night stay.

Western Lodge   MOTEL $
(☑ 970-879-1050; www.western-lodge.com; 1122 Lincoln Ave; s/d $68/94; [P][❄][📶]) The cheapest rooms in town sport an 'Avuncular '70s Cowboyist' style, clean and comfortable beds, and basic creature comforts like microwaves and minifridges. Perfect for ski bums looking to bum.

Hotel Bristol   HOTEL $$
(☑ 800-851-0872; www.steamboathotelbristol. com; 917 Lincoln Ave; d $129-149; ⊖ 📶) The elegant Hotel Bristol has small but sophisticated Western digs, with dark-wood and brass furnishings and Pendleton wool blankets on the beds. It has a ski shuttle, a six-person indoor Jacuzzi and a cozy restaurant, plus the advantage of being one of the few hotels right in the downtown area.

Rabbit Ears Motel   MOTEL $$
(☑ 800-828-7702; www.rabbitearsmotel.com; 201 Lincoln Ave; d incl breakfast $119-169; [P][❄]) A diabolically chipper, pink-neon bunny welcomes guests at this simple roadside motel. The place is smart enough to exploit its kitsch appeal, which makes many other mid-century low-rise motels so drab, by keeping the rooms bright and spotless. Rooms can be a bit smoky, but with big patios upstairs, this is still good value.

★Vista Verde Guest Ranch   RANCH $$$
(☑ 800-526-7433; www.vistaverde.com; 31100 Seedhouse Rd; per week per person from $2700; [❄][📶]) Simply put, this is the most luxurious of Colorado's top-end guest ranches. Here, you spend the day riding with expert staff, the evening around the fire in an elegantly appointed lodge, and the night in high-thread-count sheets. If you have the means, this is it.

Sheraton Steamboat Resort   HOTEL $$$
(☑ 970-879-2220; www.sheraton.com/Steamboat-Springs⃞; 2200 Village Inn Ct; d $129-179, ste $289-310; [P][⊖][❄][📶][🐾][🏊]) If skiing is paramount to your adventures here, this is a great bet. You literally walk right out of the door and onto the mountain. The remodeled amenities are standard four-star plushness: thick sheets,

flat-screen TVs and, if you're willing to pay a bit extra, great views of the mountain. After skiing, you'll love soaking in the outside tub.

Eagle Ridge Lodge
RESORT $$$

(www.steamboat.com; Eagle Ridge Dr; d from $250; P 🚗 ❄ 🛜 🐾) The style of this 40-room four-star condo-complex is clean, classic and elegant – white walls, high thread-counts, fluffy robes and stone fireplaces. In summer the huge outdoor swimming pool is delightful, and when the snow flies, the location makes it simple to get on the slopes.

🍴 Eating

Rex's American Bar & Grill
AMERICAN $

(📞 970-870-0438; www.rexsgrill.com; 3190 S Lincoln Ave; mains $11-15; ⊘ 7am-11pm; P 🐾) Grass-fed steaks, elk sausage, bison burgers and other carnivorous delights are the ticket at this place, and they're so good that you'll have to forgive the restaurant's location – attached to the Holiday Inn. Serving until 11pm, it's also the latest dinner you can have in town.

Steamboat Springs Farmers Market
MARKET $

(📞 970-846-1800; www.mainstreetsteamboatsprings.com; cnr 6th St & Lincoln Ave; ⊘ 9am-2pm Sat Jun-Sep; 🐾) 🌱 This market, held on Saturday, brings in local farmers from across northern Colorado. There are over 50 vendors selling veggies, baked goods and bread.

Backcountry Delicatessen
DELI $

(📞 970-879-3617; www.backcountry-deli.com; 635 Lincoln Ave; sandwiches $7-10; ⊘ 7am-7pm) This Colorado sandwich chain is magic: the bread and ingredients are fresh, it opens early to sell hikers and outdoorsy types box lunches, and it's staffed by a friendly crew of guys. The Timberline is a favorite around here: peanut butter, local honey and bananas.

Laundry
AMERICAN $$

(📞 970-870-0681; www.thelaundryrestaurant. com; 127 11th St; small plates $10-16, large plates $35-38; ⊘ 4:30pm-2am) This new-generation Steamboat eatery has some of the best food in town. You'll love creative takes on comfort food, charcuterie boards, big steaks, barbecue, creative presentations and pickled everything. Budget-busters will love sharing small plates – which all go a long way.

Mambo Italiano
ITALIAN $$

(📞 970-870-0500; www.mambos.com; 521 Lincoln Ave; mains $16-34; ⊘ 4-11pm) Everybody loves the Mambo. This open-kitchen concept restaurant brings new energy to Main St Steamboat. With exposed brick and an airy confidence, this may be the best Italian spot in town. Don't miss the calamari and excellent pizzas. Pastas come al dente, with a number of interesting sauce choices to go with fresh noodles.

Carl's Tavern
AMERICAN $$

(📞 970-761-2060; www.carlstavern.com; 700 Yampa St; mains $14-31) This local's favorite has great pub grub, a happening patio, live music, hot waitstaff and a raucous spirit that will get your heart thumping. It's really more bar than restaurant after 9pm, so put the kiddies to bed and get your groove on.

Winona's
BREAKFAST $$

(📞 970-879-2483; 617 Lincoln Ave; breakfast $10-15; ⊘ 7am-3pm Mon-Sat; 🐾) Arriving here during the peak breakfast hours is a mistake: Winona's creative breakfast dishes have made it the most popular breakfast joint in town. And for good reason: gooey, monstrous cinnamon rolls and plump French toast are balanced by savory treats, such as crab eggs Benedict.

Sweet Pea Market
MARKET $$

(📞 970-879-1221; www.sweetpeamarket.com; 729 Yampa St; mains $12-20; ⊘ 9am-7pm Mon-Fri, 10am-5pm Sat & Sun) 🌱 With a mission dedicated to local farmers and organic food, Sweet Pea is a welcome alternative to Steamboat's meaty scene. It stocks tons of fresh veggies and bread, and to-go items for picnics. In summer chefs also serve local, organic modern American mains in a makeshift dining room. They sometimes close shop in winter.

E3 Chophouse
STEAK $$$

(📞 970-879-7167; www.e3chophouse.com; 701 Yampa St; $30-56; ⊘ 4-9pm, brunch 8am-noon Sat & Sun in summer) Set in a glowing building overlooking the Yampa River, this steakhouse bustles to life nightly. Many just come to enjoy the happy hour, while serious dining patrons settle in around sunset. In summer don't miss an outside seat.

There's meats of all sizes and portions on the pared-back menu. Consider doing something a little more Colorado with a free-range rack of lamb or trout, if it makes the daily catch.

Harwigs
FUSION $$$

(☑ 970-879-1919; www.harwigs.com; 911 Lincoln Ave; mains $27-41; ☉ 5-10pm) This fine-dining option serves Asian-influenced French fare in elegant, candlelit environs. The mains won't blow minds – rack of lamb, duck breast with black-eyed-pea hash – but on Thai Night the prices drop and the flavors get more adventuresome. Occasionally a string quartet huddles in the corner.

Cafe Diva
FUSION $$$

(☑ 970-871-0508; www.cafediva.com; 1855 Ski Time Square Dr; mains $21-40; ☉ 5:30-10pm) Asian flavors with French preparation combine for the most exciting dinner in the Mountain Area. 'Colorado Never Ever Beef Tenderloin' comes sided with mushroom bread pudding – the best of the cold-weather menu – but in summer, fresh salads and a crab-and-tomato bisque are equally winning.

 Drinking & Entertainment

Sunpies Bistro
BAR

(☑ 970-870-3360; 735 Yampa St; ☉ noon-2am Tue-Sun; 🛜 👪) Overlooking the creek is a big backyard, where locals pack in to drink and swap tales. They can be rowdy, but it's a slice of the real Steamboat. The Texas Toothpicks (deep-fried jalapeños and onions) are a great snack at this bar and grill.

Ghost Ranch Saloon
LIVE MUSIC

(☑ 970-879-9898; http://ghostranchsteamboat. com; 56 7th St; ☉ 11am-2am Tue-Sat) The Ghost Ranch is a sure bet. Regardless of what's on stage, the crowd here is a mix of locals and visitors, and everyone seems determined to knock a few back and cut loose. The live music ranges from middling cover bands to national touring acts.

Perry Mansfield
Julie Harris Theater
PERFORMING ARTS

(http://perry-mansfield.org; 40755 County Rd 36) Keep your eyes peeled for occasional shows at this arts camp set in a bucolic setting on the way to Strawberry Hot Springs.

🛈 Tourist Information

Steamboat Springs Visitor Center (☑ 970-879-0880; www.steamboat-chamber.com; 125 Anglers Dr; ☉ 8am-5pm Mon-Fri, 10am-3pm Sat) This visitor center, facing Sundance Plaza, has a wealth of local information, and its website is also excellent for planning.

USFS Hahns Peak Ranger Office (☑ 970-879-1870; www.fs.usda.gov; 925 Weiss Dr; ☉ 8am-

5pm Mon-Sat) Rangers staff this office offering permits and information about surrounding national forests, including Mount Zirkel Wilderness, as well as information on hiking, mountain biking, fishing and other activities in the area.

🛈 Getting There & Away

Most people get into town by car from Denver via Rabbit Ears Pass on Hwy 40. Flights go in and out of the **Yampa Valley Regional Airport** (YVRA; ☑ 970-276-5000; 11005 RCR 51A), with direct flights in winter from many US destinations. The airport is in Hayden, 22 miles west of Steamboat.

Go Alpine (☑ 970-879-2800; www.goalpine. com; 1755 Lincoln Ave) This taxi and shuttle service makes several daily runs between Steamboat and Denver International Airport ($93, four hours one-way). It also makes trips to the Yampa Valley Regional Airport and operates an in-town taxi.

Greyhound Terminal (☑ 800-231-2222; www. greyhound.com; 1505 Lincoln Ave) Greyhound's US 40 service between Denver and Salt Lake City stops here, about half a mile west of town.

Storm Mountain Express (☑ 877-844-8787; www.stormmountainexpress.com) This shuttle service runs to Yampa Valley Regional Airport ($38 one-way) and beyond, though trips to DIA and Vail get very pricey.

🛈 Getting Around

Steamboat Springs consists of two major areas: the relatively regular grid of central Old Town which straddles US 40, and the newer warren of winding streets at Steamboat Village, centered on the Steamboat Mountain Resort ski area on Mt Werner southeast of town. US 40 is known as Lincoln Ave through Old Town.

Steamboat Springs Transit (☑ 970-879-3717, for pick-up in mountain area 970-846-1279; http://steamboatsprings.net) runs a free bus service along Lincoln Ave from 12th St in the west to Walton Creek Rd in the east. It also goes up Mt Werner Rd to the gondola. Though infrequent, it will also take you to a handful of towns to the west; the cost is $6 each way to Craig, $5 to Hayden and $3.50 to Milner. Check with the visitor center for seasonal schedules.

Many locals just bike around in the summer, with a fun bike path taking you from Old Town to Steamboat Village.

Oak Creek
☑ 970 / POP 892 / ELEV 7428FT

Oak Creek has the feel of Colorado back in the 1960s. The former coal town now serves as a bedroom community for people too weird, too cheap or too fringe to live in nearby Steamboat, just 30 miles north of here. There are a few vacation rentals in the town's Victorian homes, but mostly people just pass through for the day on the way to Stagecoach Reservoir or Flat Tops Wilderness (p173), having dinner at the pub, and strolling through mining-day artifacts at the museum or along Main St. Things might just change if they reopen a much-anticipated ski area at nearby Stagecoach Reservoir. Get here while the fringe still roams free.

◉ Sights & Activities

Tracks and Trails Museum   MUSEUM
(www.tracksandtrailsmuseum.com; 129 E Main St; ☉10am-noon & 1-3pm Tue-Sat summer only) Hop into this museum for a history lesson on lettuce farmers, trains and coal, baby, coal. The outside mining exhibit is the real draw.

Routt National Forest   HIKING
(www.fs.usda.gov/mbr) **FREE** Adventure opportunities abound in Routt National Forest. One of the best ways to access this massive swatch of open forest is heading up from Oak Creek to Gore Pass. Along the way you'll find a few established forest service campsites, primitive camping off the main road, trails, hikes, mountain bikes, ATV tracks and lots of spots to shoot guns at stumps (and hopefully not people).

★★ Festivals & Events

DitchFest   MUSIC
(http://ditchfestoc.com; Decker Park; $20-25; ☉Aug) Bust out the Hula-Hoop at this free-form arts and music festival, which showcases the best talent Routt County has to offer.

✖ Eating

Circle R Gastropub   AMERICAN $$
(☎970-736-1018; www.circlergastropub.com; 202 S Sharp St; mains $12-20; ☉4pm-2am Thu-Sat; ✖) ⊘ The decidedly funky Gastropub is part bar, part slow-picking bluegrass joint, part sophisticated eatery, and a central nexus of the town's local scene. Dinner is served with laser light shows in the background, and features a rotating menu that focuses on locally sourced vegetables and meats.

The steaks are ridiculously good – and sophisticated presentation is unexpected and rewarding for real foodies.

ⓘ Getting There & Away

Oak Creek is about 30 miles south of Steamboat on Hwy 131.

Craig

☑970 / POP 9464 / ELEV 6198FT

Lying on the north bank of the Yampa River between the towns of Meeker and Steamboat Springs, Craig is little more than a pit stop on the way to or from Colorado's northwest corner. The downtown stands at the junction of roads leading elsewhere: US 40 goes east–west between Steamboat Springs and Dinosaur National Monument; Hwy 789/13 runs north through desolate, rolling hills near the Wyoming Border; and 394 follows the Yampa River south to Meeker.

The main drag is Yampa Ave, but its taxidermy shops, automotive suppliers and liquor stores offer a fairly grim stroll. There are big box stores and several grocers, handy for stocking up for a trip out west.

◉ Sights & Activities

Museum of Northwest
Colorado   MUSEUM
(☎970-824-6360; www.museumnwco.org; 590 Yampa Ave; ☉9am-5pm Mon-Fri, 10am-4pm Sat; ✖) **FREE** The hats, chaps and saddles in the cowboy collection are the highlight of this community museum. But it's the handcrafted and etched spurs and hand-tooled boots that are the most cherished artifacts. It also has a small bookshop on hand with volumes on local history.

Marcia Car   MUSEUM
(cnr E Victory Way & Washington St; ☉8am-5pm Mon-Fri Jun-Aug; ✖) **FREE** This private rail car was commissioned in 1906 by David Moffat, a prominent Denver banker who owned a number of gold mines. He was also instrumental in connecting Colorado to the national rail system. You can arrange tours at the **Moffat County Visitors Center** (☎800-864-4405; 360 6 Victory Way).

Cedar Mountain   HIKING
Probably the best hike out of town, this 3.5-mile round-trip hike takes you up Cedar Mountain. To get here, head west from Craig on Hwy 40 and turn north on County Rd 7. Drive north for about five miles to the signed access to Cedar Mountain on the right.

✖ Eating

Carelli's Pizza   PIZZA $
(☎970-824-6868; 465 Yampa Ave; mains $5-12; ☉11am-9pm Mon-Sat; ✳❀✖) This simple pizza joint has an outdoor patio and a local family-friendly crowd. Pizza is the specialty,

DETOUR: ROCK ART SITES

An isolated coal and oil town on Hwy 64, Rangely is about 56 miles west of Meeker and about 90 miles north of Fruita and Grand Junction via Hwy 139. Visitors to nearby Dinosaur National Monument may wish to detour through Rangely to access the very fine rock art sites along Hwy 139 just south of town – look for self-guided tour brochures along Hwy 64 East and West – but Rangely itself is not much of a destination.

but they also make a enormous *stromboli* and serve plates of slightly dressed-up Italian fare. All told, an excellent way for hikers to carb-up before a trip into the wilderness.

ℹ Getting There & Away

⇒ **Yampa Valley Regional Airport** (p169) is midway between Craig and Steamboat Springs.

⇒ Buses from the **Craig Greyhound Depot** (🖉970-824-5161; 470 Russell St) serve Denver ($52, six hours) and Salt Lake City ($69, 6½ hours).

Dinosaur National Monument

🖉970 / ELEV 4800FT

At the end of desolate stretches of black top in the sparsely populated northwest corner of the state, Dinosaur National Monument is arguably Colorado's most remote destination, but for travelers fascinated by prehistoric life on earth, it is worth every lonely mile. It's one of the few places on earth where you can reach out and touch a dinosaur skeleton, snarling in its final pose, petrified eternally in rock and stone.

Although dinosaurs once inhabited much of the earth, only a few places have the proper geological and climatic conditions to preserve their skeletons as fossils. Paleontologist Earl Douglass of Pittsburgh's Carnegie Museum discovered this dinosaur fossil bed, one of the largest in North America, in 1909. Six years later President Woodrow Wilson acknowledged the scientific importance of the area, which straddles the Utah–Colorado border, by declaring it a national monument.

Aside from the quarry, there's lots to see here. The monument's starkly eroded canyons provide the visitor with scenic drives, hiking, camping and river running.

◉ Sights & Activities

While the fossils are pretty cool, hiking through this desolate wild space is out of this world. There are a few short trails, mostly leaving from the visitor center (p172), but you can also hike off-trail here, heading across sandstone to find adventures big and small. Bring lots of water and sun protection, plus a map and compass if you plan to go far.

★**Dinosaur National Monument** PARK (www.nps.gov/dino; off Hwy 40, Vernal; 7-day pass per vehicle $20; ⊗24hr) Straddling the Utah-Colorado state line, Dinosaur National Monument protects one of North America's largest dinosaur fossil beds, discovered here in 1909. Though both states' sections are beautiful, Utah has the bones. Don't miss the Quarry Exhibit, which is an enclosed, partially excavated wall of rock with more than 1600 bones protruding.

In summer, hours may be extended a little and you will have to take a shuttle to see the quarry; out of season you may be required to wait until a ranger-led caravan of cars is scheduled to drive up. From below the quarry parking lot, follow the Fossil Discovery Trail, a 2.4 mile round-trip, to see a few more giant femurs sticking out of the rock. The rangers' interpretive hikes are highly recommended. Plus there's easily accessible Native American rock art to see on the Utah side.

In Colorado, the Canyon Area is at a higher elevation – with some stunning overlooks – but is closed due to snow until late spring. Both sections have numerous hiking trails, interpretive driving tours (brochures for sale), Green or Yampa river access and campgrounds ($8 to $15 per campsite). The Quarry portion of the park is 7 miles north of Jensen, UT, on Hwy 149. The Canyon Area is roughly 30 miles east, outside Dinosaur, CO.

Dinosaur Quarry Exhibit Hall ARCHAEOLOGICAL SITE (www.nps.gov/dino; per vehicle $20; ⊗8am-7pm Memorial Day–Labor Day, to 4:30pm rest of year) The indoor highlight of the national monument, the dinosaur quarry wall shows off some 1500 dinosaur bones – you can see everything from allosaurus to stegosaurus. The Jurassic strata containing the fossils gives a glimpse of how paleontologists transform solid rock into the beautiful skeletons seen in museums, and how they develop

CANYON PINTADO NATIONAL HISTORIC DISTRICT

It's well worth adding a few hours to the trip between Grand Junction and Dinosaur National Monument in order to spend a few moments at **Canyon Pintado National Historic District** (www.blm.gov; CO 139; ⊘24hr) communing with these spectral, mysterious images – ghostly birds and life-size flutists. The paintings, left as inscrutable messages from the region's early settlers, create Colorado's most desolate, haunting gallery.

The images are attributed to two of Douglass Canyon's first communities: the Fremont Culture, who lived here from about AD 1 to 1300, and the Ute, who lived here from around 1300 to 1881. It was the journal of Silvestre Vélez de Escalante, a Franciscan missionary who came through on the famed Dominguez-Escalante expedition of 1776, that first named this corridor Cañyon Pintado (Painted Canyon).

Look for green-and-white Bureau of Land Management (BLM) rods that indicate the sites along Hwy 139.

scientifically reliable interpretations of life in the remote past. Ranger-led walks, talks and tours explain the site; information can also be gleaned from brochures, audio-visual programs and exhibits.

Fossil Discovery Trail ARCHAEOLOGICAL SITE
(vehicle passes $10; 🛈) This short interpretive trail is excellent for families as it's only 2.4 miles round-trip and you can reach out and touch the bones of dinosaurs. Regardless of your knowledge or understanding of paleontology, this is a stunning walk through some 65 million years of history.

Adrift Adventures RAFTING
(☏800-824-0150; https://adrift.com; 9500 E 6000 South, Jensen, UT) Head out into the riverine wilderness of Dinosaur National Monument on the Green and Yampa Rivers on one-day runs down Split Mountain Gorge; four-day expeditions on the Green's Gates of Lodore; or five days down Yampa Canyon.

🛌 Sleeping

There are no lodges in the monument, but Vernal, UT, has a good selection of motels and restaurants, and Dinosaur, CO, has a couple of each. There are designated backcountry campsites only on the **Jones Hole Trail**; otherwise wilderness camping is allowed anywhere at least one-quarter mile from an established road or trail. Lots of restrictions about backcountry camping apply, so you should register at a visitor center or ranger station. Backcountry permits are free.

Green River Campground CAMPGROUND $
(☏435-781-7700; Blue Mountain Rd; tent & RV sites $18; ⊘mid-Apr–early Oct) Dinosaur National Monument's main campground is 5 miles

east of Dinosaur Quarry along Blue Mountain Rd, with 88 sites. It has bathrooms and drinking water but no showers or hookups. A park host will sell firewood.

Split Mountain Campground CAMPGROUND $
(☏435-781-7700; Blue Mountain Rd; group sites $40, if water is not available $6) Larger groups can try Split Mountain Campground, where you'll find four group sites along the river.

Jensen Inn B&B $$
(☏435-789-5905; www.thejenseninn.com; 5056 S 9500 East, Jensen; r incl breakfast $100-125; @🛰🐾) If your destination is Dinosaur National Monument, book at the comfortable, home-style Jensen Inn B&B, three miles north of Jensen, off Hwy 40.

ℹ️ Information

Dinosaur National Monument is a 210,000-acre plot that straddles the Utah–Colorado state line. Monument headquarters and most of the land is within Colorado, but the quarry (the only place to see fossils protruding from the earth) is in Utah. There are several drives with scenic overlooks and interpretive signs, leading to a number of trailheads for short nature walks or access to the backcountry.

Information is available from **Dinosaur National Monument Headquarters Visitor Center** (☏970-374-3000; 4545 E Hwy 40; ⊘8am-5pm May-Sep, 9am-5pm Sep-May) – sometimes called the Canyon Visitor Center. It has an audio-visual program, exhibits and a bookstore. There's also a visitor center at **Dinosaur Quarry** (p171). Entrance to the monument headquarters visitor center is free, but entrance to other parts of the monument (including Dinosaur Quarry) is $20 per private vehicle and $10 for cyclists or bus passengers.

❶ Getting There & Away

The monument is 88 miles west of Craig via US 40 and 120 miles east of Salt Lake City, UT, by I-80 and US 40. Dinosaur Quarry is 7 miles north of Jensen, UT, on Cub Creek Rd (Utah Hwy 149). Monument headquarters is just off US 40 on Harpers Corner Dr, about 4 miles east of the town of Dinosaur.

Dinosaur

☑ 970 / POP 350 / ELEV 5922

Just a few miles east of the Utah border, on the doorstep of Dinosaur National Monument, Dinosaur is easy to skip. In an effort to capitalize on its location by the monument, the town changed its name from Artesia in the mid-1960s and gave the streets dinosaur-themed monikers. Junk car lots and forlorn homesteads dot the rolling hills of this windswept landscape.

Only a few things entice travelers to hit the brakes on the way through town. But in an America of roadside attractions, stopping a while to chat with the characters that inhabit the town may just make your day.

❶ Information

The well-stocked **Colorado Welcome Center** (☑ 970-374-2205; 101 E Stegosaurus St; ⊘ 8am-6pm Memorial Day–Labor Day, 9am-5pm Labor Day–Memorial Day, closed Jan & Feb; 📶 ⊕) has maps for scenic drives, and information on area rafting and camping.

❶ Getting There & Away

Dinosaur is just 2.5 miles west of Dinosaur National Monument. It sits on the intersection of Hwys 40 and 64. The intersection of loneliness is just down the road.

Meeker

☑ 970 / POP 2400 / ELEV 6239FT

The picturesque seat of Rio Blanco County, Meeker takes its name from infamous government agent Nathan Meeker, whose arbitrary destruction of a Ute racetrack precipitated a fatal confrontation in 1879. Contemporary Meeker is a small oil town, surrounded by sagebrush country where Greek American sheepherders graze huge flocks for their wool. Not many people stop here, but those who do are rewarded with fun hometown Americana, and easy access to day trips on the White River and journeys into Flat Tops Wilderness Area.

◉ Sights & Activities

Flat Tops Wilderness Area   AREA
Flat Tops wilderness sits in the White River and Routt National Forests. It protects some 230,000 acres of designated wilderness. There's over 160 miles of trail and 100-plus lakes and ponds in this wilderness.

White River Museum   MUSEUM
(☑ 970-878-9982; www.meekercolorado.com; 565 Park St; ⊘ 9am-5pm summer, 10am-4pm winter; 📶) **FREE** There's a rambling collection of eclectic Western memorabilia here: bearskin coats, a couple of peace pipes and Nathan Meeker's printing press.

JML Outfitters   OUTDOORS
(☑ 970-878-4749; www.jmloutfitters.com; 300 County Rd 75; half-day trail rides from $55, day pack trips from $300; 📶) Hosts multiday adventures into the Flat Top Wilderness on horseback, allowing guests to ride between a string of camps and get far into the brush. The excursions are rustic, but with horses, guides and a camp cook, it's a luxurious way to feel like you've worked for it. The riders here also have lots of programs for kids.

White River   CANOEING
There is excellent fishing on the primarily flat-water sections of the White River out of town. Another run further down outside of Rangely takes you clear into Utah on 100-miles of desert river, easily done in a canoe or stand up paddleboard.

🛏 Sleeping & Eating

★ **Meeker Hotel**   HISTORIC HOTEL **$$**
(☑ 970-878-5255; www.meekerhotel.com; 560 Main St; r/ste $80/125; ⊜ 📶) Gary Cooper and Teddy Roosevelt both stayed in Meeker's best hotel, which dates back to 1896. The themed rooms have Western motifs. Some have been carefully updated, like the Billy the Kid Room, while others still have a way to go.

Mexican House   MEXICAN **$$**
(624 Market St; dishes $10-18; ⊘ 11am-9pm) Try modern favorites like shrimp tacos as well as traditional enchiladas and fajitas at this decent little Mexican joint.

❶ Getting There & Away

On the north bank of the White River near the junction of Hwy 13 and Hwy 64, Meeker is 45 miles south of Craig and 42 miles north of Rifle. The Flat Tops Scenic Byway is a stunning 82-mile drive through the wilderness to Yampa.

Vail, Aspen & Central Colorado

Includes ➜

Idaho Springs 175
Georgetown 178
Winter Park 179
Frisco 185
Breckenridge 190
Copper Mountain . . . 200
Vail 201
Glenwood Springs . . . 216
Carbondale 220
Aspen 222
Salida 238
Buena Vista 241
Leadville 246

Best Places to Eat

➜ Tennessee Pass Cookhouse (p249)

➜ Matsuhisa (p233)

➜ Breckenridge Distillery (p197)

Best Places to Stay

➜ Devil's Thumb Ranch (p181)

➜ Tennessee Pass Sleep Yurts (p248)

➜ Avalanche Ranch (p237)

Why Go?

If you ask us where you can find the most trillion-dollar sights, where you can run the gnarliest rivers and charge the sickest runs, and where you can make one hike that is sure to save your citified soul within a single afternoon, we would take out the map of Colorado, trim the edges and point right to the center. Because here's where you'll find more magic per square mile than anywhere else in the state.

It's the stomping ground of war heroes and X Games athletes and the hideaway of billionaires, ski bums and gonzo fugitives. It's also patrolled by bear, elk, hummingbird and eagle, laced by trail, rail and river, and linked by free transport, epic bike paths and more friendly smiles than seems reasonable. But then again, of course people are smiling. They get to *live* here.

When to Go
Vail

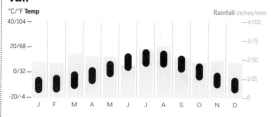

Jan–Mar Classic Colorado: fresh powder, blue skies and epic runs all day long.

Jun–Aug Long, sunny days are great for hiking, biking, paddling and outdoor concerts.

Sep & Oct Terrific lodging deals and last-gasp high-country camping amid golden aspens.

DENVER TO SUMMIT COUNTY

If you've had visions of powder or been eyeballing that snow-capped Front Range that looms magnificently above the Denver streets, then don't be surprised if you suddenly swerve onto I-70 west and hit the gas, winding your way to the doorstep of one of the greatest stretches of mountain paradise in the US. Whether you've come to ski, hike, cycle or drive the scenic byways, this is the gateway to adventure, big sky and good times – and you'll be back in Denver in time for dinner.

Idaho Springs

⚑ 303 / POP 1685 / ELEV 7526FT

Most people who are only in Denver for a limited time can barrel up the road to Idaho Springs for a quick taste of Colorado's rough-and-tumble gold-rush history. The rowdy gaggle of prospectors, gunslingers and rapscallions who rushed here to get rich in 1859 have been mostly replaced by a notably more genteel crowd of day-tripping skiers, hikers and bikers on blindingly chromed-up Harleys, but the historic buildings along Miner St retain the creaking floors and antique character of the city's colorful past.

◉ Sights

Mt Evans   MOUNTAIN
(Hwy 103; per car $10; ⊙ late May–early Oct) The pinnacle of many visitors' trips to Colorado is a drive to the alpine summit of Mt Evans, less than an hour west of Denver's skyscrapers. It was opened in 1930 and remains the highest paved road in North America. Be prepared for cool weather, even when Denver is baking hot. The road only opens in summer when conditions are safe for driving.

St Mary's Glacier   GLACIER
(Fall River Rd) Wildflowers and windswept trails, boulders and snowfields – these are the disproportionately big rewards for the easy hike up to St Mary's Glacier. It's a quick day escape from Denver, and the modest elevation gains, short distance (half-mile) and summer snow and ice make it ideal even for the littlest hikers. Although the area gets fairly busy on summer weekends, the views on a clear day are remarkable, and a scramble around the lake will bring you to the glacier itself.

☞ Tours & Activities

Clear Creek offers the closest white-water rafting to Denver, with the season usually running from June (most intense) through August (mildest). Stop by the visitor center for hiking, biking and snowshoeing tips; the website www.clearcreekcounty.org also has a good list of trails. Indian Springs has geothermal pools in a cave, though the facilities are just so-so.

Indian Springs Resort & Spa   HOT SPRINGS
(⚑ 303-989-6666; www.indianhotsprings.com; 302 Soda Creek Rd; day pass $21-23; ⊙ 7:30am-10:30pm) These hot springs are the closest soak to Denver, but if you have the time you're better off driving further for more up-to-date facilities. The geothermal pools, located in a cave, are separated by sex and are clothing-optional. Bring your own towels (one for the cave and one to dry off with). A mineral pool is also onsite.

Phoenix Mine   HISTORY
(⚑ 303-567-0422; www.phoenixmine.com; Trail Creek Rd, exit 239 off I-70; tour adult/child $10/5, gold panning $5; ⊙ 10am-6pm) One of two gold-mine tours in the area (the other is actually a mill), this one gets you underground with a former miner and is reasonably priced, too. Afterwards you can pan for gold in the stream – you won't find anything, but kids love it. Call ahead in winter and bring your own headlamp if you have one.

AVA Colorado Rafting   RAFTING
(⚑ 970-423-7031; www.coloradorafting.net; 431 Chicago Creek Rd; trips adult/child from $54/49; ⊙ Jun-Aug; ☉) One of several outfitters in town, offering a range of short rafting trips on Clear Creek (class III to class V), as well as ziplining packages.

A&A Historical Trails   HORSEBACK RIDING
(⚑ 303-567-4808; www.aastables.com; 608 Virginia Canyon Rd; 1hr ride $40, additional hour $30) Traveling through Virginia Canyon is a beautiful way to soak in the history of the area. Guided rides include a visit to the canyon's historic graveyards. Note that the stables are located several miles outside Idaho Springs – see the website for directions.

🛏 Sleeping

The Clear Creek Ranger District runs seven USFS campsites in the area; there is also plenty of dispersed camping in the National Forest. Stop by the visitor center (p178) for a

Central Colorado Highlights

1 **Breckenridge** (p190) Skiing from the tip-top of Peak 8 all the way down into the historic mining town.

2 **Aspen** (p222) Hiking to the Maroon Bells, hobnobbing with the stars and reveling in that Rocky Mountain magic.

3 **Vail** (p201) Toasting the powder in the legendary back bowls.

4 **Monarch Crest Trail** (p238) Mountain biking along the Continental Divide on one of the world's epic rides.

5 **Buena Vista** (p241) Paddling white water on the fast and furious Arkansas River.

6 **Mt Elbert** (p247) Climbing to the top of Colorado's highest peak.

7 **Copper Mountain** (p200) Hopping on a snowcat for a ride up Tucker Bowl.

8 **10th Mountain Division Hut Trip** (p228) Exploring the backcountry in modest luxury on a hut-to-hut trip.

9 **Mt Evans** (p175) Driving alongside nimble mountain goats on the highest paved road in North America.

10 **Crystal** (p221) Hiking to a postcard-perfect ghost town.

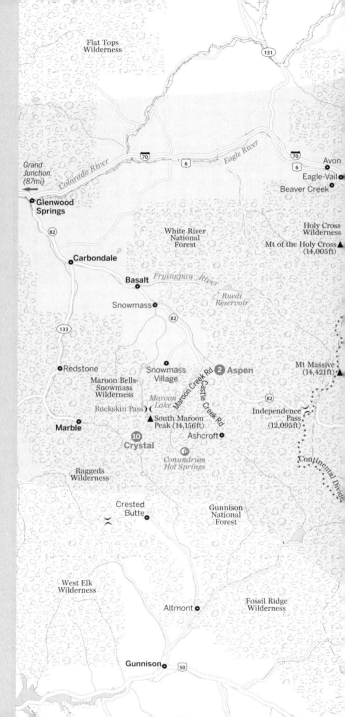

map and suggestions. Given the proximity to both Denver and Summit County, however, there's no real reason to stay here.

Echo Lake Campground CAMPGROUND $
(☑ 877-444-6777; www.recreation.gov; Squaw Lake Rd; tent & RV sites $19; ☺ Jun-Aug; ⛟) This popular USFS campground at the foot of Mt Evans is up at 10,600ft, so bring a hat and warm sleeping bag. It has both tent and RV sites along with water and toilets. Reserve.

✖ Eating & Drinking

Idaho Springs has a decent selection of restaurants catering to the steady stream of drivers headed back and forth between Denver and the mountains.

Two Brothers Deli CAFE $
(☑ 303-567-2439; www.twobrothersdeli.com; 1424 Miner St; sandwiches $6-10.50; ☺ 6am-7pm Mon-Fri, to 6pm Sat & Sun; ☏☑) The coziest cafe in town, this is an excellent option for refueling with an espresso, a smoothie or a quick meal. Breakfast wraps, fresh sandwiches and baguette pizzas are served throughout the day.

Smokin Yard's BBQ BARBECUE $
(☑ 303-567-9273; www.smokinyards.com; 2736 Colorado Blvd; BBQ from $7; ☺ 11am-9pm; ☏) Texas-style brisket, Carolina pulled pork, all-you-can-eat ribs on Monday and $2 cans of PBR ensures the parking lot here is perpetually full. Stop by for beef sliders and local brews on tap during happy hour. It's located well east of the historic district.

Buffalo Restaurant & Bar AMERICAN $$
(☑ 720-502-3121; www.buffalorestaurant.com; 1617 Miner St; mains $13-18; ☺ 11am-10pm) The buffalo burger – all-natural, free of antibiotics and growth hormones – is the way to go at this Western-style place on the main drag. The historic building gets lively at lunch, when people pack in under the bright skylights for plates of standard American fare.

Tommyknocker Brewery BREWERY
(☑ 303-567-4419; www.tommyknocker.com; 1401 Miner St; ☺ 11am-10pm; ⛟) Sores of medals from beer competitions hang over the sunlit dining space here in a testament to the expert brews. Pub food runs from buffalo burgers to brats and sauerkraut.

**Westbound & Down
Brewing Company** BREWERY
(☑ 720-502-3121; www.westboundanddown.com; 1617 Miner St; ☺ 11am-10pm) The smell of

malted barley greets you as you walk through the door into this modern space with long communal tables, brewing equipment in the back and a full dining menu from the adjacent Buffalo Restaurant (p178).

ℹ Tourist Information

Idaho Springs Visitors Center & Museum
(☑ 303-567-4382; www.visitidahospringscolorado.com; 2060 Miner St; ☺ 9am-5pm Sep-May, 8am-6pm Jun-Aug; ⛟) The visitor center contains a small but interesting display of mining history and equipment, along with some Ute artifacts. It also serves as the Clear Creek ranger office; pick up hiking and camping information here.

ℹ Getting There & Away

Almost halfway between Denver and several big ski resorts along I-70, Idaho Springs makes for a good pit stop on your way to the mountains – particularly when traffic on the interstate slows to a crawl.

Georgetown

☑ 303 / POP 1028 / ELEV 8530FT

Smaller and more soulful than Idaho Springs, historic Georgetown's mix of Victorian architecture, second-hand bookshops and cafes make it a pleasant stopover on the way up or down I-70. In summer, the town gets buzzing thanks to the day-trippers and hikers headed up the Guanella Pass Scenic Byway.

◉ Sights & Activities

Hamill House MUSEUM
(☑ 303-569-2840; www.historicgeorgetown.org; 305 Argentine St; adult/child $7/5; ☺ by appt) Originally built in 1867, this residence was renovated as a mountain estate in the late 1870s by William Hamill, who made his fortune in silver mining. Tours provide a glimpse of residential life and local tastes in a 19th-century mining town.

★**Guanella Pass
Scenic Byway** SCENIC DRIVE
Built atop an old wagon road that once connected the silver-mining towns of Georgetown and Grant, this 22-mile drive (11 miles to the pass) climbs up to 11,669ft, and is an excellent staging point for fishing excursions and alpine hikes. Sightings of bighorn sheep and mountain goats are not uncommon.

From the pass you can ascend **Mt Bierstadt** (14,060ft; 7 miles round-trip), one of the most popular fourteeners along the

Front Range. A shorter and less crowded option is Silver Dollar Lake (3 miles round-trip): this inspiring trail is mostly above the tree-line and graced with a galaxy of tiny wildflowers in summer. The trailhead is located just past Guanella Pass Campground, at 11,000ft. The pass itself closes in winter, though the road is usually plowed past the Silver Dollar Lake trailhead.

Georgetown Loop Railroad   RAIL
(☑888-456-6777; www.georgetownlooprr.com; 646 Loop Dr; adult/child 3-15yr $26/19; ☺May-Oct) Chugging along this loop is an entertaining way to leave the I-70 corridor and enjoy expansive views over Clear Creek Valley. The ride is short – only 15 minutes each way, with a pause to tour a mine in between – but the scenery from one of the open passenger cars is breathtaking.

🛏 Sleeping & Eating

There are a handful of USFS campsites, as well as free dispersed camping, off of the Guanella Pass byway. Stop by the visitor center (p178) in Idaho Springs for ranger recommendations.

Georgetown has a couple of casual cafes and restaurants that make for a nice break.

Lucha   MEXICAN $
(☑303-569-2300; www.luchacantina.com; 606 6th St; mains $11-16; ☺11am-11pm; 🛜🍴👶) The most atmospheric spot in the old downtown area, Lucha's turn-of-the-century digs were once the legendary Red Ram, frequented by the likes of Clint Eastwood and other Hollywood gunslingers. Today it serves up fresh, home-made Mexican and American staples, from fish tacos to jalapeño buffalo burgers.

Coopers on the Creek   AMERICAN $
(☑303-569-5088; 1500 Argentine St; mains $9-14; ☺11am-8pm Tue-Sun) With a menu of elk tartare and brats, duck poutine and bison ribs, this is arguably the best choice for famished hikers and skiers. Pull up a seat at the copper bar for happy-hour draft beers and cocktails. It's located at the entrance to town.

ⓘ Tourist Information

Georgetown Visitor Center (☑303-569-2300; www.georgetown-colorado.org; 1491 Argentine St; ☺9am-5pm)

ⓘ Getting There & Away

Georgetown is located off I-70, 45 miles west of Denver.

Winter Park

☑970 / POP 946 / ELEV 9000FT

Located less than two hours from Denver, unpretentious Winter Park Resort is a favorite with Front Rangers, who drive here to ski fresh tracks each weekend. Beginners can frolic on miles of powdery groomers while experts test their skills on Mary Jane's world-class bumps.

The congenial town is a wonderful base for year-round romping. Most services are found either in the ski village, which is actually south of Winter Park proper, or strung along US 40 (the main drag), which is where you'll also find the visitor center. Follow Hwy 40 and you'll get to Fraser – essentially the same town – then Tabernash and eventually the back of Rocky Mountain National Park.

🏃 Activities

In addition to downhill and cross-country skiing, Winter Park has some 600 miles of mountain-biking trails for all levels. The paved 5.5-mile Fraser River Trail runs through the valley from the ski resort to Fraser, connecting to different trail systems. Pick up trail maps at the visitor center (p182). You can even bike in winter, too – it's known as fatbiking.

Winter Park Resort   SNOW SPORTS
(☑970-726-1564; www.winterparkresort.com; Hwy 40; lift ticket adult/child $149/89; 👶) Located about 1 mile before town, Winter Park covers six main territories (3081 acres) and has a maximum vertical drop of more than 3000ft. It's most famous for those leg-crushing black-diamond bumps on Mary Jane, though there's plenty here to explore.

Trestle Bike Park   MOUNTAIN BIKING
(☑970-726-1564; www.trestlebikepark.com; 85 Parsenn Rd; day pass adult/child $46/34; ☺10am-5pm mid-Jun–Sep) When the snow melts, Winter Park turns into Trestle Bike Park, featuring three lifts and over 40 miles of free-ride trails for all levels. You can rent bikes (from $130, including gear) and sign up for lessons.

Devil's Thumb Ranch   SKIING, HORSEBACK RIDING
(☑970-726-8231; www.devilsthumbranch.com; 3530 County Rd 83; trail passes adult/child $22/10, horseback riding $95-175; 👶) Located north of Fraser, this ranch (p181) offers an abundance of outdoor adventure. In the

> ### DRIVING I-70
>
> Although I-70's mountain stretch can be downright scenic, the interstate – particularly on weekends and in bad weather – often resembles more of a parking lot than a highway. If you're trying to beat the traffic, check out www.cotrip.org or goi70.com, or the smartphone apps Waze or Colorado Roads Mobile, to get the latest on road conditions.

winter Nordic fiends descend for a scenic 65-mile network of groomed cross-country trails. Lessons and rentals are available, and they offer ice skating and fatbiking, too. In the summer it's all about the horseback riding and mountain biking on 5000 acres of Colorado high country.

Rollins Pass   SCENIC DRIVE, HIKING
(USFS Rd 149; ☉mid-Jun–mid-Nov) A popular though rugged 14-mile 4WD road leads almost to the top of this 11,660ft pass (now closed), which is famous for its railroad history. In the mid-1860s, JA Rollins established a toll wagon-road over the pass from Nederland and Rollinsville; early in the 20th century David H Moffat's Denver, Northwestern & Pacific Railway crossed the Continental Divide here.

Berthoud Pass   HIKING, SNOW SPORTS
(www.berthoudpass.com; Hwy 40) The site of one of Colorado's first ski resorts (1937–2002), Berthoud Pass (11,307ft) remains a popular spot for backcountry skiers and snowshoers. There is significant avalanche danger here, however, so don't even think about going out unless you have the proper gear and training. **Friends of Berthoud Pass** (www.berthoudpass.org) offers free avalanche courses in winter.

Colorado Adventure Park   SNOW SPORTS
(www.coloradoadventurepark.com; 566 County Rd 721; tubing per hr $22; ☉10am-10pm mid-Dec–Mar) If you or the kids need a break from skiing, the town's two tubing hills (practically right next to each other) may be calling your name. This one has a fire pit for parents and tubing runs sorted by difficulty.

Epic Mountain Sports   ADVENTURE SPORTS
(☑970-726-2868; www.epicmountainsports.com; 78941 Hwy 40; ski rental from $25, bike rental 4/8hr from $30/35; ☉8am-7pm Dec-Mar, shorter hours rest of year; ⊕) Takes care of all your ski,

snowboard and biking rental needs. They also rent snowshoes and backcountry gear (skins, avalanche beacons and probes).

☞ Tours

Dog Sled Rides
of Winter Park   DOG SLEDDING
(☑970-387-8326; www.dogsledridesofwinterpark.com; 1410 Co Rd 5; from $189; ☉Dec–mid-Apr) If you want the full-on dog-sledding experience, this is the place to go to, with five 45-minute rides (about 5 miles) a day. They also offer kennel tours and cart rides in summer.

Snow Mountain Ranch
Dog Sledding   DOG SLEDDING
(☑970-887-2152; www.snowmountainranch.org; 1101 Co Rd 53; guest/nonguest $30/70; ☉8:30am Mon & Sat Dec–mid-Apr) A more affordable option for those wanting to try out dog sledding, this is a short (2 miles) but nonetheless entertaining course at Snow Mountain Ranch (p181).

★ Festivals & Events

Springtopia   MUSIC
(www.winterparkresort.com; Hwy 40; ☉Apr) Held throughout the last month of the ski season, Springtopia is a wave goodbye to the gods of snow. Après-ski concerts, pond-skimming races (where you combine skis and icy water) and discount lift tickets for all.

King of the Rockies   CYCLING
(www.epicsingletrack.com; Fraser River Trail; ☉late Aug) The finale of the Epic Singletrack Race Series, this was the first – and remains the best – of a long summer of mountain-bike races.

Winter Park Jazz Festival   MUSIC
(☑888-409-5974; www.playwinterpark.com; Hideaway Park; ☉mid-Jul) A two-day jazz festival held in Hideaway Park in downtown Winter Park, which has been known to attract the occasional big name.

⌂ Sleeping

Robber's Roost   CAMPGROUND $
(Hwy 40; tent & RV sites $20; ☉mid-Jun–Aug; ⊛) About 5 miles outside of Winter Park on the road up to Berthoud Pass, this campsite has a partially secluded location along the Fraser River, with an elevation of 9800ft. There are 11 first-come, first-served nonelectric sites here, which usually fill up on weekends. Note that there is no drinking water available.

Idlewild Campground CAMPGROUND $
(Hwy 40; tent & RV sites $20; ☉ late May–Sep; 🐕)
While Idlewild, 1 mile south of town, may
not have the most secluded location, it's connected to the Fraser River Trail – and thus
Winter Park's extensive network of mountain biking trails – making it a very popular
choice. There are 24 first-come, first-served
nonelectric sites.

Broome Hut HUT $
(☏ 970-925-5775; www.grandhuts.org; Hwy 40,
Mile 240; adult/child $35/17.50; ☉ year-round)
Broome Hut is the first project in the Grand
Huts system that will eventually link up
Berthoud Pass with Grand Lake further
north, which will open up new terrain for
backcountry skiers and hikers. Like other
backcountry huts, you must reserve months
in advance for winter. Broome Hut is located
on the west side of Berthoud Pass; it sleeps
up to 16 people.

TimberHouse Ski Lodge LODGE $$
(☏ 866-726-3050; www.timberhouseskilodge.com;
Winter Park Dr; dm $99, d from $210; ☉ Dec–mid-
Apr; P @ 🛜) A ski-in hostel? Yes, this groovy
wooden mountain lodge is set at the base of
the ski resort on the Billy Woods Trail. Sleep
in a four- or six-person dorm, or grab a pri-
vate room with shared or private bathroom.
Rates include breakfast, dinner, tea and
shuttles to the village. It's hard to find, so get
directions first.

Vasquez Creek Inn HOTEL $$
(☏ 970-722-1188; www.vasquezcreekinn.com; 78746
Hwy 40; r week/weekend $120/180; ❄ 🛜) An in-
timate 15-room hotel, the Vasquez Creek Inn
has a touch of the Old World in its tiled bathroom floors and antique decor. There's an
outdoor hot tub by the creek, an Italian cafe
and a more formal Italian restaurant inside.

Trailhead Inn HOTEL $$
(☏ 970-726-8843; www.trailheadinn.com; 78572
Hwy 40; r week/weekend $120/180; ❄ 🛜 🐕)
A swanky refurbished motel, the Trailhead
Inn is an excellent midrange option, with re-
claimed-timber decor and wildlife watercolors
on the walls. The saltwater pool and hot tub
add to the appeal; breakfast is included.

Snow Mountain Ranch CABIN, CAMPGROUND $$
(☏ 970-887-2152; www.ymcarockies.org; 1101 Co
Rd 53; r from $139, tent sites from $40, yurts $99;
🛜 🐕) For an inexpensive family getaway
in the Rockies, this YMCA can't be beat. Located 14 miles north of Winter Park off Hwy

40, it has a plethora of activities year-round,
from horseback riding, mountain biking
and challenge courses in summer to over 60
miles of cross-country trails in the winter
(rental equipment available), plus tubing,
fatbiking and even dog sledding (p180).

Even if you're not sleeping here, it's worth
checking out for the daytime activities.

**Vintage Resort &
Conference Center** HOTEL $$
(☏ 866-239-3994; www.winterparkresort.com; 100
Winter Park Dr; r summer/winter from $129/189;
P ❄ 🛜 🐕) This 'vintage' hotel is actual-
ly in the resort's main parking lot, but for
skiers the location is better than it sounds.
In the morning you can simply hop on the
Village Cabriolet for direct access to the lifts.
Rooms are simple (think pine furnishings),
but there's a pool and many rooms have
kitchenettes and fireplaces.

★**Devil's Thumb Ranch** LODGE $$$
(☏ 800-933-4339; www.devilsthumbranch.com;
3530 County Rd 83; bunkhouse $119-149, lodge r
from $270, cabins from $450; ❄ 🛜 🐕) 🍴 The
classiest digs in the Winter Park area, this
high-altitude ranch is a fantastic base for
year-round activities (p179). Accommodations are plush, but not out of reach. The
self-service bunkhouse has the cheapest
rates, while the cowboy-chic lodge is a must
for a romantic weekend escape. Cabins are
a good bet for groups or for more privacy.

Note that the road in is unpaved; ensure
conditions are suitable for your vehicle in
the winter. Reserve well in advance. Only
certain cabins are pet-friendly.

🍴 Eating

★**Pepe Osaka's Fish Taco** JAPANESE $
(☏ 970-726-7159; www.pepeosakas.com; 78707 US
Hwy 40; 2 tacos $13-15; ☉ 4-9pm daily plus noon-
3pm Sat & Sun) You like sushi. You like fish tacos. And as it turns out, you love sushi tacos,
because...why not? At this almost-but-not-
quite Nikkei eatery (that's Japanese-Peruvian
cuisine if you haven't been keeping up), dig
in to some outstandingly spicy tuna tacos, ahi
poke ceviche tacos and blackened mahi-mahi
al pastor tacos. All served with delish fried
plantains and margaritas.

Rise & Shine Bakery CAFE $
(☏ 970-726-5530; www.riseandshinewp.com; Park
Place Plaza, 78437 Hwy 40; mains $7-14; ☉ 7am-
2pm; 🛜 🐕) Locals park their dogs out front
of this funky cafe, then head in for pastries,

AVALANCHE

For serious skiers and snowboarders, the lure of fresh powder and untracked backcountry terrain is a powerful temptation, a chance to experience that heady rush of feel-good dopamine that momentarily overrides the rest of the brain's circuitry. Unfortunately, the risks associated with backcountry skiing are hardly inconsequential – if you get caught in an avalanche, the odds are good that you won't survive.

While it's convenient to believe that most avalanche victims are naive and unprepared, Colorado's unstable snowpack does not discriminate: in the April 2013 avalanche at Loveland Pass, the state's deadliest in 50 years, not only were all the victims experienced, one was even a certified avalanche instructor.

Nevertheless, if you're going out of bounds, you need to know how to minimize risk: get trained, carry the necessary equipment and check the daily avalanche forecasts from the **Colorado Avalanche Information Center** (http://avalanche.state.co.us).

rich lattes, salads and sandwiches on home-baked bread. Wi-fi is temperamental.

Fontenot's Seafood & Grill SEAFOOD, CAJUN **$$**
(☑970-726-4021; www.fontenotswp.com; 78336 US Hwy 40; mains lunch $11-16, dinner $20-27; ☺11am-9pm Mon-Fri, 9am-9pm Sat & Sun) This place has been bringing New Orleans' tasty brand of seafood love to Winter Park for over 20 years. It has everything from fried okra and steamed mussels to crawfish and crab cakes – and these are just the starters. Main courses include catfish and shrimp (fried, of course), crawfish étouffée and gumbo.

Brickhouse 40 GREEK, AMERICAN **$$**
(☑970-887-3505; 318 E Agate Ave; mains $10-25; ☺11am-9pm) A stylish if sometimes erratic bistro with a Greek leaning in nearby Granby. It serves pizza, gyros, rack of lamb, and Greek yogurt and doughnuts for dessert. It's not your typical laid-back Colorado mountain restaurant and you won't find any microbrews on tap, but there's an air of elegance and some good wine in the cellar.

Tabernash Tavern MODERN AMERICAN **$$$**
(☑970-726-4430; 72287 US Hwy 40; mains $25-62; ☺4-9pm Tue-Sat) 🍴 One of the best restaurants in the Winter Park orbit. Set in Tabernash, just north of Fraser, this place is loved for its creativity and use of fresh local ingredients. The menu includes inspired offerings as diverse as buffalo short-rib ragù with black-pepper gnocchi and Korean barbecued pork chops served with watermelon kimchi. Reservations recommended.

🍷 Drinking & Entertainment

There are several pubs throughout town, geared primarily toward the après-ski and dinner crowd.

Idlewild Distillery DISTILLERY
(☑970-281-5773; www.idlewildspirits.com; 78737 Hwy 40, Unit 1100A; ☺2-11pm Wed-Mon) This cozy, red-walled bar and distillery features excellent cocktails made from their own spirits, plus small plates to munch on.

Foundry Cinema & Bowl CINEMA
(☑970-363-7161; www.foundry-wp.com; 22 Second St; ☺4-11pm Mon-Fri, 1-11pm Sat & Sun) Movies, bowling, wood-fired pizzas and beer guarantee fun for all ages.

❶ Tourist Information

Winter Park Visitor Center (☑970-726-4118; www.winterpark-info.com; 78841 Hwy 40; ☺9am-5pm) For maps, tips and last-minute room reservations.

❶ Getting There & Away

Winter Park gets kudos for being one of the few big ski resorts to offer free parking near the base of the mountain for day-trippers.

Amtrak (☑800-872-7245; www.amtrak.com; 205 Fraser Ave) The California Zephyr from Denver's Union Station stops in Fraser ($46, two hours, departs 8:05am) at the unstaffed depot on the corner of Fraser and Railroad Aves. The **Winter Park Express** ($39) runs on weekends and holidays, January through March, leaving from Denver at 7am and arriving at 9am; the return trip leaves Winter Park at 4:30pm.

Greyhound (☑800-231-2222; www.greyhound.com; 78841 US Hwy 40) Buses from Denver ($18, two hours) stop at the visitor center on US 40 in Winter Park.

Home James Transportation Services (☑800-359-7503; www.ridehj.com; adult/child $72/36) Offers door-to-door shuttle service between Winter Park and Denver International Airport (two hours).

SnowStang (www.ridebustang.com) Colorado's state-run bus service, Bustang, launched a pilot ski bus program in 2016. The first year saw 6am Saturday departures from the Federal Center RTD Station in Denver direct to Winter Park. Tickets were $45 round-trip.

ℹ Getting Around

Winter Park's free shuttle system, **The Lift** (www.wpgov.com), runs from the ski resort through town to Fraser; buses come every 10 to 15 minutes from 7:30am to 2am (hours vary with season). There are numerous stops.

Loveland Pass

🚗 303 / ELEV 11,990FT

The alpine scenery in the Front Range is breathtaking enough, but it's not until you make it to Loveland Pass that you really begin to feel that Rocky Mountain magic. The gateway to Summit County, the pass is flanked by a ski resort on either side – Loveland (p183) and Arapahoe Basin (p189) – and offers easy access to above-treeline hiking in the summer months.

The opening of the Eisenhower Tunnel in 1973 made the pass more of a scenic detour than a necessity (except for hazmat trucks), but if you're not in a rush, the hairpin turns bring inspiring views. It remains open year-round, though it can be treacherous in winter and will close in bad weather.

Aside from backcountry camping, there are no sleeping options here.

The only dining options here are the cafeterias, grills and bars at Loveland Ski Area (p183), which are open only in season.

🏃 Activities

Loveland Ski Area   SNOW SPORTS

(🚗 303-571-5580; www.skiloveland.com; I-70, exit 216; adult/child $71/30; ☺ Nov-Apr; 🚐) One of Colorado's older ski resorts (opened 1943), Loveland may be smaller than its neighbors, but its old-school vibe, wide-open runs, cheaper lift tickets and proximity to Denver (53 miles) guarantee enduring popularity. With a base elevation of 10,800ft, much of the terrain is above the treeline, meaning gorgeous views when the sun shines but bitterly cold winds in bad weather.

To ski off the Continental Divide, take Chair 9 up to 12,700ft – from here you can then catch a ride on the free Ridge Cat (pick up your pass first at the base) along the ridge to Loveland's high point. Access is via I-70 (exit 216).

Mt Sniktau & Grizzly Peak   HIKING

(Hwy 6; ☺ Jun-Oct) Accessible from the Loveland Pass parking lot, the short, 2-mile jaunt to **Mt Sniktau** (13,234ft) is a relatively easy hike and a good way to experience the thrill of hiking above the tree line without having to work (too much) for it. It can get pretty windy up here, so dress appropriately.

ℹ Getting There & Away

Loveland Pass is located on Hwy 6, which leaves I-70 at exit 216 on the east side and exit 205 (Silverthorne) on the west side.

The **Ski Bus** (🚗 720-924-6686; www.frontrangeskibus.com; adult/child $45/38; ☺ Wed-Sun) runs from Denver to Loveland five days a week, leaving from Union Station at 7am and the Wooly Mammoth Park-and-Ride (I-70, exit 259) at 7:30am. The return trip leaves Loveland at 3:45pm.

SUMMIT COUNTY

Home to two big-time ski resorts, the Blue River and historic Breckenridge, the aptly named Summit County is close enough to Denver for a day trip but far enough away to feel like you've truly escaped the Front Range sprawl. In summer, cyclists enjoy the endless miles of paved bike paths that connect the major towns, while hikers scale the peaks in high country.

ℹ Getting There & Away

Summit County sits along I-70, just west of the Eisenhower Tunnel. It's a mere 70-mile drive from Denver, though weekend traffic is often bumper-to-bumper and slow going at peak times.

Colorado's state-run bus service, **Bustang** (🚗 800-900-3011; www.ridebustang.com; 1010 Meadow Dr; 🛜), launched a pilot ski bus program in 2016 called SnowStang. The first year saw 6am Saturday departures from the Federal Center RTD Station in Denver, traveling direct to three Summit County destinations: Breckenridge, Keystone and A-Basin. Tickets were $45 round-trip at time of research.

More conveniently, several shuttles link Denver International Airport with Frisco, Dillon, Breckenridge, Keystone and Copper Mountain (two hours):

Colorado Mountain Express (🚗 800-525-6363; www.coloradomountainexpress.com; adult/child $66/33; 🛜)

Summit Express (🚗 855-686-8267; www.summitexpress.com; adult/child $64/32)

Peak 1 Express (🚗 855-467-3251; www.mountainshuttle.com; adult/child $60/30; 🛜)

ⓘ Getting Around

Summit Stage (☑970-668-0999; www.summitstage.com) Summit County's handy free bus service links Frisco, Dillon, Breckenridge, Keystone and Copper Mountain year-round. In winter, direct buses (Swan Mountain Flyer) run from Breckenridge to A-Basin via Keystone. In summer, bike racks (3 bikes max, dawn to dusk only) are attached to the front of buses.

Fresh Tracks (☑970-453-7433; www.freshtrackstransportation.com; to Vail $35-45) Shuttles between all the major Summit County resorts and Vail, as well as doing Denver airport runs.

Dillon

☑970 / POP 920 / ELEV 9111FT

The twin box-store towns of Dillon and Silverthorne are the first exit after passing through the Eisenhower Tunnel. While Dillon can't compete with the historic appeal of Frisco or Breckenridge, the marina and enormous Dillon Reservoir are certainly picturesque and a big draw for boaters in summer. One of Summit County's fabulous paved bike paths passes the dam and wraps around the north side of the reservoir on the way to Frisco, while the Outlets at Silverthorne draw in shoppers eager to find a deal on dozens of brand names.

🏃 Activities

Dillon Marina   WATER SPORTS
(☑970-468-2403; www.dillonmarina.com; 150 Marina Dr; 2-/4hr boat rental from $130/225; ⊙8:30am-6pm late May–Sep) Dillon's main draw in summer is the terrific marina, where you can rent motorboats, sailboats and kayak and SUP boards. If taking a sailboat, you should plan on shoving off after 11am, when the breeze generally picks up. Pontoons and runabout powerboats are best in the morning. The marina's Tiki Bar has a fab deck looking out over the reservoir.

Cutthroat Anglers   FISHING
(☑970-262-2878; www.fishcolorado.com; 400 Hwy 9, Silverthorne; half-day trips from $215; ⊙7am-7pm) River reports, gear, a variety of guided trips, fly-fishing lessons and free casting clinics.

🛏 Sleeping

Dillon offers more affordable motel-style lodging in winter than the resort towns, though don't expect anything flashy.

Prospector Campground   CAMPGROUND $
(☑877-444-6777; www.recreation.gov; Swan Mountain Rd; tent & RV sites $20; ⊙mid-May–Sep; 🐾) Dillon's main USFS campground (107 sites) is located on the south side of Dillon Reservoir, away from the traffic. It has a boat ramp and tent and RV sites, but no electrical hookups and little shade. You cannot swim in the reservoir.

Dillon Inn   MOTEL $
(☑970-262-0801; www.dilloninn.com; 708 E Anemone Trail; r summer/winter from $106/166; ❄🛜🐾) Were it not for its tremendous orientation toward those massive Buffalo and Red Mountains to the west, this stuccoed and boxy inn might not be worth considering. But it does have an indoor pool and hot tub. Rooms are simple, clean and decent value.

Ptarmigan Lodge   MOTEL $$
(☑800-842-5939; www.ptarmiganlodge.com; 652 Lake Dillon Dr; r summer/winter from $110/135; ❄🛜) The only place to stay in Dillon that looks out over the lake, rooms at the Ptarmigan Lodge all have unbroken views from their doorway. Otherwise it's a fairly plain motel disguised meekly as a lodge. Look for the Best Western sign.

Eating

Sauce on the Blue   ITALIAN $$
(☑970-468-7488; www.sauceontheblue.com; 358 Blue River Parkway, Silverthorne; lunch mains $10, pizza & pasta $12-21, dinner mains $15-32; ⊙11:30am-9pm) Backing onto the Blue River and fashioned with industrially chic decor (think reclaimed barn planks, steel siding and polished concrete floors), Silverthorne's sophisticated Italian has fast become a local favorite. Pizzas and pasta dishes come in single and family sizes – rigatoni and sausage is the specialty – or opt for a traditional main like chicken Marsala. Pizzas are half-price during happy hour.

Arapahoe Cafe & Pub   CAFE $$
(☑970-468-0873; www.arapahoecafe.com; 626 Lake Dillon Dr; mains lunch $8-11, dinner $9-24; ⊙7am-2pm & 4-10pm) The Arapahoe Cafe began life in the 1940s as a roadside cafe and motel, and it's still the grooviest place to eat pretty much any meal in Dillon. The breakfasts are filling and original, with offerings such as pork tamales and eggs – best enjoyed on the lakeview patio (weather permitting). The funky basement pub is a fun diversion after sundown.

Red Mountain Grill
AMERICAN **$$**

(☑ 970-468-1010; www.redmountaingrill.com; 703 E Anemone Trail; mains $12-22; ☺ 11am-11pm Mon-Fri, from 10am Sat & Sun; 🎄) Another of Colorado's endless grill houses. This one serves pizza and green-chili burgers all day, and Korean barbecue ribs and lobster ravioli after 5pm. The interior, with wrought-iron chandeliers and massive mountain views through floor-to-ceiling windows, makes for an attractive place to burn some hours.

Mint
STEAK **$$$**

(☑ 970-468-5247; www.mintsteakhouse.com; 347 Blue River Pkwy, Silverthorne; steaks $28-45; ☺ 5-10pm) Built in 1862, this still-dark, still-dusty saloon has tons of character, and is known for its grill-your-own steaks. That's right. You order and receive rare meat and grill it on a communal grill with the rest of the herd. If only such a gimmick came with a discount. Alas, not the best deal but certainly fun.

🍷 Drinking & Entertainment

★**Dillon Dam Brewery**
BREWERY

(☑ 970-262-7777; www.dambrewery.com; 100 Little Dam St; ☺ 11:30am-11:30pm; 🐾) This brewpub is one of Summit County's best and is certainly the most popular bar in town. The menu augments typical pub fare with dishes like pecan-crusted red trout in a maple-bourbon glaze, and pan-seared honey-sriracha salmon. There's weekly live music, and, naturally, twelve kinds of suds on tap, from a session IPA to a blackberry sour.

The place is especially busy on game days, when the circle bar, in view of the vats and several flat-screen TVs, is packed and patrolled by attentive staff.

Skyline Cinema
CINEMA

(☑ 970-468-6355; www.skyline8.com; 312 Dillon Ridge Rd; adult/child $10.25/7; ☺ 1:45-9:30pm) The only cinema in the area attracts moviegoers from Breck, Frisco and Keystone.

ℹ Tourist Information

USFS Ranger Office (☑ 970-468-5400; www. fs.usda.gov; 680 Hwy 9, Silverthorne; ☺ 8am-4:30pm Mon-Fri) Information on camping and hiking in Summit County. The office is located north of I-70 in Silverthorne.

ℹ Getting There & Away

Dillon is 70 miles west of Denver via I-70, exit 205, then 1 mile south on US 6.

Lake Dillon Water Taxi (☑ 970-486-0250; www.lakedillonwatertaxi.com; 150 Marina Dr;

adult/child one-way $10/8, bike surcharge $1; ☺ 11am-5pm Mon-Fri, 10am-6pm Sat & Sun; 🐾) The Dillon Reservoir ferry service runs between the marinas in Frisco and Dillon. Dogs and bikes welcome.

Frisco
☑ 970 / POP 2821 / ELEV 9097FT

It's almost startling to find such a cute turn-of-the-20th-century mining town, set high in the Rockies, ringed by peaks, and with another vast sculpted range flexing all the way to Breckenridge – not because it's strange to find such a soothing, tempting setting in the central Rockies, but rather because Frisco stands alone, flaunting its 19th-century history, rather than kneeling at the foot of some recently developed ski resort. Yet it's still within 30 minutes of Vail and 10 to 20 minutes of Loveland, Arapahoe Basin, Copper Mountain, Keystone and Breckenridge.

Historic Main St is a six-block stretch where you'll find almost everything you could need. There are cute inns and good restaurants, and it dead-ends at the scenic Dillon Reservoir, where you'll find a small marina. Laid-back and welcoming, with ample free parking year-round, there are a lot of reasons to fall for Frisco.

◉ Sights & Activities

Frisco Historic Park & Museum
MUSEUM

(www.townoffrisco.com; 120 Main St, cnr 2nd Ave; ☺ 10am-4pm Tue-Sat, to 2pm Sun) **FREE** Set on the site of the original town saloon in 1889, and later converted into the town's second school in 1901, this museum features a number of historical displays, including one on the Ute nation, a diorama of the original Ten Mile Canyon railroad that fed and connected the mining camps of Leadville and Frisco, and a historic map of Colorado (c 1873).

★**Summit County Bike Path**
CYCLING

(www.summitbiking.org) Frisco is Summit County's hub for fabulous paved bike paths. From the Frisco Marina you can wrap most of the way around the reservoir to Dillon (7.5 miles), for a great family trip with minimal elevation gain, and then on to Keystone (13.5 miles, 1200ft elevation gain) – or pedal around the other side and up to Breckenridge (9.5 miles, 500ft elevation gain).

Pioneer Sports
OUTDOORS

(☑ 970-668-3668; www.pioneersportscolorado. com; 842 N Summit Blvd; ski rental adult/child from

COLORADO'S BEST SNOWCAT SKIING

Ready to leave the lift lines behind and plunge through untracked powder in the backcountry bowls? Thrill-seekers should grab their avalanche beacons and fat skis for one of these snowcat tours:

Keystone (p188) Runs two separate operations: Outback Ridge ($10 per ride) and the full-day tour ($285). Powder skis/boards and lunch provided for the latter.

Copper Mountain (p200) Ride up to Tucker Mountain for soft turns and all the terrain you can handle – and best of all, rides are free (Friday to Sunday).

Chicago Ridge Snowcat Tours (p248) Ski Cooper's snowcat gets you to 2600 acres of backcountry terrain and 2000ft of vertical. Lunch, powder skis/boards, avalanche beacons and après-ski provided ($349).

Vail Powder Guides (p206) A very full day of guided backcountry skiing at Vail Pass ($500). Includes skis/boards and a yurt lunch.

Powder Addiction (☑970-726-5442; www.powderaddiction.com; off Hwy 40; $475) Only 45 minutes from Denver, this outfit provides access to 2600 acres off of Jones Pass. Avalanche gear, skis/boards, lunch and beer provided ($475).

Monarch Mountain (p239) Has 1000 acres of backcountry terrain at Mirkwood Basin, No Name Bowl and Waterdog Ridge. Lunch and skis/boards provided ($375).

Loveland (p183) After you ride Lift 9 up to the Continental Divide, head north and hop on the free Ridge Cat (Wednesday to Sunday) to take you to Loveland's highest point (13,010ft) and double-black terrain.

$18/13, bikes half-/full-day from $25/48; ⊙8am-6pm; ⋒) Good rates on ski, snowboard, snowshoe, sled and bike rentals. They also run a free Vail Pass shuttle if you opt for the full-day bike rental.

Peak One   HIKING
(Mt Royal Trailhead; ⊙Jun-Oct) A trail runs straight out of town, taking you to the beginning of the Tenmile Range. You can make this as short or long as you like, but either way get ready to sweat. It's 1.5 miles up to the ridge, where the trail forks; head right (north) to Mt Royal (10,052ft) for the easy summit.

Frisco Nordic Center
& Adventure Park   SNOW SPORTS
(☑970-668-2558; www.townoffrisco.com; 616 Recreation Way; adult/child $20/15; ⊙9am-5pm Dec–mid-Apr; ⋒) The Frisco Nordic Center offers about 25 miles of cross-country ski trails on the Dillon Reservoir peninsula east of Frisco. Lessons and rentals are available, as are snowshoes. A tubing hill ($26 per hour) is also located here and offers a good diversion for kids. The main parking lot is off Hwy 9, about 1 mile east of Frisco.

Frisco Marina   WATER SPORTS
(☑970-668-4334; www.townoffrisco.com; 902 E Main St; 2hr rental canoe/motorboat/sailboat from $40/65/120; ⊙8:30am-6pm late May–Sep; ⋒) The small marina at Frisco Bay, a small finger wandering off Dillon Reservoir, bobs with dozens of sailboats and motorboats available to rent in two- and four-hour intervals. Kayaks, canoes and stand-up paddleboards are also available (go before noon), with numerous channel islands looming at the edge of the bay providing shelter for paddlers when winds kick up 2ft swells.

☞ Tours

KODI Rafting   WATER SPORTS
(☑970-668-1548; www.whitewatercolorado.com; 908 Summit Blvd; half-day trips adult/child from $65/59; ⊙mid-May–mid-Sep; ⋒) Summit County doesn't have Colorado's best white water, but local outfitters can take you there. Alternatively, trips on the local Blue River and Clear Creek run in June and July only. Children must be seven or older. KODI also runs stand up paddleboarding trips on the Colorado River.

Trouts Fly Fishing   FISHING
(☑970-668-2583; www.troutsflyfishing.com; 309b Main St; half-day trip from $295; ⊙10am-6pm) Set on Main St is Frisco's best fly-fishing guide and retailer, open year-round, even when the rivers are ice. It takes anglers to the Blue River and across Colorado for half-day trips and full-day float trips. Rental gear available.

Sleeping

Frisco makes for a convenient and often inexpensive base from which to visit Summit County, though accommodations are limited.

Peak One Campground CAMPGROUND $
(☎877-444-6777; www.recreation.gov; Peninsula Recreation Area; tent & RV sites $22.50; ⏲late May–Sep; 🐾) Frisco's main campground (80 sites) is located on the southwest shore of the reservoir. Both tent and RV sites are available, though there are no electric hookups. If you can't get a spot here, the nearby **Pine Cove campground** (tent and RV sites $20) is first come, first served.

Inn on Galena B&B $$
(☎970-668-3224; www.friscoinnongalena.com; 106 Galena St; r winter/summer $230/150; P ❄ @ ☎) A very friendly B&B with serene atmosphere and 15 wonderfully comfortable rooms. Two hot tubs, afternoon wine and cheese, and a gourmet breakfast up the appeal.

Frisco Lodge B&B $$
(☎800-279-6000; www.friscolodge.com; 321 Main St; r winter/summer from $149/140; P ❄ ☎) On the main drag is Frisco's oldest hotel, which has been receiving guests since it first opened as a stagecoach stop in 1885. The main lodge is the original log cabin (some rooms with shared bathrooms); there's also a 1960s annex. All rooms are lovingly detailed with antiques and Victorian-inspired flourishes; full breakfast and afternoon wine and cheese are included.

Hotel Frisco INN $$
(☎970-668-5009; www.hotelfrisco.com; 308 Main St; r winter/summer from $159/139; P ☎) Comfortable and modern, the rooms here all have two-toned paint jobs, moldings and wall-mounted flat-screen TVs. King rooms are largest and brightest, and some have direct access to the hot tub on the back porch. Queen rooms are smaller and sometimes have no windows.

Eating

In addition to a handful of good local eateries, Frisco also has a number of supermarkets – stock up here if you're renting a Summit County condo. Whole Foods (p187) is a good option, with an adjacent liquor store.

★ **Lost Cajun** CAJUN $
(☎970-668-4352; www.thelostcajun.com; 204 Main St; mains $10-17; ⏲11am-9pm; ☎ 👪) Convivial waitstaff and a festive Louisiana soundtrack greet hungry diners here. First-timers are rewarded with five samples to help them decide (or prolong indecision) – tasty offerings from the open kitchen include jambalaya, chicken and sausage gumbo and some seriously good lobster bisque. Abita beer seals the deal. There are now several branches in Colorado, but this was the first.

Whole Foods SUPERMARKET $
(☎970-668-9400; 261 Lusher Ct; ⏲8am-9pm) A branch of the national chain is Summit County's most diverse grocery store, with plenty of eat-in and takeout options to boot.

Log Cabin AMERICAN $
(☎970-668-3947; www.logcabinfrisco.com; 121 Main St; mains $7-14; ⏲7am-2:30pm) Every town has one – the unequivocal champion of all things breakfast. In Frisco, it's Log Cabin. Come for sassy, no-nonsense servers, bomb French toast, gold-medal-worthy huevos rancheros, and pan-fried Cajun trout and eggs.

Himalayan Cuisine INDIAN $
(☎970-668-3330; 409 Main St; lunch buffet $8, dinner $13-16; ⏲11am-2:30pm & 5-9:30pm Mon-Sat, 5-9:30pm Sun) No, the name doesn't leave a lot to the imagination, but so what? Here's a little ray of Himalayan sunshine in the Rockies and a welcome change from burgers and pizzas.

Butterhorn Bakery & Cafe CAFE $
(☎970-668-3997; www.butterhornbakery.com; 408 Main St; mains $8-11; ⏲7:30am-2:30pm; 🌶 👪) This fun, bright and funky pastel-brushed diner is always packed for breakfast and lunch. In addition to house-baked breads, bagels and croissants, it does great breakfasts, salads and a variety of sandwiches, from BLTs to muffalettas (New Orleans–style sandwiches) and turkey Reubens, plus a couple of vegan options.

Bagali's ITALIAN $$
(☎970-668-0601; www.bagalisfrisco.com; 320 Main St; pizzas $12-15, mains $20-35; ⏲4-9pm; 👪) This cute bistro serves tasty artisan pizzas and specialties such as Colorado bass in brown butter and linguine with mussels and shrimp.

Vinny's ITALIAN $$$
(☎970-668-0340; www.vinnysfriscorestaurant.com; 310 Main St, 2nd fl; pub mains $10-16, dinner mains $20-32; ⏲2-10pm Tue-Sun) The locals' choice for tasty mains (such as duck confit)

and authentic pasta dishes – best enjoyed at the small bar – which has a devoted following and is always loads of fun. Reserve for a table in the more formal dining room.

Drinking & Nightlife

Prosit BAR
(970-668-3688; www.prostfinebeers.com; 313 Main St; 11am-10pm) Frisco's welcoming Bavarian beer hall boasts pretzels, a great selection of bratwurst (from elk and bison to veggie and frankfurters) and plenty of German beers on tap or by the bottle.

Island Grill BAR
(970-668-9999; www.islandgrillfrisco.com; 900 E Main St; 11:30am-7pm late May–early Sep) Overlooking Frisco Bay, this all-outdoor marina bar has a fantastic rooftop deck and downstairs patio bar. It stakes its reputation on blended island cocktails, New Belgium beers on tap and reggae on the stereo. It occasionally has live music. (There's food too, but you're better off eating elsewhere.)

Information

Information Center (800-424-1554; www.townoffrisco.com; 300 Main St; 9am-5pm;) Frisco's visitor center is set in the town's original town hall.

Getting There & Away

From Denver, take I-70 west 72 miles to exit 203 (the commercial center) or exit 201 (Main St). Buses arrive at the Transit Center in Frisco's commercial center; you'll need to catch a free **Summit Stage** (p184) bus to Main St or elsewhere in Summit County.

Bustang (p183) Hop on the CDOT bus to Frisco at Denver's Union Station; two departures daily at 3:10pm and 5:40pm ($12, 1¾ hours).

Greyhound (800-231-2222; www.greyhound.com; 1010 Meadow Dr) Buses traveling I-70 on the way to and from Denver ($15, 1¾ hours) stop in Frisco.

Lake Dillon Water Taxi (970-486-0250; www.dillontaxi.com; Main St & Summit Blvd; adult/child $10/8, bike surcharge $1; 11am-5pm Mon-Fri, 10am-6pm Sat & Sun;) Dillon Reservoir's ferry service runs between the marinas in Frisco and Dillon. Dogs and bikes welcome.

Keystone Resort

970 / POP 1079 / ELEV 9280FT

In operation since 1970, Keystone is a family-oriented ski resort on the Snake River 5 miles east of Dillon on US Hwy 6. Almost all of its accommodations, restaurants and services are owned and operated by a single company (the eerily ubiquitous Vail Resorts). As a result, the base area lacks the character and variety of nearby Breckenridge – although it's been well planned and is easy to make reservations and get information.

The main base area is known as River Run Village; a second base area is Mountain House, which serves true beginners and is less crowded. Although you can access some 100 miles of bike trails from Keystone, it's mostly a ghost town in summer.

Tours & Activities

Keystone Ski Area SNOW SPORTS
(www.keystoneresort.com; Hwy 6; adult/child $146/85; 8:30am-4pm Nov–mid-Apr, to 8pm most days Dec-Mar;) Keystone is known as a family-friendly resort with plenty of groomed greenies and blues (and an enormous snow fort), but don't be fooled into thinking that the terrain here is tame – with 3087 skiable acres and a 3128ft vertical drop, it's unlikely you'll get bored, regardless of your ability. There are three main mountains: Dercum (frontside), the Outpost and the Outback; it's also the only Summit County resort to offer night skiing.

Keystone Nordic Center SNOW SPORTS
(970-496-4275; www.keystoneresort.com; 155 River Course Dr; adult/child $15/free, rental packages $23; 9am-4pm Dec–Mar) Nine miles of groomed trails for cross-country skiing and snowshoeing, plus access to trails in the White River National Forest. It's located between the ski resort and Dillon.

Keystone Snowcat Tours SNOW SPORTS
(970-496-4386; www.keystoneresort.com; full-day tour $285) Access Keystone's most remote and challenging terrain on a full-day snowcat tour (12 people max). Includes lunch and powder-ski rentals; you should be comfortable skiing any type of terrain. Book well in advance.

Sleeping

Keystone has six main village areas, all of which offer a variety of condo-style lodging booked through the resort. A free shuttle system serves all villages in winter. If you prefer hotel-style rooms, try the Keystone Lodge & Spa (p189) or the Inn at Keystone (p189).

Ski Tip Lodge B&B $$$

(☑970-496-4950; 764 Montezuma Rd; r from $270; [P][🐾]) A historic 1800s stagecoach stop with an authentic log-cabin ambience and 10 country-style rooms. Breakfast is included, but it's the dinner that has everyone raving.

Inn at Keystone HOTEL $$$

(☑970-496-4825; www.keystoneresort.com; 23044 Hwy 6; r from $259; [P][🐾][🍽]) Though it's not the most luxurious choice, the Inn at Keystone is located at Mountain House, meaning you can walk to the beginner lifts.

Keystone Lodge & Spa HOTEL $$$

(☑970-496-2316; www.keystoneresort.com; 22101 Hwy 6; r from $249; [P][🐾][🍽][🏊]) At Lakeside Village. Offers hotel-style accommodations with comfortable rooms, pool and spa, with shuttles to take you to and from the slopes.

✖ Eating

There are more than 30 restaurants sprinkled throughout the resort, though the offerings are all fairly tame.

Inxpot CAFE $

(www.inxpot.com; 195 River Run Rd; mains $12; ⏱7am-5pm Sun-Tue, to 9pm Wed-Sat) This groovy, hippie-run, rock 'n' roll coffeehouse does righteous breakfast sandwiches and jet-fueled coffee, plus soups and sandwiches for lunch. It has a book nook, too.

Kickapoo Tavern AMERICAN $$

(☑970-468-0922; www.kickapootavern.com; 129 River Run Rd; mains lunch $12-19, dinner $19-25; ⏱11am-10pm; [🍺]) Your basic, friendly Colorado eatery, with veggie, buffalo and beef burgers, brisket sandwiches, rib baskets, wraps and burritos. Located at the base of the gondola in River Run.

Ski Tip Lodge AMERICAN $$$

(☑800-354-4386; 764 Montezuma Rd; 4-course meal $74; ⏱5:45pm & 8pm mid-Nov–mid-Apr & Jun-Aug) A veritable piece of Rocky Mountain history, this delightful, 19th-century log-cabin stagecoach stop has a roaring fire inside and delectable cuisine on the menu. Think herb-crusted Colorado lamb chops with black garlic risotto, or chai-spice smoked duck breast with green-onion barley. Reserve ahead for one of the two evening sittings.

❶ Getting There & Away

Keystone is located 75 miles west of Denver. Take exit 205 (Silverthorne) off I-70 and follow Hwy 6 east – don't go over Loveland Pass unless you plan on taking the scenic route. There are several free parking lots.

Summit County's free bus service (p184) links Keystone with Breckenridge and Arapahoe Basin in winter (via the Swan Mountain Flyer route) and with Dillon and Silverthorne year-round.

Arapahoe Basin Ski Area

☑970 / ELEV 10,780FT

Simple and rugged, this downbeat, old-school ski resort known as A-Basin has a 'don't bother me with the latest ski fashion, just get me onto the mountain' character. Offering up some of North America's highest in-bounds ski terrain, this is the local pick to ride, especially when temps warm up enough for large tailgate cookouts and parties in the parking lot. It's the last resort standing in spring, often staying open into June.

There are no accommodations at A-Basin.

Arapahoe Basin Ski Area SNOW SPORTS

(☑970-468-0718; www.arapahoebasin.com; Hwy 6; lift pass adult/child 6-14yr $92/45; ⏱9am-4pm Mon-Fri, from 8:30am Sat & Sun) Filled with steeps, chutes and walls, A-Basin can't be beat for thrilling descents. The back bowl, known as Montezuma, is where you'll find two dozen or so hair-raising intermediate-to-expert runs. The Jump is the biggest, baddest run on Montezuma, beginning with a 10ft drop off the mountain's ledge onto a steep 35-degree slope.

Black Mountain Lodge, the complex with all of A-Basin's dining options, runs a Full Moon Snowshoe Dinner Series ($70 to $88), where you can hike beneath the full moon and dine from lavish buffets inspired by the great mountain ranges of the world.

The lodge's Sixt Alley Bar is an après-ski favorite, with legendary Bloody Marys.

❶ Getting There & Away

A-Basin is located 80 miles west of Denver. Take exit 205 (Silverthorne) off I-70, and follow Hwy 6 east past Keystone. Going via Loveland Pass is shorter in terms of distance, though the drive itself is often longer and the pass closes in bad weather.

Summit County's free **bus service** (p184) links A-Basin with Breckenridge and Keystone in winter, on the Swan Mountain Flyer route.

Breckenridge

☎ 970 / POP 4648 / ELEV 9600FT

Set at the foot of the marvelous Tenmile Range, Breck is a surviving mining town with a vibrant historic district. The down-to-earth vibe is a refreshing change from Colorado's glitzier resorts, and the family-friendly ski runs and gold-nugget history make it Summit County's most atmospheric destination. Regardless of whether it's snow or shine, the BreckConnect Gondola up to the base of Peak 8 is where the fun begins.

The vast, hulking mountains here rise and fall, merging seamlessly into one another to present a perfect alpine backdrop. Laced with ski runs and hiking trails and stitched together with pine groves, they blaze gold in the morning, glow pink at dusk and fade into a deep shadowy blue as the sky pales then darkens, revealing endless stars best viewed from a frothing hot tub next to the roaring Blue River.

Like other Central Rockies towns, Breckenridge was blessed twice with sought-after natural resources. The first time, the masses came searching for gold buried in the peaks surrounding town. The second time it was for the snow-capped mountains themselves.

It all started with the discovery of gold along the South Platte River and in nearby Idaho Springs in 1859. Later that same summer, gold was discovered along the Blue River, which bisects present-day Breck. Now, where there's miners there's will be whiskey; the first bar, the Gold Pan Saloon, opened on Main St in 1859. It still stands and is the longest-tenured business in town. For the next several decades the town grew, acquired the first post office between the Continental Divide and Salt Lake City, saw the Southern Pacific Railroad arrive in town and nurtured its share of historic characters – folks like Edwin Carter and Barney Ford, an escaped slave turned pioneer, then entrepreneur, then politician.

In 1945, the Country Boy Mine, the last of its breed, closed down; without jobs or industry the population of Breckenridge crashed to just over 300 people in 1960. Then in July 1961 a permit was granted to build and open a ski resort in the mountains behind Breckenridge. The first lift opened on December 16, 1961, and more than 17,000 skiers visited Peak 8 that first season. Peak 9 opened in 1971 and 10 years later the world's first high-speed quad lift opened on Peak 9.

The resort innovated further in 1984 when it became the first ski resort open to snowboarders. (It even hosted the first Snowboarding World Cup on Peak 10 in 1985.) In 1997 Breckenridge and Keystone merged with Vail and Beaver Creek to form the present-day conglomerate, Vail Resorts.

◉ Sights

Breckenridge's intriguing boomtown history – well preserved by the unsung heroes at the Breckenridge Heritage Alliance (www.breckheritage.com) – means there's a lot to see here. Start with the displays in the visitor center (p199), set in a 19th-century log cabin.

★ **Barney Ford Museum** MUSEUM
(www.breckheritage.com; 111 E Washington Ave; suggested donation $5; ⏱ 11am-3pm Tue-Sun, hours vary seasonally) FREE Barney Ford was an escaped slave who became a prominent entrepreneur and Colorado civil-rights pioneer, and made two stops in Breckenridge (where he ran a 24-hour chop stand serving delicacies such as oysters) over the course of his incredibly rich, tragic and triumphant life. He also owned a restaurant and hotel in Denver. The museum is set in his old home, where he lived from 1882 to 1890.

Boreas Pass VIEWPOINT
(Boreas Pass Rd; ⏱ Jun-Oct) Originally known as Breckenridge Pass (11,481ft), this road first began serving stagecoaches in 1866 when prospectors flooded into the area from South Park looking for gold. In 1882, a narrow-gauge railway replaced the wagon road and remained in operation until 1937. Although the upper section across the Continental Divide is unpaved, you can easily drive up in summer and in fall for spectacular views.

Lomax Placer Mine MINE
(☎ 970-453-9767; www.breckheritage.com; 301 Ski Hill Rd; gold panning $10; ⏱ 11am-4pm Tue-Sun mid-Jun–Aug; 🅿) Here's a chance to pan for gold, learn how old-mining-town chemists assayed the valuable claims and check out the actual sluices and flumes used in placer (surface) mines. This site, which was active in the 1860s, also gives visitors the chance to sniff around a miner's cabin, complete with wood-burning stove, musical instruments,

snowshoes, pack saddles and other sundry items needed for survival.

Edwin Carter Discovery Center   MUSEUM
(www.breckheritage.com; 111 N Ridge St; suggested donation $5; ☉11am-3pm Tue-Sun, hours vary seasonally; 🖐) **FREE** This award-winning museum sheds light on a pioneer lured west by the Pike's Peak Gold Rush in 1858. He reached the Blue River valley in 1860. An original environmentalist, he noticed the impact of mining on wildlife early on, documenting genetic deformities (such as two-headed animals) that he suspected were linked to leaching toxins.

Breckenridge Arts District   GALLERY
(www.breckcreate.org; S Ridge St & E Washington Ave; ☉hours vary) This block-long stretch of historic Breckenridge is where you'll find a burgeoning arts scene. It has a live-work art space for visiting artists, a ceramics studio (Quandary Antiques Cabin) and exhibition space in buildings like the Breckenridge Theatre (p199). Some permanent sculptures are on display outside the buildings. Check the website for events, exhibitions and workshops.

High Line Railroad Park   HISTORIC SITE
(www.breckheritage.com; 189 Boreas Pass Rd; suggested donation $5; ☉11am-4pm Tue-Sun mid-Jun–Aug; P) **FREE** This isn't much of a park, but it is notable for its display of a vintage narrow-gauge rotary plow and the locomotives that powered it up the famed, rugged, gut-wrenching Boreas Pass railroad to keep gold-mining production open. This rail was a lifeline to miners, go-it-alone and corporate alike. Engine No 9 is on display year-round. It's also known as Rotary Snowplow Park.

Summit Ski Museum   MUSEUM
(www.breckheritage.com; 308B S Main St; suggested donation $5; ☉11am-3pm Tue-Sun, hours vary seasonally) **FREE** This small museum celebrates the first ski town in Colorado – that would be Breck – and the first century of Summit County skiing. There's a documentary video, vintage skis and gear, and the obligatory exhibit on the 10th Mountain Division.

Blue River Plaza   PLAZA
(201 S Main St; P) A beautifully landscaped riverside plaza with ample seating looking out onto the numbered peaks. There is sculpture, a 19th-century wagon, a small toddler sandbox and a murmuring stretch of the Blue River; the Breckenridge Visitor Center (p199) and bike path are just off the plaza. It's a fine place to sip coffee in the sun.

🏃 Activities

Thanks to its endless peaks and adventure opportunities, Breckenridge is easily the highlight of Summit County. Ski groomed runs and high-alpine bowls, snowshoe cross-country, ascend 14,000ft summits, race over miles of mountain-biking trails, go white-water rafting or fish the Blue River.

Breckenridge offers excellent opportunities to get out and explore the Tenmile and Mosquito Ranges. In addition to the hikes listed here, the visitor center (p199) hands out descriptions of other popular options. Alternatively, check out www.summitcountyexplorer.com.

You can rent bikes at the base of Peak 8 or in town; rental shops will be able to suggest plenty of rides, as there are over 200 miles of mountain-bike trails in the area. For pure downhill, take the chairlift from the base of Peak 8 (p193) and get ready for 1500 vertical feet of descent.

Summit County's fabulous network of paved bike paths wrap around the Dillon Reservoir, stretching from Keystone to Breckenridge to Vail, and are definitely worth exploring. From Breck to Frisco is 9.5 miles along the Blue River, with only 550ft of elevation change. **Breck Sports** (☎970-455-0215; www.breckenridgesports.com; 127 S Main St; rental skis/boards from $48/53, bikes adult/child from $47/34; ☉8am-9pm; 🖐) runs shuttles ($30) to the top of Vail Pass, from where you can cycle 21.5 miles back to town. If you run out of steam along the way, you can always catch a lift on the Summit Stage (p184) in Frisco, which is equipped with bike racks.

★ Breckenridge Ski Area   SNOW SPORTS
(☎800-789-7669; www.breckenridge.com; lift ticket adult/child $171/111; ☉8:30am-4pm Nov–mid-Apr; 🖐) Breckenridge spans five mountains (Peaks 6 to 10), covering 2900 acres and featuring some of the best beginner and intermediate terrain in the state, as well as plenty of exhilarating high-alpine runs and hike-to bowls. There are also four terrain parks and a superpipe.

You access the mountain from the free **BreckConnect Gondola**, which runs from downtown Breckenridge Station (Watson Ave) and serves the Nordic Center, Peak 7

Breckenridge

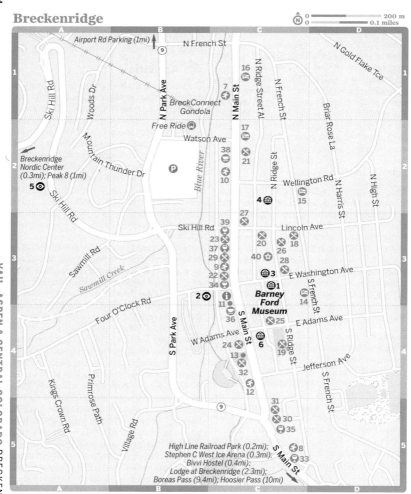

and Peak 8; a shuttle serves Peaks 9 and 10 at the southern end of town. Lift tickets can be exchanged for a Keystone pass and if you buy a three-day pass or longer, you also get access to Vail and Beaver Creek. In summer, the activity park Epic Discovery (p193) takes over part of the mountain.

★ **Quandary Peak** HIKING
(www.14ers.com; County Rd 851) Known as Colorado's easiest fourteener, Quandary Peak is the state's 15th-highest peak at 14,265ft. Though you'll see plenty of dogs and children, 'easiest' may be misleading – the sum-

mit remains 3 grueling miles from the trailhead. Go between June and September.

Avalanche Sports OUTDOORS
(☑ 970-453-1461; www.av-sports.com; 540 S Main St; rental skis & boards adult/child from $28/16, bikes adult/child from $35/25; ☺ 8am-8pm winter, 8:30am-5:30pm summer) This local rental outfit has good deals on quality skis, boards and full-suspension mountain bikes, plus snowshoes and fatbikes in the winter. There's another **branch** (☑ 970-453-4019; www.av-sports. com; 315 N Main St; rental skis & boards adult/ child from $28/16, bikes adult/child from $35/25;

Breckenridge

◉ Top Sights
1 Barney Ford Museum.............................. C3

◉ Sights
2 Blue River Plaza B3
3 Breckenridge Arts District..................... C3
4 Edwin Carter Discovery Center C2
5 Lomax Placer Mine................................. A2
6 Summit Ski Museum............................... C4

◯ Activities, Courses & Tours
7 Avalanche Sports......................................C1
8 Avalanche Sports.................................... C5
9 Breck Sports.. C3
10 Carvers.. C2
11 Historic Walking Tours........................... C3
12 Main Street Sports C4
13 Mountain Angler C4

◯ Sleeping
14 Abbett Placer Inn C3
15 Fireside Inn C2
16 Great Western Lodging............................C1
17 Woodwinds Lodging................................ C2

◯ Eating
18 Amazing Grace... C3

19 Breckenridge Market & Liquor C4
20 Briar Rose...C3
21 Canteen Tap House C2
22 Clint's Bakery & Coffee House C3
23 Columbine Cafe C3
24 Crepes à la Cart C4
25 Ember..C4
26 Fatty's C3
27 Giampietro C3
28 Hearthstone C3
29 Modis...C3
30 Park & Main..C5
31 South Ridge Seafood..............................C5
32 Wasabi C4

◯ Drinking & Nightlife
33 Breckenridge Brewery............................C5
34 Breckenridge Distillery Tasting
Room...C3
35 Cecilia's..C5
36 Crown..C4
37 Downstairs at Eric's C3
38 Kava Cafe C2
39 Motherloaded Tavern C3

◯ Entertainment
40 Breckenridge Theatre..............................C3

⊙ 8am-8pm winter, 8:30am-5:30pm summer) near the gondola.

Epic Discovery   AMUSEMENT PARK
(☑ 800-985-9842; www.epicdiscovery.com; Peak 8; day pass 3-7yr/8yr & up from $47/68; ⊙ Jun & Jul; ☝) Breck's eco-minded summer fun park combines learning about the local ecosystems with a laundry list of made-for-thrills activities, including a big-air bungee trampoline, climbing walls, ropes course, an eight-zipline tour, three alpine slides and the new 2500ft forest coaster.

Breckenridge Bike Trails   CYCLING
(☑ 970-453-5000; www.breckenridge.com; day pass $18/30; ⊙ 9:30am-5:30pm Jul–mid-Sep) In summer, mountain bikers can haul their bikes up the Colorado Super Chair from the base of Peak 8 to the 11,000ft Vista Haus summit and cruise (or fly, depending on the run) down one of 11 designated trails, two of which wander over to Peak 9.

McCullough Gulch   HIKING
(off County Rd 851; ⊙ Jun-Oct) This 2.8-mile round-trip hike is short enough for families, though huffing up the 1000ft of elevation gain will require some perseverance. Luckily you'll have plenty of scenery along the way: the meandering streams that you

follow from the trailhead eventually turn into thundering falls and, after that, a glacial lake.

Carvers   OUTDOORS
(☑ 800-568-7010; www.breckenridgeskishop.com; 203 N Main St; rental skis adult/child from $25/$18, boards adult/child $35/25, bikes per day $29-65; ⊙ 8am-8pm Dec–mid-Apr, 9am-6pm mid-Apr–Nov; ☝) A terrific indie bike and ski shop, Carvers has a bit of everything, including high-end bikes, boards, skis, boots, snowshoes, CamelBaks and disc-golf sets (not joking). It does overnight repairs, is just a short walk from the gondola, and offers a better selection than the big conglomerates. Reserve ahead for good discounts.

Main Street Sports   OUTDOORS
(☑ 970-453-1777; www.mainstreetsports.com; 401 S Main St; ski & board rental adult/child from $28/19; ⊙ 8am-8pm; ☝) A family-owned business since it opened in 1991, this is a Spyder concept store, which means it rents demo skis and snowboards, and sells all the latest Spyder ski apparel, too. Reserve rentals ahead for good deals.

Mohawk Lakes   HIKING
(Spruce Creek Rd; ⊙ Jun-Oct) Deep-green Lower Mohawk is tucked onto a tundra shelf

BRECKENRIDGE SKI TRIPS

When Main St is at 9600ft and the peaks are so plentiful that the founders went with numbers over names, you know the skiing is going to be absurdly good. In winter, which starts early here, it's all about the snow. If you're up for some backcountry travel, **Boreas Pass Road** (p190) is a good spot to strap on the snowshoes or cross-country skis. It's 6.4 miles from the parking lot (at the winter road-closure point) to the pass; there are other trails up there, as well.

Thanks to the long and relatively flat green runs on Peaks 8 and 9, the Breckenridge Ski Area has always been known as a great family mountain and a terrific place to learn. But if you're ready to step it up a notch, don't fret – there are plenty of adrenaline-addled diversions higher up on the resort's five towering peaks.

The one experience experts won't want to miss is a ride on the **highest chair lift** in North America, the Imperial Express (12,840ft). This drops you off just below the summit of Peak 8, from where you can traverse north along the ridge to Whale's Tail and Peak 7 Bowl, or steel yourself for the short, steep and lung-crushing hike up to the true summit (don't drop your gear!), where the views and terrain are simply spectacular. From here you can drop into the Imperial Bowl or the extreme Lake Chutes.

A favorite intermediate or 'blue' run is Cashier on Peak 9. Another great intermediate run on Peak 7 is Wire Patch, featuring a series of 'rollers' – mini-hills, not moguls. In 2013, the resort opened Peak 6 to skiers, adding access to three new bowls, two of which offer high-alpine intermediate terrain. There are three terrain parks, including a SuperPipe, on Peak 8.

There's a favorite expression around Breck: 'There's no friends on powder days.' And you certainly won't catch locals waiting around for anyone when it starts dumping. They'll be skiing through the trees on Peak 10, where the glades are legendary.

with the ruins of a miner's cabin just below. An outstanding, if slightly exposed, campsite is just south of the cabin. Upper Lake views are an even more spectacular moonscape: marbled rocks, stunted trees, inky lake views. That clear buzz is the quiet roar of the cosmos. It's 7 miles round-trip.

The trailhead is 1.2 miles up Spruce Creek Rd; the turnoff is 2.4 miles south of Breckenridge on Hwy 9 (towards Hoosier Pass).

Stephen C West Ice Arena   SKATING
(📞 970-547-9974;   www.breckenridgerecreation.com; 189 Boreas Pass Rd; adult/child $8/6, skate rental $4; ⏱ hours vary; 👪) An attractive, lodge-like arena south of town houses indoor and outdoor (October to April) ice rinks. It's usually open for public skating daily – and drop-in hockey once or twice a week – but check the website for the latest schedule.

Breckenridge Nordic Center   SNOW SPORTS
(📞 970-453-6855;   www.breckenridgenordic.com; 1200 Ski Hill Rd; adult/child $20/15; ⏱ 9am-4pm Nov–mid-Apr; 👪🎿) Breckenridge's Nordic Center has nine cross-country trails and five snowshoe trails set beneath the base of Peak 7. You can get here via the free town bus, the gondola (plus a short hike) or by car. Equipment rental costs $22/17 for an adult/child.

Tours

Arkansas Valley Adventures   RAFTING
(📞 800-370-0581; www.coloradorafting.net; adult/child from $54/49; ⏱ May-Sep; 👪) Arkansas Valley Adventures runs rafting trips down the legendary Arkansas and Colorado Rivers, as well as the mellower Clear Creek and Blue River (May, June and July only). The Arkansas and Colorado put-ins are about an hour's drive from Breckenridge. Children must be six and weigh at least 50lb. They also run ziplining, fly-fishing and horseback-riding trips.

Mountain Angler   FISHING
(📞 800-453-4669; www.mountainangler.com; 311 S Main St; guided fishing trips per person from $210; ⏱ 7am-9pm mid-Jun–Sep, shorter hours rest of year) Anglers will want to drop into this shop tucked inside a Main St mall. It offers a wide range of outdoor clothing, fishing gear and guided fly-fishing and float trips on the Blue, Eagle, Colorado, Arkansas and Platte Rivers.

Historic Walking Tours   WALKING
(📞 970-453-9767;   www.breckheritage.com; 203 S Main St; adult/child $10/5; ⏱ tours 11am & 1:30pm Wed-Sun, Sat & Sun only off-season) There are 250 historic structures in

Breckenridge, making it one of the oldest surviving cities in the Central Rockies. On this tour, which meets 10 minutes ahead at the visitor center (p199), you'll visit old miners' cabins, a saloon boarding house and a few museums, too.

Other walking tours include the Haunted Breck Tour, Saloon Tour and the Preston Ghost Town Hike. Check the website for seasonal schedules.

🎊 Festivals & Events

Quirky parades, feats of athletic, creative and culinary agility and ingenuity, and plenty of night music – Breckenridge knows how to throw a party.

Breckenridge Music Festival   MUSIC
(☑970-453-9142; www.breckenridgemusicfestival. com) Something of a kid sibling to the Aspen Music Festival (p228), the Breckenridge Music Institute and National Repertory Orchestra offer both summer and winter seasons of stunning classical music at the **Riverwalk Center**, a heated amphitheater on the Blue River. There are more than 50 orchestral concerts and chamber recitals each summer, and a half-dozen dates during the shorter winter season.

**International Snow Sculpture
Championship**   ART
(www.gobreck.com; ⊘ Jan-Feb) The International Snow Sculpture Championship begins in mid-January and lasts for three weeks. It starts with Technical Week, when the snow blocks are made, continues with Sculpting Week, when the sculptures are created and then judged by the public, and concludes with Viewing Week, when the sculptures decorate the River Walk.

Fourth of July   FIREWORKS, PARADE
(www.gobreck.com; ⊘ July 4) Breckenridge throws one hell of an Independence Day party. There's a parade, a 10km trail run, a 50-mile mountain bike race, and a free concert and fireworks to wrap it all up.

Ullr Fest   CULTURAL
(www.gobreck.com; ⊘ Jan) The Ullr Fest celebrates the Norse god of winter, with a wild parade and four-day festival featuring a fatbike race, a town-wide talent show and a bonfire.

Spring Fever   CULTURAL
(www.gobreck.com) From mid-March through closing day, Spring Fever offers a range of events, from concerts and competitions to chili cook-offs, an Easter-egg hunt and celebrity athlete shindigs.

Mardi Gras   PARADE
(www.gobreck.com; ⊘ Feb) Breck's take on Mardi Gras features a Fat Tuesday parade down Main St followed by a brass-band concert.

Breck Bike Week   CYCLING
(www.gobreck.com; ⊘ Jun) This festival on two wheels in late June includes skills clinics, demo gear displays and guided tours.

🛏 Sleeping

On the whole, Breckenridge is more affordable than Vail and Aspen and a good choice for families and budgeteers. Most accommodations are condo-style, so reserve early for a room in a B&B or hostel. By far the easiest way to compare different rental properties is via the town tourism website www.gobreck. com. The closest USFS campsites are near Frisco.

★**Bivvi Hostel**   HOSTEL $
(☑970-423-6553; www.thebivvi.com; 9511 Hwy 9; dm winter/summer from $85/29; P ⊛ 🛜) A modern hostel with a log-cabin vibe, the Bivvi wins points for style, friendliness and affordability. The four- to six-person dorm rooms come with private lockers, en suites and complimentary breakfast; chill out in the funky common room or out on the gorgeous deck, equipped with a gas grill and hot tub. Private rooms are also available.

To get here, take the Free Ride (p199) brown route from town or the gondola; it runs from roughly 6:30am to 11:30pm in winter.

Fireside Inn   B&B, HOSTEL $
(☑970-453-6456; www.firesideinn.com; 114 N French St; summer/winter dm $35/45, d from $80/99; P ⊛ @ 🛜) A good bet for budget travelers in Summit County, this chummy hostel and B&B is a find. All guests can enjoy the chlorine-free barrel hot tub, fridge and microwave, movie nights and the snuggly resident dog; the pricier rooms get breakfast in the morning. The English hosts are a delight. It's a 10-minute walk to the gondola in ski boots.

Section House   HUT $
(☑970-925-5775; www.summithuts.org; Boreas Pass; per person $38; ⊘ Nov-Apr) 🏃 One of four Summit County huts, the Section House (sleeps 12) is located at the top of Boreas

Pass Rd (p190) and is a favorite destination for backcountry skiers. It was originally built in 1882 to house railroad workers, abandoned after the line closed in the 1930s and restored in the '90s. A wood-burning stove, mattresses and solar-powered lighting are available.

Like all huts, you should reserve months in advance to secure a spot. The more intimate **Ken's Cabin** ($75 per night) is next door.

⭐ Abbett Placer Inn
B&B $$

(☎970-453-6489; www.abbettplacer.com; 205 S French St; r winter/summer from $179/129; P ❄ @ 🛜) This violet house has five large rooms decked out with wood furnishings, iPod docks and fluffy robes. It's very low-key. Warm and welcoming hosts cook big breakfasts and guests can enjoy an outdoor Jacuzzi deck and use of a common kitchenette. The top-floor room has massive views of the peaks from a private terrace. Check-in is from 4pm to 7pm.

Great Western Lodging
ACCOMMODATION SERVICES $$

(☎888-453-1001; www.gwlodging.com; 322 N Main St; condos summer/winter from $170/200; ❄ 🛜) Arguably the best and most refined of the rental agencies in Breckenridge. It has a portfolio of 150 homes and condos on the slope side of Main St, with an emphasis on ski-in, ski-out and walk-in, walk-out properties. Two-night minimum in summer; four-night minimum in winter.

Woodwinds Lodging
ACCOMMODATION SERVICES $$$

(☎800-403-6744; www.woodwindsbreck.com; 300 N Main St; condos summer/winter from $125/240; P ❄ 🛜) Offers one- to four-bedroom homes and condos in the flats and on the hill (including some ski-in, ski-out spots). Most require a three-night minimum stay in summer and four-night minimum stay in winter. Check-in is at the office on N Main St.

Lodge at Breckenridge
HOTEL $$$

(☎970-453-9300; www.thelodgeatbreckenridge.com; 112 Overlook Dr; r winter/summer from $300/200; P @ 🛜 ❄) High above town off of Boreas Pass Rd, this hotel's draw is the breathtaking panoramas, which look out over snow-capped peaks and acres of alpine forest. Rooms are comfortable (if a bit dated) in their rustic look; make sure you opt for a mountain-view room.

Eating

Kitchens here like to flex their creative muscles, although not everyone's an Iron Chef in the upper echelons – hit après-ski specials (4pm to 6pm) for the best deals.

Crepes à la Cart
CRÊPES $

(www.crepesalacarts.com; 307 S Main St; crepes $7-14; ⊙9am-11pm Sun-Thu, to 2pm Fri & Sat) It's Breck's most popular snack stand: you can't miss this yellow gypsy cart on Main St – or the line snaking down the block in front of it. Sweet and savory crepes are made to order and folded up in the iconic Parisian wedge, but when it gets busy, *mon dieu,* the wait can be very long.

Park & Main
SANDWICHES $

(☎970-453-9493; www.parkandmainfood.com; 500 S Main St; sandwiches $8.50-15.50; ⊙7:30am-9pm; 🍴) This bright industrial space is a welcome addition to the Breck cafe scene. It runs the gauntlet of world sandwich styles, from pressed paninis on ciabatta bread and a prosciutto-laced croque monsieur (aka grilled ham-and-cheese) to Vietnamese banh mi and even roasted-beet sliders and quinoa salad. Lots of free-range-egg creations get the day started right.

Clint's Bakery & Coffee House
CAFE $

(☎970-453-2990; www.clintsbakery.com; 131 S Main St; sandwiches $5-8.50; ⊙7am-8pm; 🛜) The coolest coffeeshop in town, where brainy baristas will steam up anything from a chalkboard full of latte and mocha flavors and dozens of loose-leaf teas. If you're hungry, the downstairs bagelry (closes at 3pm) stacks burly sandwiches and tasty breakfast bagels with egg and ham, lox, sausage and cheese. Good pastries, too.

Amazing Grace
VEGETARIAN $

(☎970-453-1445; www.amazinggracebreckenridge.com; 213 Lincoln Ave; mains $9.50-10.50; ⊙7am-3pm) 🍃 This tiny house is Breck's premier pick (indeed, perhaps the only pick) to scoff hummus sandwiches, spicy tofu salads, smoothies and other healthy, vegetarian-friendly fare.

Fatty's
AMERICAN, PIZZA $

(☎970-453-9802; www.fattyspizzeria.com; 106 S Ridge Rd; pizzas $11-13, mains $9.50-22; ⊙11am-10pm) Fatty's is true to its moniker: even the 10in pizza can feed two. It's a local dive with a sports bar that can get rowdy come dark. In summer you can sit outside on the patio and people-watch.

Columbine Cafe
BREAKFAST $

(☑970-547-4474; 109 S Main St; mains $8-12; ⊙7:30am-1:30pm; 🖨) If you're looking for a more tasteful, flavorful breakfast dive, duck into this cozy stonewall nook. It does huevos rancheros; Texas-style French toast flavored with vanilla, cinnamon and nutmeg; and eggs Benedict six ways.

Breckenridge Market & Liquor
SUPERMARKET $

(311 S Ridge St; ⊙8am-10pm) Conveniently located in the center of town – though you're better off stocking up in Frisco if you're doing your own cooking.

★ Breckenridge Distillery
AMERICAN $$

(☑970-547-9759; www.breckenridgedistillery.com; 1925 Airport Rd; small plates $10-18; ⊙4-9pm Tue-Sat) Served in a big-city-cool dining space, the eclectic menu at this distillery (p198) follows the delightful whims of former DC chef Daniel O'Brien, jumping from the sublime *cacio e pepe* (Roman spaghetti and cheese) to chicken-liver profiteroles or dates and mascarpone without missing a beat. It's mostly small plates, perfect for sharing over the top-notch cocktails.

Giampietro
ITALIAN, PIZZA $$

(☑970-453-3838; www.giampietropizza.com; 100 N Main St; mains $9-24, pizzas from $16.50; ⊙11am-10pm; 🖨) Dig into some consistently good, honest and soulful New York–style pizza. It's sold by the slice and (16in) pie, along with dishes such as baked ziti with sausage, eggplant parmesan and lunch subs. It's all served in a bright corner room, decorated with those kitschy red-checkered tablecloths. Family-sized orders (takeout only) are also available with 24-hour notice.

Canteen Tap House
AMERICAN $$

(☑970-453-0063; www.thecanteenbreck.com; 208 N Main St; mains $11.50-24; ⊙11am-10pm) There's nothing quite like reinventing the wheel, and the uber-popular Canteen does just that: all your favorite ski-town staples are here, from burgers (beef, veggie, bison and chicken) and flatbreads to Korean BBQ tacos, turkey BLTs and grilled salmon and steak. Pair it up with a zingy cocktail or one of 14 Colorado beers on tap.

Wasabi
JAPANESE $$

(☑970-453-8311; www.wasabi-breckenridge.com; 311 S Main St; lunch mains $8-15, dinner mains $15-30, sushi plates $16.50-35.50; ⊙noon-2pm Wed-Fri, 5pm-close Tue-Sun) If you're salivating for sushi, maki rolls or udon noodles, this family-run hole-in-the-wall will definitely satisfy. The chef keeps it simple and affordable, especially at lunch when he offers teriyaki tofu and chicken bowls for a song ($8); the Volcano Bowl, piled high with wasabi tuna, salmon or albacore ($13), is the best deal in the house.

The fish served here is the same as at Matsuhisa (p233) and Osaki's (p210) and is shipped in daily from Narita. It's located in the shopping center.

Hearthstone
MODERN AMERICAN $$$

(☑970-453-1148; www.hearthstonebreck.com; 130 S Ridge St; mains $26-45; ⊙4pm-late; 🖨) 🍴 One of Breck's favorites, this restored 1886 Victorian churns out creative mountain fare such as blackberry elk and braised buffalo ribs with tomatillos, roasted chilies and polenta. Fresh and delicious, it's definitely worth a splurge, or hit happy hour (4pm to 6pm) for $5 plates paired with wine.

You can dine in the oh-so-burgundy dining room or, preferably, on the three tiered patios out front when the weather cooperates. Book ahead.

South Ridge Seafood
SEAFOOD $$$

(☑970-547-0063; www.southridgeseafoodgrill.com; 500 S Main St; mains $15-35; ⊙4pm-late) The kitchen whips up some delectable dinner entrees (grilled trout with lemon-thyme aioli, teriyaki-glazed ahi with udon), but it's the après-ski scene that garners the most acclaim, with winning small plates (oysters, clam chowder, butternut-squash ravioli) that go for as little as $3.

Briar Rose
STEAK $$$

(☑970-453-9948; www.briarrosechophouse.com; 109 Lincoln Ave; mains $25-47; ⊙4-10pm; 🖨) Set in a magnificent Old West frame and on the site of Breck's original saloon, this spot is named after the famed Briar Rose gold mine on Peak 10. And while it's first and foremost a chop house, small plates (think *shishito* peppers, raclette, mussels and escargot) are served in the dining room and saloon. Fine dining doesn't get any more atmospheric in Breckenridge.

Ember
FUSION $$$

(☑970-547-9191; www.emberbreck.com; 106 E Adams Ave; mains $23-33; ⊙4pm-late) Great jazz on the sound system, strange glowing floral-art around the room and creative combinations on the plate. Appetizers include pheasant tacos with chèvre and pizza with brie and pickled blueberries. Mains include

ALMA & HOOSIER PASS

Follow Hwy 9 south from Breckenridge and after 11 miles of steady climbing, you'll come to **Hoosier Pass** (11,539ft) and the Continental Divide. From here you'll be looking out over the South Park basin, a high-altitude prairie where the bison once roamed. On the other side of the pass is funky **Alma**, the highest incorporated town in the United States, standing at an elevation of 10,578ft. It's surrounded by four fourteeners, thousand-year-old bristlecone pines and scores of old mining claims. If you want to explore, follow the unpaved Buckskin Rd (County Rd 8) 6 miles west toward Kite Lake (high-clearance 4WD is recommended for the last mile).

lamb osso buco with banana purple rice and scallops with a passion-fruit hollandaise.

Modis MODERN AMERICAN **$$$**
(☑ 970-453-4330; www.modisbreck.com; 113 S Main St; mains $20-42; ☺ 3-10pm) A groovy, fusion-leaning spot on the main drag, Modis does imaginative dishes like Eastern fried chicken with orange sauce and kohlrabi slaw, or seared Brussels sprouts with persimmon compote and Spanish ham. Solid wine list. Not cheap, but loved widely.

🍷 Drinking & Entertainment

All the Colorado haunts of the moment are well represented in Breck. Microbrewery? Check. Basement sports bar? Check. Edgy new-school pub? Check. Kava cafe? You bet.

★ Crown CAFE
(☑ 970-453-6022; www.thecrownbreckenridge.com; 215 S Main St; ☺ 7:30am-8pm; 🛜) Breck's living room might as well be at the Crown, a buzzing cafe-cum-social hub. Grab a mug of Silver Canyon coffee and a sandwich or salad, and catch up on all the latest gossip.

Downstairs at Eric's BAR
(www.downstairsaterics.com; 111 S Main St; ☺ 11am-midnight; 👪) Locals flock to this game-room-style basement joint, a Breckenridge institution, for the brews, burgers and delicious mashed potatoes. There are over 100 beers (20 on tap) to choose from and plenty of sports bar–arcade action.

Broken Compass Brewing BREWERY
(☑ 970-368-2772; www.brokencompassbrewing.com; 68 Continental Ct; ☺ 11:30am-11pm) Set in an industrial complex at the north end of Airport Road, the Broken Compass is generally regarded as the best brewery in Breckenridge. Fill up with a pint of their Coconut Porter or Chili Pepper Pale and sink back with a couple of friends in the old chairlift.

They run a shuttle every two hours between the brewery and town.

Breckenridge Distillery DISTILLERY
(☑ 970-547-9759; www.breckenridgedistillery.com; 1925 Airport Rd; ☺ 11am-9pm Tue-Sat, to 6pm Sun & Mon) Billed as the world's highest distillery, this place is worth visiting for a tour (half-hourly, 11am to 5:30pm) and 'tastings for tips' – their specialty is bourbon, but they also infuse vodka and rum and blend a mean bitter. If you don't want to drive out to Airport Rd, there's also a small tasting room (p199) in town.

Kava Cafe CAFE
(www.kavabreck.com; 209 N Main St; ☺ 8am-2pm Thu-Tue) This hole-in-the-wall and historic log-cabin cafe is the kind of place in which ragged miners may have procured dry goods back in the day. These days it makes sandwiches and coffee, but is notable for its specialties: made-to-order minidoughnuts and a 12oz cup of kava ($7.50).

Kava is a Polynesian root that's been used ceremonially for centuries. Funky, earthy and served at room temperature, this drink is a natural upper and a great way to get a pleasant buzz.

Breckenridge Brewery BREWERY
(☑ 970-453-1550; www.breckbrewpub.com; 600 S Main St; ☺ 11am-11pm; 🛜) With seven malty aromatic brews being cooked up in the kettles directly behind the bar, you know what this is all about. Sample happy-hour goodness with agave wheat, vanilla porter and a double IPA. Pub grub is served all day and late into the night.

Cecilia's CLUB
(☑ 970-453-2243; www.cecilias.tv; 520 S Main St; ☺ 2pm-2am) Ski bums love to rag on Cecilia's, but that doesn't stop them from flocking to this long-established party spot when the mood is right. It has a large dancefloor with

mostly DJ-spun grooves (and occasional live acts) and three bars. A bit of a frat-boy scene.

Breckenridge Distillery
Tasting Room DISTILLERY
(☑970-547-9759; www.breckenridgedistillery.com; 137 S Main St; ⊙11am-9pm Tue-Sat, to 6pm Sun & Mon) The local distillery's (p198) shop and tasting room (free, but tips appreciated); located in the heart of town across from the Visitor Center.

Motherloaded Tavern PUB
(☑970-453-2572; www.motherloadedtavern.com; 103 S Main St; ⊙11:30am-2am) The choice dive in Breckenridge isn't even all that divey. Sure, it's a bare-bones tavern, but it also attracts the local hipsters and anyone else who dreams of a tasty comfort food alongside hot, steaming boozy sips. Surprisingly, there are no microbrews on tap, so it'll have to be a Pabst. There's live music every Thursday through Saturday night.

Breckenridge Theatre THEATER
(☑970-485-2164; www.backstagetheatre.org; 121 S Ridge St) This vibrant, long-running theater is part of the art district and stages new and classic shows.

ℹ Information

Visitor center (☑877-864-0868; www. gobreck.com; 203 S Main St; ⊙9am-6pm; 🛜) Along with a host of maps and brochures, this center has a pleasant riverside museum that delves into Breck's gold-mining past.

ℹ Getting There & Away

Breckenridge is 80 miles west of Denver via I-70 exit 203, then Hwy 9 south. The main skier parking lots ($12 Friday to Sunday, $5 Monday to Thursday) are located at the base of the gondola; they are free in summer. You can also find small metered lots scattered throughout town. A free park-and-ride lot works for skiers just up for the day; it's located on Airport Rd north of town and is connected to the gondola via shuttle.

Summit Stage (p184) Summit County's free bus service links Breckenridge with Keystone and A-Basin in winter (Swan Mountain Flyer) and with Frisco year-round. It leaves from Breckenridge Station.

ℹ Getting Around

Free Ride (☑970-547-3140; www.breckfreeride.com; 150 Watson Ave; ⊙8am-11:45pm) Nine free bus routes serve the town and ski area. Buses depart from Breckenridge station next to the gondola.

Fairplay
☑719 / POP 679 / ELEV 9953FT

South Park's main settlement was originally a mining site and supply town for Leadville (pack burros briefly clopped back and forth over the 13,000ft Mosquito Pass to the west), and you can stop here to visit South Park City (p199), a re-created 19th-century Colorado boomtown. Get a taste of life back in the good-old, bad-old days of the gold rush through the 40 restored buildings on display, which range from the general store and saloon to a dentist's office and morgue. And yes, *South Park* fans, Fairplay does bear more than a passing resemblance to the hometown of Kyle, Cartman and the boys.

◉ Sights & Activities

South Park City HISTORIC SITE
(www.southparkcity.org; 100 4th St; adult/child 6-12yr $10/4; ⊙9am-7pm mid-May–mid-Oct, shorter hours May & Oct) South Park City has nothing to do with Cartman, Kyle, Stan or Kenny. It's a collection of 35 original buildings, built in the 1870s and 1880s in places like Fairplay, Alma, Como and the surrounding South Park area. All were restored and moved to this site in the late 1950s to better preserve the structures and publicize the region's history.

Rocky Mountain Land Library LIBRARY
(www.landlibrary.org; 37612 Hwy 9, Buffalo Peaks Ranch) If you're a fan of libraries, you'll want to check out this 1862 ranch, which is currently being renovated to accommodate some 32,000 volumes about the West. The aim is to eventually turn it into a retreat, though the earliest any accommodations will be ready is 2018. A series of writing and art workshops is currently being held each Saturday throughout the summer (June through August).

Platte Ranch HORSEBACK RIDING
(☑719-836-1670; Hwy 9; 2hr/half-day ride $70/135) If you've been itching to slide your boots into some stirrups, the Platte Ranch gets great reviews and offers guests a bona fide cowboy experience with rides through open country on an actual working ranch. Reserve ahead.

🛏 Sleeping & Eating

A handful of simple hotels are scattered around town, though there's little reason to spend the night here.

There are several predictable eating options on Front St in Fairplay.

Brown Burro Cafe
DINER $

(☑ 719-836-2804; 706 Main St; mains $8-12; ⊙ 6am-2pm Wed-Sun) The local log-cabin greasy spoon does American and Mexican classics for breakfast and lunch.

ℹ Getting There & Away

Fairplay is 21 miles south of Breckenridge on Hwy 9 and 86 miles west of Denver on Hwy 285. If you're looking for a scenic alternative to I-70, Hwy 285 is as pretty as they come and offers a good backdoor option to Breckenridge and Buena Vista. Hoosier Pass to Breckenridge stays open year-round.

Copper Mountain

☑ 970 / POP 316 / ELEV 9712FT

Opened in 1972, this picturesque, self-contained resort southwest of Frisco was the last addition to Summit County ski country. Set high on the eastern slope of Vail Pass along the Colorado Trail, it's surrounded by high, jagged peaks with long runs carved between evergreens and copious powder in the gorgeous back bowls. In summer there's everything from snowboard camps, hiking and mountain biking to golf, and you can almost always hear that ever-present rush of Copper Creek over the roar of the nearby highway.

🏃 Activities

★ Woodward Barn
ADVENTURE SPORTS

(☑ 970-239-0401; www.woodwardcopper.com; 505 Copper Rd; drop-in/intro sessions $39/49, skate & bike session $12; ⊙ 2-8pm mid-Nov–mid-Apr; 🚹) Little shredders who want to learn their way around a terrain park can take their parents to this way-cool 19,000-sq-ft playground, a year-round snowboard, skate and BMX training camp complete with trampolines, skate parks, jumps and, thankfully, foam pits. It serves all levels of athlete, from beginners to the young and sponsored. The mandatory intro class grants you access to drop-in sessions.

Copper Creek Golf Course
GOLF

(☑ 866-677-1663; www.coppercolorado.com; 85 Wheeler Pl; peak season 9/18 holes $59/89; ⊙ 8am-5:50pm Jun-Sep) An affordable and scenic 18 holes are yours to play here. Check in at the Athletic Club between the two villages as you enter the resort.

Copper Mountain
SNOW SPORTS

(☑ 866-841-2481; www.coppercolorado.com; Hwy 91; adult/child $150/85; ⊙ 9am-4pm, from 8:30am Sat & Sun Nov–mid-Apr; 🚹) The base village may be a bit too planned for some, but even the staunchest critics wouldn't thumb their noses at the mountain itself. Rising 2601ft up to the 12,313ft summit, Copper has 2490 acres of terrain, carved with over 140 trails equally divided among beginners, intermediate, advanced and expert skiers. No chichi Vail attitude here – Copper takes you back to skiing's play-hard roots.

Summer at Copper
OUTDOORS

(☑ 866-841-2481; www.coppercolorado.com; activities $12-15, day pass $49; ⊙ 10am-5pm, to 7pm Sat mid-Jun–mid-Sep; 🚹) All the usual activities are on offer in summer: there's mountain biking ($20), a climbing wall, miniature golf and go-cart race track, plus a new forest coaster is in the works. The American Eagle lift (10am to 4pm) leaves you at Solitude Station, where you can have a BBQ lunch and take one of the hiking trails. The chairlift is free, provided you've already spent $12 at the resort.

★ Festivals & Events

Copper Country Music Festival
MUSIC

(www.coppercountryfest.com; ⊙ Labor Day weekend) Copper Mountain's much loved music-and-arts festival hosts a range of events around the Labor Day weekend, with arts-and-crafts exhibitions, pony rides for the kids and diverse music acts on the lineup.

🛏 Sleeping

All lodging here comes in condo form. There are three companies that manage the properties: Copper Lodging (p201), Copper Vacations (p201) and Carbonate Lodging (p201).

The sauna-equipped Janet's Cabin is a fabulous destination for backcountry skiers, mountain bikers and hikers, run by the 10th Mountain Division Hut Association (p228). It's located along the Colorado Trail, five (winter) to seven (summer) miles west of Copper. Reservations essential.

All properties are rated from 2-Peak to 5-Peak. The rating system corresponds to price, but also to property management. Two- and 3-Peak are the cheapest, and their owners can decorate these condos any way they want, which may be why you're waking up next to a picture of someone's Aunt

Edna on the nightstand; they also tend to be more dated. A 4-Peak rating means the condos are almost always more standardized, with features such as granite counters and flat-screen TVs. The nicest are the 5-Peak properties, which have all been recently remodeled and can get downright lavish.

Copper Lodging ACCOMMODATION SERVICES $$
(☑888-760-7561; www.coppercolorado.com; condos from $200; P✻☎❄) Books lodging at Copper Mountain, which is generally in condos.

Copper Vacations ACCOMMODATION SERVICES $$
(☑800-525-3887; www.coppervacations.com; condos from $200; P✻☎☎) This accommodations management company rents a variety of condos.

**Carbonate
Lodging** ACCOMMODATION SERVICES $$
(☑800-526-7737; www.coppermtnlodging.com; condos from $200; P✻☎) Rents a selection of condos at Copper Mountain.

✖ Eating

Eating and drinking options here are pretty basic, though we love that you can ski up to a food truck and igloo-block bar at 11,355ft – that would be Chuck's Wagon Haus at the base of the Rendezvous lift.

Endo's Adrenaline Cafe CAFE $$
(☑970-968-3070; 209 Ten Mile Circle; mains $13-25; ◷8am-8pm; ❧) A laid-back but still hard-rocking place on the main village plaza. It has kayaks dangling from the ceiling, while snowboarding stills and flat-screen TVs decorate the walls. The menu is mostly sandwiches and wraps, but it does have a few departures from the usual fare, such as stewed beef cheeks and stuffed trout.

Incline Bar & Grill AMERICAN $$
(☑970-968-0200; www.inclinegrill.com; Copper Mountain Village; mains lunch $10-16, dinner $16-36; ◷11am-9pm; ☎) Set strategically at the base of Copper Mountain, steps from the American Eagle lift, this bar and grill has a roomy interior, a patio with tables overlooking the slopes and several earthy microbrews on tap.

❶ Getting There & Away

Copper Mountain is 77 miles west of Denver at I-70, exit 195. Free parking is available.

The **Ski Bus** (☑720-924-6686; www.frontrangeskibus.com; adult/child $45/38; ◷Wed-Sun) runs from Denver to Copper Moun-

tain five days a week, leaving from Union Station at 7am and the Wooly Mammoth Park-and-Ride (I-70, exit 259) at 7:30am. The return trip leaves Copper at 3:30pm.

The Summit Stage (p184) provides free bus service throughout Summit County, via the Frisco Transfer Center.

VAIL & THE HOLY CROSS WILDERNESS

Tucked between the remote Eagles Nest Wilderness to the north and the Holy Cross Wilderness to the west, Vail is a universe unto itself. Famous for its massive, stylish ski resort, this is the place where many come to indulge in their deepest, darkest, powder-filled fantasies. Your pockets don't have to be flush with cash to enjoy the dramatic scenery, however; the surrounding wilderness areas are truly magnificent and a great place to find inspiration, free of charge.

Vail

☑970 / POP 5311 / ELEV 8120FT
Blessed with peaks, graced with blue skies and fresh powder, carved by rivers and groomed with ski slopes and bike trails, Vail is the ultimate Colorado playground. The real draw has always been Vail Mountain, a hulking, domed mass of snow-driven euphoria that offers more terrain than anywhere else in the US: 1500 acres of downhill slopes on the north face and 3500 acres of back-bowl bliss.

Factor in Vail's gourmet offerings, well-coiffed clientele and pretty young powder-fueled staff and you have an adrenaline-addled yuppie utopia. Indeed, stress does not cling to the bones for long here...until you get the bill. And even then you'll have had such a remarkable time skiing, hiking, biking and horseback riding that the memories will last far longer than the icy splash of buyer remorse. Just remember going in that this is North America's most expensive ski resort.

◉ Sights

Located between the remote Eagles Nest Wilderness to the north and the Holy Cross Wilderness to the west, Vail is a world unto itself. Renowned for its huge, stylish ski resort, this is the place where many come to indulge in their powder-filled fantasies. You don't have to be fabulously wealthy to

Vail

400 m
0.2 miles

N

Riva Glen

Vail Stables
(0.3mi)

Spraddle Creek Rd

Eagle County Regional
Transportation Authority

Spraddle Creek

Spraddle Creek

Betty Ford
Alpine Gardens (0.3mi);
Ford Amphitheater (0.3mi);
S Frontage Rd E
East Vail (3mi);
S Frontage Rd E

Vail Valley Dr

Vail Valley Dr

17

Gore Creek Dr

Hanson Ranch Rd

16

Vail Nature
Center (0.5mi)

Mill Creek Cir

Mill Creek

E Meadow Dr

13

P

1

21

18

31

6

Mill Creek Cir

Riva Catwalk

25

22

Bridge St

29

Gondola
One

Grand Army Hwy

Village
Center Rd

10

27

23

26

32

Vail Transportation
Center

15

E Meadow Dr

Willow Bridge Rd

Gore Creek Dr

Mill Creek Rd

12

Willow Pl

Willow Rd

N Frontage Rd W

28

24 19

14

Vail Rd

Vail Rd

Forest Rd

Mill Creek Rd

Mill Creek Rd

S Frontage Rd W

W Meadow Dr

Beaver Dam Rd

Rockledge Rd

6
70

E Lionshead Cir

Middle Creek

4

W Meadow Dr

Gore Creek

Beaver Dam Cir

Beaver Dam Rd

Forest Rd

Forest Rd

11

Rockledge Rd

9

30

5

20

Beaver Dam Rd

Gore Creek

Forest Rd

6
70

2

Vail

◎ Sights
1 Colorado Ski Museum G2

◎ Activities, Courses & Tours
2 Bike Valet A1
3 Buzz's Ski Shop G3
  Christy Sports .... (see 29)
4 Dobson Ice Arena C1
5 Gore Creek Fly Fishermen A2
6 Summer at Vail G4
7 Troy's Ski Shop G3
8 Vail Mountain F4

◎ Sleeping
9 Arrabelle A2
10 Austria Haus F3
11 Lodge at Lionshead B2
12 Lodge Tower F3
13 Mountain Haus G3
14 Sebastian Hotel E2
15 Solaris F2
16 Tivoli Lodge G3
17 Vail Mountain Lodge G3

◎ Eating
18 Big Bear Bistro G3
   bōl .... (see 15)

19 Campo de Fiori E2
20 El Sabor A2
21 La Cantina F2
   Little Diner .... (see 2)
22 Loaded Joe's F3
   Matsuhisa .... (see 15)
   Moe's Original BBQ .... (see 2)
23 Mountain Standard F3
24 Osaki's E2
25 Russell's G3
26 Sweet Basil F3
   Tavern on the Square .... (see 9)
27 Up the Creek F3
28 Vail Farmers Market E2
29 Vendetta's F3

◎ Drinking & Nightlife
30 Garfinkels A2
31 Los Amigos G4
32 Root & Flower F3
   The George .... (see 13)
   Vail Brewing .... (see 15)
   Yeti's Grind .... (see 15)

◎ Entertainment
   Cinebistro .... (see 15)

enjoy the dramatic scenery, however; the surrounding wilderness areas are magnificent and a brilliant place to find inspiration, free of charge.

Colorado Ski Museum MUSEUM
(www.skimuseum.net; 3rd fl, Vail Village parking lot exit; suggested donation $3; ⊙10am-6pm; 🅿️) **FREE** Humble but informative, this museum takes you from the invention of skiing to the trials of the 10th Mountain Division, a decorated WWII alpine unit that trained in these mountains. There are also hilarious fashions from the past, as well as the fledgling **Colorado Ski & Snowboard Hall of Fame**. The museum runs tours ($5) on Fridays from 1pm to 3pm.

Betty Ford Alpine Gardens GARDENS
(www.bettyfordalpinegardens.org; 522 S Frontage Rd; ⊙dawn-dusk; 🅿️) **FREE** The highest botanical gardens in the US. Stop by for a soothing stroll past rock gardens, native alpine plants and collected species from as far as the Himalayas. The new Education Center is worth a stop, and there's occasionally some sort of activity going on, from yoga and butterfly launches to public tours and plant sales.

🏃 Activities

The draw to Vail is no secret. It's the endless outdoor activities in both winter and summer that make this resort so attractive. Do remember that the mud season (mid-April through May, plus November) holds little attraction for visitors – you can't ski; nor can you get up into the mountains to hike around.

True, with 5289 acres of ski terrain available it's tough to play favorites, but here are a few things to keep in mind as you explore the mountain. Beginners should stick to the groomed front side; the Gopher Hill Lift (#12) and Little Eagle Lift (#15) areas are best for first-timers. Other good green runs include **Lost Boy** in Game Creek Bowl and the **Tin Pants** and **Sourdough** in the Sourdough Express Lift (#14) area. Kids will dig the various adventure zones, which include banked turns and tunnels, so make sure to seek these out to break up the monotony of bunny hill-style runs. If they've had enough of skiing, head for Adventure Ridge (p204) at the top of the Eagle Bahn Gondola, with tubing, kids snowmobiling, ski biking and free snowshoe tours.

Some good intermediate runs are **Slifer Express**, **Cappuccino** and **Christmas** in the Mountaintop Express Lift (#4) area. **Northwoods**, in the Northwoods Express Lift (#11) area, **Avanti**, **Lodgepole** and **Columbine** in the Avanti Express Lift (#2) area and **Dealer's Choice** in Game Creek Bowl are also great. Intermediate skiers also love the wilder **Blue Sky Basin** (behind the back bowls), with runs such as Grand Review and In the Wuides. Free tours of Blue Sky Basin meet daily at Henry's Hut at 11am, across from Patrol HQ.

For advanced skiers, the backside is where the action is, with its **seven legendary bowls**: Sun Down, Sun Up, China, Siberia, Teacup and Inner and Outer Mongolia. The wide-open, spruce-dotted slopes here include favorites like **Over Yonder** (Sun Up), **Forever** (Sun Down) and **Bolshoi Ballroom** (Siberia). **Steep & Deep** and **Lover's Leap** in Blue Sky Basin are two other home runs. The options are seemingly infinite and you can ski a week here without ever covering your tracks.

Trickster snowboarders can find three terrain parks on the front side, including a superpipe that's home to the US Open Snowboarding Championships (p207).

★ Vail Mountain   SNOW SPORTS

(☑970-754-8245; www.vail.com; lift ticket adult/child $189/130; ☺9am-4pm Nov–mid-Apr; ⊕) Vail Mountain is our favorite in Colorado, with 5289 skiable acres, 195 trails, three terrain parks and (ahem) the highest lift-ticket prices on the continent. If you're a Colorado ski virgin, it's worth experiencing your first time here – especially on a bluebird fresh-powder day. Multiday tickets are good at three other resorts (Beaver Creek, Breck and Keystone).

Vail Pass Recreation Area   SNOW SPORTS

(day/season pass $6/40; ☺mid-Nov–May) Off I-70 (exit 190), Vail Pass is one of the top winter backcountry destinations in the state. The 55,000 acres are shared-access, for both motorized (snowmobiles) and non-motorized (skiers and snowboarders) users. In addition to the trails groomed by the forest service, you can access four backcountry huts from here. (You must have avalanche gear if you enter the backcountry.)

Booth Falls & Booth Lake Trail   HIKING

(Booth Falls Rd) A 2-mile hike to the 60ft **Booth Falls** follows USFS Trail 1885 into the Eagles Nest Wilderness Area. The trailhead is off N Frontage Rd west of I-70 exit 180 (East Vail). Continue beyond the falls to encounter meadows filled with wildflowers and views of the Gore Range. The trail continues to **Booth Lake**, 4.1 miles from the trailhead, and climbs about 3000ft.

Vail to Breckenridge Bike Path   CYCLING

(www.summitbiking.org) This paved, car-free bike path stretches 8.7 miles from East Vail to the top of Vail Pass (elevation gain 1831ft) before descending 14 miles into Frisco (it's 9 miles more if you go all the way to Breckenridge). If you're only interested in the downhill, hop on a shuttle from Bike Valet (p205) and enjoy the ride back to Vail.

Alpine Quest Sports   WATER SPORTS, CLIMBING

(☑970-926-3867; www.alpinequestsports.com; 34510 Hwy 6, Edwards; ☺9am-6pm) This is Vail's top backcountry-adventure kayaking resource with gear, rentals and a full kayak and SUP school with beginner, intermediate and advanced classes. It also outfits rock- and ice-climbers with gear and tips, and has telemark and AT skis, splitboards and snowshoes for rent. It's located in Edwards, west of Vail.

Vail Golf Club   GOLF

(☑970-479-2260; www.vailrec.com; 1778 Vail Valley Dr; 9/18 holes May-Oct $60/100) Hemmed in by Gore Creek and tucked up against the White River National Forest, this 18-hole par-71 course nestled at 8200ft elevation is a fine place to hit a small white ball. Reservations are vital in summer and can be made 60 days in advance. The pro shop can set you up with rentals, lessons and a cart.

Epic Discovery   ADVENTURE SPORTS

(☑970-496-4910; www.epicdiscovery.com; day pass Ultimate/Little Explorer $94/54; ☺10am-6pm Jun-Aug, Fri-Sun only Sep; ⊕) Vail's trailbreaking new summer venture is a combination of family adventure park and nature center. There are plenty of adrenaline-piqued activities to keep the screams coming – such as ropes courses, a gravity-powered mountain coaster, a climbing wall and a four-hour zipline tour ($199) – but added to the mix are interpretive elements designed to educate participants about the local ecology.

Adventure Ridge Winter   SNOW SPORTS

(☑970-754-8245; www.vail.com; ☺1-7pm Tue-Sat; ⊕) At the top of the Eagle Bahn Gondola (Lionshead), Adventure Ridge is the center of family fun. Obviously it's all about snow in winter, which can mean tubing ($45 per three runs), kids' snowmobiling ($25 per person) and ski biking ($95 tours, ages 10 and up). Hours for each activity are sometimes different, so check ahead of time.

Zip Adventures
ADVENTURE SPORTS

(📞970-926-9470; www.zipadventures.com; 4098 Hwy 131, Wolcott; per person $170; ◷May-Nov) Here's your chance to fly over a rugged canyon at well over 30mph, 200ft above a gushing creek. With six zipline tours set up over Alkali Canyon and distances ranging from 150ft to 1000ft long, you'll get plenty of time to work on your primal scream. Easy and exhilarating, the two-hour romp is worth the splurge.

It's located in Wolcott, 21 miles west of Vail on I-70.

Dobson Ice Arena
SKATING

(📞970-479-2271; www.vailrec.com; 321 E Lionshead Circle; adult/child $6/5, skate rental $3; ◷hours vary; ♿) Located at the entrance to the Lionshead ski resort, this aging yet more-than-adequate rink offers public skate times (see schedule online). There are also much smaller outdoor rinks in Vail Village and Lionshead.

Bike Valet
CYCLING

(📞970-476-7770; www.bikevalet.net; 616 W Lionshead Cir; bike rental per day from $50; ◷9am-6pm; ♿) Bike Valet is one of two independently owned bike shops in Lionshead. Rent cruisers, kids bikes and full-suspension mountain bikes or sign up for a shuttle up to Vail Pass ($49, bike included). In winter it's Ski Valet, offering tuning services and season-long ski lockers.

Vail Nordic Center
SNOW SPORTS

(📞970-476-8366; www.vailnordiccenter.com; 1778 Vail Valley Dr; day pass adult/child $10/free; ◷9am-5pm Dec-Mar; ♿) Vail's cross-country skiing resource offers lessons and gear rental for aspiring Nordic skiers. You can also rent snowshoes. There are 10 miles of trails; ask about backcountry access, too.

Christy Sports
OUTDOORS

(📞970-476-2244; www.christysports.com; 293 Bridge St; rental bikes/skis per day from $45/40; ◷10am-6pm summer, 8am-8pm winter; ♿) This Colorado chain has stores at most resorts as well as major cities throughout the state. They rent and sell skis, boards and bikes, along with outdoor clothing and gear. Quality varies with the price.

Buzz's Ski Shop
SNOW SPORTS

(📞970-476-3320; 302 Gore Creek Dr; rental skis adult/child from $21/15, boards from $29; ◷Nov–

mid-Apr; ♿) In tiny, corporate Vail, a laid-back place like Buzz's feels like a breath of fresh powder. Techs are knowledgeable, prices are among the cheapest on the mountain, the equipment is solid, and it's just a few minutes' walk to the Gondola in Vail Village. It's only open during the winter season; it also does rentals.

Troy's Ski Shop
CYCLING, SNOW SPORTS

(📞970-476-8769; www.troysskishop.com; 392 Hanson Ranch Rd; ski/bike rental per day from $44/50; ◷9am-6pm; ♿) Independently owned and with friendly staff, Troy's rents high-end, full-suspension mountain bikes in summer and the best skis and boards on the mountain in winter.

Summer at Vail
HIKING, BIKING

(📞970-754-8245; www.vail.com; gondola adult/child $36/18, bike haul adult/child $41/23; ◷9:30am-6pm Jun-Aug, Fri-Sun only Sep) Vail has plenty to offer after the snow melts. Start with a scenic gondola ride up to the top of Gondola One or Eagle Bahn, from where you'll find a choice of activities. Six short hiking trails climb to incredible views and 52 miles of mountain-biking trails traverse the mountain. Four restaurants spoiled with views keep everyone fed.

👣 Tours

Vail Nature Center
HIKING

(📞970-479-2291; www.walkingmountains.org; 601 Vail Valley Dr; family hikes from $30; ◷Jun-Sep) The Nature Center offers guided tours all summer long, from full-day backcountry hikes to more family-oriented activities. Free creekside nature tours run on Sundays; other popular kids activities include wildflower walks and evening trips to the beaver pond or stargazing with s'mores. There are also four short interpretive trails open to the public.

Gore Creek Fly Fishermen
FISHING

(📞970-476-5042; www.gorecreekflyfisherman. com; 675 Lionshead Pl, Bldg A; half-day/full-day trips per person $280/375; ◷8am-6pm) This Lionshead fly-fishing shop and outfitter will set you up with new and used gear for rent or purchase. You can also get Gore Creek fishing tips and sign up for half-day and full-day fishing trips on gold-medal waters. Don't miss the free casting clinics at 10:30am daily in summer.

Bearcat Stables
HORSEBACK RIDING

(📞970-926-1578; www.bearcatstables.com; 2701 Squaw Creek Rd, Edwards; 1/2/4hr ride

SHRINE PASS

Halfway between Copper Mountain and Vail is Shrine Pass (11,178ft), accessed via an 11.5-mile dirt road/ski trail that cuts south of Vail's Blue Sky Basin to link up with the town of Red Cliff along Hwy 24. In summer, this is a very popular multiuse trail: you can drive it, bike it (three to four hours), use an ATV, and, of course, go hiking – Shrine Mountain Trail is 4.2 miles round-trip; the trailhead is 2.25 miles up the road. From Julia's Deck (Mile 3.75) you have good views of Mount of the Holy Cross. Biking is the most interesting option because once you hump the pass (2.5 miles in), it's all downhill to Red Cliff. If you have two cars you can set up a shuttle; otherwise sign up for a bike tour with Bike Valet (p205) in Vail.

In winter this area is known as the Vail Pass Recreation Area (p204) and is equally interesting. It's used by both snowmobilers and backcountry skiers and boarders (often teaming together for the uphills), but with 55,000 acres of wilderness and 52 miles of nonmotorized trails, you should be able to find some seclusion. The forest service grooms 50 miles of trails back here, allowing you to get between Shrine Pass, Red Cliff and a third access point, Camp Hale (p246). Additionally, there are four huts (p228) in the area (Shrine Mountain, Fowler, Jackal and Janet's Cabin) for overnight trips. It goes without saying that avalanche gear and training are a must. If you've got the cash, Vail Powder Guides (p206) run a memorably full day of snowcat skiing here.

To get here, take the Vail Pass exit (190) off I-70, or park in Red Cliff or Camp Hale on Hwy 24. The Minturn ranger office (p212) has maps and trail descriptions for the area – you must pick up a map before you go, as it's quite likely you'll get lost without one. In Red Cliff, stop off at Mango's (p214) for a meal or drink.

$60/90/160; ☺ by reservation) One of the best horseback operations in the Vail Valley, Bearcat offers one- and two-hour rides, as well as four-hour backcountry rides, four-day rides to Aspen and horse-drawn sleigh rides in winter. Trips are always fairly intimate, with an eight-person maximum. Children must be seven or older.

Vail Stables   HORSEBACK RIDING
(☑ 970-445-8204; www.vailstables.com; 915 Spraddle Creek Rd; rides $70-355; ☺ May-Sep) This family-run stable offers horse-riding classes and camps for kids, and one- to three-hour rides in the Gore Range. Kids need to be six and over and at least 40in tall.

Paragon Guides   OUTDOORS
(☑ 970-926-5299; www.paragonguides.com; 210 Edwards Village Blvd, Unit B107, Edwards) Guides take guests on hut-to-hut ski tours (p229) and backcountry skiing day trips in winter, and climbing, mountain-biking and mountaineering trips in summer.

Apex Mountain School   OUTDOORS
(☑ 970-949-9111; www.apexmountainschool.com; 51 Eagle Rd, Avon) This Avon-based outfitter runs local ice-climbing and backcountry skiing tours in winter and climbing and mountaineering trips in summer. It also hosts a variety of classes and Wilderness First Responder certification courses.

Vail Powder Guides   SNOW SPORTS
(☑ 719-486-6266; www.vailpowderguides.com; Vail Pass; per person $500; ☺ mid-Dec–Apr) For an unparalleled backcountry experience, try out snowcat skiing in the Vail Pass Recreation Area (p204). It's pricey, but you'll be able to get in 10 to 12 runs of untouched powder on a day to remember. Fat skis and boards are included, as is a good lunch in their yurt.

Vail Valley Paragliding   ADVENTURE SPORTS
(☑ 970-845-7321; www.vailvalleyparagliding.com; per person $205-275) Here's your chance to fly high above the Rocky Mountains. Join one of the tandem flights, which launch in the morning and occasionally in the afternoon. You'll lift off at 8700ft and, if the winds are cooperative, you might fly as high as 14,000ft. Duration varies, but an hour is common. Dress warmly – it gets cold in heaven.

✯ Festivals & Events

Spring Back to Vail   CULTURAL
(www.vail.com/events; ☺ mid-Apr) This weekend party officially closes the ski season with a series of free concerts and barbecues.

There's always a big hitter for the Friday night concert – Wyclef Jean and Jimmy Cliff have been headliners. The annual pond-skimming championships (involving a ski jump and an icy pond) might be the highlight though.

Taste of Vail
FOOD & DRINK

(☑ 970-401-3320; www.tasteofvail.com; festival pass $430; ☺ Apr) For more than 20 years this gourmet festival in early April has offered some of the best mountain cuisine you can imagine. The main event is the grand tasting and auction, with every Vail restaurant included, but the lamb cook-off and après-ski wine tasting run a close second.

Vail Film Festival
FILM

(☑ 970-306-6843; www.vailfilmfestival.org; festival pass/ticket $50/10; ☺ Apr) It's not the biggest indie film fest on the block, but it brings plenty of star power. Past attendees include Kevin Smith, Paul Rudd, Olivia Wilde and Harold Ramis.

Snow Daze
MUSIC

(www.vail.com/events; ☺ Dec; 👫) Held annually in early December, this early-season party once marked the official opening of Vail Mountain. Now it's just one of the biggest early-season ski-town parties on the continent. Headliners include big acts like Wilco.

Burton US Open Snowboarding Championships
SPORTS

(www.vail.com/events; ☺ Feb-Mar) Catch Shaun White, Chloe Kim and all your favorite aerial shredders at the longest-running slopestyle and halfpipe championships in the world.

🛌 Sleeping

Aside from camping, don't expect to find any budget or midrange lodging in Vail. Expect to pay minimum $400 during ski season. For the most part, you're paying for location, and location only: a lot of the lodging is condo-style, and so it can be hit or miss. For cheaper alternatives, check out the options in Minturn.

Gore Creek Campground
CAMPGROUND $

(☑ 877-444-6777; www.recreation.gov; Bighorn Rd; tent sites $22; ☺ mid-May–Sep; 👫) This campground at the end of Bighorn Rd has 19 tent sites with picnic tables and fire grates nestled in the woods by Gore Creek. There is excellent fishing near here – try the Slate Creek or Deluge Lake trails; the latter leads to a fish-packed lake. The campground is 6 miles east of Vail Village via exit 180 (East Vail) off I-70.

★ Sebastian Hotel
HOTEL $$$

(☑ 800-354-6908; www.thesebastianvail.com; 16 Vail Rd; r winter/summer from $800/300; 🅿 ❄ 🛜 🏊 🐕) Deluxe and modern, this sophisticated hotel showcases tasteful contemporary art and an impressive list of amenities, including a mountainside ski valet, luxury spa and 'adventure concierge.' Room rates dip in the summer, the perfect time to enjoy the tapas bar and spectacular pool area, with hot tubs frothing and spilling over like champagne.

Solaris
CONDO $$$

(☑ 970-476-9000; www.solarisvail.com; 141 E Meadow Dr; r winter/summer from $1500/715; 🅿 ❄ 🛜 🏊) A stay in one of Vail's finest properties comes with a personal assistant on call to arrange all the details such as shopping, restaurant reservations and equipment rental. Lodging is in one- to four-bedroom condos, all of which are modern and luxurious (think Frette linens and Sub-Zero appliances). Morning pastries, coffee and après-ski are complimentary. Minimum stay required.

Vail Mountain Lodge
HOTEL $$$

(☑ 888-794-0410; www.vailmountainlodge.com; 352 E Meadow Dr; r winter/summer from $435/250; 🅿 ❄ 🛜 🏊) With only 20 rooms and seven condos, this is about as boutique as Vail gets. Decor is rustic and simple, but rooms are nonetheless plush, featuring gas fireplaces and featherbeds, heated bathroom floors and deep soaking tubs. Stays include breakfast, free access to the on-site **Vail Athletic Club** (and all drop-in classes) and indoor and outdoor hot tubs.

The cherry on the cake is the gourmet fave **Terra Bistro** restaurant, located just downstairs.

Lodge at Lionshead
LODGE $$$

(☑ 800-962-4399; www.lodgeatlionshead.com; 380 E Lionshead Circle; studios winter/summer from $475/215; 🅿 ❄ 🛜 🏊) Friendly and unpretentious, this lodge offers a wide variety of private condos from studios (with pull-down beds) to four-bedroom luxury units. You'll need to book a minimum two to seven days, depending on the month.

Arrabelle
HOTEL $$$

(☑ 888-688-8055; http://arrabelle.rockresorts.com; 675 Lionshead Pl; r winter/summer from $845/419; 🅿 ❄ 🛜 🏊 🐕) The grand dame of Lionshead, the Arrabelle is a massive, chalet-style resort with a stone-and-marble lobby, top-shelf service and a variety of accommodations, from hotel rooms to four-bedroom luxury condos. All have flat-screen TVs, Bose sound systems, plush linens and marble baths. Book months in advance for discounts.

Lodge Tower   CONDO **$$$**
(✆ 970-476-9530; www.lodgetower.com; 200 Vail Rd; r winter/summer from $450/239; P ❄ 🛜 ⛷) This tower holds privately owned one-, two- and three-bedroom condos, but you can rent studios, too (locked-off bedrooms within a condo). Each is decorated in a different style so your furnishings will always be a surprise, though all multibedroom units have kitchens and fireplaces. Breakfast is included; four-night minimum in winter.

Mountain Haus   CONDO **$$$**
(✆ 800-237-0922; www.mountainhaus.com; 292 E Meadow Dr; r winter/summer from $405/195; P ❄ @ 🛜 ⛷ 🐾) A laid-back spot near the village entrance. Rooms aren't huge but some have fireplaces, king-sized beds, balconies and a view from the upper reaches, and they are relatively up-to-date. It has a hot tub, fitness center, pool and complimentary breakfast. One of the better deals in Vail.

Austria Haus   HOTEL **$$$**
(✆ 866-921-4050; www.austriahaushotel.com; 242 E Meadow Dr; r winter/summer from $500/280; P ❄ 🛜 ⛷) One of Vail's longest-running properties, the Austria Haus offers both hotel rooms and condos (more information at www.austriahausclub.com), so make sure you're clear on what you're signing up for. In the hotel, charming details such as wood-framed doorways, Berber carpet and marble baths make for a pleasant stay. Fuel up at the generous breakfast spread in the morning.

Tivoli Lodge   HOTEL **$$$**
(✆ 800-451-4756; www.tivolilodge.com; 386 Hanson Ranch Rd; r winter/summer from $419/319; P ❄ 🛜 ⛷) The only family-run lodging in town, this hotel boasts personable staff and an excellent slope-side location, with hot tubs literally at the base of the mountain. While the room decor is nothing to blog about, all have kitchenettes and exude comfort. Quirky hotel fact: the owners' son Buddy won the Indy 500 in 1996. Kids under 12 stay free.

Hotel Talisa   DESIGN HOTEL **$$$**
(✆ 800-420-2424; www.hoteltalisa.com; 1300 Westhaven Dr; r winter/summer from $1250/550;

P ❄ 🛜) Vail's newest hotel is certainly a step up when compared with some of the town's aging condos, though the modern design and amenities comes at a hefty price. It's ski-in, ski-out, with a chairlift on the property. It's located west of Lionshead and is more secluded than Vail's other accommodations options.

✖ Eating

Although Vail lacks the depth and breadth of Denver's restaurant scene, it's nonetheless one of the top spots in Colorado for a gourmet meal. During the summer, a vibrant farmers market (p208) is held in front of the Solaris complex (E Meadow Dr) on Sundays.

★ Westside Cafe   DINER **$**
(✆ 970-476-7890; www.westsidecafe.net; 2211 N Frontage Rd; mains $9-16; ☺ 7am-3pm Mon-Wed, to 10pm Thu-Sun; 🛜 🚗) Set in a West Vail strip mall, the Westside is a local institution. It does terrific all-day-breakfast skillets – like the 'My Big Fat Greek Skillet' with scrambled eggs, gyro, red onion, tomato and feta served with warm pita – along with all the usual high-cal offerings you need before or after a day on the slopes. Also has a grab-and-go counter.

La Cantina   MEXICAN **$**
(✆ 970-476-7661; Vail Village Parking Garage, Level 3; mains $6-12.50; ☺ 11:30am-9pm) Located beneath the Transportation Center and next to the Ski Museum, it should come as no surprise that Vail's cheapest meal has a rather quirky location right at the exit of the parking garage. But no matter – where else are you going to find a salsa bar and (passable) $6 burritos?

Moe's Original BBQ   BARBECUE **$**
(✆ 970-328-0177; www.moesoriginalbbq.com; 616 W Lionshead Cir; plates $9-14; ☺ 11am-9pm) You'll put on some pounds at this blues-driven barbecue chain, but the unpretentious roadhouse vibe is a refreshing change from the rest of the resort. Plates get you one main (smothered in BBQ sauce) and two sides – wash it down with a can of PBR.

Vail Farmers Market   MARKET **$**
(www.vailfarmersmarket.com; E Meadow Dr; ☺ 10am-3:30pm Sun mid-Jun–Sep) This farmers market and art show, located on Meadow Dr in the heart of the Vail Village, was established in 2001. You can grab any number of items for your condo kitchen, including

fresh-picked organic produce, fresh-baked breads, German pastries, local meats, fresh halibut, mountain honey and art from dozens of local artists and artisans.

There are more than 120 vendors in all.

Loaded Joe's
CAFE **$**

(☑ 970-479-2883; www.loadedjoes.com; 227 Bridge St; breakfast/lunch mains from $6.50/8; ☺ 6:30am-2am; 🖐) Almost under the bridge, this low-key underground cafe serves bagels and breakfast burritos, espressos and soy lattes, and sandwiches and smoothies for lunch and dinner. You can sip and munch beneath the cedars as the creek wakes you up with its gentle hum. Serves beer and wine, too.

Big Bear Bistro
SANDWICHES **$**

(☑ 970-445-1007; www.bigbearbistro.com; Hanson Ranch Rd; breakfast/lunch sandwiches from $8/11; ☺ 8am-5pm; 🖐) Unless your accommodations include a morning buffet, this is where to go for breakfast. It serves gourmet coffee, tasty breakfast burritos and some damn good sandwiches at lunch. We suggest the 'Masterpiece' – it comes with prosciutto, capocollo, salami, maple-glazed ham, balsamic-tinged arugula, banana peppers and cracked-pepper aioli.

The Little Diner
DINER **$**

(☑ 970-476-4279; www.thelittlediner.com; 616 W Lionshead Cir; mains $8-13; ☺ 7am-1:45pm) The most popular place for breakfast at the resort is the Little Diner in Lionshead. Huevos rancheros, sweet and savory crepes, biscuits and gravy – it's all made from scratch in the open kitchen. No reservations though, so arrive early if you want to make it to the slopes in time for the first lift.

Yellowbelly
SOUTHERN US **$**

(☑ 970-343-4340; www.yellowbellychicken. com; 2161 N Frontage Rd, Unit 14; mains from $5; ☺ 11am-9pm; 🖥🖐) Man, is this fried chicken good. We could tout the healthy aspects (non-GMO, free-range, veggie-fed birds), but it's the dynamite gluten-free batter that earns this place hidden in West Vail its stars. Accompany spicy, tender pieces of chicken with sides (Brussels-sprout slaw, citrus quinoa, mac and cheese), or order an entire rotisserie bird for the whole gang.

bōl
AMERICAN **$$**

(☑ 970-476-5300; www.bolvail.com; 141 E Meadow Dr; mains $18-27; ☺ 2pm-1am; 🖥🖐) Half hip eatery, half space-age bowling alley, bōl is the most unusual hangout in Vail. You can go bowling in the back ($105 to $300 per hour!), but it's the eclectic menu that's the real draw: creations range from lamb lollipops and blue corn–crusted chiles rellenos to duck-confit gnocchi.

Vendetta's
ITALIAN **$$**

(☑ 970-476-5070; www.vendettasvail.com; 291 Bridge St; pizzas from $15, mains lunch $10-15, dinner $20-33; ☺ 11am-late; 🖐) In overpriced and borderline-snooty Vail, this throwback pizza joint wins for aroma, ambience and, well, pizza. It does steaks and chops and also pasta dishes, but the pies – also sold by the slice – are what hit the spot.

El Sabor
MEXICAN **$$**

(☑ 970-477-4410; www.elsaborvail.com; 660 West Lionshead Pl; mains $10-25; ☺ 8am-10pm) Located right next to the Eagle Bahn Gondola, El Sabor wins points more for its location than its cuisine. You can find some decent $9 specials (Tamale Tuesdays) here on weekdays; otherwise, hit happy hour for the best prices.

★ Sweet Basil
AMERICAN **$$$**

(☑ 970-476-0125; www.sweetbasilvail.com; 193 Gore Creek Dr; mains lunch $18-22, dinner $27-48; ☺ 11:30am-2:30pm & 6pm-late) 🍴 In business since 1977, Sweet Basil remains one of Vail's top restaurants. The menu changes seasonally, but the eclectic American fare, which usually includes favorites such as Colorado lamb and seared Rocky Mountain trout, is consistently innovative and excellent. The ambience is also fantastic. Reserve.

★ Game Creek Restaurant
AMERICAN **$$$**

(☑ 970-754-4275; www.gamecreekvail.com; Game Creek Bowl; 3-/4-course meal $99/109; ☺ 5:30-9pm Tue-Sat Dec-Apr, 5:30-8:30pm Thu-Sat & 11am-2pm Sun late Jun–Aug; 🖊🖐) This gourmet destination is nestled high in the spectacular Game Creek Bowl. Take the Eagle Bahn Gondola to Eagle's Nest and staff will shuttle you (via snowcat in the winter) to their lodge-style restaurant, which serves an American-French menu with stars like wild boar, elk tenderloin and succulent leg of lamb. Reserve.

The Tenth
AMERICAN **$$$**

(☑ 970-754-1010; www.the10thvail.com; Look Ma Run, Mid Vail; mains $26-34; ☺ 9am-2:30pm Dec–mid-Apr, 11am-2:30pm Fri-Sun late Jun–Aug; 🖊🖐) And you thought ski-lodge fare had to be tasteless frozen burgers and microwaved

ON-MOUNTAIN DINING

Two of Vail's best restaurants aren't in the village at all, but high up on the mountain, with unrivaled settings and great views.

The Tenth (p209)

Game Creek Restaurant (p209)

nachos. No longer: the Tenth ratchets up Vail's ski-in, ski-out dining up a notch, with a smorgasbord of gourmet alpine cuisine. Think porcini and Colorado bass, elk chili with goat cheese and Spatzle with pork bratwurst. Or you could just have a brick-oven pizza.

If you're in a hurry to get back on the slopes, opt for the express menu in the lounge. Reservations recommended.

Mountain Standard   AMERICAN $$$
(✆970-476-0123; www.mtnstandard.com; 193 Gore Creek Dr; mains lunch $16-23, dinner $28-45; ⏰11:30am-10pm; 🔊) A casual spin-off of Sweet Basil (p209) – located out front – Mountain Standard has a lovely riverside setting that spills out onto the patio in warmer weather. The open kitchen focuses on the grill (rotisserie chicken with heirloom tomatoes, grilled trout with key-lime butter), with a raw bar (oyster shooters, tuna crudo) and salads to even it out.

Osaki's   JAPANESE $$$
(✆970-476-0977; www.osakivail.com; 100 E Meadow Dr; sushi per piece $4-7, rolls $7.50-11; ⏰5:30pm-late Tue-Sun) A star disciple of both his grandfather and Nobu Matsuhisa (yes, *that* Matsuhisa (p210)), Osaki worked in the Aspen restaurant before opening up this hole-in-the-wall temple, long Vail's go-to sushi spot. It retains its intimate (some say crowded) interior and the sushi is definitely excellent, but there's no doubt the master's high-profile emergence practically next door has raised the stakes. Reserve.

Up the Creek   AMERICAN $$$
(✆970-476-8141; www.vailupthecreek.com; 223 Gore Creek Dr; mains lunch $12-18, dinner $28-43; ⏰11am-9pm) 🍃 A long-standing local favorite set alongside Gore Creek, this restaurant boasts great lunchtime deals (turkey and Brie sandwich with orange-cranberry relish) and more substantial dinners (ribs with bacon-smoked mac and cheese and

asparagus). Produce is organic, and the vibe unpretentious and friendly. Opt for the patio seating in sunny weather.

Matsuhisa   JAPANESE $$$
(✆970-476-6628; www.matsuhisarestaurants.com; 141 E Meadow Dr; mains $29-42, sushi per piece $6-15; ⏰6-10pm) Legendary chef Nobu Matsuhisa has upped Vail's culinary standards with this modern, airy space in the heart of the Solaris complex. Expect traditional sushi and tempura alongside his signature 'new-style' sashimi – Matsuhisa opened his first restaurant in Peru and incorporates South American influences into his cuisine. Star dishes include black cod with miso and scallops with jalapeño salsa. Reserve.

Tavern on the Square   PUB FOOD $$$
(✆970-754-7704; http://arrabelle.rockresorts.com; 675 Lionshead Pl; mains $17-41; ⏰7am-10pm) Part of the Arrabelle (p207), the Tavern is a typical resort restaurant. The food is decent, but all in all unspectacular.

Campo de Fiori   ITALIAN $$$
(✆970-476-8994; www.campodefiori.net; 100 E Meadow Dr; mains $21-49; ⏰5:30pm-late) It's a splurge, but then all of Vail is a splurge – and this is a worthy one. Where else in town can you slurp black mussels and follow it up with lobster ravioli, and then follow that with NY strip or a Colorado lamb rack? The risotto *dello chef* ain't bad either.

Russell's   STEAK $$$
(✆970-476-6700; www.russellsvail.com; 228 Bridge St; mains $33-63; ⏰5:30-10pm) If you're looking for center-cut Angus, beef ribs or surf-and-turf in pressed-tablecloth environs, this intimate steakhouse is a good choice. Sides are extra.

🍷 Drinking & Nightlife

Although you can certainly indulge in champagne and rare bottles of Châteauneuf-du-Pape here, Vail also has a handful of cafes and bars offering good deals, particularly during happy hour.

Yeti's Grind   CAFE
(✆970-476-1515; www.yetisgrind.com; 141 E Meadow Dr, Suite 108; ⏰7am-7pm) Vail's best coffee comes from this indie cafe on the ground floor of the Solaris complex. Beans are roasted by City on a Hill (p249) in Leadville; there are also breakfast burritos and panini sandwiches. It also serves beer and wine come evening.

Garfinkels   PUB

(☎970-476-3789; www.garfsvail.com; 536 E Lionshead Cir; ☺11am-midnight) In Lionshead, this wooden lodge–style pub has a wide deck overlooking Vail Mountain. It also has a pool table, a killer circle bar with Dale's Pale Ale and Colorado Native on tap, and a dozen flat-screen TVs showing all the sports you could want.

Root & Flower   WINE BAR

(☎970-763-5101; www.rootandflowervail.com; 225 Wall St; ☺4pm-midnight) Celebrate in style with wines by the glass (helpfully divided into categories such as 'crisp and clean' or 'wood and weight') or cocktails, paired with cheese and *salumi* plates at Vail's most elegant happy hour.

The George   PUB

(☎970-476-2656; 292 E Meadow Dr; ☺3pm-2am) With a happy hour that runs to 9pm, you know this underground lair is going to be popular. In addition to a variety of drinks under $5, you can also fill up on all the usual pub sandwiches for $11 – and have change left over for the pool table afterwards.

Vail Brewing   BREWERY

(☎970-470-4622; www.vailbrewingco.com; 141 E Meadow Dr; ☺11am-10pm) Plenty of small-batch local brews and a sunny terrace are a reason to celebrate at the taproom of this Eagle-based brewery.

Vail Ale House   BAR

(www.vailalehouse.com; 2161 N Frontage Rd; ☺11:30am-midnight) This is really the only local place to sample Colorado's diverse selection of craft beers. Enjoy 20 great picks on tap from Avery (Boulder), Great Divide (Denver), Left Hand (Longmont) and Ska (Durango), among others. In West Vail.

Los Amigos   BAR

(☎970-476-5847; www.losamigosvail.com; 400 Bridge St; ☺11:30am-10pm) If you want views, tequila, and rock and roll with your après-ski ritual, come to Los Amigos. The Mexican food is decent at best, but the happy-hour prices and slope-side seating more than make up for any culinary shortcomings.

☆ Entertainment

Ford Amphitheater   CONCERT VENUE

(☎970-476-5612; www.vvf.org; 530 S Frontage Rd E) This picturesque outdoor amphitheater with lawn seating is the site of numerous summer concerts. It's a 10-minute walk east of Vail Village.

Cinebistro   CINEMA

(☎970-476-3344; www.cinebistro.com; 141 E Meadow Dr; adult/child $14/13; ☺noon-8pm)

THE VAIL DREAM

Long before two WWII vets who were hooked on powder hiked Vail Mountain to scout the possibility of a new ski resort halfway between Denver and Aspen – the only resort of its kind at the time – the Gore Range was home to Colorado's nomadic Ute Indians, who used to trek from the arid rangeland into the alpine country to beat the summer heat. However, white settlers thirsty for gold arrived in the mid-19th century and the Utes were pushed out.

During WWII the army founded Camp Hale, a training center off present-day Hwy 24. This is where the famous 10th Mountain Division – America's only battalion on skis – lived and trained. These troops fought hard in the Italian Alps, and when they came home, many became big players in the burgeoning ski industry.

Peter Seibert was one of them. He became part of the Aspen Ski Patrol, then became the manager of the Loveland Basin Ski Area – one of Colorado's oldest ski resorts. Together with his friend Earl Eaton, who was a lifelong skier and ski-industry veteran, Siebert climbed Vail Mountain in the winter of 1957. After one long look at those luscious back bowls, these men knew they'd struck gold.

At the time Vail Mountain was owned by the forest service and local ranchers. Seibert and Eaton recruited a series of investors and lawyers and eventually got a permit from the forest service and convinced nearly all of the local ranchers to sell. Much of the construction budget was raised by convincing investors to chip in $10,000 for a condo unit and a lifetime season pass.

Opening day was on December 15, 1962. Conditions were marginal, but the dream was alive. And if you'd skied there that day you would have paid $5 for a day pass and explored nine runs, accessed by two chairs and one gondola.

Located in the Solaris complex is Vail's slick contemporary cinema, with three premium theaters outfitted with cush seats and a bar and restaurant in the lobby; place your order and they'll serve you in the theater.

ℹ Information

Vail Visitor Center (☑970-477-3522; www. vailgov.com; 241 S Frontage Rd; ⊙8:30am-5:30pm winter, to 8pm summer; 🛜) Provides maps, last-minute lodging deals and activities and town information. It's located next to the Transportation Center. The larger **Lionshead welcome center** is located at the entrance to the parking garage.

Vail has free public wi-fi that is accessible throughout the village areas and in Gondola One.

ℹ Getting There & Away

The resort has two large base areas: **Vail Village** and **Lionshead**. **West Vail** (north of I-70) is 3 miles west of Vail Village; it's where you'll find grocery stores, pharmacies and the like.

If you're driving here, note that the I-70 exits are as follows: Vail Village and Lionshead (exit 176) and West Vail (exit 173). The base areas are traffic-free; most drivers park at the Vail Village Parking Garage ($25 per day in winter, free first two hours and in summer) before entering the pedestrian mall area near the chairlifts. Lionshead is a secondary parking lot (same rates) about half a mile to the west.

If you're cutting costs, you can try parking in West Vail along Frontage Rd (in front of the strip mall) and then taking **Vail Transit** (p212), but free spots are limited.

Eagle County Airport (EGE; ☑970-328-2680; www.flyvail.com; 217 Eldon Wilson Dr, Gypsum) This airport is 35 miles west of Vail and has services to destinations across the country (many of which fly through Denver) and rental-car counters.

All buses arrive and depart from the **Vail Transportation Center** (☑970-476-5137; 241 S Frontage Rd).

Bustang (☑800-900-3011; www.ridebustang. com; 🛜) Two daily buses to Vail ($17, 2½ hours) leave Denver's Union Station at 3:10pm and 5:40pm.

SnowStang Bustang's pilot ski bus program launched in 2016. The first year saw 6am Saturday departures from the Federal Center RTD Station in Denver direct to Vail for $60 round trip.

Greyhound (☑800-231-2222; www.greyhound. com; 🛜) Buses traveling along the I-70 corridor stop at Vail en route from the Denver Bus Station ($20, 2½ hours).

ℹ Getting Around

Vail has fine public transportation: it's free, it goes where you need to go and it operates at short intervals. Traveling by bus here is thus faster and more convenient than most car trips.

There are a number of car-rental companies at the Eagle County Regional Airport serving Vail and the surrounding area.

Eagle County Regional Transportation Authority (www.eaglecounty.us; per ride $4, to Leadville $7) ECO buses offer affordable transport to Beaver Creek, Minturn and even Leadville. Buses run from roughly 5am to 11pm; check the website for the exact schedule. Buses leave from the Vail Transportation Center (p212).

Vail Transit (☑970-477-3456; www.vailgov. com; ⊙6:30am-1:30am) Loops through all the Vail resort areas – West Vail (both North and South), Vail Village, Lionshead and East Vail, as well as Ford Park and Sandstone. Most buses have bike and ski racks and all are free.

Colorado Mountain Express (☑800-525-6363; www.coloradomountainexpress.com; 🛜) Shuttles to/from Denver International Airport ($92, three hours) and Eagle County Airport ($51, 40 minutes).

Fresh Tracks (p184) Runs to/from Breckenridge and other Summit County resorts.

High Mountain Taxi (☑970-524-5555; www. hmtaxi.com; airport service $142; ⊙24hr) Vail's signature taxi service serves the entire valley from Vail to Eagle, and is equipped for pets, kids, skis and snowboards. The airport service seats six people. Book online or call.

Minturn

☑970 / POP 1035 / ELEV 7861FT

Squeezed between the burgeoning luxury condominium and resort developments of Vail and Beaver Creek, Minturn is a wonderful respite in Eagle County. This small railroad town along the Eagle River was founded in 1887 and its shops and homes retain the coziness and charm of a place that really has been around for a while. If you prefer real town ambience over faux Tyrolean architecture and fur coats, Minturn makes an excellent base.

🏃 Activities

Minturn and Red Cliff (located about 10 miles further south on US 24) are gateways to the Holy Cross Wilderness Area, where you'll find some of the most spectacular hiking in the area. Anyone heading up to the region should first check in with the Holy

THE MINTURN MILE

If you're itching to head off the grid, consider the Minturn Mile. One of the most famous 'out-of-bounds' ski runs in the world, it's accessible from the top of chairs 3 or 7 on Vail Mountain.

At the top of the turn on Lost Boy, stay left and hike up to Ptarmigan Ridge. Here you can take the access gate and begin a descent of 3 miles to Minturn. Advanced skills are a must as you'll encounter a wide range of terrain – starting in a bowl and veering through the trees. At about the midway point you'll find the 'beaver ponds,' a terrific place to take a break and catch your breath before hitting the Luge, an old fire road that gets narrow in spots and will lead you the rest of the way down.

Know that you'll be skiing into an area beyond the resort boundaries – it is *not* patrolled. If you get injured, you'll be on your own, and if you require rescue it will come at considerable expense. It's best to ski along with someone who has prior knowledge of the terrain and route, and be sure to have proper gear, equipment and an updated report on conditions (if you go too early in the season the thin coverage could be a nightmare). It is, by all accounts, a magnificent experience – one of the best in the Vail swirl – and requires a toast at the Minturn Saloon (p214) upon arrival.

Cross Ranger Office (✆970-827-5715; www.fs.usda.gov/whiteriver; 24747 Hwy 24; ☺9am-4pm Mon-Fri). Do not head into the wilderness area without the proper information and appropriate equipment.

Half Moon Pass Trail   HIKING
(Tigiwon Rd; ☺mid-Jun–Oct) The classic ascent of the 14,005ft Mount of the Holy Cross (p30), this 10.8-mile round-trip hike is best done as an overnight if you plan on making the summit, but you can also simply hike up to Half Moon Pass (1.5 miles) for a short day hike (you won't see the cross from here, though). Over a dozen campsites are located 2.8 miles in.

Notch Mountain Trail   HIKING
(Tigiwon Rd; ☺Jun 21–Oct) This strenuous hike climbs over 2700ft to Notch Mountain (13,077ft), leaving many gasping for air. It's a 10.2-mile round trip that can be done in five to seven hours, but you'll be rewarded with sublime views of the Bowl of Tears and the snowy cross on Mount of the Holy Cross (through mid-July) to the west.

Minturn Anglers   FISHING
(✆970-827-9500; www.minturnanglers.com; 102 Main St; half-day wade trips from $295; ☺10am-6pm) Guides take newbies along one of eight rivers, including Gore Creek and the Upper Eagle. They also offer free lessons outside the Solaris in Vail Village from 9am to 5pm daily (June to September), rental equipment and fishing camps for kids.

🛏 Sleeping

With a hostel and a reasonably priced B&B, Minturn is an obvious accommodations choice for mere mortals skiing in Vail or Beaver Creek. Half Moon Campground (p213), at the base of the Half Moon Pass Trail, is one of several first-come, first-served campgrounds in the region. There are also five backcountry huts run by the 10th Mountain Division Hut Association (p228).

Half Moon Campground   CAMPGROUND $
(Tigiwon Rd; tent sites $13; ☺Jun 21–Sep) Located at the trailheads for Notch Mountain and Half Moon Pass, this a popular base camp for overnight hikers in the Holy Cross Wilderness. To get here, take the turnoff to Tigiwon Rd (USFS Rd 707, opens June 21), 3 miles south of Minturn. A high-clearance vehicle is recommended for the rough 8-mile journey to the Fall Creek Trailhead.

Bears are active here; take proper food-storage precautions.

Bunkhouse   HOSTEL $
(✆970-827-4165; www.vailbunkhouse.com; 175 Williams St; dm winter/summer $100/64; ⓟ🛜) The Ikea-chic Bunkhouse features 30 custom-built pods – cozy, enclosed bunk beds that allow for a level of privacy not generally found in most hostels. There are also two private quads that can convert to a king-size bed upon request. Perks include a kitchen and individual lockers (bring your own lock). ECO buses (p212) run between Minturn and Vail for the car-less.

★ **Minturn Inn**   B&B $$

(☑970-827-9647; www.minturninn.com; 442 Main St; r summer/winter from $150/200; 🅿🛜) If you don't need to be at the heart of the action in Vail, the rustic Minturn Inn should be your pick. Set in a 1915 log-hewn building in Minturn, this cozy B&B turns on the mountain charm with handcrafted log beds, river-rock fireplaces and antlered decor. Reserve one of the newer River Lodge rooms for private Jacuzzi access.

✕ Eating

Kirby Cosmo's   BARBECUE $

(☑970-827-9027; www.kirbycosmos.com; 474 Main St; mains $7.50-15; ⊙11:30am-9pm; 🛜) This casual Carolina barbecue spot is located at the south end of town, toward Leadville. It's the best choice for a tasty affordable meal, with stalwarts like pulled-pork sandwiches, jalapeño poppers, short ribs and buffalo burgers. There are also a couple of Colorado beers on tap at the pinewood bar – need we say more?

Mango's   AMERICAN $

(☑970-827-9109; www.mangosmountaingrill.com; 166½ Eagle St, Red Cliff; mains $6-14.50; ⊙11am-8pm) Hidden in the outdoor mecca of Red Cliff, you can't miss this supergroovy, family-owned, three-story mountain pub with a fabulous roof deck. They do fish tacos and blackened-fish sandwiches, and host occasional live music on the 2nd floor, where you'll also find the pool table.

It also hosts the annual **Man of the Cliff** (www.manofthecliff.com; Red Cliff; $5; ⊙Oct), a wacky, strength-based contest where individuals and groups compete in events like wood chopping, archery, two-man cross cut, axe throw and keg toss. It's an homage to the timber days and proceeds benefit a local charity.

Nicky's Quickie   GREEK $

(☑970-827-5616; www.nickysquickie.com; 151 Main St; mains $8.25-11.75; ⊙11am-9pm; 🍴) The place to come if you're passing through and need something fast. It does a classic gyro pita (Nicky's Quickie) and a creative falafel that includes artichoke hearts and sun-dried tomatoes (Nicky's Crispie).

🍸 Drinking & Nightlife

Sticky Fingers   CAFE

(☑970-827-5353; 132 Main St; ⊙7:30am-5pm; 🛜) A great little cafe and bakery – get your breakfast burrito and latte fix in the morning, and sandwiches and smoothies in the afternoon.

Minturn Saloon   BAR

(☑970-827-5954; www.minturnsaloon.com; 146 Main St; ⊙3-11pm) Sit by the crackling fireplace and knock back margaritas with everyone else who came down the Minturn Mile at this historic après-ski hangout. It posts regular updates of Minturn Mile (p213) conditions on its Facebook page.

ℹ Information

Holy Cross Ranger Office (p212) Info on camping and hiking in the Holy Cross Wilderness. The office is 1 mile north of Minturn, shortly after you exit I-70.

ℹ Getting There & Away

Minturn is 8 miles southwest of Vail on Hwy 24 (I-70, exit 171). ECO buses (p212) connect with Vail; check the schedule online or pick up info at the **Vail Transportation Center** (p212).

Beaver Creek

☑970 / POP 6447 (AVON) / ELEV 8100FT

Breach the regal gates in Avon and you'll emerge onto a private mountain road skirting a picturesque golf course as it climbs to the foot of a truly spectacular ski mountain. Beaver Creek feels like one of those delicious secrets shared among the rich kids, and it is indeed a privilege to ski here.

Today the perfectly maintained grounds and neo-Tyrolean buildings lend a certain looming grandeur. Beaver Creek is a mellower, more conservative place than Vail and typically an older scene. It's the kind of destination where grandparents bring the whole family to enjoy a slew of all-natural adventures.

🏃 Activities

Beaver Creek Mountain   SNOW SPORTS

(☑970-754-0020; www.beavercreek.com; Village Rd; adult/child $189/130; ⊙9am-4:30pm; ⛷) Beaver Creek isn't exactly a ghost town in the summer, but it's no secret that the winter rules. The mountain boasts a 4040ft vertical rise serviced by 16 lifts, with 150 trails through aspen forest and a wide variety of ski terrain. The posh reputation keeps away some – but that just means more powder for you.

Red Sky Golf Club   GOLF

(☑970-754-8425; www.redskyranch.com; 376 Red Sky Rd; 18 holes $255; ⊙mid-May–Oct) Thirty-six holes of award-winning Tom Fazio and Greg Norman–designed fairway nirvana is available to guests of all Beaver Creek resorts (and a handful of Vail lodges, too). The courses are separated by a massive ridge, which, according to the Red Sky folks, serves as a wildlife corridor for deer and elk.

Beaver Creek Summer Adventure Center
OUTDOORS

(970-754-5373; www.beavercreek.com; Village Rd; chairlift adult/child $36/18, with bike $42/24; 9:30am-4:30pm mid-Jun–Aug, Sat & Sun only Sep;) Summertime fun in Beaver Creek features chairlift rides, mountain biking, kids' ropes courses, disc golf and hiking.

McCoy Park Nordic Center
SNOW SPORTS

(970-754-5313; www.beavercreek.com; Beaver Creek Village; adult/child $38/26; 8:45am-4pm mid-Dec–Mar;) McCoy Park is a 20-mile playground for snowshoers and cross-country and skate skiers, where groomed and rustic trails cross pine forests, aspen groves and open glades. Nestled between Beaver Creek and Bachelor Gulch at the top of the Strawberry Park lift (#12), it has terrific views of three mountain ranges.

Lakota Guides
RAFTING

(970-845-7238; www.lakotaguides.com; 411 Metcalf Rd, Avon; adult/child from $99/82; May-Sep;) Lakota Guides is a reputable river outfitter serving Vail and Beaver Creek. It can get you on all the nearby rivers – the Eagle, Arkansas and Colorado – and also offers ziplining and other activities. It's based in Avon (9 miles west of Vail). The age requirement for children depends on the river.

Sleeping

It's all luxury accommodations here. Figure on an extra $50 to $100 on top of the room rate for the resort fee, valet parking and taxes.

Park Hyatt
RESORT $$$

(970-949-1234; www.beavercreek.hyatt.com; 136 East Thomas Pl; d winter/summer $800/300;) Definitely the star of Beaver Creek Village, this splashy hotel spills out to the foot of the mountain, practically kissing the Buckaroo Express gondola. Rooms don't quite match the location's pizzazz, but they are plush, with French windows and a private terrace. The outdoor pool and fire pits are tucked into a little gulch at the top of the village.

Westin Riverfront Resort & Spa
RESORT $$$

(970-790-6000; www.starwoodhotels.com; 126 Riverfront Ln; d winter/summer from $560/265;) Perched on the Eagle River, this Avon-based resort is connected by both gondola and public shuttle to nearby Beaver Creek. There's a lovely, modern mountain lodge motif in the lobby accentuated by soaring ceilings and full-height windows with epic mountain views – it's arguably the most stylish choice in the area.

Rooms are likewise tastefully indulgent, with wood floors in the foyer, a sitting area, a flat-screen TV above the fireplace, a kitchenette (in some), king beds and fabulous views. It rents multiroom condos, too. The sole detractor is that it's not slope side.

Ritz Carlton
RESORT $$$

(970-748-6200; www.ritzcarlton.com; 130 Daybreak Ridge; d winter/summer from $950/350;) Previously listed as a top Colorado resort by *Travel & Leisure;* included on Condé Nast's gold list; lauded for family- and pet-friendliness and a prized wedding destination – the Ritz Carlton, it's fair to say, won't disappoint. It's all about skiing in and out of luxury here and it's as grand and secluded as a 220-room hotel can be.

It's located in Bachelor Gulch, west of Beaver Creek village.

Eating

Beaver Creek's ski village has the usual array of resort dining options (though the freshly baked cookies served daily at 3pm are a nice touch), plus some gourmet destinations on the mountain itself. For a better choice of restaurants, drive downhill to the town of Avon.

Ticino
ITALIAN $$

(970-748-6792; www.ticinorestaurantavon.com; 100 W Beaver Creek Blvd; lunch $11-15, dinner $15-39; 11am-9pm Mon-Fri, 5-9pm Sat & Sun;) This casual Italian is one of several good choices in Avon, with housemade pasta, pizza, subs and traditional *secondi* like osso buco. There's a sun-drenched patio for alfresco dining and *limoncello* to end your meal on just the right note.

Dusty Boot
PUB FOOD $$

(970-748-1146; www.dustyboot.com; St James Pl; mains lunch $13-20, dinner $16-39; 11am-10pm;) This friendly saloon keeps it real. This food may not be for health nuts, but it's damn tasty. The burgers (including portobello burgers), handcut steaks and shaved prime-rib sandwiches are all recommended. And the regulars here? All locals.

★ **Beano's Cabin**   MODERN AMERICAN **$$$**
(☑970-754-3463; www.beanoscabinbeavercreek.com; 5 courses per person $107; ⊙5-10pm Dec-Apr, 5-10pm Wed-Sat Jun-Sep; 📶🅱) Beaver Creek's can't-miss destination restaurant involves a 20-minute open-air sleigh ride through the snowy night to a glowing cabin on the slopes, warm from a crackling fire and with a kitchen turning out local classics such as Colorado rack of lamb and almond-crusted trout. In summer, you have the option of arriving via wagon ride or a one-hour horseback trip.

❶ Getting There & Away

Avon is 9 miles west of Vail, just off I-70 (exit 167); its transport options are similar. Most visitors fly to Denver International Airport and either rent a car or hop on a shuttle (p212) to Beaver Creek. Major carriers also fly into Eagle County Airport (p212), 26 miles west.

The Beaver Creek resort operates a useful and free private shuttle, and Avon's transit department operates a free Gondola Express shuttle for those coming up to ski for the day (if you're driving, the daily parking fee is $35).

Eagle County Regional Transportation Authority operates ECO buses (p212) that link Avon with Vail and Eagle. If you need a cab, High Mountain Taxi (p212) serves Beaver Creek and the Vail Valley.

ASPEN & THE MAROON BELLS

Located at the south end of the Roaring Fork Valley, Aspen is Colorado at its most sublime (the scenery) and glamorous (the people). Although you can get here over Independence Pass in summer, for most of the year the town is hemmed in by the towering Sawatch Range and the rugged Elk Mountains, with the only access via Hwy 82, south of I-70. Glenwood Springs, at the north end of the highway, is commonly referred to as 'down valley,' while Aspen is considered to be 'up valley.'

Glenwood Springs

☑970 / POP 9837 / ELEV 5763FT
Let's start with the fun stuff. Doc Holliday – gunfighter, gambler, Wild West legend and, uh, dentist – died here. Why he came here is the first clue to Glenwood Springs' long-standing appeal: thermal hot springs.

In Holliday's day they were thought to have restorative powers; he hoped they'd ease his chronic respiratory ailments. Perched at the confluence of the Colorado and Roaring Fork Rivers at the end of gorgeous Glenwood Canyon, the hot springs have been a travel destination for centuries. Ute Indians sat in steamy thermal caves, which they called *yampah* ('great medicine'). A mild climate and a range of summer and winter activities have rounded out the city's appeal, but the springs remain the town's primary draw.

Glenwood Springs also represents an inexpensive down-valley alternative to Aspen and Vail – it's only one hour from each, which makes it a reasonable budget base for some of Colorado's best skiing.

◉ Sights

**Glenwood Caverns
Adventure Park**   AMUSEMENT PARK, CAVE
(☑970-945-4228; www.glenwoodcaverns.com; 51000 Two Rivers Plaza Rd; amusement park adult/child $54/49, tram & cave tour adult/child $29/24; ⊙9am-9pm with seasonal variations) This family-oriented destination lumps together several attractions at once: the **Fairy Caves** (once billed as the eighth wonder of the world), a full-on amusement park, and a tram ride 1300 ft up to the top of **Iron Mountain**. The regular cave tour is probably the main attraction here: this is the largest cave in Colorado open to the public.

Linwood Cemetery   CEMETERY
(Pioneer Cemetery; cnr 12th St & Bennett Ave) Established in 1886, this is where John Henry 'Doc' Holliday was allegedly laid to rest in November 1887 (debate about this persists, since some scholars claim the ground would have been frozen). Harvey 'Kid Curry' Logan, a member of the gang headed by Butch Cassidy and the Sundance Kid, is also here. It's a 0.5-mile hike uphill from 12th and Bennett.

Frontier Historical Museum   MUSEUM
(☑970-945-4448; www.glenwoodhistory.com; 1001 Colorado Ave; adult/child $5/free; ⊙10am-4pm Mon-Sat May-Sep, shorter hours rest of year) Tucked into a quiet, leafy neighborhood, this community museum has an excellent collection of historic photos and old maps. The staff are history buffs: they host the annual Linwood Cemetery Ghost Walk.

🏃 Activities

The visitor center (p219) has a town map that also details all the nearby hiking and

DOC HOLLIDAY'S LAST LABORED BREATH

It's appropriate that the hike to this memorial at Linwood Cemetery might leave you breathless: the life of the legendary man underfoot was shaped by labored breathing. Seeking relief for tuberculosis (then known as 'consumption'), John Henry 'Doc' Holliday (1851–87) moved west from his native Georgia. He set up a dental practice in Texas, but the wheezing scared away patients. Turning to gambling and hanging out in saloons, Holliday met Wyatt Earp, with whom he participated in the most famous shoot-out of Western lore at the OK Corral.

Biographers portray Holliday as a hot-tempered vagabond with a rapacious, caustic wit evident even in his last moments. Lying infirm in a hotel on the site of the current Hotel Colorado he gazed bemusedly at his bare feet and said, 'Well I'll be damned. This is funny.' No legendary gunfighter ever expected to die with his boots off.

Despite the monument, Holliday's exact place of burial is unknown: the records were lost when the cemetery was moved from an earlier location down the hill.

cycling trails. For more in-depth information, stop by the USFS Ranger Office (p219).

★ **Glenwood Hot Springs & Spa of the Rockies**　HOT SPRINGS, SPA
(☑ 970-947-2955; www.hotspringspool.com; 401 N River St; adult/child $23.25/14.25, lower rates off-peak; ⊙ 7:30am-10pm, from 9am off-peak; ⚐) Glenwood Springs' main attraction, these hot springs pump out 3.5 million gallons of mineral water a day, flowing through two main pools: the 400ft-long big pool at 90°F (32°C) and the 100ft-long small pool at 104°F (40°C). A resort for over 125 years now, it has plenty of other amenities: namely a spa, hotel, water slides and mini-golf.

Sunlight Mountain Resort　SNOW SPORTS
(☑ 800-445-7931; www.sunlightmtn.com; 10901 County Road 117; adult/child $57/45; ⊙ 9am-4pm; ⚐) Twelve miles south of Glenwood Springs on Garfield County Rd 117, this small ski area ensures business by offering good deals for families and intermediate skiers – this is one of the least expensive spots to ski in Colorado. There's also cross-country skiing, snowshoeing and ice-skating areas.

There's a shuttle (one-way $5) to the hill from the Hot Springs Lodge (p218) and Hotel Colorado (p218). Equipment and rentals are available at the mountain or in town at Sunlight Ski & Bike Shop.

Sunlight Ski & Bike Shop　OUTDOORS
(☑ 970-945-9425; www.sunlightmtn.com; 309 9th St; rental skis adult/child from $25/20, bikes per hr/day $8/25; ⊙ 9am-7pm; ⚐) In summer, this downtown shop rents standard bikes, tandems, mountain bikes and a selection of children's bikes. It also runs a shuttle ($34)

to Bair Ranch and Hanging Lake to let you pedal back. In winter, it has all the snow gear you need.

Canyon Bikes　CYCLING
(☑ 800-439-3043; www.canyonbikes.com; 319 6th St; bike rental per day adult/child $32/24; ⊙ 8am-8pm Jun-Aug; ⚐) The paved 16-mile biking, hiking and in-line-skating trail through Glenwood Canyon starts one block from this downtown bike shop. It's a great option for families too, as it operates a shuttle (adult/child $40/30, includes bike) to save you the work of pedaling uphill.

Yampah Spa　HOT SPRINGS, SPA
(☑ 970-945-0667; www.yampahspa.com; 709 E 6th St; incl towel rental $15; ⊙ 9am-9pm) Entering these caves feels like descending into one of Dante's layers of hell, at least in terms of temperature. It's hot – damn hot: 110°F (43°C) to be exact. Mineral-rich spring waters run along the cave floors at a temperature of 125°F (52°C), filling the interior with hot steam.

First developed by the Ute hundreds of years earlier for therapeutic purposes, the natural caves have been a commercial facility since the 1880s, and though they've been widened and slightly remodeled in the years since, they still have a primeval feel. Additional spa treatments are available.

Iron Mountain Hot Springs　HOT SPRINGS
(☑ 970-945-4766; www.ironmountainhotsprings. com; 281 Centennial St; adult/child $25/17; ⊙ 9am-10pm) Soak in your pick of 16 outdoor mineral pools set along the Colorado River, as well as a larger family pool. It's a pleasant setup, but also very close to the highway.

👉 Tours

Blue Sky Adventures
RAFTING

(☑ 877-945-6605; www.blueskyadventure.com; 319 6th St; half-day adult/child $55/45; ⊙ May-Aug; 🚐) One of the most established rafting companies in town, Blue Sky operates both half- and full-day trips through the Shoshone rapids on the Colorado River. Those who don't have a thirst for white water can try out one of the scenic float trips. Inflatable kayaks ($30) are available as well.

Rock Gardens Rafting
RAFTING

(☑ 800-958-6737; www.rockgardens.com; 1308 County Rd 129; half-day adult/child from $52/42; ⊙ May-Aug; 🚐) This reputable operator in Glenwood Springs runs half- and full-day adventures on the Shoshone section of the Colorado River. It also rents out inflatable kayaks and offers combo raft and bike/zipline packages. It's off of I-70 at exit 119.

Roaring Fork Anglers
FISHING

(☑ 800-781-8120; www.roaringforkanglers.com; 2205 Grand Ave; half-day wade trips from $250; ⊙ 8:30am-5:30pm) This full-service fly shop has been operating on the local rivers for 30 years. In addition to guided half- and full-day trips, it also offers two-hour lessons for $120 and up-to-date river reports.

Up Tha Creek
RAFTING

(☑ 970-947-0030; www.upthacreek.com; 309 9th St; adult/child from $55/49; ⊙ May-Aug; 🚐) This smaller outfit has some unusual trips in its lineup, including beginner trips on less-crowded sections of the Colorado (South Canyon and Little Gore) as well as the extreme class V Gore Canyon. It also runs several sections of the Roaring Fork and even the Crystal River near Aspen. Definitely worth looking into if you want something different.

🛏 Sleeping

Glenwood's sleeping options are largely of the chain variety. If you're camping, you're better off heading up valley.

Glenwood Springs Hostel
HOSTEL $

(☑ 970-945-8545; www.hostelcolorado.com; 1021 Grand Ave; dm $30, r $45; ⊙ Oct-Jun; @ 🛜) This hostel hasn't been renovated in ages and hence rooms here are cramped and run-down. But if you need to save your nickels and dimes, it's the cheapest deal you'll find in the Aspen area. The common spaces have some character, but the clientele is much more long-term residents than fellow travelers.

Hotel Colorado
HOTEL $$

(☑ 800-544-3998; www.hotelcolorado.com; 526 Pine St; d from $119; P 🅿 🛜 ❄) Understandably nicknamed the 'Grand Dame,' this imposing 19th-century hotel has rooms that have seen better days, but the ghosts of its past residents (presidents and gangsters, heiresses and gunmen) make for a remarkably unique stay.

Sunlight Lodge
LODGE $$

(☑ 970-945-5225; www.sunlightlodge.com; 10252 County Rd 117; d $109-159; ⊙ seasonal; ❄) A stone's throw from Sunlight Mountain Resort's ski area, this adorable mountain lodge has 20 Western-style rooms with quilted beds and inviting fireplaces, around which guests congregate. Somehow, the hustle of the outside world doesn't make it through the door – there are no TVs and no cellphone reception, and when it's blanketed by snow, it achieves a languid coziness.

Glenwood Hot Springs Lodge
HOTEL $$

(☑ 800-537-7946; www.hotspringspool.com; 415 E 6th St; r from $229; P ❄ 🛜 ❄) The obvious choice if you're coming here specifically for the hot springs, the on-site hotel is as luxurious as Glenwood gets. Rooms are generic but quite comfortable. All packages include pool access and a full breakfast. Book in advance.

🍴 Eating

If you're exploring on foot and get hungry, make for 7th St off Grand Ave – it has the highest concentration of restaurants.

⭐ Slope & Hatch
TACOS $

(☑ 970-230-9652; www.slopeandhatch.net; 208 7th St; mains $7-12; ⊙ 11am-9pm Mon-Fri, 9am-9pm Sat & Sun) Glenwood is lucky enough to be blessed with not just one but two quality taco spots. This one is the funky, chef-driven place, where you can get Cajun andouille fries and craft beer alongside two mouthwatering tacos (eg margarita grilled shrimp with pineapple-jalapeño salsa or curried lamb and sweet potato). They also serve natural hot dogs and bowls of green chili.

Bluebird Cafe
CAFE $

(☑ 970-384-2024; www.bluebirdcafeglenwood.com; 730 Grand Ave; sandwiches $8.50-9.50; ⊙ 7am-6pm Mon-Sat, to 5pm Sun; 🛜) 🌱 This organic coffee shop serves up veggie breakfast burritos and a decent lunch menu of simple sandwiches and homemade soup. Folk bands occasionally pop up outside the front window and in the summer there's breezy outdoor seating.

Sweet Coloradough
BAKERY, SANDWICHES $

(☑970-230-9056; www.sweetcoloradough.com; 2430 S Glen Ave; sandwiches $3-12; ⊙6am-2pm Wed-Mon) Great little indie bakery on the road up valley (look for the old police car parked out front), with cronuts, eclairs, fine doughnuts and lots of bagel sandwiches for breakfast and lunch.

Taqueria El Nopal
MEXICAN $

(☑970-945-7311; www.taquerianopalglenwood.net; 2902 Hwy 82; tacos from $2.50; ⊙10am-9pm Tue-Sun; P 🛜) With Salvadorian *pupusas* (thick stuffed tortillas) and a tasty variety of tacos, the offerings here go well beyond the usual Col-Mex fare. They also serve housemade *horchata* (a sweet cinnamon and rice-milk drink), but it's the freshly made tortillas that seal the deal. It's located on Hwy 82 at the southern edge of town, just past 29th St.

★Pullman
AMERICAN $$

(☑970-230-9234; www.thepullmangws.com; 330 7th St; mains $12-23; ⊙11am-3:30pm & 4:30-9:30pm Mon-Fri, from 10am Sat & Sun; 🛜 🍴) 🍴 This casual industrial space is easily Glenwood Springs' hippest hangout, with bare filament bulbs hanging over the tables and an open kitchen in the back. Dishes tend to have a creative twist, landing somewhere between modern American (farro salad with kale, *queso fresco* and cranberries) and upmarket Italian (butternut-squash agnolotti).

Juicy Lucy's Steakhouse
STEAK $$$

(☑970-945-4619; www.juicylucyssteakhouse.com; 308 7th St; lunch $10.25-12.75, dinner $16.75-36.50; ⊙11am-9:30pm) Despite the cornball name, people love Lucy's because staff cook the meat well and eschew the macho brass-fitted steakhouse posture for a small-town-cafe feel. It serves game and fish dishes and has a good wine list, but the side of cheesy au gratin potatoes nearly steals the show.

🍷 Drinking & Entertainment

Glenwood Canyon Brewing Company
BREWERY

(☑970-945-1276; www.glenwoodcanyon.com; 402 7th St; ⊙11am-10pm) You'll do better to eat elsewhere, but the beers here are fresh and the night scene is lively. The lighter beers on the spectrum – particularly the Hanging Creek Honey Ale and Red Mountain ESB – are the best, though the fresh root beer is also truly outstanding.

Glenwood Vaudeville Revue
THEATER

(☑970-945-9699; www.gvrshow.com; 915 Grand Ave; adult/child $24/16) This popular two-hour dinner show is Glenwood's main entertainment option, with comedy sketches, singing and dancing. Shows are usually held on Friday and Saturday; dinner is à la carte.

ℹ️ Information

USFS Ranger Office (☑970-945-2521; www.fs.usda.gov; 900 Grand Ave; ⊙8am-4:30pm Mon-Fri) Information about camping and hiking in the surrounding White River National Forest.

Visitor center (☑970-945-6580; www.visitglenwood.com; 802 Grand Ave; ⊙9am-5pm Mon-Fri, 10am-4pm Sat & Sun) Assists with booking rooms and activities.

ℹ️ Getting There & Away

Glenwood Springs is 159 miles west of Denver and 87 miles east of Grand Junction along I-70. Hwy 82, which runs up valley to Aspen, meets I-70 here. The installation of a new bridge at the entrance to town is expected to disrupt traffic into Glenwood, Aspen and elsewhere up valley through the first half of 2018; check for the latest updates and plan accordingly.

Amtrak (☑800-872-7245; www.amtrak.com; 413 7th St) The *California Zephyr* stops daily at the Glenwood Springs Amtrak Station. Trips to and from Denver ($44, 5¾ hours) happen once daily.

Bustang (☑800-900-3011; www.ridebustang.com; 🛜) The Bustang runs between Glenwood Springs and Denver once daily ($28, four hours). It leaves Denver at 5:40pm and the South Glenwood BRT Station (Hwy 82, near 27th St) at 7:05am.

Greyhound (☑800-231-2222; www.greyhound.com; 51171 Hwy 6) Alta Convenience serves as the unstaffed station in Glenwood Springs, with service along I-70 to Denver ($30, 3½ hours).

ℹ️ Getting Around

Roaring Forks Transit Authority (☑970-925-8484; www.rfta.com) With several lines, this network of public transportation serves the Roaring Fork Valley, from Glenwood Springs ($1 in town) to Aspen ($7), passing several ski areas in winter and connecting to the **Maroon Bells shuttle** (www.rfta.com; Aspen Highlands; adult/child $8/6; ⊙8am-4:30pm Jun 15–Aug, Fri-Sun only Sep–Oct 6) in summer.

Ride Glenwood Springs (☑800-659-3656; www.ci.glenwood-springs.co.us; day pass $1; ⊙7am-8pm) Buses operate on the half-hour between the Glenwood Springs Mall and the

Roaring Forks Marketplace at the south end of town. Check the city website for routes and schedules.

Carbondale

📍 970 / POP 6574 / ELEV 6171FT

Dominated by the magnificent, twin-peaked Mt Sopris (12,965ft) rising up from the valley floor, Carbondale is without a doubt the most charismatic spot to cool your engine when traveling the Roaring Fork Valley. This historic settlement with an artsy, earthy community,provides a refreshing counterpoint to the glitz and upmarket leanings of Aspen. It's hardly your typical American town, but Main St is still the place to be: take a wander to find excellent restaurants, a good selection of consignment stores and a handful of bars. There's great mountain biking in the area, though you'll need your own wheels.

5Point Film Festival FILM
(www.5pointfilm.org; ☺Apr) Carbondale's film festival has gradually acquired a name for itself as the Sundance of adventure cinema. Films aren't of the testosterone-driven 'look at me' variety, but instead explore inspiration and transformation as experienced in the great outdoors. In late April.

🛏 Sleeping

Carbondale's sleeping options are largely of the apartment-rental variety, although there is also a B&B and farmstay.

Cedar Ridge Ranch FARMSTAY $$
(📞970-963-3507; www.cedarridgeranch.com; 3059 County Rd 103; yurts $215; 🔊🐾) Possibly Colorado's only glamping opportunity, this cool farmstay/artist workspace is one-of-a-kind and offers the opportunity to sleep in either a large safari tent or a yurt, each equipped with everything you need for a thoroughly comfortable stay. Two-night minimum in summer. The ranch is 6.5 miles northeast of Carbondale.

Dandelion Inn B&B $$
(📞970-963-3597; www.dandelioninnco.com; 66 N 2nd St; r $110-170; 🅿❄🔊) Remodeled in 2016, this welcoming B&B has four personalized rooms and stylish common areas. Relatively inexpensive but plenty comfortable, it's a pleasant alternative to staying in Aspen – an excellent midvalley option. Several bikes on loan.

✖ Eating

For a small town, Carbondale has a fantastic selection of restaurants, from Thai and upscale Italian to a smoothie shop and local food co-op for groceries.

⭐**Carbondale Beat** HEALTH FOOD $
(📞970-963-5613; www.thecarbondalebeat.com; 968 Main St; mains $6-13; ☺9am-4pm Tue-Sat) Get your probiotics fix at this charming bay-window cafe specializing in organic shakes loaded with bee pollen, cacao nibs, açaí berries, coconut water and like. They've also got kombucha and mate on tap, along with açaí bowls, open-face ciabatta sandwiches and soba salads.

Village Smithy AMERICAN $
(📞970-963-9990; www.villagesmithy.com; 26 S 3rd St; mains $7-12; ☺7am-2pm) For the best breakfast in town – pancakes that droop over the edge of your plate, skillets and scrambles with a Southwestern flavor, and the adventurous McHuevos – make for the historic blacksmith shop that locals adore. Juicy burgers and salads are served at lunch.

Phat Thai THAI $$
(📞970-963-7001; www.phatthai.com; 343 Main St; mains $14-18; ☺5-9pm Mon-Sat; 🖊) 🍴 It may not be Chiang Mai, but you're not going to find any naysayers here. Great food and cool decor (exposed brick walls, curvy counter seating) make this a very hip spot, and it gets busy every night of the week. Expect Thai classics, Vietnamese and Malaysian specialties, and a few native Colorado twists for the locavores.

🍷 Drinking & Entertainment

There are plenty of places here to grab a pint of Colorado's finest, including the local brewery (p220).

Carbondale Beer Works BREWERY
(📞970-704-1216; www.carbondalebeerworks.com; 647 Main St; ☺11am-11pm Fri-Mon, 1:30-11pm Tue-Thu) As they say, make beer, not war, and Carbondale's local brewery is doing a fine job of that. Swing by to sample some of their contributions to the peace movement, along with guest ciders, brews and kombucha, too.

Pour House BAR
(📞970-963-3553; 351 Main St; ☺11am-11pm; 🔊) An 1890s original, the Pour House is a happy-hour favorite and low-key choice for a drink, with six-shooters and a Winchester behind the bar, Annie Oakley posters on the wall and TVs to catch the big game.

CRYSTAL GHOST TOWN

One of Colorado's most famous ghost towns, Crystal is also one of the most photogenic, though it is smack in the middle of nowhere – which is certainly a good thing, as long as you're up for the detour.

The first mining in the area took place in the 1860s, but access was so poor it wasn't until the 1880s that it really picked up. By 1893 there were a half-dozen mines producing silver, lead and zinc, and the population spiked at several hundred. Despite having been virtually abandoned by 1915, there are several fairly intact structures still standing, including the iconic Crystal Mill, a turn-of-the-century power generator.

To get here, you'll need to pass through tiny Marble, whose quarry (still in operation) has supplied stone to some of the most famous statuary in the US, including the Lincoln Memorial and Tomb of the Unknown Soldier. Out West Guides (p237) runs a variety of horseback-riding and fishing trips from town.

Marble is located 28 miles south of Carbondale, about 6 miles up County Rd 3. After Marble the dirt road to Crystal is another 6 miles, but you'll need a high-clearance 4WD vehicle to make the trip; it is accessible only from June to November. If your car isn't up to the task, contact Crystal River Jeep Tours (p237) or consider hiking it. The road continues on to Crested Butte, but is in very poor condition and is not recommended. Budget three or four hours for a visit to Crystal.

★ **Steve's Guitars** LIVE MUSIC
(☑970-963-3304; www.stevesguitars.net; 19 N 4th St) On weekend nights, this unassuming guitar shop turns into an intimate one-room venue where the focus is all about enjoying great, usually acoustic, music. Shows at this community favorite start around 8:30pm on Friday and/or Saturday nights, but it's best to turn up earlier if you want a seat. The cover charge varies, so bring cash.

❶ Tourist Information

Carbondale Chamber of Commerce (☑970-963-1890; www.carbondale.com; 520 S 3rd St; ☺9am-5pm Mon-Fri) Check the town website for lodging tips and upcoming events.

Aspen-Sopris Ranger District (☑970-963-2266; 620 Main St; ☺9am-4:30pm Mon-Fri) For info on hiking, biking, camping and other activities in the White River National Forest.

❶ Getting There & Away

Carbondale is 13 miles south of Glenwood Springs and 29 miles northwest of Aspen on Hwy 82. **RFTA** (p236) runs regular buses up and down the valley.

Basalt

☑970 / POP 3857 / ELEV 6611FT

Aspen's humble neighbor and down-to-earth little sibling has plenty to flaunt. Set at the confluence of the Fryingpan and Roaring Fork Rivers, it's framed by gold-medal trout waters, making this cute but humble town something of a fly-fishing paradise – most Aspen outfitters will bring you down here to cast. Also on the river is a white-water park, constructed in 2017, for kayakers and stand-up paddlers to play in.

The town is tiny but blessed with a historic main-street strip, plenty of tasty dining options and a couple of cute boutiques (read: not Louis Vuitton or Prada). It's only 20 minutes from the Four Mountain slopes and another 20 to artsy Carbondale down valley; stock up on groceries and outdoor gear at the newer Willits Town Center, 4 miles northwest on Hwy 82. Basalt is also the gateway to little-visited Hunter-Fryingpan Wilderness area.

⌂ Sleeping

Basalt itself offers little apart from a few motels, but there's a Westin just down valley, and numerous camping options to the east along the Fryingpan River and at Ruedi Reservoir, including the Chapman Campground.

Chapman Campground CAMPGROUND $
(☑877-444-6777; www.recreation.gov; Fryingpan Rd; tent & RV sites $23-25; ☺late May–early Oct; ◉) Located upstream from Ruedi Reservoir (good for boaters), this is one of six campgrounds along the Fryingpan River. It's fairly developed as far as USFS campgrounds go, with volleyball courts, a horseshoe pit and some seriously good fishing holes nearby.

Water is available, but no electrical hookups. It's 29 miles east of Basalt.

Basalt Mountain Inn
MOTEL $$

(☑970-927-4747; www.basaltmountaininn.com; 220 Midland Ave; r $120-175; P🐾) If you're not after anything fancy, this is one of the most affordable places to stay in the Aspen area. Renovated in 2014, the decor is fresh and the suites come with wet bars and sleeper couches.

Element Basalt-Aspen
HOTEL $$$

(☑970-340-4040; www.elementbasaltaspen.com; 499 Market St; r winter/summer from $250/170; P❄🐾♿🐾) 🧺 If you don't need to be in Aspen, this Westin property offers comfortable modern studios at comparatively affordable rates. Located in the new, purpose-built Willits Town Center, what the area lacks in atmosphere it makes up for in convenience (eg you can walk to two supermarkets). It's 20 miles from Aspen on Hwy 82; free bikes on loan.

✖ Eating

There are a handful of good dining options in town, mostly along Midland Ave.

★ Free Range Kitchen & Wine Bar
AMERICAN $$

(☑970-279-5199; www.freerangebasalt.com; 305 Gold Rivers Ct; small plates $9-15, mains $16-24; ⊙11:30am-2:30pm & 5:30-9pm) 🧺 Working uniquely with local farmers and ranchers, the recently opened Free Range Kitchen merits a trip down from Aspen. Pair a glass of peppery Gigondas with small-plate favorites like beef empanadas, blackened haricots verts with crispy garlic, pan-fried cheese with mushrooms and tapenade...suffice it to say, you can't go wrong with anything on the menu here. *Bon appetit!*

Riverside Grill
PUB FOOD $$

(☑970-927-9301; 181 Basalt Center Circle; mains $13-24; ⊙11am-10pm) The most atmospheric place to eat and grab a beer in Basalt is this old timber warehouse that opens directly onto the Fryingpan River. Flat-screens show sports, and the menu has a good array of well-prepared pub food.

Cafe Bernard
BISTRO $$$

(☑970-927-4292; www.cafebernard.net; 200 Midland Ave; mains lunch $10-15, dinner $22-31; ⊙7:30am-2pm Tue-Fri, 8am-1pm Sat & Sun, 6pm-late Tue-Sat) Owned by a French chef, this is one of the town's cutest, most beloved restaurants. Set on the main drag, it's a good spot to indulge in Gallic fare without breaking the bank: look for escargots, trout *almandine* and, for a bit of variety, curried shrimp. It serves breakfast and reasonably priced lunch as well.

ℹ Getting There & Away

Basalt is 18.5 miles northwest of Aspen and 23.1 miles southeast of Glenwood Springs on Hwy 82. RFTA (p236) runs regular buses up and down the valley.

Aspen

☑970 / POP 6658 / ELEV 7908FT

Here's a unique town, unlike anyplace else in the American West. It's a cocktail of cowboy grit, Euro panache, Hollywood glam, Ivy League brains, fresh powder, live music and lots of money. It's the kind of place where no matter the season you can bring on a head rush in countless ways. Perhaps you dropped into a near-vertical run in the Highland Bowl, or huffed up to the top of Buckskin Pass in under three hours. It could also come while relaxing at the local music festival, peering down into a ginormous superpipe or ripping around a banked turn on a mountain bike.

Whatever you've seen, heard or done, there is one common Aspen cure-all. Simply take your body to the moonlit hot tub and leave your head behind. But do bring a bottle. After all, Aspen is nothing if not a place of extravagance, indulgence and excellence.

⊙ Sights

Aspen, like most towns in the Rocky Mountains, is less about seeing and more about doing and experiencing. But with a handful of outstanding art venues downtown, a cutting-edge environmental center and two nearby ghost towns, this is the most culturally happening spot west of Denver.

Christopher Martin Gallery
GALLERY

(☑970-925-7649; www.christophermartingallery.com; 525 E Cooper Ave; ⊙11am-6pm Tue-Sun) Local artist Christopher Martin specializes in reverse glass painting, a technique that dates back to the Middle Ages. Stop by for a peek at his dynamic swirls of color on acrylic discs and rectangles.

Boesky West
GALLERY

(☑212-680-9889; www.marianneboeskygallery.com; 100 S Spring St; ⊙10am-6pm Tue-Sat, noon-

5pm Sun) Opened in 2017, this is the Western outpost of Marianne Boesky's Manhattan gallery, displaying the works of emerging artists over two floors.

Ashcroft
GHOST TOWN

(www.aspenhistory.org; Castle Creek Rd; $5; ⊙ guided tours mid-Jun–Sep) The access point to the breathtaking Castle Creek Valley is the ghost town of Ashcroft, a silver-mining town founded in 1880. What remains are mostly miners cottages (log cabins with tin roofs), a couple of broken-down wagons stranded in the waist-high grass, a post office and a saloon.

At its height in 1893 about 2500 people worked here, but the silver veins were quickly exhausted and by 1895 the town's population plummeted to 100 residents. To get here, drive half a mile west of town on Hwy 82 to the roundabout and follow Castle Creek Rd south for 12.2 miles.

Aspen Art Museum
MUSEUM

(☑970-925-8050; www.aspenartmuseum.org; 637 E Hyman Ave; ⊙10am-6pm Tue-Sun) **FREE** Opening in 2014, the art museum's striking new building features a warm, lattice-like exterior designed by Pritzker Prize winner Shigeru Ban, and contains three floors of gallery space. There's no permanent collection, just edgy, innovative contemporary exhibitions featuring paintings, mixed media, sculpture, video installations and photography by artists such as Mamma Andersson, Mark Manders and Susan Philipsz. Art lovers will not leave disappointed. Head up to the roof for views and a bite to eat at the cool cafe.

Independence
GHOST TOWN

(www.aspenhistory.org; Hwy 82; $5; ⊙ guided tours mid-Jun–Aug) Just 16 miles east of Aspen, at the foot of Independence Pass (p224), this gold-mining boom town turned ghost town started as a tented camp in the summer of 1879, when one lucky miner struck gold on the Fourth of July. Operated and preserved by the Aspen Historical Society (p228), the site offers the chance to see the remains of the old livery, the general store and a miners cabin or three.

Peter Lik
GALLERY

(☑970-925-1820; www.lik.com; 406 E Hopkins Ave; ⊙9am-10pm) Displays the work of the self-taught Australian photographer. Lik focuses on vibrant panoramic landscapes, with a fine selection of local Aspen shots that sometimes appear to be in 3D.

Baldwin Gallery
GALLERY

(☑970-920-9797; www.baldwingallery.com; 209 S Galena St; ⊙10am-6pm Mon-Sat, noon-5pm Sun) A two-floor gallery, the Baldwin opened in 1994 and specializes in contemporary American art. It's among the best in the Rocky Mountains.

Galerie Maximillian
GALLERY

(☑970-925-6100; www.galeriemax.com; 602 E Cooper Ave; ⊙10am-8pm Mon-Sat, 11am-7pm Sun) Come here for famous 20th-century names from Chagall to Lichtenstein, mixed in with works from contemporary American and British artists.

Ice Age Discovery Center
MUSEUM

(☑970-922-2277; www.snowmassiceage.com; Snowmass Village Mall; ⊙10am-5pm; ⊕) **FREE** In October 2010, a bulldozer working near Snowmass unearthed the tusk of a female mammoth. Spurred by this unusual discovery, the Denver Museum of Nature & Science (p69) moved in for the next 10 months to conduct its largest-ever fossil excavation, resulting in the discovery of some 36,000 bones from 52 different Ice Age animals (including camels, sloths and mastodons – distant relatives of the mammoths).

Rio Grande Park
PARK

(www.aspenrecreation.com; Rio Grande Pl; ⊕) Aspen's biggest public park runs along the river and is bisected by the Rio Grande Trail for 2.1 miles. The park is home to an enticing skate park, outdoor basketball courts, a huge athletic field perfect for football or frisbee, an art museum and sculpture garden, and the John Denver Sanctuary (another garden).

🏃 Activities

Aspen, for all its money, taste and eccentricity, owes its current status to the surrounding slopes. Above all, this is a ski town and one of the best in America, with four mountains accessible from a single lift ticket – each offering a different flavor and an adventurous twist. But downhill is not the town's only gift.

★ Aspen Snowmass Ski Resort
SNOW SPORTS

(☑800-525-6200; www.aspensnowmass.com; 4-mountain lift ticket adult/child $164/105; ⊙9am-4pm Dec–mid-Apr; ⊕) OK, the top winter activity here is pretty much a given: the pursuit of powder, and lots of it. The Aspen Skiing Company runs the area's four resorts – Snowmass (p226), best all-around choice,

Aspen

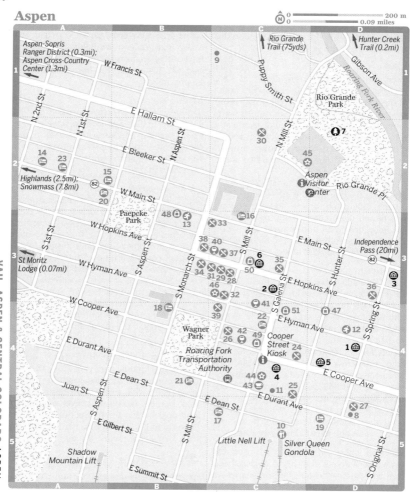

VAIL, ASPEN & CENTRAL COLORADO ASPEN

with the most terrain and vertical; Aspen (p226), intermediate/expert; the Highlands (p226), expert; and Buttermilk (p226), beginner/terrain parks – which are spread out through the valley and connected by free shuttles.

Both Aspen and Snowmass are also open in summer (lift ticket $22; mid-June to September) for hiking, mountain biking, concerts and activities.

★ Maroon Bells   HIKING, SKIING

If you have but one day to enjoy a slice of pristine wilderness, spend it in the shadow

of Colorado's most iconic mountains: the pyramid-shaped twins of North Maroon Peak (14,014ft) and South Maroon Peak (14,156ft). Eleven miles southwest of Aspen, it all starts on the shores of Maroon Lake, an absolutely stunning spot backed by the towering, striated summits.

★ Independence Pass   SCENIC DRIVE

(Hwy 82; ⊙ late May–Oct) Looming at 12,095ft, Independence Pass connects Aspen with Twin Lakes and is one of the more high-profile passes along the Continental Divide. The hairpin-turn views are gorgeous but a downright

Aspen

◎ Sights
1 Aspen Art Museum................................ D4
2 Baldwin Gallery C3
3 Boesky West... D3
4 Christopher Martin Gallery.................... C4
5 Galerie Maximillian D4
6 Peter Lik C3
7 Rio Grande Park.. D2

◎ Activities, Courses & Tours
8 Aspen Bike Tours & Rentals................. D5
9 Aspen Center for Environmental
    Studies C1
10 Aspen Mountain.. C5
    Aspen Paragliding............................(see 8)
11 Aspen Trout Guides & Outfitters.......... C4
12 Hub D4
13 Ute City Cycles... B3

◎ Sleeping
14 Annabelle Inn.. A2
15 Hotel Aspen A2
16 Hotel Jerome... C3
17 Hyatt Grand Aspen C5
18 Limelight Hotel... B4
19 Little Nell D5
20 Molly Gibson Lodge................................. A2
21 Mountain Chalet Aspen B4
22 Residence Hotel....................................... C4
23 Tyrolean Lodge A2

◎ Eating
24 520 Grill... C4
    BB's Kitchen...................................(see 4)
25 Big Wrap... C4
26 Bosq.. C4

27 Butchers Block D5
28 Cache Cache.. C3
29 Campo de Fiori C3
30 Clark's.. C2
31 Jimmy's.. C3
32 Justice Snow's.. C3
33 Matsuhisa... C3
34 Meat & Cheese... B3
35 Peach's Corner Cafe C3
    Pyramid Bistro...............................(see 48)
36 Spring Cafe.. D3
37 Steakhouse No 316.................................. C3
38 White House Tavern.................................. B3
39 Wild Fig C4

◎ Drinking & Nightlife
40 Aspen Brewing Co.................................... C3
41 HOPS... C4
    J-Bar..(see 16)
42 Red Onion... C4
43 Victoria's Espresso & Wine Bar............. C4

◎ Entertainment
44 Belly Up.. C4
    Isis Theatre.....................................(see 6)
45 Theatre Aspen C2
46 Wheeler Opera House.............................. C3

◎ Shopping
47 Aspen Saturday Market D4
48 Explore Booksellers B3
49 Kemosabe... C4
    Little Bird ....(see 4)
50 Radio Boardshop....................................... C3
    Silver Peak....................................(see 24)
51 Ute Mountaineer....................................... C4

distraction for drivers, so save contemplation of the summer snowfields and knife-edged peaks for the designated pullouts. Look for the ghost town of Independence (p223) on the way up.

Crested Butte Hike   HIKING
Ready for an adventure? You can walk (almost) from Aspen to Crested Butte. With roughly 11 miles and 3000ft of elevation gain you'll be gasping for oxygen, but the summer wildflowers and Maroon Bells panoramas are more than adequate compensation. Start at the Maroon Bells shuttle drop-off, head up to Crater Lake and then continue to **West Maroon Pass** (12,480ft).

Stillwater   WATER SPORTS
If you've a hankering to try out stand up paddle surfing (SUP), this mellow section of the Roaring Fork River is a gem. Put-in is just east of Aspen at the Wildwood School;

you'll then float downstream for several hours through the **North Star Nature Preserve**, taking out at Rainbow Bridge. You can also inner-tube it, but either way, you'll need two cars (or bikes).

Conundrum Hot Springs   HOT SPRINGS, HIKING
(Conundrum Creek Rd) The steaming Conundrum Hot Springs, west of Castle Peak (14,265ft), are the reward for 8.5 miles of tough climbing on the **Conundrum Creek Trail** (USFS Trail 1981). As it's hugely popular, the Forest Service is drafting new visitation guidelines (including a possible permit system) following a sharp uptick in visitation, which has essentially resulted in the area getting completely trashed.

The several pools here have outrageous alpine views, including glimpses of steep avalanche chutes and waterfalls, and are certainly a worthy destination (although it's now more of a party spot than a rejuvenating one). Be sure to check in with the ranger office (p236) before planning an overnight trip here.

Hunter Creek Trail HIKING, BIKING

(www.aspenrecreation.com) Accessible from town, the easy Hunter Creek Trail follows Hunter Creek northeast for about 4 miles and links up with a plethora of other trails, including the popular network at nearby **Smuggler Mountain** (10,700ft). The trails here are open to both hikers and mountain bikers.

To get to the trailhead, follow N Mill St across the river and then right onto Lone Pine Rd. You can also walk here from ACES.

Snowmass SNOW SPORTS

(☑800-525-6200, 970-923-0560; www.aspensnowmass.com; 4-mountain lift ticket adult/child $164/105; ⊙late Nov–mid Apr; ☝) With the most terrain (3332 acres) and vertical drop (4406ft) in the Four Mountains (p230), Snowmass wins for variety. From beginner runs to cliffs and headwalls, even intermediates can get above tree line and enjoy untouched powder in the glades. It's 9 miles west of Aspen, with its own vibrant village area and a good choice of accommodations and restaurants.

Buttermilk SNOW SPORTS

(☑970-925-1220, 800-525-6200; www.aspensnowmass.com; Hwy 82; 4-mountain lift ticket adult/child $164/105; ⊙Dec–Mar; ☝) Popular with snowboarders of all levels, Buttermilk has the best park and pipe. Located just 2 miles west of Aspen proper, it has 44 trails across 470 acres. With a 22ft superpipe, riders who want to jump and try out their bag of tricks can do so to their hearts' content. The resort is also an ideal playground for newbie riders and skiers.

Aspen Highlands SNOW SPORTS

(☑800-525-6200, 970-920-7009; www.aspensnowmas.com; Prospector Rd; 4-mountain lift ticket adult/child $164/105; ⊙Dec–early Apr) Aspen Highlands resort, 2 miles southwest of town, is a web of 122 trails on 1040 acres of uncrowded terrain that's revered by many locals and accessed via five ski lifts. The highlight here is the gorgeous **Highland Bowl**, a stunning hike-to area for extreme skiers with a peak elevation 700ft above the lifts. Free snowcats also serve the bowl.

Aspen Mountain SNOW SPORTS

(☑970-925-1220, 800-525-6200; www.aspensnowmass.com; 601 E Dean St; 4-mountain lift ticket adult/child $164/105; ⊙late Nov–mid-Apr) Aspen, or Ajax, is an athlete's mountain, offering more than 3000ft of steep vertical drop right from the front door of the Little Nell (p229). There's no beginner terrain here, just 675 acres of bumps, trees and World Cup–worthy runs served by the **Silver Queen Gondola** (in 1946 it was the single-seat Lift 1, the longest chairlift in the world).

Aspen Paragliding ADVENTURE SPORTS

(☑970-925-6975; www.aspenparagliding.com; 426 S Spring St; tandem flights $275; ⊙flights 6:45am, 8:15am & 10:15am) Feel like flying? This paragliding outfitter runs tandem flights year-round. During the summer, flights take off from the Silver Queen Gondola on Aspen Mountain. In winter, liftoff is either from Sam's Knob on the top of Snowmass or on Aspen Mountain. Private instruction and group courses are also available.

Snowmass Bike Park MOUNTAIN BIKING

(☑800-525-6200; www.aspensnowmass.com; bike haul $42; ⊙10am-4pm mid-Jun–Sep; ☝) Yeehaw! A good 3000ft of downhill and 50 miles of mountain bike trails at Snowmass guarantee good times in the summer. Most trails are accessible from either the Elk Camp Gondola or Elk Camp Lift. Some of the classic cross-country trails, such as Government and Tom Blake, don't require a lift ticket.

Check out www.rfmba.org or ask around at rental shops for other good singletrack rides in and around the valley.

Cathedral Lake Trail HIKING

(Ashcroft) Particularly stunning in autumn when the aspens shimmer gold, the Cathedral Lake hiking trail is one of the most popular in Aspen – though with 2000ft of elevation gain over 3 miles, it's definitely no walk in the park.

Aspen-Snowmass Nordic
Trail System SNOW SPORTS

(☑970-429-2039; www.aspennordic.com) **FREE** This European-style village-to-village trail system incorporates over 60 miles of free trails that link up the towns of Aspen, Snowmass, Woody Gulch and Basalt. The hub is the local golf course, where you'll find the **Aspen Cross-Country Center** (☑970-925-2145; www.utemountaineer.com;

39551 Hwy 82; ski rental adult/child $25/10; ⊙9am-5pm Dec-Mar), which rents out equipment and gives lessons.

Rio Grande Trail · CYCLING
(www.riograndetrail.com; Puppy Smith St) This bike trail rambles for 42 mostly paved miles along a former railroad corridor from Aspen to Glenwood Springs, passing through Basalt and Carbondale. Access it north of the Aspen Center for Environmental Studies.

Ute City Cycles · CYCLING
(🖉970-920-3325; www.utecitycycles.com; 231 E Main St; bike rental per 24hr $95; ⊙10am-5pm) A high-end road- and mountain-bike retailer, this place also offers limited rentals from its demo fleet: there's nowhere else in town where you can rent $6500 Orbea road bikes or $2700 Yeti mountain bikes. Rentals are $95 per day with a two-day maximum; no reservations. Staff can also point you in the direction of Aspen's best cycling.

Hub · CYCLING
(🖉970-925-7970; www.hubofaspen.com; 616 E Hyman Ave; bike rental per day from $89; ⊙9am-6pm) This long-running bike shop has recently changed owners and locations, but still rents cruisers, full-suspension mountain bikes and carbon-fiber road bikes. They'll also offer advice on the best road routes and single tracks plying Aspen and Smuggler Mountains, the Montezuma Basin, and Pearl and Independence Passes.

🕝 Tours

★Aspen Center for Environmental Studies · OUTDOORS
(ACES; 🖉970-925-5756; www.aspennature.org; 100 Puppy Smith St, Hallam Lake; ⊙9am-5pm Mon-Fri; 👪) **FREE** The Aspen Center for Environmental Studies is a 25-acre wildlife sanctuary that hugs the Roaring Fork River and miles of hiking trails in the Hunter Creek Valley. With a mission to advance environmental conservation, the center's naturalists provide free guided hikes and snowshoe tours, raptor demonstrations (eagles and owls are among the residents) and special programs for youngsters.

Maroon Bells Outfitters · HORSEBACK RIDING
(🖉970-920-4677; www.maroonbellsaspen.com; 3125 Maroon Creek Rd; 1hr rides from $75) Saddle up at this working ranch down the slope from the Maroon Bells Wilderness Area. Shorter rides (one hour to full-day trips) head into the spectacular Maroon Bells Wilderness (p224), while overnight rides ($850) take you all the way to Crested Butte (p225).

Aspen Expeditions · OUTDOORS
(🖉970-925-7625; www.aspenexpeditions.com; 133 Prospector Rd, Suite 4115) Based in the Aspen Highlands ski area, this guiding company is notable for its adventurous itineraries: some stellar hiking, mountaineering and rock-climbing trips to some of Aspen's most spectacular destinations, as well as ice climbing and cross-country and downhill ski trips in winter. It also runs level-one and -two avalanche courses.

Ashcroft Ski Touring · SNOW SPORTS
(🖉970-925-1044; www.pinecreekcookhouse.com; 11399 Castle Creek Rd; adult/child $25/15; 👪) This local Nordic outfitter serves 20 miles of groomed trails through 600 acres of backcountry – it's a bit more wild than your typical Nordic center. The mountain backdrop is spectacular, the Ashcroft ghost town (p223) eerie. Rent classic cross-country ski equipment, ski gear or snowshoes. Individual and group lessons, as well as snowshoe and ski tours, run daily.

Aspen Trout Guides & Outfitters · FISHING
(🖉970-379-7963; www.aspentroutguides.com; 520 E Durant Ave; half-day trips from $250; ⊙9am-5pm) Based out of Hamilton Sports Pro Shop (summer only), this has been Aspen's top fly-fishing outfitter since 1981. Trips to the Fryingpan and Roaring Fork Rivers; Maroon, Castle and Hunter Creeks; or nearby lakes, including Thomas, Blue and Little Gem, are customized to clients' wishes and include casting instruction. Family trips also available.

Blazing Adventures · OUTDOORS
(🖉800-282-7238; www.blazingadventures.com; 48 Upper Village Mall, Snowmass; 👪) A popular Snowmass-based outfitter that will get you in a raft, kayak or jeep, or on a bike or high-altitude ridge at sunset. It's located in the upper (main) mall and consistently gets rave reviews, most notably for the white-water-rafting trips on the nearby Colorado River. There's another location in Aspen.

Aspen Bike Tours & Rentals · CYCLING
(🖉888-448-2330; www.aspenbikerentals.com; 430 S Spring St; half/full-day adult from $35/45, child from $22/29; ⊙9am-6pm; 👪) Easily the

most laid-back bike shop in town – shaved legs and lycra bravado are nowhere to be found here. Along with premium road and mountain bikes for rent, it also has a network of private guides who can set you up on terrific mountain-biking tours onto trails seldom glimpsed by tourists. They also rent SUP boards (half-/full-day $60/90).

Aspen Historical Society TOURS
(✏ 970-920-5770; www.aspenhistory.org; tours $10-25) Sign up for local walking, biking and skiing tours of historic Aspen and around. It also runs visits to several small specialist museums ($10), including the Wheeler/ Stallard Museum and the Holden Marolt Mining & Ranching Museum.

✦✦ Festivals & Events

X Games SPORTS
(http://xgames.espn.com; ☉ Jan) Buttermilk is one of the homes of the Winter X Games and the place to see some of the world's top extreme athletes. From slopestyle and superpipe competitions to bike cross and snowmobile snocross, entertainment is guaranteed. In late January.

Jazz Aspen Snowmass MUSIC
(✏ 970-920-4996; www.jazzaspen.org; ☉ Jun & Labor Day) This festival is true to its jazz roots, with horn players such as Christian McBride and Nicholas Payton and crooners such as Harry Connick Jr and Natalie Cole gracing the Benedict Music Tent or downstairs at the Little Nell in the week leading up to the Fourth of July. A second concert series is held over Labor Day weekend.

Aspen Music Festival MUSIC
(✏ 970-925-9042; www.aspenmusicfestival.com; ☉ Jul & Aug) Every summer for the past 60 years, some of the best classical musicians from around the world have come to play, perform and learn from the masters of their craft. Students form orchestras led by world-famous conductors and perform at the Wheeler Opera House (p235) or the Benedict Music Tent, or in smaller groups on Aspen street corners.

Food & Wine Classic FOOD & DRINK
(www.foodandwine.com; ☉ Jun) Three days of culinary celebs, eating, drinking and hobnobbing with tastemakers makes this one of Aspen's top events. Satellite events include concerts, a 5K run and more, so even if you can't get one of the $1550 passes (they sell out months in advance), there's plenty

to entertain. Lodging can be tough to find during this weekend. In mid-June.

🛏 Sleeping

Aspen is a cute town to nest in – and although pricey, it's still more affordable than Vail. If the prices make you balk, consider a down-valley option in Basalt, Carbondale or Glenwood Springs. In summer, camping is a great option. Wherever you stay, especially if you're car-camping, make sure to reserve well in advance.

★10th Mountain Division Hut Association HUT $
(✏ 970-925-5775; www.huts.org; per person $33) This organization manages a system of over 30 backcountry huts across Colorado – a few with wood-burning saunas. Most are connected by 350 miles of trails ideal for cross-country skiing and snowshoeing in the winter and mountain biking and hiking in the summer. The majority are located between Vail and Aspen, but there are growing networks in Summit and Grand counties.

★Difficult Campground CAMPGROUND $
(✏ 877-444-6777; www.recreation.gov; Hwy 82; tent & RV sites $24-26; ☉ mid-May–Sep; 🐾) The largest campground in the Aspen area, Difficult is one of four sites at the foot of Independence Pass and the only one that takes reservations. Located 5 miles west of town, it also has the lowest altitude (8000ft). Higher up are three smaller campgrounds: Weller, Lincoln Gulch and Lost Man. Water is available, but no electrical hookups for RVs.

St Moritz Lodge HOSTEL $
(✏ 970-925-3220; www.stmoritzlodge.com; 334 W Hyman Ave; winter/summer dm $83/74, d $302/233; 🅿 ❄ @ 🛜 🏊) St Moritz is the best no-frills deal in town. Perks include a heated outdoor pool and grill overlooking Aspen Mountain, and a lobby with games, books and a piano. The European-style lodge offers a wide variety of options, from quiet dorms to two-bedroom condos; the cheapest options share bathrooms. There's a guest kitchen downstairs.

Silver Bell Campground CAMPGROUND $
(✏ 877-444-6777; www.recreation.gov; Maroon Creek Rd; tent & RV sites $15; ☉ late May–Sep; 🐾) If you want to pitch a tent near the Maroon Bells but don't have time to get into the backcountry, this is your spot. There are three small campgrounds along the access road, all of which take reservations; the

10TH MOUNTAIN DIVISION HUT-TO-HUT TRIPS

Exploring the Colorado wilderness is already quite an adventure in summer, but imagine the thrill of gliding through the backcountry on skis: just you, your friends and quiet snowfall blanketing the mountainside. Well, thanks to the 10th Mountain Division Hut Association, which manages a system of over 30 huts (some with wood-burning saunas), it can be done – without having to spend the night in a snow cave.

The huts are connected by a 350-mile trail network ideal for cross-country skiing and snowshoeing in the winter, and mountain biking and hiking in the summer. The majority are located between Vail Pass and Aspen (10th Mountain Huts and Braun Huts), but there are growing networks in Summit and Grand counties. You'll be out in the wilderness, so you should be a decent backcountry skier and be familiar with avalanche safety before reserving a bunk. It's best to go as a group (some huts only accept group reservations), with at least one experienced leader who knows how to find a trail in a storm.

So how do you sign up for all this winter fun? The catch, of course, is securing reservations: these huts are incredibly popular and space is limited. Winter reservations for the following year begin with a member-only lottery on March 1 (annual membership $35). Call-in reservations for non-members open up on June 1. In other words, you have to plan your trip six to 12 months in advance and be somewhat flexible with your dates (avoiding weekends is key).

Summer is generally easier to arrange, though not all huts are open; call-in reservations for the following year open October 1.

other two are Silver Bar and Silver Queen. Water is available, but there are no electrical hookups for RVs.

Tyrolean Lodge   LODGE $$
(☑ 970-925-4595; www.tyroleanlodge.com; 200 W Main St; r winter/summer from $220/190; P ✳ 🛜) One of the few midrange lodges in Aspen, the Tyrolean is a popular, family-owned option, located within walking distance of downtown. The white condo-style building is adorned with a giant bronze eagle and crossed skis mounted on the outside walls; built to resemble a Native American version of an Austrian ski lodge, it's hard to miss.

Annabelle Inn   HOTEL $$
(☑ 877-266-2466; www.annabelleinn.com; 232 W Main St; r winter/summer from $249/200; P ✳ @ 🛜) Personable and unpretentious, the cute and quirky Annabelle Inn resembles an old-school European-style ski lodge in a central location. Rooms are cozy without being too cute, and come with flat-screen TVs and warm duvets. We enjoyed the after-dark ski-video screenings from the upper-deck hot tub (one of two on the property); a good breakfast is included.

Wildwood Snowmass   LODGE $$
(☑ 970-923-8400; www.wildwoodsnowmass. com; 40 Elbert Ln, Snowmass; r winter/summer from $199/89; P 🛜 🏊 ♨) Given a slick, colorful makeover in 2012, the

Wildwood's 145 rooms are still motel-like in their layout and comfort level – renovations were mostly skin-deep – but if you're OK with that, then it's a groovy, affordable choice located a five-minute walk from the slopes. No air-con in summer.

★ Little Nell   HOTEL $$$
(☑ 970-920-4600; www.thelittlenell.com; 675 E Durant Ave; r winter/summer from $1200/700; P ✳ 🛜 🏊 ♨) A legendary ski-in, ski-out Aspen landmark offering understated, updated elegance and class at the foot of Aspen Mountain. Gas-burning fireplaces, high-thread-count linens and rich color schemes make up the recently refreshed modernist decor. There are fabulous Balinese pieces in the lobby and hallways decorated with wonderful ski photography. The Ajax Tavern is primo for après-ski; Element 47 serves gastronomic cuisine.

★ Limelight Hotel   HOTEL $$$
(☑ 855-925-3025; www.limelighthotel.com; 355 S Monarch St; r winter/summer from $500/250; P ✳ 🛜 🏊 ♨) Sleek and trendy, the Limelight's brick-and-glass modernism reflects Aspen's vibe. Rooms are spacious, with stylish accoutrements: granite washbasins, leather headboards and mountain views from the balconies and rooftop terraces.

ASPEN SKI TRIPS

With four sublime mountains to choose from there's no way you can ski all the terrain in the Aspen Snowmass Ski Resort (p223) in a few days, but if you follow our lead, you'll find your bliss wherever you ski.

Snowmass With the most terrain in Aspen and superb views of the Maroon Bells from the top of Elk Camp, Snowmass is the best all-around choice. The best beginner run is **Assay Hill**: it's short, typically free of crowds and sloped perfectly for newbies. Access it via the Assay Hill lift or the Elk Camp Gondola. The top intermediate choice is **Sneaky's**: offering sweeping views of the Roaring Fork Valley, this wide-open cruiser is the perfect blue groomer, and those looking for a challenge can ski into powder and trees on either side of the run at anytime. Access it from the Sheer Bliss or Big Burn lifts. Any run in the **Cirque** or the **Hanging Valley Headwall** will suit the adrenaline set. Make the 10-minute hike to the top of Headwall and head down Roberto's to **Strawberry Patch**, where you can often find fresh powder. It's accessed via the High Alpine lift. There are three terrain parks here.

Aspen Mountain Accessed from town, Aspen (or Ajax) is the only mountain with no beginner terrain. It can get crowded, so expect bumps. Intermediate skiers and riders will dig **Ruthie's**, a wide-open groomed run with sweeping views; this is the same terrain that has been skied by Women's World Cup racers for the past fifteen years. Local tip: stay skier's right at the top of Ruthie's and you'll head into the **Jerry Garcia Shrine**, accessed from the FIS and Ruthie's lifts. **Walsh's**, on the other hand, is for experts – it's steep, deep and breathtaking (visually and physically), with jaw-dropping views of Independence Pass.

Aspen Highlands You know all those amazing promo shots of beautiful people joyfully hiking atop an exposed snow-covered ridge with skis hoisted on one shoulder and incredible alpine scenery in the background? That's here. Although there are some beginner and intermediate runs here (**Apple Strudel**, accessed by the Exhibition lift, and the groomed **Golden Horn** run to Thunderbowl), the Highlands is all about extreme skiing in the stunning hike-to **Highland Bowl**: expect chutes, vertiginous drop-offs and glades. Try **G-4** for a steep, deep tree run and **Hyde Park** for one of the longest bump-and-tree runs you've ever taken. It's accessed by Loge Peak and Deep Temerity lifts, then hop a free snowcat ride part-way or just hike it.

Buttermilk Beginners here head to **Westward Ho** via the Summit Express and West Buttermilk Express. The Summit Express and Upper Tiehack lifts take intermediate skiers to the blue runs at **Buckskin**; the best advanced terrain is **Buttermilk Park**, starting on Jacob's Ladder. This is where you can ski/ride the same hits and 22ft superpipe as Shaun White, Julia Marino and all your favorite X Games athletes. You read that right: this is one of the venues for the **Winter X Games** (p228).

Additional perks include shuttles that run to all the slopes and a fab breakfast.

A new Limelight is slated to open next to the Snowmass (p226) gondola in time for the 2018 ski season.

Hotel Aspen HOTEL **$$$**
(☑970-925-3441; www.hotelaspen.com; 110 W Main St; r winter/summer from $400/300; P❋🐾📶♨🐾) The hip Hotel Aspen is one of the better picks in town, with a casual vibe and affordable luxury. Modern decor features rust-hued walls, a wet bar and stylish furnishings – if you go for the fireplace suite, you'll also have access to your own private solarium. Whichever room you choose, the heated pool and frothing hot tubs are another plus.

Across the street is its sister property, the Molly Gibson Lodge.

Molly Gibson Lodge HOTEL **$$$**
(☑970-925-3434; www.mollygibson.com; 101 W Main St; r winter/summer from $400/270; P❋@📶♨🐾) One of two tasteful good-value properties across from each other on the edge of downtown. Rooms are redone regularly, which means fresh paint, lush linens and Venetian blinds; it's all very mod and Ikea-ish but with an upscale slant. Some rooms are huge, with fireplaces and

massive hot tubs. Online deals lower the rates. Breakfast and happy hour included.

The sister property is the Hotel Aspen.

Residence Hotel   BOUTIQUE HOTEL **$$$**
(📞 970-920-6532; www.aspenresidence.com; 305 S Galena St; r winter/summer from $400/200; P 🛜 🐾) Affectionately dubbed 'the Harry Potter Hotel,' the Residence is certainly the most unique place to lay your head in town. Consisting of one- to three-bedroom apartments, each suite here is endearingly bizarre, from leopard-print carpeting and portraits of French nobility to overly verdant house plants and antique furnishings. The owner, Terry Butler, is quintessential Aspen and quite a trip.

Hotel Jerome   HOTEL **$$$**
(📞 855-331-7213; www.hoteljerome.com; 330 E Main St; r winter/summer $1175/905; P ❄ 🛜 🏊 🐾) Superb service and relaxed elegance are trademarks at this historic hotel. A long-time favorite with Aspen's old-money crowd, the Jerome occupies a landmarked 1889 brick building constructed during Colorado's silver heyday, in addition to the adjacent historic Aspen Times building, which it began renovating in 2017. Rooms are individually decorated with period antiques, double-marble vanities and baths with oversized tubs.

Beds feature lots of pillows and fluffy, feather-down comforters for cold winter nights. If you just want to enjoy the view, sink into one of the armchairs facing Aspen Mountain. The hotel also has a great bar (p234) and lobby, where a hand-carved fireplace is the centerpiece and guests dine on fish and game served by friendly waiters. A new underground speakeasy is part of the current renovation project.

Those interested in the building's storied history can sign up for a tour with the Aspen Historical Society (p228).

Hyatt Grand Aspen   HOTEL **$$$**
(📞 970-429-9100; www.hyatt.com; 415 E Dean St; studio/1BR from $579/1219; P ❄ 🛜 🐾) Soak in your private hot tub on your private deck and take in the gorgeous mountain views at sunset – the perfect way to end a perfect Aspen day. Specializing in pampering, the Hyatt provides pure luxury and the service and location are spot on. Right next to the Silver Queen Gondola, so you couldn't ask for a better slope-side location.

Mountain Chalet Aspen   HOTEL **$$$**
(📞 970-925-7797; www.mountainchaletaspen.com; 333 E Durant Ave; r winter/summer from $274/209; P ❄ 🛜 🏊) Just two short blocks from the gondola, the Mountain Chalet has a great location. Rooms at this family-run hotel are a bit outdated and bland, but clean and comfortable nevertheless. The hot tub and sauna are perfect after a long day on the slopes. The best deals here are the apartment suites ($749), which sleep six.

Westin Snowmass   HOTEL **$$$**
(📞 970-923-8200;   www.westinsnowmass.com; 100 Elbert Ln; r winter/summer from $400/150; P ❄ 🛜 🏊 🐾) Opened in 2012, the ski-in, ski-out Westin delivers the most comfort for your money in Snowmass. The 253 rooms are spacious and feature modern alpine decor: think varnished wooden headboards, contemporary art on the walls and a beige-and-tan color scheme. Parking is in addition to the resort fee.

Viceroy   HOTEL **$$$**
(📞 970-923-8000;   www.viceroysnowmass. com; 130 Wood Rd; studios winter/summer from $625/276; P ❄ 🛜 🏊 🐾) This is another popular choice in Snowmass, with ski-in, ski-out convenience in winter and affordable luxury in summer. Here you'll find stylish studios and condos steeped in glamor, with high ceilings, full kitchens, deep soaking tubs, mosaic showers, seagrass wallpaper, fireplaces and flat-screen TVs.

🍴 Eating

For a mountain town, Aspen has a refreshingly diverse culinary scene. From hole-in-the-wall sandwich joints to top-shelf sushi, pop-up bone-broth stands and grass-fed, locally sourced beef, you should have no problem replenishing your calorie count in style after an action-packed day. You'll generally need to reserve a table for dinner.

Big Wrap   SANDWICHES **$**
(📞 970-544-1700; 520 E Durant Ave, Suite 101; wraps $7.60; ⏰ 10am-6pm Mon-Sat; 🍴) One of Aspen's most beloved spots for a quick, cheap meal, the Big Wrap's creative and vaguely healthy concoctions have won over legions of fans. In addition to Thai-, Mexican- and Greek-inspired wraps, there are also tacos, salads and smoothies. It's located downstairs from the main sidewalk on Hunter St (despite the Durant St address). Cash only and no seating.

Peach's Corner Cafe

CAFE $

(www.peachscornercafe.com; 121 S Galena St; mains $9-13; ⊙7am-5pm Mon-Sat; 🛜📶🚺) This busy organic cafe is good for affordable coffee and a quality meal at any time of the day. When the sun shines – which is often – everyone decamps to the patio seating out front. Look for monster slices of quiche, yummy pizzas, sandwiches and smoothies.

Fuel

CAFE $

(📶970-923-0091; 45 Village Sq, Snowmass; mains $6-9; ⊙7am-3:30pm) This hard-rocking Snowmass cafe does two things exceptionally well: jet-fueled espresso and world-class breakfast burritos. It also has protein bars and energy food to keep you going on the slopes and ridgelines no matter what the season, as well as bagels, paninis, wraps and smoothies.

520 Grill

SANDWICHES $

(📶970-925-9788; www.520grill.com; 520 E Cooper Ave; sandwiches & salads $9-12; ⊙11am-9pm Mon-Fri, to 5:20pm Sat & Sun; 🛜📶) A (mostly) healthy (kinda) fast-food grill, if there is such a thing. Sandwiches are creative, spicy concoctions. The achiote chicken is grilled and piled on the pita with roasted red peppers, avocado and cheese. The Veg Head is an alchemy of roasted portobello mushrooms and garlic, with a pepper medley dressed in balsamic.

Butchers Block

DELI $

(📶970-925-7554; www.butchersblockaspen.com; 424 S Spring St; sandwiches $9.50-11.75; ⊙8am-6pm) The depth and breadth of the gourmet spirit of this ski-town deli is striking. Here you'll find Gruyère, Roquefort and chèvre, wild salmon and sashimi-grade ahi, caviar and gourmet olive oil, maple-glazed walnuts, dried mangoes, good deli sandwiches, and terrific roast chicken and salads. It's open until 6pm, but stops making sandwiches at 5pm.

Clark's

SUPERMARKET $

(📶970-925-8046; www.clarksmarket.com; 300 Puppy Smith St; ⊙7am-10pm) The local grocery store has locations in Aspen and Snowmass, and offers all the organic, gourmet necessities that you'll need to stock up your Aspen kitchen in style.

★ Meat & Cheese

DELI $$

(📶970-710-7120; www.meatandcheeseaspen.com; 319 E Hopkins Ave; mains $14-34; ⊙10am-9pm) 🍴 By all means stop by to browse the artisan offerings in the gourmet deli, but don't leave without nibbling on a plate of cheese and charcuterie, beet-and-chèvre salad or a Vietnamese chicken noodle bowl. This true farm-to-table establishment grew out of the nearby **Avalanche Cheese Company,** but while the produce may be local, their culinary expertise spans the globe.

★ Ranger Station

PUB FOOD $$

(📶970-236-6277; www.rangerstation.org; 100 Elbert Ln, Snowmass; mains $9-18; ⊙11am-8pm winter, shorter hours in summer) This place is much more a bar than a restaurant, but given the dearth of dining choices in Snowmass, you may as well eat here too. The stars of the show are the 10 New Belgium beers on tap, but where else can you get Bavarian pretzels with yummy dipping sauces, ciabatta-style grilled cheese or bison chili? Ski-in, ski-out. Yes!

★ Pyramid Bistro

CAFE $$

(📶970-925-5338; www.pyramidbistro.com; 221 E Main St; mains lunch $12-18, dinner $19-29; ⊙11:30am-9:30pm; 🍴) 🍴 Set on the top floor of Explore Booksellers (p235), this gourmet veggie cafe serves up some delightful creations, including sweet-potato gnocchi with goat's cheese, red-lentil sliders and quinoa salad with avocado, goji berries and sesame vinaigrette. Definitely Aspen's top choice for health-conscious fare.

Spring Cafe

VEGETARIAN $$

(📶970-429-8406; www.springcafe.org; 119 S Spring St; mains $12-17; ⊙7am-5pm; 🍴) Vegetarian-friendly juice bar and cafe, with a good choice of tofu scrambles, tempeh burgers, seitan fajitas and plenty of greens. Service can be disorganized and the $9 smoothies seem pricey even for Aspen, but quibbles aside, it's one of the better options for a healthy meal.

Justice Snow's

AMERICAN $$

(📶970-429-8192; www.justicesnows.com; 328 E Hyman Ave; mains lunch $12-18, dinner $17-26; ⊙11am-2am Mon-Fri, 9am-2am Sat & Sun; 🛜📶) 🍴 Located in the historic Wheeler Opera House (p235), Justice Snow's is a retro-fitted old saloon that marries antique wooden furnishings with a deft modern touch. Although nominally a bar – the speakeasy cocktails are the soul of the place – the affordable and locally sourced menu (a $12 gourmet burger – in Aspen!) is what keeps the locals coming back.

White House Tavern
SANDWICHES **$$**

(📋970-925-1007; www.aspenwhitehouse.com; 302 E Hopkins Ave; mains $17-24; ⊙11:30am-9pm) As American as a crispy chicken sandwich and kale salad, the White House is a premier lunch stop with a casually elegant atmosphere. Sit in booths, at the bar or outside to savor a choice of gourmet sandwiches that are even more delicious than they sound. No reservations, so arrive early or be prepared to wait.

★Matsuhisa
JAPANESE **$$$**

(📋970-544-6628; www.matsuhisarestaurants. com; 303 E Main St; mains $29-42, 2 pieces sushi $8-12; ⊙5:30pm-close) The original Colorado link in Matsuhisa Nobu's iconic global chain that now wraps around the world, this converted house is more intimate than its Vail sibling and still turns out spectacular dishes such as miso black cod, Chilean sea bass with truffle and flavorful uni (sea urchin) shooters.

Jimmy's
AMERICAN **$$$**

(📋970-925-6020; www.jimmysaspen.com; 205 S Mill St; mains $17.50-58; ⊙5:30-11:30pm) Jimmy's is a soulful tequila bar and steakhouse that attracts a very A-list crowd. Settle into a booth and check out the guest graffiti on the wall in the main dining room, or skip the high-priced grill and try to wrangle a spot at the perpetually packed bar, which serves a cheaper menu and 105 types of tequila and mescal.

Bosq
AMERICAN **$$$**

(📋970-710-7299; www.bosqaspen.com; 312 S Mill St; mains $32-68; ⊙5:30-11pm) Of Aspen's new dinner destinations, Bosq is perhaps the most unique, with a playful modern menu that reflects the travels and culinary interests of chef Barclay Dodge. Expect dishes like salmon crudo with cucumber ceviche, red-mole tacos, Colorado lamb in a goat-cheese crema and even sweet-and-sour eggplant and Peking duck.

BB's Kitchen
AMERICAN **$$$**

(📋970-429-8284; www.bbskitchen.com; 525 E Cooper Ave, 2nd fl; mains lunch $15-22, dinner $32-42; ⊙11:30am-10pm, from 10am Sat & Sun) A long-standing local darling, this 2nd-floor patio is the best spot for a leisurely gourmet brunch (think lobster Benedict or wild-morel omelet). This isn't show food – the chef-owners are committed to quality, down to curing their own meats. For dinner, slip into a red booth for duck confit toast,

pork-belly steamed buns or caramelized sea scallops over grits.

Steakhouse No 316
STEAK **$$$**

(📋970-920-1893; www.steakhouse316.com; 316 E Hopkins Ave; mains $30-68; ⊙5:30-10:30pm) The Steakhouse is one of Aspen's 'it' destinations, drawing a crowd even in the shoulder season. There's nothing complicated on the menu here, just a choice selection of cuts grilled to perfection, coupled with sauces such as cognac peppercorn, chimichurri and black-truffle butter. Reserve.

Pine Creek Cookhouse
AMERICAN **$$$**

(📋970-925-1044; www.pinecreekcookhouse.com; 12700 Castle Creek Rd; winter prix-fixe dinner with ski tour/sleigh $100/130, à la carte $16-68; ⊙lunch & dinner Dec-Mar & mid-Jun–Sep; 🚗🚼) 🍴 This log-cabin restaurant, located 1.5 miles past Ashcroft ghost town (p223) at the end of Castle Creek Rd (about 30 minutes from Aspen), boasts the best setting around. In summer you can hike here; in winter it's cross-country skis or horse-drawn sleigh in the shadow of glorious white-capped peaks. Sample alpine delicacies like house-smoked trout, buffalo tenderloin and grilled elk brats.

Cache Cache
BISTRO **$$$**

(📋970-925-3835; www.cachecache.com; 205 S Mill St; prix-fixe menu $38; ⊙5:30pm-close) One of several chic eateries in this gourmet-inclined brick minimall. The stylish modern dining room opens up completely to the colorful courtyard, which features dangling baskets of flowers. The limestone bar and glassed-in wine cellar are also striking, but it's the bistro menu that you'll remember: steamed mussels, escargot, beef tartare and osso buco.

Wild Fig
AMERICAN **$$$**

(📋970-925-5160; www.thewildfig.com; 315 E Hyman Ave; mains $25-42; ⊙5:30-10:30pm) This bright, tiled dining room and patio edged with flower boxes packs plenty of gourmet cheer. It does a nightly risotto, a tender grilled-octopus salad and an enticing fig-glazed duck breast. The small plates are also worth considering – we loved the marinated figs with pancetta, the pan-seared scallops and the fire-roasted clams with chorizo.

Campo de Fiori
ITALIAN **$$$**

(📋970-920-7717; www.campodefiori.net; 205 S Mill St; mains $23-49; ⊙from 5:30pm) Authentic Italian cooking and festive Mediterranean flair have been the mainstay of this minimall kitchen for more than a decade. The menu is seasonal, the gnocchi is housemade, and the seafood – especially the calamari – is excellent. It's located on the bottom level of the shopping complex.

 Drinking & Nightlife

While Aspen's nightlife drifts more toward house parties, there are plenty of choices for designer cocktails, a bottle of Bouchard Père & Fils, or a simple pint, depending on your preferences. Be on the lookout for the traveling champagne bar on Aspen's slopes.

Victoria's Espresso & Wine Bar

CAFE, WINE BAR

(☏ 970-920-3001; www.aspenespressobar.com; 510 E Durant St; ⏰ 7am-7pm; 🛜) Victoria's serves up delish pastries, wine by the glass, full breakfasts and tempting curries and cheese plates for afternoon grazing, but the must-try here is the vanilla latte. Made with housemade syrup crafted from real vanilla bark, it isn't too sweet – just immediately and completely addictive.

Red Onion

PUB

(☏ 970-925-9955; www.redonionaspen.com; 420 E Cooper Ave; ⏰ 11am-2am; 🍴) Open since 1892, this saloon has a distinct mountain-bistro flair. The food is decent for a saloon, with elk Bolognese and bacon-and-jalapeño mac and cheese; plus the kitchen stays open well into the night.

HOPS

CRAFT BEER

(☏ 970-925-4677; www.hopsculture.com; 414 E Hyman Ave; ⏰ 11:30am-11pm) With 30 craft beers on tap, plus more by the bottle, this is Aspen's love letter to hop-heads. Falafel sandwiches and bison chili fries will soak up the excess alcohol as you work your way through the drink menu.

Woody Creek Tavern

PUB

(☏ 970-923-4585; www.woodycreektavern.com; 2 Woody Creek Plaza, 2858 Upper River Rd; ⏰ 11am-10pm) Enjoying a 100% agave tequila and fresh-lime margarita at the late, great gonzo journalist Hunter S Thompson's favorite watering hole is well worth the 8-mile drive – or Rio Grande Trail (p227) bike ride – from Aspen. The walls at this rustic funky tavern, a local haunt since 1980, are plastered with newspaper clippings, photos of customers and paraphernalia.

The lunch menu features salads, low-fat but still juicy burgers and popular Mexican food, including some quality guacamole. The dinner menu is less imaginative, but there's plenty of alcohol – 11 gallons of margaritas a day can't be wrong.

J-Bar

BAR

(www.hoteljerome.com; 330 E Main St; ⏰ 11:30am-2am; 🛜) Once Aspen's premier saloon, this bar was built into the Hotel Jerome (p231) in 1889 and remains full of historic charm. It's packed with everyone from local shopkeepers to Hollywood stars.

Aspen Brewing Co

BREWERY

(☏ 970-920-2739; www.aspenbrewingcompany. com; 304 E Hopkins Ave; ⏰ noon-late; 🛜) With five signature flavors and a sun-soaked balcony facing the mountain, this is definitely the place to unwind after a hard day's play. Brews range from the flavorful This Year's Blonde and high-altitude Independence Pass Ale (its IPA) to the mellower Conundrum Red Ale and the chocolatey Pyramid Peak Porter.

☆ **Entertainment**

★ Belly Up

LIVE MUSIC

(☏ 970-544-9800; www.bellyupaspen.com; 450 S Galena St; cover varies; ⏰ hours vary) Long the top nightspot in Aspen, Belly Up has built and maintained its street cred by bringing the best live acts to the Aspen people. That means everything from local bluegrass bands to hip-hop globalist K'NAAN and up-close throwdowns with the latest stars, like 21 Pilots.

No matter who you see, the room will be intimate and alive with great sound. Easily the best venue this side of Denver.

Aspen Santa Fe Ballet

DANCE

(☏ 970-920-5770; www.aspensantafeballet.com; 335 High School Rd) Founded in Aspen in 1996 and with a second home in Santa Fe, this company is known for its innovative contemporary dance performances by classically trained dancers. There are summer and winter performances at the District Theatre (in the elementary school).

Theatre Aspen

THEATER

(☏ 970-300-4474; www.theatreaspen.org; 470 Rio Grande Pl; 🍴) A nonprofit theater and drama school that hosts classes, workshops and periodic productions (mostly in the summer and early autumn) from its gorgeous, tented complex in the heart of Rio Grande Park (p223). Matinees include bonus views of the nearby mountains; evening productions play beneath a starry sky. Check website for details of upcoming shows and see one if you can.

Wheeler Opera House   PERFORMING ARTS
(✆970-920-5770; www.aspenshowtix.com; 320 E Hyman Ave; ☺box office noon-5pm Mon-Fri) Built in 1887, one of Aspen's oldest and finest examples of Victorian architecture has been a working theater since it first opened, with the exception of the 30 or so years during which things were interrupted by fire, depression and reconstruction. Part of Aspen's postwar revival, it still presents opera, films, concerts and musicals.

Isis Theatre   CINEMA
(✆877-789-6684; www.metrotheatres.com; 406 E Hopkins Ave; adult/child $11/7.75) The only movie house in Aspen proper plays first-run Hollywood fare, but thankfully spices up the blockbusters with an occasional pinch of art-house and foreign cinema. (This is Aspen, after all.)

🛍 Shopping

Aspen is for the professional shopper. Part Malibu, part Rodeo Dr, part Champs-Élysées, this is Colorado's only luxury-brand haute couture strip. Everything from high-end hoodies to pro-grade outdoor gear to designer bling is available. That said, you won't find many local boutiques here. If Louis Vuitton's not your thing, head down valley to Basalt or Carbondale.

Silver Peak   DISPENSARY
(✆970-925-4372; www.silverpeakapothecary.com; 520 E Cooper Ave; ☺11am-7pm) If you were to take your mother out shopping for marijuana (so Mom, are you more sativa or indica?), this bright, inviting boutique downtown would definitely be your first choice. Everything here is beautifully packaged, from the well-coiffed sales team and buds in spotless glass apothecary jars to the gourmet-looking gummies and miniwaffle cookies.

Ute Mountaineer   SPORTS & OUTDOORS
(✆970-925-2849; www.utemountaineer.com; 210 S Galena St; ☺9am-9pm) All the outdoor gear you need, plus maps and guidebooks to get you where you want to go. If you're interested in alpine touring (aka AT or 'uphilling') you can rent a full setup ($75) here, including fat skis, skins, touring boots and avalanche gear.

ASPEN ART GALLERIES

Among the inevitable 'Western' galleries selling hackneyed cowboy paintings and the like are a few jewels for serious art lovers.

Baldwin Gallery (p223)

Galerie Maximillian (p223)

Boesky West (p222)

Peter Lik (p223)

Christopher Martin Gallery (p222)

Anderson Ranch Art Center (✆970-923-3181; www.andersonranch.org; 5263 Owl Creek Rd, Snowmass; ☺hours vary)

You can uphill at all the Aspen resorts for free, though the regulations vary. Pick up the gear the night before.

Aspen Saturday Market   MARKET
(S Hunter St, E Hopkins Ave & E Hyman Ave; ☺8:30am-3pm mid-Jun–mid-Oct) 🍴 This market blooms on Saturday mornings. It's more than just a farmers market, though self-caterers can grab their organic fruits and veggies, artisan cheese and locally raised beef, bison and elk here. It also has tons of crafts, including handmade soap, silver jewelry and fixed-gear bikes built with vintage frames.

Kemosabe   CLOTHING
(✆970-925-7878; www.kemosabe.com; 434 E Cooper Ave; ☺10am-5pm) The sister to Vail's cowboy apparel depot, Kemosabe vends the same handmade boots and Stetson hats – steam-shaped to please. Expect friendly faces, a stuffed buffalo head, gleaming belt buckles and a bluegrass soundtrack.

Explore Booksellers   BOOKS
(✆970-925-5336; www.explorebooksellers.com; 221 E Main St; ☺10am-9pm; 🛜) A sweet and intimate local bookshop, the kind that must survive if humanity is to preserve its literate soul. Little alcoves are stacked with biographies, history, adventure and nature tomes, new and classic literature, and the staff tips are rock-solid. By far the best excuse in Aspen to put down the screen and turn a page.

Little Bird   CLOTHING
(✆970-920-3830; www.thelittlebirdinc.com; 525 E Cooper Ave; ☺10am-6pm Mon-Sat, noon-5pm Sun) This gem of a consignment store has new

and vintage luxury designer scarves, dresses, handbags, shoes and more. Gucci, Jimmy Choo, Blahnik – all the handsome boys are here. You can bargain too – if staff have had the gear for more than 30 days, you may strike a deal. (But it still won't be cheap. You are in Aspen, after all.)

Radio Boardshop   SPORTS & OUTDOORS
(☑970-925-9373; www.radioboardshop.com; 400 E Hopkins Ave; ⊙10am-6pm) On the shortlist for the coolest shop in Aspen, this place does stylish top-shelf skateboards and snowboards, and sells the gear, shoes and boots to match. It's a mom-and-pop store with style to spare.

❶ Information

MEDIA

Aspen Times (www.aspentimes.com) The local paper has a decent website packed with relevant local and regional news and events.

MEDICAL SERVICES

Aspen Valley Hospital (☑970-925-1120; www.aspenvalleyhospital.org; 401 Castle Creek Rd; ⊙24hr) A small but up-to-the-minute community hospital with 24-hour emergency services.

TOURIST INFORMATION

Aspen-Sopris Ranger District (☑970-925-3445; www.fs.usda.gov/whiteriver; 806 W Hallam St; ⊙8am-4:30pm Mon-Fri) The USFS Aspen-Sopris Ranger District operates about 20 campgrounds and covers Roaring Fork Valley and from Independence Pass to Glenwood Springs, including the Maroon Bells Wilderness. Come here for maps and hiking tips.

Aspen Visitor Center (☑970-925-1940; www.aspenchamber.com; 425 Rio Grande Pl; ⊙8:30am-5pm Mon-Fri) Located across from Rio Grande Park.

Cooper Street Kiosk (cnr E Cooper Ave & S Galena St; ⊙10am-6pm) Maps, brochures and magazines.

TRAVEL AGENCIES

Ski.com (☑800-908-5000; www.ski.com; 210 Aspen Airport Business Center, Suite AA; ⊙hours vary) An online travel agency offering discounted all-inclusive ski and snowboard packages that include everything from flights to lodging to rentals and lift tickets.

❶ Getting There & Away

Aspen is 41 miles south of Glenwood Springs on Hwy 82. From Denver, it's 200 miles via I-70 and Hwy 82. The road to Aspen via Independence Pass is only open from late May to early November.

Aspen-Pitkin County Airport (ASE; ☑970-920-5380; www.aspenairport.com; 233 E Airport Rd; ☎) Four miles northwest of Aspen on Hwy 82, this spry airport has direct year-round flights from Denver, as well as seasonal flights direct to eight US cities, including Los Angeles and Chicago. Several car-rental agencies operate here. A free bus runs to and from the airport, departing every 10 to 15 minutes.

Colorado Mountain Express (☑800-525-6363; www.coloradomountainexpress.com; adult/child to DIA $120/61.50; ☎) Runs frequent shuttles to/from the Denver International Airport (four hours).

❶ Getting Around

If your hotel doesn't have parking, save yourself the hassle of street parking and head straight for the town parking garage (per hour/day $1.50/15) next to the visitor center on Rio Grande Pl. Skiers not staying in Aspen can go to the free Park-and-Ride lot on Brush Creek Rd (Rodeo Lot), which is opposite the turnoff for Snowmass off Hwy 82; the free shuttles here serve all mountains.

High Mountain Taxi (☑970-925-8294; www.hmtaxi.com; airport to/from Aspen $19-30; ⊙24hr) Serves the airport and offers Aspen-area metered fare services 24 hours a day. Taxis seat up to six people and are equipped with child seats.

Maroon Bells Shuttles (☑307-690-8856; www.maroonbellsshuttles.com) If you're doing a one-way hike, bike ride or river trip, contact this shuttle service to help arrange transport.

Roaring Fork Transportation Authority (RFTA; ☑970-925-8484; www.rfta.com; 430 E Durant Ave, Aspen; ⊙6:15am-2:15am; ☎) RFTA buses connect Aspen with the Highlands, Snowmass and Buttermilk via free shuttles, while the **VelociRFTA** serves the down-valley towns of Basalt ($4, 25 minutes), Carbondale ($6, 45 minutes) and Glenwood Springs ($7, one hour). Passengers must have exact change or can purchase a discounted ticket at vending machines at certain stops. Most buses are equipped with ski/bike racks; bikes are an additional $2. The Aspen depot is located at Durant Ave and Mill St at the **Rubey Park Transit Center**. RFTA also runs a shuttle to Maroon Bells (p219), which leaves from the Aspen Highlands (p226) parking lot.

Redstone

☑970 / POP 92 / ELEV 7203FT

Wedged between Chair Mountain and Mt Sopris, Redstone was a true company town, quite unlike the 'every man for himself' spirit of the Gold Rush era. Founded in 1890 by John C Osgood, multimillionaire and head of the Colorado Fuel & Iron Company, Redstone was one of the early experiments in welfare capitalism, where workers were provided with higher standards of living but discouraged from forming unions. The town was created to carbonize coal from Coalbasin Mine, and the first thing you'll see as you drive up the highway are the remains of some 50 beehive coke ovens, lined up across from the town entrance. When the mine closed in 1909, the town was virtually abandoned overnight, though new residents have since moved in over the past few decades. Hiking and fishing are the big activities here.

⊙ Sights & Activities

Redstone Castle   HISTORIC BUILDING
(☑970-963-9656; www.theredstonecastle.com; 58 Redstone Castle Ln; adult/child $15/10; ⊙tours 11am) Several of Redstone's original buildings are still standing, including the original chalet-style workers' cottages and John Osgood's personal residence, the 42-room Redstone Castle. Located 1 mile south of town on a private road, it was thoroughly renovated in 2017 and is open for tours only (check online for schedules). There are plans to open the castle as accommodations in future.

Out West Guides   HORSEBACK RIDING, FISHING
(☑970-963-5525; www.outwestguides.com; 7500 County Rd 3, Marble; horseback rides per hr from $50) This family-run guiding tour knows the area well and operates horseback rides from $50 per hour. Half-day fly-fishing expeditions start at $285 for two people.

Avalanche Ranch   HOT SPRINGS, MASSAGE
(☑970-963-2846; www.avalancheranch.com; 12863 Hwy 133; adult/child $15/10 Mon, Tue & Thu, $18/12 Fri-Sun; ⊙9am-5pm Thu-Tue) Make sure to reserve in advance for a soak in one of the three cascading geothermal pools at Avalanche Ranch. They are open to nonguests in four-hour windows, though you'll have greater access if you spend the night. Limited massage services are also available.

Penny Hot Springs   HOT SPRINGS
(Hwy 133) FREE Conveniently accessed and set in a beautiful location, these hot springs are plenty warm, though the pools are completely flooded by the river when water is high (usually spring and early summer).

Park at the unmarked pull-off after mile marker 55.

Crystal River Jeep Tours   TOURS
(☑970-963-1991; www.smithfamilycolorado.com; 575 W Park St, Marble; tours per person $60-125; ⊙Jun-Nov) This company hires rugged Jeeps to take guests to Crystal (p221), a ghost town. The sweeping panoramas of the Maroon Bells-Snowmass Wilderness Area can be breathtaking, and, even if you get jostled about like a rag doll, it's a lot more fun than fretting about a broken axle on your own car.

🛏 Sleeping & Eating

There's a cafe and general store in Redstone; the Redstone Inn also serves meals. You'll want to bring at least some food with you.

★ Avalanche Ranch   CABIN $$
(☑970-963-2846; www.avalancheranch.com; 12863 Hwy 133; cabins $85-230; 🛜🐾) This ranch is set on the back of Mt Sopris alongside Avalanche Creek (north of Redstone), with 13 cabins, three wagons and a ranch house. Cabins are well appointed with kitchens, sleeping lofts and front porches, but the real appeal are the three geothermal pools lined with river rocks. (They are open to nonguests, but you must reserve.)

Redstone Inn   HOTEL $$
(☑970-963-2526; http://redstoneinn.thegilmorecollection.com; 82 Redstone Blvd; r $90-300; ❄🐾🛜) Tucked away behind massive red cliffs, this hotel – and the tiny village of Redstone that surrounds it – occupies a little slice of Rocky Mountain heaven. It's an intimate getaway, perfect for those looking to disappear for a few days. Opened in 1902 as bachelor housing for miners, the historic inn occupies 22 acres of pristine, secluded land surrounded by national forest.

❶ Getting There & Away

Redstone is 18 miles south of Carbondale on Hwy 133 and a one-hour drive from Aspen.

SALIDA & THE COLLEGIATE PEAKS

The Arkansas River Valley, running from Leadville in the north to Salida in the south, is a picturesque slice of high-desert landscape whose natural diversity is such that

ST ELMO

An old gold-mining ghost town tucked into the base of the Collegiate Peaks, St Elmo makes for a fun excursion. The drive is the best part: the road wends its way past stands of redolent ponderosa pine, a wildlife-viewing meadow and jagged peaks before petering out at what is Colorado's best-preserved ghost town.

Of course, it wasn't about the scenery back in the good ol' days – there was gold in this here creek! Most buildings were built in or around 1881: the schoolhouse, an old mercantile building, and a miners exchange are among the best kept of the bunch.

The only catch to this spectacular setting is that St Elmo is also a staging point for ATV and snowmobile enthusiasts, who follow the forest service road up to Tincup Pass. The revving of not-too-distant engines can take away some of the charm, so try to avoid weekends.

If you've got the time and energy, you can continue on 5 miles to Hancock; the turnoff is just before St Elmo. From here it's a 3-mile hike up to the Alpine Tunnel – a failed attempt to get a railroad through the mountain – and amazing views from the Continental Divide. Ready to tackle it on bike? Sign up for a tour with Absolute Bikes in Salida.

If you want to have the place to yourself, stay the night: the Ghost Town Guest House (p243) is a local B&B (really!), and there are three very popular USFS campgrounds on the way up. They're all nice, but Chalk Lake (p243) has a choice location with views of Mt Princeton. Reservations are essential. Just before the turnoff to the campground is a parking lot for the Agnes Vaille trail (on your right), a short half-mile hike up to a waterfall. It's the perfect spot to stretch your legs.

St Elmo is on County Road 162, 11.5 miles past Mt Princeton Hot Springs. The road turns to dirt about halfway up. In summer it's not a problem, but in winter or muddy weather you'll probably want a 4WD.

you never tire of looking at it. The mighty Sawatch Range, and the Collegiate Peaks in particular, are the dominant geological feature, forming the backdrop to one of the most popular stretches of white water in the entire country.

Salida

☏719 / POP 5406 / ELEV 7083FT

When a town of only about 5400 people has three microbreweries, you know something's up. The former railroad hub turned ranching community turned outdoor mecca is quintessential Colorado: mud-spattered pickup trucks cruise the streets alongside battered Subarus adorned with rooftop kayaks, and distant mighty peaks form postcard panoramas everywhere you look.

Blessed with one of the state's largest historic districts, Salida is not only an inviting spot to explore, it also has an unbeatable location, with the Arkansas River on one side and the intersection of two large mountain ranges on the other. The plan of attack here is to hike, bike or raft during the day, then come back to town to refuel with grilled buffalo ribs and a cold IPA at night.

And did we mention that the sun always shines here?

◉ Sights & Activities

Both bikers and hikers should note that some big-time trails – the Continental Divide (www.continentaldividetrail.org), the Colorado Trail (www.coloradotrail.org) and the Rainbow Trail (p342) – are within spitting distance of town. If you don't want to sweat it, a gondola can haul you from Monarch Pass nearly 1000ft up to the top of the ridge.

Salida Museum   MUSEUM
(☏719-539-7483; www.salidamuseum.org; 406½ W Rainbow Blvd; by donation; ☉1-5pm Sat & Sun) The local history museum has a small selection of artifacts and old photos. It's staffed by volunteers and not always open.

★Monarch Crest Trail   MOUNTAIN BIKING
One of the most famous rides in all of Colorado, the Monarch Crest is an extreme 20- to 35-mile adventure. It starts off at Monarch Pass (11,312ft), follows the exposed ridge 12 miles to Marshall Pass and then either cuts down to Poncha Springs on an old railroad

grade or hooks onto the Rainbow Trail. A classic ride with fabulous high-altitude views.

Monarch Mountain
SNOW SPORTS

(☑719-530-5000; www.skimonarch.com; 23715 Hwy 50; adult/child $84/40; ☺Dec–mid-Apr; ♿) Cut along the same lines as the Eldora and Ski Cooper ski resorts, Monarch is a great local mountain. Although the resort, with 800 acres, is on the small side, you'll still find lots of varied terrain, great powder and reasonably affordable fees. For a real treat, sign up for their backcountry snowcat skiing ($375). It's just below Monarch Pass, on Hwy 50.

Captain Zipline
ADVENTURE SPORTS

(☑877-947-5463; www.captainzipline.com; 1500 County Rd 45; tours from $69; ♿) This popular zipline tour takes in six cables through the high desert, some of which send you flying above some pretty deep canyons. Expect to spend two to three hours on the tour. There are also Via Ferrata tours (assisted climbing) and a large aerial challenge course. Children must be six or older.

Salida Mountain Trails
MOUNTAIN BIKING

(www.salidamountaintrails.org) If you don't want to bother with a shuttle, the best place to start riding in Salida is the Arkansas Hills Trail System just across the river (look for the giant S). Open year-round – yes, you can ride here in winter – it offers a nice variety of short rides for all levels.

Monarch Crest Tramway
CABLE CAR

(☑719-539-4091; www.monarchcrest.net; adult/child $10/5; ☺8:30am-5:30pm mid-May–mid-Sep) At the top of Monarch Pass (11,312ft), this gondola was originally opened in 1966 and hauls visitors nearly 1000ft up to the top of the ridge, where stupendous views await.

☞ Tours

★ Absolute Bikes
CYCLING

(☑719-539-9295; www.absolutebikes.com; 330 W Sackett Ave; bike rental per day $15-100, tours from $90; ☺9am-6pm; ♿) The go-to place for bike enthusiasts, offering maps, gear, advice, rentals and, most importantly, shuttles to the trailhead. Check out the great selection of guided rides, from St Elmo ghost town to the Monarch Crest.

Ark Anglers
FISHING

(☑719-539-4223; www.arkanglers.com; 7500 Hwy 50; half-day wade trip $225; ☺8am-6pm) The Arkansas is a great place to cast for trout and the Ark is the best spot to meet the local

anglers and get up-to-date reports on current river conditions. It also has a shop in Buena Vista.

Arkansas River Tours
RAFTING

(☑800-321-4352; www.arkansasrivertours.com; 19487 Hwy 50; half-/full-day adult $59/109, child $49/99; ☺May-Aug; ♿) This outfit runs from Brown's Canyon downstream, specializing in Royal Gorge trips. They have an office in Cotopaxi, 23 miles east of Salida.

🛏 Sleeping

Salida has a good hostel and hotel in town, along with a few generic motels on the outskirts. The **Arkansas Headwaters Recreation Area** (☑719-539-7289; http://cpw.state.co.us; 307 W Sackett Ave; ☺8am-5pm, closed noon-1pm Sat & Sun) operates six campgrounds (bring your own water) along the river, including Hecla Junction. Another top campground is Monarch Park, up by the pass, near the hiking and biking along the Monarch Crest and Rainbow Trails.

★ Simple Lodge & Hostel
HOSTEL $

(☑719-650-7381; www.simplelodge.com; 224 E 1st St; dm/d/q $24/60/84; 🅿 @ 🛜 🐾) If only Colorado had more spots like this. Run by the superfriendly Mel and Justin, this hostel is simple but stylish, with a fully stocked kitchen and a comfy communal area that feels just like home. It's a popular stopover for touring cyclists following the coast-to-coast Rte 50 – you're likely to meet some interesting folks here.

Hecla Junction
CAMPGROUND $

(☑719-539-7289; http://coloradostateparks.reserveamerica.com; Hwy 285, Mile 135; tent & RV sites $18, plus daily pass $7; 🐾) Located at the takeout for Browns Canyon on the Arkansas River, Hecla is a pleasant campground in the river canyon, though there can be a lot of traffic in summer. Good location for anglers, boaters and access to Salida (14 miles southeast on Hwy 285). No hookups or water available. Reserve.

Monarch Park
CAMPGROUND $

(☑877-444-6777; www.recreation.gov; off Hwy 50; tent & RV sites $18; ☺Jun-Sep; 🐾) Top pick for a subalpine setting near Salida, with views and fishing a few miles from Monarch Pass. There are a lot of fabulous hiking and biking trails up here, including the Continental Divide, the Monarch Crest and Waterdog Lakes. It's up at 10,500ft, so be prepared for cooler weather in the evening. No hookups. Reserve.

Palace Hotel
BOUTIQUE HOTEL $$

(☑719-207-4175; www.salidapalacehotel.com; 204 N F St; ste $150-240; 🅿❄🛜📺) ✏ The most atmospheric digs in Salida, the three-story Palace is an old railway hotel (1909) that was entirely renovated in 2012 by Vicki and Fred Klein. It's now a smart, solar-powered boutique option, with 14 personalized suites in vintage decor (some with claw-foot bathtubs). Some suites sleep up to four people; all include kitchenettes and continental breakfast.

✖ Eating

Eating well in Salida will not be a problem. Tapas, pho, pizza and organic cafes abound.

Seasons Cafe
CAFE $

(☑719-530-9525; www.seasonssalida.com; 300 W Sackett Ave; mains $8-12; ☺8am-8pm Fri-Mon, takeout only 6am-6pm Tue-Thu; 🚼) ✏ Riverside cafe featuring local, organic brunches on weekends, plus cocktails, beer and shared plates after 3pm. No reservations, so come with time to spare. From Tuesday through Thursday, they also do coffee and sandwiches to go.

Fritz
TAPAS $

(☑719-539-0364; 113 East Sackett St; tapas $5-10, mains $10-15.50; ☺11am-9pm; 🛜) This fun and funky riverside watering hole serves up clever American-style tapas: think three-cheese mac with bacon, fries and truffle aioli, seared ahi wontons, and brie ciabatta with date jam. It also does a mean grass-fed beef burger and other salads and sandwiches. Good selection of local beers on tap.

Little Cambodia
CAMBODIAN $

(☑719-539-6599; 135 N F St; mains $6-16; ☺11am-8pm Tue-Sat) Half brick-walled pool hall, half checkerboard-tiled restaurant, this Salida stalwart delivers the goods: pho (noodle soup), bun (cold noodle salad), fresh spring rolls, Vietnamese coffee and boba tea. Look for the daily specials, like hot-and-sour soup.

Sweetie's
SANDWICHES $

(☑719-539-4248; www.sweetiesinsalida.com; 124 F St; sandwiches $9-11; ☺10am-4pm Mon-Sat; 🚼) This uber-popular and superfriendly Salida sandwich shop makes for a good lunch – try out specialties like the Don Draper (pastrami, horseradish Havarti, roasted green peppers and caramelized onions) or the Flaming Goat (bacon, chèvre, avocado, lettuce and tomato).

★ Amícas
PIZZA $$

(☑719-539-5219; www.amicassalida.com; 127 F St; pizzas & paninis $6.90-13; ☺11am-9pm Mon-Wed,

7am-9pm Thu-Sun; 🚼♿) Thin-crust wood-fired pizzas, panini, housemade lasagne and five microbrews on tap? Amícas can do no wrong. This high-ceilinged, laid-back hangout is the perfect spot to replenish all those calories you burned off during the day. Savor a Michelangelo (pesto, sausage and goat cheese) or Vesuvio (artichoke hearts, sun-dried tomatoes, roasted peppers) alongside a cool glass of Headwaters IPA.

🍷 Drinking & Nightlife

Cafe Dawn
CAFE

(☑719-539-5105; www.cafe-dawn.com; 203 W 1st St; ☺6am-6pm; 🛜) ✏ The place to go for your morning cappuccino and raspberry scone. This great community cafe is run by Phillip and Dawn out of a former Volkswagen repair shop, and features organic beans, local ingredients in the lunch menu and good lattes. Phillip has also written two local guidebooks (climbing and mountain biking), which you can find here. Cash only.

Boathouse Cantina
BAR

(☑719-539-5004; www.boathousesalida.com; 228 N F St; ☺11am-9pm; 🛜) If you can snag a table by the river, this is a pretty sweet spot. It's got 20 craft beers on tap, including local brew Elevation. The buffalo chili and fish tacos ain't bad either.

Elevation
BREWERY

(☑719-539-5258; www.elevationbeerco.com; 115 Pahlone Pkwy, Poncha Springs; ☺noon-8pm) A top pick for beer geeks, Elevation is definitely worth the drive out to Poncha Springs. Beers are rated green to double black (the latter are aged in bourbon barrels), but they all go down easy. Food truck on site.

ℹ Tourist Information

Salida Chamber of Commerce (☑719-539-2068; www.nowthisiscolorado.com; 406 W Rainbow Blvd; ☺9am-5pm Mon-Fri) General tourist info.

USFS Ranger Office (☑719-539-3591;.www.fs.usda.gov; 5575 Cleora Rd; ☺8am-4:30pm Mon-Fri) Located east of town off Hwy 50, with camping and trail info for the Sawatch and northern Sangre de Cristo Ranges.

ℹ Getting There & Away

Located at the 'exit' of the Arkansas River Valley, Salida occupies a prime location at the crossroads of Hwys 285 and 50. Indeed, this used to be a railroad hub, and you'll likely spot an abandoned line or two while exploring the area. Gunnison,

Colorado Springs, the Great Sand Dunes and Summit County are all within one to two hours' drive, provided you have your own car.

Buena Vista

719 / POP 2734 / ELEV 7954FT

With Mt Princeton (14,197ft) and the rest of the Collegiate Peaks providing a dramatic backdrop to the west, and the icy Arkansas River rushing by the boulder-filled hills east of town, Buena Vista certainly lives up to its name. Whether you're hiking, biking, paddling, hot-spring soaking or simply admiring the stupendous landscapes, this is a town that has 'adventure playground' written all over it.

Historic E Main St, the town's main drag, runs perpendicular to Hwy 24. Follow Main St (away from the mountains) to the end and you'll come to the Arkansas River. Heading west (towards the mountains) off Hwy 24 is W Main St, which turns into Rte 306 and heads up to Cottonwood Pass.

Sights

Love Meadow WILDLIFE RESERVE
(County Rd 162) Once a pioneer homestead belonging to an impressive local woman, it's now a small wildlife sanctuary. There's no access – you can only view wildlife from the parking area.

Buena Vista River Park PARK
(E Main St) FREE Take E Main St to its riverside conclusion and you'll find a park that sprawls for more than 2 miles along the Arkansas River. At its northern end are soccer fields, basketball courts, a tennis court, a humble skate park, boat-staging put-ins, and the Barbara Whipple trailhead (p242).

Cottonwood Lake LAKE
(County Rd 344; ⊙Jun-Oct) Tucked up against a stark, moonscape granite wall on one side and into a gorgeous, pine-dappled bowl on the other, this is one of the most picturesque picnic spots in the area. Reachable by car or a strenuous bike ride, it's another 3 miles on a dirt road to the left off the main County Rd 306. A good spot for fishing and paddle boarding.

Buena Vista Heritage Museum MUSEUM
(☑719-395-8458; www.buenavistaheritage.org; 506 E Main St; adult/child $5/1; ⊙10am-5pm Mon-Sat, noon-5pm Sun late May–Sep) Housed in the 1882 Chaffee County Courthouse, the museum focuses on railroad and mining exhibits

(there's a great model railroad of the Arkansas River Valley), a fashion room and school room. The past two years it has also hosted the popular *Madams of Central Colorado* show, where you can learn about life in the Palace of Joy at the turn of the 20th century.

Activities

Among the many diversions available to the thrill-seeking wanderer in Buena Vista, the top attraction is by far the Arkansas River: 99 miles of white water accessible from Main St. If you have your own boat, check out the Buena Vista Whitewater Park at the end of E Main St.

Collegiate Peaks Wilderness HIKING
Who said the Ivy League has to be stuck-up and boring? Encompassing 166,938 acres laced with 105 miles of trails, the Collegiate Peaks has the highest average elevation of any wilderness area in the US: eight peaks exceed 14,000ft, including the state's 3rd- and 5th-highest summits, Mt Harvard and La Plata Peak. (Princeton, Yale, Oxford and Columbia are the 20th, 21st, 26th and 35th respectively.)

Cottonwood Pass SCENIC DRIVE
(County Rd 306; ⊙Jun-Oct) Ever wonder what it's like to drive to the moon? Wind your way past the Collegiate Peaks Campground to Cottonwood Pass (12,126ft) – this is the Continental Divide and the border between the San Isabel National Forest on the eastern slope and the Gunnison National Forest to the west.

Mt Princeton Hot Springs Resort HOT SPRINGS, SPA
(☑719-395-2447; www.mtprinceton.com; 15870 County Rd 162; day pass adult/child $22/16; ⊙9am-10pm Mon-Thu, to 11pm Fri-Sun;) A sprawling, four-star hot-springs resort, this is a terrific destination for families. There are 30 natural pools on the property that differ in size and atmosphere, including soaking pools, an expansive swimming pool and a 400ft water slide. Many guests stay the night, but it is also possible to purchase a day pass.

Cottonwood Hot Springs HOT SPRINGS
(☑719-395-6434; www.cottonwood-hot-springs.com; 18999 County Rd 306; adult/child $20/15; ⊙8am-10pm) Take Main St across Hwy 24 and keep going up the mountain toward Cottonwood Pass, and you'll soon come to the hippiest of the Collegiate hot springs.

These renovated pools are set on leafy grounds and are relatively peaceful (albeit somewhat kitsch), with gushing fountains of hot water, dangling vines and wind chimes (but no water slide).

Barbara Whipple Trail   MOUNTAIN BIKING, HIKING
(Whipple Trail; Buena Vista River Park) Good for hikers, bikers and picnickers, this trail system is about as idyllic as town parks get. Accessed from the end of E Main St (turn north), it follows an old stage road through the arid hills and funky rock formations east of the Arkansas River, with stupendous views back towards the Collegiates (p241).

Mt Princeton   HIKING
(www.14ers.com; Mt Princeton Rd) Although experienced hikers will probably want to tackle Yale's east ridge, it can be hard to resist Princeton's dominating peaks from down below. If you have a 4WD vehicle, figure on 6.5 miles of hiking and 3200ft of elevation gain; if not, it's a grueling 13 miles and 5400ft of elevation gain. Either way, count on a long day.

Tours

★ **Rocky Mountain Outdoor Center**   OUTDOORS
(RMOC; ☑ 719-395-3335; www.rmoc.com; 23850 Hwy 285; climbing trips from $75; ⏱ 8am-6pm; ♿) The local Swiss Army knife of outdoor adventure, RMOC offers all sorts of guided activities, but is particularly good for rafting, kayaking, stand-up paddling and rock-climbing trips. If you want to learn some basic techniques, it also offers instruction in kayaking and SUP. Rent river gear here.

Mt Princeton Hot Springs Stables   HORSEBACK RIDING
(☑ 719-395-3630; www.coloradotrailrides.com; 14582 County Rd 162; 1hr ride $40) Located down the hill from the Mt Princeton Hot Springs Resort (p241), this stable offers a variety of trips, from one-hour nose-to-tail rides to overnight pack trips. Children must be five or older.

River Runners   RAFTING
(☑ 800-723-8987; www.riverrunnersltd.com; 24070 County Rd 301; half-/full-day trip adult $68/109, child $60/99; ⏱ May-Aug; ♿) Recommended river outfitter based in Buena Vista, Salida and Cañon City, and in the business of guiding trips since 1972. It does everything from placid float trips to thrilling outings on

class V rapids. In Salida they rent out tubes and SUP boards; pick up gear at their store in downtown Buena Vista.

American Adventure Expeditions   RAFTING
(☑ 719-395-2409; www.americanadventure.com; 12844 Hwy 24; half-/full-day trip adult $65/109, child $55/94; ⏱ May-Aug; ♿) This outfitter is located 2 miles south of Buena Vista on Hwy 24/285 and comes recommended by locals in the know. They also offer ziplining and horseback riding.

Wilderness Aware Rafting   RAFTING
(☑ 800-462-7238; www.inaraft.com; 12600 Hwys 24/285; half-/full-day trip adult $67/103, child $57/88; ⏱ May-Aug; ♿) This adventure company operates 2 miles south of Buena Vista, offering rafting trips, horseback riding, mountain biking and more.

Noah's Ark   RAFTING
(☑ 719-395-2158; www.noahsark.com; 23910 Hwy 285; half-/full-day trip adult $66/94, child $53/83; ⏱ May-Aug) One of the larger river outfitters in the Buena Vista–Salida swirl, offering a range of trips that run every bit of the Arkansas.

Sleeping

The indoor sleeping options in Buena Vista are limited, though what's here is generally excellent. Campgrounds, in contrast, abound: the Arkansas River has Railroad Bridge and Ruby Mountain, Cottonwood Pass has the Collegiate Peaks, and the road to St Elmo and Mt Princeton Hot Springs has three campgrounds, including Chalk Lake.

Collegiate Peaks Campground   CAMPGROUND $
(www.reserveamerica.com; Hwy 306; tent & RV sites $20; ⏱ mid-May–Sep; ♥) Aptly named, this is a good base from which to summit the nearby peaks, including Yale and Turner. You can also get on the Colorado and the Ptarmigan Lake Trails, or simply fish for trout in Middle Cottonwood Creek. The campground is located 11 miles due west of Buena Vista at an altitude of 9800ft. Reserve ahead.

Railroad Bridge   CAMPGROUND $
(☑ 719-539-7289; www.coloradostateparks.reserveamerica.com; County Rd 371; tent & RV sites $18, plus day pass $7; ⏱ year-round; ♥) Just after passing through the series of blasted tunnels on a dirt road, you'll find Elephant Rock and the first of two campgrounds nestled among

giant boulders and the abandoned railway line. The first, on the left, is free primitive camping. There are no toilets, but the Arkansas River, nearby bolted climbs and massive mountain views are hard to beat.

Three miles past this spot is the Arkansas Headwaters' (p239) Railroad Bridge campground, which has a similar landscape, toilets and is better maintained. Neither site has water.

To get here, turn north on Colorado Ave off E Main St and keep going.

Chalk Lake Campground CAMPGROUND $
(☑ 877-444-6777; www.recreation.gov; County Rd 162; tent & RV sites $20; ⊙ mid-May–Sep; ▣) One of three campgrounds in between the Mt Princeton Hot Springs and the St Elmo ghost town, with nice tent sites by the creek. It's 13 miles southwest of Buena Vista at an elevation of 9000ft; the nearby trailhead provides access to the Colorado Trail. The other two nearby campgrounds are Mt Princeton and Cascade. No hookups.

Ruby Mountain CAMPGROUND $
(☑ 719-539-7289; www.coloradostateparks. reserveamerica.com; County Rd 300; tent & RV sites $18, plus day pass $7; ⊙ year-round; ▣) A popular put-in for Brown's Canyon rafting trips, Ruby Mountain is a pretty, heavily used campsite 9 miles south of Buena Vista off Hwy 285. In addition to river access, this is the only place from which you can hike or bike into the Brown's Canyon National Monument. No water or hookups.

★ Liars' Lodge B&B B&B $$
(☑ 719-395-3444; www.liarslodge.com; 30000 Co Rd 371; r from $168, cabins $305; ☎) This airy, spectacularly set log cabin is perched on a finger of the Arkansas River, so close that the river will sing you to sleep. It has five rooms and a cabin, which sleeps up to five people. Breakfast is served on an outstanding riverside terrace, weather permitting. This place represents outstanding value and is easily the best in Buena Vista, so reserve ahead.

Surf Chateau HOTEL $$
(☑ 719-966-7048; www.surfchateau.com; 1028 Wave St; r $200-240; ⓟ ❄ ☎ ▣) Funky and modern, the river-stone Surf Chateau is the anchor of Buena Vista's up-and-coming South Main district on the banks of the Arkansas. Split-level lofts are set in English-looking row houses; more traditional rooms have patios overlooking the river. A new addition is due to be completed in 2018, with more accommodations, a concert space and a pool.

Ghost Town Guest House B&B $$
(☑ 719-395-2120; www.ghosttownguesthouse. com; County Rd 162, St Elmo; r incl 2 meals $175-195; @ ☎) While ghosts are not guaranteed, you can still spend the night in St Elmo's best-preserved ghost town, St Elmo. The three rooms are decked out with period furnishings, and Sharon and Chuck provide breakfast and dinner (picnic lunches are available upon request). In wet or snowy weather, 4WD is recommended.

✖ Eating

Like neighboring Salida, Buena Vista has gone through a culinary renaissance in the past few years, with a number of new restaurants – and, in particular, food trucks – springing up on Main St.

Evergreen Cafe DINER $
(☑ 719-395-8984; www.evergreencafebv.com; 418 US Hwy 24; mains $6.75-11; ⊙ 6:30am-2pm Mon-Fri, to 1pm Sat & Sun; ▣ ▣) ◑ Fun and funky, this canary-yellow train car of a diner on Hwy 24 north of Main St is where you'll find some seriously tasty offerings, such as brownie sundaes, smoothies and sinful bread pudding, not to mention killer organic omelets, melts, burgers and salads.

Bearded Lady FOOD TRUCK $
(☑ 719-838-1549; www.thebeardedladyfarmtofork. com; 410 East Main St; 3 tacos $9.25; ⊙ 7:30am-8pm Thu-Sat, to 2pm Sun & Mon late May–Sep) Street tacos, empanadas and fruit *paletas* (popsicles) with ingredients straight from the Crowded Acre family farm. Look for the blue school bus.

House Rock Kitchen AMERICAN $
(☑ 719-966-2326; www.houserockkitchen.com; 421 E Main St; mains $11-16; ⊙ 11am-8:30pm; ▣) ◑

① LOCAL FARMERS MARKETS

The Central Colorado Foodshed Alliance (www.foodshedalliance. com) runs farmers markets from June through mid-October in Buena Vista (3pm to 7pm on Fridays) and Salida (8am to 12:30pm on Saturdays). They're a great resource for more information on locally grown food in Central Colorado. See the website for details.

RAFTING THE ARKANSAS

The headwaters of the Arkansas are Colorado's best-known stretch of white water, with everything from extreme rapids to mellow ripples. Although most rafting companies cover the river from Leadville to the Royal Gorge, the most popular trips descend through Brown's Canyon National Monument, a 16-mile stretch that includes class III to IV rapids (rafting is the principal way to visit the monument). If you're with young kids or just looking for something more low key, Bighorn Sheep Canyon is a good bet. Those after more of an adrenaline rush can head upstream to the Numbers or downstream to the Royal Gorge (p318), both of which are class IV to V. If you'd like to go solo, most outfitters also rent duckies (inflatable kayaks).

Water flow varies by season, so time your visit for late May or early June for a wilder ride – by the time August rolls around, the water level is usually pretty low. If you're rafting with kids, note that they need to be at least six (sometimes older, depending on the trip/outfitter) and weigh a minimum of 50 pounds.

Most companies are based just south of Buena Vista, close to where Hwys 24 and 285 diverge, and typically also offer full-day packages that include adventure parks, rock climbing or horseback riding in addition to rafting. The larger ones have Cañon City locations as well. We recommend the following:

American Adventure Expeditions (p242)

Arkansas River Tours (p239)

Noah's Ark (p242)

River Runners (p242)

Wilderness Aware Rafting (p242)

An outdoor fire pit, sofa, local band, horseshoes and bocce ball – eating at HRK is a bit like hanging out at a backyard BBQ. The menu ranges from house-smoked pork and beef brisket to jicama-orange salad, hot sandwiches, greens and monster bowls like the Moroccan, with quinoa tabbouleh, roasted beets, *chermoula* (herb sauce), avocado, and raisin-lemon sauce.

Buena Vista Farmers Market　　MARKET $
(www.ccfa.coop; S Main Town Sq; ⊙3-7pm Fri Jun-Oct) A small gathering of local, organic farmers gets together with musicians and hungry locals to form a fun and tasty summer market.

Asian Palate　　ASIAN $$
(☎719-395-6679; www.theasianpalate.com; 328 E Main St; mains $15-20; ⊙5-9pm; ⊕) Eclectic Asian fare is what passes for haute cuisine in Buena Vista. Dishes such as Massaman curry, pork *larb* and beef with udon noodles are typical kitchen fare, while raw morsels appear from the sushi bar. All are served in minimalist environs – think high-beamed ceilings and burgundy walls strategically cracked to reveal swatches of original brick.

 Drinking & Entertainment

There's no shortage of quality watering holes in Buena Vista. Jailhouse bars, breweries and distilleries all vie for your patronage.

★**Buena Vista Roastery**　　CAFE
(☎719-966-5500; www.buenavistaroasterycafe.com; 409 E Main St; ⊙7am-6pm; ☎) Known among locals as the Roastery, this wonderful, aromatic cafe sells fair-trade and organic beans, supporting local nonprofit organizations through its Coffees for a Cause program. It's a nice space with patio seating and delectable pastries available throughout the day.

Deerhammer　　DISTILLERY
(☎719-395-9464; www.deerhammer.com; 321 E Main St; ⊙4-10pm Wed-Sun) Single-malt whiskey, gin and brandy are the winning trifecta at Buena Vista's distillery. Stop by for an Old Fashioned and mosey on out to the patio, where you'll find rye-bread sandwich melts at the Viking food truck.

Eddyline Restaurant & Brewery　　PUB
(☎719-966-6000; www.eddylinepub.com; 926 S Main St; ⊙11am-9pm; ☎⊕) With sunny patio seating just steps from the Arkansas River, it's no surprise this South Main brewpub is a

local hangout. The food – wood-fired pizzas and grass-fed local beef – is solid, if unspectacular. You can't go wrong with the seven beers on tap, however.

To get here, take E Main St to the end of town, then follow the signs south.

Commanche Drive In CINEMA
(☎719-395-2766; www.comanchedrivein.com; 27784 County Rd 339; adult/child $8/4; ☉late May–early Sep) This historic 1966 drive-in movie theater is one of only eight remaining in Colorado. It's located 3 miles west of Buena Vista.

🛈 Getting There & Away

Buena Vista is 93 miles west of Colorado Springs and 35 miles south of Leadville on Hwy 24, and 25 miles north of Salida on Hwy 285.

Twin Lakes
🗐 719 / POP 171 / ELEV 9200FT

An alternative to staying in Leadville, Twin Lakes is a gorgeous historic mining camp set on the shores of the largest glacial lakes in Colorado, at the base of the sinuous climb to Independence Pass. Fed by steady stagecoach lines, this was log-cabin mining country in the late 19th century, and a convenient rest stop between Aspen and Leadville. First called Dayton during the 1860s gold rush, it was renamed Twin Lakes in 1879 when the silver rush revived the village.

⦿ Sights & Activities

Several historic structures still stand on the lake shore, including the **Red Rooster Tavern** (aka the town brothel), now the visitor center. On the south shore of the main lake is **Interlaken**, the vestiges of what was once Colorado's largest resort, built in 1889. The ruins have good signage and you can even walk inside and explore the abandoned buildings. You can get here along the Colorado and Continental Divide trails; it's about 5 miles round-trip with little elevation gain. The turnoff for the Interlaken trailhead is 0.6 miles after you turn onto Hwy 82, after Lost Canyon Rd.

The cross-country skiing and snowshoeing in the area is magnificent (though you'll have to bring your own gear). In summer, you can fish and boat on the lakes. Canoe rentals are available in the village.

If you're up for some higher-altitude views, La Plata Peak and Independence Pass lie just west of town.

La Plata Peak HIKING
(www.14ers.com; ☉Jun-Sep) La Plata Peak's (14,336ft) **Ellingwood Ridge** is a fun challenge for experienced hikers. At 9.5 miles round-trip, this is a particularly long hike because of the time needed to navigate the complex class-3 route. The trailhead is at South Fork Lake Creek Rd on the eastern side of Independence Pass, past Twin Lakes. Start early!

🛏 Sleeping

Twin Peaks Campground CAMPGROUND $
(Hwy 82; tent & RV sites $19; ☉Jun–mid-Sep; 🐾) No connection to David Lynch, the first-come, first-served Twin Peaks Campground looks out over the Sawatch Range and is a good base for those hiking the Continental Divide Trail, Mt Elbert or La Plata Peak. The elevation here is 9600ft.

Parry Peak Campground CAMPGROUND $
(Hwy 82; tent & RV sites $17; ☉Jun–mid-Sep) Parry Peak Campground is a fantastic campground set 2.5 miles west of Twin Lakes – it's perfect for those hiking La Plata Peak. There's no potable water, so bring your own.

Twin Lakes Inn HOTEL $$
(☎719-486-7965; www.thetwinlakesinn.com; 6435 Hwy 82; r incl breakfast $109-149; ☉late May–Sep; 🖥) Over 130 years old, this green-shuttered inn was reopened in 2013 after three years of restoration. Some rooms are on the small side and not all have private bathrooms, but you can't argue with the lakeside location. The downstairs **restaurant** (lunch mains $7 to $12, dinner mains $16 to $26) and saloon is the main hangout in Twin Lakes.

Twin Lakes Roadhouse Lodge LODGE $$
(☎719-486-9345; www.twinlakescolorado.com; 6411 Hwy 82; r incl breakfast $108-155, bungalows $235; ☉late May–Sep; 🐾🖥) This is the first inn you'll see if you're driving up Hwy 82 from the southeast. A sweet log cabin has been given tasteful add-ons and crafted into a whitewashed wooden house overlooking the upper lake. Views from the front porch are positively immobilizing, and that gurgling fountain only adds to the ambience. They also serve dinner.

❶ Getting There & Away

Twin Lakes is 37 miles from Aspen, just over Independence Pass (open late May through October) on Hwy 82. Hwy 24 is just east of the lakes, providing access to Leadville (22 miles north) and Buena Vista (26 miles south).

Leadville

📷 719 / POP 2595 / ELEV 10,152FT

Formerly Cloud City, Leadville was once Colorado's 2nd-largest city (population 40,000) and a quintessential Wild West town, where fortunes were made and lost overnight, swindlers ruled the roost and Doc Holliday got into a shootout with the law and won.

Today, Leadville may feel slightly abandoned, but there's adventure to be had in these hills. You can climb the two tallest peaks in Colorado, run a 100-mile race, mountain bike for 24 hours straight, cross-country ski to a gourmet meal or simply hop on a historic train to glimpse wildflowers. Well, what are you waiting for?

History

It was silver, not gold, that brought riches to the lucky few in Leadville, but after the bottom dropped out of the silver market in 1893, the city took a serious nosedive. Other minerals kept Leadville alive, however, particularly after the discovery of molybdenum (atomic number 42), which was extremely popular in wartime as it helped to reinforce steel; Germany, Japan and the Soviet Union were the three biggest customers of Climax Mine during the 1930s. Unsurprisingly, the US government subsequently designated Climax (located atop Hwy 91 and still in operation) the nation's most important mine in the following decade.

◉ Sights

Tabor Opera House   HISTORIC BUILDING
(📷 719-486-8409; www.taboroperahouse.net; 308 Harrison Ave; adult/child $8/2; ⊙ 10am-5pm Mon-Sat Jun-Aug) Built in 1879 by multimillionaire Horace Tabor, this was once one of the premier entertainment venues in all of Colorado, if not the West, and hosted the likes of Houdini, Oscar Wilde and Anna Held. You can visit the interior on a tour; there are also occasional performances.

Camp Hale   MEMORIAL
(Hwy 24) About 16 miles north of Leadville on Hwy 24, just over Tennessee Pass, lies the former US Army facility Camp Hale. Established in 1942, it was created specifically for the purpose of training the 10th Mountain Division, the Army's only battalion on skis. At its height during WWII, there were over 1000 buildings and some 14,000 soldiers housed in the meadow here.

Matchless Mine   HISTORIC SITE
(📷 719-486-1229; www.mininghalloffame.org; E 7th Rd; adult/student with tour $12/10, without tour $6/5; ⊙ noon-4:45pm mid-May–Sep) This is where silver magnate and Colorado senator Horace Tabor made and then lost millions in the 1880s, and where his glamorous and sensational wife, Baby Doe, eventually froze to death after spending the last three decades of her life in poverty.

Healy House Museum & Dexter Cabin   MUSEUM
(📷 719-486-0487; www.leadvilletwinlakes.com; 912 Harrison Ave; adult/child $6/free; ⊙ 10am-4:30pm late May–Sep) Two of Leadville's oldest surviving homes are decked out with the owners' original gear, plus period pieces resembling what they may have enjoyed. The Dexter Cabin was the original home of wealthy gold-mining investor James V Dexter. The much grander 1878 Greek Revival home, now known as Healy House, was built by August R Meyer.

National Mining Hall of Fame   MUSEUM
(www.mininghalloffame.org; 120 W 9th St; adult/student $12/10; ⊙ 9am-5pm, closed Mon Nov-Apr; 🅿) Although it sounds both cheesy and dreary, this is a surprisingly informative museum, with mineral displays, gold-mining dioramas, a mock-up coal mine and an introduction to the local mining industry. Kids will find enough here to stay entertained for an hour or two.

Leadville Heritage Museum   MUSEUM
(📷 719-486-1878; www.leadvilletwinlakes.com; 102 E 9th St; adult/child $6/3; ⊙ 10am-5pm May-Oct; 🅿) This middling museum includes an art gallery, Victorian artifacts from the late 19th century, a 10th Mountain Division display, dioramas explaining early mining history and our favorite piece: that rusted mining car right out front.

🏃 Activities

There's a reason that one of the largest mountain bike races in the world – the Leadville Trail 100 (p248) – happens here. There

INDEPENDENCE PASS

Looming at 12,095ft, Independence Pass (p224) is one of the more high-profile mountain passes along the Continental Divide. Perhaps it's the proximity to Aspen (just 20 miles away on Hwy 82), or maybe it's the celeb quotient. (Kevin Costner lives on its western slope.) But we think it's the drive itself.

A narrow ribbon of road swerves above the timberline with gentle then hairpin turns. Views range from pretty to stunning to downright cinematic, and by the time you glimpse swaths of snow along the ridges just below the knife edge of peaks you'll be living in your own IMAX film. Late season you'll see everyone from bow hunters dressed in camo gear and last-gasp family vacationers (or a cocktail of the two) to two kinds of bikers: unshaven Harley riders with frayed bedrolls on the tailgate, and leg-shaven millionaire road bikers with iPhones in their saddle bags.

A paved nature trail wanders off the parking area at the top of the pass. It's tundra country up here, so dress warmly and stay on trails lest you cause decades of unknowable damage in a single step.

If you've got some mountaineering experience, consider climbing 14,336ft La Plata Peak (p245), the state's 5th highest. The trail leaves from South Fork Lake Trailhead on the eastern slope of Independence Pass. There are two routes to the top: the mellower Northwest Ridge and the more challenging class III Ellingwood Ridge (give yourself extra time for route finding). Both routes are roughly 9.5 miles round-trip with over 4000 feet of elevation gain. Start early and note that this is definitely not a climb for beginners.

There are some great eastern slope campgrounds to stay at if you're here to hike – there are other trails to explore. Both Parry Peak Campground (p245), 2.5 miles west of Twin Lakes (bring your own water), and the stunning Twin Peaks Campground (p245), nestled at the base of two peaks, have great locations and are first-come, first-served.

are simply so many trails that you could bike for weeks and never retrace your path.

Mosquito Pass (p248) presents a unique opportunity to ride above 13,000ft in treeless alpine scenery. This extremely challenging 7-mile ascent follows E 7th St from Leadville. If you're on a one-way trip, you can continue on to Alma.

Another good destination where you can enjoy panoramic vistas is Hagerman Pass (p248) (11,925ft), west of Leadville. Riders follow a relatively easy railroad grade on USFS Rd 105 for 7 miles to Hagerman Pass from the junction on the south bank of Turquoise Lake Reservoir. On the way you pass Skinner Hut (p248), maintained by the 10th Mountain Division Hut Association.

An easy ride follows the shoreline trail on the north side of Turquoise Lake Reservoir for 6 miles between Sugar Loaf Dam and May Queen Campground. Another follows the Colorado Trail north from Tennessee Pass for 2.5 miles to Mitchell Creek. For other suggestions, visit Cycles of Life bike shop.

★ **Mineral Belt Trail**   MOUNTAIN BIKING, SKIING
(www.mineralbelttrail.com) The paved, 12-mile Mineral Belt Trail is a great place to start

exploring Leadville on bike or foot, looping around town past historic points of interest and beautiful scenery. It's also open to cross-country skiers in winter.

★ **Mt Elbert**   HIKING
(www.14ers.com; ☉ Jun-Sep) Colorado's tallest peak and the second-highest in the continental US, Mt Elbert (14,433ft) is a relatively gentle giant. There are three established routes to the top, none of which are technical. The most common approach is via the northeast ridge; it's a 9-mile round-trip hike with 4700ft of elevation gain, so expect to spend most of the day.

Cycles of Life   MOUNTAIN BIKING
(☑ 719-486-5533; www.colbikes.com; 309 Harrison Ave; bike rental per day $25-100; ☉ 10am-6pm Mon-Sat, to 4pm Sun; ☻) Great rental shop with everything you need to hit the trail in all seasons, including fat tires (there are actually eight miles of groomed singletrack in winter) and cross-country skis. They will happily recommend great area rides.

Mt Massive   HIKING
(www.14ers.com; ☉ Jun-Oct) The state's second-tallest peak, Mt Massive (14,421ft)

lives up to its name: it has four summits and a 3-mile-long ridge, giving it more total area above 14,000ft than any other peak in the state. From Hwy 24, it dominates the western horizon.

Mosquito Pass   MOUNTAIN BIKING

Huff and puff all the way up to this pass (13,186ft) east of town. The 7-mile ascent is rugged and only for those in great cycling shape. Follow E 7th St from Leadville. On the other side, you can continue down into the town of Alma.

Hagerman Pass   MOUNTAIN BIKING

Enjoy the panoramas riding easy railroad grade to Hagerman Pass (11,925ft), west of Leadville. It's 7 miles on USFS Rd 105 from the south bank of Turquoise Lake Reservoir.

Ski Cooper   SNOW SPORTS

(☑ 800-707-6114; www.skicooper.com; Hwy 24; lift ticket adult/child $52/32; ⊙ 9am-4pm Dec–mid-Apr; ⊕) Ski Cooper offers about 400 acres of skiable terrain, a dedicated snowboard terrain park, and backcountry thrills through the snowcat tours on Chicago Ridge ($349). It's small but affordable, and a great place for beginning and intermediate skiers and boarders. It's just north of Leadville on Hwy 24, at Tennessee Pass.

Tennessee Pass
Nordic Center   SNOW SPORTS

(☑ 719-486-1750; www.tennesseepass.com; Hwy 24; trail pass adult/child $15/10; ⊙ 8:30am-5pm Dec–mid-Apr; ⊕) Snowshoers and cross-country skiers come here to get their Leadville fix. Some 15 miles of groomed trails extend from the base of Ski Cooper, but the highlight is the 1-mile haul to your favorite gourmet yurt: the Tennessee Pass Cookhouse.

Leadville, Colorado
& Southern Railroad   RAIL

(☑ 866-386-3936; www.leadville-train.com; 326 E 7th St; adult/child $37/20; ⊙ late May–early Oct) Originating in Leadville, the LC&S follows the old Denver, South Park & Pacific, and Colorado & Southern lines to the Continental Divide. Time it right and you'll see fields of wildflowers give way to panoramas across the Arkansas River Valley. All trips are 2½ hours; engine and caboose seating costs extra.

☆ Festivals & Events

★ **Leadville Trail 100**   CYCLING
(www.leadvilleraceseries.com; ⊙ Aug) The Leadville 100, held in August, is one of the most

famous and longest mountain-bike races in the world: 100 miles of lung-crushing, adrenaline-fueled riding on the old silver-mining roads that go from 9200ft to 12,424ft and back again. But the Leadville Trail races are not just about the mountain bikers.

🛏 Sleeping

All in all, Leadville offers fairly inexpensive lodging, including a hostel, historic hotel and a string of chain motels on the outskirts of town. There are a lot of campgrounds in the area, particularly around Turquoise Lake and in the Halfmoon Recreation Area in the Mt Massive Wilderness.

Leadville Hostel   HOSTEL $

(☑ 719-486-9334; www.leadvillehostel.com; 500 East 7th St; dm/d from $23/60; @ 🛜 🐾) A true travelers hostel, this place is one of the coziest budget choices in the state. Guests get the run of the place, which includes two common areas, a downstairs games room and movie niche, and a large kitchen. It's within reach of several ski resorts: Cooper, Copper Mountain and Vail. Towels and wi-fi cost extra.

Delaware Hotel   HOTEL $

(☑ 800-748-2004; www.delawarehotel.com; 700 Harrison Ave; tw/d Sep-Jul from $65/85, Aug from $80/120; ⊙ mid-May–Oct; P 🌸 🛜 🐾) This antique-strewn Victorian mining-era hotel dates back to 1886 and has a slightly eccentric atmosphere. The innkeeper enjoys her burlesque hat and gloves, and the old-style rooms feature high ceilings and lace curtains. It's nothing fancy, but certainly solid value.

Skinner Hut   HUT $

(☑ 970-925-5775; www.huts.org; Hagerman Pass Rd; per person $33) Maintained by the 10th Mountain Division Hut Association, Skinner (11,620ft) has one of the steepest and most difficult winter approaches in the hut system. Cyclists and hikers can call for reservations from July through September. The hut sleeps 16 people.

★ **Tennessee Pass Sleep Yurts**   YURT $$
(☑ 719-486-8114; www.tennesseepass.com; Tennessee Pass; per yurt $245) Sleeping in the backcountry has never been so luxurious. With a woodburning stove, kitchenette and even luggage delivery and room service, this is a great way to enjoy all the magic of a quiet winter night without having to wake up with frostbitten toes. Yurts sleep up to six people and are located 1.3 miles from the Tennessee Pass Nordic Center.

Part of the appeal is that you have to ski, snowshoe or hike in: gear can be rented at the Nordic Center, and the yurts are a great base for exploring the Tennessee Pass trail system. You can cook your own meals, but ordering dinner from the cookhouse (mains $15 to $24) is highly recommended.

✕ Eating

High Mountain Pies   PIZZA $
(☑719-486-5555; 115 W 4th St; pizzas from $12; ☻11:30am-10pm; ☑) An ultra-popular pizza joint with great toppings. Unfortunately, seating is limited, so make sure you either arrive early or order to go.

El Mexicano   MEXICAN $
(1903 N Poplar St; tacos $1.65, burritos $4.25; ☻11:30am-8pm Tue-Sat) Located in what is surely one of the world's most picturesque Safeway parking lots, this food truck at the north entrance of town prepares savory tacos and burritos filled with chicken, carne asada, carnitas or adovada (marinated pork), plus excellent green- and red-chili tamales (both with pork). There's nowhere to sit, but the food is damn good.

Tennessee Pass Cafe   CAFE $
(☑719-486-8101; www.tennesseepasscafe.com; 222 Harrison Ave; mains $10-16; ☻11am-9pm; ☑⊞) ✐ This artsy cafe has the most inventive menu in town, with organic specials ranging from buffalo shepherd's pie and baked trout to sweet-potato gnocchi and pizza. (It's unrelated to the Tennessee Pass Cookhouse.)

Quincy's   AMERICAN, STEAK $
(☑719-486-9765; 416 Harrison Ave; mains from $8; ☻5-9pm) Readers of the local Leadville *Herald Democrat* voted this steakhouse set in a historic building their favorite restaurant, and it's likely to be for the prices as much as for the meat: steaks cost from $8, while prime-rib dinners are $13.

★ **Tennessee Pass
Cookhouse**   MODERN AMERICAN $$$
(☑719-486-8114; www.tennesseepass.com; Tennessee Pass; lunch $12-18, 4-course dinner $89; ☻lunch Sat & Sun, dinner Dec–mid-Apr, dinner only Thu-Sun late Jun–Sep; ☑) If you've never had a gourmet dinner in a yurt before, this is your chance. Diners get to hike, snowshoe or cross-country ski 1 mile to the yurt, where an elegant four-course meal featuring elk tenderloin, local rack of lamb and rainbow trout awaits. Departures are from

the Tennessee Pass Nordic Center (p248), at the base of Ski Cooper. Reservations only.

⬤ Drinking & Nightlife

Periodic Brewing   BREWERY
(☑720-316-8144; www.periodicbrewing.com; 115 E 7th St; ☻3-9pm Mon-Thu, noon-9pm Fri-Sun) There aren't many breweries up above 10,000 feet, which makes Periodic something of an anomaly. Hoppy and dark beers predominate, but there is also cider on tap and food in the kitchen. You can also find their beers at another local anomaly: the recreational oxygen bar O2.

City on a Hill   CAFE
(☑719-486-0797; www.cityonahillcoffee.com; 508 Harrison Ave; ☻6am-6pm; ☎) Freshly roasted beans and delectable espresso drinks are available in this attractive coffeehouse with high ceilings, exposed brick walls and comfy couches. It serves sandwiches, soups, pastries and freshly baked quiches, and is one of the few spots in town with free wi-fi.

O2   CRAFT BEER
(☑719-299-5250; 401 Harrison Ave; ☻3-10pm Mon-Fri, noon-10pm Sat & Sun) If you're feeling a little light-headed, you can acclimatize with some oxygen while knocking back cocktails, infused moonshine and beers from Periodic Brewing. They also serve pasta.

ℹ Tourist Information

Leadville Ranger District (☑719-486-0749; 810 Front St; ☻8am-4pm Mon-Fri) Has information, books and topo maps on Mt Massive, Mt Elbert and other USFS lands in the area. Pick up info on camping here.

Leadville Visitor Center (☑719-486-3900; www.leadvilletwinlakes.com; 809 Harrison Ave; ☻10am-4pm summer, closed Mon winter; ☎) Grab maps and brochures here.

ℹ Getting There & Away

Leadville is 23 miles southwest of Copper Mountain (via Hwy 91), 38 miles south of Vail (Hwy 24) and 34 miles north of Buena Vista (Hwy 24).

Bus services run to Summit County and Vail in the morning, and return in the evening:

ECO (☑970-328-3520; www.eaglecounty.us; per ride $7) Links Leadville with Vail (one hour), leaving twice in the early morning and returning twice in the late afternoon.

Summit Stage (☑970-668-0999; www.summitstage.com; per ride $5) The Lake County Link connects Leadville with Copper Mountain and Frisco (20 to 50 minutes), leaving twice in the morning and returning three times in the evening.

VAIL, ASPEN & CENTRAL COLORADO LEADVILLE

Mesa Verde &
Southwest Colorado

Includes ➜

Mesa Verde
National Park 251

Mancos. 256

Cortez &
the Four Corners 257

Telluride 261

Ridgway 268

Ouray & the
Million Dollar Hwy . . 269

Silverton 273

Durango 275

Pagosa Springs. 281

Creede 284

Lake City 287

Crested Butte 288

Grand Junction. 301

Fruita 303

Best Places to Eat

➜ Tacos del Gnar (p269)

➜ Chop House (p266)

➜ Secret Stash (p291)

Best Places to Stay

➜ Willowtail Springs (p256)

➜ Mancos Inn & Hostel (p256)

➜ Kelly Place (p258)

Why Go?

The West at its most rugged, this is a landscape of twisting canyons and ancient ruins, with burly peaks and gusty high desert plateaus. Centuries of boom and bust, from silver to real estate, tell part of the story. There's also the lingering mystery of its earliest inhabitants, whose relics have been found at the abandoned cliff dwellings in Mesa Verde National Park.

Southwestern Colorado can be a heady place to play. Some of the finest powder skiing in the world melts to reveal winding singletrack and hiking trails in summer. Vineyards are sprouting up on the western slope. A sense of remove keeps the Old West alive in wooden plank saloons and aboard the chugging Durango railroad.

With all that fresh mountain air, local attitudes – from the ranch hand to the real-estate agent – are undoubtedly relaxed. Dally a bit under these ultra-blue skies and you will know why.

When to Go
Durango

Jun–Aug Prime time for hiking and camping in the legendary San Juans.

Sep–Nov Cool days in the desert and fewer crowds in Mesa Verde.

Dec–Apr Powder hounds hit the famed slopes of Telluride.

Mesa Verde National Park

ELEV 7000FT–8000FT

More than 700 years after its inhabitants disappeared, Mesa Verde retains an air of mystery. No one knows for sure why the Ancestral Puebloans left their elaborate cliff dwellings in the 1300s. It's a wonderland for adventurers of all sizes, who can clamber up ladders to carved-out dwellings, see rock art and delve into the mysteries of ancient America.

Mesa Verde National Park occupies 81 sq miles of the northernmost portion of the mesa. Ancestral Puebloan sites are found throughout the park's canyons and mesas, perched on a high plateau south of Cortez and Mancos.

The National Parks Service (NPS) strictly enforces the Antiquities Act, which prohibits the removal or destruction of any antiquities and prohibits public access to many of the 4000 known Ancestral Puebloan sites.

History

A US army lieutenant recorded the spectacular cliff dwellings in the canyons of Mesa Verde in 1849–50. The large number of sites on Ute tribal land, and their relative inaccessibility, protected the majority of these antiquities from pothunters.

The first scientific investigation of the sites in 1874 failed to identify Cliff Palace, the largest cliff dwelling in North America. Discovery of the 'magnificent city' occurred only when local cowboys Richard Wetherill and Charlie Mason were searching for stray cattle in 1888. The cowboys exploited their 'discovery' for the next 18 years by guiding both amateur and trained archaeologists to the site, particularly to collect the distinctive black-on-white pottery.

When artifacts started being shipped overseas, Virginia McClurg of Colorado Springs was motivated to embark on a long campaign to preserve the site and its contents. McClurg's efforts led Congress to protect artifacts on federal land, with the passage of the Antiquities Act establishing Mesa Verde National Park in 1906.

◉ Sights

The park entrance is off US 160, midway between Cortez and Mancos. From the entrance, it's about 21 miles to park headquarters, Chapin Mesa Museum and Spruce Tree House. Along the way are Morefield Campground (4 miles), the panoramic viewpoint at Park Point (8 miles) and the Far View Lodge (about 11 miles). Towed vehicles are not allowed beyond Morefield Campground.

If you only have time for a short visit, check out the Chapin Mesa Museum and try a walk through the Spruce Tree House, where you can climb down a wooden ladder into the cool chamber of a kiva.

Mesa Verde rewards travelers who set aside a day or more to take the ranger-led tours of Cliff Palace and Balcony House, explore Wetherill Mesa (the quieter side of the canyon), linger around the museum or participate in one of the campfire programs run at Morefield Campground.

★ **Mesa Verde National Park** NATIONAL PARK
(970 529 4465; www.nps.gov/meve; 7-day car/ motorcycle pass Jun-Aug $20/10, Sep-May $15/7; P ♿ 🐾) 🅿 A fascinating, if slightly eerie, national park. Anthropologists will love it here; Mesa Verde is unique among American national parks in its focus on maintaining this civilization's cultural relics rather than its natural treasures. The park also offers plenty of hiking, skiing, snowshoeing and mountain-biking options. Visitors can camp out or stay in luxury at the lodge.

★ **Cliff Palace** ARCHAEOLOGICAL SITE
(www.recreation.gov; Cliff Palace Loop; 1hr guided tour $5; ♿) 🅿 The only way to see the superb Cliff Palace is to take the hour-long ranger-led tour. The tour retraces the steps taken by the Ancestral Puebloans – visitors must climb down a stone stairway and four 10ft ladders. This grand engineering achievement, with 217 rooms and 23 kivas, provided shelter for 250 to 300 people.

Balcony House ARCHAEOLOGICAL SITE
(www.recreation.gov; Cliff Palace Loop; 1hr guided tour $5; P ♿) 🅿 Tickets are required for the one-hour guided tours of Balcony House, on the east side of the Cliff Palace Loop. A visit is an adventure that will challenge anyone's fear of heights or small places. You'll be rewarded with outstanding views of Soda Canyon, 600ft below the sandstone overhang that once served as the ceiling for 35 to 40 rooms.

Long House ARCHAEOLOGICAL SITE
(www.recreation.gov; Wetherill Mesa Rd; 1hr guided tour $5; ◷ May-Aug; ♿) 🅿 On Wetherill Mesa, the magnificent Long House is the second-largest cliff dwelling in the park. A strenuous place to visit, it is only reached as part of a ranger-led guided tour (organized

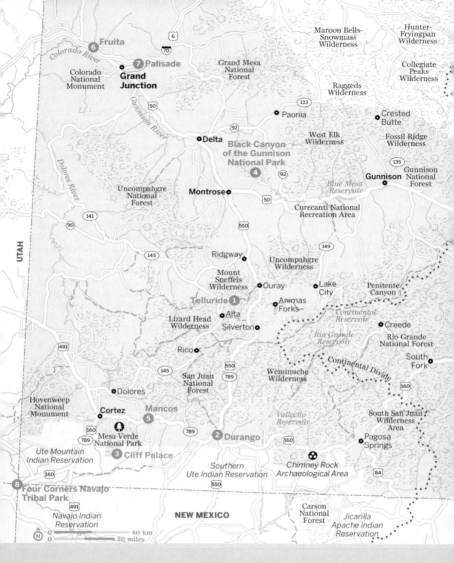

Southwest Colorado Highlights

1 Telluride Ski Resort
(p262) Carve turns on these
world-class slopes.

**2 Durango & Silverton
Narrow Gauge Railroad**
(p275) Climb aboard a vintage
steam locomotive for jaw-
dropping scenery.

3 Cliff Palace (p251)
Retrace the steps of Ancestral

Puebloans at Mesa Verde
National Park.

**4 Black Canyon of the
Gunnison National Park**
(p292) Hike the rim to peer
deep down the sheer and
shadowy canyon walls.

5 Mancos (p256) Explore
the culinary delights around
this friendly, offbeat town.

6 Fruita (p303) Ride the
desert singletrack of this
mountain-biking destination.

7 Palisade (p306) Savor the
bold reds in this unique patch
of Colorado wine country.

**8 Four Corners Navajo
Tribal Park** (p257) Driving to
the point where four states
(almost) meet.

from the visitor center). Access involves climbing three ladders – two at 15ft and one at 4ft. The 0.75-mile round-trip hike has a 130ft elevation change.

Park Point
VIEWPOINT

(off North Rim Rd) The fire lookout at Park Point is the highest elevation (8571ft) in the park and offers panoramic views. To the north are the 14,000ft peaks of the San Juan Mountains; in the northeast are the 12,000ft crests of the La Plata Mountains; to the southwest, beyond the southward-sloping Mesa Verde plateau, is the distant volcanic plug of Shiprock; and to the west is Sleeping Ute Mountain, whose profile resembles a supine human.

Wetherill Mesa
ARCHAEOLOGICAL SITE

This is the second-largest concentration of sites. Visitors may enter stabilized surface sites and two cliff dwellings, including the Long House, open from late May through August.

Chapin Mesa Museum
MUSEUM

(☎970-529-4475; www.nps.gov/meve; Chapin Mesa Rd; admission incl with park entry; ⊙8am-6:30pm Apr–mid-Oct, to 5pm mid-Oct–Apr; P⏦) The Chapin Mesa Museum has exhibits pertaining to the park and is a good first stop. Staff at the museum provide information on weekends when the park headquarters is closed.

Spruce Tree House
ARCHAEOLOGICAL SITE

(Chapin Mesa Rd; admission incl with park entry; P⏦) ✈ This Ancestral Puebloan ruin is the most accessible of the archaeological sites, although the half-mile round-trip access track is still a moderately steep climb. Spruce Tree House was once home to 60 or 80 people and its construction began around AD 1210. Like other sites, the old walls and houses have been stabilized.

During winter, there are free ranger-led guided tours at 10am, 1pm and 3:30pm.

Chapin Mesa
ARCHAEOLOGICAL SITE

The largest concentration of Ancestral Puebloan sites is at Chapin Mesa, where you'll see the densely clustered Far View Site and the large Spruce Tree House, the most accessible of sites, with a paved half-mile round-trip path.

If you want to see Cliff Palace or Balcony House, the only way is through an hour-long ranger-led tour booked in advance at the visitor center. These tours are extremely popular; go early in the morning or a day

in advance to book. Balcony House requires climbing a 32ft and 60ft ladder – those with medical problems should skip it.

Step House
ARCHAEOLOGICAL SITE

(Wetherill Mesa Rd; admission incl with park entry) ✈ Step House was initially occupied by Modified Basketmaker peoples residing in pithouses, and later became the site of a Classic Pueblo–period masonry complex with rooms and kivas. The 0.75-mile trail to Step House involves a 100ft descent and ascent.

Activities

Given the historical nature of the park, backcountry access is specifically forbidden and fines are imposed on anyone caught wandering off designated trails or entering cliff dwellings without a ranger. Please respect the regulations so that these fragile and irreplaceable archaeological sights and artifacts remain protected for centuries to come.

When hiking in Mesa Verde always carry water and avoid cliff edges. Trails can be muddy and slippery after summer rains and winter snows, so wear appropriate footwear. Most park trails, except the Soda Canyon Trail, are strenuous and involve steep elevation changes. Hikers must register at the respective trailheads before venturing out.

Spruce Canyon Loop Trail
HIKING

This 2.1-mile trail begins at Spruce Tree House and descends to the bottom of Spruce Tree Canyon. It's a great way to see the canyon bottoms of Mesa Verde.

Petroglyph Loop Trail
HIKING

This 2.8-mile trail is accessed from Spruce Tree House. It follows a path beneath the edge of a plateau before making a short climb to the top of the mesa, where you'll have good views of the Spruce and Navajo Canyons. This is the only trail in the park where you can view petroglyphs.

Tours

The NPS and the park concessionaire Aramark run various organized tours for walkers as well as small-group bus tours.

Wetherill Mesa Bike & Hike Adventure
HIKING

(per person $15; ⊙departs 9:45am late May–early Sep; ⏦) ✈ This six-hour, 9-mile ranger-led walking and biking tour views rock art, cliff dwellings and the Long House. It includes a total of three miles of walking. Binoculars are recommended as there's superb views

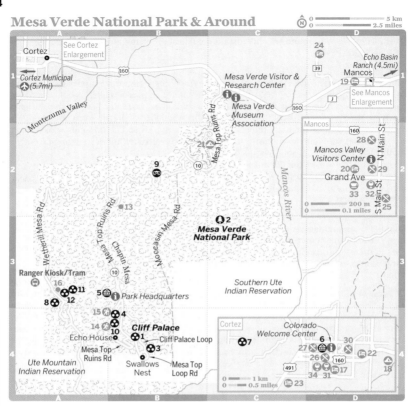

across the canyon to multiple cliff dwellings. Bring your own bike.

Aramark Mesa Verde   HIKING, TOURS
(☑ 970-529-4421; www.visitmesaverde.com; Mile 15, Far View Lodge; adult $42-48) The park concessionaire offers varied guided private and group tours throughout the park daily from May to mid-October. Book online or at the office in Far View Lodge.

🛏 Sleeping

There are plenty of accommodation options in nearby Cortez and Mancos, and Mesa Verde can be visited as a day-trip from Durango.

Within the national park, visitors can stay in luxury at the lodge, or rough it camping. Overnight stays give convenient access to the many sites during the best viewing hours, participation in evening programs and the pleasure of watching the sunset

over Sleeping Ute Mountain from the tranquility of the mesa top.

Morefield Campground   CAMPGROUND $
(☑ 970-529-4465; www.visitmesaverde.com; Mile 4; tent/RV sites $30/40; ⊙ May-early Oct; 🐾) 🌿 The park's camping option, located 4 miles from the entrance gate, has 445 regular tent sites on grassy grounds conveniently located near Morefield Village. The village has a general store, a gas station, a restaurant, showers and a laundry. It's managed by Aramark. Dry RV campsites (without hookup) cost the same as tent sites.

Far View Lodge   LODGE $$
(☑ 970-529-4421, toll-free 800-449-2288; www.visit mesaverde.com; Mile 15; r $124-177; ⊙ mid-Apr–Oct; 🅿❄✲📶🐾) On a mesa top 15 miles inside the park entrance, this tasteful Pueblo-style lodge has 150 Southwestern-style rooms, some with kiva fireplaces. Don't miss sunset over the mesa from your private balcony. Standard

Mesa Verde National Park & Around

◎ Top Sights
1 Cliff Palace	B4
2 Mesa Verde National Park	C3

◎ Sights
3 Balcony House	B4
4 Chapin Mesa	B4
5 Chapin Mesa Museum	A3
6 Cortez Cultural Center	D4
7 Crow Canyon Archaeology Center	C4
8 Long House	A3
9 Park Point	B2
10 Spruce Tree House	B4
11 Step House	A3
12 Wetherill Mesa	A3

◎ Activities, Courses & Tours
13 Aramark Mesa Verde	B2
Come Dance Tonight	(see 27)
Kokopelli Bike & Board	(see 6)
14 Petroglyph Loop Trail	A4
15 Spruce Canyon Loop Trail	A4
16 Wetherill Mesa Bike & Hike Adventure	A3

◎ Sleeping
17 Best Western Turquoise Inn & Suites	D4

18 Cortez-Mesa Verde KOA	D4
19 Enchanted Mesa Motel	D1
Far View Lodge	(see 13)
20 Mancos Inn & Hostel	D2
21 Morefield Campground	C2
22 Retro Inn	D4
23 Tomahawk Lodge	C4
24 Willowtail Springs	D1

◎ Eating
25 Absolute Baking & Cafe	D2
26 Burger Boy	D4
Far View Terrace Café	(see 13)
27 Farm Bistro	D2
Metate Room	(see 13)
28 Millwood Junction	D2
29 Olio	D2
Pepperhead	(see 27)
Stonefish Sushi & More	(see 27)
30 Tequila's Mexican Restaurant	D4

◎ Drinking & Nightlife
31 Blondie's	D4
32 Columbine Bar	D2
33 Fahrenheit Coffee Roasters	D2
34 Main Street Brewery & Restaurant	D4

rooms don't have air con (or TV) and summer daytimes can be hot. You can even bring your dog for an extra $10 per night.

✖ Eating

There's fine dining, a small market and a cafe in the park, but campers will be happiest if they come stocked with provisions.

Far View Terrace Café CAFE $
(☏970-529-4421, toll-free 800-449-2288; www.visitmesaverde.com; Mile 15; mains $8; ◷7-10am, 11am-3pm & 5-8pm May–mid-Oct; �🖉🖶) Housed in Far View Lodge, this self-service place offers reasonably priced meals and a convenient espresso bar. Don't miss the house special: the Navajo Taco.

Metate Room MODERN AMERICAN $$$
(☏800-449-2288; www.visitmesaverde.com; Mile 15, Far View Lodge; mains $20-36; ◷7-10am & 5:30-9:30pm Apr–mid-Oct, 5-7:30pm mid-Oct–Mar; 🖉🖶) ✎ With an award in culinary excellence, this upscale restaurant in the Far View Lodge offers an innovative menu inspired by Native American food and flavors. Interesting dishes include stuffed poblano chilies, prickly pear pork belly and cold smoked trout.

ℹ Tourist Information

Mesa Verde Museum Association (☏970-529-4445, toll-free 800-305-6053; www.mesaverde.org; ◷8am-6:30pm Apr–mid-Oct, to 5pm mid-Oct–Mar; 🖶) Attached to the Chapin Mesa Museum, this nonprofit organization sponsors research activities and exhibits. It has an excellent selection of materials on the Ancestral Puebloans and modern tribes in the American Southwest, and has related books and souvenirs for sale.

Mesa Verde Visitor & Research Center (☏970-529-5034, 800-305-6053; www.nps.gov/meve; ◷8am-7pm Jun–early Sep, to 5pm early Sep–mid-Oct, closed mid-Oct–May; 🛜🖶) This huge visitor center has water, wi-fi and bathrooms, in addition to information desks selling tickets for tours of Cliff Palace, Balcony House or Long House. It also displays museum-quality artifacts.

Park Headquarters (☏970-529-4465; www.nps.gov/meve; Chapin Mesa Rd; 7-day park entry per vehicle $15, cyclists, hikers & motorcyclists $8; ◷8am-5pm Mon-Fri; 🖶) Located 21 miles from the road entrance. Offers road information and the word on park closures (many areas are closed in winter), though your first stop should be the visitor center.

ⓘ Getting There & Away

Although there are some operators running tours to and around Mesa Verde National Park from Durango – 36 miles to the east; contact the **Durango Welcome Center** (p281) – most people visit with a private car or motorcycle. Vehicular transport is necessary to get to the sites from the front park gate as well as to get between them.

ⓘ Getting Around

The Mesa Verde National Park entrance is off US 160, midway between Cortez and Mancos.

South from park headquarters, Mesa Top Rd consists of two one-way circuits. Turn left about a quarter mile from the start of Mesa Top Rd to visit Cliff Palace and Balcony House on the east loop.

From the junction with the main road at Far View Lodge, the 12-mile mountainous Wetherill Mesa Rd snakes along the North Rim, acting as a natural barrier to tour buses and indifferent travelers. The road is open only from Memorial Day in late May to Labor Day in early September.

Mancos

📞 970 / POP 1360 / ELEV 7028FT

Santa Fe eat your heart out. With a growing gallery scene, chilled desert vibe and its own special brand of quirk, Mancos is worth a stop. Wander amid the boutiques, artists co-op and landmark buildings and kick back for some charming and eclectic eats. Mesa Verde National Park is just 7 miles to the west, so if visiting the park is on your itinerary, staying in Mancos makes an appealing stopover.

From June through September, the town puts on **Grand Summer Nights**, a series of gallery walks that local restaurants and shops also participate in. It's held the last Friday of the month.

🛏 Sleeping

★ Mancos Inn & Hostel   HOSTEL $
(📞970-533-9164; www.mancosinn.com; 200 W Grand Ave; dm $35, r without/with bathroom from $60/75; 🛜) For a bargain stay in downtown Mancos, these homey digs could not be lovelier. There's a large, modern kitchen, comfortable living room with games and a powerful telescope and rooms with original art. A small four-bed dormitory has palette beds suspended on chains (yes, they'll hold).

★ Jersey Jim Lookout Tower   CABIN $
(📞970-533-7060; www.fs.usda.gov/recarea/san juan/recarea/?recid=44040; r $40; ⊙mid-May–mid-Oct) How about spending the night in a former fire-lookout tower? Standing 55ft above a meadow 14 miles north of Mancos at an elevation of 9800ft, this place is on the National Historic Lookout Register and comes with an Osborne Fire Finder and topographic map. But no water.

The tower accommodates up to four adults (bring your own bedding) and must be reserved long in advance; there's also a two-night minimum stay. The reservation office opens on the first workday of March (1pm to 5pm) and the entire season is typically booked within days.

Enchanted Mesa Motel   MOTEL $
(📞970-533-7729; www.enchantedmesamotel. com; 862 W Grand Ave; r $82; 🅿🛜) Hipper than most independent motels, this place has shiny lamps and solid wooden furniture, along with king- and queen-size beds. There's a big playground out front for the kids. Best of all, you can play a game of pool while waiting for your whites to dry – there's a billiards table in the laundry room!

Echo Basin Ranch   RANCH $$
(📞970-533-7000; www.echobasin.com; County Rd M; cabins $149-295; 🐴) Traveling with horse? Stop for the night at Echo Basin Ranch, an affordable, unstructured dude ranch. The cheaper A-frame cabin accommodation is very cool (as long as you don't mind rustic, and by that we mean basic). We love the pitched roof and big windows – very Rocky Mountain high.

★Willowtail Springs   LODGE, CABIN $$$
(📞800-698-0603; www.willowtailsprings.com; 10451 County Rd 39; cabins $239-269; 🅿🛜) Peggy and Lee, artist and t'ai chi master, have crafted a setting that inspires and helps you to slow down to the pace of their pond's largemouth bass. These exquisite camps sit within 60 acres of gardens and ponderosa forest. Two immaculate cabins and a spacious lake house (sleeping six) feature warm and exotic decor including a real remnant beehive.

🍴 Eating

★ Absolute Baking & Cafe   BREAKFAST, SANDWICHES $
(📞970-533-1200; www.absolutebakery.com; 110 S Main St; mains $7-11; ⊙7am-2pm; 🛜🚸) 🍴 The screen door is always swinging open at this town hot spot with giant breakfasts. Try the green chili on eggs – it's made from scratch, as are the organic breads and pastries. Lunch includes lavender lemonade, salads,

big sandwiches and local, grass-fed beef burgers. Grab a bag for the trail, but don't forgo a square of gooey, fresh carrot cake.

Millwood Junction   STEAK $$
(✆970-533-7338; www.millwoodjunction.com; cnr Main St & Railroad Ave; mains $8-27; ⏲11am-10:30pm; ⏺) Folks come from miles around to this popular steak and seafood joint, especially for Friday night's seafood buffet. It often doubles as a club, showcasing live music.

Olio   CAFE $$$
(www.oliomancos.com; 114 W Grand Ave; mains $20-38; ⏲4-9pm Tue-Sat; ✍) This friendly, upscale cafe is the spot to hit for a glass of wine and cheese boards with fig jam. Highlights include deviled eggs, and light items like watermelon salad, and local lettuce served with shaved fennel, cherries and aged balsamic. In addition to being pretty original, they also cater well to vegan and gluten-free diets.

🍸 Drinking & Nightlife

Fahrenheit Coffee Roasters   CAFE
(201 W Grand Ave; ⏲6:30am-5pm Mon-Sat; 📶) Imbued with the aroma of fresh-roasted beans, this quality espresso house also serves slices of homemade pie and cheap breakfast burritos to go. It also provides an interesting atmosphere, with small-talking locals, outdoor sofas and Oz-like art installations.

Columbine Bar   BAR
(✆970-533-7397; 123 W Grand Ave; ⏲10am-2am) Established in 1903, one of Colorado's oldest continuously operating bars is still going strong. Think divey old saloon. The mounted animal heads keep watch as you shoot pool.

ℹ Tourist Information

Mancos Valley Visitors Center (✆702-533-7434; www.mancosvalley.com; 101 E Bauer Ave; ⏲9am-5pm Mon-Fri) offers extensive information on local attractions and activities.

ℹ Getting There & Away

Mancos sits between Cortez and Durango. You'll need your own vehicle to explore the area.

Cortez & the Four Corners
📍970 / POP 8570 / ELEV 6201FT

Cortez is replacing its strip malls and rifle shops with natural food stores and upscale sport shops, putting a new sheen on the old-time downtown. With good reason: its location 10 miles west of Mesa Verde

National Park and 40 miles from the Four Corners makes it a logical base with quiet appeal. Mountain bikers will covet the hundreds of great singletrack rides nearby. For those intrigued with ancient ruins, the Ute Mountain Tribal Park is an interesting foray into lesser-known sites. The downtown has some thriving businesses: three great restaurants on just one city block proves it. The surrounding desert is also a pleasure, with surprises like archaeological sites and the occasional desert winery.

◉ Sights

Cortez Cultural Center   MUSEUM
(✆702-565-1151; www.cortezculturalcenter.org; 25 N Market St; ⏲10am-5pm Mon-Sat) **FREE** Exhibits on the Ancestral Puebloans, as well as art displays, make this museum worthy of a visit if you have a few hours to spare. The adjoining Cultural Park is an outdoor space where Ute, Navajo and Hopi tribe members share their cultures with visitors through dance and crafts demonstrations. Weaving demonstrations and Ute mountain art also are displayed and visitors can check out a Navajo hogan.

Guy Drew Vineyard   WINERY
(www.guydrewvineyards.com; 19891 Rd G; ⏲10am-6pm Tue-Sat) A fun stop if you are in the area, this well-regarded, small, family-run vineyard has informal tastings in the straw-bale farm kitchen. Owned by happy corporate dropouts, it may have only 13 years of production under its belt but it has lots of good stories to tell.

Crow Canyon
Archaeology Center   ARCHAEOLOGICAL SITE
(✆970-565-8975; 800-422-8975; www.crowcanyon.org; 23390 Rd K; adult/child $60/35; ⏲9am-5pm Wed & Thu Jun–mid-Sep; ⏺) This cultural center, about 3 miles north of Cortez, offers a day-long educational program that visits an excavation site west of town. Programs teach the significance of regional artifacts and are an excellent way to learn about Ancestral Puebloan culture firsthand.

Four Corners Monument   MONUMENT
(✆928-871-6647; www.navajonationparks.org; $5; ⏲8am-7pm May-Sep, to 5pm Oct-Apr) Don't be shy: do a spread eagle for the camera on top of the four corners marker that signifies you're in four states at once. It's a good image, even if not 100% accurate – government surveyors admitted that the marker is almost

HOVENWEEP NATIONAL MONUMENT

While ruins abound in the Southwest, the six prehistoric villages of Hovenweep are worth exploring for a few hours or more. Built between AD 1200 and 1300, structures include towers perched on canyon rims and balanced on boulders. From US 160/US 666 south of Cortez, turn at the sign for the Cortez Airport onto Montezuma County Rd G, which follows McElmo Canyon west through red-rock country north of Sleeping Ute Mountain and Ute tribal lands. At the Utah border you cross onto the Navajo Reservation and can expect sheep, goats or even cattle on the road. A signed road to the monument turns right (north) from McElmo Creek.

2000ft east of where it should be, but it is a legally recognized border point marking the intersection of Arizona, New Mexico, Utah and Colorado.

🏃 Activities

Kokopelli Bike & Board CYCLING
(☎970-565-4408; www.kokopellibike.com; 130 W Main St; all-day bike rental $35-55; ⊙9am-6pm Mon-Fri, to 5pm Sat) The friendly staff at Kokopelli are happy to talk trail with riders, and also rent out and repair mountain bikes and fat bikes. As a bonus it doubles as a damn good coffee shop with locally made pastries and strong espresso! Rentals include helmet, air pump, water bottle and tools. For trip planning, visit the website for trail descriptions.

Come Dance Tonight DANCING
(☎970-564-9771; www.millenniumcentercortez. com; 30 W Main St; drop-in dance lessons $10; ⊙hours vary) Behind the trophy-cluttered windows, this nondescript storefront opens onto a surreal world, where Friday nights find couples cha-cha-ing across the wide wooden floor along to the buoyant clapping of Denise. There's also country and Latin dancing. A ballroom studio and social club that seems from another era, this is a truly weird and awesome scene.

🛏 Sleeping

Cortez has heaps of budget motels along its main drag, and rates and rooms are much the same at most. In winter prices drop by almost 50%.

Tomahawk Lodge LODGE $
(☎970-565-8521, 800-643-7705; www.angelfire. com/co2/tomahawk; 728 S Broadway; r from $65; 🛜🐾) Friendly hosts welcome you at this clean, good-value place. It feels more personable than the average motel, and offers coffee and pastries in the morning. A few rooms allow pets, but they might be a little intimidated by the sweet pony-sized Great Danes kept by the host.

Cortez-Mesa Verde KOA CAMPGROUND $
(☎970-565-9301; www.koa.com/campgrounds/ cortez; 27432 E Hwy 160; sites $38-100, cabins $69; ⊙Apr-Oct; 🛜🐾) The only campground in town not right next to a highway or dedicated to RVs. Tepee lodgings are considered luxury and cabins come without bathrooms but with the option of air-conditioning for a few dollars more.

★ Kelly Place B&B $$
(☎970-565-3125; www.kellyplace.com; 14663 Montezuma County Rd G; r & cabins $125-215, 2-person campsite/RV sites $45/55; 🐾🛜) 🌿 A rare gem B&B with archaeological ruins and desert trails with nary another soul in sight. Founded by late botanist George Kelly, this lovely adobe-style lodge sits on 40 acres of orchards, red-rock canyon and Indian ruins abutting Canyon of the Ancients, 15 miles west of Cortez. Rooms are tasteful and rates (even camping) include an enormous buffet breakfast.

Retro Inn MOTEL $$
(☎970-565-3738; www.retroinnmesaverde.com; 2040 E Main St; d $115-149) This classic roadside motel has been revamped to 1950s splendor. We love the rooms in popsicle colors and a grassy strip with cooking grills. Big flat-screen TVs, thick mattresses, irons, coffee makers, microwaves and fridges make it fully modern. There's also a large continental breakfast featuring fruit, yogurt and eggs.

Best Western Turquoise Inn & Suites HOTEL $$
(☎970-565-3778; www.bestwestern.com; 535 E Main St; r from $148; 🅿🐾❄🛜🐾) With two swimming pools to keep the young ones entertained, this is a good choice for families (kids stay free, and the restaurant has a

kiddy menu). Rooms are spacious, with two-room suites for bigger families. If you're exploring Mesa Verde all day and just want an affordable and clean, if slightly bland, hotel, it will do the trick.

✕ Eating

★ Pepperhead   SOUTHERN US $

(☑ 970-565-3303; www.pepperheadcortez.com; 44 W Main St; mains $7-15; ⊙ 11am-9pm Tue-Sat; ➍) A haven of smoky Southwestern spice, this favorite sits in a colorful room adorned by a beautiful mural. Start with a grapefruit margarita – it's tart perfection. Also worthwhile are the *posole* (hominy stew), thin steaks *tampequeña* and delicious *chiles rellenos* (stuffed peppers) made with the famous Rocky Ford variety. End with some warm *sopapillas* (fry bread) dripping in local honey.

Stonefish Sushi & More   JAPANESE $

(☑ 970-565-9244; 16 W Main St; rolls $3-12; ⊙ 11am-2pm & 4:30-9pm Tue-Sat) With blues on the box and a high tin ceiling, this is sushi for the Southwest. Specialties like potstickers with prickly-pear chili and Colorado rancher seared beef and wasabi liven things up. Cool light fixtures, black tiles and globe-shaped fish tanks behind the bar complete the scene.

Tequila's Mexican Restaurant   MEXICAN $

(☑ 970-565-6868; 1740 E Main St; mains $8-14; ⊙ 11am-10pm; ➍) Good-tasting food at bargain prices draws the crowds on any given night. Though a chain, it does a great job. The chicken *mole*, seafood tacos and *carne asada* (grilled, sliced beef) all win raves, as do margaritas with fresh lime juice. Expect a wait on weekends.

Navajo Fry Bread Cart   SNACK $

(Four Corners Navajo Tribal Park; fry bread $3; ⊙ 11am-5pm) Vendors have set up around the edge of the Four Corners Navajo Tribal Park selling food, Native American crafts and jewelry and knickknacks. You can nosh on a flat piece of fried dough from this cart, to your right as you exit the parking area.

Burger Boy   BURGERS $

(☑ 970-565-7921; 400 E Main St; mains $5-11; ⊙ 11am-8pm Jun-Aug; ➍) From gum-chomping high-school girls to cheapie trays of burgers and fries, this drive-in is no throwback: it's the real deal. The service is so sweet and the experience is so classically mid-century American that it matters none if most of the food goes from the deep freezer to the deep fryer.

Farm Bistro   CAFE $$

(☑ 970-565-3834; www.thefarmbistrocortez.com; 34 W Main St; lunch mains $9-12, dinner mains $12-23; ⊙ 11am-3pm Mon-Wed, 7am-9pm Thu-Sat; ➋) 🌱 With a mantra of 'mostly local, mostly organic,' this brick cafe with mismatched seat-yourself tables is a hub for healthy appetites. On the menu are grass-fed beef burgers with tomato jam, zucchini fritter salad and homemade green chili with a worthy zing. Ingredients come from an organic farm down the road in Mancos. Vegan and gluten-free options available.

🍷 Drinking & Nightlife

Main Street Brewery & Restaurant   PUB

(☑ 970-544-9112; 21 E Main St; ⊙ 3:30-10pm) The excellent German-style house-brewed beers are listed on the wall, right next to the cheery hand-painted murals at this cozy place. Pub grub (mains $8 to $15) ranges from Southwestern cuisine to requisite burgers and pizzas. Kick it up in the downstairs game room, where you can enjoy a beer and some billiards.

Blondie's   BAR

(☑ 970-565-4015; www.blondiespubandgrub. net; 45 E Main St; ⊙ 11am-2am) If you're lucky, there's a bike rally that's pulled in here for some cold ones and a few shots of Jager, and a local band that goes by the name Gods of Thunder is about to take the stage. If these rough-cut pine walls could speak, they'd probably have a dirty mouth.

ℹ Tourist Information

Colorado Welcome Center (☑ 970-565-4048; 928 E Main St; ⊙ 9am-5pm Sep-May, to 6pm Jun-Aug) has maps, brochures and some excellent pamphlets on local activities like fishing and mountain biking.

ℹ Getting There & Away

Cortez Municipal Airport (☑ 970-565-7458; 22874 County Rd F) is 2 miles south of town off US 160/666 and has daily flights to Denver.

Your best bet to explore the area is via private vehicle. In the extreme southwest corner of the state, Cortez is easier to reach from either Phoenix, AZ, or Albuquerque, NM, than from Denver, 379 miles away by the shortest route.

East of Cortez, US 160 passes Mesa Verde National Park on the way to Durango, the largest city in the region, 45 miles away. To the northwest, Hwy 145 follows the beautiful Dolores River through the San Juan Mountains on an old

UTE MOUNTAIN INDIAN RESERVATION

Ute people once inhabited this entire region, from the San Luis Valley west into Utah, and, after a series of forced relocations and treaties from the 1860s to 1930s, control only this small strip of land in the dry high plains of the Colorado Plateau. **Ute Mountain Tribal Park** (☏ 970-749-1452; www. utemountaintribalpark.info; Morning Star Lane; half-day/full-day tours per person $29/48, transfer $12; ☺ by appointment) encompasses several archaeological sites, including petroglyphs and cliff dwellings, but can only be accessed through half- and full-day guided tours (arranged through the tribal park), which include lots of rough and dusty driving over back roads.

The relationship between Utes and the federal government is one of conflict and ongoing tension. The Ute tribe won their first rights for potable water on this arid reservation in 1988.

The tribe operates the Ute Mountain Casino, Hotel & Resort (☏ 800-258-8007; www.utemountaincasino.com; 3 Weeminuche Dr; r $80-225), near Sleeping Ute Mountain.

Rio Grande Southern narrow-gauge route over Lizard Head Pass to Telluride, 77 miles distant.

Dolores

☏ 970 / POP 945 / ELEV 6936FT

Scenic Dolores, sandwiched between the walls of a narrow canyon of the same name, is the size of a pea. Come for the treasure trove of Native American artifacts or to visit the sublime river of the same name – only rafted in spring. On a more permanent basis, the McPhee Lake boasts the best angling in the Southwest.

◎ Sights

Anasazi Heritage Center   MUSEUM
(☏ 970-882-5600; www.mesaverde.com/ anasazi; 27501 Hwy 184; admission $3, Dec-Feb free; ☺ 9am-5pm Mar-Nov, 10am-4pm Dec-Feb; ℗ ✦) The Bureau of Land Management (BLM) manages the Anasazi Heritage Center, a good stop for anyone touring the area's archaeological sites. It's 3 miles west of town, with hands-on exhibits such as weaving, corn grinding, tree-ring analysis and an introduction to the way in which archaeologists examine potsherds. Entrance is free with an America the Beautiful national parks pass (p366).

McPhee Lake   LAKE
The second-largest body of water in Colorado, McPhee Lake is one of the top fishing spots in the San Juan basin. With the best catch ratio in southern Colorado, it's great for new anglers. The artificial reservoir is 8 miles long and 2 miles wide, stretching north and west of town. Fishers should have a valid Colorado fishing license.

Art Girls' Studio   ARTS CENTER
(200 S 4th St; ☺ 10am-5pm Tue-Sat) This fully decked-out quilt and crafts shop is a do-it-yourselfer's dream. Classes are offered, finished products such as art quilts are on sale and some of the stock, such as Japanese quilting patches, is truly original.

⊨ Sleeping

Rio Grande Southern Hotel   HOTEL $
(☏ 866-882-3026; www.rgshotel.com; 101 S 5th St; r $69-79; ☎) Norman Rockwell prints and an old-world front desk welcome guests at this National Historic Landmark where Zane Gray wrote *Riders of the Purple Sage* (in room 4). Today it's a bit misshapen; in fact, you might be turned away if the host is napping. Features include a cozy library and small, antique-filled guest rooms.

Outpost Motel   MOTEL $
(☏ 800-382-4892, 970-882-7271; www.dolores outpostmotelco.com; 1800 Central Ave; RV sites $35, d $70, cabins $125-150; ☎✦) At the east end of town, this friendly riverside motel has small but clean rooms with pine beds and quilts, as well as cabins. Some rooms have kitchenettes and the courtyard features a pleasant little wooden deck overlooking the Dolores River. The motel also takes RVs.

Dolores River RV Park   CAMPGROUND $
(☏ 970-882-7761; www.doloresrivercampground. com; 18680 Hwy 145; tent/RV sites $27/39, cabins $60-110) This riverside campground has pleasant but overpriced sites, 1.5 miles east of town. The small cabins are the best deal going.

Circle K Guest Ranch   MOTEL $
(☏ 970-562-3826; www.ckranch.com; 27758 Hwy 145; tent/RV sites $25/35, d $55-70, cabins $149-189; ℗) South of Rico, this largely

utilitarian riverside ranch is popular with family reunions. There's a home-style restaurant serving family-friendly meals, plus there's horses to ride (from $43 per hour). Lodgings are sprawled out but include simple private cabins, worthwhile renovated motel rooms, dated and basic lodge rooms (very cheap) and a place to park the RV.

✖ Eating & Drinking

Rio Grande
Southern Restaurant   GERMAN $
(☏ 866-882-3026; www.rgshotel.com; 101 S 5th St; mains $9-17; ⊙ 7am-8pm Wed-Sat; 🍺) Downstairs from the historic hotel, this welcoming dining room functions as a German restaurant with generous portions of bratwurst and Wiener schnitzel. Repeat customers swear it's the best German food in the region. You can also let off some steam on Karaoke Sundays (2pm to 8pm).

★ **Dolores River Brewery**   BREWERY
(☏ 970-882-4677; www.doloresriverbrewery.com; 100 S 4th St; pizzas $9-13; ⊙ 4pm-late Tue-Sun) Welcome to Dolores nightlife, with live bluegrass bands and cask-conditioned ale. Hickory wood-fired pizzas are the specialty here, with toppings like goat's cheese, chipotle peppers and grilled eggplants spicing it up. Drawing patrons from Cortez, it's easily the best pizza in the Four Corners region, and worth the torturous wait (entertain yourself with a pint or two).

ℹ Tourist Information

For information, the **Dolores Visitor Center** (☏ 800-807-4712, 702-882-4018; 421 Railroad Ave; ⊙ 9am-5pm Mon-Fri) can help with lodging and activities, while the **USFS Dolores Ranger Station** (☏ 970-882-7296; www.fs.usda.gov/sanjuan; 29211 Hwy 184; ⊙ 8am-5pm Mon-Fri) handles the San Juan National Forest.

ℹ Getting There & Away

Dolores is 11 miles north of Cortez on Hwy 145, also known as Railroad Ave. There's no public transportation to the region, so visitors will need their own set of wheels.

Rico

☏ 970 / POP 260 / ELEV 8825FT

At the base of a steep climb to Telluride, Rico (meaning 'rich') was founded when prospectors sought silver in the hills. Local wags will claim that it is Colorado's last boom town.

Today it's a stretch-your-legs stop with lodgings at bargain rates unthinkable in glam Telluride next door. Stiff Ute resistance thwarted the first efforts at mining here. When the Utes signed the Brunot Agreement to effectively surrender the entirety of the San Juan Mountains in 1878, miners came rushing back. A boom from the Enterprise Lode brought some 5000 residents at the town's peak in 1892, but the timing was too late. Things went bust with the Silver Panic of 1893, and the town all but folded up. There's a few historic buildings and the Van Winkle Headframe and Hoist Structure, a towering piece of mining equipment alongside the road, which makes a quick photo op.

Summer brings fabulous fishing along the Dolores River (which runs through town). Anglers score big with cutthroat, rainbow and brown trout. You can also hike the 9-mile loop from the top of Lizard Head Pass to the base of Lizard Head Peak, a crumbling 13,113ft tower of rock. Aside from that, it's mostly a place to gas up and move on.

For accommodations, keep going until Telluride.If you hope to stop in tiny Rico, you will need private transportation.

Telluride

☏ 970 / POP 2320 / ELEV 8750FT

Surrounded on three sides by mastodon peaks, exclusive Telluride is quite literally cut off from the hubbub of the outside world. Once a rough mining town, today it's dirtbag-meets-diva – mixing the few who can afford the real estate with those scratching out a slope-side living for the sport of it. The town center still has palpable old-time charm, though locals often villainize the recently developed Mountain Village, whose ready-made attractions have a touch of Vegas. Yet idealism remains the Telluride mantra. Shreds of paradise persist with the town's free box – where you can swap unwanted items (across from the post office) – the freedom of luxuriant powder days and the bonhomie of its infamous festivals.

◉ Sights & Activities

You don't have to be a skier to appreciate Telluride, but loving the outdoors is a must. The town is surrounded by epic alpine scenery. Ajax Peak, a glacial headwall, rises up behind the village to form the end of the U-shaped valley. To the right (or south) on Ajax Peak, Colorado's highest waterfall,

Bridal Veil Falls, cascades 365ft down; a switchback trail leads to a restored Victorian powerhouse atop the falls. To the south, Mt Wilson reaches 14,246ft among a group of rugged peaks that form the Lizard Head Wilderness Area.

Telluride Historical Museum   MUSEUM

(☑ 970-728-3344; www.telluridemuseum.org; 201 W Gregory Ave; adult/student $5/3; ☉ 11am-5pm Mon-Sat, 1-5pm Sun) This Smithsonian-affiliated museum features the geologic history of the region as well as background on local mining history and native cultures. While you're here, check out the Telluride Blanket, an intact artifact from Ancestral Puebloans dated between AD 1041 and 1272.

Ride with Roudy   HORSEBACK RIDING

(☑ 970-728-9611; www.ridewithroudy.com; County Rd 43Zs; 2hr ride from $85; ☉ Mon-Sat; ☖) Offers all-season trail rides through the surrounding hills. Roudy moved here as 'one of the old hippies' in the 1970s and has been leading trips for 30 years. Just don't show up wearing shorts! His rugged hospitality recalls Telluride's yesteryear. Call for an appointment and pricing details.

Paragon Ski & Sport   OUTDOORS

(☑ 970-728-4525; www.paragontelluride.com; 213 W Colorado Ave; bike rental $35-55) Paragon has branches at three locations in town and a huge selection of rental bikes. Guided trips include a popular 17-mile downhill on Lizard Head Pass. It's a one-stop shop for outdoor activities in Telluride.

Telluride Ski Resort   SNOW SPORTS

(☑ 888-288-7360, 970-728-7533; www.telluride skiresort.com; 565 Mountain Village Blvd; adult/child full-day lift ticket $124/73) Known for its steep and deep terrain – with plunging runs and deep powder at the best times – Telluride is a real skier's mountain, but dilettantes love the gorgeous San Juan mountain views and the social town atmosphere. Covering three distinct areas, the resort is served by 16 lifts. Much of the terrain is for advanced and intermediate skiers, but there's still ample choice for beginners.

Telluride Ski & Snowboarding School   SNOW SPORTS

(☑ 970-728-7507; www.tellurideskiresort.com; 565 Mountain Village Blvd; ☖) If you'd like to sharpen your skills, the Telluride Ski Resort offers private and group lessons with good teachers through this school; classes for children and sessions specific to women, with women instructors, are available.

Telluride Nordic Center   SNOW SPORTS

(☑ 970-728-1144; www.telluridetrails.org; 500 E Colorado Ave) Provides Nordic instruction and rentals on public cross-country trails in Town Park, as well as along the San Miguel River and the Telluride Valley floor west of town.

Telluride Flyfishers   FISHING

(☑ 970-728-4440, 800-294-9269; www.telluride flyfishers.com; 213 W Colorado Ave; half-day fly-fishing $265) This outfit offers fishing guides and instruction on walking and wading trips on the San Juan and Dolores rivers.

Jud Wiebe Trail   HIKING

This favorite 3-mile trail is a grind, but it's also gorgeous. You'll pass through aspen groves and get high above town while obtaining 1140ft of vertical gain. It starts at the north end of Aspen St and ends by Tomboy Rd.

☞ Tours

★ Ashley Boling   HISTORY

(☑ 970-798-4065, 970-728-6639; per person $20; ☉ by appointment) Local Ashley Boling has been giving engaging historical walking tours of Telluride for over 20 years. They last over an hour and are offered year-round. Rates are for a minimum of four participants, but he'll cut a reasonable deal for two or more. By reservation.

Telluride Mountain Guides   ADVENTURE SPORTS

(☑ 970-728-6481; www.telluridemountainguiding. com; half-day rock-climbing per person $175) Guides backcountry skiing, mountaineering, hiking, rock and ice climbing with experienced leaders. Perhaps their biggest sell is Telluride's Via Ferrata route, a half-day that takes you traversing sheer rock faces with the aid of bolted steps and handholds while wearing safety harnesses and helmets. Rates are based on two participants and drop with more.

Telluride Outside   ADVENTURE

(☑ 970-728-3895; www.tellurideoutside.com; 121 W Colorado Ave; SUP tour $120; ☉ 8am-noon & 1:30pm-5:30pm) In business for over 30 years, this longtime local operation is the go-to guide service for fly-fishing, mountain-bike tours, 4WD tours, rafting and more. Their guided river stand-up paddleboarding tours are a great summer activity. In winter there's snowmobile tours. Check the website for fishing reports and blog.

Telluride

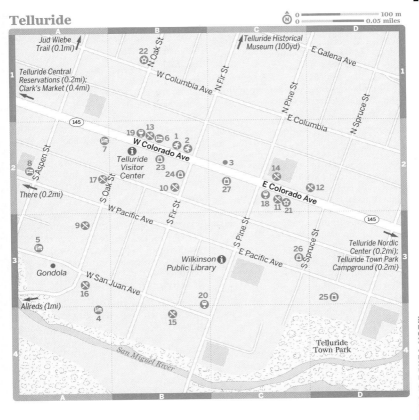

Telluride

Activities, Courses & Tours
1 Paragon Ski & Sport B2
2 Telluride Flyfishers B2
3 Telluride Outside C2

Sleeping
4 Camel's Garden A4
5 Hotel Columbia A3
6 New Sheridan Hotel B2
7 Telluride Alpine Lodging A2
8 Victorian Inn A2

Eating
9 221 South Oak A3
10 Baked in Telluride B2
11 Brown Dog Pizza C2
12 Butcher & the Baker D2
13 Chop House
   Cosmopolitan ....(see 5)
14 La Cocina de Luz C2

15 La Marmotte B4
16 Oak A3
17 Tacos del Gnar A2

Drinking & Nightlife
18 Last Dollar Saloon C2
19 New Sheridan Bar B2
20 Smugglers Brewpub B3

Entertainment
21 Fly Me to the Moon
   Saloon C2
22 Sheridan Opera House B1

Shopping
23 Between the Covers B2
24 Over the Moon B2
25 Scarpe D3
26 Telluride Bud Co C3
27 Telluride Sports C2

✦ Festivals & Events

★ Mountainfilm
FILM

(www.mountainfilm.org; ⊙ May) An excellent four-day screening of outdoor adventure and environmental films, with gallery exhibits and talks, held on Memorial Day weekend. Events (some free) are held throughout Telluride and Mountain Village.

Telluride Bluegrass Festival
MUSIC

(☎ 800-624-2422; www.planetbluegrass.com; 4-day pass $235; ⊙ late Jun) This festival attracts thousands for a weekend of top-notch rollicking alfresco bluegrass. Stalls sell all sorts of food and local microbrews to keep you happy, and acts continue well into the night. Camping out for the four-day festival is very popular. Check out the website for info on sites, shuttle services and combo ticket-and-camping packages – it's all very organized!

Telluride Mushroom Festival
FOOD & DRINK

(www.telluridemushroomfest.org; ⊙ late Aug) Fungiphiles sprout up at this festival which brings together the best mushroom hunters, chefs and even those in the know of their drug potential.

Telluride Film Festival
FILM

(☎ 603-433-9202; www.telluridefilmfestival.com; ⊙ early Sep) National and international films are premiered throughout town, and the event attracts big-name stars. For more information on the relatively complicated pricing scheme, visit the film-festival website.

Brews & Blues Festival
BEER, MUSIC

(www.tellurideblues.com; 3-day pass $200; ⊙ mid-Sep) Telluride's festival season comes to a raucous end at this event, where blues musicians take to the stage and microbrews fill the bellies of fans.

🛏 Sleeping

Aside from camping, there's no cheap lodging in Telluride. If staying in the summer or winter peak seasons, or during one of the city's festivals, you'll pay dearly. Off-season rates drop quite a bit, sometimes up to 30%. If you're coming during festival time, contact the festival organizers directly about camping.

Some of the huge properties in Mountain Village offer decent online rates, but none has the character of the smaller hotels downtown.

Most skiers opt to stay in vacation rentals – there are scores of them. If you're interested in booking a room in one, the most reputable agency is **Telluride Alpine Lodging** (☎ 888-893-0158; www.telluridelodging.com; 324 W Colorado Ave).

★ Telluride Town Park Campground
CAMPGROUND $

(☎ 970-728-2173; 500 E Colorado Ave; campsite with/without vehicle space $28/17; ⊙ mid-May–mid-Oct; ☆ 🏊) Right in the center of town, this convenient creekside campground has 43 campsites, along with showers, swimming and tennis. Sites are all on a first-come, first-served basis, unless it is festival time (consult ahead with festival organizers). Fancy some nightlife with your camping? Why not.

Matterhorn Campground
CAMPGROUND $

(☎ 970-327-4261; Hwy 145; sites $18; ⊙ May-Sep) Ten miles south of Telluride, this USFS campground has well-maintained sites, as well as shower and toilet blocks. It's a good option if you arrive during a festival and other lodging options are full.

Sunshine Campground
CAMPGROUND $

(☎ 970-327-4261; off Hwy 145; sites $18; ⊙ late May-late-Sep) Located in the Uncompahgre National Forest, this campground is the closest to Telluride. It has 15 first-come, first-serve campsites.

Hotel Columbia
HOTEL $$

(☎ 970-728-0660, toll-free 800-201-9505; www.columbiatelluride.com; 300 W San Juan Ave; d/ste from $195/319; ☆ 🅿 ❄ ☆ ☆ 🏊) ⭐ Since pricey digs are a given, skiers might as well stay right across the street from the gondola. Locally owned and operated, this stylish and swanky hotel pampers. Store your gear in the ski and boot storage and head directly to a room with espresso maker, fireplace and heated tile floors. With shampoo dispensers and recycling, it's also pretty eco-friendly.

Other highlights include a rooftop hot tub and fitness room. Breakfast is included, but food at the connected Cosmopolitan (p266) is also excellent.

New Sheridan Hotel
HOTEL $$

(☎ 800-200-1891, 970-728-4351; www.newsheridan.com; 231 W Colorado Ave; d from $223; ☆ 🏊) Elegant and understated, this historic brick hotel (erected in 1895) provides a lovely base camp for exploring Telluride. High-ceilinged rooms feature crisp linens and snug flannel throws. Check out the hot-tub deck with mountain views. In the bull's eye of downtown, the location is perfect, but some rooms are small for the price.

Victorian Inn
LODGE **$$**

(☑970-728-6601; www.victorianinntelluride.com; 401 W Pacific Ave; r from $169; ➠❄🐾) The smell of fresh cinnamon rolls greets visitors at one of Telluride's better deals, offering comfortable rooms (some with kitchenettes) and a hot tub and dry sauna. Best of all, there are fantastic lift-ticket deals for guests. Kids aged 12 years and under stay free, and you can't beat the downtown location.

Camel's Garden
HOTEL **$$$**

(☑970-728-9300; www.camelsgarden.com; 250 W San Juan Ave; r from $250; P➠❄🐾🦮) This modern and luxurious choice is located at the base of the gondola. The lobby is filled with local artwork and the large rooms feature custom-crafted furniture and Italian marble bathrooms with oversized tubs. Don't miss the giant 25ft hot tub on the top level. The complex also features restaurants, bars and spa treatments.

Inn at Lost Creek
BOUTIQUE HOTEL **$$$**

(☑970-728-5678; www.innatlostcreek.com; 119 Lost Creek Lane, Mountain Village; r $275-500; ➠🐾) This lush boutique-style hotel in Mountain Village knows cozy. At the bottom of Telluride's main lift, it's also very convenient. Service is personalized, and impeccable rooms have alpine hardwoods, Southwestern designs and molded tin. There are also two rooftop spas. Check the website for packages.

Lumière
HOTEL **$$$**

(☑907-369-0400, 866-530-9466; www.lumiere hotels.com; 118 Lost Creek Lane, Mountain Village; d from $250; P➠❄@🐾🦮) In Mountain Village, this ski-in, ski-out luxury lodge commands breathtaking views of the San Juans. This plush option boasts seven-layer bedding, Asian-inspired contemporary design and suites with top-of-the-line appliances that few probably even use. But even with the hip sushi bar and luxuriant spa menu, its greatest appeal is zipping from the slopes to a bubble bath in minutes.

✖ Eating

Meals and even groceries can be pricey in Telluride, so check out the food carts and the taco truck on Colorado Ave with picnic table seating for quick fixes. Gaga for sustainability, many local restaurants offer grass-fed beef or natural meat; we indicate those with the greatest commitment to sustainability.

For fine dining, it's best to reserve ahead as early as possible in winter and summer.

Clark's Market
MARKET

(www.clarksmarket.com; 700 W Colorado Ave; ⏰7am-9pm) Put the condo kitchenette to good use after picking up supplies at Clark's, the nicest market in town. It stocks specialty goods and scores of treats, with fresh fruit and deli meats.

Tacos del Gnar
MEXICAN **$**

(☑970-728-7938; www.gnarlytacos.com; 123 S Oak St; mains $7-14; ⏰noon-9pm Tue-Sat; 🌱) The second outlet of a no-nonsense taco shop that puts flavor ahead of frills. Its fusion-style tacos, borrowing from Korean BBQ and Asian flavors, will make your taste buds sing. Do it.

Butcher & the Baker
CAFE **$**

(☑970-728-3334; 201 E Colorado Ave; mains $10-14; ⏰7am-2pm Mon, to 9:30pm Tue-Sat, 8am-2pm Sun; 🖐) 🍃 Two veterans of upscale local catering started this heartbreakingly cute cafe, and no one beats it for breakfast. Generous sandwiches with local meats are the perfect takeout for the trail and there are heaps of baked goods and fresh sides.

Baked in Telluride
BAKERY **$**

(☑970-728-4775; www.bakedintelluride.com; 127 S Fir St; mains $6-14; ⏰5:30am-10pm) Don't expect ambience. This cafeteria-style Telluride institution serves up XL doughnuts, mom's meatloaf, sourdough wheat-crust pizza and some hearty soups and salads. The front deck is a fishbowl of local activity and the vibe is happy casual.

La Cocina de Luz
MEXICAN, ORGANIC **$$**

(www.lacocinatelluride.com; 123 E Colorado Ave; mains $9-19; ⏰9am-9pm; 🌱) 🍃 As they lovingly serve two Colorado favorites (organic and Mexican), it's no wonder that the lunch line runs deep at this healthy taquería. Order the *achiote* pulled pork and you might be full until tomorrow. Delicious details include a salsa and chip bar, handmade tortillas and margaritas with organic lime and agave nectar. With vegan and gluten-free options, too.

Oak
BARBECUE **$$**

(The New Fat Alley; ☑970-728-3985; www.oaks telluride.com; 250 San Juan Ave, base of chair 8; mains $11-23; ⏰11am-10pm; 🖐) You can pick something off the chalkboard or just take what the other guy has his face in – a cheap and messy delight. Go for the pulled-pork sandwich with coleslaw on top. Do it right by siding it with a bowl of crispy sweet-potato fries. The beer specials are outrageous.

Brown Dog Pizza   PIZZA **$$**
(📌970-728-8046; www.browndogpizza.net; 10 E Colorado Ave; pizzas $10-22; ⊙11am-10pm) The pizza? It's chewy and crusty, but the crowd makes the place interesting. Ten minutes after you belly up to the bar for a slice and a cheap pint of Pabst, you'll be privy to all the local dirt. It's one of the most affordable meals on the strip.

⭐ **Chop House**   MODERN AMERICAN **$$$**
(📌970-728-4531; www.newsheridan.com; 231 W Colorado Ave, New Sheridan Hotel; mains $26-62; ⊙5pm-2am) With superb service and a chic decor of embroidered velvet benches, this is an easy pick for an intimate dinner. Start with a cheese plate, but from there the menu gets Western with exquisite elk shortloin and ravioli with tomato relish and local sheep-milk ricotta. Top it off with a flourless dark chocolate cake in fresh caramel sauce.

Breakfasts are gourmet and particularly noteworthy too.

221 South Oak   MODERN AMERICAN **$$$**
(📌970-728-9505; www.221southoak.com; 221 S Oak St; mains $30-48; ⊙5-10pm; 🖋) A great pick, this is an intimate restaurant in a historic home, with a small but innovative menu spinning world flavors with fresh ingredients. Dishes are flavorful and usually based on meat, fish and seafood, with ample vegetable accents. There's also a vegetarian menu with depth and diversity. Tuesdays have two-for-one mains.

Inquire about Chef Eliza Gavin's appetizer and wine pairing classes that teach cooking techniques and the art of wine pairing, with sampling included.

Cosmopolitan   MODERN AMERICAN **$$$**
(📌970-728-0660; www.cosmotelluride.com; 300 W San Juan Ave, Hotel Columbia; mains $26-49; ⊙5pm-late) 🖋 The on-site restaurant at the Hotel Columbia is one of Telluride's most respected for fine modern dining with a twist – can you resist Himalayan yak ribeye or lobster corn dogs? The food is certainly inventive, and cheap if you come at happy hour (5pm to 6pm), when sushi and cosmos are half-price.

La Marmotte   FRENCH **$$$**
(📌970-728-6232; www.lamarmotte.com; 150 W San Juan Ave; mains $28-44; ⊙5:30pm-late Tue-Sat) Seasonal plates of French cuisine, white linen and candlelit warmth contrast with this rustic 19th-century icehouse. Dishes like the coq au vin with bacon mashed potatoes are both smart and satisfying. There are some organic options and an extensive wine list. Parents should check out the Friday-night winter babysitting options.

Allreds   CONTEMPORARY AMERICAN **$$$**
(📌970-728-7474; www.allredsrestaurant.com; gondola station St Sophia; mains $29-49; ⊙5:30-9:30pm, bar 5-11:30pm) Midway up the gondola, Allreds stuns with San Juan mountain panoramas – though the bar boasts the best views. Upscale and very exclusive, it emphasizes Coloradan and organic ingredients, and has five-course dinners with wine pairings. Those with smaller budgets can still indulge: hit the bar for sunset drinks with glorious handcut truffle fries and burgers. Summer alpenglow peaks just before 8pm.

🍷 **Drinking & Nightlife**

There's more good times to be had in Telluride than the rest of southern Colorado combined. Bring your wallet; those drinks aren't free or even close. Live bands spark it up.

There   COCKTAIL BAR
(📌970-728-1213; www.therebars.com; 627 W Pacific Ave; mains $4-18; ⊙5pm-midnight) A hip social alcove for cocktails and nibbling, plus weekend brunch. On a comic-book-style menu, East meets West in yummy lettuce wraps, duck ramen and sashimi tostadas, paired with original hand-shaken drinks. We liked the Jalapeño Kiss.

New Sheridan Bar   BAR
(📌970-728-3911; www.newsheridan.com; 231 W Colorado Ave, New Sheridan Hotel; ⊙5pm-2am) It's rush hour for beautiful people, though in low season you'll find real local flavor and opinions. In summertime, beeline for the breezy rooftop. Old bullet holes in the wall testify to the plucky survival of the bar itself, even as the adjoining hotel sold off chandeliers and antiques to pay the heating bills when mining fortunes waned.

Telluride Brewing Co   MICROBREWERY
(📌970-728-5094; www.telluridebrewingco.com; 156 Society Dr; ⊙noon-7pm Mon-Sat, to 5pm Sun) For good brews and local atmosphere among the shiny metal vats, head to this warehouse between town and the Mountain Village. Their Face-Down Brown has won gold medals twice at the Great American Beer Festival.

Last Dollar Saloon BAR
(☑970-728-4800; www.lastdollarsaloon.com; 100 E Colorado Ave; ⊙3pm-2am) All local color – forget about cocktails and grab a cold can of beer at this longtime late-night favorite, which is popular when everything else closes. With pool tables and darts.

Smugglers Brewpub PUB
(☑970-728-5620; www.smugglersbrewpub.com; 225 S Pine St; ⊙11am-10pm; ⋒) Beer-lovers will feel right at home at casual Smugglers, a great place to hang out, sample local brew and eat fried stuff. With at least seven beers on tap, it's a smorgasbord, but go for the chocolatey Two Plank Porter or the Smugglers' Scottish Strong Ale.

☆ Entertainment

Fly Me to the Moon Saloon LIVE MUSIC
(☑970-728-6666; 132 E Colorado Ave; ⊙3pm-2am) Let your hair down and kick up your heels to the tunes of live bands at this saloon, the best place in Telluride to party hard.

Sheridan Opera House THEATER
(☑970-728-4539; www.sheridanoperahouse.com; 110 N Oak St; ⋒) This historic venue has a burlesque charm and is always the center of Telluride's cultural life. It hosts the Telluride Repertory Theater, and frequently has special performances for children.

🛍 Shopping

Between the Covers BOOKS
(☑970-728-4504; www.between-the-covers.com; 224 W Colorado Ave; ⊙9am-5pm Sun-Thu, to 6pm Fri & Sat) Bookworms flock to this homey shop with a big selection of local interest, creaking floors and a doting staff. Check online for readings and events. Local secret: the coffee counter in back turns out a mean espresso milkshake.

Telluride Sports SPORTS & OUTDOORS
(☑970-728-4477; www.telluridesports.com; 150 W Colorado Ave; ⊙8am-8pm; ⋒) There are branches and associated shops in Mountain Village, making this the biggest network of outdoor suppliers in town. It covers everything outdoors, has topographical and USFS maps, sporting supplies and loads of local information.

Telluride Bud Co DISPENSARY
(☑970-239-6039; www.telluridebc.com; 135 S Spruce St; ⊙9am-7pm) There's more than one pot shop in Telluride but this one is touted for its broad selection of products. Like everything else in Telluride, it's more expensive than shops elsewhere.

Scarpe CLOTHING
(☑970-728-1513; www.shopscarpe.com; 250 E Pacific Ave; ⊙10am-7pm) The hand-picked selection of women's shoes, skirts and accessories makes Scarpe the best clothing boutique in town. Things here feel timeless, designed by a fleet of names that includes a good number of locals.

Over the Moon CHEESE
(www.overthemoontelluride.com; 200 W Colorado Ave; ⊙11am-5pm Mon-Sat, noon-5pm Sun) Over the alleyway, this gourmet wine and cheese shop would be a boon to Wallace and Gromit. Cheeses are organized by country of origin, plus it offers fig confit, truffled honey and charcuterie.

❶ Tourist Information

Telluride Central Reservations (☑888-355-8743; 700 W Colorado Ave; ⊙9am-5pm Mon-Sat, 10am-1pm Sun) Handles accommodations and sells festival tickets.
Telluride Library (☑970-728-4519; www.telluridelibrary.org; 100 W Pacific Ave; ⊙10am-8pm Mon-Thu, to 6pm Fri & Sat, noon-5pm Sun; ☎⋒) Good resource for maps and local information, with some free public events.
Telluride Visitor Center (☑888-353-5473, 970-728-3041; www.telluride.com; 230 W Colorado Ave; ⊙10am-5pm winter, to 7pm summer) Info in all seasons.

❶ Getting There & Away

In ski season **Montrose Regional Airport** (p298), 65 miles north, has direct flights to and from Denver (on United), Houston, Phoenix and limited cities on the east coast.

Commuter aircraft serve the mesa-top **Telluride Airport** (TEX; ☑970-778-5051; www.tellurideairport.com; 1500 Last Dollar Rd), 5 miles east of town – weather permitting. At other times, planes fly into Montrose.

Thanks to its box canyon location, there's only one way to drive into town on a paved road.

❶ Getting Around

Colorado Ave, also known as Main St, has most of the restaurants, bars and shops. You can walk everywhere, so if you have a vehicle, leave it at the intercept parking lot at the south end of Mahoney Dr (near the visitor center) or at your lodgings. Visitors can use the bike path for bicycle and foot travel.

From town you can reach the ski mountain via two lifts and the **gondola** (S Oak St; ⊙7am-midnight; 🏃). Located on S Oak St, the gondola also links Telluride with Mountain Village, the base for the Telluride Ski Resort. Located 7 miles from town along Hwy 145, Mountain Village is a 20-minute drive east, but only 12 minutes away by gondola (free for foot passengers).

The **Galloping Goose** (☑970-728-5700; www.telluride-co.gov; ⊙7am-9pm) has bus routes downtown and to nearby communities. The **Telluride Express** (☑970-728-6000; www.tellurideexpress.com; to Montrose adult/child $53/31) shuttles from town to Telluride Airport, Mountain Village or Montrose airport; call to arrange pick-up.

Ridgway

☑970 / POP 930 / ELEV 6985FT

Ridgway, with its local quirkiness, zesty history and outrageous views of Mt Sneffels, is hard to just blow through. Recreation lies every which way. Right on the outskirts is the gorgeous Ralph Lauren Ranch, though nearby Forest Service trails for hiking and backcountry skiing will give you the same backdrop without the elite price tag. The town also served as the location for John Wayne's 1969 cowboy classic, *True Grit*.

👁 Sights & Activities

Ridgway Railroad Museum   MUSEUM
(☑970-626-5181; www.ridgwayrailroadmuseum.org; 150 Racecourse Rd; ⊙10am-6pm May-Sep, reduced hours Oct-Apr; 🚹) **FREE** Ridgway was the birthplace of the Rio Grande Southern Railroad, a narrow-gauge rail line that connected to Durango with the 'Galloping Goose,' a kind of hybrid train and truck that saved the struggling Rio Grande Southern for a number of years.

The volunteers who staff the museum are true railroad zealots – one even reconstructed a Galloping Goose engine outside from photos and sketches. The permanent collection has maps, historical photos and a really cool diorama of the Pleasant Valley Trestle and Motor #2. It's also the de facto historical museum for the town, and it has good brochures for a short self-guided tour.

★ **Chicks Climbing & Skiing**   CLIMBING
(☑970-325-3858; www.chickswithpicks.net) This group is dedicated to getting women onto the rocks and ice, giving instruction for all-comers (beginners included) about pursuits such as rock-climbing, bouldering and iceclimbing. The programs change frequently and often involve multiday excursions or town-based courses. Men are included on some activities, but most are women-only.

**San Juan Hut
System**   SNOW SPORTS, MOUNTAIN BIKING
(☑970-626-3033; www.sanjuanhuts.com; per person $30) Experienced cross-country skiers will appreciate the strong series of basic huts along a 206-mile route stretching from Telluride west to Moab, Utah. In summer these huts, equipped with bunks and cooking facilities, are popular with mountain bikers. Book well in advance, as huts fill quickly.

Orvis Hot Springs   HOT SPRINGS
(☑970-626-5324; www.orvishotsprings.com; 1585 County Rd 3; per hour/day $18/22) The attractive rock pools make this outdoor, clothing-optional hot spring hard to resist. Yes, it does get some exhibitionists, but the variety of soaking areas (100°F to 114°F) mean you can probably find the perfect spot. It's 9 miles north of Ouray, outside Ridgway.

**Ridgway State
Park & Recreation Area**   FISHING
(☑970-626-5822; www.parks.state.co.us/parks/ridgway; 28555 US Hwy 550; $7; ⊙dawn-dusk) Fishing aficionados should head to Ridgway State Park and Recreation Area, 12 miles north of town. The reservoir here is stocked with loads of rainbow trout, as well as German brown, kokanee, yellow perch and the occasional large-mouth bass. There are also hiking trails and campsites.

**Rigs Fly Shop
& Guide Service**   FISHING, OUTDOORS
(☑970-626-4460, toll-free 888-626-4460; www.fishrigs.com; 1075 Sherman St; half-day fishing tours from $270; ⊙7am-7pm; 🚹) Rigs Fly Shop offers guided fly-fishing tours out of Ridgway from half-day beginners' trips to multi-day camp outs for more experienced anglers. Rigs also does white-water rafting and other soft-adventure itineraries in and around southwest Colorado. Costs drop significantly with the number of guests.

🛏 Sleeping

**Ridgway State
Park & Recreation Area**   CAMPGROUND **$**
(☑800-678-2267; www.parks.state.co.us/parks/ridgway; 28555 US Hwy 550; tent/RV/yurt sites $20/26/80) With almost 300 sites, the three campgrounds here offer good availability with gorgeous water views, hiking and

fishing. Tent campers have 25 walk-in sites, but the path is short and there are wheelbarrows to transport your stuff. Or check out the cool canvas yurts. Rest rooms have coin-operated showers and there's a playground for kids. Book online or over the phone.

★**Chipeta Solar
Springs Resort** LODGE **$$$**
(☑970-626-3737; www.chipeta.com; 304 S Lena St; r from $225; ☺🐾🗫) This Southwestern adobe-style complex is a swanky, upscale lodge dedicated to erasing your everyday cares. Rooms feature hand-painted Mexican tiles, rough-hewn log beds and decks with a view. There are wonderful public areas on the property.

Have a read in the Great Room or a chat in the solarium, or head out to the hot tubs on the property for a quiet soak. The on-site spa features treatments developed by the Utes and daily yoga classes. Check Chipeta's website for ski, soak and stay deals, where you can ride the slopes at Telluride, soak in the hot springs pools in Ouray and spend the night in Ridgway.

✖️ **Eating & Drinking**

★**Tacos del Gnar** MEXICAN **$**
(☑970-626-9715; www.gnarlytacos.com; 630 Sherman St; mains $7-14; ☺11am-9pm Tue-Sat; ✎) Started by two chefs discontented with the snooty world of fine dining, this delicious riff on the taco truck delivers big time. Whether you're eating Korean short-rib tacos with kimchi or crisp panko-crusted mahi mahi with ginger slaw, these bad boys sing with flavor. The ambience is fast-casual. There's also gluten-free options and beer or canned wine available.

Colorado Boy PIZZA **$**
(602 Clinton St; pizzas $12; ☺4-9pm Tue-Sun) Baking goat's-cheese pizzas with fennel sausage and serving craft beer by the barrel, congenial Colorado Boy is a boon to locals, who rush to claim the outdoor picnic tables early. Wash the artisan pizza down with the house-brewed Irish Red, with caramel and toffee notes, or a Mexican Coke.

Kate's Place BREAKFAST **$**
(☑970-626-9800; 615 W Clinton St; mains $9-14; ☺7am-2pm; ✦) Consider yourself lucky if the morning starts with a chorizo-stuffed breakfast burrito and white cheddar grits from Kate's: it's the best breakfast joint for miles.

The restaurant's dedication to local farmers, cute and colorful interior and bubbly waitstaff seal the deal.

Thai Paradise THAI **$$**
(☑970-626-2742; 146 N Cora St; mains $12-16; ☺11am-2pm Mon-Fri, 5-9pm Mon-Sun) Serving up all the standard curries in light, spicy and fragrant preparations, this tiny house of flavor is a hit. Pad Thai, crispy duck and tempura round out the menu, with brown rice and Asian beers also on offer. If it's warm out, you can enjoy the few tables set on the outdoor patio.

True Grit Cafe AMERICAN **$$**
(☑970-626-5739; 123 N Lena St; mains $8-22; ☺11am-9pm; ✦🖼) Scenes from the original *True Grit* were filmed at this appropriately named cafe and watering hole. It's a kind of shrine to John Wayne, with pictures and memorabilia hung on the walls. Quarter-pound burgers, tasty chicken and fried steaks are served, and a crackling fire warms patrons in the winter.

Cimmaron Coffee House CAFE
(☑970-626-5858; 380 Sherman St; snacks $3; ☺7am-6pm) Coffee addicts collect at this unassuming cafe and bookstore to get a fix and a smothered breakfast burrito. There are also smoothies. With patio seating.

ℹ️ **Tourist Information**

Ridgway Area Chamber of Commerce
(☑800-220-4959, 970-626-5181; www.ridgwaycolorado.com; 150 Racecourse Rd; ☺9am-5pm Mon-Fri) Has a lot of information about local activities.

ℹ️ **Getting There & Away**

Ridgway sits at the crossroads of US 550, which goes south to Durango, and Hwy 62, which leads to Telluride. The downtown area is tucked away on the west side of the Uncompahgre River. The town is best accessed with a private vehicle.

Ouray & the Million Dollar Hwy

POP 1015 / ELEV 7760FT

With gorgeous icefalls draping the box canyon and soothing hot springs dotting the valley floor, Ouray (you-ray) is privileged, even for Colorado. For ice climbers it's a world-class destination, but hikers and 4WD fans can also appreciate its rugged and sometimes stunning charms. The town is a well-preserved quarter-mile mining village sandwiched between imposing peaks.

Ouray is named after the legendary Ute chief who maintained peace between the white settlers and the crush of miners who descended on the San Juan Mountains in the early 1870s. Ouray relinquished the Ute tribal lands, preventing the slaughter of his people.

◉ Sights

Box Canyon Falls   WATERFALL
(off Box Canyon Rd; adult/child $4/2; ⊙8am-8pm Jun-Aug; P 🚻) 🅿 This is a popular short walk from town, or you can drive to the signposted parking lot off Box Canyon Rd. The waterfall is 285ft high and issues thousands of gallons of water each minute over a spectacular drop. The immediate area around the falls is rich in birdlife – the protected black swift nests in the rock face. The falls are within Box Canyon Park, which has a modest entry fee.

Ouray County Museum   MUSEUM
(☑970-325-4576; www.ouraycountyhistorical society.org; 420 6th Ave; adult/child $7/3; ⊙10am-4:30pm Mon-Sat, noon-4:30pm Sun, closed Dec 1-Apr 14; 🚻) Little Ouray, 'the Switzerland of America,' is very picturesque and littered with old houses and buildings. The visitors center and museum issue a free leaflet with details of an excellent walking tour that takes in two dozen buildings and houses constructed between 1880 and 1904. The collection is mostly of interest to those fascinated by local history.

🏃 Activities

Bird-watchers come to Ouray to spot rare birds. The Box Canyon Falls have the USA's most accessible colony of protected black swifts. There are surprising numbers of unusual birds in town, including warblers, sparrows and grosbeaks. The visitor center has resources for bird-watchers, and the excellent Buckskin Booksellers (p272) has books and guides.

There are stacks of things to do in and around Ouray. Remember that Ouray falls within the purview of tour and activities providers in nearby Ridgway, Montrose and Silverton, and even Durango and Gunnison – so check what's on offer in those towns as well.

★ Ouray Hot Springs   HOT SPRINGS
(☑970-325-7073; www.ourayhotsprings.com; 1200 Main St; adult/child $18/12; ⊙10am-10pm Jun-Aug, noon-9pm Mon-Fri & 11am-9pm Sat & Sun Sep-May; 🚻) For a healing soak or kiddish fun, try the recently renovated historic Ouray Hot Springs. The natural springwater is crystal-clear and free of the sulphur smells plaguing other hot springs. There's a lap pool, water slides, a climbing wall overhanging a splash pool and prime soaking areas (100°F to 106°F; 37.7°C to 41.1°C). The complex also offers a gym and massage service.

★ Million Dollar Highway   SCENIC DRIVE
The whole of US Hwy 550 has been called the Million Dollar Hwy, but more properly it's the amazing stretch south of Ouray through the Uncompahgre Gorge up to Red Mountain Pass at 11,018ft. The alpine scenery is truly awesome and driving south towards Silverton positions drivers on the outside edge of the skinny, winding road, a heartbeat away from free-fall.

Some credit the name to a roadbed rich in valuable gold ore. Others say it cost $1 million per mile to build. Vehicles traveling north sit more snugly on the inside edge. Passing abandoned mine head-frames and slag piles from the former Idarado Mine, much of the road is cut into the mountainsides and gains elevation in tight hairpin turns and S-bends. The brooding mountains loom large and close, their bulk and flanks intimidating, with snow clinging to their lofty misty peaks even in high summer. In good weather the road is formidable. In drizzle or rain, fog or snow, the Million Dollar Hwy south of Ouray is downright scary, so take care.

Perimeter Trail   HIKING
A six-mile hiking circuit that loops you around town on the hillsides, taking in Cascade falls, the Box Canyon and a cool remnant miner's tunnel. Put aside 2.5 to 4 hours. Most hikers park across the street from Ouray Hot Springs and start there, but there are many points on the edge of town to pick up the trail.

It's especially handy if there's still snow in the high country.

Ouray Ice Park   CLIMBING
(☑970-325-4061; www.ourayicepark.com; County Rd 361; ⊙7am-5pm mid-Dec–Mar; 🚻) FREE Enthusiasts from around the globe come to ice climb at the world's first public ice park, spanning a 2-mile stretch of the Uncompahgre Gorge. The sublime (if chilly) experience offers something for all skill levels. Get instruction through a local guide service.

👉 Tours

San Juan Mountain Guides   CLIMBING, SKIING
(☑800-642-5389, 970-325-4925; www.ouray
climbing.com; 725 Main St; ⬥) Ouray's own
professional guiding and climbing group is
certified with the International Federation
of Mountain Guides Association (IFMGA).
It specializes in ice- and rock-climbing and
wilderness backcountry skiing.

San Juan Scenic Jeep Tours   4WD, FISHING
(☑970-325-0089; www.sanjuanjeeptours.com;
206 7th Ave; adult/child half-day $59/30; ⬥) The
friendly folks at the Historic Western Hotel
operate a customized Jeep-touring service.
Abandoned ghost towns of the old mining
days are always popular, as are off-road
tours of the nearby peaks and valleys. Hiking, hunting and fishing drop-offs and pick-
ups can be arranged.

Ouray Mule & Carriage Co   TOURS
(☑970-708-4946; 834 Main St; adult/child $15/10;
⊙afternoons Jun-Aug; ⬥) The mule-drawn
coach you see clip-clopping along Ouray's
main streets is the nine-person dray that
takes visitors (and locals) around on interpretive tours of the old town. Departures go
at 1pm, 3pm, 5pm and 7pm, with charters
available for larger groups.

✨ Festivals & Events

Ouray Ice Festival   CULTURAL
(☑970-325-4288; www.ourayicefestival.com; donation for evening events; ⊙Jan; ⬥) The Ouray
Ice Festival features four days of climbing
competitions, dinners, slide shows and clinics. There's even a climbing wall set up for
kids. You can watch the competitions for
free, but various evening events require a
donation to the ice park. Once inside, you'll
get free brews from popular Colorado micro-
brewer New Belgium.

🛏 Sleeping

**Amphitheater Forest
Service Campground**   CAMPGROUND $
(☑877-444-6777; www.recreation.gov; US Hwy
550; tent sites $20; ⊙Jun-Aug) With great tent
sites under the trees, this high-altitude campground is a score. On holiday weekends a
three-night minimum applies. South of town
on Hwy 550, take a signposted left-hand turn.

**Historic Western
Hotel, Restaurant & Saloon**   HOTEL $
(☑970-325-4645; www.historicwesternhotel.com;
210 7th Ave; r without/with bath $55/105; P🛜)

Open by reservation in shoulder season,
this somewhat threadbare Wild West board-
inghouse serves all budgets. Huge, floral
widow's-walk rooms are straight out of a
Sergio Leone flick, with saggy beds and a
clawfoot tub in room. It's probably wise to
skip the cramped shared-bath rooms. The
saloon serves affordable meals and grog under a wall of mounted game.

★ **Wiesbaden**   HOTEL $$
(☑970-325-4347; www.wiesbadenhotsprings.com;
625 5th St; r $132-347; ⊛🛜🏊) Quirky, quaint
and new age, Wiesbaden even boasts a nat-
ural indoor vapor cave, which, in another
era, was frequented by Chief Ouray. Rooms
with quilted bedcovers are cozy and roman-
tic, but the sunlit suite with a natural rock
wall tops all. In the morning, guests roam in
thick robes, drinking the free organic coffee
or tea, post-soak or awaiting massages.

The on-site Aveda salon also provides
soothing facials to make your mountain
detox complete. Outside there's a spacious
hot-spring pool (included) and a private,
clothing-optional soaking tub with a water-
fall, reserved for $35 per hour.

Beaumont Hotel   HOTEL $$
(☑970-325-7000; www.beaumonthotel.com; 505
Main St; r from $189; P⊛) With magnificent
four-post beds, clawfoot tubs and hand-
carved mirrors, this 1886 hotel underwent
extensive renovations to revive the glamour
it possessed a century ago. Word has it that
Oprah stayed here, and you'll probably like
it too. It also has a spa and boutiques, but
due to the fragile decor, pets and kids under
16 years old are not allowed.

**Box Canyon Lodge
& Hot Springs**   LODGE $$
(☑800-327-5080, 970-325-4981; www.box
canyonouray.com; 45 3rd Ave; r $189; 🛜) 🗲 It's
not every hotel that offers geothermal heat-
ing, not to mention pineboard rooms that
are spacious and fresh, and spring-fed barrel
hot tubs – perfect for a romantic stargazing
soak. With good hospitality that includes
free apples and bottled water, it's popular, so
book ahead.

Ouray Victoria Inn   HOTEL $$
(☑970-325-7222, toll-free 800-846-8729; www.
victorianinnouray.com; 50 3rd Ave; d from $120;
P⊛🛜) Refurbished in 2009, 'The Vic' has
a terrific setting next to Box Canyon Park on
the Uncompahgre River near Ouray Ice Park.
Rooms have cable TV, fridges and coffee

makers, some with balconies and splendid views. Kids will appreciate the deluxe swing set with climbing holds. Rates vary widely by season, but low-season rates are a steal.

St Elmo Hotel HOTEL **$$**
(970-325-4951, toll-free 866-243-1502; www.stelmohotel.com; 426 Main St; d $140-220;) Effusively feminine, this 1897 hotel is a showpiece of the Ouray museum's historic walking tour. Nine unique renovated rooms have floral wallpaper and period furnishings. Guests have access to a hot tub and sauna and there's even some of Ouray's best dining, Bon Ton Restaurant, on-site downstairs.

Eating

Maggie's Kitchen BURGERS **$**
(970-325-0259; 520 Main St; mains $8-12; 11am-5pm Tue-Thu, to 8pm Fri-Sun) Visit this graffiti-bombed hole-in-the-wall for sloppy burgers and fries. Options seem endless, but a serrano chile and bacon burger could easily fortify a day on the ice. In summer, enjoy sitting on the large deck.

Buen Tiempo Mexican Restaurant & Cantina MEXICAN **$$**
(970-325-4544; 515 Main St; mains $11-21; 5:30-10pm Mon-Fri, 11:30am-10pm Sat & Sun;) This good-time spot bursts with bar-stool squatters and booths of families. From the chili-rubbed sirloin to the *posole* with warm tortillas, Buen Tiempo delivers. Start with a signature margarita with chips and spicy homemade salsa. End with a satisfying scoop of deep-fried ice cream. But to find out how the dollars got on the ceiling, it will cost you.

Outlaw Restaurant AMERICAN **$$**
(970-325-4366; 610 Main St; mains $12-34; 4:30pm-close;) Ouray's oldest, this convivial bar-restaurant specializes in door-stopper steaks cut and cooked to your liking. There's a select wine list and menu of cocktails as well as ubiquitous Colorado microbrewed beers. The decor is fun – a wall is covered with sports memorabilia, antiques and, allegedly, John Wayne's hat.

O'Briens Pub & Grill PUB FOOD **$$**
(970-325-4386; www.obriensouraycolorado.com; 726 Main St; mains $10-18; 11am-midnight) Somewhere between the thick soups and greasy plates, this classic pub fare gets motors started. Perhaps for the lack of pretension, or the very friendly service, it's among the most popular haunts in town, packing in locals and visitors alike. Happy hour is daily from 4pm to 6pm.

Bon Ton Restaurant FRENCH, ITALIAN **$$$**
(970-325-4419; www.bontonrestaurant.com; 426 Main St; mains $16-40; 5:30-11pm Thu-Mon, brunch 9:30am-12:30pm Sat & Sun;) Bon Ton has been serving supper for a century in a beautiful room under the historic St Elmo Hotel. The French-Italian menu includes specialties like roast duck in cherry peppercorn sauce and tortellini with bacon and shallots. The wine list is extensive and the Champagne brunch comes recommended.

Drinking & Nightlife

Ouray Brewery BREWERY
(970-325-7388; www.ouraybrewery.com; 607 Main St; 11am-9pm) With chairlift bar stools and a rooftop deck to spy on Main St, this pub is something of a flytrap for visitors; in fact, there is a notable lack of locals around. The brewery offers a brew sample tray and growlers to go.

KJ Wood DISTILLERY
(970-325-7295; www.kjwooddistillers.com; 929 Main St; 3-9pm Fri & Sat) Considering the slim opening hours here, you would think Prohibition is still in. Nevertheless the gold-medal-winning Jinn is probably worth a stop at this atmospheric tasting room. If gin's not your drink, check out the whiskey made with Colorado barley and blue corn.

Silver Eagle Saloon BAR
(617 Main St; 5pm-2am) With an 1886 barback and Wild West attitude to spare, this smoky saloon is a favorite of locals. Unless you're smoking (smoking is legal since it's grandfathered in to tobacco-sale sites), the only thing to do is drink. No food is served but bartenders display an expert pour. It boasts the only pool table in town, though it will take gumption to play.

Shopping

Buckskin Booksellers BOOKS
(970-325-4071; www.buckskinbooksellers.com; 505 Main St; 9am-5pm Mon-Sat) This excellent bookstore exemplifies the passion locals have for their town and area. Buckskin carries a huge amount of books on local history, mining and geology, as well as birding books, guidebooks and hiking and camping information. There are antique books and

collectibles, old photographs and ephemera, as well as a great range of fiction titles.

There are also plush armchairs where you're invited to sit and read a while before you buy.

❶ Tourist Information

Ouray Visitors Center (☑970-325-4746, 800-228-1876; www.ouraycolorado.com; 1230 Main St; ⊙9am-6pm Mon-Sat, 10am-4pm Sun; ☎) Located behind the Ouray hot-springs pool.

❶ Getting There & Away

Ouray is on Hwy 550, 70 miles north of Durango, 24 miles north of Silverton and 37 miles south of Montrose. There are no bus services in the area and private transportation is necessary.

Silverton

☑970 / POP 630 / ELEV 9318FT

Ringed by snowy peaks and steeped in the sooty tales of a tawdry mining town, Silverton would seem more at home in Alaska than the Lower 48. But here it is. For those into snowmobiling, biking, fly-fishing or just basking in some very high-altitude sunshine, Silverton delivers.

It's a two-street town, but only one is paved. Greene St is where you'll find most businesses (think homemade jerky, fudge and feather art). Still unpaved, notorious Blair St – renamed Empire – runs parallel to Greene. During the silver rush, Blair St was home to thriving brothels and boozing establishments. In summer, Silverton hosts crowds off the Durango-bound steam train, selling them boatloads of trinkets. In winter, snowmobiles provide transportation, and town becomes a playground for intrepid travelers, mostly powder hounds.

Just getting here from Ouray on the Million Dollar Hwy (p270) is one of Colorado's best road trips.

◎ Sights

Mining Heritage Center MUSEUM
(☑970-387-5838; www.sanjuancountyhistorical society.org; 1559 Greene St; adult/child $8/3; ⊙9am-5pm Jun-Oct; ℗☻) This specialist museum is dedicated to Silverton's mining history. Old mining equipment is displayed and there's a re-created blacksmith shop.

Mayflower Gold Mill HISTORIC BUILDING
(☑970-387-0294; www.silvertonhistoricsociety. org; County Rd 2; adult/child $8/free; ⊙10am-4pm Jun-Sep; ℗☻) This mill was once a major employer in Silverton. Stop in to see how miners extracted gold and minerals from the ore. The Aerial Tram House is a highlight of the self-guided tour.

Silverton Museum MUSEUM
(☑970-387-5838; www.silvertonhistoricsociety. org; 1557 Greene St; adult/child $8/3; ⊙10am-4pm Jun-Oct; ℗☻) Installed in the original 1902 San Juan County Jail, the Silverton Museum has an interesting collection of local artifacts and ephemera.

☆ Activities

★Silverton Railroad Depot RAIL
(☑970-387-5416, toll-free 877-872-4607; www. durangotrain.com; 12th St; deluxe/adult/child round-trip from $189/89/55; ⊙departures 1:45pm, 2:30pm & 3pm; ☻) You can buy one-way and round-trip tickets for the brilliant Durango & Silverton Narrow Gauge Railroad (p275) at the Silverton terminus. The Silverton Freight Yard Museum is located at the Silverton depot. The train ticket provides admission two days prior to, and two days following, your ride on the train.

The train service offers combination train-bus return trips (the bus route is much quicker). Tickets are also available on the website. Hikers use the train to access the Durango and Weminuche Wilderness trailheads.

★Silverton Mountain Ski Area SKIING
(☑970-387-5706; www.silvertonmountain.com; State Hwy 110; daily lift ticket $59, all-day guide & lift ticket $159) Not for newbies, this is one of the most innovative ski mountains in the US – a single lift takes advanced and expert backcountry skiers up to the summit of an area of ungroomed ski runs. Numbers are limited and the mountain designates unguided and the more exclusive guided days.

The lift rises from the 10,400ft base to 12,300ft. Imagine heli-skiing sans helicopter. You really need to know your stuff – the easiest terrain here is comparable to skiing double blacks at other resorts.

Kendall Mountain Recreation Area SKIING
(☑970-387-5522; www.skikendall.com; Kendall Pl; daily lift tickets adult/child $25/17; ⊙11am-4pm Fri & Sat Dec-Feb; ☻) Managed by the town, with just one double 1050ft chairlift and four runs, all of them suitable for beginners. People goof around on sleds and tubes. It's cheap and family-friendly. Skis, tubes, sleds

MESA VERDE & SOUTHWEST COLORADO SILVERTON

and snowboards can be rented from the Kendall Mountain Community Center.

Tours

San Juan Backcountry
DRIVING

(☑ 970-387-5565, toll-free 800-494-8687; www.sanjuanbackcountry.com; 1119 Greene St; 2hr tour adult/child $60/40; ☺ May-Oct; 🚗) 🦯 Offering both 4WD tours and rentals, San Juan Backcountry can get you out and into the brilliant San Juan Mountain wilderness areas around Silverton. The tours take visitors around in modified open-top Chevy Suburbans.

Old Hundred Gold Mine Tour
TOURS

(☑ 970-387-5444, toll-free 800-872-3009; www.minetour.com; County Rd 4a; adult/child $19/10; ☺ hourly 10am-4pm May 15-Oct 15; 🚗) Fifteen minutes east of town, the hour-long Old Hundred Mine Gold Tour is hugely popular. A tram travels a third of a mile into a tunnel where passengers alight. Tour around the old gold-mine workings with drilling demonstrations and 1930s-era mining machinery. Panning for gold is included in the tour price – an area is regularly 'salted' with gold dust.

The tour is totally wheelchair accessible.

🛏 Sleeping

Silver Summit RV Park
CAMPGROUND $

(☑ 970-387-0240, toll-free 800-352-1637; www.silversummitrvpark.com; 640 Mineral St; RV sites $42; ☺ May 15-Oct 15; 🅿🛜🐾) Like so much else in Silverton, Silver Summit is a mixed business also running rental Jeeps out of the RV park headquarters. The park has good facilities, including a laundry, hot tub and fire pit. Tents can set up on the paved drive, but it's not ideal.

Blair Street Hostel
HOSTEL $

(☑ 970-387-5599; www.blairstreethostel.com; 1025 Blair St; dm $25-30, r $64-71, ste $189; 🛜) History is thick here, but the beds are a little tired. The renovated four-person suite is in fine shape. There's a backyard fire pit, a grill and communal showers for dorm visitors or passing Colorado Trail hikers. Laundry service too. Kids not allowed.

Inn of the Rockies
at the Historic Alma House
B&B $$

(☑ 970-387-5336, toll-free 800-267-5336; www.innoftherockies.com; 220 E 10th St; r $129-173; 🅿😊❄) Opened by a local named Alma in 1898, this inn has nine unique rooms furnished with Victorian antiques. The hospitality is first-rate and its New Orleans–inspired breakfasts, served in a chandelier-lit dining room, merit special mention. Cheaper rates are available without breakfast. There's also a garden hot tub for soaking after a long day.

Wyman Hotel
B&B $$

(☑ 877-504-5272; www.thewyman.com; 1371 Greene St; d from $175; ☺ closed Nov; 😊🛜) A handsome sandstone on the National Register of Historic Places, this just-revamped 1902 building offers sleek rooms with muted colors and a fine-tuned minimalist touch. It's a stylish alternative to the usual bric-a-brac approach. Check out the historic caboose alongside a gravel patio out back.

Red Mountain
Motel & RV Park
MOTEL, CAMPGROUND $$

(☑ 970-382-5512, toll-free 800-970-5512; www.redmtmotelrvpk.com; 664 Greene St; motel r from $80, cabins from $70, RV/tent sites $43/27; 🅿😊🛜🐾) This year-round operation covers everything from tent camping and RV facilities to cabins and motel rooms. The tiny log cabins stay warm and make good use of their limited space with a double bed, a bunk, a tiny TV and a fully outfitted kitchenette. The managers are friendly and keen to make sure guests and customers have a good time.

Also on offer are Jeep and ATV hire and guided tours, snowmobiling, fishing and hunting. The river, with good fishing, is just a few minutes' walk away. Pet-friendly.

Bent Elbow
HOTEL $$

(☑ 970-387-5775, toll-free 877-387-5775; www.thebent.com; 1114 Blair St; d $132-152; 🅿🛜) Located on notorious Blair St, these creaky rooms once served as a bordello. For what you get these days, prices are a little steep, but the decoration is pleasingly quaint and Western. Dine on okay Western fare at the restaurant, a cheerful dining room with a gorgeous old wood shotgun bar.

🍴 Eating

Grand Restaurant & Saloon
AMERICAN $$

(☑ 970-387-5527; 1219 Greene St; mains $8-26; ☺ 11am-3pm May-Oct, occasional dinners 5-9pm; 🚗) Stick with the burgers and club sandwiches at this atmospheric eatery. The player piano and historic decor are a big draw. The full bar is well patronised by locals and visitors alike.

Handlebars
AMERICAN $$

(☑ 970-387-5395; www.handlebarssilverton.com; 117 W 13th St; mains $10-22; ☺ 10:30am-9pm

May-Oct;) Steeped in Wild West kitsch, this place serves worthy baby-back ribs basted in a secret BBQ sauce, and other Western fare. The decor, a mishmash of old mining artifacts, mounted animal heads and cowboy memorabilia, gives this place a ramshackle museum-meets-garage-sale feel. After dinner, kick it up on the dance floor to the sounds of live rock and country music.

⚲ Drinking & Nightlife

★ Rum Bar
BAR

(☑ 970-769-8551; www.silvertonrumbar.com; 1309 Greene St; mains $6-14; ⊙ 11am-2am) This regional favorite delivers rum bliss in a spacious minimalist bar on Greene St. On a summer day, score a seat on the rooftop deck. Bartenders here can talk you into anything, crafting exotic cocktails with homemade syrups and award-winning rum. Note: low-season hours change.

Avalanche Brewing Co
PUB

(☑ 970-387-5282; www.avalanchebrewing.com; 1067 Blair St; ⊙ 11am-9pm Mon, Thu & Fri, to 10pm Sat & Sun) In a cute blue cottage fenced by cast off skis, this diminutive pub does its own microbrews (not brewed on-site) and pizzas.

❶ Tourist Information

Silverton Chamber of Commerce & Visitor Center (☑ 970-387-5654, toll-free 800-752-4494; www.silvertoncolorado.com; 414 Greene St; ⊙ 9am-5pm; ☀) provides information about the town and surrounds.

❶ Getting There & Away

Silverton is on Hwy 550 midway between Montrose, about 60 miles to the north, and Durango, some 48 miles to the south.

Other than private car, the only way to get to and from Silverton is by using the Durango and Silverton Narrow Gauge Railroad (p275), or the private buses that run its return journeys.

Durango

☑ 970 / POP 17,600 / ELEV 6580FT

An archetypal old Colorado mining town, Durango is a regional darling that's nothing short of delightful. Its graceful hotels, Victorian-era saloons and tree-lined streets of sleepy bungalows invite you to pedal around soaking up all the good vibes. There is plenty to do outdoors. Style-wise, Durango is torn between its ragtime past and a cool, cutting-edge future where townie bikes, caffeine and farmers markets rule.

The town's historic central precinct is home to boutiques, bars, restaurants and theater halls. Foodies will revel in the innovative organic and locavore fare that is making it one of the best places to eat in the state.

But there's also interesting galleries and live music that, combined with a relaxed and congenial local populace, make it a great place to visit. Durango is also an ideal base for exploring the enigmatic ruins at Mesa Verde National Park, 35 miles to the west.

⚹ Activities

All sorts of outdoor activities can be arranged in this hub for travel and soft adventure. Listen for the train drivers riding the steam whistles of the locomotives traveling the famous 1882 Durango & Silverton Narrow Gauge Railroad, issuing plumes of steam as they pull into the town's historic railyards.

★ Durango & Silverton Narrow Gauge Railroad
RAIL

(☑ 970-247-2733; www.durangotrain.com; 479 Main Ave; return adult/child 4-11yr from $89/55; ⊙ May-Oct; ☀) Riding the Durango & Silverton Narrow Gauge Railroad is a Durango must. These vintage steam locomotives have been making the scenic 45-mile trip north to Silverton (3½ hours each way) for more than 125 years. The dazzling journey allows two hours for exploring Silverton. This trip operates only from May through October. Check online for different winter options.

Duranglers
FISHING

(☑ 970-385-4081, toll-free 800-347-4346; www.duranglers.com; 923 Main Ave; 1-/2-person day trip $375/425) It won't put the trout on your hook, but Duranglers will do everything to bring you to that gilded moment, serving beginners to experts.

Big Corral Riding Stable
HORSEBACK RIDING

(☑ 970-884-9235; www.vallecitolakeoutfitter.com; 17716 County Rd 501, Bayfield) Highly recommended by locals, this outfitter does day rides and overnight horseback camping for the whole family in the gorgeous Weminuche Wilderness. If you're short on time, try the two-hour breakfast ride (including sausage, pancakes and cowboy coffee) with views of Vallecito Lake. Located 26 miles northeast of Durango.

Soaring Tree Top Adventures ZIPLINE
(☑ 970-769-2357; www.soaringcolorado.com; $529; ☝) If taking the train to Silverton seems like a small adventure, stop along the way for the longest ziplining course in the US. The 27 zip lines range up to 1400 feet in length, and run across the Animas River with views of the San Juans. There's no access by road, but the cost includes train travel in a special deluxe car.

Durango Rivertrippers RAFTING
(☑ 970-259-0289, toll-free 800-292-2885; www.durangorivertrippers.com; 720 Main Ave; 2hr trip adult/child $39/32; ☝) This family-operated outfit is the oldest accredited rafting operator in Durango and highly reputed. It offers various river-rafting trips on the Delores and Animas Rivers, from two-hour family runs to six-day wilderness adventures.

Purgatory SNOW SPORTS
(☑ 970-247-9000; www.purgatoryresort.com; 1 Skier Pl; lift tickets adult/child from $89/55; ☉ mid-Nov–Mar; ☝) Durango's winter highlight is 25 miles north on US 550. The resort offers 1200 skiable acres of varying difficulty, and boasts 260in of snow per year. Two terrain parks offer plenty of opportunities for snowboarders to catch big air. Check local grocery stores and newspapers for promotions and two-for-one lift tickets and other specials before purchasing directly from the ticket window.

Mild to Wild Rafting RAFTING
(☑ 970-247-4789, toll-free 800-567-6745; www.mild2wildrafting.com; 50 Animas View Dr; trips from $59; ☉ 9am-5pm; ☝) In spring and summer white-water rafting is one of the most popular sports in Durango. Mild to Wild Rafting is one of numerous companies around town offering rafting trips on the Animas River. Beginners should check out the one-hour introduction to rafting, while the more adventurous (and experienced) can run the upper Animas, which boasts Class III to V rapids.

Trimble Spa & Natural Hot Springs SPRING, MASSAGE
(☑ 970-247-0111, toll-free 877-811-7111; www.trimblehotsprings.com; 6475 County Rd 203; day pass adult/child $19/13; ☉ 9am-9pm Sun-Thu, to 10pm Fri & Sat; ☝) If you need a pampering massage or just a soak in some natural hot springs after hitting the slopes or mountain-bike trails, this is the place. Qualified massage therapists can work out those knotted muscles and tired limbs with treatments ranging from acupressure to trigger-point myotherapy. Five miles north of Durango.

Phone or check the website for last-minute specials, which sometimes include two-for-one deals and other discounts.

★★ Festivals & Events

San Juan Brewfest BEER
(http://sanjuanbrewfest.com; Buckley Park; $30; ☉ late Aug) Showcasing 30-odd specialist brewers from Durango, around Colorado and interstate, this annual festival is a highlight. Official judging takes place late in the afternoon but all attendees (must be aged 21 and over to taste) get to vote for the San Juan Brewfest's People's Choice award. There are bands and food and a carnival atmosphere.

🛏 Sleeping

After rural southwestern Colorado, Durango is the jackpot for lodgings with something for most budgets.

Siesta Motel MOTEL $
(☑ 970-247-0741; www.durangosiestamotel.com; 3475 N Main Ave; d from $85; ℗☍☀☎) This family-owned motel is one of the town's cheaper options – sparkling clean and spacious but admittedly dated. If you're self-catering, there's a courtyard with a barbecue grill.

★ Rochester House HOTEL $$
(☑ 970-385-1920, toll-free 800-664-1920; www.rochesterhotel.com; 721 E 2nd Ave; d $169-229; ☍☀☎☎) Influenced by old Westerns (movie posters and marquee lights adorn the hallways), the Rochester is a little bit of old Hollywood in the new West. Rooms are spacious, with high ceilings. Two formal sitting rooms, where you're served cookies, and a breakfast room in an old train car, are other perks at this pet-friendly establishment.

Check out the free summer concert series on Wednesdays at 4:30pm, in the courtyard.

General Palmer Hotel HOTEL $$
(☑ 970-247-4747, toll-free 800-523-3358; www.generalpalmer.com; 567 Main Ave; d $165-275; ☀@☎) With turn-of-the century elegance, this 1898 Victorian has a damsel's taste, with pewter four-post beds, floral prints and teddies on every bed. Rooms are small but elegant, and if you tire of TV, there's a collection of board games at the front desk. Check out the cozy library and the relaxing solarium.

Adobe Inn
MOTEL **$$**
(☑970-247-2743; www.durangohotels.com; 2178 Main Ave; d $120; ⊜❄@🖘) Locally voted the best-value lodging, this friendly motel gets the job done with clean, decent rooms and friendly service. You might even be able to talk staff into giving their best rate if you arrive late at night. Check out the Durango tip sheet.

Strater Hotel
HOTEL **$$**
(☑970-247-4431; www.strater.com; 699 Main Ave; d $185-269; ⊜❄@🖘) The past lives large in this historical Durango hotel with walnut antiques, hand-stenciled wallpapers and relics ranging from a Stradivarius violin to a gold-plated Winchester. Rooms lean toward the romantic, with comfortable beds amid antiques, crystal and lace. The boast-worthy staff go out of their way to assist with inquiries.

The hot tub is a romantic plus (reserved by the hour), as is the summertime melodrama (theater) the hotel runs. In winter rates drop by more than 50%, making it a virtual steal. Look online.

★ Antlers on the Creek
B&B **$$$**
(☑970-259-1565; www.antlersonthecreek.com; 999 Lightner Creek Rd; r from $249; 🅿🖘) Tuck yourself into this peaceful creekside setting surrounded by sprawling lawns and cottonwoods and you may never want to leave. Between the spacious main house and the carriage house there are seven tasteful rooms with jetted tubs, plush bed linens and gas fireplaces. There's also a decadent three-course breakfast and hot tub in the outdoor gazebo. It's open year-round.

✗ Eating
This foodie town has options ranging from Western pub fare to exquisite fine dining.

★ James Ranch
MARKET **$**
(☑970-385-9143; www.jamesranch.net; 33800 US Hwy 550; mains $5-18; ⊙11am-7pm Mon-Sat) A must for those road-tripping the San Juan Skyway, the family-run James Ranch, 10 miles out of Durango, features a market and an outstanding farmstand grill featuring the farm's own organic grass-fed beef and fresh produce. Steak sandwiches and fresh cheese melts with caramelized onions rock. Kids dig the goats.

Burger and band nights are held every Thursday from July to October. There's also yoga hosted on the terraces in summer. A two-hour farm tour ($25) is held several times per week in summer.

★ Cream Bean Berry
ICE CREAM **$**
(☑970-903-1300; http://creambeanberry.com; 1021 Main Ave; ice cream $4; ⊙noon-9pm) Handmade, organic and local, the artful frozen treats created here taste like happiness. It's also inventive – with flavors, some seasonal, like salted caramel, beet poppyseed and peach cardamom. It's the creation of a journalist who grabbed inspiration sampling the *helados* of Mexico.

Living Tree
HEALTH FOOD **$**
(☑970-286-0227; www.thelivingtreesaladbar.com; 680 Main Ave; mains $7-12; ⊙10am-8pm; ☑) If oversized salads made to order and kombucha on tap sound good, you've found your spot in the crowded Durango restaurant scene. There's a rotating menu of fermented foods and organic greens to boot.

Doughworks
BREAKFAST **$**
(☑970-247-1610; www.durangodoughworks.com; 2653 Main Ave; mains $8-11; ⊙6am-2pm) For mammoth breakfasts or diner-style lunch, this busy hub by the high school has your back. A brisk takeout business offers bagels and doughnuts, with about a dozen self-serve coffee stations to keep you caffeinated. Or grab a booth and peruse the large menu. For some kick, add the homemade green chili to a burrito or egg sandwich.

Durango Diner
DINER **$**
(☑970-247-9889; www.durangodiner.com; 957 Main Ave; mains $7-18; ⊙6am-2pm Mon-Sat, to 1pm Sun; ☑🖘) To watch Gary work the grill in this lovable greasy spoon is to be in the presence of greatness. Backed by a staff of button-cute waitresses, Gary's fluid, graceful wielding of a Samurai spatula turns out downright monstrous plates of eggs, smothered potatoes and plate-sized French toast. The best diner in the state? No doubt.

Homeslice
PIZZA **$**
(☑970-259-5551; www.homeslicedelivers.com; 441 E College Dr; slice $5; ⊙11am-10pm) Locals pile into this no-frills pizza place for thick pies with bubbly crust, and Sriracha sauce on the side. It has gluten-free crust options and salads too, plus patio seating.

Olde Tymers Café
BURGERS **$**
(☑970-259-2990; www.otcdgo.com; 1000 Main Ave; mains $8-13; ⊙11am-10pm; ☑🖘) Voted Durango's best burger by the local paper, Olde

Durango

100 m
0.05 miles

Animas River

Animas Brewing (0.5mi);
Durango Public Library (0.9mi)

San Juan Brewfest
(160yd)

E 11th St

Camino Del Rio

550

Narrow Guage Ave

Main Ave

W 10th St

E 10th St

W 9th St

E 9th St

W 8th St

E 8th St

W 7th St

E 7th St

Main Ave

Narrow Guage Ave

E 2nd Ave

San Juan-Rio Grande
National Forest
Headquarters (1mi)

W College Dr

E College Dr

Homeslice (0.1mi);
Greyhound Bus Station (0.5mi)

E 5th St

Gazpacho (166yd)

7

14

9
20

11

1

18

8

22

3

17

5

6

13

12

15

16
19

4

21

10

2

Durango

Activities, Courses & Tours
1 Duranglers...C3
2 Durango & Silverton Narrow Gauge
   Railroad..B7
3 Durango Rivertrippers C5

Sleeping
4 General Palmer Hotel............................B6
5 Rochester House D5
6 Strater Hotel...C5

Eating
7 Cream Bean Berry..................................D1
8 Cyprus Cafe...D5
9 Durango Diner..C2
10 East by Southwest...............................C6
11 El Moro C2
12 Jean Pierre Bakery B6

13 Living Tree...C5
14 Olde Tymers Café...................................D2
15 Ore House...C6

Drinking & Nightlife
16 Bookcase & the Barber C6
   Diamond Belle Saloon ....(see 6)
17 Eno...D5
18 Steamworks Brewing.............................D4

Entertainment
   Henry Strater Theatre ....(see 6)

Shopping
19 2nd Avenue Sports................................D6
20 Maria's Bookshop...................................D2
21 Pedal the Peaks.....................................C6
22 Sante..C5

Tymers is popular with the college crowd, especially on Monday's $5.50-burger nights. Well-priced American classics are served at cozy booths under pressed-tin ceilings in a big open dining room or on the patio outside. Ask about the cheap daily specials.

★ **El Moro**   GASTROPUB **$$**
(☑970-259-5555; www.elmorotavern.com; 945 Main Ave; mains $10-30; ⊙11am-midnight Mon-Fri, 9am-midnight Sat & Sun) There are two reasons to come here: drinking damn good custom cocktails at the bar or dining on some innovative small plates like Korean fried cauliflower, cheeses, housemade sausages and fresh salads. It's ground zero for Durango hipsters but really aims to please all.

Cyprus Cafe   MEDITERRANEAN **$$**
(☑970-385-6884; www.cypruscafe.com; 725 E 2nd Ave; mains $18-28; ⊙11:30am-2:30pm & 5-9pm Mon-Sat; 🐾) ✎ Nothing says summer like live jazz on the patio at this little Mediterranean cafe, a favorite of the foodie press. With a farm-to-table philosophy, it offers locally raised vegetables, wild seafood and natural meats. Favorites include warm duck salad with almonds and oranges, and Colorado trout with quinoa pilaf.

East by Southwest   FUSION, SUSHI **$$**
(☑970-247-5533; www.eastbysouthwest.com; 160 E College Dr; sushi $4-15, mains $12-28; ⊙11:30am-3pm & 5-10pm Mon-Sat, 5-10pm Sun; ✎🐾) ✎ Low-lit but vibrant, this place is packed with locals on date night. Skip the standards for goosebump-good sashimi with jalapeño or rolls with mango and wasabi honey. Fish

is fresh and endangered species are off the menu. Fusion plates include Thai, Vietnamese and Indonesian, well matched with creative martinis or sake cocktails. The best deals are the happy-hour food specials (5pm to 6:30pm).

Kennebec Café   AMERICAN **$$**
(☑970-247-5674; www.kennebeccafe.com; 4 County Rd 124, Hesperus; mains $12-34; ⊙11am-3pm & 5-9pm Tue-Fri, 8am-3pm & 5-9pm Sat & Sun) This romantic countryside cafe flaunts Euro style with American overtones. Think tasty and creative – chef Miguel Carrillo serves up Duck Two Ways (seared with a pomegranate glaze) and poblano chilies stuffed with strip steak. Weekend brunch makes playful twists on old favorites, best enjoyed on the patio. It's located in Hesperus, 10 miles west of Durango on Highway 140.

Jean Pierre Bakery   FRENCH, BAKERY **$$**
(☑970-247-7700; www.jeanpierrebakery.com; 601 Main Ave; lunch mains $11-17, dinner mains $17-25; ⊙8am-9pm; ✎🐾) A charming patisserie serving mouthwatering delicacies made from scratch. Breakfasts are all-out while dinner is a much more formal affair. Prices are dear, but the soup-and-sandwich lunch special with a sumptuous French pastry (we recommend the sticky pecan roll) is a deal.

Gazpacho   MEXICAN **$$**
(☑970-259-9494; www.gazpachodurango.com; 431 E 2nd Ave; mains $11-28; ⊙11:30am-10pm Mon-Sat, to 9pm Sun; ✎🐾) A crowd pleaser, this tiled quasi–New Mexican restaurant dishes up local beans, savory *carne*

adovada (red chili pork) and green chili cheeseburgers. Families love it and the friendly bar is a good spot to grab a margarita and fresh, hot sopaipillas. Also has good gluten-free and vegetarian options, like the vegan burger piled high with smoked chilies.

Ore House
STEAK $$$

(☑ 970-247-5707; www.orehouserestaurant.com; 147 E College Dr; mains $25-75; ⊙ 5-10pm; 🚼) The best steakhouse in town, with food served in casual and rustic environs. Order a hand-cut aged steak, or try the steak, crab leg and lobster combo known as the Ore House Grubsteak, easily serving two people. The meat is natural and antibiotic-free, and organic vegetables are the norm. There's also a large wine cellar.

🍷 Drinking & Nightlife

Durango knows how to party. There's a heap of live music venues and bars with a focus on brewpubs, apt for its setting as a university town.

★ Bookcase & the Barber
COCKTAIL BAR

(☑ 970-764-4123; www.bookcaseandbarber.com; 601 E 2nd Ave, suite B; ⊙ 2pm-midnight) This modern speakeasy may be Durango's sexiest nightcap, hidden behind a heavy bookcase, with exquisite cocktails worth the $12 price tag and a dimly lit allure. Enter via the barbershop, but you'll need the password (found somewhere on their Facebook page). Try a spicy paloma celosa (jealous dove), a perfect tease of tequila, grapefruit and ancho chili

★ Ska Brewing Company
BREWERY

(☑ 970-247-5792; www.skabrewing.com; 225 Girard St; mains $9-15; ⊙ 9am-9pm Mon-Fri, 11am-9pm Sat, to 7pm Sun) Big on flavor and variety, these are the best beers in town. Although the small, friendly tasting-room bar was once mainly a production facility, over the years it's steadily climbed in the popularity charts. Today it is usually jam-packed with friends meeting for an after-work beer.

Despite the hype, the place remains surprisingly laid-back and relaxed. Ska does weekly BBQs with live music and free food; call for dates – they are never fixed.

81301 Coffee
COFFEE

(☑ 970-385-1941; www.81301coffee.com; 3101 Main Ave #1; ⊙ 6:30am-6pm; 🛜) The best brew in Durango hails from this small batch roaster. Stop by for a latte and homemade pastry on your way up valley or grab a bag of beans to brighten up your road trip.

Eno
CAFE, WINE BAR

(☑ 970-385-0105; 723 E 2nd Ave; ⊙ 11am-9pm Mon-Sat) Serving excellent pour-over coffee by day and dangerous cocktails at night, this tiny house is an intimate spot to socialize. The award-winning 'alpenglow' pairs local rum with muddled cucumber, mint and hibiscus. Highlights include deviled eggs and the Colorado cheese plate, though big appetites should go elsewhere. The later happy hour (8pm to 10pm) makes it a good after-dinner spot.

Steamworks Brewing
BREWERY

(☑ 970-259-9200; www.steamworksbrewing.com; 801 E 2nd Ave; ⊙ 11am-midnight Mon-Thu, to 2am Fri-Sun) Industrial meets ski lodge at this popular microbrewery, with high sloping rafters and metal pipes. It has a large bar area, as well as a separate dining room with a Cajun-influenced menu. At night there are DJs and live music.

Animas Brewing
MICROBREWERY

(☑ 970-403-8850; www.animasbrewing.com; 1560 E 2nd Ave; ⊙ 11am-9pm Tue-Thu & Sun, to 10pm Fri & Sat, 4-9pm Mon) If you so happen to be biking the creek path, stop by this adjacent brew pub packed with locals. There's a pleasant patio and garlic hot wings that beg a cold pint (or two).

Durango Brewing Co
BREWERY

(☑ 970-247-3396; www.durangobrewing.com; 3000 Main Ave; ⊙ tap room 11am-10pm Mon-Fri, 10am-10pm Sat & Sun) Newly revamped with a pleasant outdoor deck, this place pleases all – including serious beer fans who concentrate on the brews. There are taproom tastings and it's open seven days a week.

Diamond Belle Saloon
BAR

(☑ 970-376-7150; www.strater.com; 699 Main Ave; ⊙ 11am-late) A rowdy corner of the historic Strater Hotel, this elegant old-time bar has waitresses flashing Victorian-era fishnets and live ragtime that packs out-of-town visitors into standing room only at happy hour (4pm to 6pm). The food isn't an attraction. Also in Strater, the Office serves cocktails in an upscale and much more low-key atmosphere.

☆ Entertainment

Henry Strater Theatre
LIVE MUSIC

(☑ 970-375-7160; www.henrystratertheatre.com; 699 Main Ave) Internationally renowned, producing old-world music-hall shows, live bands, comedy, community theater and more for nearly 50 years.

Shopping

Maria's Bookshop BOOKS
(☑970-247-1438; www.mariasbookshop.com; 960 Main Ave; ⊙9am-9pm) Maria's is a good general bookstore – independently owned and well stocked. It does e-reader orders too.

Sante DISPENSARY
(☑970-375-2837; www.santecolorado.com; 742 ½ Main Ave; ⊙9am-9pm Sun-Wed, to 9:45pm Thu-Sat) This medical and recreational marijuana dispensary is considered one of Colorado's best.

Pedal the Peaks SPORTS & OUTDOORS
(☑970-259-6880; www.pedalthepeaks.biz; 598b Main Ave; all-day bike rental $25-85; ⊙9am-6pm Mon-Sat, to 5pm Sun; ⊕) ⦿ This specialist bike store offers the works from mountain- and road-bike sales and rentals to custom-worked cycles, trail maps and accessories. The staff are all hard-core riders, and their friendly advice and local knowledge are second to none.

2nd Avenue Sports SPORTS & OUTDOORS
(☑970-247-4511; www.2ndavesports.com; 600 E 2nd Ave; ⊙9am-6pm Mon-Sat, to 5pm Sun) Skiing and extensive cycling and mountain-biking gear for sale and rental.

❶ Tourist Information

Durango Public Library (☑970-375-3380; www.durangopubliclibrary.org; 1900 E 3rd Ave; ⊙9am-8pm Mon-Wed, 10am-5:30pm Thu, 9am-5:30pm Fri & Sat; ⊛) A handy resource for regional information.
Durango Welcome Center (☑970-247-3500, toll-free 800-525-8855; www.durango.org; 802 Main Ave; ⊙9am-7pm Sun-Thu, to 9pm Fri & Sat; ⊛) An excellent information center located downtown. There is a second **visitor center** (☑800-525-8855; www.durango.org; 111 S Camino del Rio) south of town, at the Santa Rita exit from US Hwy 550.
San Juan-Rio Grande National Forest Headquarters (☑970-247-4874; www.fs.fed.us/r2/sanjuan; 15 Burnett Ct; ⊙9am-5pm Mon-Sat) Located a half-mile west of Durango off US Hwy 160. Offers camping and hiking information and maps.

❶ Getting There & Away

Durango lies at the junction of US Hwys 160 and 550, 42 miles east of Cortez, 49 miles west of Pagosa Springs and 190 miles north of Albuquerque in New Mexico.
Durango-La Plata County Airport (DRO; ☑970-247-8143; www.flydurango.com; 1000 Airport Rd) The regional airport is 18 miles southwest of Durango via US Hwy 160 and Hwy 172. Both United and American Airlines have direct flights to Denver; American flies to Dallas-Fort Worth and Phoenix.
Durango Transit (☑970-259-5438; www.getarounddurango.com; 250 W 8th St; fares $1-2) Runs local bus routes around the city and to nearby destinations.
Greyhound Bus Station (☑970 259 2755; www.greyhound.com; 250 E 8th Ave) Serves the region and beyond.

❶ Getting Around

All Durango buses are fitted with bicycle racks. The **Main Avenue Trolley** (www.durangotransit.com; Main Ave; fare $1; ⊙7am-10pm Jun-Aug, to 7pm Sept-May) loops downtown every 20 minutes along Main Ave to the north end of town at Animas View Dr and Hwy 550.

Pagosa Springs

 / POP 1838 / ELEV 7126FT
Pagosa Springs may appear to serve up a large slice of humble pie, but it has the bragging rights to the biggest snowfall in Colorado – at Wolf Creek Ski Area – nearby. Pagosa, a Ute term for 'boiling water', refers to the other local draw: hot springs. Natural thermals provide heat for some residents. Sunny and cheerful, it has become a popular spot for retirees seeking warmer climes.

⦿ Sights

Weminuche Wilderness Area NATURE RESERVE
Named for a band of the Ute tribe, the Weminuche Wilderness Area is the most extensive wilderness in Colorado, with an area of more than 700 sq miles. The Weminuche extends west along the Continental Divide from Wolf Creek Pass to the Animas River near Silverton. Along the Continental Divide National Scenic Trail (USFS Trail 813), you will find many secluded hiking opportunities as the trail travels 80 miles of the Weminuche Wilderness between Wolf Creek Pass and Stony Pass.

One trail of particular interest leads to an undeveloped natural hot spring west of the Divide. To reach **Wolf Creek Pass Hot Spring** take USFS Trail 560 west from the Divide, descending more than 6 miles through the Beaver Creek drainage to the

West Fork headwaters of the San Juan River. The spring, with more than 100°F (38°C) water, is to the right on USFS Trail 561, about half a mile above the trail junction.

Visitors should have maps of both the Rio Grande and San Juan National Forests. Ranger stations for the Rio Grande National Forest are in either Del Norte or Creede; the nearest San Juan National Forest ranger station is in Pagosa Springs. From June to July of 2013, the West Fork Complex fire, caused by lightning strikes and strong winds, burned over 100,000 acres, some within this area.

Chimney Rock
Archaeological Area   ARCHAEOLOGICAL SITE
(☑ off-season 970-264-2287, visitor cabin 970-883-5359; www.chimneyrockco.org; Hwy 151; guided tours adult/child $12/5; ☉ 9am-4:30pm mid-May–late Sep, additional evening hours for special events; ♿) Designated an Archaeological Area and National Historic Site in 1970, these 4000 acres within the San Juan National Forest hold remains of 100 permanent structures at the base of two large red-rock buttes. Like the architects of the elaborate structures in Chaco Canyon – with which this community was connected – the people of the Chimney Rock Archaeological Area were dedicated astronomers and this was a place of spiritual significance.

Today the rock monuments remain, though the thriving religious and commercial center has been reduced to sketches in stone. The largest pair of buildings, the Great Kiva and Great House, are impressive examples of Chacoan architecture.

Fred Harman Art Museum
& the Red Ryder Roundup   MUSEUM
(☑ 970-731-5785; www.harmanartmuseum.com; 85 Harman Park Dr; adult/child $3/0.50; ☉ 10:30am-5pm Mon-Sat; 🅿 ♿) The Red Ryder's image might be lost on today's whippersnappers, but Fred Harman's comic book hero was born in Pagosa Springs, and today Harman's home is a small museum. It's a kitschy and off-beat roadside attraction, but Harman himself is often on hand to show you around his studio.

Pagosa Springs' biggest annual event is the Red Ryder Roundup, a carnival with a rodeo and art show that ends in fireworks. It's held near 4th of July.

🏃 Activities

★ Springs Spa   HOT SPRINGS
(☑ 970-264-4168; www.pagosahotsprings.com; 165 Hot Springs Blvd; adult/child from $30/17;

☉ 7am-midnight; ♿ 🧖) These glorious pools along the San Juan River have healing, mineral-rich waters from the Great Pagosa Aquifer, the largest and deepest hot mineral spring in the world. Artificial pools look fairly natural, and the views are lovely. Temperatures vary from 83°F to 111°F (28°C to 44°C).

Wolf Creek Ski Area   SNOW SPORTS
(☑ 970-264-5639; www.wolfcreekski.com; US 160; lift ticket adult/child $66/37; ☉ Nov–mid-Apr; ♿) Boasting Colorado's highest annual snowfall, little old Wolf Creek Ski Area offers a white-carpet ride without comparison. Steep and deep, it's awesome for advanced skiers and boarders, with waist-high powder after a big storm blows through.

Located 25 miles north of Pagosa Springs on US Hwy 160, this family-owned ski area gets over 465in of light and dry powder per year – that's 150in more than Vail. Eight lifts service 70 trails, from wide-open bowls to steep tree glades. The on-site ski school has lessons for beginners and children.

For cross-country skiing, many backcountry and groomed trails that lead into quiet, pristine forest are available. It's some of the most remote Nordic skiing in the state. Contact the USFS Pagosa Ranger Station (p283) for details.

Long considered a Colorado secret, its distance from major airports and big urban areas has reinforced its happy isolation. There are no lodgings on-site, so it's not a destination ski area. Your best bet is to stay in Pagosa Springs, on the west side of the pass, or South Fork, on the east.

Pagosa Outside   RAFTING
(☑ 970-264-4202; www.pagosaoutside.com; 350 Pagosa St; full day Upper Piedra $150; ☉ 10am-6pm, reduced hours in winter; ♿) Check out this outfitter's springtime white-water trips (class III) on the San Juan and Piedra Rivers. The most exciting travels Mesa Canyon, ideal to sight eagles and other wildlife. Rivers mellow in summer and the focus turns to river tubing ($15 for two hours), mountain-biking trips, including a thrilling singletrack route at Turkey Creek, and equipment rentals ($35 per day).

🛏 Sleeping

Since the springs are a year-round draw, hotels in the area hold their rates fairly steady. A number of motels and new hotels sprawl out from the town center on US 160. Usually the equation is fairly straightforward:

the further away from the hot springs, the better the deal.

Alpine Inn Motel
MOTEL **$**

(☑970-731-4005; www.alpineinnofpagosasprings. com; 8 Solomon Dr; d $80; P ❄ @ 🛜) A converted chain motel, this roadside option is excellent value. The rooms, each with dark carpet and balconies, are a standard size, but the owners are great guides to the local area and there's a deluxe continental breakfast.

★ Fireside Inn Cabins
CABIN **$$**

(☑888-264-9204; www.firesidecabins.com; 1600 E Hwy 160; cabins from $155; P 🐾 ❄ 🛜) Hands down our favorite place in town – each log cabin comes with a Weber grill and planters of wildflowers. Pine interiors have immaculate kitchenettes, quilts and flat-screen TVs. The San Juan River flows through the property. Equestrians can use the corral, and the games available at the central office are great for families.

Springs Resort & Spa
SPA HOTEL **$$**

(☑800-225-0934; www.pagosahotsprings.com; 165 Hot Springs Blvd; r from $209; ❄ 🛜 🏊 🐾) 🌿 This classic hot springs resort is revamped to serve a growing public. The hotel features a spa, offers ski packages and welcomes pets. The cheapest rooms are nothing special, while sprawling deluxe rooms feature thicker mattresses, higher thread-count sheets and kitchenette. The newest addition is a LEED-certified luxury building, called the Ecoluxe Hotel, with plenty of sheen and green credentials.

🍴 Eating & Drinking

Pagosa Baking Company
BAKERY **$**

(☑970-0264-9348; www.pagosabakingcompany. com; 238 Pagosa St; rolls & muffins $3; ⊘7am-2pm Mon-Tue, to 6pm Wed-Sun; 🚼) It's dead charming: they use all local ingredients and set up a space to chat over coffee in the front room of a bright yellow Victorian. Breakfast burritos, good muffins and quiche make it busy in the morning. And they make a bread of the day.

Pagosa Brewing Company
PUB FOOD **$**

(☑970-731-2739; www.pagosabrewing.com; 118 N Pagosa Blvd; mains $7-15; ⊘11am-10pm; 🚼) Brewmaster Tony Simmons is a professional beer judge, and the Poor Richard's Ale is brewed according to historical standards – the corn and molasses mix is inspired by the tipple of Ben Franklin. After a few, move on to a menu of made-from-scratch pub food, at this, Pagosa's fun dinner spot.

★ Riff Raff Brewing Co
MICROBREWERY

(☑970-264-4677; 274 Pagosa St; ⊘11am-10pm) 🌿 Pagosa's thermal waters heat the building and provide the spring water for the beers brewed on-site. But don't come just for the eco-credentials. There's live music, locally raised yak burgers and pints of green chile ale. Sunny days were made for sprawling on the shady deck with views of the main drag.

ℹ Tourist Information

Pagosa Springs Area Chamber of Commerce (☑970-264-2360; www.visitpagosasprings. com; 105 Hot Springs Blvd; ⊘9am-5pm Mon-Fri) A large visitor center across the bridge from US Hwy 160 with information on lodging, activities and restaurants.

USFS Pagosa Ranger Station (☑970-264-2268; 180 Pagosa St; ⊘8am-4:30pm Mon-Fri) Recreation resource with info on the San Juan National Forest.

ℹ Getting There & Away

Pagosa Springs sits east of Durango, on US 160 at the junction with US 84 south to New Mexico. The historic downtown, with most of the visitor services, is near the intersection of Hot Springs Blvd and US 160. Condos and vacation rentals flank a winding series of roads 2 miles to the west, over a small rise. The town and its surrounding areas are best accessed with your own vehicle.

South Fork

☑719 / POP 370 / ELEV 8300FT

The appeal of visiting South Fork is hardly evident in the low-slung stretch of buildings along US 160, 31 miles west of Monte Vista. But its position at the confluence of the South Fork and Rio Grande Rivers makes it an excellent base from which to fish the Gold Medal waters of the Rio Grande.

In ski season, South Fork is a more affordable lodging alternative than Pagosa Springs for skiers at Wolf Creek. Exceptional backcountry hiking in the Weminuche Wilderness of the Rio Grande National Forest, Colorado's largest pristine area, is readily accessible from trailheads near South Fork. An abundance of nearby campgrounds also attracts vacationers who want to enjoy a forested mountain setting.

🅾 Sights & Activities

Coller State Wildlife Area
PARK

(Hwy 149) The grassy riverbanks in the Coller State Wildlife Area attract elk, deer and moose in winter. You can see bighorn sheep throughout the year on the south-facing Palisade cliffs extending from the Coller State Wildlife Area to Wagon Wheel Gap. At the gap, golden eagles soar above the cliff faces and fish the Rio Grande.

From South Fork, follow Hwy 149 toward Creede for about 7 miles, where there's a sign on the left; turn there and you enter the area after a couple hundred yards.

Mountain Man Rafting & Tours RAFTING
(8200 Mountain Sports; ☑ 719-658-2663; www.mountainmantours.com; 30923 W Hwy 160; Rio Grande half-day adult/child $65/55) Guided mountain-bike tours and bike rentals are offered here, as well as rafting tours and equipment rental, and guided river fishing.

🛏 Sleeping

Ute Bluff Lodge MOTEL $
(☑ 719-873-5595, 800-473-0595; www.utebluff lodge.com; 27680 US Hwy 160; d from $75, cabins $75-185; ℙ ⊜ ❄) This impeccably clean hotel is the best option in town. Run by a South Carolina transplant named Debbie, the rooms have new carpet, wood paneling and a great location on the border of USFS land, where there are hiking trails. A few moderately priced cabins offer a good option for families.

Spruce Lodge B&B $
(☑ 719-873-5605, 800-228-5605; www.spruce lodges.com; 29431 US Hwy 160; r $69-99; 🛜) Bed and breakfast with shared bathroom are on offer at this woodsy lodge with a relatively plush Jacuzzi room. It's about 1 mile east of the visitors center.

Blue Creek Lodge LODGE, CABIN $
(☑ 719-658-2479; www.bluecreeklodgesouthfork. com; 11682 Hwy 149; d $67, cabins $106-243, RV sites $30) This lodge, 7 miles up the road from South Fork, is a faux-rustic B&B, restaurant and beauty salon. It's housed in a former saloon with lots of deer heads on the wall, and offers a juicy chicken-fried-steak breakfast.

Chinook Lodge & Smokehouse MOTEL $$
(☑ 888-890-9110, 719-873-9993; www.chinook lodge.net; 29666 US Hwy 160; cabins $90-155; ℙ) Carnivorous folk will appreciate this lodge and smokehouse, where copious meats are smoked on the premises (sample its amazing beef jerky). Guests stay in rustic, century-old cabins, most with handsome rock fireplaces and kitchens.

✖ Eating

Bear Claw Bakery BAKERY $
(☑ 719-580-5333; 29411 US Hwy 160; snacks $4; ⊙ 7am-2pm Mon-Sat) Sticky buns thick with cinnamon are the mainstay of this friendly, no-frills bakery, but there's plenty else to tempt a traveler.

Two Rivers BBQ BARBECUE $$
(☑ 719-657-1122; www.tworiversbbq.co; 29411 US Hwy 160; mains $9-24; ⊙ 11am-9pm; 👶) Enjoy the warm welcome of this casual eatery just off the main road. Come with an appetite: from slow-smoked brisket to half-pound green chile burgers and fried pickles, there's some serious eating to be done. Wash it down with the Trashy Blonde on tap. Also child-friendly, with a special kids' menu.

Rockaway Cafe CAFE $$
(☑ 719-873-5581; 30333 US Hwy 160; mains $14-38; ⊙ 7am-6pm; 🛜 👶) This humble, friendly diner sends out a good breakfast of big pancakes and enormous cups of coffee. For dinner, the fresh grilled trout doesn't disappoint. If you are headed into the wilderness and need to do a little planning, it also has complimentary wi-fi and a little book exchange.

❶ Tourist Information

South Fork Chamber of Commerce (☑ 719-873-5512, toll-free 800-571-0881; www.southfork.org; 29803 W Hwy 160; ⊙ 9am-5pm Mon-Fri, 10am-4pm Sat & Sun Jun-Aug) Information on outdoor activities and lodging.

❶ Getting There & Away

At South Fork, US Hwy 160 turns south from the Rio Grande toward Wolf Creek Pass 18 miles away, and Hwy 149 continues upstream 21 miles to Creede before crossing the Continental Divide to Lake City. This remote area is accessed by private vehicle.

Creede

☑ 719 / POP 400

Welcome to the mountainous middle of nowhere. Creede is an unanticipated beauty, the only incorporated city in Mineral County, which joins neighboring Hinsdale County as one of Colorado's least-populated counties: each has fewer than 900 people. Mineral County dug its wealth from the ground: underfoot are huge reserves of silver, lead and zinc. From 1988 all the silver mines here ceased operation and became tourist attractions. Today you can tour the rugged mining landscape north of town where tremendous mills cling to spectacular cliffs. Below the vertical-walled mouth of Willow Creek Canyon, narrow Creede Ave is a mix of galleries and shops in historic buildings.

For scenic beauty, the surroundings are difficult to beat. Untrammeled trails into the immense surrounding wilderness areas provide beauty and solitude, as well as access to unique sights like the bizarre volcanic spires and pinnacles of the Wheeler Geologic Area.

◉ Sights

Wheeler Geologic Area　　　NATURE RESERVE
Part of the La Garita Wilderness, the dramatic stone formations of the Wheeler Geologic Area were carved by wind and rain into volcanic tuff framed by evergreen forest. Rocks resemble rows of sharp animal teeth, and bear names like City of Gnomes, White-Shrouded Ghosts and Dante's Lost Souls. It's a spectacular and fairly strenuous full-day hike in a remote setting at 11,000ft near the Continental Divide.

Wheeler is accessible by hiking (7 miles) or via a grueling 14-mile 4WD road from Creede.

North Clear Creek Falls　　　WATERFALL
Twenty-five miles west of Creede and only 0.5 miles from signs on Hwy 149, these impressive falls are visible from an overlook on the fenced edge of a deep gorge. From the parking area, a short walk over the ridge away from the falls takes you to another viewpoint above the sheer-walled canyon with Bristol Head in the distance.

Far below your feet a metal aqueduct carries Clear Creek away from its natural course to the Santa Maria Reservoir as part of a massive effort to regulate the flow of the Rio Grande headwaters.

Creede Underground
Mining Museum　　　MUSEUM
(☑719-658-0811; www.undergroundmining museum.com; 407 N Loma Ave; adult/child $7/5; ☉10am-4pm Jun-Aug, to 3pm Sep-May, closed weekends Dec-Feb; ▦) Opened in 1992, this fascinating museum was hewn from the ground by mine workers, and the tours, which really bring home the grim reality of life in the mines, are also led by miners. It's a chilling exhibit in more ways than one: with the temperature a steady 51°F (11°C) year-round, visitors are advised to bring jackets.

Creede Historic Museum　　　MUSEUM
(☑719-658-2303; http://museumtrail.org/creede historicmuseum.asp; 17 S Main St; adult $2; ☉10am-4pm late May-early Sep) Mineral treasures attracted miners by the trainload, but this museum chronicles the more intriguing opportunists and scoundrels who arrived to take advantage of Creede's short-lived prosperity. It's housed in the former railroad depot, behind City Park.

✷ Activities

Hiking options are nearly limitless within the extensive Weminuche and La Garita Wilderness Areas on either side of the Rio Grande Valley. A good source of information if you wish to explore the Continental Divide east of Stony Pass is Dennis Gebhardt's *A Backpacking Guide to the Weminuche Wilderness*. You can rent hiking packs and tents at **San Juan Sports** (☑888-658-0851, 719-658-2359; 102 S Main St; ☉10am-5pm).

Rafting tours and equipment rental are available from Mountain Man Rafting & Tours (p284).

Rio Grande　　　RAFTING
Below Wagon Wheel Gap, scenic float trips with a few rapids and quality fishing are the primary attractions of the 20-mile run to South Fork. A good place to put in along Hwy 149 is the Goose Creek Road Bridge immediately west of the gap. During high water, rafters should beware the closely spaced railroad bridge abutments at Wagon Wheel Gap.

East Bellows Trail　　　HIKING
(Trail 790; Wheeler Geologic Area) This USFS trail is a 17-mile round-trip hike. It climbs nearly 2000ft from the Hanson's Mill campground to the base of the Wheeler geologic formations. The trail affords some great views and there are lots of places to camp along the way.

To get to the trailhead, drive southeast along Hwy 149 for slightly more than 7 miles and turn left on USFS Rd 600 (Pool Table Rd). Continue along this road for 9½ miles to Hanson's Mill campground. From Hanson's Mill there is also a 14-mile 4WD road that leads to the area.

Bachelor Loop　　　SCENIC DRIVE
Bouncing along 17-mile Bachelor Loop, a tour of the abandoned mines and town sites immediately north of Creede is a fun DIY adventure and a good way to punish the rental

car. The route offers outstanding views of La Garita Mountains (San Luis Peak is 14,014ft) and Rio Grande Valley.

Sections of the road are very narrow and steep, but not difficult, so long as the road is dry and you drive slowly. It's well sign-posted and easy to follow with a booklet ($1) from the Chamber of Commerce.

Rio Grande Angler FISHING
(☑ 719-658-2955; www.southforkanglers.com; 13 S Main St; 2hr lesson for 2 $200; ☉10am-6pm Mon-Sat Jun-Aug) Recommended for fishing supplies, information and guide services.

🛏 Sleeping

Soward Ranch RANCH $
(☑ 719-658-2295; 4698 Middle Creek Rd; cabins $126-300; ☉May-Oct) About 8 miles southwest of Creede, this beautiful centennial ranch has been operated by the same family for more than 100 years. Guests can enjoy fishing from four lakes as well as 4 miles of trout creek on the 1500-acre property. Twelve cabins range in price depending on size and amenities.

Take Hwy 149 southwest for 7 miles, turn left on Middle Creek Rd, continue for a mile and when you get to the fork in the road, bear right, following the signs to the ranch.

★ Aspen Inn INN $$
(☑ 719-658-0212; 123 N Main St; r $102-125; 🛜 🐾) A stunner, this refurbished 2nd-story hotel overlooking Main St still has the old-time scuffs from spurs on the floor. But that's all. Rooms have been revamped to let in light and show off the brickwork. Each is different, with huge nature murals, cozy ruffled bedding and high style befitting a whole other price range. Does not offer breakfast.

Creede Hotel B&B HOTEL $$
(☑ 719-658-2608; www.creedehotel.com; 120 N Main St; d $105-115) With some throwback charm, this 1892 hotel has four rooms with private bathrooms. Both the hotel and its excellent restaurant are closed October to May.

Antlers Rio Grande Lodge RANCH $$
(☑ 719-658-2423; www.antlerslodge.com; 26222 Hwy 149; d from $149, cabins from $150, RV sites $48; ☉mid-May-Oct; 🛜) Families are welcome at Antlers Ranch. Some 5 miles southwest of Creede, there's motel-style rooms and cabins on both banks of the Rio Grande. Cabins are also rented at a weekly rate and amenities include a riverside hot tub.

Creede Snowshoe Lodge MOTEL $$
(☑ 719-658-2315; www.creedesnowshoe.com; cnr 202 E 8th & Hwy 149; d $119; P 🛜 🐾) Rates at this clean, friendly place, on the southeast edge of town, include a continental breakfast and, unlike a lot of places around, it's open all year.

Wason Ranch RANCH $$$
(☑ 719-658-2413; www.wasonranch.com; 19082 Hwy 149; d $350, cabins from $325, 3-night minimum) Two miles southeast of Creede, this ranch has two-bedroom cabins equipped with kitchenettes (available May through October). Riverside cottages with three bedrooms and two baths are available year-round with a minimum stay of three nights. The ranch also offers fly-fishing lessons, fishing guides and a dory (boat).

🍴 Eating

Arps CAFE $
(☑ 719-658-2777; www.eatatarps.com; 112 N Main St; mains $9-14) Touting comfort food, Arps is a stylish cafe serving up mac 'n' cheese, fried okra, curried chicken sandwiches and thick Angus burgers. The spare decor is accented with handsome moose murals and antler decor – a modern take on the tired old Western theme. Locals and visitors love the place.

Cascada Bar & Grill TEX-MEX $$
(☑ 970-658-1033; www.cascadagrill.com; 981 La Garita St; mains $8-21; ☉8am-9pm) In an adobe-style building on the edge of town, this place serves traditional breakfasts as well as grilled specialties and usually tasty Mexican fare. Their drinks (tequila being the house spirit of choice) are known as the best in town.

ℹ Tourist Information

Creede/Mineral County Chamber of Commerce (☑ 800-327-2102, 719-658-2374; www.creede.com; 904 S Main St; ☉8am-5pm Mon-Sat Jun-Aug, from 9am Mon-Fri Dec-Feb) Friendly local information.

USFS Divide District Ranger Station (☑ 719-658-2556; cnr E 3rd St & Creede Ave; ☉8:30am-4pm Mon-Fri mid-Apr–Nov) Recreation information about Weminuche and La Garita wilderness areas, portions of the Colorado Trail and the Continental Divide Trail, Wolf Creek Ski Area, Wheeler Geologic Area and the historic mining district of Creede.

ℹ Getting There & Away

There's no public transportation here. Creede is 23 miles northwest of South Fork on the Silver

Thread National Scenic Byway, which follows Hwy 149 for 75 miles between South Fork and Lake City.

Lake City

📞 970 / POP 400 / ELEV 8671FT

It's hard to believe that the 'flyspeck' seat of Hinsdale County was once known as the Metropolis of the Mines. But back in the 1870s, while so many other mining towns would swell and dwindle with the prosperity of the lodes, Lake City boasted a population of 5000 people. Settlers built Greek and Gothic Revival buildings and tree-lined streets that reflected a nostalgia for their homes back east. Today less than a fifth of that population remains, making this remote town a quiet base for exploring the mountains.

⊙ Sights & Activities

Slumgullion Slide   LANDMARK

In AD 1270 a catastrophic earth flow moved almost 5 miles down the mountainside and dammed the Gunnison River to form Lake San Cristobal, Colorado's second-largest lake. The land is still moving, but it has slowed down, advancing between 2ft and 20ft per year. It's best viewed in the morning from Windy Point Overlook, south of Lake City off Hwy 149, at 10,600ft.

This active section of the slide, whose name comes from the yellowish mud's resemblance to the watery miner's stew, is mostly barren, and spotted in patches with forests of crooked trees. Another good view is from the top of Cannibal Plateau Trail (USFS Trail 464), the site where prospector Alfred Packer is said to have eaten his companions for dinner. The trailhead is below Slumgullion Campground, off Cebolla Creek Rd.

Hinsdale Haute Route   OUTDOORS

(📞970-944-2269; www.hinsdalehauteroute.org; yurts $110, summer per person $20) For cross-country skiing or overnight summer hiking, check out the Hinsdale Haute Route, a nonprofit that maintains sleeping yurts on the Continental Divide between Lake City and Creede. Among the niche of hut-to-hut recreation, this system has a flawless reputation for the scenery and the quality of the huts.

Even novice skiers can enjoy the 2 miles of backcountry travel from Hwy 149 to an overnight stay at the first yurt. The yurts

sleep up to eight people, and have cooking facilities. Winter rates are for the entire yurt.

Three Rivers Resort   RAFTING

(📞970-641-1303, toll-free 888-761-3474; www.3 riversresort.com; 130 County Rd 742, Almont; rafting from $50; 🚣) This place offers river-rafting trips from serene floats down the Gunnison River (suitable for all ages) to adrenaline-fueled class IV Lake Fork River runs, and everything in between. Its lodge has two- to eight-berth cabins.

🛏 Sleeping

Lake City's comfortable digs for travelers range from camping to lodges and motels.

There are a couple of private campgrounds in town, but the state and federal land nearby is a better option. Dispersed camping is available on USFS lands along Henson Creek immediately east of town. Free BLM riverside campsites are available at the Gate, 20 miles north next to Hwy 149, and at Gateview and Redbridge along Lake County Rd 25, which continues beside the river where Hwy 149 turns east from the river course.

Additional primitive campsites are available by continuing east on Cebolla Creek Rd, where rarely used trails enter La Garita Wilderness Area in the Gunnison National Forest's Cebolla Ranger District.

Raven's Rest   HOSTEL $

(📞970-944-7119; www.theravensresthostel.com; 207 Gunnison Ave; dm $26; 📶) A godsend to through-hikers coming off the Colorado Trail, this clean bunkhouse has a small guest kitchen and a dozen bunks with weary mattresses and a set of stall showers ($5 for non-guests). If no one is there, the service is DIY – go through the gate to the backyard for instructions. The website has information on trail closures too.

Pleasant View Resort   RESORT $

(📞970-944-2262; www.pleasantviewresort.net; 549 S Gunnison Ave; cabins from $89; 🅿) A good option for cabins just outside of town to the south. The small cabins are wood paneled and immaculately kept, and there's a swing set for the kids. They also rent out Jeeps.

Wupperman Campground   CAMPGROUND $

(📞970-944-2225; County Rd 33; sites $15) This campground on Lake San Cristobal is a good option for those who want to be near the water. No reservations accepted.

Elkhorn RV Resort
& Cabins
CAMPGROUND **$**

(☑970-944-2920; www.elkhornrvresort.com; 713 N Bluff St; cabins $62, tent/RV sites $26/39; P 🛜) Try this place for RV hookups; there's also some utilitarian tent camping and simple 'camping cabins,' which come without linens.

Inn at the Lake
MOTEL **$$**

(☑936-499-1323; www.innatthelake.org; 600 County Rd 33; d $135-160; P 🛜 ❄ 🛜) On the shores of Lake San Cristobal, this is a log-fitted motel where potted flowers sway in the breeze. It has 10 rooms, all of which enjoy a view of the water.

Matterhorn Motel
MOTEL **$$**

(☑970-944-2210; www.matterhornmotel.com; 409 Bluff St; r from $119; 🛜 ❄) Our favorite motel in the downtown area is the Matterhorn, a smartly remodeled 1940s motel with red trim and scalloped siding, where some rooms have kitchenettes.

✖ Eating

Chillin'
CAFE **$**

(☑970-944-0287; 205 Gunnison Ave; mains $5-11; ⏱7am-4pm; 🛜) This friendly internet cafe and eatery bustles with locals and travelers. Dine on Texas toast or huevos rancheros in the morning or an assortment of well-crafted sandwiches (we like the BLT on sourdough) for lunch. There's also seating on the shady porch.

Lake City Bakery
BAKERY **$**

(☑970-944-2613; 922 Hwy 149; snacks $2-7; ⏱7am-4pm) Customers buzz in on their ATVs for fresh doughnuts, goopy cinnamon rolls and egg sandwiches.

Climb Elevated Eatery
AMERICAN **$$**

(☑970-944-5566; www.climbeatery.com; 808 Gunnison Ave; lunch mains $12-14, dinner mains $14-40; ⏱11am-9pm Tue-Sat, 9am-8pm Sun) Fresh cut truffle fries, elk carpaccio and quinoa power bowls are some of the exotic treats you wouldn't expect to find in this forgotten corner of Colorado. Climb is a welcome addition to a town well versed in burgers and beers, though yes, you can get Angus beef here too – all natural, of course.

🛍 Shopping

Sportsman Outdoors
& Fly Shop
SPORTS & OUTDOORS

(☑970-944-2526; www.lakecitysportsman.com; 238 S Gunnison Ave; bike/tent/car camping kit rental per day $26/25/125; ⏱7am-7pm Jun-Aug,

9am-6pm Tue-Sat Sep-Dec, 10am-4pm Jan-May) This full-service outfitter is a godsend in Lake City. It rents camping and fishing gear and bikes, with cheaper rates after the first night. They offer tons of local information and lead trips into the area.

ℹ Tourist Information

Lake City/Hinsdale County Chamber of Commerce (☑800-569-1874, 970-944-2527; www.lakecity.com; 800 Gunnison Ave; ⏱9am-3pm Mon-Sat) Visitor information, including USFS and BLM coverage.

ℹ Getting There & Away

Lake City is on Hwy 149 (Gunnison Ave in town), 47 miles south of the intersection with US 50, which in turn leads east to Gunnison and west to Montrose. It lies west of the Continental Divide at Spring Creek Pass and the giant **Slumgullion** (p287) landslide. To the west rises Uncompahgre Peak and four others peaks over 14,000ft, creating a barrier between Lake City and Ouray. This wall of mountains is crossed only by the USFS Alpine Byway, which requires 4WD vehicles or a mountain bike and a strong pair of legs. From Lake City it's 50 miles south on Hwy 149 to Creede. For travel in the area, a private vehicle is necessary and 4WD is worth consideration since there are plenty of trails around.

Crested Butte

☑970 / POP 1520 / ELEV 8885FT

Powder-bound Crested Butte has retained its rural character better than most Colorado ski resorts. Ringed by three wilderness areas, this remote former mining village is counted among Colorado's best ski resorts (some say the best). The old town center features beautifully preserved Victorian-era buildings refitted with hip shops and businesses. Two-wheel traffic matches the laid-back, happy attitude.

In winter, the scene centers on Mt Crested Butte, the conical ski mountain emerging from the valley floor. But come summer, these rolling hills become the state wildflower capital (according to the Colorado State Senate), and many mountain bikers' fave for sweet alpine singletrack.

⊙ Sights

★ Crested Butte
Center for the Arts
ARTS CENTER

(☑970-349-7487; www.crestedbuttearts.org; 606 6th St; admission varies; ⏱10am-6pm; P 🛗) With a magnificent recent expansion, the arts

SCENIC DRIVES: SAN JUAN ROUTES

If you have a high-clearance 4WD and four-wheeling skills, these rugged routes are a blast. Jeep tours may also be available.

Alpine Loop Demanding but fantastic fun, this 63-mile drive into the remote and rugged heart of the San Juans begins in Ouray and travels east to Lake City before looping back. Along the way you'll cross two 12,000ft mountain passes, with spectacular scenery and abandoned mining haunts. Allow six hours.

Imogene Pass Every year, runners tackle this rough 16-mile mining road, but you might feel that driving it is enough. Ultra-scenic, it connects Ouray with Telluride. Built in 1880, it's one of the San Juans' highest passes, linking two important mining sites. In Ouray, head south on Main St and turn right on Bird Camp Rd (City Rd 361). Pass Bird Camp Mine, once one of the San Juans' most prolific, climbing high into the mountains. There are stream crossings and sheer cliff drops – a total adrenaline rush! Eventually the route opens onto high alpine meadows before the summit of Imogene Pass (13,114ft). Descending toward Telluride, you will pass the abandoned Tomboy Mine, which once had a population as large as present-day Ouray. The pass is open in summer; allow three hours one-way.

center hosts shifting exhibitions of local artists and a stellar schedule of live music and performance pieces. There's always something lively and interesting happening here.

Crested Butte Mountain Heritage Museum
MUSEUM

(☏ 970-349-1880; www.crestedbuttemuseum.com; 331 Elk Ave; adult/child $5/free; ⊙ 10am-6pm summer, noon-6pm winter; P ♿) In one of the oldest buildings in Crested Butte, this museum is a worthwhile visit to see a terrific model railway. Exhibits range from geology to mining and early home life.

Crested Butte Cemetery
CEMETERY

(Gothic Rd) Many of the town's pioneers are buried in the cemetery, about 0.25 miles north of town towards Mt Crested Butte. Also interred here are 59 miners who died in the Jokerville Mine explosion of 1884, many of them boys and adolescents.

🏃 Activities

★ Crested Butte Mountain Resort
SKIING

(☏ 970-349-2222; www.skicb.com; 12 Snowmass Rd; lift ticket adult/child $111/100; ♿) One of Colorado's best, Crested Butte is known for open tree skiing, deep powder and few crowds. Catering mostly to intermediates and experts, the resort sits 2 miles north of the town at the base of Mt Crested Butte. Surrounded by forests, rugged peaks, and the West Elk, Raggeds and Maroon Bells-Snowmass Wilderness Areas, the scenery is breathtaking.

In summer there's lift access for mountain bikers (day passes adult/child $43/37).

Alpineer
MOUNTAIN BIKING

(☏ 970-349-5210; www.alpineer.com; 419 6th St; bike rental per day $25-75) Serves the mountain-biking mecca with maps, information and rentals. There's a great selection of men's and women's clothing. It also rents out skis and hiking and camping equipment.

Crested Butte Nordic Center
SKIING

(☏ 970-349-1707; www.cbnordic.org; 620 2nd St; day passes adult/child $20/free; ⊙ 8:30am-5pm; ♿) With 50km of groomed cross-country ski trails around Crested Butte, this center issues day and season passes, manages hut rental and organizes events and races. Ski rentals and lessons are available, in addition to ice-skating, snowshoeing and guided tours of the alpine region.

Fantasy Ranch
HORSEBACK RIDING

(☏ 970-349-5425, toll-free 888-688-3488; www.fantasyranchoutfitters.com; 935 Gothic Rd; 1½hr rides $75; ♿) Offers short trail rides (for guests over seven years and under 240lbs), wilderness day rides and multiday pack trips. One highlight is a stunning ride from Crested Butte to Aspen round-trip.

Irwin Guides
OUTDOORS

(☏ 970-349-5430; www.irwinguides.com; 330 Belleview Ave; ⊙ 8am-5pm) Guide service for hard-core backcountry skiing, ice climbing or mountaineering. With over a decade of experience, these guys can get you into (and out of) some seriously remote wilderness. They can also provide equipment.

Adaptive Sports Center OUTDOORS

(☑970-349-2296; www.adaptivesports.org; 10 Crested Butte Way) This nonprofit group is dedicated to providing opportunities for people with disabilities to participate in outdoors activities and adventure sports.

✦ Festivals & Events

★ Crested Butte Arts Festival ART

(☑970-349-1184; www.crestedbutteartsfestival. com; Elk Ave; ⊙Jul/Aug; 🚻🐾) For 38 years the Crested Butte Arts Festival, in late July or early August, has drawn huge crowds and hundreds of artists, musicians and food and wine vendors to Elk Ave for a wonderful free street party. Artists from all over the US come to display and sell their weird and wonderful works.

🛏 Sleeping

Visitors to Crested Butte can stay either in the main town, which is better for restaurants and nightlife, or in one of the many options at the mountain resort. Some of the Mt Crested Butte hotels and apartment buildings close over the spring and fall, but others offer great discounts – check the websites, compare prices and bargain. If you've come for the wildflowers, hiking or mountain-biking, you can do very well at these times.

Crested Butte Mountain
Resort Properties ACCOMMODATION SERVICES

(CBMR Properties; ☑888-223-2631; www.skicb.com) This property-management group, part of the Crested Butte Mountain Resort, handles reservations for dozens of the lodges, hotels and apartment buildings at Mt Crested Butte.

Crested Butte International Hostel HOSTEL $

(☑970-349-0588; toll-free 888-389-0588; www. crestedbuttehostel.com; 615 Teocalli Ave; dm $37, r $104-115; 🛜) For the privacy of a hotel with the lively ambience of a hostel, grab a room here, one of Colorado's nicest hostels. The best private rooms have their own baths. Dorm bunks have reading lamps and lockable drawers, and the communal area has a stone fireplace and comfortable couches. Rates vary with the season, with winter being high season. Extended stays attract discounts.

Inn at Crested Butte BOUTIQUE HOTEL $$

(☑970-349-2111; toll-free 877-343-211; www.innat crestedbutte.com; 510 Whiterock Ave; d $199-249;

🅿❄🛜) This refurbished boutique hotel offers intimate lodgings in stylish and luxurious surrounds. With just a handful of rooms, some opening onto a balcony with views over Mt Crested Butte, and all decked out with antiques, flat-screen TVs, coffee-makers and minibars, this is one of Crested Butte's nicest vacation addresses.

Elevation Hotel & Spa HOTEL $$

(☑970-349-2222; www.elevationresort.com; 500 Gothic Rd; r from $159; 🅿) At the base of Crested Butte Mountain Resort and just steps from a major chairlift, this swanky address offers oversized luxury rooms ready for first call on powder days. The slope-side deck is the spot for brews by the fire pit while you watch snowboarders whiz by. Check online for specials, particularly at the start or end of the season.

Nordic Inn INN $$

(☑800-542-7669; www.nordicinncb.com; 14 Treasury Rd; d $160; 🛜🐾) In 1963 this Swiss-style inn was the first lodging in Crested Butte. Its newest incarnation as a stylish stopover with a huge outdoor hot tub is most welcome. There's 28 rooms with mostly king-sized beds, flat-screen TVs and Nespresso machines, all run by a very affable South African.

★ Ruby of Crested Butte B&B $$$

(☑800-390-1338; www.therubyofcrestedbutte. com; 624 Gothic Ave; d $149-299, ste $199-499;) Thoughtfully outfitted, down to the bowls of jellybeans and nuts in the stylish communal lounge. Rooms are brilliant, with heated floors, flat-screen TVs with DVD players and DVD selections, iPod docks and deluxe linens. There's also a Jacuzzi, a library, a ski-gear drying room and use of retro townie bikes. Hosts help with dinner reservations and other services.

Pets get first-class treatment that includes their own bed, bowls and treats.

🍴 Eating

This mountain town bursts with good fine dining and casual options. In winter, reserve ahead for dinner.

Third Bowl ICE CREAM $

(☑970-349-2888; 201 1/2 Elk Ave; snacks $4-6; ⊙8:30am-10pm) Homemade ice cream and doughnuts draw out the whole Crested Butte community for something sweet. Delightful options include goat's cheese strawberry and cowboy coffee. There's also non-dairy options made with almond or co-conut milk. It's up the stairs.

Izzy's CAFE $
(218 Maroon Ave; mains $9-11; ⊙7am-1pm Wed-Mon) Start your day right with breakfast from this buzzing cafe. Latkes, egg dishes and homemade bagels are all done up right. Don't skip the sourdough made with a 50-year-old starter. It's on the alley by the creek between Maroon and Elk Aves.

The Last Steep AMERICAN $
(☑970-349-7007; http://thelaststeep.com; 208 Elk Ave; mains $10-14; ⊙11am-11pm Sun-Thu, to midnight Fri & Sat; ⊛) When locals want an affordable bite out, they come to this down-home eatery for burgers, teriyaki tofu bowls and coconut shrimp. It's family-run with options for all, including a kids' menu.

★ **Secret Stash** PIZZA $$
(☑970-349-6245; www.thesecretstash.com; 303 Elk Ave; mains $12-18; ⊙8am-late; 🅿⊛) With phenomenal food, the funky-casual Stash is adored by locals, who also dig the original cocktails. The sprawling space was once a general store, but now is outfitted with teahouse seating and tapestries. The house specialty is pizza; its Notorious Fig (with prosciutto, fresh figs and truffle oil) won the World Pizza Championship. Start with the salt-and-pepper fries.

Avalanche Bar & Grill PUB FOOD $$
(www.avalanchebarandgrill.com; 15 Emmons Rd; mains $9-30; ⊙7:30am-9pm winter, from 11:30am summer; 🅿⊛) One of the favorite après-ski venues, Avalanche is right on the slopes and has a big menu of American comfort foods (tuna melts, burgers, club sandwiches, pizzas), as well as an impressive lineup of desserts and beverages. There's a kids' menu too.

Soupçon FRENCH $$$
(☑970-349-5448; www.soupcon-cb.com; 127 Elk Ave; mains $39-47; ⊙6-10:30pm) 🚭 Specializing in seduction, this petite French bistro occupies a characterful old mining cabin with just a few tables. Chef Jason has worked with big NYC names and keeps it fresh with changing menus of local meat and organic produce. Reserve ahead.

🍷 **Drinking & Nightlife**

Merrymaking is serious business in the Butte – head out for craft cocktails, regular tap beer or live music.

★ **Montanya** BAR
(www.montanyarum.com; 212 Elk Ave; snacks $3-12; ⊙11am-9pm) The Montanya distillery receives wide acclaim for its high-quality rums. Its basiltini, made with basil-infused rum, fresh grapefruit and lime, will have you levitating. There are also tours, free tastings and worthy mocktails.

Camp 4 Coffee COFFEE
(www.camp4coffee.com; 402 1/2 Elk Ave; ⊙5am-midnight) Grab your caffeine fix at this serious local roaster, the cutest cabin in town, shingled with license plates (just as local miners once did when they couldn't afford to patch their roofs).

Bonez COCKTAIL BAR
(☑970-349-5118; www.bonez.co; 130 Elk Ave; ⊙4-10pm Sun-Thu, from noon Fri & Sat) Don your flannels and trucker hat to hit this hip alcove for tequila flights and tacos. While the food isn't all that, it's the place for a stiff and sometimes fiery drink, like the Scorpion with habanero, pineapple and tequila.

Princess Wine Bar WINE BAR
(☑970-349-0210; 218 Elk Ave; ⊙8am-midnight) Intimate and perfect for conversation while sampling the select regional wine list. There's regular live acoustic music featuring local singer-songwriters. A popular après-ski spot.

☆ **Entertainment**

Crested Butte Mountain Theatre THEATER
(☑970-349-0366; www.cbmountaintheatre.org; 403 2nd St) The best local and community theatre. For deals, check out dress-rehearsal shows.

Eldo Brewery LIVE MUSIC
(☑970-349-6125; www.eldobrewpub.com; 215 Elk Ave; cover charge varies; ⊙3pm-late, music from 10:30pm) With a great outdoor deck, this lively microbrewery doubles as the club where most out-of-town bands play. The pub grub is just OK, but the beats are deadly.

🛍 **Shopping**

Big Al's Bicycle Heaven SPORTS & OUTDOORS
(☑970-349-0515; www.bigalsbicycleheaven.com; 207 Elk Ave; rentals per day $21-72; ⊙9am-6pm) The place to come for bicycle rentals or purchases. Options range from townie rides for cheaper rates to high-performance mountain bikes and fat bikes on the high end, but no road bikes. Staff are knowledgeable and helpful.

Townie Books BOOKS

(☎ 970-349-7545; www.towniebookscb.com; 414 Elk Ave; ⊙ 7am-10pm) A great local bookstore featuring guides, maps, a slew of local authors and a coffee shop on the side. You can also find original gifts that transcend the usual bric-a-brac.

Soma Wellness Lounge DISPENSARY

(☎ 970-349-6640; www.somacolorado.com; 423 Belleview Ave; ⊙ 9am-8pm) With helpful budtenders and lots of different strands and edibles, Soma is considered a professional dispensary for recreational marijuana, with outlets in other Colorado locations too.

Christy Sports SPORTS & OUTDOORS

(☎ 970-349-6601, toll-free 877-754-7627; www. christysports.com; 620 Gothic Rd #150; ⊙ 8am-6pm) Christy Sports has ski equipment, snowboards, snowshoes and clothing for hire and sale.

Black Tie Ski Rentals SPORTS & OUTDOORS

(☎ 970-349-0722, toll-free 888-349-0722; www. blacktieskis.com; 719 4th St, unit A; ⊙ 7:30am-10pm winter) Black Tie hires out skis, skiing equipment and snowboards.

❶ Tourist Information

The **Visitor Center** (☎ 970-349-6438; www. crestedbuttechamber.com; 601 Elk Ave; ⊙ 9am-5pm) is just past the entrance to town on the main road and stocks loads of brochures and maps.

❶ Getting There & Away

Crested Butte is about four hours' drive from Denver, and about 3½ hours from Colorado Springs. Head for Gunnison on US 50 and from there head north for about 30 minutes to Crested Butte on Hwy 135.

Several bus lines serve Crested Butte, offering free shuttle services to the mountain resort; frequency varies with the season, so see the respective websites for schedules.

Alpine Express (RTA; ☎ 970-641-5074; www. alpineexpressshuttle.com)

Mountain Express (☎ 970-349-7318; www. mtnexp.org)

Black Canyon of the Gunnison National Park

The Colorado Rockies are known for their mountains, but the Black Canyon of the Gunnison National Park is the inverse geographic feature – a massive yawning chasm etched out over millions of years by the Gunnison River and volcanic uplift. Here a dark, narrow gash above the Gunnison River leads down a 2000ft chasm as eerie as it is spectacular. No other canyon in America combines the narrow openings, sheer walls and dizzying depths of the Black Canyon, and a peek over the edge evokes a sense of awe (or vertigo). In just 48 canyon miles, the Gunnison River loses more elevation than the entire 1500-mile Mississippi. This fast-moving water, carrying rock and debris, is powerfully erosive. Without the upstream dams, the river would carry five times its current volume.

History

This massive canyon has presented an impassable barrier to human beings since they first trod these lands. Utes had settlements along Black Canyon's rim, but there's no evidence of human habitation within the chasm itself. Early Spanish records of sojourns through this part of the country make no mention of the gorge. John W Gunnison, who was commissioned to survey the Rockies for a future Pacific railroad, sought a crossing over the river that would later bear his name. He bypassed the canyon in 1853 and continued west until he and his party were massacred near Lake Sevier, Utah, by Utes (though there are some who believe they were killed in a Mormon conspiracy).

The 1871 Hayden geological survey – again seeking a route for a Pacific railroad – was the first to document the canyon. By 1900 settlers seeking water for irrigating crops in the nearby Uncompahgre Valley looked to the river as a source. In 1901 Abraham Fellows and William Torrence floated through the canyon on rubber mattresses, traveling 33 miles in nine days. By 1905 construction of the 5.8-mile Gunnison Diversion Tunnel had begun and it still provides water to farms today.

Though moves were afoot to protect the canyon as a national park as early as the 1930s, it took until 1999 for its park status to be declared, protecting 14 of the canyon's 48 miles.

◉ Sights & Activities

Black Canyon of the Gunnison National Park NATIONAL PARK

(☎ 970-641-2337; www.nps.gov/blca; 7-day admission per vehicle/pedestrians & cyclists $15/7) This 32,950-acre park is a black canyon so sheer, deep and narrow, sunlight only touches the canyon floor when the sun is directly overhead. The intense Gunnison River is prime fishing territory.

Gunnison River
FISHING

The Gunnison River, designated as Gold Medal Water and Wild Trout Water, offers some of the best fishing in Colorado. However, strict regulations are enforced to maintain this status. The best access to the river is down the summer-only East Portal Rd. Anglers can also access the river from steep tracks leading into the canyon (for the fit only).

East Portal Road
SCENIC DRIVE

(☺summer only) For easy access to the Gunnison River, take this steep route that also goes through Curecanti National Recreation Area. The opening season for the road is weather-dependent (when it snows and when it melts), so check the latest reports before setting off.

South Rim Road
SCENIC DRIVE

This 6-mile road visits 11 overlooks at the edge of the canyon, some reached via short trails up to 1.5 miles long (round-trip). At the narrowest part of Black Canyon, Chasm View is 1100ft across yet 1800ft deep. Rock climbers are frequently seen on the opposing North Wall. Colorado's highest cliff face is the 2300ft Painted Wall.

To challenge your senses, cycle along the smooth pavement running parallel to the rim's 2000ft drop-off. You definitely get a better feel for the place than you do trapped in a car.

North Vista Trail
HIKING

This 7-mile round-trip is relatively flat for much of the way. If you don't have the time to go all the way to Green Mountain, make it halfway to Exclamation Point for some of the best inner-canyon views. The trail starts at the North Rim Ranger Station.

Oak Flat Loop
HIKING

A strenuous 2-mile round-trip that takes you exploring below the rim. Start near the South Rim Visitor Center and loop right, descending through a grove of aspen to another signed junction and go left, through Gambel oak scrub to some great views. Pets are not allowed.

🛏 Sleeping & Eating

The park has three campgrounds although only one is open all year round. Water is trucked into the park and only the East Portal Campground has river-water access. Firewood is not provided and may not be collected in the national park – campers must bring their own.

Visitors should bring their own provisions, as there are no services here. Depending on where you are coming from, supplies could be purchased and gas topped off in Delta, Montrose or Gunnison. Follow instructions on-site for safe food storage in bear country.

North Rim Campground
CAMPGROUND $

(www.nps.gov/blca; North Rim Rd; tent sites $16; ☺May–mid-Oct) Popular with climbers, this shady 11-site campground has easy access to rim views. Sites have picnic table and fire pits. There's a pit toilet and water.

East Portal Campground
CAMPGROUND $

(☑970-249-1915; www.nps.gov/blca; East Portal Rd; sites $8; ☺May–mid-Oct) At the end of the steep East Portal Rd, within the canyon walls, is this shaded campground with 15 sites, pit toilets, tables and fire grills.

ℹ Tourist Information

South Rim Visitor Center (☑970-249-1915, 800-873-0244; www.nps.gov/blca; South Rim Dr; ☺8am-6pm late May-early Sep, 8:30am-4pm late Sep-early May) is located two miles past the park entrance on South Rim Dr. The more remote **North Rim Ranger Station** (North Rim; ☺8:30am-4pm, closed mid-Nov–mid-Apr) is accessed via Hwy 92 from Delta.

ℹ Getting There & Away

Access with a private vehicle. The park is 12 miles east of the US 550 junction with US 50. Exit at Hwy 347 – well marked with a big brown sign for the national park – and head north for 7 miles.

Curecanti National Recreation Area

The Gunnison River, which once flowed freely through the canyons, is now plugged by three dams creating the Curecanti National Recreation Area. Its official title, the Wayne N Aspinall Storage Unit, is more apt – named for a US representative, in office between 1948 and 1973, who never met a water project he did not like. Many RVs are strangely attracted to the bleak and windy shores of chilly Blue Mesa Reservoir, which Curecanti surrounds. The calm waters of the

Blue Mesa are popular with windsurfers, as well as boating and fishing families. Stunning landforms that survived immersion are the unsinkable Curecanti Needle and Dillon Pinnacles, a volcanic breccia capped by welded tuff.

There are no entrance fees for Curecanti, unless entering through the main entrance of the Black Canyon of the Gunnison National Park.

Tours

Morrow Point Boat Tour BOATING
(970-641-2337, ext 205; adult/child $24/12; 10am & 12:30pm Wed-Mon;) The popular boat tour is run by the National Park Ranger Service, and takes visitors on a gentle 1½-hour tour through the upper Black Canyon on a 42-seat pontoon. Access the Pine Creek boat dock via a 1½-mile round-trip trail with 232 steps. The trailhead is just off Hwy 50, between Montrose and Gunnison, at the 130-mile marker. Bookings essential.

The views from the boat are superb and the ranger delivers a commentary on the stunning scenery and wildlife. Allow an hour to walk from the trailhead to the boat dock.

Sleeping

Curecanti has 10 campgrounds, and some, such as Elk Creek and Lake Fork, are developed, with showers and flush toilets, while others are more basic. For hikers there are also small campgrounds at the end of the Curecanti Creek Trail (2 miles) and Hermit's Rest Trail (3 miles). The latter descends 1800ft, so be prepared for a steep climb back out.

Elk Creek CAMPGROUND $
(970-641-2337; www.nps.gov/cure; US 50; sites $16-22;) A bleak treeless area nonetheless popular with family and boating folk. There are 160 sites arrayed around four road loops; Loops A and D may be reserved in advance, and only Loop D offers electric hookups. There are showers, flush toilets (mid-May to mid-September only, otherwise pit toilets), tables and fire grates. With a marina and boat ramp. Booking fees ($3) apply to advance reservations.

Lake Fork CAMPGROUND $
(970-641-2337; www.nps.gov/cure; US 50; sites $16) Near the Blue Mesa Dam, Lake Fork camping area offers showers (summer only), pit toilets, marina and boat ramp, and a

visitor center that opens intermittently in summer. There are 90 sites (no electric hookups), which may be reserved for a fee ($3).

Tourist Information

There are information centers at Cimarron and Lake Fork, which only operate from late May to late September.

Part of the Black Canyon of Gunnison National Park, the **Elk Creek Visitor Center** (970-641-2337, ext 205; www.nps.gov/cure; 102 Elk Creek Rd; 8am-6pm late May-early Sep, to 4:30pm rest of year) is the main office serving the Curecanti National Recreation Area.

Getting There & Away

Access is by private vehicle only. It's on US 50, six miles west of the junction with Hwy 149 to Lake City.

Gunnison

970 / POP 5875 / ELEV 7703FT

While not a destination for vacationers, affable Gunnison has become more than the ranch town of yesteryear, with great recreation access and affordable lodgings and meals. In winter a free shuttle bus plies between Gunnison and Crested Butte continuously each day, and staying off the mountain can make skiing vacations a little less expensive.

This western town is home to the handsome campus of Western State College of Colorado, which opened in 1911. The giant W on the hill southeast of town is a reference to the college. However, a walk through the older residential neighborhoods will reveal numerous Victorians and masonry homes. Long ago Ute tribes hunted on the plains surrounding the present-day town of Gunnison in summer.

Sights & Activities

Pioneer Museum MUSEUM
(970-641-4530; www.gunnisonpioneermuseum.com; 803 E Tomichi Ave; adult/child $10/3; 9am-5pm Memorial Day–mid-Sep;) Definitely worth a stop for auto aficionados, with 16 buildings crammed with old cars and carts, tools and trains, and a fascinating telephony display. The Model T and Model A Fords bookend the auto collection against the 1960s cruisers and sedans.

Johnson Building HISTORIC SITE
(124 N Main St) The Johnson Building was erected in 1881 and traded as a restaurant

from 1901, originally as the Royal Cafe and later as the Johnston Restaurant until 1985. It's now a gallery and antique store downstairs, with offices upstairs.

Smith Opera House HISTORIC SITE
(114 N Boulevard St) FREE The old Smith Opera House is indeed an oddity. It was built in 1882 and is rather bovine in its proportions and outlook. The building opened in 1883, but within a year was sold in a repossession sale and divided up into apartments. Its design, a homely mash-up of Italianate and Victorian styles, now serves as office space.

It's not clear whether opera was ever performed in the Smith Opera House.

Scenic River Tours RAFTING
(970-641-3131; www.scenicrivertours.com; 703 W Tomichi Ave; Taylor River full-day $98;) With a varied excursion schedule, this rafting provider travels to scenic sections of the Gunnison River for family-friendly rafting trips and the Taylor and Lake Fork Rivers for more dramatic action. There are age and weight restrictions for Class III-plus white-water. Fishing trips and rock-climbing are also offered.

Sleeping

Wanderlust Hostel HOSTEL $
(970-901-1599; www.thewanderlusthostel.com; 221 N Boulevard St; dm $25, d $45-57;) A find! Think bright and clean rooms, a garden with pickable berries and grill, and a large and well-equipped communal kitchen. Amy, the owner, is an adventure guide with an encyclopedic knowledge of the area and a cute hostel dog. At festival times, guests can raid the incredible costume closet. Emphasis on sustainability and loaner bikes for guests.

Alpine Inn HOTEL $
(970-641-2804; toll-free 866-299-66; www.gunnisonalpineinn.com; 1011 W Rio Grande Ave; d from $66;) A good budget choice, this super-clean remodel has a range of rooms with nice bedding, cable TV and hearty breakfasts that include biscuits, gravy and eggs. There's an indoor pool and pets are welcome.

Tall Texan Campground CAMPGROUND $
(970-641-2927; www.rvpark.com; 194 County Rd 11; tent sites $22, RV $38, cabins $85-100;) In 10 acres off the Crested Butte road north of Gunnison, this place has RV hookups, cabins and sites for campers with tents.

Eating & Drinking

Twisted Fork INTERNATIONAL $
(970-641-1488; www.twistedforkgunnison.net; 206 N Main St; mains $8-15; 11am-9pm;) This is new-school Gunnison: healthy dishes rocking Asian influences alongside craft cocktails. The Korean beef bowl combines heat and well-seasoned greens. There's also lettuce wraps, noodle bowls and wagyu beef burgers cooked to order with spicy steak fries. Linger on the sprawling deck overlooking the vegetable garden beds. There's gluten-free options and organic and natural foods when possible.

Firebrand Deli SANDWICHES $
(970-641-6266; 108 N Main St; sandwiches $8-10; 7am-3pm Wed-Sun;) If you're after healthy breakfast and lunchtime eating in Gunnison, it's hard to go past the Firebrand Deli. The freshly made sandwiches are always terrific with a great selection of breads and fillings. Vegetarians (who have it hard in Gunnison) get more than lip service.

Garlic Mike's ITALIAN $$
(970-641-2493; www.garlicmikes.com; 2674 State Hwy 135; mains $15-31; 5pm-late;) Just north of Gunnison on the road to Crested Butte, this place has long been a town favorite. For rural Colorado, it's a pretty authentic taste of Italy. Mike Busse, chef and restaurateur, has won awards and appears on Colorado radio. Try the shrimp scampi, with garlic and shrimp tossed in fresh linguine.

High Alpine Brewery BREWERY
(970-642-4500; www.highalpinebrewing.com; 111 N Main St; 11am-11pm Sun-Wed, to midnight Thu-Sat;) Come sundown, this is the place to be, chilling on the 2nd-story terrace overlooking the main drag. Quaffable house beers include a poblano chile ale with bite and chocolate maple porter. Thin-crust pizzas and fresh salads make it a good choice for meals as well. Check the website for dates for live acoustic music, jazz and other entertainment.

Shopping

Rock & Roll Sports SPORTS & OUTDOORS
(970-641-9150; www.rockandrollsports.com; 608 Tomichi Av; 9am-6pm Mon-Sat) Gunnison's best bike shop can tune your ride and also supplies gear for climbing and skiing pursuits. Check their calendar for cycling events.

🛈 Tourist Information

Gunnison Chamber of Commerce (📞 970-641-1501, toll-free 800-323-2453; www.gunnisonchamber.com; 500 E Tomichi Ave; ⏰ 8am-5pm Mon-Fri) Pick up a self-guided historic walking tour booklet, maps of area mountain-bike trails and lists of accommodations and activities.

🛈 Getting There & Away

The **Gunnison Airport** (GUC; 📞 970-641-2304; www.gunnisoncounty.org/airport; 519 Rio Grande Ave) is under renovation but is expected to open in the near future, with seasonal service to Denver and Houston. You can still rent vehicles at the airport from **Avis** (📞 970-641-0263; www.avis.com; 711 W Rio Grande Ave; ⏰ 9am-5pm), **Budget** (📞 970-641-4403; www.budget.com; 711 W Rio Grande Ave; ⏰ 9am-1pm) or **Hertz** (📞 970-641-2881; www.hertz.com; 711 W Rio Grande Ave; ⏰ 9am-5pm).

Nearby attractions are best accessed via private vehicle but you can get to Crested Butte with the free **Mountain Express** (Gunnison Valley RTA; 📞 970-349-5616; www.gunnisonvalleyrta.org; ⏰ 6:30am-8pm) shuttle or the private **Dolly's Mountain Shuttle** (📞 970-349-2620, 970-209-9757; www.crestedbutteshuttle.com; to Crested Butte from $115; 🚲), which also serves area trailheads.

Denver is about 3½ hours' drive away, while Colorado Springs is about three hours. Gunnison lies on US Hwy 50, 65 miles east of Montrose and 34 miles west of Monarch Pass. The highway to the Divide is a scenic trip following Tomichi Creek.

Montrose

📞 970 / POP 19,015 / ELEV 5974FT

Montrose is an agricultural center and a wholesale supply point for Telluride, 65 miles to the south. With the lofty San Juan Mountains to the south, the Black Canyon of the Gunnison National Park to the east, the Grand Mesa to the north and the Uncompahgre Plateau to the west, it's a handy starting point for adventure. Historic buildings provide the old center with atmosphere, which is distinctly missing on the north–south US 550 route with huge chain stores, motels and fast-food restaurants.

Though rather perfunctory, there are some good museums, antique stores and a clutch of decent restaurants. But perhaps the best reason to stay in Montrose is to day-trip to the awesome Black Canyon of the Gunnison National Park and to pursue mountain biking on the Uncompahgre Plateau.

◉ Sights

The vestiges of the old town can be found along Main St and near the old Denver and Rio Grande Railroad Depot on N Rio Grande Ave. Some of the buildings date from the early 1880s, although the grander edifices were constructed around the turn of the 20th century as Montrose moved from frontier railroad town to significant financial center. A set of 12 interpretive signs is installed in the historic five-block central area around Main St.

★ **Ute Indian Museum**   MUSEUM
(📞 970-249-3098; www.historycolorado.org/museums/ute-indian-museum-0; 17253 Chipeta Rd; adult/child $4.50/2; ⏰ 9am-4:30pm Tue-Sat, 11am-4:30pm Sun; 🅿 👶) 🚲 One of the few American museums dedicated to one tribe. The Ute are the traditional people of western Colorado. The museum is situated on a homestead that belonged to legendary Uncompahgre Ute chief Ouray and his wife Chipeta. A visitors center is attached to the museum.

Museum of the Mountain West   MUSEUM
(📞 970-249-4162; www.mountainwestmuseum.com; 68169 E Miami Rd; adult/child $10/5; ⏰ 8:30am-4:30pm Mon-Sat; 🅿 👶) On display are a staggering number of pieces from the 1880s to the 1930s. There's a re-created Old West town replete with storefronts, a saloon, drugstore and doctor's surgery. The original Diehl Carriage Works building is where 1919–26 world heavyweight boxing champion Jack Dempsey trained.

Montrose County Historical Museum   MUSEUM
(📞 970-249-2085; www.montrosehistory.org; 21 N Rio Grande Ave; adult/child $7/4; ⏰ 9am-4:30pm Fri & Sat, 11am-4pm Sun mid-May–mid-Oct; 🅿 👶) 🚲 Installed in the old Denver and Rio Grande Railroad Depot, this interesting museum has a vast collection of pioneer-era furniture and memorabilia. There are tools and farm equipment, and the children's area has lots of dolls and toys. It's an interesting place to spend a hour or two pondering the way things were.

Cimarron Railroad Exhibit   HISTORIC SITE
(www.nps.gov/cure; US Hwy 50, Cimarron; 🅿 👶) **FREE** A restored old steam locomotive, boxcar and caboose sit on a narrow-gauge bridge crossing the Cimarron River, the last piece of railroad infrastructure from the

Denver and Rio Grande Narrow Gauge Railroad. The exhibit is within the Curecanti National Recreation Area, about 20 miles east of Montrose.

Bryant Building   HISTORIC BUILDING
(428 E Main St) The Bryant Building was erected in 1890. To its west and east are the 1908 SH Nye Building and the 1906 Thomas Hotel – all handsome brick edifices of the city's early years.

Lott's Hotel   HISTORIC BUILDING
(401 E Main St) The Lott's Hotel building has been standing here since 1883. It's the oldest grand building in Montrose.

🏃 Activities

Montrose Skate Park   SKATING
(540 S Rio Grand Ave; 🚻) **FREE** If you've got your deck or rollerbades, head for Montrose Skate Park, 15,000 sq ft of concrete action judged one of the best in the USA by *Thrasher Magazine*.

BMX Complex   CYCLING
(☎970-417-1824; 1001 N 2nd St; 🚻) **FREE** This excellent BMX complex is located at the Montrose County Fairgrounds. The local BMX community is very welcoming to new and visiting riders.

Toads Guide Shop   FISHING
(☎970-249-0408; www.toadsguideshop.com; 309 E Main St; half-day tours from $225; 🚻) 🎣 This angler's shop provides customized guided fly-fishing tours to the Gunnison and Uncompahgre Rivers and beyond.

🛏 Sleeping

For the most part Montrose's sleeping options are dominated by the big motel chains, but there are terrific B&Bs and a few places to pitch a tent or hook up an RV. There are several camping areas around Montrose run by the Bureau of Land Management and the National Park Service; ask at the Montrose Chamber of Commerce & Tourism (p298) for more information.

Black Canyon Motel   MOTEL $
(☎970-249-3495, toll-free 800-348-3495; www.blackcanyonmotel.com; 1605 E Main St; d $86; 🅿❄❅🛜🐾) East Main St heading into Montrose is lined with chain motels. This is one of the few independents, offering good lodgings at a reasonable price and very welcoming service. It's spotless, with some

family rooms and complimentary breakfast. Some pets OK.

Cedar Creek RV Park   CAMPGROUND $
(☎970-249-3884, toll-free 877-425-3884; www.cedarcreekrv.com; 126 Rose Lane; tent sites/RV $23/44, cabins from $52; 🅿🛜🐾) One of several RV parks in Montrose, this facility is well equipped. Includes a coin-laundry and a designated area for pets.

Canyon Creek Bed & Breakfast   B&B $$
(☎970-249-2886, toll-free 877-262-8202; www.canyoncreekbedandbreakfast.com; 820 E Main St; d $142; 🅿❄❅🛜🐾) This beautiful 1909 house on the town's busy main street has been carefully refurbished into an immaculate B&B with an outdoor hot tub. Each of the three suites is uniquely decorated. Flatscreen TVs and a wine hour welcome wagon are some of the perks on offer.

🍴 Eating

The no-fuss dining scene in Montrose can be refreshing after hitting the ski resorts – there's plenty of good fare on offer.

Montrose Farmers Market   MARKET
(☎970-209-8463; www.montrosefarmersmarket.com; cnr Main St & Uncompaghre Ave; ⊙9am-1pm Sat May-Oct; 🅿🚻) On Saturdays the Montrose Farmers Market is held at Centennial Plaza in downtown Montrose. Depending on the harvest, you might find local produce, cheeses and some artisan crafts.

★ Colorado Boy   PIZZA $
(☎970-240-2790; 320 E Main St; mains $8-12; ⊙11:30am-9pm; 🚻) Worth stopping at even if you're just passing through, this wonderful spot dishes up spinach salads and amazing, mouthwatering pizzas with names like Molto Carne (for meat-lovers!) or Rustica, with artichokes and capicola. The setting, a bare but refurbished spot with worn brick and carved tin ceilings, offers a cool ambience to match.

Don Gilberto   MEXICAN $
(☎970-874-8040; 16367 S Townsend Ave #14; mains $3-12; ⊙7am-7pm Mon-Sat) In a small shopping plaza, this unassuming and authentic Mexican restaurant does enchilada plates oozing with cheese and overstuffed tacos in warm corn tortillas. For fast casual, it's a no-brainer. Plus, you can get up to date on all the high-school gossip while dining in an ornate booth.

Pahgre's ITALIAN $

(☑970-249-6442; www.pahgres.com; 1541 Oxbow Dr; mains $10-13; ⏱11am-8pm Sun-Thu, to 9pm Fri & Sat; 🖉🚼) Serving pizzas, paninis, salads and pasta, Pahgre's is a favorite among Montrose locals. Try the pizzas (our picks are the Motherlode or the Blue Mesa). A healthy range of inventive salads offers vegetarians some genuine choices come dinnertime.

Stone House SEAFOOD $$$

(☑970-240-8899; www.stonehousemontrose.com; 1415 Hawk Pkwy; mains $16-33; ⏱11am-10pm; 🚼) With prompt, affable service and a menu as long as your arm, the Stone House offers a catalog of Modern American, Italian and Caribbean-style dishes. Fresh fish and seafood are specialties, and prime beef comes in 8oz, 12oz or 14oz cuts.

Camp Robber SOUTHERN US $$$

(☑970-240-1590; www.camprobber.com; 1515 Ogden Rd; mains $12-38; ⏱11am-9pm Mon-Sat, 9am-2pm Sun; 🚼) Fine-dining without attitude, Camp Robber's eclectic menu offers Americana tricked-up with contemporary New Mexican and Italian accents. The signature dish is the green-chili pistachio-crusted pork medallions served in a rich cream sauce. 'Camp Robber' refers to the gray jaybird that pilfers campers' provisions.

🍷 Drinking & Nightlife

Horsefly Brewing Co PUB

(☑970-249-6889; 846 E Main St; ⏱11am-9pm Sun-Thu, to 11pm Fri & Sat) This very popular brewhouse and barbecue hut serves baskets of nachos, hot wings and burgers alongside pitchers of its signature Tabano Red. It has pleasant outdoor patio seating and bluegrass on the speakers.

Coffee Trader CAFE

(☑970-249-6295; 845 E Main St; ⏱6am-7pm Mon-Fri, 7am-7pm Sat & Sun) In a big old house with a lovely shaded patio, this caffeine stop offers frozen and hot coffee drinks and Italian sodas, as well as some pastries and breakfast burritos.

🛍 Shopping

Montrose is renowned for its antique stores; pick up the detailed *Montrose Antique Trail* brochure from the Montrose Chamber of Commerce & Tourism.

Cascade Bicycles SPORTS & OUTDOORS

(☑970-249-7375; www.cascadebicyclesllc.com; 21 N Cascade Ave; ⏱10am-6pm Mon-Fri, to 4pm Sat)

This local bike shop has been outfitting cyclists and supporting local cycling events for years. For rentals and great local advice on mountain biking, touring and BMX, talk to the friendly owners.

ℹ Tourist Information

Montrose Chamber of Commerce & Tourism (☑970-249-5000; www.visitmontrose. com; 1519 E Main St; ⏱9am-5pm) Right near the outskirts of town as you approach from the east. The friendly folks can help you out with itineraries and information on outdoor activities and Montrose's historical points of interest.

Bureau of Land Management (☑970 240 5300; www.blm.gov; 2465 S Townsend Ave; ⏱8am-16:30pm; 🚼) has camping and hiking information.

ℹ Getting There & Away

Montrose Regional Airport (MTJ; ☑970-249-3203; www.montroseairport.com; 2100 Airport Rd) is a small regional airport that serves the public of Telluride and Crested Butte ski resorts. United Express flies daily from Denver, plus has direct flights from Houston. American Airlines flies from Dallas and Chicago during winter.

ℹ Getting Around

Montrose Airport has rental-car agencies represented on site, including **Avis** (☑970-240-4802; www.avis.com; 2100 Airport Rd; ⏱9am-7:15pm & 10:15-10:45pm Wed-Mon, 9am-5pm & 10:15pm-10:45pm Tue), **Budget** (☑970-249-6083; www.budget.com; 2100 Airport Rd; ⏱8am-11pm Sun-Fri, to 9pm Sat), **Hertz** (☑970-240-8464; www.hertz.com; 2100 Airport Rd; ⏱9am-5pm & 10-11pm) and **Enterprise** (☑970-252-8898; www.enterprise.com; 2100 Airport Rd; ⏱8am-11pm).

Delta

☑970 / POP 8860 / ELEV 4890FT

Once known as Uncompahgre, Delta is the gateway to the north rim of Black Canyon of the Gunnison National Park. It's a small crossroads town that travelers to southwest Colorado can hardly miss, though in recent times its population has doubled. It's also home to a large state prison, which along with a number of empty storefronts, may lend to the town's general lack of sparkle. It's worth checking out the lovely postwar-style murals along Main St, which depict the region's agricultural tradition.

Sights

Dry Mesa
Dinosaur Quarry
NATURAL FEATURE

(970-874-6638; Uncompahgre National Forest; P) FREE Within the borders of the Uncompahgre National Forest, this bone-rich area yielded one of the most diverse Jurassic vertebrate collections in the world. Over a dozen different dinosaurs have been unearthed here since the first dig in 1971, including the terrifying Torvosaurus and various birds, crocodiles and mammals.

The quarry is located 26 miles southwest of Delta on the Uncompahgre Plateau. A short hike will also bring you to a Ute rock-art site. For visitor information, inquire at the USFS forest station.

Fort Uncompahgre
HISTORIC BUILDING

(970-874-7566; www.fortuncompahgre.org; 205 Gunnison River Dr; adult/child $5/3; 9am-3pm Apr-Sep;) Delta's history as a frontier outpost comes alive with a self-guided tour behind the rough timber walls of this 1828 fort. Allow about an hour for a visit.

Sleeping & Eating

Delta isn't so pretty, but its location makes it a likely pit stop. There are any number of mid-century roadside motels along the central corridor, but there's a better selection in nearby Montrose (p296).

A few good restaurants will keep your hunger at bay in Delta.

El Tapatio
MEXICAN $

(970-874-4100; 353 Main St; mains $8-12; 10am-10pm Sun-Thu, to 11pm Fri & Sat) The bright booths are ornately carved, and the plates of Mexican food are moderately priced. Lunch deals, like the green chile and cheese-smothered enchiladas Suizas are both filling and satisfying. Pair them with *aguas frescas* (fresh fruit drinks).

Daveto's
ITALIAN $

(970-874-8277; 520 Main St; mains $5-13; 11am-9pm Tue-Sat;) This place has generous plates of pasta, big pizzas and inexpensive lunches. It also goes boldly where few Italian restaurants dare tread: into the Mexican-Italian fusion. Mexican calzone anyone?

Entertainment

Tru Vu Drive-In
CINEMA

(970-874-9556; 1001 Hwy 92; tickets $8.50; late May-Sep;) When the evening air is warm and dusk falls on Delta, this historic drive-in has a magical atmosphere. It is one of the few remaining such facilities in Colorado, and there are only a handful in the entire USA. Check out Tru Vu's Facebook page to find out what's showing.

Tourist Information

Delta Chamber of Commerce (970-874-8616; www.deltacolorado.org; 301 Main St; 9am-5pm Mon-Fri;) has area brochures and maps.

USFS Grand Mesa, Uncompahgre & Gunnison National Forest Headquarters (970-874-6600; 2250 US 50; 9am-4:30pm Mon-Fri) offers recreation information.

Getting There & Away

Most attractions are outside Delta, meaning a car is practically essential. The **Delta TNM&O/Greyhound Station** (970-874-9455; 270 E Hwy 92) serves the region and adjoining states.

Delta lies 40 miles southeast of Grand Junction and 21 miles northwest of Montrose via US 50.

Paonia

970 / POP 1435 / ELEV 5674FT

A worthy stop between Carbondale and Montrose, rural Paonia has the right mix of quirkiness, calm and Wild West tradition. The city's founder wanted to name the town 'Paeonia,' the Latin name for the peony flower, but according to local legend an austere postmaster wouldn't allow the city moniker to have so many vowels.

For its size, Paonia offers a surprising combination of natural beauty, working-class society and liberal culture. It's the home of *High Country News,* one of the country's most outspoken environmental publications. Surrounded by farms and wildlands, it also has a bundle of late-19th-century buildings in superb condition. Coal mining is still a significant local industry. Today most of its residents are a mix of coal miners, farmers (also cultivating the state's newest cash crop – pot) and boomers gone off the grid.

Eating

Enjoy the classic mountain fare ranging from baked goods to hearty country dinners. In summer look for farm stands selling fresh produce and fruit.

Backcountry Bistro
CAFE $

(970-527-5080; 210 3rd St; mains $3-8; 7am-2pm Mon-Thu, to 9pm Fri, 8am-3pm Sat & Sun;)

The town meeting spot is this shoebox cafe serving strong coffee alongside fresh and organic baked goods and sweet-potato breakfast burritos. If it's hot, go for the ginger or mint house lemonade, with herbs plucked from the garden the moment you order. Breakfast is served all day.

Flying Fork Cafe & Bakery   RESTAURANT, BAKERY **$$**
(☑ 970-527-3203; www.flyingforkcafe.com; 101 3rd St; mains $11-22; ☺ 5:30-9pm Wed-Sun) ✦ Chef Kelly Steinmetz' seasonal menu has an Italian accent; the vegetarian lasagna was a dining highlight of the summer. For something lighter, try the gourmet salads with local greens or thin-crust pizza. The bakery has sandwiches and baked goods to go.

❶ Tourist Information

Paonia Chamber of Commerce (☑ 970-527-3886; www.paoniachamber.com; 130 Grand Ave; ☺ 10am-noon & 1-3pm Thu-Sat) A good source of local information.

USFS Paonia Ranger Station (☑ 970-527-4131; 403 N Rio Grande Ave; ☺ 8am-4pm) For recreation information.

❶ Getting There & Away

The historic downtown – all 10 or so blocks of it – is just south of the highway. As you descend into the valley of the North Fork River, the Grand Mesa flanking one side and Mt Lamborn towering on the other, Hwy 133 runs right through town. It's best to travel by private transportation.

Colorado National Monument

The Colorado National Monument is the crown jewel of the Western Slope, where the setting sun alights otherworldly red-rock formations. Hike its starkly beautiful landscape or watch from camp as lightning storms roll across the distant plains.

These canyons rise from the Uncompahgre Uplift of the Colorado Plateau, 2000ft above the Grand Valley of the Colorado River, to reveal a stunning view. The twinkling lights of Grand Junction, the green strip of the Colorado River, the black ribbon of I-70, the tree-lined farm fields of the Grand Valley – these are all far below, together a memorable juxtaposition of Colorado's ancient geological past and modern present.

Once dinosaur country, this 32-sq-mile scenic wonder is one of the most rewarding side trips possible from an interstate highway, well worth a detour by car but even better for backcountry exploration.

◉ Sights & Activities

Most trails starting on Rim Rock Dr are relatively short, such as the half-mile **Coke Ovens** hike or the quarter-mile **Devils Kitchen**. The numerous canyons are more interesting, but rugged terrain makes loop hikes difficult or impossible; a steep descent from the canyon rim means an equally steep ascent on the return.

We recommend a car or bicycle shuttle, since some trailheads outside the park are reached most easily from Hwy 340, the Broadway/Redlands Rd between Fruita and Grand Junction.

If you have half a day and lots of ambition, it's interesting to make for **Rattlesnake Arches**, the largest collection of natural arches anywhere outside Arches National Park. Getting there is tricky, since the arches can be accessed by trailheads in the Bureau of Land Management (BLM) Black Ridge Wilderness Area or within the national monument. Inquire about directions at the BLM office in Grand Junction (p303) or the Saddlehorn Visitor Center (p301).

Colorado National Monument   PARK
(☑ 970-858-3617, ext 360; www.nps.gov/colm; Hwy 340; per vehicle per week $15; ☺ 24hr, visitor center 9am-6pm) A huge red rock mesa standing sentinel over the Grand Junction metropolis, the monument offers exceptional hiking, camping and road biking.

Monument Canyon Trail   HIKING
Perhaps the monument's most rewarding trail, the 6-mile Monument Canyon Trail leads from Rim Rock Dr down to Hwy 340, past many of the park's most interesting natural features, including the Coke Ovens, the Kissing Couple and Independence Monument.

Liberty Cap Trail   HIKING
This full-day hike links up with the steeper Ute Canyon Trail to form a 14-mile loop.

🛏 Sleeping & Eating

Sleep in nearby Grand Junction or camp at Saddlehorn Campground.

There are no restaurants in the park, but it's a quick day or half-day trip from Grand Junction. Bring your own picnic.

Saddlehorn Campground
CAMPGROUND $

(☑ 970-858-3617; www.nps.gov/colm; Rim Rock Dr; tent & RV sites $20) The only organized camp in the monument has good car camping with expansive views. It's easy for RVs and near the visitor center.

❶ Tourist Information

Saddlehorn Visitor Center (☑ 970-858-3617; www.nps.gov/colm; Rim Rock Dr; ⊙ 9am-6pm Mon-Sun Jun-Oct, low season hours vary) For information and backcountry camping permits.

❶ Getting There & Away

To reach the monument, travel by private vehicle or bicycle. The visitor center is 16 miles from downtown Grand Junction (up steep canyon roads).

Grand Junction

☑ 970 / POP 59,800 / ELEV 4586FT

Grand Junction is as utilitarian as its name suggests. Near two major rivers, its intersecting highways are built over centuries-old trading routes. It's admittedly not much to look at. Amid one of Colorado's most fertile agricultural zones, Grand Junction is a cow town at heart – despite being western Colorado's main urban hub. It's worth browsing downtown Main St, revamped into a pleasant pedestrian mall with fountains, benches and sculptures that capture some small-town atmosphere away from the sprawl.

◉ Sights & Activities

Most of the banner sights of the area are actually outside city limits. The sightseeing action in the town itself is concentrated in the pleasant downtown. The self-explanatory Art on the Corner program makes for a pleasant stroll along Main St.

Some of Colorado's finest mountain biking is to be had around Grand Junction. Those with even a cursory interest would be remiss not to spend a of couple hours exploring.

Major trails include the 142-mile Grand Junction to Montrose Tabeguache Trail (pronounced 'tab-a-watch'), and the Kokopelli Trail outside Fruita. While doing the full length of any of these trails requires extensive preparation, both offer plenty of loops and other shorter ride possibilities.

If time is short, go up the road to Fruita, where numerous sights are an easy pedal north of the village.

Western Colorado Botanic Gardens
GARDENS

(☑ 970-248-3288; www.westerncoloradobotanical gardens.org; 655 Struthers Ave; adult/child/student & senior $5/3/4; ⊙ 10am-5pm Tue-Sun; P) The Orchid Display is the jewel in the crown of this small community botanic gardens, which takes an hour to leisurely stroll through.

Museum of Western Colorado
MUSEUM

(☑ 970-242-0971; www.museumofwesternco.com; 462 Ute Ave; adult/child $7/4; ⊙ 9am-5pm Tue-Sat; 🖈) The most impressive of Grand Junction's sites, this well-arranged museum is the largest in the region, featuring impressive multidisciplinary displays on regional history (such as the awesome Thrailkill Collection of firearms) and special exhibits. Look for the modern bell tower downtown, the most central of the museum's three facilities.

Adventure Bound USA
WATER SPORTS

(☑ 800-423-4668, 970-245-5428; www.adventure boundusa.com; 2392 H Rd; day trip from $90; 🖈) This excellent operator is fully licensed on all BLM and NPS land and runs extended excursions on isolated, pristine sections of western Colorado's rivers. Day trips raft the Ruby and Horsethief Canyons. The Yampa River multiday offers great rapids and excellent scenery, running through Dinosaur National Monument following the route of mid-19th-century explorer John Wesley Powell.

🛏 Sleeping

Grand Junction has abundant accommodations. If you're blowing through town on the highway, the I-70 exit for Horizon Dr is downright silly with hotels from just about every major chain. The walkable downtown is more pleasant, with higher-end chains flourishing. Nice B&Bs occupy the outskirts.

Skip Grand Junction's RV-loaded private camping for some of the excellent state and national land in the area.

James M Robb Colorado River State Park
CAMPGROUND $

(☑ 970-434-3388; www.parks.state.co.us; tent/ RV sites $18/28; P) Conceived as a 'string of pearls' along the Colorado, it's five small parks in one. The Fruita Section is within walking distance of Dinosaur Journey (p304) and has over 60 sites, including a nice loop for tents along a small lake.

Castle Creek B&B
B&B $$

(☑ 970-241-9105; www.castlecreekbandb.com; 638 Horizon Dr; d $125-155; P ⊖ ✻ 🛜) From the

MESA VERDE & SOUTHWEST COLORADO GRAND JUNCTION

driveway, Castle Creek looks like little more than an enormous suburban mansion, but the details are spot on – independent entrances, chocolates on the pillow, a big selection of movies, popcorn by the microwave, and a hot tub from which to take in the fresh night air. Adults-only, the spacious grounds allow for a quiet stay.

Grand Junction Bookcliffs Bed & Breakfast
B&B $$

(970-261-3938; www.grandjunctionbnb.com; 3153 F Rd; d $115-150; P❀✿❖🐾) North of town, this family-operated B&B has immaculate country-style rooms. Though on a busy road, it's an excellent alternative to Grand Junction's mostly bleak hotels. Rooms are bright and cozy, and there's a backyard and nearby park for the kids to run around.

Eating

★ Pablo's Pizza
PIZZA $

(970-255-8879; www.pablospizza.com; 319 Main St; mains $6-12; 11am-8:30pm Sun-Thu, to 9pm Fri & Sat; 🐾👶) 🌱 These creative pies are easily the best pizza in town and we love the bike-to-dinner incentives. With sidewalk seating and a small-town vibe, this place serves steaming thin-crust pizzas. Pair with a microbrew. With gluten-free options.

Cafe Sol
CAFE $

(970-986-3474; www.cafesolgj.com; 420 Main St; mains $7-15; 8am-3:30pm) This cute downtown cafe is crushing it with its tempting selection of salads (like bleu fig with prosciutto and greens), fresh smoothies and satisfying panini sandwiches. Breakfasts are also creative. Has good options for vegans and the gluten-free crowd.

Dream Café
BREAKFAST $

(970-424-5353; 314 Main St; breakfast $6-12; 6:45am-2:30pm Mon-Sun; 👶) Hit this bright, sleek cafe for Grand Junction's best breakfast. Our favorite of the five eggs Benedict dishes is the California Dreamin' Bene, topped with red peppers, avocado, asparagus and hollandaise. For something sweet, opt for the pineapple upside-down pancakes.

Main Street Bagels
BAGELS, DELI $

(970-241-2740; www.mainstreetbagels.net; 559 Main St; sandwiches $7-10; 6:30am-6:30pm Mon-Sat, 7am-2:30pm Sun; 📶👶) A big open space with communal guitars hung up on the wall, this is where the town comes to gossip, clack away at their laptops and sip coffee. The sandwiches and bagels make

tasty, quick carb-loading lunches before hitting the trails outside town.

Zen Garden Asian Grill & Sushi Bar
PAN-ASIAN $

(970-254-8898; www.zengardengrandjunction. com; 2886 North Ave; mains $7-14; 11am-9:30pm) Zen Garden serves up plates of sushi with oddball attitude, lo mein and Thai curries. The boxed lunches are good value, and the warmly lit, intimate atmosphere is great when the weather is nasty.

Nepal Restaurant
INDIAN, NEPALESE $$

(970-242-2233; www.nepalgj.com; 356 Main St; mains $10-22, lunch buffet $9; 11am-2:30pm & 5-9pm Mon-Sat; 🐾) In a town without much ethnic food, the Nepalese lunch buffet fills a niche. There are plenty of vegan dishes as well.

Il Bistro Italiano
ITALIAN $$

(970-243-8622; www.ilbistroitaliano.com; 400 Main St; mains $14-20; 4:30-9pm Mon-Sun) Seasonal homemade pasta, lovingly made by Brunella Gualerzi, puts this rustic provincial Italian place on the radar of pasta aficionados. The dining area features exposed brick and white tablecloths.

Blue Moon Bar & Grille
AMERICAN $$

(970-242-4506; www.bluemoongj.com; 120 N 7th St; mains $10-21; 11am-2am Mon-Sat) With a cute retro setting, this hopping grill serves up classic fare like burgers, salads and prime rib Huge sandwiches come with curly fries and there's a laundry list of bottle beers and microbrews on offer.

★ 626 on Rood
MODERN AMERICAN $$$

(970-257-7663; www.626onrood.com; 626 Rood Ave; mains $16-45; 3-10pm) 🌱 Elegant and inventive, this is contemporary American at its best, like whole plates of stunning heirloom tomatoes in season, house-made mozzarella and lobster mac 'n' cheese. Artful mains change with the seasons and are paired with an excellent wine list. Servers know their stuff and can highlight regional wines, many of which are sustainable and biodynamic.

Drinking & Entertainment

Brewpubs and live music make the Junction a decent place to overnight if you are itching for a night out.

★ Kannah Creek Brewing Company
BREWERY

(970-263-0111; www.kannahcreekbrewingco. com; 1960 N 12th St; 11am-10pm Sun-Thu, to

11pm Fri & Sat) Kannah's Broken Oar is probably the best IPA on the Western Slope, and the Black Bridge Stout – an Irish-style dry stout with lots of depth – isn't fooling around either. Students from Mesa State, beer lovers and mountain bikers pack this place to drink and eat off the menu of calzone and brick-oven pizza in creative combos.

Mesa Theater & Club CLUB
(☑970-241-1717; www.mesatheater.com; 538 Main St; ⊙hours vary) With occasional live music, this small theater serves more as a nightclub, popular with students from the local university. The website details upcoming events.

Rockslide Brewery BREWERY
(☑970-245-2111; www.rockslidebrewpub.com; 401 Main St; ⊙11am-midnight Mon-Sat, 8am-11pm Sun) Though locals like it more for the beer than the food, Rockslide has a huge patio and is an amiable place on summer weekends.

Avalon Theatre CINEMA, LIVE MUSIC
(☑970-263-5700; www.tworiversconvention.com/avalon; 645 Main St; ⊙hours vary; ⛴) This historic theater hosts art-house films, comedy shows and live music. It might be the only venue that can boast hosting both composer John Philip Sousa and pop songstress Pat Benatar. During movies, it serves beer and wine.

🛍 Shopping

REI SPORTS & OUTDOORS
(☑970-254-8970; www.rei.com/stores/grand-junction; 644 North Ave; ⊙10am-8pm Mon-Fri, to 6pm Sat, 11am-5pm Sun) It's not as mammoth as some of the other sporting-goods outlets in town, but for camping and climbing, REI sells the best gear and the enthusiastic staff give the best advice.

Summit Canyon Mountaineering SPORTS & OUTDOORS
(☑970-243-2847, 800-360-6994; www.summitcanyon.com; 461 Main St; ⊙9am-7pm Mon-Sat, 10am-5pm Sun) You're in good hands here: the bearded dude behind the desk greets you as 'bro' andbreaks down the region's climbs. Stocks backpacking gear, kayak and stand up paddleboard (SUP) rentals, books and maps.

Grand Valley Books BOOKS
(☑970-424-5437; 350 Main St; ⊙10am-7pm Mon-Sat, to 4pm Sun) By exchanging store credit for used books, this downtown shop is a godsend for avid readers. It has a big selection of titles about regional history, Native American culture and the West.

ⓘ Tourist Information

BLM Grand Junction Field Office (☑970-244-3000; www.blm.gov; 2815 H Rd; ⊙8am-4:30pm Mon-Fri) Information on Bureau of Land Management lands.

USFS Grand Junction Ranger District Office (☑970-242-8211; 764 Horizon Dr; ⊙8am-5pm Mon-Fri) Offers national forest information.

Visitors Center (☑970-244-1480, toll-free 800-962-2547; www.visitgrandjunction.com; 740 Horizon Dr; ⊙8:30am-6pm Mon-Sat, from 9am Sun; 🅟) This volunteer-staffed information center is a quick minute from the highway.

ⓘ Getting There & Away

Grand Junction is on I-70, 248 miles west of Denver and 30 miles east of the Utah state line.

Grand Junction Amtrak (www.amtrak.com; 339 S 1st St; to Denver from $67; ⊙ticket office 9am-6pm) Amtrak's daily *California Zephyr* between Chicago, IL, and Oakland, CA, stops at the passenger depot; there's a small information booth here.

Grand Junction Regional Airport (Walker Field Airport, GJT; ☑970-244-9100; www.gjairport.com; 2828 Walker Field Dr) Grand Junction's commercial airport is 6 miles northeast of downtown. Flights connect to six cities in the western US, including Las Vegas, Phoenix and Los Angeles, but most flights go to and from Denver.

Greyhound Station (☑970-242-6012; www.greyhound.com; 230 S 5th St) Bus services to Denver (five hours, $47), Las Vegas, NV, and Salt Lake City, UT.

ⓘ Getting Around

Grand Valley Transit (GVT; ☑970-256-7433; www.gvt.mesacounty.us; 525 S 6th Street; fare $1.50; ⊙5:45am-6:15pm Mon-Sat) serves the city and region.

For car hire, Hertz, Avis, National and Budget have offices at the airport.

Fruita
☑970 / POP 12,700 / ELEV 4514FT

Home to some of the best singletrack in the US, modest Fruita is becoming a popular destination for mountain biking, though its trails are still less crowded than nearby Moab, Utah. It has thus far escaped a dire fate as an extended suburb of Grand Junction. Its cute two-block 'downtown' has traveler services that wisely cater to cyclists, beyond the odd antique shop and Saturday farmers market. The town is also the gateway to the 550-mile Dinosaur Diamond Prehistoric Hwy, a recent addition to the Scenic & Historic Byways network, which leads north to Dinosaur National Monument and into Utah.

◎ Sights & Activities

The singletrack rides around Fruita are some of the best in the West, drawing serious enthusiasts from afar. The dry, mild high-desert climate allows for a long riding season that stretches from late April to mid-November.

You can ride 142 miles of dirt to Moab on the Kokopelli Trail, but there's tons of options in two areas near town: the 18 Road area, more suited to beginners, and the Kokopelli area trails, best for high-intermediates and experts. Maps are available at Fruita's bike shops.

Dinosaur Journey   MUSEUM
(☑970-858-7282; www.museumofwesternco.com; 550 Jurassic Ct; adult/child $9/5; ☺ 9am-5pm Mon-Sun May-Sep, 10am-4pm Mon-Sat & from noon Sun Oct-Apr; ⚑) This small museum has a fantastic collection of scary animatronic dinos that snort steam and jerk around, bestial skeletons and interesting multimedia demonstrations. It's a little bit corny at times, but thrilling for the younger members of the party.

Kokopelli Trail   MOUNTAIN BIKING
This 128-mile trail stretches from outside Fruita to Moab in Utah. It's epic, with miles of ruggedly beautiful terrain. It requires careful planning and a multiple-day commitment. The start is in Loma, Colorado.

Trail Through Time   HIKING
(www.blm.gov; I-70, exit 2, McInnis Canyons National Conservation Area; ☺ dawn-dusk) **FREE** The best of four interpretive dinosaur trails around Fruita. On this 1.5-mile loop you can learn loads about the prehistoric landscape from interpretive signs, touch in-situ bones and, in summer, check out the active Mygatt-Moore Quarry.

Over the Edge Sports   CYCLING
(www.otefruita.com; 202 E Aspen Ave; bicycle rental $49-89; ☺ 9am-6pm) This is the store that put Fruita on the map. A full-service bike shop, which offers guided rides like the Kokopelli Trail and advocates for responsible trail use.

Fruita Paleontological Area   HIKING
(www.blm.gov; Horsethief Rd, off Kings View Rd; ☺ dawn-dusk) **FREE** Maybe it's the desolation of the dry, rumbling country; maybe it's the lack of anything man-made in your view.

Whatever the reason, it seems entirely possible to imagine dinosaurs roaming Fruita Paleontological Area. A half-mile loop trail leads past good interpretive signs explaining the six types of dinosaurs found here during 100 years of off-and-on excavation.

🛏 Sleeping & Eating

If you're looking for an overnight in town, there are national chain hotels on the south side of I-70, off the Fruita exit. Camping on Bureau of Land Management (BLM) land is available but is very sought-after by mountain bikers – try to find a campsite as early as possible in the day.

Balanced Rock Motel   MOTEL $
(☑970-858-7333, ext 4; www.balancedrockmotel. com; 126 S Coulson St; d $65; ❄🐾) Tidy and well maintained, the independent Balanced Rock is an excellent value for the price. The two-story, exterior-access motel is popular with mountain bikers.

★**Hot Tomato Cafe**   PIZZA $
(☑970-858-1117; www.hottomatocafe.com; 124 N Mulberry St; small pizzas $12-16; ☺ 11am-9pm Tue-Sat) 🚲 This pizza joint and cyclist hangout is run by Jen and Anne, a pair of bike enthusiasts who espouse a sustainable business ethos. Pizza comes in thick slices, there's a good salad selection and a row of Colorado beer on tap. When it gets late, there's a fun scene on the small outdoor patio.

Aspen Street Coffee   CAFE $
(☑970-858-8888; 136 E Aspen Ave; dishes $2-8; ☺ 6:30am-5pm Mon-Sat, 7am-1pm Sun; 🐾) With simple wraps, strong coffee and homemade granola, this is a great spot to stock up before the ride.

ℹ Tourist Information

Fruita (www.fruita.org) The homepage for the city of Fruita details local attractions, lodgings and events.
GoFruita.com A useful local tourism website.

ℹ Getting There & Away

You'll need your own private vehicle or bicycle to explore these parts.

Palisade

☑ 970 / POP 2635 / ELEV 4728FT
Famous for growing Colorado's best peaches, this small town owes its luck to a warm, dry microclimate that later turned out to also be

ideal for vineyards. Bordeaux-style grapes do well here, though you will find a bit of everything on offer. Relatively new on the scene, Palisade vineyards cannot compare to those in Napa Valley, but they do offer a fun outing into this blue-sky farmland. Palisade also offers good mountain biking that's not yet widely known with the newly developed Palisade Rim Trail.

Utes were the first inhabitants of the Grand Valley, followed by white settlers around 1881. Today it's a pleasant small town with a farm feel and entrepreneurs focused on developing the accoutrements of a wine-country culture.

◉ Sights & Activities

★ Suncrest Orchard, Alpacas and Fiber Mill   FARM
(☑970-464-4862; www.suncrestorchardalpacas. net; 3608 E 1/4 Rd; tour $10; ☉9am-5pm Tue, Thu & Sat; P👭) If cute were currency, Mike and Cindy McDermott would be sitting on a gold mine with their combination Alpaca and lavender farm. While Mike patiently explains the fiber processing, kids stand agape before the inquisitive beasts. You can also sample alpaca trekking. The on-site store, with its selection of natural yarns, hats and stuffed bears, has one-of-a-kind gifts.

★ Colterris Winery at the Overlook   WINERY
(☑970-464-1150; www.colterris.com; 3548 E 1/2 Rd; tour $4; ☉10am-5pm Jun-Oct) Sold in Colorado's finest restaurants, Colterris sits in a league of its own – as a sip of its earthy, balanced Cabernet Sauvignon confirms. The inviting tasting patio has cheese with wine pairings, and the servers are very knowledgable. The three-hour tour (reserve ahead) takes you from the vines to the packing shed, with beautiful river views.

High Country Orchards   FARM
(☑970-464-1150; www.highcountryorchards.com; 3548 E 1/2 Rd; ☉10am-5pm; P👭) While campaigning for the 2008 presidential election, the Obamas picked up a box of peaches at this family-operated outfit. The tractor tours are a fun way for families to get out into the fields and the on-site store stocks yummy peach salsa.

Maison La Belle Vie Winery   WINERY
(☑970-464-4959; www.maisonlabellevie.com; 3575 G Rd; ☉11am-5pm Mon-Sat; P) Owner John Barbier is a gregarious oenophile of the most lovable sort and his 'House of Beautiful Life' produces some of the area's finest Cab, Syrah and Rosé. On site there's also Amy's Courtyard, an elegant little space that doubles as a piano bar.

Sage Creations Organic Farm   FARM
(☑970-464-9019; www.sagecreationsorganicfarm. com; 3555 E Rd; ☉9am-4pm Thu-Sun) Tour this organic farm and pick your own lavender from its gorgeous fields. The lavender eye pillows make great gifts. It also sells bags of juicy cherries and heirloom tomatoes. The farm is generous about sharing growing tips with do-it-yourselfers.

Little Book Cliffs Wild Horse Range   WILDLIFE RESERVE
(☑970-244-3000; P) FREE One of three federally designated areas for wild horses in the United States, over 100 wild horses get the run of some 30,000 acres of craggy canyons and plateaus. To catch a glimpse of them, get ready for the grueling 10¼-mile Tellerico Loop, which rises 2300ft from the canyon floor to the top of the Bookcliffs.

It's 2.2 miles from I-70 on a dirt road that leads behind Mt Garfield.

Carlson Vineyards   WINERY
(☑970-464-5554; www.carlsonvineyards.com; 461 35 Rd; ☉10am-6pm Mon-Sun) When the hunt for the state's fine wine leads to this pole building, your expectations might take quite a dip. But if Carlson's reds are nothing special, this family winery rewards the search with fine whites and interesting fruit-based wines, including one from Palisade peaches. It's Colorado's third-oldest winery, with expansive views.

Rapid Creek Cycles & Sports   CYCLING
(☑970-464-9266; www.rapidcreekcycles.com; 237 S Main St; per day from $39; ☉9am-6pm Mon-Sat, 10am-4pm Sun) Rents out cruisers, mountain bikes and electric bikes, which can be handy for touring wine country.

🛏 Sleeping & Eating

★ Wine Valley Inn   B&B $$
(☑970-464-1498; www.winevalleyinnpalisade.com; 588 West 1st St; d $149-169; ❋🛜) From the wraparound porch to the comfortable quilted beds and clawfoot tubs, this welcoming Victorian inn is pure romance. In a quiet neighborhood setting, this is the ideal base for wandering the vineyards. With hospitable hosts and a pleasant 24-hour hot tub in a private, landscaped garden. Adults only.

TOURING WINE COUNTRY

Colorado's tiny wine region boasts the surreal backdrop of the wide Colorado River, red-rock canyons and big blue skies. Here hot summers and volcanic soil produce wines that are as bold as the surroundings.

According to locals, Palisade is the smallest town in the USA with an all-of-the-above approach to producing booze: a winery, meadery, distillery and brewery all within the city borders. Exploring area wineries and orchards makes for a fun weekend trip, though you can enjoy more peace if you go midweek. All offer free tastings, some have extensive tours (for a small fee), available with reservations.

Across from the town plaza, **Rapid Creek Cycles** offers bikes apt for touring the vineyards. It also has John Hodge's handy area map. To vineyard-hop in air-conditioned comfort, contact **American Spirit Shuttle** (970-523-7662; www.americanspiritshuttle.net; per person $40; noon-4pm Sat Apr-Nov), with scheduled four-stop tours of the Grande Valley AVA wineries. The Palisade Tourism Board and **Chamber of Commerce** have handy maps you can download from their websites. You can also find useful information at www.coloradowine.com.

Colorado Wine Country Inn HOTEL $$
(970-464-5777; www.coloradowinecountryinn.com; 777 Grande River Dr; d $202, ste $278; P ✳@🛜🏊) More chain hotel than B&B, this newish 80-room lodging sits right next to I-70. Hopefully, the pool and white rocking chairs looking out on surrounding vineyards will help you forget. Staff are helpful and there's a social atmosphere with Friday night BBQs and wine receptions for guests. The adjoining winery has self-guiding tours. With a hot buffet breakfast.

Inari's A Palisade Bistro BISTRO $$
(970-464-4911; www.inarisbistro.com; 336 Main St; mains $11-25; 5-9pm Sat & Sun) Just taking a whiff of the cheese menu makes it evident that Palisade has fine dining that's worth the trip. The seasonal menu features a dash of Mediterranean and Asian influences. The honey-soy-glazed grilled salmon is terrific.

 Drinking & Nightlife

After exploring the wineries, round off your day of drinking with a visit to the distillery and brew pub.

Palisade Brewing Company BREWERY
(970-464-1462; www.palisadebrewingcompany.com; 200 Peach Ave; sandwiches $7-13; noon-10pm) The unadorned warehouse demonstrates a single-minded focus on beer making. On nice days the patio fills up with families eating brats and paninis while listening to live music (Wednesday and Friday). The popcorn machine is a nice touch; a few salty handfuls pique your thirst for some

Dirty Hippie, a dark American wheat. Kids get homemade rootbeer.

Peach Street Distillers DISTILLERY
(970-464-1128; www.peachstreetdistillers.com; 144 Kluge Ave; noon-10pm) From the moment you size up this room – more work-a-day warehouse than an uppity tasting room – it's clear that Peach Tree is dead serious about its booze. Sure, the sign behind the bar reminds you that this is a tasting room and *not* a bar, but locals pack in. Bring in dinner from the food truck parked alongside.

If you're taking a bottle home, go for the boutique and seasonal stuff, such as limited-edition pear vodka, or Peach Goat Vodka, infused with the famous local peaches. If you're just here for a drink, the Bloody Mary is to die for.

 Tourist Information

Palisade Chamber of Commerce (970-464-7458; www.palisadecoc.com; 319 Main St; 9am-5pm Mon-Fri) Tourist information office in downtown Palisade. Website has downloads including regional maps and auto-tours.

Palisade Tourism Board (www.palisadetourism.com) This website has a useful index of lodgings, wineries, orchards and other attractions. It also lists upcoming events.

Getting There & Away

Palisade sits around 14 miles east of Grand Junction on the I-70. Palisade and its surrounding area are best accessed and explored with your own private vehicle.

Southeast Colorado & the San Luis Valley

Includes ➡

Colorado Springs ... .310
Cañon City .... .317
Florence 320
Cripple Creek 320
Manitou Springs ..... .321
Pueblo 325
Trinidad 329
Great Sand Dunes
National Park 332
Alamosa 335
San Luis .... .337
Westcliffe .... .341
Crestone 344

Best Places to Eat

➡ Marigold (p316)

➡ Adam's Mountain Cafe (p323)

➡ San Luis Valley Brewing Co (p337)

Best Places to Stay

➡ Broadmoor (p314)

➡ Garden of the Gods Resort (p314)

➡ Cliff House at Pikes Peak (p323)

Why Go?

Colorado's arid southeast is a place of high desert landscapes backed by craggy peaks and flat-topped mesas, where silvery sage and scraggly juniper morphs into the great aspens and pines of the central mountains. There's no shortage of glory-hallelujah scenery in this quiet corner of the state, and the dramatic and at times surreal vistas may leave you speechless.

There's history here, too, from dino fossils and footprints to petrified sequoias and the volcanic vestiges of a mindboggling geological timescale. This spectacular stage has also seen significant human drama, for it was here that the Santa Fe Trail hastened a cultural collision between Native Americans, Mexican pioneers, French trappers, do-or-die miners and hope-filled homesteaders.

It's this theme of natural and historical diversity – well-preserved in a wealth of museums, off-the-beaten track beauty, and a laid-back, surprisingly youthful vibe – that makes Southeast Colorado so appealing.

When to Go
Colorado Springs

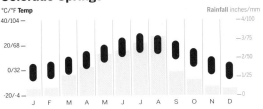

May & Jun Milder weather is perfect for exploring the high desert and dunes.

Jun–Aug Climb the peaks, bike the back roads and rock out at music festivals.

Sep & Oct Golden aspens light up Pikes Peak and the Sangres.

Southeast Colorado & the San Luis Valley Highlights

① **Great Sand Dunes National Park** (p332) Work out how all this sand got here.

② **Garden of the Gods** (p310) Marvel at the majesty of this heavenly Colorado Springs park.

③ **Phantom Canyon** (p319) Try not to pretend you're a rally driver as you navigate the twisty road to Cripple Creek.

④ **Venable-Comanche Loop Trail** (p342) Stalk a herd of bighorn sheep through the Sangre de Cristo Mountains.

⑤ **Spanish Peaks Wilderness** (p328) Hike by sheer volcanic walls that rise from the earth outside Cuchara.

⑥ **Royal Gorge** (p318) Ride the wild Arkansas River on the fringe of Cañon City.

⑦ **Penitente Canyon** (p340) Camp in the silence of the surreal desert around Del Norte.

⑧ **Cumbres & Toltec Scenic Railroad** (p338) Ooh and ahh your way into the mountains above Antonito.

⑨ **Valley View Hot Springs** (p343) Contemplate Gaia while soaking in thermal ponds with mind-blowing vistas.

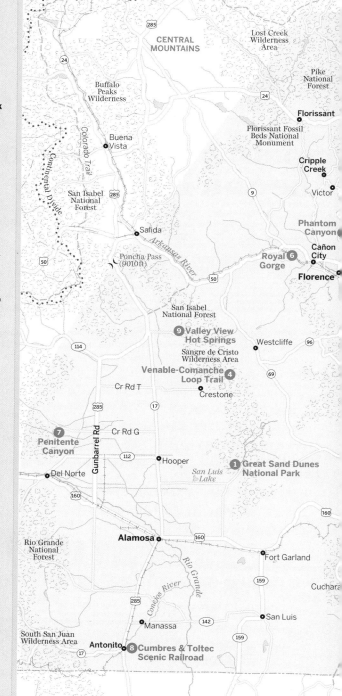

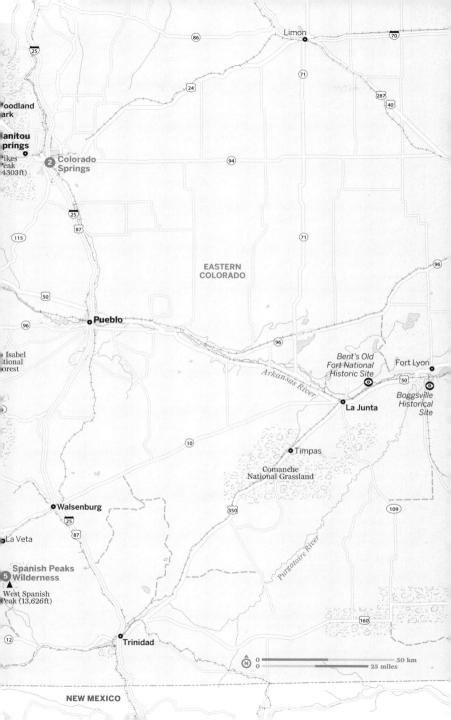

SOUTHERN FRONT RANGE

Most visitors to southeast Colorado don't venture much further than the neighboring population centers of Colorado Springs and Manitou Springs, which snuggle up to the foothills of the vast Southern Front Range. With gorgeous vistas and parks galore, each has an eclectic mix of galleries and museums and a wealth of family-friendly attractions that are activity-based, fun and informative. Throw in a vibrant dining and craft-brewery scene and there's no shortage of ways to keep occupied.

Those who do venture off the beaten track into the mountains will be rewarded with expansive wilderness, endless skies and relics of days gone by. Adventurers will want to head to Cañon City to ride the rapids of the dramatic Royal Gorge or kit up their packs to explore the area's hundreds of miles of pine-shaded or open-range walking trails.

🅘 Getting There & Away

Colorado Springs Airport (p317) is the air gateway into the southeast, with regular scheduled services to Denver, Los Angeles, San Francisco, Seattle, New York, Washington and Atlanta.

The I-25 runs straight through Colorado Springs, which is 69 miles south of Denver, then onward to Pueblo.

🅘 Getting Around

Heading west into the 'hills' of the Southern Front Range, Hwy 24 passes through Manitou Springs before weaving its way to Vail, some 165 miles away.

It's 20 miles west of Manitou Springs on Hwy 24 to Divide where Hwy 67 shoots south to Cripple Creek (19 miles), then another 27 miles to Cañon City and the Royal Gorge.

Colorado Springs

📞 719 / POP 445,830 / ELEV 6010FT

One of the nation's first destination resorts, Colorado Springs is now the state's second-largest city. Its natural beauty and pleasant climate attract visitors from around the globe, who come to ascend majestic Pikes Peak and admire the exquisite sandstone spires of the Garden of the Gods.

Comprising a sprawling quilt of neighborhoods, which can be a little confusing to navigate, Colorado Springs has many faces. It's home to three of the nation's highest security military bases, it's an evangelical stronghold, and it boasts a vibrant liberal-arts university campus.

Recently the Springs has come of its own as a year-round adventure and leisure tourism destination, with a bunch of new family-focused attractions adding to the appeal of the Front Range and its existing cache of sights, from the excellent fine-arts museum to the historic Air Force Academy and an up-and-coming restaurant scene.

🅞 Sights

★ Garden of the Gods   PARK

(www.gardenofgods.com; 1805 N 30th St; ⊗ 5am-11pm May-Oct, to 9pm Nov-Apr; P) FREE This gorgeous vein of red sandstone (about 290 million years old) appears elsewhere along Colorado's Front Range, but the exquisitely thin cathedral spires and mountain backdrop of the Garden of the Gods are particularly striking. Explore the network of paved and unpaved trails, enjoy a picnic and watch climbers test their nerve on the sometimes flaky rock.

For information on horseback rides and other activities in the park, stop off at the excellent visitor center on the way in. In the summer, Rock Ledge Ranch (p313), a living history museum near the park entrance, re-enacts life in the 19th century for Native Americans and settlers in the region.

★ Colorado Springs Fine Arts Center   MUSEUM

(FAC; 📞 719-634-5583; www.csfineartscenter.org; 30 W Dale St; adult/student $12/5; ⊗ 10am-5pm Tue-Sun; P) Fully renovated in 2007, this expansive museum and 400-seat theater originally opened in 1936. The museum's collection is surprisingly sophisticated, with some terrific Latin American art and photography, and great rotating exhibits that draw from the 23,000 pieces in its permanent collection.

Red Rock Canyon Open Space   PARK

(www.redrockcanyonopenspace.org; Hwy 24, at S 31st St; P🐾) FREE A former quarry and part of the sandstone vein that runs through the Garden of the Gods, this 787-acre park was nearly developed into a golf course and townhouses. Thanks to committed residents who fought the good fight, however, it's now a fabulous local park, where you can hike, mountain bike and rock climb, without all the tourist hoopla.

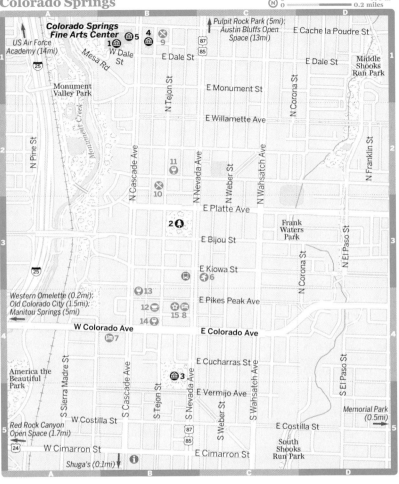

Colorado Springs

◎ Top Sights
1 Colorado Springs Fine Arts Center B1

◎ Sights
2 Acacia Park B3
3 Colorado Springs Pioneers Museum ... B4
4 Cornerstone Arts Center B1
5 Money Museum B1

✛ Activities, Courses & Tours
6 CityRock C3

🛏 Sleeping
7 Antlers B4

8 Mining Exchange B4

✕ Eating
9 La'au's Taco Shop B1
10 Poor Richard's Restaurant B2

🍷 Drinking & Nightlife
11 Brooklyn's on Boulder St B2
12 Perk Downtown B4
13 Phantom Canyon Brewing B4
14 Thirsty Parrot B4

✪ Entertainment
15 Kimball's Twin Peak Theater B4

US Air Force Academy SCHOOL

(☑719-333-2025; www.usafa.af.mil; I-25, exit 156B; ⊙visitor center 9am-5pm; Ⓟ) **FREE** A visit to this campus, one of the highest-profile military academies in the country, offers a limited but nonetheless fascinating look into the lives of an elite group of cadets. The visitor center provides general background on the academy; from here you can walk over to the dramatic chapel (1963) or embark on a driving tour of the expansive grounds.

The entrance is via the North Gate, 14 miles north of Colorado Springs on I-25.

Colorado Springs Pioneers Museum MUSEUM

(☑719-385-5990; www.cspm.org; 215 S Tejon St; ⊙10am-5pm Tue-Sat; Ⓟ) **FREE** Colorado Springs' municipal museum is set in the old El Paso County Courthouse, built in 1903. The collection and exhibition of some 60,000 pieces sums up the region's history. Particularly good is the Native American collection, which features hundreds of items from the Ute, Cheyenne and Arapaho Nations.

Austin Bluffs Open Space PARK

(www.coloradosprings.gov; ⊙5am-9pm) This beautiful reserve overlooking Colorado Springs and the Rockies beyond is strewn with distinctive rock formations dating to the Eocene period. Walking and hiking trails crisscross the park and adjacent Pulpit Rock Park (p313).

Old Colorado City Historic District AREA

The neighborhood known as Old Colorado City is where the original town was founded in 1860. It's former Wild West dens of vice (21 saloons in four blocks!) now host restaurants and souvenir shops, and the area is good for a stroll.

Cheyenne Mountain Zoo ZOO

(☑719-633-9925; www.cmzoo.org; 4250 Cheyenne Mountain Zoo Rd; adult/child $20/15; ⊙9am-5pm, last admission 4pm; Ⓟ⛪) High up on Cheyenne Mountain, the largest private zoo in the country was launched with holdovers from the private animal collection of Spencer Penrose (1865–1939), a prominent local businessman and philanthropist. Serious about conversation, the zoo is proud of its giraffe breeding program, and its animal habitats feature educational elements. There are also some nice play areas for kids.

The Mountaineer Sky Ride (adult/child $5/4), a brief chairlift experience, will give you a bird's-eye view of the entire zoo.

Will Rogers Shrine of the Sun MONUMENT

(☑719-633-9925; www.cmzoo.org; 4250 Cheyenne Mountain Zoo Rd; admission incl with zoo admission; ⊙9am-3pm; Ⓟ) Set behind the Cheyenne Mountain Zoo and those massive crenelated stone gates, on a cliff about two-thirds of the way up Cheyenne Mountain, is this tower named for Spencer Penrose's good friend Will Rogers, who died in a plane crash coincidentally around the time of its construction. There are busts of both men out front and the best Colorado Springs views in town.

World Figure Skating Museum & Hall of Fame MUSEUM

(☑719-635-5200; www.worldskatingmuseum.org; 20 1st St; adult/child $6/4; ⊙10am-4pm Tue-Fri; Ⓟ) Fans of figure skating should stop by this museum where you can glimpse snippets of past greats. You'll see their skates and outfits, and stills and video footage of some of the greatest routines ever performed.

Memorial Park PARK

(www.springsgov.com; 1605 E Pikes Peak Ave; Ⓟ⛪) Set just off downtown, with Prospect Lake surrounded by wide green lawns and ball fields, and Pikes Peak and the rest of the southern front range looming to the west, this is the city's biggest public park and the site of the Labor Day Lift Off (p313), one of America's biggest and best hot-air-balloon festivals.

Cornerstone Arts Center GALLERY

(☑719-389-6607; www.coloradocollege.edu; 825 N Cascade Ave; ⊙hours vary; Ⓟ) **FREE** Colorado College's striking, $30-million LEED–certified arts complex sits across the street from the Fine Arts Center. You'll see sculpture on the front lawn, and there's a free gallery inside and frequent guest lecturers and film screenings. Past guests have included filmmakers, prominent feminists, Buddhist masters and big-time video-game producers.

Money Museum MUSEUM

(☑719-482-9834; www.money.org; 818 N Cascade Ave; adult/student $8/6; ⊙10:30am-5pm Tue-Sat; Ⓟ) Yes, museums dedicated to coin collecting do exist. This museum, operated by the American Numismatic Association, has gold coins from the early 19th century, early commemorative coins from the turn of the 20th century and a few vintage greenbacks, too.

Old Colorado Historical Society MUSEUM
(☏719-636-1225; www.occhs.org; 1 S 24th St; ⏰11am-4pm Tue-Sat; P) FREE Located in a former Baptist church, this tiny museum and bookstore introduces visitors to the history of Old Colorado City and is a good way to add context to a wander past today's boutiques and restaurants.

Acacia Park PARK
(☏719-385-5940; www.visitcos.com/directory/acacia-park; 115 E Platte Ave; ⏰fountain splash park 11am-5pm Jun-Aug) Home to the much loved Uncle Wilbur's Fountain, a lifeguard-monitored pop jet fountain with over 200 water jets, 52 of which are part of a play area where kids can valiantly try to stem the unstoppable streams.

Rock Ledge Ranch MUSEUM
(☏719-578-6777; www.coloradosprings.gov/RockLedgeRanch; 3105 Gateway Rd; adult/child $8/4; ⏰10am-5pm Wed-Sat Jun–mid-Aug) This living history museum near the Garden of the Gods (p310) park entrance is worth a visit for those interested in the lives of Native Americans and 19th-century homesteaders in the region.

Pulp RK
(P) t-
ed to 2)
and is
suita r-
al fit at
N Ne

Banc RK
(W Co s-
torica h
is set o
City. r
Coun

Overc k
(☏719- 6
Spectr l-
10pm v
in 20 r
racetr .
Zippy e
downs e
more hard-core 2nd-floor 'speed' track. In another nice first, the track also has special go-karts made in Italy with hand controls for the mobility impaired.

CityRock CLIMBING
(☏719-634-9099; www.climbcityrock.com; 21 N Nevada Ave; climbing trips half-/full day $139/169, gym day pass $15; ⏰11am-10pm Mon-Fri, 10am-8pm Sat, noon-8pm Sun; 🚻) Learn to climb with this local association, which runs an indoor gym and leads trips to Garden of the Gods, Red Rock Canyon and Shelf Road. Rental equipment available.

US Olympic Training Center TOUR
(☏888-659-8687; www.teamusa.org; 1750 E Boulder St; ⏰9am-4:30pm Mon-Sat; 🚻) FREE Fans of Olympic sports will enjoy a guided spin through one of three official United States Olympic and Paralympic training centers (the other two are in Lake Placid and Chula Vista). This is the chief training facility for various sports, including gymnastics, judo, swimming and volleyball. It begins with an inspirational up-to-date highlight reel.

✦ Festivals & Events

★**Territory Days** FAIR
(⏰May) What began as a local barbecue in 1975 has grown into this three-day street festival held in the Historic District on Colorado Ave between 23rd and 27th Sts, over the Memorial Day weekend. The event attracts over 200 vendors and around 80,000 visitors!

Labor Day Lift Off AIR SHOW
(www.coloradospringslabordayliftoff.com; ⏰Sep) Formerly called the Colorado Springs Classic, for the past 40 years hot-air balloonists, both amateur and pro, have been launching Technicolor balloons into the sky just after sunrise for three straight days over the Labor Day weekend. You'll have to wake with the roosters to see it all, but it's definitely worth your while.

MeadowGrass MUSIC
(☏719-495-2743; www.meadowgrass.org; 6145 Shoup Rd; ⏰May) Three days of bluegrass at the La Foret retreat center, just north of Colorado Springs. For the full experience, buy a full festival/camping pass.

Great Fruitcake Toss CULTURAL
(☏719-685-5089; www.manitousprings.org; ⏰1st Sat in Jan) Don't miss the famous post-Christmas fruitcake toss, when locals make homemade slingshots to catapult the suckers. The cake that flies furthest wins. Held on the Manitou Springs High School track.

🛏 Sleeping

Colorado Springs has a wide variety of accommodation options, including some very special hotels and a glut of chain motels.

Extended Stay America   APARTMENT **$**
(Colorado Springs West; ☑ 719-266-4206; www.extendedstayamerica.com; 5855 Corporate Dr; r from $89; P ✳ 🛜) The recently renovated studio-apartment-style rooms of this well-located hotel, central to both Colorado Springs and Manitou Springs, make for a comfortable, self-contained stay and are suitable for traveling families or if you're sticking around for a few days. That said, cheap rates and long-stay-without-a-lease potential can attract all sorts – your neighbors can be hit-and-miss.

⭐ **Great Wolf Lodge**   RESORT **$$**
(☑ 844-553-9653; www.greatwolf.com/colorado-springs; 9494 Federal Dr; r incl park passes from $199; P ✳ 🛜 🏊) Colorado Springs' newest kid-friendly attraction is a winner for its fun activities, including mini-golf, climbing and bowling; its slew of cool year-round pools; and its more educational pursuits, such as the adventurous 'MagiQuest,' and the take-what-you-make 'Creation Station,' where kids (and adults!) can design and build their own soft toy. The catch: to use the park, you must stay at the resort.

Fortunately, when you add up the expense of family rooms in motels, meals, and admission fees, Great Wolf Lodge, as a one stop shop, offers excellent value. Note that while admission to the water park is included in the package, meals aren't: but there's a range of dining options to choose from under the one roof.

Mining Exchange   HOTEL **$$**
(☑ 719-323-2000; www.wyndham.com; 8 S Nevada Ave; r from $149; P ✳ 🛜) Opened in 2012 and set in the former turn-of-the-century bank where Cripple Creek prospectors traded in their gold for cash (check out the vault door in the lobby), the Mining Exchange takes the prize for Colorado Spring's most stylish hotel. Twelve-foot-high ceilings, exposed brick walls and leather furnishings make for an inviting, contemporary feel.

Antlers   HOTEL **$$**
(☑ 719-955-5600; www.antlers.com; 4 S Cascade Ave; d/ste from $189/269; P ✳ 🛜) While it doesn't look much from the outside, the interior of the Antlers has a 'masculine-chic' vibe, with lots of dark wood, chocolate leather, and chunky, comfortable, high-end furnishings. Of its 273-rooms and surprisingly large number of suites (22), most have excellent views, and the downtown Colorado Springs location is unsurpassed.

Staybridge Suites   HOTEL **$$**
(☑ 719-590-7829; www.ihg.com; 7130 Commerce Center Dr; apt from $169; P ✳ 🛜 🏊) Located to the north of the city, in the vicinity of the US Air Force Academy, these winning-formula chain apartments – in studio, one- and two-bedroom variations, with added extras such as evening socials and a decent breakfast spread – offer excellent value. Friendly, professional staff help round out the offering.

Academy Hotel   HOTEL **$$**
(☑ 719-598-5770; www.theacademyhotel.com; 8110 N Academy Blvd; d from $119; P 🛜 🏊) The closest hotel to the US Air Force Academy has kept on top of its game, undertaking regular updates to ensure its rooms stay spick and span for its high turnover of guests, so you can be sure of comfortable beds, fast internet and friendly service.

Drury Inn & Suites   HOTEL **$$**
(☑ 719-598-2500; www.druryhotels.com; 1170 Interquest Pkwy; r from $179; P ✳ 🛜) At the northern end of town, convenient for the Air Force Academy, you'll find this smart, well-managed and well-maintained hotel with large, comfortable rooms that come with plenty of little extras: a microwave, free breakfast, evening snacks and even some free long-distance calls.

⭐ **Broadmoor**   RESORT **$$$**
(☑ 855-634-7711; www.broadmoor.com; 1 Lake Ave; r from $295; P ✳ 🛜 🏊 🏊) One of the top five-star resorts in the US, the 744-room Broadmoor sits in a picture-perfect location against the blue-green slopes of Cheyenne Mountain. Everything here is exquisite: acres of lush grounds and a lake, a glimmering pool, world-class golf, myriad bars and restaurants, an incredible spa and ubercomfortable guest rooms (which, it must be said, are of the 'grandmother' school of design).

There's a reason that hundreds of Hollywood stars, A-list pro athletes and nearly every president since FDR have made it a point to visit.

⭐ **Garden of the Gods Resort**   RESORT **$$$**
(☑ 719-632-5541; www.gardenofthegodsclub.com; 3320 Mesa Rd; d/ste from $309/459; P ✳ 🛜 🏊)

Under new management, with ongoing expansion, and having just completed the renovation of all its luxury hotel rooms and suites and the construction of an enormous day-spa facility, the resort wing of the Garden of the Gods Club is giving the competition (known for its historic elegance) a run for its old-money.

A resort fee of $30 per day applies for the duration of your stay.

Lodge at Flying Horse RESORT $$$
(☑ 844-768-2684; www.lodgeatflyinghorse.com; 1880 Weiskopf Point; d from $329; P❄️🛜🏊) Colorado Springs' newest accommodations are up there with its finest. Set within the grounds of the exclusive Flying Horse community and complementing its world-class golf course, athletic club and spa, the 'Rocky Mountains Tuscan'–styled lodge's 48 plush, luxuriously appointed guest rooms are more likely to motivate you to stay in than to do a circuit at the gym.

Cheyenne Mountain Resort RESORT $$$
(☑ 719-538-4000; www.cheyennemountain.com; 3225 Broadmoor Valley Rd; d from $299; P❄️🏊) Boasting a glorious position overlooking Cheyenne Mountain, this woodsy, lodge-like resort with its country-life furnishings, fireplaces, fitness center, day spa and a range of dining options has an air of indulgence about it. You'll certainly feel much more at home here with someone special than if you were flying solo.

A resort fee of $28 per day applies for the duration of your stay.

✖️ Eating

In recent years, Colorado Springs has followed Denver's lead and started to gain traction as a culinary destination. You can enjoy a wide variety of cuisine here, from fast food to fine dining, and a range of world flavors.

Thunder and Buttons PUB FOOD $
(☑ 719-446-9888; www.thunderandbuttons.com; 2415 W Colorado Ave; mains $6-13; ⏱ 11am-2am; ❄️) One of the coolest spots in Old Colorado City, this richly atmospheric divey bar and grill has old dark-wood furnishings, exposed brick walls and a local following. The menu offers the usual pub grub, but the award-winning elk chili is worth dropping in for.

Shuga's CAFE $
(☑ 719-328-1412; www.shugas.com; 702 S Cascade Ave; dishes $8-9; ⏱ 11am-midnight; 🛜) If you thought Colorado Springs couldn't be hip, stroll to Shuga's, a Southern-style cafe with a knack for knockout espresso drinks and hot cocktails. Cuter than a button, this little white house is decked out in paper cranes and red vinyl chairs; there's also patio seating. The food – brie BLT on rosemary toast, Brazilian coconut shrimp soup – comforts and delights. Don't miss vintage-movie Saturdays.

Burrowing Owl VEGAN $
(☑ 719-434-3864; www.burrowingowllounge.com; 1791 S 8th St; dishes $6-12; ⏱ 4pm-2am; P🅿️) 🌱 This cozy neighborhood joint bills itself as social, sustainable and vegan, and it's more like a hangout than a restaurant, where people come to sit, sip chai or an organic brew and enjoy tasty vegan small plates and bar snacks. Very cool.

Western Omelette BREAKFAST $
(☑ 719-636-2286; www.westernomelette.com; 16 S Walnut St; mains $4-10; ⏱ 6am-3pm; P) If you're hungover after a big night, do as the locals do and head here for a green chile cure. The Mexican breakfast dishes, including the huevos rancheros (with green chile, of course), are greasy-spoon fare. It's a big place completely lacking in character, which oddly gives the restaurant its charm.

La'au's Taco Shop HAWAIIAN, MEXICAN $
(☑ 719-578-5228; www.laaustacoshop.com; 830 N Tejon St; dishes $6-10; ⏱ 11am-9pm; 🅿️🛜) Tucked into Spencer Center, near Colorado College, this creative Hawaiian taco shack offers tasty, fast and healthy fare in the form of taco, bowl, (massive) burrito or salad. Choose your protein (shrimp, steak, mahi, chicken or pork), and your salsa and toppings style (Baja, Kona, Hilo or Maui) and grab some coconut flan for dessert.

Poor Richard's Restaurant AMERICAN $
(☑ 719-632-7721; www.poorrichardsdowntown. com; 324 1/2 N Tejon St; pizza slices from $4.50, mains $6-12; ⏱ 11am-9pm; 🛜) Hit up Poor Richard's Restaurant for an additive-free meal. The casual restaurant is well-known for its delicious, hand-tossed, New York–style pizzas made from crispy white, wheat or spelt crust, as well as fresh build-your-own salads with more than 30 ingredient choices. Kids will dig the indoor playground in the back.

La Baguette CAFE $
(☑ 719-577-4818; www.labaguette-co.com; 2417 W Colorado Ave; mains $6-12; ⏱ 7am-6pm Mon-Sat,

8am-5pm Sun) A cute hole-in-the-wall cafe that bakes some of the best, if not the best, baguettes and croissants in the city – no small feat, given the altitude. It also does tasty, rustic soups and salads.

★**Pizzeria Rustica** PIZZA $$
(🕿719-632-8121; www.pizzeriarustica.com; 2527 W Colorado Ave; pizzas $12-24; ⊙noon-9pm Tue-Sun; 🅿✚) Wood-fired pizzas, locally sourced ingredients and a historic Old Colorado City locale make this bustling pizza joint the place to make a beeline for when you have a craving for pie. Its popularity means that it's always smart to make dinner reservations when possible.

★**Marigold** FRENCH $$
(🕿719-599-4776; www.marigoldcafeandbakery.com; 4605 Centennial Blvd; mains lunch $8-13, dinner $11-24; ⊙bistro 11am-2:30pm & 5-9pm, bakery 8am-9pm Mon-Sat) Way out by the Garden of the Gods is this buzzy French bistro and bakery that's easy on both the palate and the wallet. Feast on delicacies such as snapper Marseillaise, garlic-and-rosemary rotisserie chicken, and gourmet salads and pizzas, and be sure to leave room for the double (and triple!) chocolate mousse cake or the lemon tarts.

★**Uchenna** ETHIOPIAN $$
(🕿719-634-5070; www.uchennaalive.com; 2501 W Colorado Ave, Suite 105; mains $12-22; ⊙noon-2pm & 5-8pm Tue-Sun; 🅿✚✚) Chef Maya learned her recipes from her mother before she moved to America, and you'll love the homey cooking and family-friendly vibe at this authentic Ethiopian restaurant. Go for well-spiced meat or veg options and mop everything up with the spongy injera.

Jake & Telly's GREEK $$
(🕿719-633-0406; www.greekdining.com; 2616 W Colorado Ave; mains lunch $9-14, dinner $16-28; ⊙11:30am-9pm; 🕿✚) One of the best choices in Old Colorado City, this Greek eatery looks and sounds slightly touristy – lots of Greek monument murals on the walls and themed music on the stereo – but the food is absolutely delicious. It does a nice Greek-dip sandwich, as well as traditional dishes such as souvlaki, dolmas and spanakopita.

★**Blue Star** MODERN AMERICAN $$$
(🕿719-632-1086; www.thebluestar.net; 1645 S Tejon St; mains $21-38; ⊙3pm-midnight; 🅿✚) One of Colorado Springs' most popular gourmet eateries, the Blue Star is in the gentrifying Ivywild neighborhood just south of downtown. The menu at this landmark spot changes regularly, but always involves fresh fish, top-cut steak and inventive chicken dishes, flavored with Mediterranean and Pacific Rim rubs and spices.

🍷 Drinking & Nightlife

The downtown Tejon St strip, between Platte and Colorado Aves, is where most of the after-dark action happens. Although Colorado Springs isn't as happening as Denver to the north, it's certainly on the up, with some new breweries and bars bringing a bit of big-city culture to town.

Trinity Brewing Co BREWERY
(🕿719-634-0029; www.trinitybrew.com; 1466 W Garden of the Gods Rd; ⊙11am-10pm Sun-Wed, to midnight Thu-Sat; 🕿) ✚ Inspired by Belgium's beer cafes, the ecofriendly Trinity Brewing Co is a cool addition to the Colorado Springs pub scene. Owned by two self-admitted beer geeks, it serves 'artisanal beers' (made from rare ingredients and potent amounts of alcohol) and has a veggie-friendly menu – though don't expect miracles from the kitchen.

Look for the brewery in a strip mall one block west of Centennial Blvd.

Phantom Canyon Brewing BREWERY
(🕿719-635-2800; www.phantomcanyon.com; 2 E Pikes Peak Ave; ⊙11am-1am; 🕿) In an old exposed warehouse building saved from the wrecking ball in 1993, this local brewery serves a variety of pints in a casual atmosphere with wood floors and furnishings. It's not the best brewery in town, but it's definitely the most central. Locals flock to the upstairs billiards room at night.

Brooklyn's on Boulder St COCKTAIL BAR
(🕿719-415-3115; www.brooklynsonboulder.com; 110 E Boulder St; ⊙4-10pm Wed, 5pm-midnight Thu-Sun) Cousins Nick and Ian are living their dream, having opened Colorado Springs' first gin distillery (Lee Spirits Co), the tasting room of which operates as a speakeasy for folks visiting this 'fine haberdashery.' Hint: ring the doorbell.

Bristol Brewing Co BREWERY
(🕿719-633-2555; www.bristolbrewing.com; 1604 S Cascade Ave; ⊙11am-10pm; 🕿) Although a bit out of the way in southern Colorado Springs, this brewery – which in 2013 spearheaded a community market center in the shuttered Ivywild Elementary School – is

worth seeking out for its Laughing Lab ale and pub grub from the owner of the gourmet Blue Star (p316).

Perk Downtown CAFE
(📞 719-635-1600; www.theperkdowntown.com; 14 S Tejon St; ⊙ 6am-10pm Mon-Fri, 7am-11pm Sat, to 9pm Sun; 📶) With a fantastic rooftop boasting unobstructed views of Colorado Springs' signature mountain, Pikes Peak, Perk is a favorite regional coffee shop. Read a magazine, write a novel or just enjoy a chat with friends in the cozy 2nd-floor lounge or on the rooftop deck when the weather's nice. It also serves sandwiches.

Thirsty Parrot BAR
(📞 719-884-1094; www.facebook.com/thirsty parrotcos; 32 S Tejon St; ⊙ 4pm-2am Tue-Sat) However cheeseball this place looks – and it certainly does look it – it does provide a blast of much-needed nightlife on Tejon St when DJs spin dance music on Fridays.

Jives Coffee Lounge CAFE
(📞 719-445-1841; 16 Colbrunn Ct; ⊙ 7am-11pm Sun-Thu, to midnight Fri & Sat; 📶) Easily the hippest hand on the Old Colorado City stretch, this large brick-walled coffee lounge has ample sofas, wi-fi, and a bandstand featuring regular live music (weekends) and a Wednesday open-mic night. It does coffee and a selection of all-fruit, no-sugar smoothies. Food is limited.

☆ Entertainment

Kimball's Twin Peak Theater CINEMA
(📞 719-447-1945; www.kimballstwinpeak.com; 113 E Pikes Peak Ave; adult/child $9/6.50; ⊙ screenings 2:30-8:30pm) Staffed by artsy movie geeks, this downtown indie cinema offers beer-drinking, wine-swilling, and first-run foreign and independent films.

Loft PERFORMING ARTS
(📞 719-445-9278; www.loftmusicvenue.com; 2506 W Colorado Ave; ⊙ hours vary) This Old Colorado City spot features diverse artists in an underground performance space sans liquor license. There's usually one show per week and swing dancing once a month.

🛍 Shopping

Colorado Springs Flea Market MARKET
(📞 719-380-8599; www.csfleamarket.com; 5225 E Platte Ave; ⊙ 7am-4pm Sat & Sun) Colorado Springs' year-round flea market has up to 1000 vendors hawking almost anything you

could think of, as well as live entertainment and a variety of food trucks.

❶ Tourist Information

Colorado Springs Convention and Visitors Bureau (📞 719-635-7506; www.visitcos.com; 515 S Cascade Ave; ⊙ 8:30am-5pm; 📶) A well-stocked resource for all things Southern Colorado.

❶ Getting There & Away

A smart alternative to Denver, **Colorado Springs Airport** (COS; 📞 719-550-1900; www.flycos. com; 7770 Milton E Proby Pkwy; 📶) is served principally by United and Delta, with flights to 11 major cities around the country. There is no public transportation into town, however, so you'll have to rent a car or take a cab.

Up to six **Greyhound** (📞 800-231-2222; www. greyhound.com) buses a day ply the route between Colorado Springs and Denver (from $10, 90 minutes), departing from the **Colorado Springs Downtown Transit Terminal** (📞 719-385-7433; 127 E Kiowa St; ⊙ 8am-5pm Mon-Fri).

❶ Getting Around

All street parking is meter only; if you have your own wheels, bring lots of quarters.

Reliable **Mountain Metropolitan Transit** (📞 719-385-7433; www.coloradosprings.gov/ department/91; per trip $1.75, day pass $4) buses serve the entire Pikes Peak area. Bus 3 is the most useful, running from downtown Colorado Springs through Old Colorado City and on to Manitou Springs. Maps and schedule information is available online. Exact change only.

The **Yellow Cab** (📞 719-777-7777; www.yccos. com) fare from the airport to the city center is about $35. It's about $55 to Manitou Springs.

Cañon City

📞 719 / POP 16,340 / ELEV 5332FT
Recent investment in regional tourism has meant that rafting the Royal Gorge or being incarcerated in one of the area's 13 prisons (you read that right) are no longer the only reasons people come to town. Granted, they're still the main reasons, but not the only ones.

Yes, there's no getting around it: Cañon City is a prison town. Most of the town's population work in the incarceration business in some capacity. There's even a prison on the main street. While these facts do give the place a certain vibe, you can't downplay the beauty of the majestic Rockies that abut the town, nor the striking, adrenaline-delivering Royal Gorge just outside it. The area offers some spectacular scenic drives and two excellent new museums.

◉ Sights

★ Royal Gorge Bridge & Park BRIDGE

(☎719-275-7507; www.royalgorgebridge.com; 4218 County Rd 3A; adult/child $26/21; ☉10am-7pm mid-Jun–mid-Aug, reduced hours rest of the year; ♿) In 1929 this 1260ft-long suspension bridge was built across the 950ft-deep Royal Gorge, which stretches for 10 miles west of Cañon City. The bridge and surrounding area became a popular tourist attraction until a wildfire in 2013 ravaged the Royal Gorge landscape and destroyed the vast majority of park attractions, miraculously sparing the bridge. The park has since been rebuilt and features aerial gondolas, rides and a theater. For daredevils, additional zipline and skycoaster packages are available (from $89).

General admission includes access to the park, the bridge, and all attractions except the zipline, skycoaster and special events.

★ Royal Gorge
Dinosaur Experience MUSEUM

(☎719-275-2726; www.dinoxp.com; 44895 W Hwy 50; ☉9am-6pm Mon-Sat, noon-6pm Sun) More than three years in gestation, this dinosaur of an experience hatched in 2016 and comes highly recommended for fans of the Jurassic period and anyone interested in the evolution of life on the planet. Featuring interactive science-focused displays, the opportunity to get hands-on with genuine dinosaur fossils, life-size fossil casts and convincing animatronic beasties. A multistory ropes course completes the fun.

Museum of Colorado Prisons MUSEUM

(☎719-269-3015; www.prisonmuseum.org; 201 N 1st St; adult/child $8/6; ☉10am-6pm; P♿) Set in the original women's prison, right outside the stone walls of the territorial prison, each of the 30 cells is decked out with a different exhibit. The coup de grace is the vintage gas chamber.

Prospect Heights HISTORIC SITE

(4th St) When United Artists were making John Wayne Westerns in Cañon City, this is where they lived and worked. A turn-of-the-20th-century Colorado Fuel & Iron company town before Hollywood came and went, Cañon City was legally dry, so the drinkers, like Wayne and cowboy actor Tom Mix, came down to this area to drink and fight. You'll see remnants of the old stone jail and brick storefronts. To get here follow 4th St from Main over the river and across the tracks.

Centennial Park PARK

(Griffin Ave; ☉dawn-dusk; P☻) Connected by footbridge to the Whitewater Kayak & Recreation Park, this place is called 'duck park' by locals, thanks to the numerous web-footed residents. There's a great wide lawn, outdoor grills and picnic tables, making it a perfect place for a family picnic.

Royal Gorge Museum
& History Center MUSEUM

(☎719-269-9036; www.rgmhc.org; 612 Royal Gorge Blvd; ☉10am-4pm Wed-Sat; ♿) FREE Good for that rare rainy day is this municipal museum, which introduces the region's early history. In 2013 it incorporated the local dinosaur museum collection (it's here indefinitely), consisting of a stegosaurus cast and a few skull replicas. Visits are by tour only.

Garden Park
Fossil Area ARCHAEOLOGICAL SITE

(☎719-269-8500; 3501-3767 Garden Park Rd) The second-largest Jurassic graveyards in Colorado, and still one of the largest in North America, these are the quarries that spawned the Bone Wars and produced such dinosaur stars as stegosaurus, diplodocus and allosaurus back in the late 1800s. They're still standing in the Smithsonian today. The world's most complete Stegosaurus skeleton was excavated here in 1992.

🏃 Activities

★ River Runners RAFTING

(☎800-723-8987; www.whitewater.net; 44641 Hwy 50; half-/full day from $57/105) Since its amalgamation with other local operators, River Runners has grown to have the widest range of rafting packages available.

★ Royal Gorge Route Railroad RAIL

(☎888-724-5748; www.royalgorgeroute.com; 330 Royal Gorge Blvd; adult/child from $44/39; ☉9am, 12:30pm, 3:30pm, 6:30pm Jun-Sep, reduced hours Oct-May) In 1999, following a 32-year hiatus, passenger service on the Royal Gorge Route, a 12-mile segment of the old D&RG train line, was restored. Visitors can make the two-hour ride in carriages or open-air observation cars from Cañon City to Parkdale and back through the majestic gorge. Riding these rails along the Arkansas River is unforgettable.

★ **Shelf Road** SCENIC DRIVE
(www.goldbeltbyway.com) An old stagecoach
road that once connected Cañon City with
Cripple Creek, much of this drive – with its
red earth, low-growing piñon pines and juniper, and sheer limestone cliffs – feels like
you've entered the set for an old Western. The
final 8 miles of this 26-mile road are unpaved
and definitely not for those with vertigo.

★ **Phantom Canyon** SCENIC DRIVE
(www.goldbeltbyway.com) Even if you weren't
planning on heading to Cripple Creek, this
incredible 35-mile drive might make you
change your mind – anyone with a sense
of adventure and history will enjoy this
trip. It follows a sinuous old railroad grade
(the Florence & Cripple Creek; 1894–1912)
through gorgeous red sandstone cliffs and
blasted-out tunnels to historic Victor.

Raft Masters RAFTING
(☑719-275-6645; www.raftmasters.com; 2315 E
Main St; half-/full day from $35/105; ⛵) This op-
erator has been guiding folks along the rapids of the Arkansas River since 1989.

Echo Canyon River Expeditions RAFTING
(☑800-755-3246; www.rafftecho.com; 45000 Hwy
50; half-/full day from $67/114) Offers a range of
tours, including one suitable for all ages.

Arkansas River Tours RAFTING
(☑800-321-4352; www.arkansasrivertours.com;
Hwy 50, Cotopaxi; half-/full day from $50/100)
Operating from just outside the hamlet of
Cotopaxi, this operator has a range of tour
packages.

🛏 Sleeping

Cañon City is no pageant winner, and as
almost all sleeping options are right on the
highway, you'd be better off spending the
night in Salida or Florence if possible.

America's Best Value Inn MOTEL **$**
(☑719-275-3377; www.americasbestvalueinn.com;
1925 Fremont Dr; r from $79; P✳🛜🏊) Rooms
are decent value and three-star quality with
fresh paint, a rather nice shower head and
crown moldings. Family units are huge with
two queen beds and a sofa, but you do get
Hwy 50 traffic noise here. The sign outside
says 'Royal Gorge Lobby.'

Sand Gulch Campground CAMPGROUND **$**
(www.blm.gov; Red Canyon Rd; tent sites $8)
This first-come, first-served BLM-managed
campground is north of Cañon City on Red

Canyon/Shelf Rd and is mostly used by
climbers; the desert location is ideal. There
is no water here. A similar site, the Banks, is
further north.

Hampton Inn HOTEL **$$**
(☑719-269-1112; www.canoncity.hamptoninn.com;
102 McCormick Pkwy; r from $159; P✳🛜🏊🐾)
Stark and solitary at the eastern end of
town, this standard Hampton Inn is the
most comfortable choice in town, with large
rooms and an included breakfast.

★ **Royal Gorge Cabins** CABIN **$$$**
(☑800-748-2953; www.royalgorgecabins.com;
45054 W Hwy 50; tents/cabins from $150/345) Lo-
cated 8 miles west of Cañon City, the area's
newest lodgings, brought to you by the folks
at Echo Canyon River Expeditions, comprise
a selection of stylish, super-comfy, self-contained one- and two-bedroom cabins and
rustic glamping tents in a beautiful location.
You'll need to book in advance if you don't
want to miss out.

✗ Eating

El Caporal MEXICAN **$**
(☑719-276-2001; 1028 Main St; mains $6-14;
⏱11am-9pm; ⛵) This funky, family-owned
diner serves up decent Mexican fare. Tuck
into carne asada, grilled chicken dinners
with refried beans, rice and guacamole, tasty
chicken *tacos al carbon,* enchiladas, burritos, chimichangas and a fine *arroz con pollo*
(chicken with rice). The tortilla and green
chili soups get rave reviews, too.

Oak Creek Grade General Store AMERICAN **$**
(☑719-783-2245; 1009 County Rd 277; meals
$8-16; ⏱8am-2pm Sep-May, 8am-2pm & 4-10pm
Jun-Aug; ⛵) Midway between Cañon City
and Westcliffe, this historic general store
and steakhouse pours the Old West atmosphere on thick. In the summer it hosts
bluegrass sessions for a Saturday-night
dinner show, which brings together the
area's best pickers.

ℹ Tourist Information

The **San Carlos Ranger District** (☑719-269-
8500; www.fs.usda.gov; 3028 E Main St; ⏱8am-
4pm Mon-Fri) office, which shares space with
the **Bureau of Land Management** (☑719 269-
8500; www.blm.gov; 3028 E Main St; ⛵), can
offer camping and hiking tips and has topographical maps for the Spanish Peaks Wilderness, Gold
Belt Byway and the southern Sangre de Cristos
Mountains.

ⓘ Getting There & Away

Cañon City is on US 50, 40 miles west of Pueblo and 60 miles east of Salida.

There's no public transportation in, out or around town, save for organized tour buses heading to the Gorge.

Florence

📋 719 / POP 3860 / ELEV 5180FT

Lying in the southeastern Colorado lowlands amid century old pastures, Florence's mountain vistas might not be as mighty as the sort that defines much of the state, but there's a simple beauty and authenticity to the town that's not just skin deep.

Here is a place working to redefine itself from a depressed farming community into a regional arts, crafts and antique lovers' hub. Folks come from across Colorado to sift through bins and hunt for gems almost every weekend, while the area's shop owners work together to promote their goods.

It's a nice cooperative movement, with 10 or so galleries and boutiques lined up on the historic Main St, and it's well worth a visit if you've come as far as Cañon City.

🛏 Sleeping & Eating

★ **Florence Rose**   B&B $$
(📋 719-784-4734; www.florencerose.com; 1305 W 3rd St; r $149-239; 🅿 ❄ �) The only B&B in Florence is an award-winner rich in history. Built in 1886, highlights include a tremendous brick kitchen with beamed ceilings, an old cerulean-tinted wood-burning stove in the dining room, period furnishings and wallpaper in the five bedrooms (each with attached bath), a sprawling garden, and the engaging hosts, of course.

Reservations are a must. It's busy in the summer and sometimes closed in the winter.

Aspen Leaf Bakery   BAKERY $
(📋 719-784-3834; 113 W Main St; baked goods from $3; ⊙ 11am-3pm Sun-Tue, 8am-4pm Wed-Sat; ❄) A very cool wood-floored bakery and kitchenware gallery with huge chunky brownies, puffy éclairs and dainty tiramisu squares. It does club sandwiches on fresh-baked breads, and sells whole loaves and homemade jams as well.

ⓘ Getting There & Away

Florence is about 10 miles southeast of Cañon City. To get here take 9th St south across the river and you'll be on State Hwy 115, which takes a rather sinuous route on its way to Florence (look out for the signs to make sure you stay on the right road).

Cripple Creek

📋 719 / POP 1180 / ELEV 9494FT

Just an hour's drive from Colorado Springs, yet worlds away, Cripple Creek hurls you back into the Wild West of yore. Its restored buildings are authentic, though it feels somewhat like a Wild West theme park, with its no fewer than nine casinos cashing in on the fact that this lucky lady had by 1952 produced a staggering $413 million in gold.

While that bounty has been all but scoured, and yesteryear's saloons and brothels have closed their doors, the theme of striking it rich still resonates, only today it's with the chiming of slot machines.

If you're not a gambler and have some time to spare, a trip to this unfortunately named town is worthwhile, if only to imagine what life was like out here way back when, and to gawk at the stunning scenery as you drive in.

◎ Sights & Activities

Florissant Fossil Beds National Monument   ARCHAEOLOGICAL SITE
(📋 719-748-3253; www.nps.gov/flfo/index.htm; 15807 County Rd 1, Florissant; ⊙ 9am-5pm) In 1873 Dr AC Peale, as part of the USGS Hayden expedition, was on his way to survey and map the South Park area, when he reputedly discovered these ancient lake deposits, which were buried by the dust and ash from a series of volcanic eruptions. Located 17 miles north of Cripple Creek, the site has since been recognized as one of the greatest collections of Eocene fossils (34 million years old) on the planet, though unfortunately most of it lies beneath your feet.

Outlaws & Lawmen Jail Museum   MUSEUM
(📋 719-689-6556; www.visitcripplecreek.com; 136 W Bennett Ave; adult/child $2/free; ⊙ 9am-5pm Thu-Sun; 🅿) This museum is set in the old Teller County Jail, which rather remarkably operated from 1901 all the way until 1992 when the ACLU filed the lawsuit that made them upgrade. You'll be able to explore the tiny 6.5ft-by-9ft cells that held six men each. The men slept on hammocks, practically on top of one another. There's even a solitary confinement cell where one of the Wild Bunch was held briefly.

Cripple Creek District Museum   MUSEUM

(☑719-689-9540; www.cripplecreekmuseum.com; 500 E Bennett Ave; adult/child $7/free; ⊙10am-5pm; ℙ) Set in an old midland train station terminal is the city's official museum. Between 1896 and 1949 the train came up from the divide four times daily. The Victorian rooms on the 3rd floor have original antiques, and on the 2nd floor you'll find mining gear and railroad memorabilia.

Cripple Creek Heritage Center   MUSEUM

(☑719-689-3289; www.visitcripplecreek.com; 9283 Hwy 67; ⊙9am-4pm; ℙ🐕) FREE This splashy 11,600-sq-ft facility is set on a ridge overlooking town and has massive mountain views. It offers a variety of interactive and interpretive displays depicting early settlement, native histories and the gold-mining boom. There are plenty of dog-walking trails with outstanding views, and your four-footed friend is allowed inside the building, too.

Mollie Kathleen Gold Mine   MINE

(☑719-689-2466; www.goldminetours.com; 9388 Hwy 67; adult/child $20/12; ⊙8:45am-6pm mid-May–Oct; ℙ) If you're not insanely claustrophobic you might want to descend the 1000ft into the vertical shaft of this disused gold mine. That's about as deep as the Empire State building is tall...

Cripple Creek & Victor Railroad   RAIL

(☑719-689-2640; www.cripplecreekrailroad.com; 520 E Carr Ave; adult/child $15/10; ⊙10am-5pm mid-May–mid-Oct; ♿) Kids love this somewhat dinky narrow-gauge railroad that runs between Cripple Creek and nearby Victor, every 45 minutes in season.

🛏 Sleeping & Eating

Cripple Creek has a campground and RV park, a B&B or two and some cheap motels, but the better rooms are found in the casino hotels.

For what could be just a sleepy forgotten gold-rush ghost town by now, you'll be able to get a decent meal here and you can even count on a little variety, courtesy of the casino trade.

❶ Tourist Information

The **Cripple Creek Heritage Center** also serves as the town's information center. If you're thinking of checking out the backroads, let a local know your plans and they'll be able to update you on the latest road conditions.

❶ Getting There & Away

Cripple Creek is 50 miles southwest of Colorado Springs on scenic Hwy 67.

If you've got a vehicle that's suitable for a little off-road driving, there's more than one road in and out. Thrill-seekers heading back to Colorado Springs might want to check out the Old Gold Camp Rd out of Victor. It's narrow, in poor shape and its tunnels are reputedly haunted, but the views are amazing. It's a hair-raising 1½ to two hours down to the Springs.

More spectacular, less terrifying and a little less haunted are Phantom Canyon (p319) and Shelf Road (p319), both of which lead to Cañon City.

Alternatively, catch the **Casino Shuttle** (Ramblin' Express; ☑719-590-8687; www.casinoshuttle.com; round-trip tickets $25; ⊙departures 7am-midnight Wed-Sun) from Colorado Springs.

Manitou Springs

☑719 / POP 5320 / ELEV 6358FT

Most travelers will naturally gravitate toward Manitou Springs, Colorado Springs' nearest neighbor, located directly beneath Pikes Peak and half-way between Colorado Springs and the Garden of the Gods. Many of the key attractions of the Colorado Springs–Manitou Springs area are located here, including a wealth of hiking tracks and the eponymous springs.

Easily navigable on foot, Manitou Springs feels like a tourist town, whereas Colorado Springs has a more residential vibe, although to many, the two towns are just extensions of one another.

⊙ Sights

★ Pikes Peak   MOUNTAIN

(☑719-385-7325; www.springsgov.com; highway per adult/child $12/5; ⊙7:30am-8pm Jun-Aug, to 5pm Sep, 9am-3pm Oct-May; ℙ) Pikes Peak (14,110ft) may not be the tallest of Colorado's 54 14ers, but it's certainly the most famous. The Ute originally called it the Mountain of the Sun, an apt description for this majestic peak, which crowns the southern Front Range. Rising 7400ft straight up from the plains, over half a million visitors climb it every year.

Its location as the easternmost 14er has contributed heavily to its place in American myth. Zebulon Pike first made note of it in 1806 (he called it 'Grand Peak,' but never made it to the top) when exploring the Louisiana Purchase, and Katherine Bates, a guest lecturer at Colorado College in 1893, wrote the original draft of *America the Beautiful* after reaching the summit.

Today there are three ways to ascend the peak: the Pikes Peak Hwy (about a five-hour round-trip), which was built in 1915 by Spencer Penrose and winds 19 miles to the top from Hwy 24 west of town; the cog railway; and on foot via the Barr Trail.

★ **Cave of the Winds**　　　CAVE
(☑ 719-685-5444; www.caveofthewinds.com; 100 Cave of the Winds Rd; adult/child Discovery Tour $21/15, Lantern Tour $31/18; ⊗ 9am-9pm Jun-Aug, 10am-5pm Sep-May; P) Set on the rim of a craggy canyon is this developed cavern concessionaire. You'll forgive the cheesy entry and elevator music because here are the stalactites and stalagmites of your dreams. Most opt for the 45-minute Discovery Tour, but the Lantern Tour goes twice as deep, gets twice as dark and lasts twice as long.

There is also a ropes course and a zipline ($20 per person), open March to October.

Manitou Cliff Dwellings　ARCHAEOLOGICAL SITE
(☑ 800-354-9971; www.cliffdwellingsmuseum.com; 10 Cliff Dwellings Rd; adult/child $10/8.50; ⊗ 9am-6pm May-Sep, reduced hours Oct-Apr; P) This set of Ancestral Puebloan cliff dwellings was carved into the red-rock hills just east of Manitou Springs off Hwy 24. You'll see the adobe facades and get a feel for the cool cave interiors with their grain-storage turrets and beamed ceilings in what is a string of half-a-dozen multiple-family homes. Talk about an efficient use of space!

Rocky Mountain Dinosaur Center　MUSEUM
(☑ 719-686-1820; www.rmdrc.com; 201 S Fairview St, Woodland Park; adult/child $11.50/7.50; ⊗ 9am-6pm Mon-Sat, 10am-5pm Sun; P ♿) This fun dinosaur center is located in Woodland Park, 14 miles west of Manitou Springs. The kids won't want to miss this private museum owned by working paleontologists, where you can watch lab techs assemble casts and clean fossils from digs across the western states, from Montana to Texas.

Mineral Springs　　　SPRING
(P) Manitou got its name from the numerous mineral springs that bubble up from limestone aquifers along Manitou Ave. In some cases, it's believed that the water is as much as 20,000 years old. Many, such as Shoshone and Cheyenne, have sipping fountains where you can sample the distinctive-tasting (OK, it's not San Pellegrino) carbonated water.

 Activities

★ **Pikes Peak Cog Railway**　　RAIL
(☑ 719-685-5401; www.cograilway.com; 515 Ruxton Ave; round-trip adult/child $40/22; ⊗ 8am-5:20pm May-Oct, reduced hours Nov-Apr; ♿) Travelers have been making the trip to the summit of Pikes Peak on the Pikes Peak Cog Railway since Zalmon Simmons had it constructed in 1891. Today's diesel-powered, Swiss-built trains make the round-trip in three hours and 10 minutes, which includes 40 minutes at the top. Make sure you bring warm clothing, no matter how hot it may be at the base.

★ **SunWater Spa**　　　SPA
(☑ 719-695-7007; www.sunwaterspa.com; 514 El Paso Blvd; soak 2hr/day pass $25/35; ⊗ 2-10pm Mon, 8am-10pm Tue-Sat, to 8pm Sun) Opened in 2015, this three-story day spa and wellness center sources its waters from Manitou's eponymous springs, deep within the earth. Decadent treatments and soothing waters await, including the opportunity to soak in open-air tubs overlooking the mountains.

Incline Trail　　　HIKING
(⊗ 6am-6pm) After a 1990 landslide washed away so much track of this former incline railway that it had to be shut down, a hectic hiking trail with sweeping views took its place, amid controversy over access rights and safety. Those issues have been resolved and the trail has reopened after extensive renovation.

Barr Trail　　　HIKING
(Hydro St) The tough 12.5-mile Barr Trail ascends Pikes Peak with a substantial 7400ft of elevation gain. Most hikers split the trip into two days, stopping to overnight at Barr Camp (p323), the halfway point at 10,200ft. The trailhead is near the Pikes Peak Cog Railway depot; parking is $5.

Colorado Wolf & Wildlife Center　WILDLIFE
(☑ 719-687-9742; www.wolfeducation.org; 4729 Twin Rocks Rd, Divide; 1hr guided tour adult/child $15/8; ⊗ Tue-Sun; ♿) Located between the hamlets of Divide and Florissant, 24 miles west of Manitou Springs off Hwy 24, this private, nonprofit wildlife sanctuary shelters three subspecies of wolf (timber, arctic and Mexican gray), two species of fox (red and swift) and coyotes.

✤ Festivals & Events

Pikes Peak International
Hill Climb SPORTS

(☑719-685-4400; www.ppihc.com; ⊘Jun) Held on the last weekend in June, this legendary car race was first launched by Spencer Penrose after he built the road to Pikes Peak. These days the cars are faster and the drivers more skilled. The course along Pikes Peak Toll Road is 12.42 miles in total, beginning at 9390ft just uphill from the tollgate.

Emma Crawford
Festival & Coffin Races CULTURAL

(www.emmacrawfordfestival.com; Manitou Ave; ⊘Oct) In 1929 the coffin of Emma Crawford was unearthed by erosion and slid down Red Mountain. Today coffins are decked out with wheels and run down Manitou Ave for three hours on the Saturday before Halloween.

🛏 Sleeping

Manitou Springs has an awesome collection of retro motels complete with original 1960s and '70s neon signage, but you'll find a wider range and higher standard of accommodations in Colorado Springs.

Barr Camp CAMPGROUND $

(www.barrcamp.com; tent sites/lean-tos/cabin dm $12/$20/$33; ☀) At the halfway point on the Barr Trail, about 6.5 miles from the Pikes Peak summit, you can pitch a tent, shelter in a lean-to or reserve a bare-bones cabin. The campground has drinking water and showers; dinner ($8) is available Wednesday to Sunday. Reservations are essential and must be made online in advance. It's open year-round.

Eagle Motel HOTEL $

(☑719-685-5467; www.eaglemotel.com; 423 Manitou Ave; d from $79; P❄🖤) This hotel is spick and span, but has a grassroots, down-to-earth vibe, and is billed as a 'smoker-friendly hotel.' This is also Colorado, so we take that to mean it's generally a very friendly, open-minded and tolerant place. Great location. Nice rooms. Nice price. Easy!

Days Inn HOTEL $

(☑719-685-1312; www.daysinn.com/hotel/17759; 120 Manitou Ave; d from $89; P❄🖤) This stock-standard chain hotel is one of the better examples of the brand: it's well managed, well located, built in the last 10 years and won't blow your budget.

★ **Cliff House**
at Pikes Peak BOUTIQUE HOTEL $$

(☑719-785-1000; www.thecliffhouse.com; 306 Canon Ave; r from $159; P❄🖤) Nestled at the foot of Pike's Peak, the Cliff House started as a 20-room boarding house and stagecoach stop in 1844. Today this luxurious country inn offers the discriminating traveler a Victorian boutique experience, complete with fabulous mountain vistas and rooms styled in late-1800s decor.

Avenue Hotel B&B $$

(☑719-685-1277; www.avenuehotelbandb.com; 711 Manitou Ave; r incl breakfast from $120; P❄🖤) This Victorian mansion, on a hill in downtown Manitou Springs, began as a boarding house in 1886. One hundred years later, it reopened as the city's first B&B. Decorated in warm colors, the seven rooms, reached via a fantastic three-floor, open-turned staircase, have claw-foot tubs, lush fabrics and canopied wrought-iron beds.

Families should ask about the bigger Carriage House, which has a private kitchen.

✗ Eating

There's a handful of restaurants in Manitou Springs, but you'll find a far broader range to choose from in Colorado Springs.

Heart of Jerusalem Cafe MIDDLE EASTERN $

(☑719-685-1325; www.heartofjerusalemcafe.com; 718 Manitou Ave; mains $7-18; ⊘11am-9pm Mon-Sat, to 8pm Sun; 🖤) This fabulous Middle Eastern greasy-spoon haunt is exactly the kind of place you wouldn't expect to find in Manitou Springs. It does savory shawarma and falafel sandwiches, as well as tasty kebab plates. There's also a delectable veggie plate, with hummus, tabouleh, falafel, dolmas, and warm pita seasoned with za'atar spice mix.

Pikes Peak Chocolate
& Ice Cream ICE CREAM $

(☑719-685-9600; www.pikespeakchocolate.com; 805 Manitou Ave; cones from $3; ⊘10am-10pm) The place to refuel in Manitou Springs, with local Josh and John's ice cream, espresso and smoothies.

★ **Adam's**
Mountain Cafe MODERN AMERICAN $$

(☑719-685-1430; www.adamsmountain.com; 934 Manitou Ave; mains $9-21; ⊘8am-3pm Mon & Sun, 8am-3pm & 5-9pm Tue-Sat; 🖤🖤) This slow-food cafe makes for a lovely stop. Breakfast includes orange-almond French toast and huevos rancheros. Lunch and dinner are more eclectic, with offerings such as Moroccan chicken, pasta gremolata and grilled watermelon salad. The interior is airy and attractive with marble floors and exposed rafters, and there's patio dining and occasional live music, too.

PJ's Stagecoach Inn
AMERICAN $$

(☑719-685-9400; www.facebook.com/stage coachinn; 702 Manitou Ave; mains $14-26; ⊙11am-8pm Mon-Thu, to 9pm Fri-Sun; P 📶) On your right-hand side as you enter downtown Manitou Springs, you won't miss the historic stagecoach out front (it's usually covered with kids). Inside this historic cabin on the creek there's burgers (buffalo and beef) and hot turkey sandwiches at lunch, and a host of steaks, ribs and seafood at dinner.

Craftwood Inn
AMERICAN $$$

(☑719-985-9400; www.craftwood.com; 404 El Paso Blvd; mains $20-44; ⊙5-11pm; P ❄) If you're hungry for wild game, then this is the place for you. It has elk, buffalo, antelope, ostrich, pheasant and quail. (And some vegetarian dishes, too.)

🍷 Drinking & Entertainment

Manitou Springs is sleepy after dark. Head in to Colorado Springs if you feel the need to dance the night away.

★Swirl
WINE BAR

(☑719-345-2652; www.swirlismybar.com; 717 Manitou Ave; ⊙noon-10pm Sun-Thu, to midnight Fri & Sat) Behind a stylish bottle shop, this nook bar is pleasantly intimate. The garden patio has dangling lights and vines, while the interior features antique armchairs and a fireplace. If you're feeling peckish, sample the tapas and homemade pasta.

Manitou Penny Arcade
ARCADE

(☑719-685-9815; 900 Manitou Ave; ⊙10am-10pm; 📶) If you or someone you love is the type that adores a vintage arcade (you know the kind: they miss games like Pole Position and Ski Ball, Galaga and Out Run, Supershot and air hockey), this sprawling complex, stretched between Canon and Manitou Avenues, is for you. And it might even help ween the kids off modern video games. Or not.

❶ Tourist Information

Manitou Springs Chamber of Commerce
(☑719-685-5089; www.manitousprings.org; 354 Hwy 24; ⊙8:30am-5pm) Staff can help with all your questions about hiking, biking and getting into the great outdoors.

❶ Getting There & Away

Manitou Springs is 6 miles west of Colorado Springs along Hwy 24.

From mid-May to mid-September, free shuttle buses run along Manitou Ave and between Manitou Springs and Manitou Incline/Cog Railway, about every 20 minutes from 8am to 6pm.

THE SANTA FE TRAIL

For those who like to walk along the old wagon ruts of history, back to a time when finding yourself in this part of the world meant facing a daily fight for survival, driving the Santa Fe Trail will be a rewarding opportunity for reflection and contemplation. For others, it's a pretty and lonely drive with a series of don't-blink-or-you'll-miss-'em historical markers along the highway.

Either way, this section of the Santa Fe Trail is one of great natural beauty and contrasts. From the wild, sun-drenched prairie around Bent's Fort to the high mesas and billowing clouds outside Trinidad on the New Mexico border and the ancient volcanic walls of the twin Spanish Peaks near La Veta, this long-traveled route provides a good mix of history and natural wonder.

History

One of the great overland trade routes of the 19th century, the Santa Fe Trail stretched from Missouri to New Mexico (a Mexican province from 1821 to 1848), bringing manufactured European and American goods west, and Mexican silver and Native American jewelry, blankets and furs east. The 800-mile route took seven to eight weeks to cross with a covered wagon, and was defined by monotony and hardship. Near Dodge City in Kansas, the route divided: the southern road (Cimarron Route) cut down into New Mexico, and was shorter but more dangerous, due to a lack of water and hostile Native Americans. The northern road (Mountain Route) continued through Bent's Fort and Trinidad in Colorado and was longer but safer. With the expansion of the railroad west, trade along the route eventually diminished, coming to a close in 1880. You can drive the route today, following Hwys 56, 50 and 350.

ⓘ Getting There & Away

Trinidad and Pueblo are the gateway towns to the region with road, bus and rail connections to elsewhere in the state and beyond.

Pueblo

📋 719 / POP 108,423 / ELEV 4695FT

When America first expanded west, one pioneer at a time, the Arkansas River – which bisects Pueblo – was the border between the United States and Old Mexico. Following the Mexican–American War (1846–48), developers began turning this eastern Colorado market town into a railroad hub and steel manufacturing center. It went on to become Colorado's second-largest city and eventually earned the moniker Pittsburgh of the West, thanks to the success of Colorado Fuel & Iron.

However, business flagged after WWII and with the steel market crash in 1982, Pueblo's steady decline turned into a free fall, which has only recently abated. But all that history makes for an interesting downtown wander. Seventy buildings and places are listed in the national historic registry, and plaques have been installed detailing local history along Grand and Union Aves, between 1st and B Sts.

◎ Sights

★ El Pueblo History Museum MUSEUM
(📋 719-583-0453; www.historycolorado.org; 301 N Union Ave; adult/child $5/4; ⊙10am-4pm Tue-Sat; 🅿🚻) Set on central plaza, the original site of Fort Pueblo (an American fort established in 1842 and held until 1854, when a Ute and Apache raid on Christmas Day caused the fort to be abandoned), this airy, modern museum with a stunning interior houses treasures from the Pueblo past.

★ Buell Children's Museum MUSEUM
(📋 719-295-7200; www.sdc-arts.org; 210 N Santa Fe Ave; adult/child $8/6; ⊙11am-4pm Tue-Sat; 🚻) This is the place to climb into classic cars, jam to old rock and roll, build bridges, swim with jellyfish, create magical fairy lands and discover the power of numbers while exploring exhibits that help kids learn with a smile on their faces. It should appeal to kids up to the age of 14.

★ Bent's Old Fort
National Historic Site HISTORIC SITE
(www.nps.gov/beol; 35110 Hwy 194; adult/child $3/2; ⊙8am-5:30pm Jun-Aug, 9am-4pm Sep-May;

🅿) Set just north of the Arkansas River, this was once the natural and official border between the US and Old Mexico (until 1846), and was once a cultural crossroads. The old adobe fort, with its timber-beamed ceilings, has been beautifully restored. It's staffed by knowledgeable guides in period clothing (dressed like old trappers and with an Old West twang).

Picketwire Dinosaur Tracksite HISTORIC SITE
(📋 719-384-2181; www.fs.usda.gov/recarea/psicc/recarea/?recid=77620; 1420 E 3rd St, La Junta; adult/child $15/10.50; ⊙by reservation May, Jun & Sep–mid-Oct; 🚻) The 0.25-mile Picketwire Dinosaur Tracksite is the largest documented site of its kind in North America, with as many as 1300 visible dinosaur tracks. Some 150 million years ago, two types of dinosaurs, allosaurus and apatosaurus, migrated along the muddy shoreline of a large prehistoric lake. If you intend to drive to visit the site, you must reserve a guided auto tour through La Junta Ranger District, which begins at 1420 E 3rd St, La Junta, 69 miles south of Pueblo.

Nature & Raptor
Center of Pueblo WILDLIFE RESERVE
(📋 719-549-2414; www.natureandraptor.org; 5200 Nature Center Rd; per car $3; ⊙grounds 6am-10pm daily, raptor center 11am-4pm Tue-Sun; 🅿🚻) Riverside trails, reptile displays, picnic and playground areas, and a raptor center bring people beneath the cottonwoods on the Arkansas River. The raptor program began in 1981 to assist the Department of Wildlife in rehabilitating injured birds of prey. The turnoff for Nature Center Rd is 3 miles west of downtown, north of the Pueblo Ave Bridge.

Pueblo Union Depot NOTABLE BUILDING
(📋 719-544-0020; www.pueblouniondepot.com; 132 W B St; ⊙9am-5pm; 🅿🚻) **FREE** Still standing proudly on the railway, this historic 1880s structure has been refurbished and reclaimed as a shopping mall and law-office complex of sorts. But there is a case of historical artifacts by the back door on the ground floor, as well as 'American Only' signs by the old waiting room (a throwback to the anti-Mexican segregation of yore).

Sand Creek Massacre
National Historic Site MEMORIAL
(www.nps.gov/sand; cnr County Rd 54 & County Rd W; ⊙9am-4pm; 🅿) **FREE** On November 29, 1864, Colorado Volunteer soldiers attacked

an encampment of Cheyenne and Arapaho along Sand Creek. Led by Chief Black Kettle, the Native Americans had been assured that moving to this site would ensure their safety. According to eye witnesses, 163 people were killed, including 110 women and children. This site was dedicated in 2002.

Camp Amache HISTORIC SITE
(☑719-734-5492; www.santafetrailscenicand historicbyway.org/amache.html; Hwy 50, Granada; ☺museum by appointment; Ⓟ🚻🐕) FREE Just east of Lamar, this WWII Japanese internment camp in Granada covered 1 sq mile with 29 block barracks at its peak. Most of the 7567 prisoners (ever fans of the euphemism, politicians called them 'evacuees') were brought here from the farmlands of central California, and two-thirds of them were born in California, meaning they were US citizens. All you'll see here is a stone memorial, an old camp cemetery and overgrown concrete foundations that stand out on the silent prairie.

Boggsville Historic Site HISTORIC SITE
(☑719-456-0453; Hwy 101; ☺10am-4pm Fri-Sun May, 10am-5pm daily Jun-Oct) FREE The Boggsville Historic Site, about 16 miles east of Bent's Fort and 2 miles south on Colorado Hwy 101, nestled on the Purgatoire River, was pioneer Kit Carson's homestead and trading center, which he built in the 1860s. Eventually it became the first county seat for Bent County when the railroad arrived in 1873. The site comprises old wagons under the cottonwoods, a cabin and a decrepit old barn, and newer, yet still historic, homes.

Rosemount Museum MUSEUM
(☑719-545-5290; www.rosemount.org; 419 W 14th St; adult/child $6/4; ☺10am-3:30pm Tue-Sat Feb-Dec; 🅟) Pueblo's premier historic attraction is this three-story, 37-room Victorian mansion, constructed in 1893 of pink rhyolite stone. It contains elaborate stained glass and elegant original furnishings. The top floor features an Egyptian mummy and other assorted booty from philanthropist Andrew McClelland's global travels during the early 20th century.

Pueblo Railway Museum MUSEUM
(☑719-251-5024; www.pueblorailway.org; 201 W B St; adult/child$4/3; ☺10am-4pm Tue-Sat; 🅟) A somewhat decentralized museum with exhibits set up in a corner of the Southeastern Colorado Heritage Center, an old freight warehouse opposite Union Station. It also owns vintage railcars and engines on the tracks behind the old Union Depot.

Sangre de Cristo Art Center MUSEUM
(☑719-295-7200; www.sdc-arts.org; 210 N Santa Fe Ave; adult/child $5/4; ☺11am-4pm Tue-Sat) Set

FORTS & TRAGEDIES OF THE SANTA FE TRAIL

Just north of the Arkansas River, the adobe **Bent's Old Fort National Historic Site** (p325) was a former fur trading post and the official border between the US and Old Mexico until 1846. It has been beautifully restored and is staffed by knowledgeable guides in period clothing.

A further 16 miles east, then 2 miles south on Hwy 101 the **Boggsville Historic Site** (p326), a former homestead and trading center, became the first county seat for Bent County when the railroad arrived in 1873.

The Bents did build another fort in 1853 (known as Bent's New Fort or Fort Wise), which was a profitable trading post until 1857, when a Colorado gold strike and the resulting land grab, coupled with the mass slaughter of bison by Americans and Europeans, spurred unrest among the Native Americans of the plains. As a result, the US cavalry built Fort Fauntleroy on the site to protect settlers.

Later renamed **Fort Lyon**, it was from here that on November 29, 1864, John Chivington led the Colorado Volunteers in a dawn attack on Chief Black Kettle and his band, who had been told they would be safe if they moved to this desolate reservation. Over 150 Cheyenne and Arapaho men, women and children were slaughtered and their corpses grotesquely mutilated, bringing a new wave of conflict to the Santa Fe Trail. The event is commemorated at the Sand Creek Massacre National Historic Site (p325).

Today Fort Lyon is used as a treatment facility for homeless folks battling addictions, but you can still view the building from the outside. Since it's construction, this isolated fortress has also had incarnations as a sanitarium, psychiatric hospital and a prison.

Fort Lyon is located 19 miles east of Bent's Old Fort along Hwy 50.

in three brick buildings, housing seven galleries that feature both fine and regional historical arts and crafts, this is more than just Pueblo's art museum. It's also an arts center with more than 100 music, dance and fine-arts classes each quarter. Admission also includes entrance to the Buell Children's Museum (p325).

Riverwalk WATERFRONT
(101 S Union Ave; pedal boats per 30min $10, gondola tours $5; ⊙ boat rental & tours Sat & Sun May-Aug; ⊛) **FREE** A pedestrian-friendly and peacefully lazy channeled slice of the Arkansas – the rest of it is running more fiercely underground – this is the center of historic Pueblo. There are sidewalks on both sides of the river and plenty of shady seating. It runs for about four blocks and during the summer months you can book pedal boats or take a gondola tour.

The city hosts occasional concerts and events here, too.

🛏 Sleeping

With few exceptions, Pueblo's sleeping options are chain offerings. Eagleridge Blvd in north Pueblo, just off the I-25, has more than half-a-dozen familiar names.

Edgar Olin House B&B $
(☑ 719-544-5727; www.olin-house.com; 727 W 13th St; r from $89; P ❀ 🕾) This three-story brick home is set in Pueblo's architecturally interesting, though somewhat dilapidated, historic residential district. With period furnishings in the Victorian interior and welcoming hosts, this is the finest place to stay in Pueblo.

Santa Fe Inn HOTEL $
(☑ 719-543-6530; www.santafeinnpueblo.com; 730 N Santa Fe Ave; d from $65; P ❀ 🕾) There's something cool about how old-school this unfussy motor inn is, plonked right in the middle of Pueblo. Rooms are dated and a little drab, but not tacky, and are spotlessly clean.

Hampton Inn HOTEL $$
(☑ 719-543-6500; www.hamptoninn.hilton.com; 4790 Eagleridge Circle; r from $119; ❀ 🕾 ⬚) If you'd rather not nest downtown, Eagleridge Circle in north Pueblo has more than a half-dozen chain options, with this Hampton Inn (by Hilton) at the top end of the scale.

✖ Eating

Bingo Burger BURGERS $
(☑ 719-225-8363; www.bingoburger.com; 101 Central Plaza; burgers $6-13; ⊙ 11am-8pm Mon-Sat; ⊛) A locally owned downtown burger joint – conveniently right across from the History Museum – Bingo only uses grass-fed lamb and beef produced in the region, and it does chicken and portobello burgers, too. Cheese options include blue and goat's cheese, shakes and malts are made with Hopscotch ice cream, and it has both sweet potato and regular fries.

Papa Jose's MEXICAN $
(☑ 719-545-7476; 320 S Union Ave; mains $7-18; ⊙ 11am-8pm Mon-Sat; ⊛) Here's a dirty little Colorado secret: the Mexican food is very often underwhelming. But this town, called Pueblo and down south of the Arkansas River, was part of Mexico until relatively recently. Translation: feel free to get your hopes up, because Papa Jose's will oblige.

Hopscotch Bakery BAKERY $
(☑ 719-542-4467; 333 S Union Ave; sandwiches $6-8; ⊙ 7am-4pm Tue-Sat; ⊛) If you are just passing through long enough to see a few sights and grab a bite to eat, make that bite happen here. Hopscotch does fresh pastries and quiche of the day, cookies and tarts, and some terrific gourmet sandwiches with capicola ham, chicken breast, and balsamic vinegar–soaked portobello. It also makes its own ice cream. No seating.

Franco's Bistro BISTRO $
(☑ 719-583-6216; 210 N Santa Fe Ave; mains $7-15; ⊙ 9am-7pm Tue-Sat; P ✏) Locals love Franco's at the Sangre de Cristo Art Center for its hearty renditions of Italian favorites served in a fun, family-friendly environment and at seriously low prices.

dc's on b street BISTRO $$
(☑ 719-584-3410; www.dcsonbstreet.1wp.com; 115 W B St; mains lunch $8-14, dinner $12-25; ⊙ 11am-2pm Mon & Tue, 11am-2pm & 5:30-9pm Wed-Sat) This cute B St bistro (located in the old Coors Building) offers some of the best eats in town. It does a terrific Reuben on marbled rye and a Poulet Pueblo with tomato chutney for lunch, and fancier fare for dinner. Think steak au poivre, Colorado lamb and lemon-pepper fettuccine. It's several blocks south of the Riverwalk.

GREAT DIKES OF THE SPANISH PEAKS

Some of the Kapota band of the Ute tribe aptly referred to the volcanic Spanish Peaks as *wahatoya* – 'breasts of the earth.' Spanish and American travelers relied on these twin sentinels to guide their approach to the Front Range across the eastern Great Plains.

On closer inspection, you'll find hundreds of magnificent rock walls radiating like fins from the peaks. Called 'dikes,' they were formed from fissures, surrounding the volcanic core, being filled up with magma, later turning into solid rock as it cooled. Subsequent erosion has exposed the dikes, leaving a peculiar landscape of abrupt perpendicular rock walls protruding from the earth. This is the largest collection of such dikes in the world.

For an opportunity to see wildlife and wildflowers, you can explore the great dikes on foot by following the Wahatoya Trail along the saddle between the East and West Spanish Peaks, or from the road along scenic Hwy 12, which intersects the dikes at several different points.

ⓘ Tourist Information

The **Pueblo Chamber of Commerce** (☑ 800-233-3446; www.pueblochamber.org; 302 N Santa Fe Ave; ⊙ 8am-5pm Mon-Fri) can assist with tourism-related inquiries.

The **Pueblo Ranger Office** (☑ 719-553-1400; www.fs.usda.gov/psicc; 2840 Kachina Dr, off Hwy 50; ⊙ 8:30am-4pm Mon-Fri) supervises the San Isabel and Pike National Forests and the Comanche Grasslands to the east.

ⓘ Getting There & Around

Pueblo is 112 miles south of Denver and 45 miles south of Colorado Springs at the crossroads of I-25 and US 50.

Greyhound operates bus services north to Colorado Springs (from $9, one hour) and south into New Mexico from the **Greyhound Bus Depot** (☑ 800-231-2222; www.greyhound.com; 123 Court St).

Pueblo Memorial Airport (☑ 719-553-2760; 31201 Bryan Circle; 🖈) has limited domestic connections to Las Vegas and Denver.

The compact bus network run by **Pueblo Transit** (☑ 719-553-2727; www.pueblo.us; 123 Court St; 🖈) has 12 routes covering most of the city.

La Veta

☑ 719 / POP 760 / ELEV 7013FT

Undiscovered Colorado at its finest, historic La Veta is a little town beautifully framed by high country ranges at the base of the stunning Spanish Peaks. Complete with all the magnificence of the best of the Rockies, with a dash of small-town charm (and minus the crowds of better-known hamlets), prepared to be wooed by La Veta, where paved streets are outnumbered by churches.

It would take a serious effort to get lost in La Veta – its compass-oriented grid is divided by north–south Main St (Hwy 12). Most businesses are at the north end near the old narrow-gauge railroad.

⊙ Sights & Activities

★ **Spanish Peaks Wilderness**   HIKING
(www.spanishpeakscountry.com; ⊙ Jun-Oct; 🖈) Long before you make it into La Veta, the twin Spanish Peaks, named for their past life as part of Old Mexico, loom majestically over the valley. The East Peak is 12,708ft high, while the West Peak soars to 13,625ft. With incredible vertical stone dikes erupting from the earth like some kind of primordial fence line, these mountains are ripe for hiking adventures.

Francisco Fort Museum   MUSEUM
(☑ 719-742-5501; www.franciscofort.org; 306 S Main St; adult/child $5/free; ⊙ 10am-4pm Tue-Sat, 11am-3pm Sun Jun-Aug) This museum is set on the site of the original 1862 fort, with a couple of the real-deal buildings still left. It was built by 12 men as a base of operations for settlement, trade and 'Indian protection' – meaning protection from Native Americans, which involved attacking the Ute and surrounding tribes.

SPACe Gallery   GALLERY
(Gallery in the Park; ☑ 719-742-3074; www.spanish peaksarts.org; 132 W Ryus St; ⊙ hours vary) **FREE** More than 24 artists display paintings, pottery, glasswork and weavings at this cooperative gallery built in 1983 by the origins of what has become the Spanish Peaks Arts Council. It's a two-minute walk east of Railroad Park.

Walsenburg Mining Museum   MUSEUM
(☑ 719-738-1992; www.cityofwalsenburg.net/walsenburg-mining-museum; 112 W 5th St, Walsenburg; adult/child $2/1; ⊙ 10am-4pm Mon-Fri, to

1pm Sat) This museum is the only reason to stop in Walsenburg on the way to or from the Spanish Peaks. Set in the old jailhouse (built in 1896), it's a monument to the struggle for labor laws in the Colorado mining industry, in the days leading up to the 1913 Ludlow Massacre.

Sleeping & Eating

Monument Park Lake Resort CAMPGROUND $
(✆719-868-2226; www.monumentlakeresort.com; 4789 Hwy 12; tent & RV sites from $20, cabins & lodges from $109; ⊗mid-May–mid-Sep; 🅿) The popular Monument Park Lake Resort has camping and RV sites, as well as showers and a coin-operated laundry. There are also lodge rooms and cabins decorated in Southwestern style. The resort's restaurant serves decent home-style American food. The resort is only open in the summer, though you can fish here year round ($8 day pass per vehicle).

Purgatoire Campground CAMPGROUND $
(✆877-444-6777; www.recreation.gov; off Hwy 12; tent sites $16; ⊗May–mid-Oct; 🅿🐾) There are three campgrounds in the Spanish Peaks Wilderness Area; Purgatoire is the only one that you can reserve. It's located 4 miles west of Monument Lake, off Hwy 12, at the base of the Sangre de Cristos.

Yellow Pine Guest Ranch RANCH $$
(✆719-742-3528; www.yellowpine.us; 15890 Hwy 12, Cuchara; cabins from $110; ⊗May-Oct; 🅿🐾🐾) The Yellow Pine is located up in Cuchara, where you can rent cute red cabins (accommodating two to eight people) perfectly oriented for marvelous valley, meadow and West Peak views. There are horse professionals to take you riding ($30 per hour), old wagon wheels lining the driveway and a stream meandering through the property.

La Veta Inn HOTEL $$
(✆719-742-3700; www.lavetainn.co; 103 W Ryus Ave; r from $119; 🅿❄🐾) This inviting hotel has 18 comfortable rooms equipped with feather mattresses and each personalized by a different artist. Just south of the railroad tracks, it's the main place to sleep, eat and drink in town. The restaurant serves up tempting Southwestern fare.

★ Dog Bar & Grill PUB FOOD $$
(✆719-742-6366; www.dogbarcuchara.com; 34 Cuchara Ave, Cuchara; meals $9-24; ⊗11am-10pm; 🐾) With its wood bar, wide inviting patio,

pool table, live music on weekends and damn good pizzas, the Dog Bar is a Cuchara institution.

ⓘ Tourist Information
Although not officially a visitor center, the **La Veta Cuchara Chamber of Commerce** (✆719-742-3676; www.lavetacucharachamber.com; 903 S Oak St; ⊗9am-5pm Mon-Fri) should be able to help with any tourism-related inquiries you might have, while the **La Veta District Ranger Office** (✆719-742-3588; www.csfs.colostate.edu/districts/laveta-district; 303 E Moore Ave; ⊗8am-4pm Mon-Fri) can help with trail maps and information on the Spanish Peaks Wilderness.

ⓘ Getting There & Away
La Veta is 60 miles east of Alamosa on Hwy 160. There is no public transportation into the town.

Following Hwy 12 south from town will take you on the Hwy of Legends byway, which wraps around the Spanish Peaks before reaching Trinidad.

Trinidad
✆719 / POP 9130 / ELEV 6025FT
Tucked into a chimney-top mesa, quiet Trinidad sits on the Purgatoire River, which flows down from the heights of the Sangre de Cristo Mountains and the Spanish Peaks in the west. The town's past – from its origins as a Spanish outpost and Santa Fe Trail stopover to its coal-mining period when it played a central role in a groundbreaking labor dispute – is documented in its museums and on the brick-paved streets.

While the history buffs may want to take their time here, road trippers will smell adventure on the pine-tinged winds streaming down Rte 12 from Cucharas Pass on the Highway of Legends, the scenic drive that passes through the Spanish Peaks Wilderness (p328).

⊙ Sights
★ Trinidad History Museum MUSEUM
(www.coloradohistory.org; 312 E Main St; adult/child $8/3; ⊗9am-4pm Mon-Sat May-Sep) This is a lot of museum, a full city block in fact, set smack dab on Main St. There are three sights here: the adobe Baca House (1870), the French-style Bloom Mansion (1882) and the Santa Fe Trail museum.

Arthur Roy Mitchell Memorial Museum of Western Art   MUSEUM

(☑719-846-4224; www.armitchell.us; 150 E Main St; adult/child $3/free, Sun free; ☺10am-5pm Tue-Sat, noon-4pm Sun May-Sep; ◈) Also known as the 'Mitch,' this pleasant gallery was built in honor of local cowboy artist, and the origi-nal, if unofficial, town historian, AR Mitchell. Set in an old, late 19th-century department store (those tiled ceilings are original), the ground floor is the permanent collection of Mitchell's work: cowboys, horses, Western landscapes, more horses and more cowboys.

Comanche National Grassland   HISTORIC SITE

(☑719-523-6591; www.fs.usda.gov/goto/psicc/com; cnr County Rd 9 & Hwy 350, Springfield) Heading west from La Junta toward Trini-dad, you'll find this unforgiving wilderness of hip-high grasses and wild grains, rising into small hills and diving into shallow canyons. This was prime buffalo-hunting ground, and wagon trains could be easily ambushed here, too, which is why wagons would travel in staggered formations rather than follow one another in a single file. After several thousand crossings, this clay soil got worn into ruts, which can still be seen to this day...if you look hard enough.

Ludlow Massacre Memorial   MONUMENT

(County Rd 44) **FREE** In 1914 striking migrant workers were living in a large tent city in Ludlow. After a series of conflicts, the Colo-rado National Guard were called in. An en-suing clash saw the tent city razed, resulting in the deaths of 21 people – including two women and 11 children. This well-executed stone monument, just north of Trinidad, was dedicated by the United Mine Workers to tell the story.

Louden-Henritze Archaeology Museum   MUSEUM

(☑719-846-5508; 600 Prospect St; ☺10am-3pm Mon-Thu; ℗) **FREE** This small museum

---

CH...CH...CH...CHANGES

Before arriving here you'll probably hear that Trinidad is unofficially credited with being the sex-change capital of the USA. However, you won't find much evidence among the local population. Dr Stanley Biber, who passed away in 2006, was chiefly responsible for this reputation via his supposedly cash-only practice, which changed the gender of 4500 people.

---

is located on the campus of Trinidad State Junior College, north of I-25. It's only one room and the exhibits could do with some more context, but it's nonetheless a quick intro to the area's geology and prehistory. In addition to fossils and artifacts, there's even a mammoth tusk.

🏃 Activities

Southside Park   OUTDOORS

(1309 Beshore Dr; ☺8am-10pm; ◈) **FREE** This community center at the south end of Trini-dad has acres of athletic fields, a public pool and, according to the legendary Tony Hawk, one of the top skate parks in the US. The sport's longest grind is possible on the 120ft flat wall. Next to the skate park is Trinidad's disc-golf course.

Trinidad Lake State Park   OUTDOORS

(☑719-846-6951; www.parks.state.co.us; Hwy 12; vehicle pass per day $7; ◈) Three miles south-west of the city, off Hwy 12, this park sits on a bluff above the Purgatoire River, downstream from the reservoir dam. Hiking, wildlife view-ing, an interpretive nature trail, fishing, and boating on the reservoir are all available.

🛏 Sleeping

Trail's End Motel   MOTEL $

(☑719-846-4425; 616 E Main St; s/d from $48/55; ℗✳🛜) Blessed with a vintage neon sign and a nice flowery sundeck, this hole-in-the-wall motel isn't fancy, but it is great value and very friendly. Family-owned and operat-ed, it has small rooms with recently remod-eled bathrooms, satellite TV and wi-fi, and will do for a one-night pit stop.

Carpios Ridge Campground   CAMPGROUND $

(www.coloradostateparks.reserveamerica.com; Trinidad Lake State Park; tent sites $10-16, RV sites $20-24) About a mile west of the dam at Trinidad Lake State Park, this campground has flush toilets, showers and coin laundry, along with 62 sites for RVs and tents. There's a $10 booking fee if you reserve ahead.

★ Tarabino Inn   B&B $$

(☑719-846-2115; www.tarabinoinn.com; 310 E 2nd St; d from $119; 🛜✳) There are four guest rooms in this beautifully restored Italianate villa, by far the classiest sleep in Trinidad, with antique-style furnishings. The cheaper rooms on the 3rd floor share a bathroom (though they do have prime ac-cess to the top-floor widow's walk), while

HIGHWAY OF LEGENDS

Heading south from La Veta the Highway of Legends byway is a stunning scenic route that wraps around the west side of the Spanish Peaks for 66 miles before reaching Trinidad to the south. The road also offers the best access to the hiking and camping opportunities in the area.

Your first port of call is Cuchara, a one-dirt-road town snuggled among the Spanish Peaks Wilderness (p328). Here are lush, green hills crowned by the Great Dikes of the Spanish Peaks (p328): stark vertical granite walls jutting up from deep in the earth, through meadows and on mesas, against the backdrop of the Spanish Peaks – which happen to be two million years older than the Continental Divide. Grab a bite at the Dog Bar & Grill (p329) or spend a night at the Yellow Pine Guest Ranch (p329).

About 18 miles further along, and off a side-road, Purgatoire Campground (p329) is the only one of three campgrounds in the Spanish Peaks that can be reserved in advance.

Soon you'll pass through the Evergreen forests that surround Monument Park, named for a rock formation rising from the waters of its reservoir. Numerous summer activities are offered, including fishing the trout-stocked lake, horseback riding and mountain biking. The summer-only Monument Park Lake Resort (p329) has camping and RV sites, and a restaurant.

From here it's a further 38 lovely miles into Trinidad.

the two suites have private bathrooms with huge claw-foot tubs.

Holiday Inn & Suites HOTEL **$$**
(☑719-845-8400; www.holidayinn.com; 3130 Santa Fe Trail; r from $119; P✳🏚🐾🐕) This is the best of the chains that are scattered a couple of miles south of downtown. Rooms are large with a king or two queen beds, huge Samsung flat-screen TVs, free wi-fi throughout and excellent service.

✗ Eating

★The Cafe CAFE **$**
(☑719-846-7119; 135 E Main St; dishes $4-14; ⊙8am-4pm Mon-Fri, 9am-2pm Sat; 🏚🖉) This cafe, set in the Danielson Dry Goods building, is a terrific find. In the morning it does gourmet egg wraps, such as the Santa Fe (eggs, bacon, spicy corn salsa, Anaheim chili, cheese and crème fraîche) or the Farmers Market (eggs, artichoke hearts, oven-roasted tomatoes, Parmesan and creamy basil spread). For lunch, expect tantalizing sandwiches and salads.

Nana & Nano's ITALIAN **$**
(☑719-846-2696; 418 E Main St; mains $8-16; ⊙10:30am-7:30pm Wed-Sat) Given the historical connection of Italian miners to the area, it shouldn't be a surprise that there are several Italian restaurants in town. This deli is a Trinidad institution, with fine meats, specialty cheeses and homemade sandwiches.

It does tasty meatball and sausage heroes as well as a 'heavenly combo' with a roasted green chili.

The pasta dinners are less impressive, however – stick to the sandwiches.

Rino's ITALIAN **$$**
(☑719-845-0949; www.rinostrinidad.com; 400 E Main St; mains $12-28; ⊙5-9pm Wed-Sun) Situated in an antiquated stone church, Rino's is where Las Vegas meets Little Italy, and your chicken parmigiana is served by a singing waiter. No joke. Hey Frankie, keep the wine coming.

Bella Luna PIZZA **$$**
(☑719-846-2750; 121 W Main St; pizzas $11-22; ⊙11am-3pm & 5-9pm Mon & Wed-Sat, noon-6pm Sun; 🏚🚺) Wood-fired pizza in an antiquated dark-wood Main St dining room with exposed brick walls, high ceilings and good beer on tap. Locals rave.

❶ Tourist Information

The **Colorado Welcome Center** (☑719-846-9512; www.colorado.com; 309 Nevada Ave; ⊙8am-6pm Jun-Aug, to 5pm Sep-May; 🏚🚺) provides travel information on Southeast Colorado and beyond.

❶ Getting There & Away

Trinidad is 86 miles south of Pueblo on the I-25.

Greyhound buses from Trinidad run north to Pueblo ($13, 1½ hours) and onward to Colorado Springs and Denver.

Amtrak (800-872-7245; www.amtrak.com) operates a daily Southwest Chief train service between Los Angeles and Chicago that stops in Trinidad.

THE SAN LUIS VALLEY

The strange and mysterious San Luis Valley is the driest part of Colorado, hemmed in by the San Juan mountains to the west and the Sangre de Cristos to the east. Despite the seemingly barren landscape, however, the valley holds many surprises – the most famous of which is the rippling sea of sand at the Great Sand Dunes.

The valley was also the first part of Colorado to be permanently settled, when Hispanic pioneers set out from Taos in the mid-19th century to find new homesteads, and their influence still defines valley culture today.

But the most important thing of all to know is that this is one of the top areas in the world for alien sightings and abductions. Don't say we didn't warn you!

🛈 Getting There & Away

Alamosa, the region's largest city and transport hub, is located at the intersections of Hwy 17, Hwy 160 and Hwy 285, some 165 miles southwest of Colorado Springs via I-25 and Hwy 160. From Denver it's a more direct route following Hwy 285 south for 218 miles.

Fort Garland

719 / POP 440 / ELEV 7936FT

Fort Garland (1858–83) was established to protect Hispanic and white settlers in the San Luis Valley from Ute raids, and Union troops stationed here marched in a campaign against confederates in Texas during the Civil War. For a short time the outpost was under the direction of famed frontier scout Kit Carson. Though Carson successfully negotiated a period of peace with Utes, all hell broke loose after the Meeker Massacre in 1879. After that, the fort became a major base of operations in the forcible removal of Utes from the area.

Today Fort Garland – all five square blocks of it – is the first town encountered by westbound travelers in the San Luis Valley. The town's worthwhile **museum** (719-379-3512; www.historycolorado.org; 29477 Hwy 159; adult/child $5/3.50; 9am-5pm Apr-Oct, 10am-4pm Thu-Mon Nov-Mar;) is located

in the original fort and contains five of the original 22 buildings.

From Fort Garland it's 10 miles west to the Hwy 150 turnoff to Great Sand Dunes National Monument, 25 miles west to Alamosa or 16 miles south to San Luis via Hwy 159.

Great Sand Dunes National Park

ELEV 8200FT

For all of Colorado's striking natural sights, the surreal Great Sand Dunes National Park, a veritable sea of sand bounded by jagged peaks and scrubby plains, is a place of stirring optical illusions where nature's magic is on full display.

From the approach up Hwy 150, watch as the angles of sunlight make shifting shadows on the dunes; the most dramatic time is the day's end, when the hills come into high contrast as the sun drops low on the horizon. Hike past the edge of the dune field to see the shifting sand up close; the ceaseless wind works like a disconsolate sculptor, constantly amending the landscape.

Most visitors limit their activities to the area where Medano Creek divides the main dune mass from the towering Sangre de Cristo Mountains. The remaining 85% of the park's area is designated wilderness: not for the unfit or fainthearted.

◉ Sights

★**Great Sand Dunes**
National Park   NATIONAL PARK
(719-378-6399; www.nps.gov/grsa; 11999 Hwy 150; adult/child $3/free; visitor center 8:30am-5pm Jun-Aug, 9am-4:30pm Sep-May) Landscapes collide in a shifting sea of sand at Great Sand Dunes National Park, making you wonder whether a spaceship has whisked you to another planet. The 30-sq-mile dune park – the tallest sand peak rises 700ft above the valley floor – is squeezed between the jagged 14,000ft peaks of the Sangre de Cristo and San Juan Mountains and the flat, arid scrubbrush of the San Luis Valley.

UFO Watchtower   TOWER
(805-886-6959; www.ufowatchtower.com; 2502 County Rd 61; donation per car $5) Don't panic! The visiting aliens are harmless. Or mostly harmless anyway. And if you're eager for a glimpse (or perhaps want to leave an offering for a weary interstellar hitchhiker), then

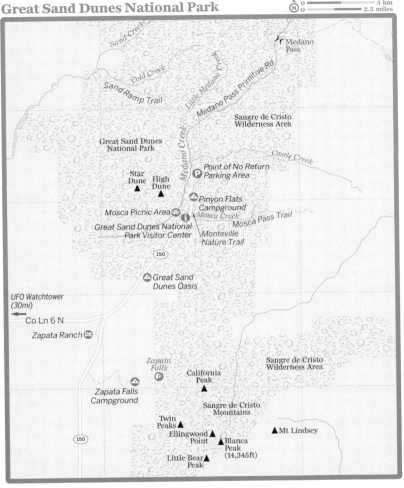

a stop at the UFO Watchtower is a must. About 15ft high, the tower is unlikely to improve your chances of actually spotting a flying saucer, but the garden and its assorted treasures is definitely something to behold.

The watchtower is located off Hwy 17 near Hooper (about 30 miles west of the national park), and is easiest to access if you're driving south toward the dunes from Salida.

San Luis State Park STATE PARK
(☎719-378-2020; www.cpw.state.co.us; 16393 Lane 6 N, Mosca) This state park is a patch of bleak terrain on the edge of the Great Sand

Dunes National Park, where dunes covered with saltbush and rabbitbrush stand in contrast to the grassy wetlands – the secondary beneficiary of this governmental largesse. Waterfowl, shorebirds and birdwatchers enjoy the recently restored wetlands.

🏃 Activities

Regardless of your chosen activity and where you go in the park, always take a hat, closed shoes, sunscreen, water, and a bandanna to protect your face if the wind picks up, and always check conditions at the Great Sand

Dunes National Park Visitor Center (p335) before setting out.

Throughout summer NPS rangers lead interpretive nature walks from the visitor center and hold evening programs at the amphitheater. This is an excellent way to learn more about the unseen world of the dunes – surprising thickets of sunflowers, burrowing owls and even tiger salamanders! Inquire at the visitor center about specific programs and times.

Inner Tubing

One of the most curious spectacles in the entire park, the snowmelt Medano Creek flows down from the Sangre de Cristos and along the eastern edge of the dunes. Peak flow is usually in late May or early June, and the rippling water over the sand creates a temporary beach of sorts, which is extremely popular with families. In years when the water is high enough (check the park website for daily water-level reports; the level of late has been very low), children can even float down the creek on an inner tube, right along the dunes. The combination of the creek's appeal and the end of the school year means that this is the park's peak season.

Hiking

There are no trails through this expansive field of sand, but it's the star attraction for hikers. Two informal hikes afford excellent panoramic views of the dunes. The first is a hike to High Dune (strangely, not the highest dune in the park), which departs from a parking area just beyond the visitor center. It's about 2.5 miles out to the peak and back, but be warned: it's not easy. As you trudge along up the hills of sand, it feels like you're taking a half-step back for every one forward. If you're up for it, try pushing on to the second worthy goal: just west of High Dune is Star Dune (750ft), the tallest in the park.

From the Great Sand Dunes National Park Visitor Center (p335), a short trail leads to the Mosca Picnic Area next to ankle-deep Medano Creek, which you must ford (when the creek is running) to reach the dunes. Across the road from the visitor center, the Mosca Pass Trail climbs up into the Sangre de Cristo Wilderness.

The area beyond the Point of No Return parking lot is a good spot to get further out into the backcountry on backpacking trips; a road theoretically leads up to Medano Pass (9982ft) at the top of the Sangres, but because of the sand it's not recommended unless you have a suitable off-road vehicle.

In midsummer, hikers should hit the hills during the early morning, as the sand can reach 140°F (60°C) during the heat of the day. Although you might think sandals would be the footwear of choice, closed-toe shoes provide better protection against the heat. Those with limited mobility can borrow a dunes-accessible wheelchair from the visitor center.

If you are hiking with children, don't let them out of your sight. It is very easy to get separated once you've entered the dunes.

Dune Sandboarding & Sledding

The heavy wooden sled may seem like a bad idea when you're trudging out to the dunes, but the gleeful rush down the slopes is worth every footstep. There's a bit of a trick to making this work. Sand conditions are best after a recent precipitation; when it's too dry you'll simply sink. Also, the best rides are had by those who are relatively light, so if you've bulked up on microbrews and steaks, don't expect to zip down the hill.

During the winter days when snow covers the dunes, the sledding is excellent. To rent a board, visit Kristi Mountain Sports (p336) in Alamosa or the Great Sand Dunes Oasis at the edge of the park.

Mountain Biking

Off-road cyclists should plan for a real slog. The unimproved roads of the park get washed over in sand and are very difficult until the road climbs the beautiful narrow valley to Medano Pass. The pass is 11 miles from the Point of No Return parking area at the north end of the paved road. A detailed mileage log for the Medano Pass Primitive Rd is available at the visitor center.

For a shorter fat-tire ride, visit the spectacular area around Zapata Falls, south of the park, which also offers outstanding views of the valley. A consortium of 13 agencies has opened 4 miles of trail in the Zapata Falls Special Recreation Area on the west flank of Blanca Peak.

Bicycle rentals, repairs and riding information are available at Kristi Mountain Sports (p336) in Alamosa.

🛏 Sleeping

For beauty at its spookiest, plan your visit during a full or new moon. Stock up on supplies, get your backcountry camping permit and hike into the surreal landscape to set up camp: bring plenty of shade and water.

There are also half-a-dozen backcountry sites that can be accessed from the Point of No Return parking lot, north of Pinyon Flats. These sites vary in terrain, from alpine and woodland to desert.

★**Zapata Falls Campground**   CAMPGROUND **$**
(☑719-852-7074; www.fs.usda.gov; BLM Rd 5415; tent & RV sites $11; ☀) Seven miles south of the national park, this campground offers glorious panoramas of the San Luis Valley from its 9000ft perch in the Sangre de Cristos. There are 23 first-come, first-served sites, but note that there is no water and that the 3.6-mile access road is steep and fairly washed out, making for slow going.

The payoff, however, is worth it, especially if you prefer a secluded location.

Great Sand Dunes Oasis   CAMPGROUND **$**
(☑719-378-2222; www.greatdunes.com; 5400 Hwy 150; tent/RV sites $25/38, cabins $55, r $100; ☺Apr-Oct; **P**@) At the park entrance, the Oasis serves as a general store, restaurant, and campground and motel. It has a convenient location and there are facilities to shower and do laundry, but overall the sites are fairly bleak. This is very much a Plan B choice. The cabins are also very spartan.

Pinyon Flats Campground   CAMPGROUND **$**
(☑888-448-1474; www.recreation.gov; Hwy 150; tent & RV sites $20; ☀) This is the official park campground, with a great location not far from the dune field. There are 88 sites here, but be warned: it is very popular and regularly fills up from mid-May through August. Half of the sites are available on a first-come, first-served basis (open year-round), the other 44 (open May to mid-November) can be reserved online.

Reserve as far in advance as possible; otherwise show up early and cross your fingers. Water and toilets are available.

Zapata Ranch   RANCH **$$$**
(☑719-378-2356; www.zranch.org; 5303 Hwy 150; d with full board $300) Ideal for horseback-riding enthusiasts, this exclusive preserve is a working cattle and bison ranch set amid groves of cottonwood trees. Owned and operated by the Nature Conservancy, the main inn is a refurbished 19th-century log structure, with distant views of the sand dunes.

ℹ Tourist Information

Stop by the informative **Great Sand Dunes National Park Visitor Center** (☑719-378-6399; www.nps.gov/grsa; 11999 Hwy 150; ☺8:30am-5pm Jun-Aug, 9am-4:30pm Sep-May; ♿) before venturing out, to learn about the geology and history of the dunes or to chat with a ranger about hiking or backcountry-camping options. A free backcountry permit is required if you're planning on being adventurous, and it pays to let the ranger know where you're going.

Be sure to ask about scheduled nature walks and nightly programs held at the amphitheater near Pinyon Flats.

ℹ Getting There & Away

Great Sand Dunes National Park is 33 miles northeast of Alamosa. To get here, travel east on US 160 for 14 miles toward prominent Blanca Peak, turn left (north) on Hwy 150 and follow the road for 19 miles to the visitor center, 3 miles north of the park entrance. You can also get here from the north, turning west off Hwy 17 onto County Ln 6 N.

Alamosa

☑719 / POP 9540 / ELEV 7543FT
The largest city in the San Luis Valley, Alamosa has a small liberal-arts university that helps to keep things fresh in what is otherwise a run-of-the-mill rural American outpost. Its greatest appeal for travelers is its convenience as a base for explorations into the Great Sand Dunes National Park.

Main St, with its small walking district, runs parallel to and one block north of Hwy 160. It's far more enjoyable to approach downtown on foot by walking along the river.

◉ Sights

★**Alamosa National Wildlife Refuge**   WILDLIFE RESERVE
(☑719-589-4021; www.fws.gov/alamosa; 9383 El Rancho Lane; ☺dawn-dusk; **P**) **FREE** This wildlife refuge on the banks of the Rio Grande is a special spot, and will give you some idea of what the valley must have looked like before it was developed for agriculture. It's best to visit at dawn or dusk, when wildlife is the most active and when you'll hear the amazing soundscape of bird calls and whistles.

San Luis Valley Museum   MUSEUM
(☑719-587-0667; www.museumtrail.org; 401 Hunt Ave; adult/child $2/free; ☺10am-4pm Tue-Sat)

RECOMMENDED HIKES IN GREAT SAND DUNES NATIONAL PARK

Montville Nature Trail

The Montville Store once stood at the foot of Mosca Pass Trail. It was built in the 1830s by fur trader Antoine Robidoux, who used the pass to transport supplies to his posts in western Colorado and eastern Utah. Many miners passed here on their way west to the San Juan Mountains. Today a half-mile trail next to Mosca Creek provides a self-guided tour through a variety of ecosystems, leading to a grand view of the San Luis Valley and the dunes. The Montville Nature Trail starts north of the visitor center, and is a good option for those visiting the area with children or who just want a quick walk.

Mosca Pass Trail

This is a moderate hike (7 miles round-trip) that climbs through meadows and stands of aspen along Mosca Creek. Near the start of the trail is a bronze plaque etched with the impression of Zebulon Pike, who described the dunes as 'appearing exactly as a sea in storm except as to color.' It begins at the Montville Nature Trail trailhead.

Zapata Falls

This short half-mile hike higher up in the Sangre de Cristos provides a refreshing change from slogging through the dunes. The falls, though small, are hidden at the end of a slot canyon and the last 150 yards are loads of fun (though not without risk), as you'll need to scramble through ankle-deep ice-cold water and over slippery rocks to get there. This is a good family hike.

Grippy water shoes are a good idea. If you want to make a day of it, you can continue on to South Zapata Lake (8 miles round-trip). The turnoff for the falls is 7 miles south of the park entrance along Hwy 150. It's a further 3.5 miles up a dirt road from here, from where you'll have an excellent view of the dunes.

Located behind the Chamber Depot, this museum has a small but well-arranged collection of 'then and now' photographs and artifacts from early farm life in the valley. Knowledgeable volunteers answer questions and can help plan excursions to historical sites.

Blanca Wetlands   WILDLIFE RESERVE
(☑719-274-8971; www.blm.gov; County Rd 2S; ⊙mid-Jul–mid-Feb) **FREE** The Bureau of Land Management has restored the wildlife habitat at Blanca Wetlands, northeast of Alamosa. Activities include fishing for bass or trout in newly created ponds and viewing waterfowl, shorebirds and other species. Hiking trails lead throughout the many marshes and ponds, but are closed in the nesting season from February 15 to July 15.

To get here from Alamosa, travel 6 miles east on Hwy 160, then 5 miles north on Alamosa County Rd 116S.

🏃 Activities & Tours

River Walk   WALKING
The river walk starts at the information depot in Cole Park and offers views of Blanca Peak and a stroll through tree-lined neighborhood streets to the downtown area.

Paths follow the Rio Grande on both banks from the information depot, but most walkers and joggers will prefer the wide, well-drained levee on the east side.

Kristi Mountain Sports   OUTDOORS
(☑719-589-9759; www.slvoutdoor.com; 3323 Main St; sandboard/bike rental per day $18/20; ⊙9am-6pm Mon-Sat) These extremely friendly folks rent bikes and sandboards and have a good selection of camping gear; the office is located west of town on Main St/Hwy 160.

⭐ **Rio Grande Scenic Railroad**   RAIL
(☑877-726-7245; www.coloradotrain.com; 610 State Ave; trips from $99) A variety of themed excursions are conducted on this fabulous scenic train that runs between La Veta and Alamosa. Check the website for dates and themes.

🛌 Sleeping

As a popular overnight stop at the convergence of three highways, Alamosa has plenty of old-school budget motels and most of the popular chain offerings, but not much else.

Comfort Inn Alamosa
MOTEL **$**

(☎719-587-9000; www.comfortinn.com; 6301 Hwy 160; d from $89; P❄☎☒☒) One of the nicer chain hotels, with a good breakfast, plasma TVs, and a pool and hot tub. There's also a coin laundry.

Valley Motel
MOTEL **$**

(☎719-589-9095; www.valleymotelalamosa. com; 2051 Main St; r from $59; ❄☎☒) This well-maintained family-run motel offers the best value option in Alamosa. It's located west of town on Hwy 160. Rates include breakfast.

✗ Eating & Drinking

There are plenty of franchise fast-food joints lining the highway at both ends of town, but you won't find too many fine-dining options here. If you're a fan of New Mexican food, you'll be spoiled for choice: the Colorado–New Mexico state line is just 33 miles south.

★ San Luis Valley Brewing Co
PUB FOOD **$$**

(☎719-587-2337; www.slvbrewco.com; 631 Main St; mains $8-22; ⊙11am-2am; ☎⟲) Housed in an old bank, the local brewery has some winning drinks on tap – notably the green-chili-infused Valle Caliente – as well as $3 margaritas during happy hour and homemade black-cherry cream soda. The food, which ranges from pub fare to pasta to Rocky Mountain trout, is better than expected.

Calvillo's
MEXICAN **$$**

(☎719-587-5500; 400 Main St; mains $9-21; ⊙8am-9pm; ☎⟲) The first place you'll see as you turn onto Main St, Calvillo's is *the* place to eat in town – mostly thanks to its legendary buffet. Chiles rellenos, enchiladas, tacos, fajitas, *chicharonnes,* and on and on...the buffet also includes agua fresca (fruit-flavored water) and dessert, and there are enough customers to ensure that fresh servings are constantly being dished out.

Milagro's Coffee House
CAFE

(☎719-589-9299; 529 Main St; ⊙7am-8pm Mon-Sat, 8am-4pm Sun; ☎⟲) This great little stop-off for travelers has wi-fi, comfy couches and a shelf of used books for sale. There are also pastries and breakfast burritos on offer, but it's better for drinks.

ⓘ Tourist Information

Alamosa County Chamber of Commerce (☎800-258-7597; www.alamosa.org; 610 State Ave; ⊙8am-5pm; ☎) is the go-to office for tourist information on the San Luis Valley, the Great Sand Dunes and beyond. Feel free to hit them up for a local perspective on all the alien hoo-haa.

ⓘ Getting There & Away

Alamosa is 72 miles west of Walsenburg and the I-25 on Hwy 160, 35 miles southwest of the Great Sand Dunes and 82 miles south of Salida on Hwy 17. Hwy 285 runs 218 miles north to Denver.

Greyhound operates infrequent bus services between Alamosa and Denver (via Salida; from $44, five hours). Pick-up is from the **Alamosa Bus Stop** (102 Hwy 160 E).

South of the central district on State Ave, **Alamosa San Luis Valley Regional Airport** (☎719-589-4848; www.sanluisvalleyairport. org; 2490 State Ave) is served by daily flights from Denver via Pueblo on Great Lakes Airline, an independent partner of United Airlines.

San Luis

☎719 / POP 630 / ELEV 7965FT

Tucked into the far southeast margin of the San Luis Valley is the town of San Luis, which happens to be Colorado's oldest settlement (1851).

Its character – today and throughout history – is largely the result of its isolation. For Spain, the upper Rio Grande was a lost province best left to the nomadic Native American tribes that Spain was unable to dominate. Under the threat of Ute raids, and far from the mercantile and spiritual centers at Taos and Santa Fe, San Luis developed as a self-sufficient outpost and largely escaped the 'progress' that revoked Hispanic tenure in other parts of the valley following the arrival of the railroad; today the town remains almost 90% Hispanic, a harbor of cultural diversity among Colorado's predominantly white population.

San Luis is worth a detour for those who want to experience the slow, scenic pace of the deep San Luis Valley.

⊙ Sights

★ San Luis Museum & Cultural Center
MUSEUM

(☎719-672-0999; 401 N Church Pl; $2; ⊙10am-4pm Mon-Fri) This handsome museum and gallery chronicles Hispanic culture in southern Colorado, in a modern building that blends sustainable concepts with traditional regional architecture. Exhibits on the Penitente Brotherhood are

MOUNTAIN STEAM: SCENIC RAILROADS

In 1880 the Denver & Rio Grande Western Rail (D&RG) completed a track over Cumbres Pass, linking Chama, NM, with Denver, CO, by way of Alamosa. The twisting, mountainous terrain was suited to narrow-gauge track, which is only 3ft wide instead of the standard gauge of 4ft 8in. Within a few years the line was extended to Durango, Farmington and the Silverton mining camp, 152 miles away. Railroad buffs encouraged Colorado and New Mexico to buy the scenic Cumbres Pass segment when the Antonito–Farmington line came up for abandonment in 1967. Their efforts led to a compact between Colorado and New Mexico to save the railway as a National Register site, and churning along its track, past hills of pine and aspen and expansive views of the high plains and mountains, makes an excellent way to spend a day.

Trains run daily, roughly from Memorial Day to mid-October, on the **Cumbres & Toltec Scenic Railroad** (p338) from Antonito and on the **Rio Grande Scenic Railroad** (p336) from Alamosa.

Dress warmly, as the unheated cars, both enclosed and semi-enclosed, can get extremely cold. Check the websites of each operator for current schedules, routes and a diverse program of themed journeys.

especially intriguing for their insight into this formerly secretive local sect of Catholicism.

★ **Stations of the Cross**　　CHRISTIAN SITE
(cnr Hwys 142 & 159) Following a path up a small hill, local sculptor Huberto Maestas' 15 dramatic life-sized statues of Christ's crucifixion are a powerful testament to the Catholic heritage of communities near the 'Blood of Christ' Mountains. The sculptures are stationed along a 1-mile pathway – an excellent chance to stretch the legs.

Viejo San Acacio　　CHURCH
(Costilla County Rd 15) The beautiful Viejo (old) San Acacio is a historic Catholic church where mass is still occasionally held. To get here, head 4 miles east of San Luis on Hwy 142, then turn left (south) on Costilla County Rd 15. The church is near Culebra Creek.

❶ Getting There & Away

San Luis is 41 miles southeast of Alamosa and 17 miles south of Fort Garland. West on Hwy 142 is Los Caminos Antiguos Byway, a scenic stretch of road along the New Mexico border dotted with mesas and chamisa shrubs. It runs through Manassa and on to Antonito.

Antonito

📞 719 / POP 780 / ELEV 7890FT
Pickup trucks with fishing tackle in the back rumble through the dusty, run-down little berg of Antonito, the only two real attractions of which are means of getting somewhere else: a historic railway to New Mexico and scenic Hwy 17, which follows the Conejos River into the Rio Grande National Forest.

◉ Sights & Activities

Jack Dempsey Museum　　MUSEUM
(📞719-843-5207; 412 Main St, Manassa; ⊙9am-5pm Tue-Sat Jun-Aug) FREE Manassa, a 10-minute drive northeast of Antonito, is home to a tiny one-room cabin where boxing legend Jack Dempsey was born as the ninth child of a poor mining family. It was a destitute childhood, but Dempsey channeled his hardship into boxing, and from 1919 to 1926 reigned as the heavyweight world champion. Boxing fans will enjoy this collection of memorabilia.

★ **Cumbres & Toltec Scenic Railroad Depot**　　RAIL
(📞888-286-2737; www.cumbrestoltec.com; 5234 Hwy 285; trips from adult/child $99/59; 🚻) Though other narrow-gauge historic trains can be found in Colorado, none of the rebuilt engines are quite as impressive as this ride – a chance to tackle the Cumbres Pass by power of steam. In 1880 the Denver & Rio Grande Western Rail completed a track over Cumbres Pass, linking Chama, NM, with Denver, CO, by way of Alamosa.

🛏 Sleeping & Eating

With lodging and campgrounds available along the beautiful Conejos River (west on Hwy 17), and no shortage of motels in

Alamosa to the north, there's little reason nor many places to stay here.

Antonito eating options are scarce and 'dining' options non-existent – it's best to stock up on supplies in Alamosa.

Dutch Mill CAFE **$**
(☏719-376-2373; 407 Main St; mains $6-15; ☺6:30am-9pm) Cheesy Mexican food and standard US dishes are available at this place, the best in town mostly because of a lack of competition.

❶ Tourist Information

Contact the **Antonito Chamber of Commerce** (☏719-376-2277; 220 Main St; ☺9am-5pm Mon-Fri) in the former railway station for tourist information.

❶ Getting There & Away

Antonito is the first town in Colorado on Hwy 285, across the Colorado–New Mexico state line, 28 miles south of Alamosa.

Conejos River & the South San Juans

If you truly want to get away from it all, the South San Juans are certainly a good option. Hwy 17 follows the Conejos River west out of Antonito and into the San Juan wilderness, providing a scenic detour over the Cumbres Pass (10,022ft) on the road to Chama and Santa Fe in New Mexico. Superb fishing, camping and hiking are the main attractions here. The volcanic character of the San Juan range from this angle is vivid, with ragged rock outcrops that rise above drivers motoring over the pass.

✖ Activities

There is a lot of good hiking and camping in the remote South San Juan Wilderness Area, a part of the Rio Grande National Forest. Don't expect a crowded trail; this area is probably the least used wilderness in southern Colorado.

The **Elk Creek Trailhead** makes for a good base; from here you can hike in to Duck Lake (3 miles) or First Meadows (2 miles); for a longer hike, continue past First Meadows to the Dipping Lakes (13 miles) and the Continental Divide Trail. Elk Creek is 24 miles west of Antonito, just off Hwy 17.

You can also access the Continental Divide Trail from the top of Cumbres Pass, near the depot.

For maps and information about these hikes and surrounding campgrounds, contact the **USFS Conejos Peak Ranger District** (☏719-274-8971; 15571 County Rd T5; ☺8am-4:30pm Mon-Fri), 11 miles north of Antonito (3 miles south of La Jara) on Hwy 285.

Specially managed Wild Trout Waters are designated by the Colorado Division of Wildlife on the uppermost Lake Fork, plus sections of the Conejos River next to the South San Juan Wilderness and below the Menkhaven Lodge for 4 miles. These streams support self-sustaining native cutthroat trout populations. The Division of Wildlife manager in Antonito prepares a map and handout on fishing the Conejos River for each season; it's available at the Antonito Chamber of Commerce and tackle shops. Alternatively, stop in at Conejos River Anglers.

Conejos River Anglers FISHING
(☏719-376-5660; www.conejosriveranglers.com; 34591 Hwy 17; half-day trips per person from $195; ☻) A good source for information on fishing conditions and specific regulations for the season. The shop also offers fishing guides for your choice of wading, hiking or horseback trips on the Conejos River and its tributaries from May to November. Cabins are available from $99 per night. It's 5 miles west of Antonito.

▣ Sleeping & Eating

There are five USFS campgrounds along Hwy 17, between Antonito and Cumbres Pass. The first three (Aspen Grove, Mogote and Spectacle Lake) are nice enough, but the scenery definitely improves the higher up into the mountains you go. Another good spot is Trujillo Meadows near the top of the pass. A reservoir stocked with trout is nearby, as is the Continental Divide.

There's barely any food vendors out here. You'll be looking after your own catering, so be sure to stock up in Alamosa or Santa Fe, NM, before setting out.

Elk Creek Campground CAMPGROUND **$**
(Hwy 17; tent sites $20; ☺Jun–mid-Sep; ☻) Elk Creek is a choice location; free dispersed camping is also available just down the road at Elk Creek Trailhead.

Conejos River Ranch LODGE **$$**
(☏719-376-2464; www.conejosranch.com; 25390 Hwy 17; lodge d from $105, cabins $150-235; ☏)

Comfortable cabins and B&B accommodations, all with private bath, are available at this ranch, 14 miles west of Antonito. Six fully equipped riverside cabins are on hand (our favorite is the bright and airy La Casita) and there are eight comfortably furnished lodge rooms. All accommodations include breakfast, and you can board horses for a small fee.

ⓘ Getting There & Away

To reach the Conejos River from Antonito, travel directly west on Hwy 17. The point at which the river first kisses the highway (after it's first crossing) is about 10 miles out of town.

Penitente Canyon

ELEV 8000FT

Penitente Canyon offers visitors the chance to climb, hike and bike among a never-ending tumble of strangely shaped giant boulders, spread out through four separate canyons. The main canyon takes its name from Los Hermanos Penitentes and is symbolized by the fading, blue-cloaked mural of the Virgin of Guadalupe painted on a canyon wall. Local legend has it that the mural was painted by three men, one of whom descended sitting on a suspended tire; the inscription reads 'Consuelo y Espiritu' (Comfort and Courage).

Some 27 million years ago, one of the largest volcanic explosions in earth's history ejected an unimaginable 1000 cubic miles of ash that over time became the rock formations you see today. After the eruption the underground chamber collapsed, forming the caldera (22 miles wide by 47 miles long!) west of Penitente, where these ancient ash formations and volcanic plugs rise like spires in a haunting landscape.

⌖ Sleeping & Eating

Accommodations are limited to the tent and RV sites of the year-round Penitente Canyon Campground.

Penitente Canyon
Campground   CAMPGROUND $
(☎719-852-7074; www.fs.usda.gov; County Road 38A; tent & RV sites $12; 🗷) There are 13 first-come, first-served tent sites at the main campground and a further eight sites at Witches Canyon. In theory there is a water pump here near the turnoff for the canyon, but play it safe and bring plenty with you. The campground is open year round.

La Garita Trading Post   AMERICAN $
(☎719-754-3755; www.lagaritagasstationandrestaurant.com; 41605 County Rd G; ⌚7am-6pm Tue-Sat, 7-11am Sun) This cash store is the closest place to stock up on supplies (gas, firewood, groceries) and get a bite to eat for breakfast or lunch. It's in La Garita (which barely qualifies as a town), 2 miles west of Penitente.

ⓘ Getting There & Away

Penitente Canyon is 7.5 miles west of Hwy 285, off County Rd 38A. From Hwy 285, take County Rd G to La Garita, then continue on County Rd 38A to Penitente. You can also get here from Del Norte, 13 miles south. Take Oak St (County Rd 112) north out of town, then turn onto County Rd 33, which will turn into County Rd 38A.

You'll pass a turnoff for a natural arch 3 miles south of Penitente. Although the arch is not particularly impressive (in addition to being quite hard to find), the drive through the caldera is quite beautiful.

Del Norte

☑719 / POP 1690 / ELEV 7879FT

Sun-bleached and lazy, Del Norte (rhymes with 'port') is a place most travelers blast through on the way to or from sites in Colorado's southwest. The town is seated next to the Rio Grande del Norte, for which it was named, in the San Juan foothills on Hwy 160.

One of Colorado's oldest towns, Del Norte was founded in 1860 and by 1873 it was a thriving supply point for mining in the San Juan Mountains, giving it both historical and scenic appeal.

Today Del Norte marks the beginning of Gold Medal fishing on the Rio Grande and is the closest 'big' town for rock climbers and hikers on their way to Penitente Canyon.

⊙ Sights & Activities

Gold-medal fishing on the Rio Grande begins a mile upstream at the Farmer's Union Canal. From here to the Hwy 149 bridge at South Fork is one of Colorado's most productive fisheries, producing 16in to 20in trout. Access the river and signed public property via the bridges on Rio Grande County Rds 17, 18 and 19, plus the Hwy 149 bridge above South Fork.

See www.fishtheupperrio.com for more information.

Fat-tire bikes are permitted on all public trails with the exception of designated wilderness areas. One ride recommended by the USFS follows an old stock driveway along an alpine ridge on USFS Trail 700 from Grayback Mountain (12,616ft) east 7 miles to Blowout Pass (12,000ft). To reach the Grayback Mountain trailhead, you have to travel about 20 miles south of Del Norte on USFS Rd 14, then continue another 5 miles on USFS Rd 330. Otherwise the dirt roads heading into the caldera area near Penitente Canyon are easy riding and offer some remarkable scenery. It is hot and dry out here, though, so come prepared.

Rio Grande County Museum & Cultural Center
MUSEUM

(☑719-657-2847; 580 Oak St; $2; ⊗10am-4pm Tue-Fri, to 2pm Sat Apr-Oct) This museum and cultural center features Pueblo and Ute rock art, Hispanic history and early photographs of Monte Vista's 'potato row' wagons loaded high with valley spuds at the turn of the 20th century. Special programs include talks and outdoor excursions led by local historians and naturalists. The museum has information for people who want to visit local rock-art sites.

🛏 Sleeping & Eating

Alongside the historical Windsor Hotel, Del Norte has a pair of budget motels on the east side of Grand Ave (Hwy 160) that offer comparably drab rooms; head up the road to Monte Vista for more options.

Del Norte has the best dining options for miles and miles and miles. You won't necessarily be spoiled for choice, but the town's need to cater to healthy outdoorsy folk means you won't be limited to greasy fry-ups (although they are still an option).

★ Windsor Hotel
HOTEL $$

(☑719-657-9031; http://windsorhoteldelnorte. com; 605 Grand Ave; r from $175; [P][❄][🛜]) This landmark 1874 hotel has been lovingly restored, from the original color schemes all the way down to the hardwood floors. The 22 rooms are simple but cozy, and the ground-floor restaurant (mains $12 to $26) is the nicest dining option west of Alamosa, with specialties such as pan-seared rainbow trout.

🍷 Drinking & Nightlife

Three Barrel Brewing Co
BREWERY

(☑719-657-0681; www.threebarrelbrew.com; 475 Grand Ave; ⊗11am-9pm) Welcome to one of Colorado's smallest breweries. It produces only 350 barrels of beer from its relatively nondescript HQ just a block off the main drag. But it's damn good beer. The 'just one more' inclination inspired by brews such Pemba Sherpa or Black Yak might be the best reason to spend the night in town.

ℹ️ Tourist Information

The **Del Norte Chamber of Commerce** (☑719-657-2845; www.delnortechamber.org; 505 Grand Ave; ⊗8:30am-5pm Mon-Fri) and **USFS Divide District Ranger Station** (☑719-657-3321; 13308 W Hwy 160; ⊗8am-4:30pm Mon-Fri) can both assist with inquiries about camping, climbing, hiking and biking in the area.

ℹ️ Getting There & Away

Del Norte is 31 miles northwest of Alamosa on Hwy 160.

SANGRE DE CRISTO MOUNTAINS

In a state full of dazzling mountains, the shark-toothed Sangre de Cristo ('Blood of Christ') range certainly holds its own. These mountains are steep and jagged, rising as much as 6000ft in about 4 miles, and three – Kit Carson, Crestone Peak and Crestone Needle – were the last of Colorado's 14ers to be summitted (Colorado College professors Albert Ellingwood and Eleanor Davis managed the feat in July 1916, after walking over 100 miles from Colorado Springs). Learn about the fourteeners at: www.14ers.com.

ℹ️ Getting There & Away

The Sangre de Cristo is a rugged range covering a vast area. The limited access points include Crestone and the Great Sand Dunes to the west, and Westcliffe to the east.

Westcliffe

☑719 / POP 580 / ELEV 7867FT

The full panorama of the rugged north–south Sangres is best viewed coming into Westcliffe on Hwy 96, where you'll see peak after jagged peak rising up dramatically from the valley floor. The town itself is a down-to-earth ranching community; outside of the bluegrass festival and rodeo in July, it's mainly of interest to travelers as the staging ground for excursions into the eastern Sangre de Cristo wilderness.

◉ Sights & Activities

Westcliffe has a historic Main St, with a few old 19th-century buildings around town. The old state bank on 2nd St is where scenes from *Comes a Horseman,* the 1978 flick starring James Caan and Jane Fonda, were shot.

There are three fourteeners here (and countless 13ers!), which include Crestone Peak (14,294ft) and Crestone Needle (14,197ft), among the toughest ascents in Colorado. Luckily there are also plenty of hikes that don't require technical expertise. Many do, however, require a high-clearance 4WD vehicle to get to the main trailhead.

Talk to the ranger offices in either Salida (p238) or Cañon City (p319) for detailed information on trails and campgrounds. For maps, try Valley Ace Hardware, south of Westcliffe on Hwy 69.

Silver Cliff Museum   MUSEUM
(☑719-783-2615; 606 Main St, Silver Cliff; ⊙1-4pm Sat & Sun Jun-Sep) **FREE** This small museum is housed in a former town hall and fire station, built in 1879. You can view relics and photographs of regional history. It's located in Silver Cliff, just east of Westcliffe.

★Venable-Comanche Loop Trail   HIKING
(www.alltrails.com/trail/us/colorado/venable-comanche-trail; ⊙Jun-Sep) For outstanding views on the crest of the Sangre de Cristo Mountains, the Comanche-Venable Loop Trail (USFS Trail 1345) is hard to beat. This is a spectacular hike – lots of granite faces, dark-blue alpine lakes and the famously exposed Phantom Terrace – but you really have to earn it. The 13-mile loop gains over 3600ft in elevation; start with Venable Canyon.

Music Pass Trail   HIKING
(www.alltrails.com/explore/trail/us/colorado/music-pass-trail; ⊙Jun-Oct) This 7.4-mile hike traverses the ridge at Music Pass (11,400ft) leading to Sand Creek Lakes on the west side of the range. The area was named by hikers who claimed to hear music made by the wind whistling through the trees. It's a 1½-mile hike to the pass from the 4WD trailhead.

South Colony Lakes Trail   HIKING
(www.alltrails.com/trail/us/colorado/south-colony-lakes-trail; ⊙Jun-Oct) Climbers use South Colony Lakes as a base camp, but the 12,000ft lakes beneath the awe-inspiring trio of Crestone Needle, Crestone Peak and Humboldt Peak also make for an excellent day hike. It's a 4.75-mile round-trip hike from the 4WD trailhead.

Rainbow Trail   HIKING
This historic trail traverses the eastern slope of the Sangre de Cristo range, stretching over 100 miles all the way from the Continental Divide near Salida to Music Pass south of Westcliffe. It's a multi-use trail in places, open for hiking, horseback riding, mountain biking and ATVs, though there are plenty of solitary sections and it certainly makes for an interesting through hike.

Wherever you go, you'll likely cross it at some point. Check with the USFS Ranger Office (p240) in Salida for various options.

Bear Basin Ranch   HORSEBACK RIDING
(☑719-783-2519; www.bearbasinranch.com; 473 County Rd 271; rides half-day $60, full-day incl lunch $120; ♿) Eleven miles east of Westcliffe, this ranch offers horseback rides on its extensive property in the Wet Mountains. All-day and multiday trips into the mountains are also available.

Cliff Lanes   BOWLING
(☑719-783-2147; www.clifflanes.com; 25 Main St; games $4, shoe rental $3; ⊙7am-9pm Mon-Fri, 8am-8pm Sat & Sun; ♿) At the west end of Main St, this bowling alley/diner is a good diversion if you're looking for a little *Big Lebowski* action and reliable diner grub.

★☆ Festivals & Events

High Mountain Hay
Fever Bluegrass Festival   MUSIC
(www.highmountainhayfever.org; ⊙mid-Jul) This town loves bluegrass, and this festival is a chance to see some of the best 'grass heads' in Colorado.

Jazz in the Sangres   MUSIC
(www.jazzarts.org; ⊙mid-Aug) Young jazz artists perform both day and night at this jazz festival, the culmination of a week-long jazz-performance camp that draws students from around Colorado.

Westcliffe Stampede Rodeo   RODEO
(www.westcliffe-colorado.com/stampede-rodeo.html; ⊙mid-Jul) A rodeo and parade are the featured events at the Custer County Fair.

🛏 Sleeping

Apart from camping, Westcliffe does not have a lot of sleeping options. Do note that the Sangres see a lot of bear activity, and the forest service recommends that you take extra precautions down here if you're camping. Abundant open campsites can be

Understand Colorado

COLORADO TODAY **346**
What happened to swing state? Colorado goes progressive, legalizing marijuana and transforming public transportation.

HISTORY **348**
From Wild West frontier to outdoor haven and ski central: Colorado has a whole lot of history.

THE ARTS **353**
Art doesn't figure in many people's concept of Colorado – let's see if we can change that.

WILDLIFE & THE LAND **356**
If you're coming here, you're probably heading outdoors. Here's a taste of what's waiting for you.

Colorado Today

From double-diamond runs to stiff espressos, Colorado is about vigor. Universities and high-tech show the state's industrious side, though even workaholics might call in sick when snow starts falling. It's no wonder that the sunny state attracts so many East Coasters and Californians. Latinos also have answered the call to shore up a huge hospitality industry. And while much of Colorado remains conservative, there's common ground in everyone's mad love for the outdoors and an inspiring and friendly can-do ethos.

Best on Film

Butch Cassidy & the Sundance Kid (1969) The seminal cliff-jumping scene was shot on the Durango & Silverton Narrow Gauge Railroad.
True Grit (1969) Set in Arkansas but filmed in the San Juan Mountains.
The Shining (1980) Inspired by the Stanley Hotel in Estes Park.
Dear Eleanor (2014) Leonardo DiCaprio produced this Sundance flick, which was filmed on the Front Range.

Best in Print

On the Road (Jack Kerouac; 1957) The Denver doldrums and the origins of road-tripper culture.
House of Rain (Craig Childs; 2007) Tracks the Anasazi in the Southwest.
Plainsong (Kent Haruf; 1999) Examines a Colorado farming community.
The Dog Stars (Peter Heller; 2012) The dark poetry of a postapocalyptic world.
Abandon (Blake Crouch; 2009) The mysterious mass abandonment of a (fictional) 19th-century gold-mining town.

The Grass is Greener

Colorado voted to legalize the recreational use of marijuana in November 2012, and became the first jurisdiction in the world (alongside Washington state) to do so. People of 21 years or older may possess under 1oz (28.35g) of marijuana or cultivate up to six plants per person for personal use. It may be consumed only within private residences, not in public. As with alcohol, consumption of pot while driving is illegal. For dispensaries, which popped up after Colorado legalized medical marijuana back in 2000, the ruling has been a cash cow. But don't expect bud to be sold alongside beer coolers. To keep a low profile with minors, dispensaries have nondescript storefronts, usually away from prime real estate.

Attitudes toward ganja had been softening around the country for some time, but Colorado's trailblazing act failed to take into account one detail: marijuana is still illegal at the federal level.

With the Trump administration in the White House, that might pose a problem. But for now it's a boon – the billion-dollar industry garnered 200 million dollars for the state in tax revenue in 2016 alone. While most states struggle to find resources, Colorado has a new cash cow funding public education, local law enforcement, substance-abuse counseling and other social services.

Cannabis legalization was supported by over 55% of voters, and most Coloradans are thrilled about the added revenue, though attitudes do vary. The coming years may prove an interesting social experiment.

The Young & The Restless

Once a mining, ranching and farming stronghold, today's Colorado is a young state getting younger, with 24% of its 5.5 million residents under the age of 18.

Most live in and around Denver, where suburban development on former farmland fueled real estate and technology booms. Some of those jobs were lost in tech busts in the late 1990s and early 2000s, but the area weathered the storm. Growth has not only sparked suburban sprawl but also urban gentrification.

Denver's once-blighted LoDo neighborhood is a poster child for urban revitalization, with hip residential lofts and strings of bars and restaurants. Young college grads flock here from across the US, with an eye toward pairing an outdoor, weekend-warrior lifestyle with a high-paying tech gig.

Another industry has gripped northern Colorado, and we aren't talking about the marijuana business. Known as the Colorado Clean Energy Cluster, there are now 32 clean-energy companies working together to promote and produce green energy in the Denver–Boulder area. In 2016 Colorado was ranked third on CNBC's Top States for Business list. It's no wonder that Google is adding a huge new Boulder campus.

In 2015 Colorado was the second-fastest-growing state in the nation, with out-of-staters coming to live the Colorado dream. There may be a low unemployment rate (3.2% in 2016), but there's also a dearth of new jobs. According to an annual report from the Colorado Center on Law & Policy, the median hourly wage has remained flat for nearly a decade, despite rising costs. Still dreaming of forging a new life out west? Best bring your piggy bank.

Red State, Blue State

Politically Colorado is a divided land, with 1.15 million registered Democrats and 1.14 million registered Republicans in 2016. How did that happen? Urban population growth. Colorado's long-standing tendency has always been to vote Republican. This conservative streak has been rooted in its evangelical base in Colorado Springs and the ranching and mining interests found scattered throughout the state.

But there are plenty of progressives here as well, particularly in Denver, Boulder and throughout the Front Range. This is how Colorado managed to vote for Barack Obama twice, and for Hillary Clinton in 2016 (with a 5% margin). In 2013 the state approved gay civil unions. Then there's current Colorado governor John Hickenlooper, a Democrat and former geologist-turned-entrepreneur who helped transform Denver's LoDo. A Quaker, he is beloved by Colorado progressives, and has promoted initiatives such as gun control, legalizing marijuana and a sustainable development program called Greenprint Denver.

Liberalism has its limits here, too. Guns are a hot-button issue. After a local man shot and killed 12 moviegoers (injuring 70 more) in an Aurora movie theater on July 20, 2012, stringent new state gun laws were passed. But gun advocates lobbied hard against restrictions and, in September 2013, two Democratic Colorado state legislators were recalled by voters for supporting the laws.

POPULATION: **5.5 MILLION**

AREA: **104,185 SQ MILES**

UNEMPLOYMENT: **3%**

NUMBER OF STATE WILDLIFE AREAS: **350**

PEAKS OVER 14,000FT: **53, 54 OR 58 (DEPENDING ON WHO'S COUNTING)**

if Colorado were 100 people

69 would be Caucasian
21 would be Latino
5 would be African American
3 would be Asian
2 would be Native American

belief systems
(% of population)

| Protestant | Catholic | Mormon |
| 43 | 16 | 2 |

| Jewish | Buddhist | other |
| 1 | 1 | 37 |

population per sq mile

COLORADO · USA · DENVER

† ≈ 55 people

History

Colorado's history is written in petroglyphs, gold dust and ski tracks. A story about the making of today's United States, it's also a parable about European domination of the New World. Ambitious adventurers and salespeople, colonizing politicians and fighters intermingled and spread slowly across Colorado, overtaking the domain of Native Americans whose complex cultures had persisted through countless generations at the time of first contact.

Pre-America

Late Paleo-Indian artifacts of the Cody Cultural Complex indicate that inhabitants relied on hunting modern bison, while around 7500 years ago some peoples switched to hunting smaller game – a likely indicator of human population pressure on the declining bison. Petroglyphs near Dinosaur National Monument date back as far as 499 BC; in total Colorado has over 56,000 prehistoric sites, dating as far back as 12,000 BC.

The most complex societies in North American antiquity, however, were the agricultural pueblos of the Colorado Plateau, where cliff dwellers left behind impressive ruins in areas like Mesa Verde – its 4300 sites, including 600 cliff dwellings, make it the largest archaeological preserve in the US. The first were built after AD 650 and the area was abandoned by 1285, probably due to instability in both social structures and the environment.

Many Native American groups occupied the Rocky Mountain region at the time of European contact. The Utes consisted of six eastern bands in Colorado, territory that stretched from the Uinta Mountains and the Yampa River in the north to the San Juan River in the south, and as far east as the Front Range.

The Denver Mint, the largest producer of coins in the world, struck and minted its first gold and silver coins on February 1, 1906. The mint was robbed of $200,000 in broad daylight on December 18, 1922.

Exploration & Settlement

The first European explorers were Spaniards moving north from Mexico. They founded Santa Fe at the end of the 16th century, and established land grants as far north as the Arkansas River in present-day Colorado. In the search for overland routes to California, the Domínguez-Escalante Expedition of 1775–76 explored the Colorado Plateau.

TIMELINE

AD 100 The region's dominant indigenous cultures emerge. The Hohokam settle in the desert, the Mogollon dwell in the mountains and valleys, and Ancestral Puebloans build cliff dwellings around the Four Corners.

1300s The entire civilization of Ancestral Puebloans living in Mesa Verde abandons this sophisticated city of cliff dwellings – just why is one of history's most enduring unsolved mysteries.

1775–76 Spanish missionaries Francisco Atanasio Domínguez and Silvestre Vélez de Escalante lead an expedition through the Colorado Plateau in search of overland routes to California.

Early-18th-century French explorers and fur traders converged on the northern plains from eastern Canada, but by the early 19th century the Spanish had moved throughout the western half of present-day Colorado, the southwestern corner of Wyoming and even shared, at least formally, occupation of parts of Montana with the British, who had established trading posts. Virtually all of New Mexico, Arizona, California, Utah and Nevada were under Spanish authority.

In 1803 the USA acquired the French territorial claim known as the Louisiana Purchase. It included the coveted port of New Orleans, virtually all of present-day Montana, three-quarters of Wyoming and the eastern half of Colorado. Then-president Thomas Jefferson invited army captain Meriwether Lewis to command an exploratory expedition; Lewis is asked his colleague William Clark to serve as co-commander. Their Corps of Discovery set forth to benefit American commerce by seeking a 'Northwest Passage' to the Pacific Ocean. Meanwhile, the expedition managed to make serious scientific observations on flora, fauna, climate and the inhabitants of the region.

Lewis and Clark's was the most successful of early US expeditions to the west; others ended in disaster. After a foray into Colorado in 1806–07, Zebulon Pike was arrested in New Mexico by Spanish police – and he never actually climbed the famous peak that bears his name.

In 1839 journalist John L O'Sullivan suggested in his essay 'Manifest Destiny' that it was white America's destiny to own the American continent from coast to coast and tip to tip, an idea that inevitably became US policy under then-president James Polk. This in turn spiked westward settlement and caused inevitable violent clashes with both Mexico – which owned southern Colorado – and native peoples. The Mexican–American War raged in the mid-1840s; by its end Charles Bent, appointed first governor of New Mexico, had been assassinated by Pueblo Indians in Taos, and his brother William was married to a Cheyenne woman in Colorado. The less-publicized Indian Wars were the euphemism for the violent subjugation of Colorado's native people by the Colorado Volunteers. The exclamation point to this process was the 1864 Sand Creek Massacre (p325).

The discovery of gold in 1859 brought more miners and pioneers. Not long after the Pony Express blazed the Overland Trail through the Pawnee Grassland to deliver the US mail, Southern families came this way after the Civil War, planting sugar beets in northeast Colorado.

Fur Trade & Emigrant Trails

In the early 1800s fur traders spread across the Rockies, trading with Native Americans and living rough lives on the frontier. They came to know the Rockies backcountry better than any other Europeans.

HISTORY FUR TRADE & EMIGRANT TRAILS

Slavery to Riches

Barney Ford was born a Virginian slave in 1822. Eventually he escaped to Chicago to study, and later settled in Breckenridge, right after the first Colorado gold strike. He became the wealthiest man in the town – opening restaurants and hotels, and funding gold explorations – and was elected to the state legislature.

Ghost Towns

Colorado has around 500 ghost towns, a legacy of the boom-and-bust cycle of the gold- and silver-mining days. Check out www.ghosttowns. com for the lowdown on all of them.

1803	1821	1846–48	1849
US President Thomas Jefferson commissions Lewis and Clark to explore the western interior – the first US overland expedition to the Pacific Coast and back.	After 11 years of war, Mexico gains independence from Spain. The US acknowledges Mexico's hegemony over most of the West, including three-quarters of Colorado.	The Mexican–American War is spurred by the United States' recent annexation of Texas; Mexicans know the event as the First US Intervention in Mexico.	Regular stagecoach service starts along the Santa Fe Trail. The 900-mile trail serves as the country's main freight route for the next 60 years, until the railway finally makes it to town.

The Santa Fe Trail (p324), launched in the early 1830s, led west through hostile country from Missouri through Kansas and Colorado. By 1833 the brothers William and George Bent had built a fort that was an oasis for pioneers traveling on the trail.

Even into the 20th century, hundreds of thousands of emigrants followed the Oregon Trail across the Continental Divide to South Pass, where they split up to reach various destinations. The Mormons came fleeing persecution in New York and the Midwest. In the late 1860s, completion of the Transcontinental Railroad across southern Wyoming slowed the inexorable march of wagon trains.

Water & Western Development

Though the lingering image of the Great American Desert, a myth propagated by explorers such as Pike and Long, had deterred agricultural settlers and urban development, Americans were beginning to think of occupying the area between the coasts.

Water was a limiting factor as cities such as Denver began to spring up at the base of the Front Range. Utopians such as Horace Greeley, who saw the Homestead Act of 1862 as the key to agrarian prosperity, planned agricultural experiments on the nearby plains. This act envisioned the creation of 160-acre family farms to create a rural democracy on the Western frontier.

Government agents encouraged settlement and development in their assessments of the region, but differed on how to bring these changes about. Two of the major figures were Frederick V Hayden of the United States Geological Survey (USGS) and John Wesley Powell, first of the Smithsonian Institute and later of the USGS. Hayden, who had surveyed the Yellowstone River area and played a major role in having it declared a national park, was so eager to promote the West that he exaggerated the region's agricultural potential.

Powell, a great figure in American history, made a more perceptive assessment of both the region's potential and its limitations. Famous as the first man to descend the Colorado River through the Grand Canyon, Powell knew the region's salient feature was aridity and that its limited water supply depended on the snowpack that fell in the Rockies. The 160-acre ideal of the Homestead Act was inappropriate for the West. His masterful *Report on the Lands of the Arid Regions of the United States* challenged the tendency toward exploiting the region's minerals, pastures and forests, and proposed distributing land according to its suitability for irrigation.

Powell recommended dams and canals to create an integrated, federally sponsored irrigation system administered by democratically elected cooperatives. Unfortunately his vision collided with the interests of

Women's Suffrage

On November 7, 1893, Colorado became the first US state – and one of the first places in the world – to adopt an amendment granting women the right to vote.

Historic Sites

Buffalo Bill Museum & Grave (Golden)

Overland Trail (Sterling)

Durango & Silverton Narrow Gauge Railroad (Durango, Silverton)

Cripple Creek & Victor Narrow Gauge Railroad (Cripple Creek)

1858	1864	1876	1879
General William H Larimer pegs out a square-mile plot of land, establishing the settlement that will eventually become Denver after gold is discovered nearby.	Colonel John Chivington leads 700 troops and militia in the infamous Sand Creek Massacre. The heads of Arapaho victims are paraded through today's LoDo district in grisly celebration.	Colorado is granted statehood, becoming the 38th state of the Union. This takes place 28 days after the US Centennial, earning Colorado its 'Centennial State' moniker.	Major Thornburgh and his officers are killed in a Ute ambush, as are Indian Agent Nathan Meeker and his 10 employees. Some women and children are taken hostage. This becomes known as the Meeker Massacre.

influential cattle barons – nor did it appeal to real-estate speculators. These interests united to undermine Powell's blueprint; what survived was the idea that water development was essential to the West.

Twentieth-century development took the form of megaprojects such as the Glen Canyon Dam on the Colorado River, and water transfers from Colorado's Western Slope to the Front Range and the plains via a tunnel under the Continental Divide. These, in turn, provided subsidized water for large-scale irrigators and electrical power for users far from their source.

Statehood & Labor Strife

American expansion in the West spread to Colorado with the discovery of gold in the mountains west of Denver in 1859. In 1861 the boundaries of Colorado Territory were defined, and President Lincoln appointed William Gilpin the first governor.

In 1870 two sets of railroad tracks reached Denver, ending Colorado's isolation. The Denver Pacific Railroad connected Denver with the Union Pacific's transcontinental line at Cheyenne, WY, and the Kansas Pacific arrived from Kansas City, MO. That same year, General William Palmer began planning the Denver & Rio Grande's narrow-gauge tracks into the mountain mining camps. The mining emphasis shifted from gold to silver during the 1870s, and mountain smelter sites like Leadville and Aspen developed into thriving population centers almost overnight.

National political expedience led to Colorado statehood in 1876, the centennial of US independence.

Disputes over working conditions for the state's miners would lead to tragedy in the early years of the next century. In 1914 labor activist

Rightwing Radicals

With so many progressives in towns such as Boulder, Denver and Aspen, it's easy to forget that Colorado has a politically radical streak, but the state birthed the rightwing militia movement of the 1990s. According to the Southern Poverty Law Center, as of 2015 Colorado had 15 hate groups operating in the state (and their numbers have grown nationally as well).

HISTORY STATEHOOD & LABOR STRIFE

FATE OF THE NATIVE AMERICANS

The US government signed treaties in the latter half of the 19th century to defuse Native American objections to expanding settlement. Huge reservations and rations were an attempt to compensate Native Americans for the loss of hunting territory. Under pressure from miners and other emigrants, the federal government continually reduced the size of the reservations, shifting many to less desirable areas.

Ute territorial sovereignty survived a bit longer than that of other Native Americans in the region, but with the influx of silver miners west of the Continental Divide in the 1870s, Chief Ouray had little option but to sign treaties relinquishing traditional lands.

In 1879, the White River Band of Utes attacked federal troops and White River Indian Agent Nathan Meeker and his family near the present-day town of Meeker. All Utes suffered vicious American reprisals. By 1881 Utes not removed to forsaken lands in Utah were left with a narrow, 15-mile-wide plateau in southwestern Colorado.

1917	1962–70s	1999	2000
William F 'Buffalo Bill' Cody dies and is buried at Mt Lookout, overlooking Denver. Today you can visit the Buffalo Bill Museum & Grave from Golden.	A series of industrial and environmental accidents combined with urbanization pressures lead to increased green activism, which pushes state and federal authorities to clean up military facilities and waste sites.	Students Eric Harris and Dylan Klebold kill 12 students and one teacher before committing suicide at Columbine High School, near Denver.	Coloradans vote for Amendment 20 in the state election, which provides for the dispensing of cannabis to registered patients. A proliferation of medical marijuana clinics ensues over the next decade.

Mary Harris 'Mother' Jones came to Trinidad to join a particularly contentious miners' strike. She was 82 years old and taking on the Rockefeller family's Colorado Fuel & Iron. The miners, mostly European immigrants, were evicted from company homes and erected a tented camp in Ludlow. Jones bonded with them and led marches through downtown, bringing the national spotlight on Colorado. Eventually she was arrested and forced into 20 days of solitary confinement while the state militia stormed and torched the tented camp, killing three miner men, two women and 11 children. The tragedy humiliated the Rockefellers and led to labor-law reformation.

Post-WWII

From its earliest days the West was the country's most urbanized region; when Colorado became a state in 1876, more than a third of its residents lived in Denver. In part, urbanization was a function of the tourist economy, as Americans, who had flocked to the national parks during the economic boom after WWII, began to appreciate the Rockies as a place to live rather than just to visit. The federal government played a role by providing employment, thanks in large part to investment in Cold War military installations such as NORAD (North American Aerospace Defense Command), a facility near Colorado Springs. People relocated to remote towns such as Telluride as communications decentralized some sectors of the economy.

Increasingly, well-educated locals and visitors in the late 1960s and early '70s expressed environmental concerns. Military facilities, such as the Rocky Mountain National Arsenal near Colorado Springs and the Rocky Flats nuclear weapons facility near Denver, came under attack by activists concerned with environmental contamination, and were declared priority clean-up sites under the federal Environmental Protection Agency's Superfund program.

Tourism is now an economic mainstay in the Rockies. The industry blossomed in the post-WWII economic boom, when veterans of the 10th Mountain Division arrived home from war and dreamed up a whole new industry: they built the state's first ski lift out of spare parts and went on to help open ski resorts in Loveland, Arapahoe Basin and eventually Vail and Aspen. While the region's natural attractions have drawn visitors since the 1870s, up until WWII it was mostly only wealthy travelers who saw the backcountry. But post-war prosperity and the improvement of roads brought larger numbers of middle-class tourists. In 2015 Colorado had a record 77.7 million visitors who spent $19 billion, an income that has become an essential contribution to the state's economy.

Museums & Stately Buildings

Black American West Museum & Heritage Center (Denver)

Byers-Evans House Museum (Denver)

History Colorado Center (Denver)

Colorado Springs Fine Arts Center (Colorado Springs)

Trinidad History Museum (Trinidad)

Barney Ford Museum (Breckenridge)

Brown Palace Hotel (Denver)

Colorado State Capitol (Denver)

Stanley Hotel (Estes Park)

Wheeler Opera House (Aspen)

Broadmoor (Colorado Springs)

Strater Hotel (Durango)

2010	2012	2013	2016–17
Fires burn for 11 days near Boulder, causing mass evacuations and property damage. Over 1000 firefighters are deployed, and 7000 acres and 169 houses are burnt.	With the passing of Amendment 64, Colorado makes recreational marijuana legal.	The 2013 Colorado Floods result from massive rainfall between September 9 and 12, killing eight people. The Front Range sustains over $1 billion of damage.	Denver votes to approve marijuana social clubs; in 2017 a handful of clubs open.

The Arts

More jock than artist, more adventurer than poet, Colorado isn't the most obvious candidate for a flourishing arts scene. But a convergence of key ingredients – transcendent natural beauty, a scrappy history and inspiration – has fostered great performances, literary movements and works of art well worth contemplating. To boot, the state's perfect summer weather has allowed outstanding cultural events such as the Colorado Shakespeare Festival and Aspen Music Festival to take the arts out into the open air.

The Mark of Ancient Cultures

The Ancestral Puebloan people lived in sandstone cliff dwellings in the Four Corners region of Colorado. Their striking architecture and handiwork included cylindrical ceremonial kivas and decorated pottery and basketry, all born from utilitarian need.

But their rock and cave paintings are something else entirely. Interpretations offered by Native American elders indicate that most have deeper meanings. On a visit to Petroglyph Point at Mesa Verde National Park, you'll see spirals, palm prints and human and animal figures. Some help to mark time; others hold more spiritual and ritualistic meaning, or display social rank. A petroglyph at Hovenweep National Monument on the Utah border has a well-known solstice marker. Shafts of sunlight strike the spiral differently at the winter and summer solstices.

Pottery, basketry and rock art played a central role in Native American life for hundreds of years. Evidence of Arapahoe, Cheyenne, Apache and Ute artifacts can be viewed in museums across the state. Ute pieces are especially prominent. On display are buffalo-hide paintings, beaded horse bags, rattles, and drums made from buffalo rawhide.

To experience ceremonial drumming, chanting and dancing in traditional dress, you'll need to find your way to a powwow. The Southern Ute's annual powwow is held in Ignacio in early September.

An Art World Emerges

Folk art was the way from the days of indigenous freedom right through to the pioneering period. While there was certainly live music, song and dance in saloons that doubled as brothels, there wasn't much of what we would now consider fine art in nascent Colorado. In fact, even as the state grew into a ranching, mining and railroad force in the first half of the 20th century, sophisticated art wasn't part of the equation.

Enter Alice Bemis Taylor, the wife of a powerful mining tycoon. She leaned on her vast connections in the New York art world and, with the help of other wealthy philanthropists, founded the Colorado Springs Fine Arts Center, where Martha Graham danced on stage in its 400-seat theater on opening night. Today the center is still arguably the best museum in Colorado.

But what about iconic Western imagery? The Denver Art Museum, which also has a vast collection of contemporary and global art, as well as the largest Native American art collection in the US, is perhaps most famous for its gallery of cowboy art, including the iconic *Long Jakes, the*

Jack Kerouac's *On the Road* set many scenes on Denver's Larimer St. Neal Cassady, the book's inspiration, once asked a friend to sort his unpaid tab at Denver's oldest continually running bar, located nearby at 2376 15th St (today called My Brother's Bar). You'll find the framed letter hanging inside.

Rocky Mountain Man by Charles Deas. The Arthur Roy Mitchell Memorial Museum of Western Art is a decidedly smaller but earnest Western art gallery in Trinidad. Also known as 'the Mitch,' it was built in honor of this local cowboy artist in a late-19th-century department store.

But what about the new West? Public art and the growth of modern-art outlets are shaking it up. Our favorite is Denver's newly inaugurated Clyfford Still Museum, featuring the breathtaking works of this major 20th century abstract impressionist.

Galleries in the West

Aspen has the most-established and best-connected art scene in Colorado, with several galleries in the historic downtown. The 212 Gallery is among the most forward-thinking, bringing a NYC edge to the mountain air.

The fledgling art scenes of Mancos and Pueblo sponsor First Friday art walks in the summer.

Summer Means Festivals

For the past 60-odd years, the Aspen Music Festival (p228) has given this town its artistic gravitas. Some of the best classical musicians from around the world come to perform and learn from the masters of their craft. Students form orchestras led by world-famous conductors and perform at the Wheeler Opera House or the Benedict Music Tent, or in smaller duets, trios, quartets and quintets on Aspen street corners. All told, more than 350 classical music events take place over eight weeks. If you're hungry to hear the best music in the sweetest venue, the Benedict is a must. And you don't even have to pay – just unfurl a blanket on the Listening Lawn.

And that's not even the only music festival worth mentioning in Aspen. Jazz Aspen Snowmass (p228) is a biannual event held at the beginning and end of the summer, featuring jazz masters such as Christian McBride, Nicholas Payton and Natalie Cole in June, and major pop and rock acts such as Wilco around Labor Day. Theatre Aspen (p234) is another annual tradition, which stages Tony-winning romantic comedies

Willie Nelson's seminal album *Red Headed Stranger* is a concept album about a fugitive Montana cowboy on the run from the law after killing his wife and her lover. Inspired by Colorado's Rocky Mountains, Nelson purportedly wrote the tracks while driving back from a ski weekend.

THE LITERARY CANON

Colorado's rebellious literary soul was led by the late, great Hunter S Thompson, the original 'Gonzo journalist' and author of *Fear and Loathing in Las Vegas*. Here's a man who ran for sheriff on the Freak Power Ticket and made his name by hanging with the Hells Angels, heckling Nixon and downing experimental-drug cocktails. Eventually he committed suicide and had his ashes blasted out of a cannon. His favorite hangout, the Woody Creek Tavern (p234), has become a fan pilgrimage site.

One of Thompson's inspirations was Jack Kerouac, who also did some time on Colorado's freight trains and downbeat street corners. Another Beat writer (and Pulitzer Prize winner) with a lasting impact was Allen Ginsberg: the author of *Howl* was a founding poet of Jack Kerouac's School of Disembodied Poetics at Boulder's Naropa University (p113), where Ginsberg taught for more than two decades.

Colorado has captured the imaginations of many other authors as well. Stephen King has set several of his bestsellers in Colorado (*The Stand, The Shining, Misery*); Wallace Stegner's masterpiece *Angle of Repose* is partly set in Leadville; and local Craig Childs has some fantastic books about the Southwest, from hairy wildlife stories in *Animal Dialogues* to the Anasazi in *House of Rain*. Set in eastern Colorado, *Plainsong,* by Kent Haruf, was a finalist in the National Book Award. And then of course there's always good old Louis L'Amour, whose frontier stories defined the Old West for many readers.

COLORADO IN THE MOVIES

Denver & Around The coming-of-age film *Dear Eleanor* (2014), a Sundance film produced by Leonardo DiCaprio, was filmed at various Front Range locations.

Creede The open range for Johnny Depp's flop *The Lone Ranger* (2013).

Telluride Tarantino's Western *The Hateful Eight* (2015) and *Darling Companion* (2012), with Diane Keaton and Kevin Kline.

Boulder Starred in both *Catch and Release* (2006) with Jennifer Garner and *About Schmidt* (2002) with Jack Nicholson.

Pikes Peak Adrenaline franchise *Furious 7* (2015) was filmed on the mountain.

Stanley Hotel This Estes Park hotel was the setting for Stanley Kubrick's *The Shining* (1980) – another Nicholson gem – though Kubrick filmed in Montana, Oregon and England.

Durango & Silverton Narrow Gauge Railroad Bakers Bridge is where Robert Redford and Paul Newman jumped into the river in *Butch Cassidy and the Sundance Kid* (1969). Durango also made a star turn in Renée Zellweger's *Nurse Betty* (2000).

Silverton Westerns and silver-screen classics brought Marilyn Monroe, Clark Gable, Anthony Quinn, James Stewart, Janet Leigh and Henry Fonda here.

Cañon City The Prospect Heights neighborhood was the defacto Western backlot of film company United Artists; *True Grit* (1969), starring John Wayne, was shot here and in Ridgway.

Glenwood Springs The crew of *Mr. & Mrs. Smith* (2005) stayed at the Hotel Colorado while filming part of the flick.

THE ARTS SUMMER MEANS FESTIVALS

and deliciously subversive musicals in a gorgeous, tented complex in the heart of Rio Grande Park, mostly in the summer and early fall.

Of course, summer music festivals aren't exclusive to Aspen. Breckenridge hosts a similar, summer-long classical music festival (p195) with free concerts along the Blue River, and Telluride hosts a bluegrass festival (p264) in June that attracts a mix of straight-up bluegrass players, up-and-coming rockers and global icons – it's worth planning your trip around.

And bluegrass isn't even what put Telluride on the map. That would be the Telluride Film Festival (p264), an iconic international event attracting 4000 cinephiles each September for a sneak peak at innovative new films. The first megahit to come out of it was *Slumdog Millionaire* (2008), and with guests like Salman Rushdie, Stephen Sondheim and Noah Baumbach, it's considered on par with Sundance, featuring indie and edgy domestic and international fare, and attended by Hollywood stars and career-makers. Festival-goers on a budget can enjoy free films, open-air cinema and conversations with influential moviemakers. There are also discounted passes to the late show. But if you want to rub elbows with Hollywood elite at the ticketed social events, you'll need to pony up.

Another solid bet is Telluride's Mountainfilm (p264), a Memorial Day festival showcasing excellent outdoor adventure and environmental films sure to whet your appetite for the San Juans, which loom over the town.

Top Public Art

Dancers (Denver)

I See What You Mean (Denver)

Stations of the Cross (San Luis)

Swetsville Zoo (Fort Collins)

Blue Mustang (Denver)

Wildlife & the Land

A quilt of arid canyons and mesas, Colorado has vast unbroken plains and a burly Rocky Mountain backbone. Much of this extraordinary landscape enjoys some protection and management by local, state and federal agencies, but industry is present too. In previous years mining took its toll; today oil and gas development via fracking has become a point of contention for public health. The other major issue: loving Colorado to death, as population growth and ski-resort developments encroach on natural habitats.

Geology

Tectonic shifts and volcanic activity known as the Laramide Revolution shook, folded and molded the Colorado landscape, where granite peaks rise nearly 10,000ft above adjacent plains. Colorado's highest point is the 14,433ft Mt Elbert. Behind the Front Range lie several scattered mountain ranges and broad plateaus; their most notable geologic feature is the spectacular Rocky Mountain Trench, a fault valley 1100 miles long.

Glaciers also shaped the land. The Laurentide Ice Sheet left deep sediments as it receded into the Arctic during the warming of the Quaternary period. A cordilleran glacier system formed at higher altitudes in the Rockies, leaving moraines, lakes, cirques and jagged alpine landforms as they melted. Their melting also formed massive rivers that eroded and shaped the state's spectacular canyons on the Colorado Plateau to the southwest.

Spanish Peaks

The Spanish Peaks, in southern Colorado near La Veta, are not part of the Rocky Mountains, but are actually extinct volcanoes.

Dinosaurs

Although dinosaurs dominated the planet for over 100 million years, only a few places have the proper geological and climatic conditions to preserve their skeletons as fossils and their tracks as permanent evolutionary place holders. Colorado is near the top of that list. If you or your loved ones are dinophiles, you've come to the right state.

Back in the *really* olden days – like during the Jurassic (208 to 144 million years ago) and Cretaceous (144 to 65 million years ago) periods – Colorado was a decidedly different place. The Rockies hadn't yet risen and Pangaea had only recently split (what's a million years?), meaning present-day Colorado was close to the equator.

Most, if not all, of the sites where fossilized dinosaur bones were found en masse are thought to have been in or near a floodplain. These areas were important water sources during wet season, but could be bone-dry in dry season. Often dinosaurs would migrate for miles and days and weeks in search of water. If they arrived at the flood plain at the wrong time of year, many simply died. Winds covered their bodies in layers of dust, and later floods further coated their bones in mud. It takes many thousands of layers of dust and mud and approximately 12,000 years for these bones to become fossils. It also takes a pressurized environment, which is why layers of water over the earth is a key (though not vital) ingredient to fossilization.

With time and pressure the porous bones begin to absorb the minerals from the dust and stone, which replace the original cell structure of the bones, turning them into fossils.

Flora

Colorado's vegetation is closely linked to climate, which in turn depends on both elevation and rainfall. Vegetation at altitude can still vary depending upon exposure and the availability of water. That's why parts of the San Juans and Spanish Peaks can look so different from the Maroon Bells and Rocky Mountain National Park.

Sparse piñon-juniper forests cover the Rockies' slopes from about 4000ft to 6000ft, while ponderosa pines indicate the montane zone between 6000ft and 9000ft, where deciduous alders, luscious white-barked aspens (whose lime-green foliage turns gold in fall), willows and the distinctive blue spruce flourish in damper areas. In the subalpine zone, above 9000ft, Engelmann spruce largely replace pine (though some stands of lodgepoles grow higher), while colorful wildflowers such as columbine, marsh marigold and primrose colonize open spaces. In the alpine zone above 11,500ft, alpine meadows and tundra supplant stunted trees, which can grow only in sheltered, southern exposures.

East of the Rockies, the Great Plains are an immense grassland of short and tall grasses, interrupted by dense gallery forests of willows and cottonwoods along the major rivers. The best example of intact savanna is found in the Pawnee National Grassland, where the Pawnee Buttes loom. A good example of eastern Colorado's riparian (riverbank) foliage is found along the Arkansas River near Bent's Old Fort on the Santa Fe Trail. Those arid zones closest to the Rockies consist of shorter species such as wheatgrass, grama and buffalo grass, which grow no higher than about 3ft.

Wildlife

Colorado wildlife correlates in part (but not completely) to elevation and climate, and the number of animals, especially that of the more mobile ones, varies seasonally. In the alpine zones, for instance, small rodents such as pikas inhabit rockfalls throughout the year, but larger

It's no myth: Colorado really does average 300 days of sun annually, and 300,000 people float down Colorado rivers every year.

WILDLIFE & THE LAND FLORA

Conservation plays an important role in Colorado's future. Contact the **Nature Conservancy** (www. nature.org) for information on current issues and volunteer opportunities. To help out in Colorado parks, contact the individual offices.

BEST DINO SITES

Before embarking on your dino-tracking tour, make sure you stop by the **Denver Museum of Nature & Science** (p69). A good primer for what you'll see in the field, the prehistoric wing has the most complete *Stegosaurus* skeleton discovered. Excellent field sites include the following:

Dinosaur National Monument (p171) The quintessential stop for dinophiles of all ages is in northern Colorado; the visitor center is set in a quarry with views of over 1500 prehistoric bones embedded in the cliff face.

Picketwire Dinosaur Tracksite (p325) The largest documented site of its kind in North America, there are as many as 1300 visible allosaurus and apatosaurus tracks, left behind as they migrated along the muddy shoreline of a large prehistoric lake in the state's southeast.

Garden Park Fossil Area (p318) Also in the southeast, this is one of Colorado's largest Jurassic graveyards. It was the stage for the so-called Bone Wars, an academic battle to discover new dinosaur species.

Dinosaur Ridge (p106) Kids love the footprints and fossils here; it's the closest dinosaur option to Denver.

COLORADO'S BEST HOT SPRINGS

From the hidden, all-natural variety that takes a full day's hike to discover to day-use private springs in historic towns and splashy resorts in the shadow of Collegiate Peaks, you'd do well to sink into some riverside bliss.

Conundrum Hot Springs (p225) Aspen locals love to hike high into the mountains above town, then slip into all-natural hot springs beneath the stars.

Strawberry Park Hot Springs (p165) Absolutely the most laid-back hot spring in the state, Strawberry Park Hot Springs is a place to check in and chill out.

Hot Sulphur Springs Resort & Spa (p162) Set beneath the looming San Juans, the Pagosa Springs namesake is an attractive private concession beloved by locals.

Mt Princeton Hot Springs (p241) A splashy, sprawling resort, bubbling with hot springs in an idyllic Collegiate Peaks location.

mammals such as Rocky Mountain elk and bighorn sheep are present only in summer.

The Great Plains have their own singular fauna, such as the swift pronghorn antelope and prairie dogs. The swift pronghorn grazes short-grass plains nearest the mountains, while the prairie dog is neither a prairie-dweller nor a dog: related to the squirrel, it lives in sprawling burrows known as prairie dog 'towns.' Species such as mule deer and coyotes range over a variety of zones from the plains to the peaks. The solitary, lumbering moose prefers riparian zones; if luck is on your side, you'll see them wading in lakes and trudging through wetlands in the Kawuneeche Valley in Rocky Mountain National Park.

The most famous animal of the Colorado plains was, of course, the magnificent buffalo (aka bison) that grazed the prairies in enormous herds until its near extinction. The bison survives in limited numbers in Wyoming, but the last-known wild buffalo in the state was killed in the South Park area in 1897. Today's Colorado bison are livestock raised for beef.

Foxes

Four species of fox are native to Colorado. Red foxes live in mountain riparian zones; gray foxes like canyons; swift foxes live in the eastern plains; and kit foxes live in the western deserts.

Bears

The black bear is probably the most notorious animal in the Rockies. Despite the name, its fur can have a honey or cinnamon tint, its muzzle can be tan, and it can even have white spots on its chest. Adult males weigh from 275lb to 450lb; females weigh about 175lb to 250lb. They measure 3ft high on all fours and can be over 5ft when standing on their hind legs. The largest populations of black bears live in areas where aspen trees propagate, and near open areas of chokecherry and serviceberry bushes. Their range can stretch to 250 sq miles.

The grizzly bear, America's largest meat eater, is classified as an endangered species in Colorado, but it is almost certainly gone from the state. The last documented grizzly in Colorado was killed in 1979.

Bighorn Sheep

Rocky Mountain National Park is a special place: 'Bighorn Crossing Zone' is a sign you're unlikely to encounter elsewhere. From late spring through summer, three or four volunteers and an equal number of rangers provide traffic control on US 34 at Sheep Lakes Information Station, 2 miles west of the Fall River Entrance Station. Groups of up to 60 sheep – typically ewes and lambs – move from the moraine ridge north of the highway across the road to Sheep Lakes in Horseshoe Park. Unlike the big, under-curving horns on mature rams, ewes grow swept-back crescent-shaped horns that reach only about 10in in length. The Sheep Lakes are evaporative ponds ringed with tasty salt deposits that attract the ewes in the morning and early afternoon after lambing in May and June. In August they rejoin the rams in the Mummy Range.

To see bighorn sheep on rocky ledges, you'll need to hike or backpack. The estimated 300 to 400 animals in the park live permanently in the Mummy Range. On the west side, an equally large herd inhabits the volcanic cliffs of the Never Summer Mountains. A smaller herd can be seen along the Continental Divide at a distance from the rim of the crater near Milner Pass; Crater Trail (which is 3 miles west of the Alpine Visitors Center on Trail Ridge Rd) follows a steep course for 1 mile to the observation point.

Elk

Seeing a herd of North American elk, or wapiti (a Native American name meaning 'white rump,' a description of the animal's rear), grazing in their natural setting is unforgettable. According to NPS surveys, about 2000 elk winter in the Rocky Mountain National Park's lower elevations, while more than 3000 inhabit the park's lofty terrain during summer months. The summer visitor equipped with binoculars or a telephoto lens is almost always rewarded by patiently scanning the hillsides and meadows near the Alpine Visitors Center. Traffic jams up as motorists stop to observe these magnificent creatures near the uppermost section of Fall River Rd or Trail Ridge Rd. Visitors are warned by signs and park rangers not to call to, harass or come in contact with the animals.

Mature elk bulls may reach 1100lb; cows weigh up to 600lb. Both have dark necks with light tan bodies. Like bighorn sheep, elk were virtually extinct around Estes Park by 1890, wiped out by hunters; in 1913 and '14 before the establishment of the park, people from Estes Park brought in 49 elk from Yellowstone. The elk's natural population increase since the establishment of Rocky Mountain National Park is one of the NPS' great successes, directly attributable to the removal of their principal predator: humans with guns.

Other Mammals

Somewhere along your journey you're likely to encounter mule deer, named for their large mule-like ears, as they browse on leaves and twigs from shrubs at sunny lower elevations. Howling coyotes commonly serenade winter campfires – lucky visitors may spy a coyote stalking small rodents. Other large carnivores such as the bobcat and mountain lion are

WILDLIFE & THE LAND WILDLIFE

Best Wildlife Viewing

Weminuche Wilderness Area

Rocky Mountain National Park

Black Canyon of the Gunnison National Park

Arapahoe National Wildlife Refuge

Maroon Bells Wilderness

GREEN SHEEN

Colorado flies the sustainability flag as a point of fervent local pride. Browse any menu and a litany of local, grass-fed, fair-trade or organic options read like a tedious send-up of *Portlandia* characters. The EPA recognizes Colorado as having some of the cleanest air and water in the country. It's also a leader in renewable energy, with more LEED-certified buildings than any other state. Colorado College boasts some of these LEED buildings, as well as a permaculture dorm and a conscientious cafeteria: over 40% of the student dining budget goes to locally sourced food.

There's more in the works, too. Denver has added light-rail transportation from Denver International Airport to downtown and a revamped Union Station. Highway 36 between Denver and Boulder is being redesigned to reward alternative transportation, with tolls imposed on single-occupant cars, an express shared-vehicle lane and dedicated bus and bike lanes (the first phase cost a cool $312 million). And not far behind, bike-share programs in Front Range cities will help maintain the state's status as the nation's slimmest.

very rarely seen. Small but ferocious long-tailed weasel hunt near their streamside dens at night.

Birds

An astounding 465 bird species have been identified in the state of Colorado. Among them are flycatchers, burrowing owls (federally listed as threatened) and great horned owls, crows, mourning doves, mountain plovers, chickadees, Canadian geese, bluebirds and cranes. The newly classified and unique Gunnison sage grouse, found in the southwest, is listed as a Species of Special Concern and is a candidate to be placed on the federal endangered species list.

There are also two types of eagle. The more prevalent golden eagle has a wingspan of 7ft and ranges throughout North America. The bald eagle only relatively recently bounced back from near extinction and remains on the endangered species list. At its low point only two or three nesting pairs nested in Colorado, but that number has increased each year (from 51 nests in 2009 to 170 in 2017, according to a federal report).

Best Birding

Rocky Mountain National Park

Pawnee National Grassland

Alamosa National Wildlife Refuge

Arapahoe National Wildlife Refuge

Chautauqua Park

Survival Guide

DIRECTORY A–Z 362

Accommodations 362

Dangers &
Annoyances 364

Discount Cards 364

Electricity 365

Embassies &
Consulates 365

Health 365

Insurance 366

Internet Access 367

Legal Matters 367

LGBT+ Travelers 367

Money 368

Opening Hours 368

Post 368

Public Holidays 368

Telephone 368

Time 368

Toilets 369

Tourist
Information 369

Travelers with
Disabilities 369

Visas 369

Volunteering 369

Work 369

TRANSPORTATION . . 370

GETTING THERE &
AWAY 370

Entering Colorado 370

Air 370

Land 371

GETTING AROUND 372

Air 372

Bicycle 372

Bus 372

Car & Motorcycle 373

Hitching 374

Train 374

Directory A–Z

Accommodations

Colorado provides a vast array of accommodation options: from pitching a tent under a starlit sky to budget motels and midrange B&Bs; and from adobe inns and historical hotels to four-star lodgings, luxurious spas and dude ranches. The most comfortable accommodations for the lowest price are usually found in that great American invention, the roadside motel.

B&Bs

Many B&Bs are high-end, romantic retreats in restored historic homes run by personable, independent innkeepers who serve gourmet breakfasts. These B&Bs often take pains to evoke a theme – Victorian, rustic etc – with amenities ranging from merely comfortable to hopelessly indulgent. Rates start around $120; the best run to more than $300. Many B&Bs have minimum-stay requirements, and some exclude young children.

European-style B&Bs can be found in Colorado: these may be rooms in someone's home, with plainer furnishings, simpler breakfasts, shared bathrooms and cheaper rates. They often welcome families.

B&Bs can close out of season and reservations are essential, especially for high-end places. To avoid surprises, always ask whether bathrooms are shared or private.

Camping & Holiday Parks

Camping is the cheapest, and in many ways the most enjoyable, approach to a Colorado vacation. Visitors with a car and a tent can take advantage of hundreds of private and public campgrounds and RV parks at prices of $13 to $34 per night. The best resource for camping is www.recreation.gov, which has information on all reservable USFS campsites.

Some of the best camping areas are on public lands (national forests, and state and national parks), including **Bureau of Land Management** (BLM; ☑800-877-8339, 303-239-3600; www.co.blm.gov; 2850 Youngfield St, Lakewood; ☺8:30am-4pm Mon-Fri; ☐28) lands. Free dispersed camping (meaning you can camp almost anywhere) is permitted in many public backcountry areas. Sometimes you can camp along a dirt road, especially in BLM and national forest areas, with sites generally marked with a tent symbol. In other places you can backpack your gear into a cleared campsite.

Information and maps are available from ranger stations or BLM offices, and may be posted along the road into the campsite. Sometimes, a free camping permit is required for backcountry camping, particularly in national parks.

Being wildfire country, fire bans are common. Look for alerts posted at trailheads and in campgrounds.

HUTS & YURTS

Colorado has an extensive system of backcountry huts and yurts that are accessed year round by trails and fire roads. These range from very basic dry cabins to more elegant affairs with solar-powered lights, automated wood-burning stoves and eco-compost toilets.

10th Mountain Division Hut Association (☑970-925-5775; www.huts.org; per person $33)

Never Summer Nordic Yurts (☑970-723-4070; www.neversummernordic.com; 247 County Rd 41, Walden; yurts $85-120)

San Juan Hut System (☑970-626-3033; www.sanjuanhuts.com; per person $30)

ONLINE RESOURCES

Camping USA (www.camping-usa.com) A great resource with more than 12,000 campgrounds in its database, including RV parks, private campgrounds, BLM areas and state and national parks.

Kampgrounds of America (KOA; ☑888-562-0000; www.koa.com) A vast national network of private campgrounds. You can purchase the annual directory of KOA campgrounds at any KOA office; it's also available for free download from their website.

Recreation.gov (☑518-885-3639, toll-free 877-444-6777; www.recreation.gov) Organizes reservations for campsites on federal land.

PRIVATE CAMPGROUNDS

Private campgrounds are usually close to towns or nearby. Most are designed for RVs; but tents can usually be erected. Camp fees are higher than for public campgrounds. Fees are usually quoted for two people per site, with additional fees for extra people (about $6 per person). Some places charge just per vehicle. Facilities can include hot showers, coin-operated laundry, swimming pool, full RV hookups, a games area, playground and convenience store.

RESERVATIONS

National forest and BLM campgrounds are usually less developed, while national park and state park campgrounds are more likely to have greater amenities. The less-developed sites are often on a 'first-come, first-served' basis, so arrive early – preferably during the week, as sites fill up fast on Friday and weekends. More developed areas may accept or require reservations. Expect summer weekend sites to be booked several weeks out.

WASTE & FACILITIES

When camping in an undeveloped area choose a site at least 200yd from water and wash up at camp, not in the stream, using biodegradable soap. Dig a 6in-deep hole to use as a latrine and cover and camouflage it well when leaving the site. Burn toilet paper, unless fires are prohibited. Carry out all trash.

Use a portable charcoal grill or camping stove; don't build new fire rings, and check on local fire policies in advance. If there already is a fire ring, use only dead and downed wood or wood you have carried in yourself. Make sure you leave the campsite as you found it.

Developed areas usually have toilets, drinking water, fire pits (or charcoal grills) and picnic benches. Some don't have drinking water, and some turn the water off out of season. It's always a good idea to have a few gallons of water when camping. These basic campgrounds usually cost about $13 to $18 a night. Some areas have showers or RV hookups and often cost $22 to $34.

Dude Ranches

Dude ranches date back to the late 19th century. Most visitors today are city-slickers looking for an escape from a fast-paced, high-tech world. You can find anything from a working-ranch experience (smelly chores and 5am wake-up calls included) to a Western-style Club Med. Typical week-long visits run from $250 to $600 per person per day, with prices including accommodations, meals, activities and equipment.

While the centerpiece of dude-ranch vacations is horseback riding, many ranches feature swimming pools and have expanded their activity lists to include fly-fishing, hiking, mountain biking, tennis, golf, skeet-shooting and cross-country skiing. Accommodations range from rustic log cabins to cushy suites with whirlpools and cable TV. Meals range from family-style spaghetti dinners to four-course gourmet feasts.

Colorado Dude & Guest Ranch Association (☑866-942-3472; www.coloradoranch.com)

Dude Ranchers' Association (☑307-587-2339; www.duderanch.org)

Hostels

Staying in a private double room at a hostel can be a great way to save money and still have privacy (although you'll usually have to share a bathroom). A private room in a Colorado hostel costs between $38 and $60. Dorm beds allow those in search of the ultimate bargain to sleep cheap under a roof; dorms cost between $18 and $28, depending on the city and time of year.

US citizens and residents can join **Hostelling International-USA** (HI-USA; ☑301-495-1240; www.hiusa.org; annual membership adult/child $28/ free) by calling and requesting a membership form or by downloading a form from the website. HI-USA doesn't have any hostels in Colorado. However, the HI card may be used for discounts at some local merchants and for local services, including some intercity bus companies.

Hotels

Except for chains, Colorado's hotels are mostly found in cities, and they're generally large and luxurious – except for a few boutique hotels, which tend to be small, understated and lavish. Prices start at around $79 and shoot up from there; ask about discounts and special packages when making reservations. Always check online first when booking a hotel.

Motels

Budget chain motels are prevalent throughout Colorado. Many motels have at-the-door parking, with exterior room doors. These are convenient, though some, especially single women, may prefer the more expensive places with more secure interior corridors.

Advertised prices are referred to as 'rack rates' and are not written in stone. Asking about specials can often save quite a bit of money, as can using online booking aggregators. Children are often allowed to stay free in their parents' room.

Rental Accommodation

Houses or condominiums can be rented for anywhere from two days to two months. This type of lodging is most often found in resort areas and almost always includes kitchens and living rooms.

Several people can lodge for the same price, so long-term rentals can be more economical than motels or hotels on a per-person basis, especially if you can cook your own food. The chambers of commerce in resort towns have information on condominium listings and can give advice on renting.

Dangers & Annoyances

➡ Like all urban areas, Colorado's cities have occasional crime and mishaps; common sense and awareness of your surrounding are the best way to steer clear of problems.

➡ Most traffic mishaps on the highway are due to driving too fast, especially in bad weather and in vehicles without sufficient traction.

➡ On trails and mountains, be sure to bring plenty of water and heed all warning signs (including weather reports and area closures, especially at ski resorts).

➡ In wildlife areas, follow instructions for what to do if you encounter animals (p366).

Discount Cards

Visitors to Colorado should look into all the standard national and international discount cards – you can find ways to shave costs off hotel rooms, meals, rental cars, museum admissions, etc.

Students

➡ Ask for a student discount whenever booking a room, reserving a car or paying an entrance fee.

➡ Discounts will generally be only 10% or so, but sometimes as much as 50%.

➡ Full-time students should consider buying a **Student Advantage Card** (www. studentadvantage.com) or an **International Student Identity Card** (www. isiccard.com).

➡ Always carry your proof of student status.

Youths

➡ Non-students up to 30 years old can get the **International Youth Travel Card** (www.isic.org), which offers similar benefits to the ISIC student card.

Seniors (Over 62)

➡ Ask for a senior discount whenever booking a room, reserving a car or paying an entrance fee.

➡ Discounts will generally be only 10% or so, but sometimes as much as 50%.

➡ Consider buying an **America the Beautiful Senior Pass** ($90; http:// store.usgs.gov/pass), which is valid for the lifetime of the pass owner and offers 50% discounts on fees such as camping on federal recreational lands.

➡ Always carry proof of age.

Over 50s

Travelers between the ages of 50 and 62 should contact the **American Association of Retired Persons** (www. aarp.org) for travel discounts, which are typically 10% to 25% off hotels, car rentals, entertainment etc.

Motorists

Card-carrying members of automobile associations are entitled to travel discounts. **AAA** (AAA; ☎866-625-3601, roadside assistance 800-222-4357; www.colorado.aaa.com; 4100 E Arkansas Ave, Denver; ⏰8:30am-5:30pm Mon-Fri, 9am-1pm Sat, roadside assistance 24hr; 🚌40, 46) has reciprocal agreements with several international auto associations, so bring your membership card from home.

Other Discounts

Other people whose status might lead to discounts are US military personnel and veterans, travelers with disabilities, children, business travelers and foreign visitors.

Discount Coupons

➡ Discount coupons can be found at every tourist locale. They always have restrictions and conditions, so read the fine print. Some are hardly worth the effort, but scour tourist information offices and highway welcome centers for brochures and fliers, and you'll find a few gems.

➡ For online hotel coupons, browse www.hotelcoupons.com.

Electricity

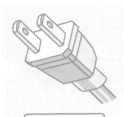

Type A
120V/60Hz

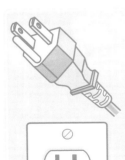

Type B
120V/60Hz

Embassies & Consulates

While there are no embassies in Colorado, a handful of countries have consulates or honorary consuls in the state; each offers a different level of assistance to travelers. Check out www.consularcorpscolorado.org for contact information.

International travelers who want to contact their home country's embassy while in the US should visit www.embassy.org, which lists contact information for all foreign embassies in Washington, DC.

Health
Before You Go
HEALTH INSURANCE

The USA offers some of the best-quality health care in the world, but it can be prohibitively expensive. International travelers should check if their regular policy covers them in the US; if it doesn't, having travel insurance to cover any sort of medical event is absolutely essential.

VACCINATIONS

No special vaccines are required or recommended for travel to or around the USA. All travelers should be up-to-date on routine immunizations.

In Colorado
AVAILABILITY & COST OF HEALTH CARE

In general, if you have a medical emergency, your best bet is to go to the nearest

hospital's emergency room or an urgent-care clinic. If the problem isn't urgent, you can call a nearby hospital and ask for a referral to a local physician, which should usually be cheaper than a trip to the emergency room. (Independent, for-profit urgent-care centers can be convenient, but may perform large numbers of expensive tests, even for minor illnesses.)

If you're heading to more remote areas of the state, it pays to be aware of the closest emergency medical services. If heading into backcountry areas, stop by the local ranger station or visitors center for information.

ENVIRONMENTAL HAZARDS

Colorado has an extraordinary range of climate and terrain, from the freezing heights of the Rockies to the searing midsummer heat of the desert tablelands. Infectious diseases will not be a significant concern for most travelers, who are unlikely to experience anything worse than a little diarrhea, sunburn or a mild respiratory infection.

High altitude is the most serious health risk. Stay hydrated, take it easy, and allow a few days to acclimatize before going really high – like to the top of one of the state's fourteeners (p30). Generally a little light-headedness and slight headaches are normal when arriving in high country. If you experience severe and continued nausea, headache and dizziness, you should consult a doctor or get to lower altitudes. Altitude sickness, including High Altitude Pulmonary Edema (HAPE)

EATING PRICE RANGES

The following price ranges refer to a main course at dinner.

$	less than $15
$$	$15–25
$$$	more than $25

and High Altitude Cerebral Edema (HACE) are concerns, especially over 8000 feet.

Sun exposure is the other big risk. Cover up and pile on the SPF sunscreen.

WILDLIFE

Always make lots of noise when traveling in the backcountry to avoid surprising a wild animal in its habitat.

Common-sense approaches to animal bites and stings are the most effective:

➡ Wear boots when hiking to protect from snakes.

➡ Wear long sleeves and pants to protect from ticks and mosquitoes.

➡ If you're bitten, don't overreact. Stay calm and seek the relevant treatment.

➡ Lyme disease can be caused by tick bites. In heavy woods it's smart to wear a hat, and check your friends for ticks at the end of the day.

ANIMAL BITES

➡ Do not attempt to pet, handle or feed any nondomestic animal. Most animal-related injuries are directly related to a person's attempt to touch or feed the animal.

➡ Any bite or scratch from a mammal, including bats, should be promptly and thoroughly cleansed with large amounts of soap and water, followed by application of an antiseptic, such as iodine or alcohol.

➡ Local health authorities should be contacted immediately for possible rabies treatment, regardless of prior immunization.

➡ It may also be advisable to start an antibiotic: wounds caused by animal bites and scratches frequently become infected.

SNAKE BITES

➡ There are several varieties of venomous snakes in Colorado; these snakes do not cause instantaneous death, and antivenins are available.

➡ Place a light constricting bandage over the bite, keep the wounded part below the level of the heart and move it as little as possible.

➡ Stay calm and get to a medical facility as soon as possible.

➡ Bring the dead snake for identification if you can, but don't risk being bitten again.

➡ Do *not* use the mythic 'cut an X and suck out the venom' trick.

MOUNTAIN LIONS

The chances of encountering an aggressive mountain lion are extremely small, but as humans encroach on their territory attacks are increasing. Avoid hiking alone in prime mountain-lion habitat and keep children within view; make lots of noise as you go. If you encounter one, raise your arms and back away slowly. Speak firmly or shout. If attacked, fight back fiercely.

BEARS

Colorado has black bears, which are smaller than grizzlies and have very few incidences of attacking humans. Still, you should never get between a mother bear and her cubs. If camping, always hang your food, lock it in a bear-proof canister or keep it in a closed car. Make noise (whistling, clapping or chatting) when hiking in bear country so you don't surprise a bear. Don't run if you encounter one – they are fast. Back away slowly and avoid eye contact.

When planning a backpacking trip, make sure you know the park safety regulations. In Rocky Mountain National Park, campers are required to bring a bear-proof canister to store food, trash and toiletries in. (If you don't want to buy one, they usually may be rented from camping stores.)

MOOSE

One of the most dangerous animals in the Colorado wilderness is the moose. Never approach a moose, make lots of noise on the trails, and back away slowly if you run into one.

HUMANS

During hunting season, wear bright colors (eg yellow or orange) and make plenty of noise while walking.

TAP WATER

Colorado has great tap water – you can drink out of the tap pretty much anywhere in the state (some people may choose to drink bottled water at places using a well). When camping, you will need to boil or purify water.

Insurance

No matter how long or short your trip, make sure you purchase adequate travel insurance before departure.

Consider coverage for luggage theft or loss and for trip cancellation. If you already have a homeowner's or renter's policy, see what it will cover and consider getting supplemental insurance to cover the rest. If you've prepaid a large portion of your trip, cancellation insurance is a worthwhile expense. A comprehensive travel insurance policy that covers all these things can cost up to 10% of the total cost of your trip.

If you will be driving, it's essential that you have liability insurance. Car-rental agencies offer insurance that covers damage to the rental vehicle and separate liability insurance, which covers damage to people and other vehicles. Most major credit cards also provide some level of insurance for rentals.

Worldwide travel insurance is available at www.lonelyplanet.com/travel-insurance. You can buy, extend and claim online anytime – even if you're already on the road.

Internet Access

➡ Accommodations, cafes, restaurants, bars etc that provide guest computer terminals for going online are identified by the internet icon; the wi-fi icon indicates that wireless access is available. There may be a fee for either service.

➡ Free or fee-based wi-fi hot spots can be found at major airports. Virtually all hotels and motels in Colorado offer wi-fi; many tourist information centers, museums, bars and restaurants offer it, too.

➡ Free public wi-fi is proliferating. Even some state parks are now wi-fi–enabled.

➡ To find more public wi-fi hot spots, search www. wififreespot.com.

➡ Public libraries have internet terminals (online time may be limited, advance sign-up required and a nominal fee charged for out-of-network visitors) and free wi-fi access.

Legal Matters

Rights

➡ People arrested for a serious offense in the US have the right to remain silent, the right to an attorney and the right to make one phone call. They are presumed innocent until proven guilty.

➡ International visitors who are arrested and don't have a lawyer or family member to help should call their country's embassy or consulate.

Recreational Marijuana

Recreational pot has been legal in Colorado since 2014, but you can't just roll a joint and start puffing away on the

street. Here's how the rules break down:

Buying

➡ You must buy cannabis from a dispensary, not some random in a bar. Only licensed dispensaries may legally sell marijuana.

➡ You must be 21+ to purchase marijuana products, and will be asked at the dispensary door to show a government-issued ID.

➡ Adults can possess up to one ounce (28g) of cannabis products at a time; lower limits for out-of-towners have been removed.

➡ You can 'gift' up to an ounce of recreational bud to another adult as long as it's done in-state.

➡ Most dispensaries are cash-only. Some have ATMs on-site.

Transporting

➡ It's illegal to transport pot across state lines, and it is not allowed in airports.

➡ Do *not* mail marijuana in any form. It can be considered a federal offense.

➡ It's illegal to drive with an open container of Mary Jane in your car. The definition of 'open container,' however, is vague; to be safe, put your dime bag in the trunk (or, in a hatchback, behind the back seats).

Using

➡ It's illegal to smoke, vape or use cannabis edibles in public areas, including parks, sidewalks, alleys, restaurants, bars and even inside dispensaries. Federal properties, like national parks, also are off-limits.

➡ It's illegal to use it in your car or in a taxi, regardless if you're a passenger. Driving while high can be prosecuted like a DUI.

➡ You can consume MJ in specially designated limousines or buses, like the ones used for cannabis tours.

➡ You can light up in your house or in someone else's house, as long as it's in an area not visible to the public (like a front porch).

➡ Some hotels allow marijuana smoking in certain rooms, and even cater to pot-tourists; be sure to ask in advance.

➡ In late 2016, Denver voters approved the creation of 'social clubs' to address the lack of public places to legally use pot, especially for visitors. Look for them to start opening once the city council hammers out the necessary regulations.

Resources

For up-to-date information on everything related to Colorado cannabis, check out the following:

➡ **The Cannabist** (www. thecannabist.co)

➡ **Colorado Pot Guide** (www.coloradopotguide. com)

Other Drugs

Possession of any kind of illicit drug – including cocaine, ecstasy, LSD, heroin, hashish, methamphetamines or more than one ounce of cannabis – is a felony potentially punishable by lengthy jail sentences. For foreigners, conviction of any drug offense is grounds for deportation.

LGBT+ Travelers

Colorado is very much a mixed bag for gay and lesbian travelers. In general cities and college towns have more progressive attitudes – Denver especially has a thriving gay and lesbian scene.

Some other areas in the state are characterized by conservative attitudes and old-school ideas of machismo. The more affluent ski areas and artsy communities are less uptight about same-sex relationships, but you still couldn't mistake the region for San Francisco.

Resources

For the latest news, events and goings-on in Denver, Boulder and beyond, check out the online edition of **Out Front Colorado** (www.outfrontonline.com), **Out Boulder County** (www.outboulder.org), and the website of **The Center** (www.glbtcolorado.org), the largest LGBT community center in the Rocky Mountain region.

Good national guidebooks include *Damron Women's Traveller*, *Damron Men's Travel Guide* and *Damron Accommodations*, with listings of gay-owned or gay-friendly accommodations nationwide. All three are published by **Damron** (www.damron.com).

Another good resource is the **Gay & Lesbian Yellow Pages** (☏800-697-2812; www.glyp.com), a directory of LGBTQ-friendly businesses.

Finally, if you believe you've been the target of discrimination or a hate crime, contact the **National Gay & Lesbian Task Force** (☏Washington, DC 202-393-5177; www.thetaskforce.org) and/or **Lambda Legal** (☏Los Angeles 213-382-7600, NYC 212-809-8585; www.lambdalegal.org), both national organizations dedicated to protecting LGBTQ civil rights.

Money

ATMs are widely available. Credit and debit cards are accepted by most businesses.

Exchange Rates

Australia	A$1	$0.79
Canada	C$1	$0.79
Eurozone	€1	$1.18
Japan	¥100	$0.91
Mexico	MXN10	$0.57
New Zealand	NZ$1	$0.73
UK	£1	$1.29

For current exchange rates, see www.xe.com.

Tipping

Generally, tipping is expected in restaurants and bars, and anytime a service has been provided. Specifically:

Bars $1 per drink

Guides 15–20% of the cost of the tour

Luggage Attendants $1–2 per suitcase

Restaurants 15–20% of the bill

Spas 20% of the treatment

Taxis 10–15% of the fare

Opening Hours

High-season hours follow. In rural areas, many businesses close on Sunday.

Banks 8:30am–5pm Monday to Friday, 9am–noon on Saturday

Bars & Pubs 4pm–midnight, to 2am on Friday and Saturday

Businesses 9am–5pm Monday to Friday

Restaurants Breakfast 7am–10:30am (weekend brunch 9am–2pm); lunch 11:30am–2:30pm; and dinner 5–9:30pm, later on weekends

Stores 10am–6pm Monday to Saturday, noon–5pm Sunday; shopping malls often extend to 8pm or 9pm

Supermarkets 7am–9pm; most cities have 24-hour supermarkets

Post

No matter how much people like to complain, the **US Postal Service** (www.usps.com) provides great service for the price. Check the website for locations throughout the state.

Private shippers such as **United Parcel Service** (www.ups.com) and **Federal Express** (www.fedex.com) are useful for sending more important or larger items.

Public Holidays

New Year's Day January 1

Martin Luther King Jr Day Third Monday of January

Presidents' Day Third Monday of February

Easter March or April

Memorial Day Last Monday of May

Independence Day July 4

Labor Day First Monday of September

Columbus Day Second Monday of October

Veterans Day November 11

Thanksgiving Fourth Thursday of November

Christmas Day December 25

Telephone

Calling Codes

Country code	☏1	
Area codes in Colorado	☏303, ☏719, ☏720, ☏970	
International access code	☏011	

Mobile Phones

Coverage can be unreliable in mountain regions. SIM cards are readily available in large stores like Walmart or Target.

➡ A prepaid SIM card can be cheaper than using your home network. Check with your carrier about rates before making calls.

➡ There are plenty of holes in coverage around the area; don't assume you'll have reception, particularly when between cities.

Time

Colorado is on Mountain Standard Time (MST), seven hours behind GMT/UTC. Colorado switches to Mountain Daylight Time, one hour later, from the second Sunday of March to the first Sunday of November.

| Denver | GMT/ UTC minus 7 hours | noon |
| Washington, DC | GMT/ UTC minus 5 hours | 2pm |

Toilets

➡ Parks and wildlife areas often have basic bathrooms near the parking lot; if there's a visitor center, head inside for flushing toilets.

➡ In cities, public toilets are hard to find. Try gas stations, libraries, department stores and supermarkets.

Tourist Information

Bureau of Land Management Colorado (BLM; ☎800-877-8339, 303-239-3600; www.co.blm.gov; 2850 Youngfield St, Lakewood; ⏰8:30am-4pm Mon-Fri; 🚌28) Provides information on historic sites, trails, and more.

Camping USA (www.camping-usa.com) A great resource, with more than 12,000 campgrounds in its database.

Colorado Parks & Wildlife (CPW; Map p78; ☎800-678-2267, 303-470-1144; www.cpw.state.co.us; 1313 Sherman St, Denver; ⏰8am-5pm Mon-Fri) Manages 42 state parks and more than 300 wildlife areas; handles camping reservations.

Colorado Road & Traffic Conditions (☎511; www.codot.gov; ⏰24hr) Has up-to-date information on Colorado traffic conditions, including cycling maps.

Colorado Travel & Tourism Authority (☎800-265-6723; www.colorado.com) Detailed information on sights, activities, etc.

Travelers with Disabilities

Travel within Colorado is getting easier for people with disabilities, but it's still not easy. Public buildings are required by law to be wheelchair-accessible and to have appropriate restroom facilities. Public transportation services must be made accessible to all, and telephone companies have to provide relay operators for the hearing-impaired. Many banks provide ATM instructions in Braille, curb ramps are common, many busy intersections have audible crossing signals, and most chain hotels have suites for guests with disabilities. Also, some ski resorts offer programs specifically designed for skiers with disabilities. Download Lonely Planet's free Accessible Travel guide from http://lptravel.to/AccessibleTravel.

A number of organizations specialize in the needs of travelers with disabilities:

➡ **Mobility International USA** (☎541-343-1284; www.miusa.org; 132 E Broadway, Suite 343; ⏰9am-4pm Mon-Fri)

➡ **Society for the Advancement of Travel for the Handicapped** (www.sath.org)

➡ **Adaptive Sports Center** (☎970-349-2296; www.adaptivesports.org; 10 Crested Butte Way)

Visas

All foreign visitors must have a visa to enter the USA unless they are Canadian citizens or part of the Visa Waiver Program.

➡ Every foreign visitor entering the USA needs a passport valid for at least six months longer than the intended stay.

➡ Apart from most Canadian citizens and those under the **Visa Waiver Program** (https://esta.cbp.dhs.gov/esta), all visitors need to obtain a visa from a US consulate or embassy abroad.

➡ For a complete list of US customs regulations, visit the official website for **US Customs & Border Protection** (www.cbp.gov).

Volunteering

Opportunities for volunteering in Colorado are many and varied. Volunteering can also provide truly memorable experiences: you'll get to interact with people and the land in ways you never would if just passing through.

There are numerous casual, drop-in volunteering opportunities in the big cities, where you can socialize with locals and help out nonprofit organizations. Check weekly alternative newspapers for calendar listings, or browse the free classified ads online at Craigslist. The public website **Serve.gov** (www.serve.gov) and private websites **Idealist** (www.idealist.org) and **VolunteerMatch** (www.volunteermatch.org) offer free, searchable databases of short- and long-term volunteer opportunities nationwide.

More formal volunteer programs, especially those designed for international travelers, typically charge a hefty fee of anywhere from $300 to $1000, depending on the length of the program and what amenities are included (eg housing or meals). None cover the costs of travel to the USA.

Work

Seasonal work is possible in national parks and other tourist sites, especially ski areas. These are usually low-paying service jobs filled by young people who are happy to work part of the day so they can play during the rest. You must be legally able to work in the US or be eligible (and sponsored) for a temporary work visa through your potential employer. For information about opportunities, contact park headquarters or local chambers of commerce well in advance of the work season.

Transportation

GETTING THERE & AWAY

Most travelers arrive in Colorado by air or car, with arrivals by bus a distant third. There is also a daily **Amtrak** train service that pulls into Denver's Union Station.

Colorado has fairly comprehensive coverage by commuter flights, although the cost may deter most travelers. On the ground, public transportation leaves much to be desired, and travelers without their own vehicles need to be patient and flexible to take advantage of the limited possibilities. The most enjoyable way to travel within the state is by car or motorbike.

Flights, tours and rail tickets can be booked online at lonelyplanet.com/bookings.

Entering Colorado

Almost all visitors to Colorado come through **Denver International Airport** (DIA).

Train The University of Colorado A Line Train departs from the airport every 15 minutes (every 30 minutes off-peak) and goes to downtown's Union Station ($9, 37 minutes).

Taxi Queue outside Ground Transportation area (to downtown should cost about $60).

Uber & Lyft Car-service drivers will meet you at passenger pick-up.

Bus RTD (☑303-299-6000; www.rtd-denver.com; per ride $2.60-4.50, day pass $5.20-9) operates SkyRide buses with frequent service between 3:30am and 1:10am to downtown Denver ($9, 55 minutes) and Boulder ($9, 70 minutes).

Shuttle SuperShuttle (☑800-258-3826; www.supershuttle.com; ⊙24hr; ☒A)

and others (rates from $33 per person) go to Denver, Boulder, Fort Collins, surrounding suburbs and parts of Wyoming. Some ski areas have shuttle services that are reasonably priced to and from Denver International Airport. Try **Colorado Mountain Express** (CME; ☑800-525-6363; www.colorado mountainexpress.com; 8500 Peña Blvd, Denver International Airport; ☎; ☒A) for trips to mountains.

Air

Airports & Airlines

Denver is the region's main air hub, although there are various alternatives if you are coming on a domestic flight. Colorado has dozens of smaller airports throughout the state. Resort airports such as Aspen, Eagle County, Yampa, Telluride and Gunnison offer direct US flights during ski season.

CLIMATE CHANGE & TRAVEL

Every form of transport that relies on carbon-based fuel generates CO_2, the main cause of human-induced climate change. Modern travel is dependent on airplanes, which might use less fuel per mile per person than most cars but travel much greater distances. The altitude at which aircraft emit gases (including CO_2) and particles also contributes to their climate change impact. Many websites offer 'carbon calculators' that allow people to estimate the carbon emissions generated by their journey and, for those who wish to do so, to offset the impact of the greenhouse gases emitted with contributions to portfolios of climate-friendly initiatives throughout the world. Lonely Planet offsets the carbon footprint of all staff and author travel.

Denver International Airport
(DIA; ☎303-342-2000; www.
flydenver.com; 8500 Peña Blvd;
⏰24hr; 🛜; 🚇A)

Aspen-Pitkin County Airport
(ASE; ☎970-920-5380; www.
aspenairport.com; 233 E
Airport Rd; 🛜)

Colorado Springs Airport
(COS; ☎719-550-1900; www.
flycos.com; 7770 Milton E Proby
Pkwy; 🛜)

**Durango-La Plata County
Airport** (DRO; ☎970-247-8143;
www.flydurango.com; 1000
Airport Rd)

Eagle County Regional Airport
(EGE; ☎970-328-2680; www.
flyvail.com; 217 Eldon Wilson Dr,
Gypsum) West of Vail.

**Grand Junction Regional
Airport** (Walker Field Airport,
GJT; ☎970-244-9100; www.
gjairport.com; 2828 Walker
Field Dr)

**Gunnison-Crested Butte
Regional Airport** (GUC; ☎970-
641-2304; www.gunnison
county.org/airport; 519 Rio
Grande Ave)

Montrose Regional Airport
(MTJ; ☎970-249-3203; www.
montroseairport.com; 2100
Airport Rd)

Telluride Regional Airport
(TEX; ☎970-778-5051; www.
tellurideairport.com; 1500 Last
Dollar Rd)

Yampa Valley Airport (YVRA;
☎970-276-5000; 11005 RCR
51A) West of Steamboat Springs.

Airlines handling the main routes
in and out of Colorado:

Alaskan Airlines (☎800-252-
7522; www.alaskaair.com)

Allegiant Airlines (☎702-505-
8888; www.allegiantair.com)

American Airlines (☎800-433-
7300; www.aa.com)

Delta (☎800-221-1212; www.
delta.com)

Frontier (☎800-432-1359;
www.frontierairlines.com)

Jet Blue (☎800-538-2583;
www.jetblue.com)

Southwest (☎800-435-9792;
www.southwest.com)

United Airlines (☎800-864-
8331; www.united.com)

Departure tax is included in
the price of a ticket.

Land
Bus
➡ **Greyhound** (☎800-231-
2222; www.greyhound.com)
runs cross-country buses
between San Francisco
and New York via Wyoming,
Denver and Chicago; and
between Los Angeles and
New York via Las Vegas,
Denver and Chicago.

➡ There are also bus services
from other eastern-seaboard
cities such as Philadelphia
and Washington, DC, and
southern cities such as
Atlanta and Miami.

➡ Fares are relatively high
and bargain airfares can
undercut buses on long-
distance routes. On shorter
routes it can be cheaper to
rent a car than to ride the
bus.

➡ Very long-distance bus
trips are often available at
bargain prices by looking
for web-only fares on the
Greyhound website.

Car & Motorcycle
➡ I-70 runs east–west across
nearly the entire length of the
USA, passing through central
Colorado.

➡ I-25 runs north–south
from New Mexico through
Colorado and ends at a
junction with I-90 in northern
Wyoming.

DRIVE-AWAYS
Drive-away agencies find
people to transport a car for
its owner from one location
to another. This can be a
cheap way to get around if
you meet eligibility requirements; applicants need a
valid license and a clean driving record. Generally drivers
pay for gas and a small
refundable deposit. You need
to be flexible about dates and
destinations when you call.
Search for drive-away and

auto transport companies
online.

Train
➡ **Amtrak** (☎800-872-7245;
www.amtrak.com) provides
cross-country passenger
services between the West
Coast and Chicago, stopping
in Denver at **Union Station**
(Map p70; ☎303-592-6712;
www.unionstationindenver.
com; 1701 Wynkoop St; 🅿;
🚌55L, 72L,120L, FF2, 🚇A, B,
C, E, W). Travelers to/from
the East Coast must make
connections in Chicago.
Amtrak trains service only a
few destinations in Colorado
besides Denver.

➡ The daily *California Zephyr*
from San Francisco (via
Emeryville, CA) passes
through Colorado en route
to Chicago. In Colorado the
train stops at Fort Morgan,
Denver's Union Station,
Fraser-Winter Park, Granby,
Glenwood Springs and Grand
Junction.

➡ The *Southwest Chief*
goes from Los Angeles
via Albuquerque and the
southern Colorado towns of
Trinidad, La Junta and Lamar
to Kansas City and Chicago.

TICKETS
Amtrak tickets may be
purchased aboard the train
without penalty if the station is not open 30 minutes
prior to boarding. Rail travel
is generally cheaper if you
purchase tickets in advance.
Round-trips are the best
value, but even these can be
as expensive as airfares.

For further travel assis-
tance, call Amtrak, surf its
website or ask your travel
agent. Note that most small
train stations don't sell tickets. Instead you must book
them with Amtrak over the
phone or buy online. Some
small stations have no por-
ters or other facilities, and
trains may stop there only if
you have bought a ticket in
advance.

➡ Amtrak offers some good-
value USA Rail Passes.

➡ Children aged between two and 15 years can travel for 50% of the adult fare when accompanied by an adult. Kids under two travel free.

➡ Seniors aged 62 years and over are entitled to a 15% discount (with some limitations) on adult fares.

➡ **AAA** (AAA; ☑866-625-3601, roadside assistance 800-222-4357; www.colorado. aaa.com; 4100 E Arkansas Ave, Denver; ◷8:30am-5:30pm Mon-Fri, 9am-1pm Sat, roadside assistance 24hr; ⬚40, 46) members get a 10% discount and students with a Student Advantage or **ISIC Card** (www.isiccard. com) get 15%. Active military personnel, their spouses and dependents get a 10% discount; Veterans Advantage card holders get 15%.

GETTING AROUND

Car Essential for exploring the state, unless you stay on the Front Range or in a ski town. Rentals are available in every town or city. Drive on the right. Colorado drivers are quite courteous – outside of Denver.

Bus Limited service, but good within Boulder, Fort Collins and Denver.

Bicycle Join locals in loving the bike-sharing programs in Denver, Boulder and Fort Collins. Bike paths in ski resort areas and cities help facilitate travel.

Train Amtrak's *California Zephyr* stops here between San Francisco and Chicago. There are a few steam-train routes.

Car Shares Uber and Lyft operate in most larger towns and all the resort areas. There are a few car-share programs in Denver, including Zipcar and Car2go.

Air

Colorado has many small commercial airports. All are served by flights out of Denver, and Grand Junction also has flights to and from Salt Lake City, UT. During ski season, resort airports offer direct flights to major cities around the US.

Bicycle

Cycling is a cheap, convenient, healthy, environmentally sound – and above all, fun – way of traveling. In Colorado, because of altitude, distance and heat, it's also a good workout.

Cycling has increased in popularity so much in recent years that concerns have risen over damage to the environment, especially from unchecked mountain biking. Know your environment and regulations before you ride. Bikes are restricted from entering wilderness areas and some designated trails, but may be used in National Park Service (NPS) sites, state parks, national and state forests and Bureau of Land Management (BLM) singletrack trails.

➡ Cyclists should carry at least a gallon of water and refill bottles at every opportunity since dehydration can be a major problem.

➡ Airlines accept bicycles as checked luggage; contact them for specific rules.

➡ City and long-haul buses and trains can carry bikes, and in the mountains shuttles are fitted with racks for skis in winter and mountain bikes in summer.

➡ Boulder, Fort Collins and Denver have bike-share programs.

➡ Rental bicycles are widely available.

➡ In Colorado's legendary mountain-biking regions the range of rental options can be bewilderingly comprehensive. Hard-tail mountain bikes rent for around $34 a day while fancy full-suspension rentals go for more like $75.

➡ Bicycles are generally prohibited on interstate highways if there is a frontage road. However, where a suitable frontage road or other alternative is lacking, cyclists are permitted on some interstates.

➡ Cyclists are generally treated courteously by motorists.

➡ Colorado currently has no legal requirement for cyclists to wear helmets (but they do reduce the risk of head injury so consider wearing one).

➡ Denver, Boulder and Summit County have some of the country's most comprehensive off-road paved trail systems.

Bus

The main bus service within the region is **Greyhound** (☑312-408-5821; www.greyhound.com; 630 W Harrison St; ⓜBlue Line to Clinton), with a network of fixed routes and its own terminal in most central cities. The company has an excellent safety record, and the buses are comfortable and usually run on time.

➡ Greyhound tickets can be bought over the phone or online with a credit card and mailed if purchased 10 days in advance, or picked up at the terminal with proper identification.

➡ Discounts apply to tickets purchased 14 or 21 days in advance.

➡ All buses are nonsmoking, and reservations are made with ticket purchases only. Regional parts of Colorado are poorly serviced by buses. Exceptions are RTD (Denver and Boulder areas), Summit County's Summit Stage, ECO (Eagle County) and Roaring Fork Transportation (around Aspen). Bike racks on buses are the norm, as are ski racks in high country.

Car & Motorcycle

One of the great ways to experience Colorado is to drive its roads and byways. The road conditions are generally very good and it's always rewarding when you point the car down an unknown back road just to see where it goes. Good maps and road atlases are sold everywhere.

The penchant Coloradans have for monster SUVs and mega motorhomes can be a little intimidating when you're putt-putting up a steep mountain road in your clapped-out compact rental car. But fellow drivers are courteous and generous with their friendly conversation at roadside diners and gas stations – 'Where you headed?' is a common opener. Tuning into local radio stations along the way is part of the immersive cultural experience.

Hire

The rental-car market is crowded and competitive, which means you can get some good deals, especially if you hire for a week or more.

With advance reservations for a small car, the daily rate with unlimited mileage is about $30 to $40; typical weekly rates are $150 to $200. Rates for midsize cars may be a tad higher. You can often snag great last-minute deals via the internet. Renting in conjunction with an airplane ticket often yields better rates, too. Try some of the booking consolidator websites.

Ask about any extra surcharges, such as fees for one-way rental and additional drivers.

Some companies won't rent vehicles to people without a major credit card; others require things such as prepayment or cash deposits. Booking can be secured with a credit card and then paid by cash or debit card.

Car-rental companies always offer extra insurance, but if you're adequately covered under a travel-insurance policy or your credit card offers its own for rentals then don't be fooled by the compelling sales pitch. Basic liability insurance is required by law and included in the basic rental price. Check with your insurance company regarding any extended coverage.

Many rental agencies stipulate that damage a car suffers while being driven on unpaved roads is not covered by the insurance they offer.

Companies operating in Colorado:

Alamo (☏800-327-9633; www. alamo.com)

Avis (☏800-831-2847; www. avis.com)

Budget (☏800-527-0700; www.budget.com)

Dollar (☏800-800-4000; www. dollar.com)

Enterprise (☏800-325-8007; www.enterprise.com)

Hertz (☏800-654-3131; www. hertz.com)

National (☏800-227-7368; www.nationalcar.com)

Thrifty (☏800-847-4389; www. thrifty.com)

Road Hazards

➡ Much of Colorado is open-range country, where livestock and deer forage along the highway. Pay attention to the roadside, especially at night.

➡ During winter months, tire chains may be required. Some roads require chains or 4WD. It's a good idea to keep a set of chains in the trunk and drive slowly.

➡ I-70 to the mountains from Denver has a tread law that requires cars driving in snow to have good tread.

➡ Other cold-weather precautions include keeping a sleeping bag, warm clothing, extra food, a windshield ice-scraper, a snow shovel, flares and an extra set of gloves and boots in the trunk for emergencies. You always need lots of windshield fluid in winter.

➡ While Colorado doesn't require motorcycle riders over 18 years to wear helmets, it's highly recommended.

➡ Weather is a serious factor, especially in winter. For road and travel information, as well as state highway patrol information by telephone, dial ☏877-315-7623.

Colorado Road Conditions (☏511; www.codot.gov; ⏱24hr)

Road Rules

➡ Speed limits on Colorado state highways range from 55mph to 65mph, and go as high as 75mph on I-70. The limit inside downtown city areas is usually 25mph, and 35mph in residential areas. On open mountain highways the speed limit is 40mph.

➡ Texting from cell phones while driving is prohibited, and drivers under the age of 18 years are prohibited from using cell phones.

➡ Colorado's highway patrol is famously intolerant of speeding. If you're consistently flouting the speed limit you'll get booked.

➡ Seat belts are required for the driver and front-seat passenger and for all passengers on highways and interstates.

➡ On motorcycles, helmets are required for anyone under 18.

➡ Driving while impaired (DWI) is defined as having a blood-alcohol level of 0.05% or above; driving drunk will probably land you in jail and definitely earn you heavy fines.

➡ Driving while high on marijuana is also prohibited. Drivers with more than 5 nanograms of THC in their blood can be prosecuted under DUI terms.

Hitching

Hitchhiking is pretty easy in Colorado. You cannot thumb for rides directly on the interstate, but will instead need to wait on the on-ramp. Pedestrians on the highway must walk in the opposite direction of traffic.

Hitchhiking is never entirely safe, and we don't recommend it. Travelers who hitch should understand that they are taking a small but potentially serious risk.

Train

Rail service within Colorado is very limited beyond the interstate options.

Tourist trains include the **Durango & Silverton Narrow-Gauge Railroad** (Map p278; ☑970-247-2733; www.durangotrain.com; 479 Main Ave; return adult/child 4-11yr from $89/55; ⊙May-Oct) in southern Colorado, the **Georgetown Loop** (☑888-456-6777; www.georgetownlooprr.com; 646 Loop Dr; adult/child 3-15yr $26/19; ⊙May-Oct), the **Cumbres & Toltec Scenic Railroad** (☑888-286-2737; www. cumbrestoltec.com; 5234 Hwy 285; trips from adult/child $99/59) from Antonito to Chama in New Mexico, **Amtrak** (☑800-872-7245; www.amtrak.com) rides between Denver and Winter Park and up to Glenwood Springs, and the **Pikes Peak Cog Railway** (☑719-685-5401; www.cograilway.com; 515 Ruxton Ave; round-trip adult/child $40/22; ⊙8am-5:20pm May-Oct, reduced hours Nov-Apr) in Manitou Springs. Although they are tourist trains, the Durango and Cumbres lines allow hikers and anglers access to wilderness areas.

Behind the Scenes

SEND US YOUR FEEDBACK

We love to hear from travelers – your comments keep us on our toes and help make our books better. Our well-traveled team reads every word on what you loved or loathed about this book. Although we cannot reply individually to your submissions, we always guarantee that your feedback goes straight to the appropriate authors, in time for the next edition. Each person who sends us information is thanked in the next edition – the most useful submissions are rewarded with a selection of digital PDF chapters.

Visit **lonelyplanet.com/contact** to submit your updates and suggestions or to ask for help. Our award-winning website also features inspirational travel stories, news and discussions.

Note: We may edit, reproduce and incorporate your comments in Lonely Planet products such as guidebooks, websites and digital products, so let us know if you don't want your comments reproduced or your name acknowledged. For a copy of our privacy policy visit lonelyplanet.com/privacy.

WRITER THANKS

Benedict Walker

First and foremost, I'm forever grateful to Alex Howard, my destination editor on the other side of the planet, who found a space for me on this gig, knowing I loved the mountains, and who dealt with some weird challenges I threw at him with an air of calm and an absence of judgment. Thanks to Brad, my beautiful friend from Missoula, who reminded me that while many men wage wars, some put out fires, and some paint pictures with words. And thanks to the aliens of Nevada and Colorado for pushing me out of my comfort zone. It's a beautiful world out there, whatever we choose to focus on. And there is always more...

Loren Bell

To all of my family and friends on the way who provided hot tips, cold beer, and warm support – thank you, your friendships make this all worthwhile. To Kari: I don't know how you put up with me during these projects, but your patience must be deeper than Grand Prismatic Spring – your beauty certainly is. Finally, to Hawkeye: I know you can't read, but having you by my side was the highlight of the trip. You're a good boy.

Carolyn McCarthy

Many thanks to the fine people of southern Colorado whose help and hospitality in mud season is highly appreciated. My gratitude goes out to Dave and Lyn

in Telluride, Angela and Jim in Ouray and Katie in Durango. Gracias to Sandra for her contributions to the hiking portion of the trip. Hasta la proxima, Colorado!

Christopher Pitts

Huge thanks to Debbie Lew for her Summit County connections, Melissa Wisenbaker in Aspen, Sara Stookey in Snowmass and Sally Gunter in Vail. Also many thanks to the rest of the Colorado team for input, ideas and updates.

Greg Benchwick

This book wouldn't be possible without the support and love of my family. First and foremost, there's little Violeta 'Monkey Face' Benchwick, who continues to research the world with her wayward Daddy. Thanks, too, to Sarah for making the trip to Estes and beyond, and to the lovely editors, writers and big thinkers at Lonely Planet.

Liza Prado

Sincere thanks to the extraordinary LP team, especially Alex Howard and my co-authors. Special thanks to my Coloradan friends Meghan Howes, Alexia Eslan, Samantha Lentz, Kate McGoldrick, Paisley Johnson, Darin Pitts and Rob Roberts for the inside scoop on some of your favorite places. Mil gracias to Mom, Dad, Joe, Elyse and Susan for your loving help with the kids. Big thanks to Eva and Leo for waiting so patiently for family movie night. And to Gary, thank you for your boundless love and support...you make my world turn.

ACKNOWLEDGEMENTS

Climate map data adapted from Peel MC, Finlayson BL & McMahon TA (2007) 'Updated World Map of the Köppen-Geiger Climate Classification', Hydrology and Earth System Sciences, 11, 163344.

Cover photograph: Colorado National Monument, Michele Falzone/Getty ©

THIS BOOK

This 3rd edition of Lonely Planet's *Colorado* guidebook was researched and written by Benedict Walker, Loren Bell, Carolyn McCarthy, Christopher Pitts, Greg Benchwick and Liza Prado. The previous edition was written by Carolyn McCarthy, Greg Benchwick and Christopher Pitts.

This guidebook was produced by the following:

Destination Editor Alexander Howard

Product Editors Ronan Abayawickrema, Kate Mathews

Regional Senior Cartographer Alison Lyall

Book Designer Gwen Cotter

Assisting Editors Imogen Bannister, Michelle Bennett, Pete Cruttenden, Ali Lemer, Rosie Nicholson, Sarah Stewart, Ross Taylor, Saralinda Turner, Maja Vatrić

Cover Researcher Brendan Dempsey-Spencer

Thanks to Hannah Cartmel, Heather Champion, Grace Dobell, Evan Godt, Victoria Harrison, Sandie Kestell, Kate Mansell, Genna Patterson, Valerie Stimac, Greg Thilmont, Angela Tinson, Bill Weir

Index

10th Mountain Division 191, 203, 211, 229, 246

A
accommodations 362-4, *see also individual locations*
adventure sports 38-9
air travel 370-1, 372
Alamosa 335-7
Alma 198
amusement parks
　Elitch Gardens 74-6
　Epic Discovery 193
　Glenwood Caverns Adventure Park 216
　Howler Alpine Slide 166
　Lakeside Amusement Park 76
　Overdrive Raceway 313
　Water World 76
animals 357-60
Antonito 338-9
aquariums 71
Arapahoe Basin Ski Area 189-90
archaeological sites 357
area codes 21, 368
Arkansas River 14, 244, **14**
art galleries, *see* galleries
arts 353-5
Aspen 11, 222-36, **224**, **5**, **11**
　accommodations 228-31
　activities 223-7
　drinking 234
　entertainment 234-5
　events 228
　festivals 228
　food 231-4
　information 236
　nightlife 234
　shopping 235-6
　sights 222-3

Map Pages **000**
Photo Pages **000**

　tours 227-8
　travel to/within 236
Aspen Music Festival 26
ATMs 368
avalanches 182

B
backcounty permits 142
backpacking, *see* hiking & backpacking
ballooning 166
Basalt 221-2
bathrooms 369
bears 358, **154**
Beaver Creek 214-16
beer 22-3, *see also* microbreweries
beer festivals 116, 264, 276
bicycling 14, 37, 39, 77, 372
bighorn sheep 358-9, **154-5**
birds 360
bird-watching 360
Black Canyon of the Gunnison National Park 18, 292-3, **18**
boating 145, 160
books 346, 353
Boreas Pass 190
Boulder 10, 59, 107-35, **108**, **110-11**, **116-17**, **10**
　accommodations 107, 117-20
　activities 113-15
　children, travel with 120
　climate 107
　courses 115
　drinking 125, 127
　entertainment 127
　events 115-17
　festivals 115-17
　food 107, 120-5
　highlights 108
　history 108-9
　information 131
　itineraries 114
　nightlife 125, 127

　shopping 127-31
　sights 109-13
　tours 115
　travel seasons 107
　travel to/within 131-2
　walking tours 126, **126**
Boulder Creek Festival 25-6, 115
Boulder Reservoir 109
Brainard Lake 150
Breckenridge 16, 190-9, **192**, **16**
　accommodations 195-6
　activities 191-4
　drinking 198-9
　entertainment 198-9
　events 195
　festivals 195
　food 196-8
　information 199
　sights 190-1
　tours 194-5
　travel to/within 199
breweries, *see* microbreweries
budget 21, 362, 365
Buena Vista 241-5
business hours 368
bus travel 371, 372

C
Cache la Poudre River 157-9
camping 362-3
canoeing, 40, 163, 173, *see also* rafting
Cañon City 317-20
Canyon Pintado National Historic District 172
Carbondale 220-1
car travel 371, 373, *see also* scenic drives
caves 216
cell phones 20, 368
central Colorado 60, 174-249, **176-7**
　accommodations 174

　food 174
　highlights 176-7
children, travel with 56-8, 120
Clark, William 349
climate 20, **20**
Cody, William F 'Buffalo Bill' 351
coffee 128
Colorado National Monument 11, 300-1, **11**
Colorado Springs 310-17, **311**
　accommodations 314-15
　activities 313
　drinking 316-17
　entertainment 317
　events 313
　festivals 313
　food 315-16
　nightlife 316-17
　shopping 317
　sights 310-13
　tourist information 317
　travel to/within 317
Conejos River 339-40
consulates 365
Copper Mountain 200-1
Cortez 257-60
costs 362, 365
Cottonwood Lake 241
Cottonwood Pass 41-2, 241, **48**
courses
　climbing 114, 268
　cooking 77, 115
　kayaking 77
　skiing 167, 180
coyotes 322, 359, **155**
Craig 170-1
Creede 284-7
Crested Butte 288-92
Crestone 344
Cripple Creek 320-1
cross-country skiing 141-2, *see also* skiing & snowboarding

INDEX C–G

Crystal 221
Curecanti National Recreation Area 293-306
currency 20, 368
cycling, see bicycling
Aspen 227-8
Boulder 114, 115
Breckenridge 193
Fort Collins 151
Frisco 185
Glenwood Springs 217
Golden 104
Grand Lake 160
Rocky Mountain National Park 141
Salida 239
southwest Colorado 14
Steamboat Springs 166
Vail 204, 205

D

Del Norte 340-1
Delta 298-306
Dempsey, Jack 338
Denver 9, 59, 62, 63-102, **64, 66-7, 70, 78, 9**
accommodations 62, 81-4
activities 77
climate 62
courses 77
drinking 89-93
entertainment 93-7
festivals 79-81
events 79-81
food 62, 84-9
highlights 64
itineraries 72
medical services 100
nightlife 89-93
shopping 97-100
sights 63-77
tourist information 100
tours 78-9
travel seasons 62
travel to/within 100-2
walking tour 75, **75**
websites 63
Dillon 184-5
Dinosaur 173
Dinosaur National Monument 13, 171-3, **13**
Dinosaur Ridge 106
dinosaurs 356-7

disabilities, travelers with 369
distilleries 24, **23**
dog sledding 180
Dolores 260-1
driving, see car travel
dude ranches 12, 57, 363, **12**
Durango 17, 275-81, **278**, **17**
Durango & Silverton Narrow Guage Railroad 14, 275, 373, **15**

E

economy 346-7
electricity 365
elk 359, **155**
El Pueblo History Museum 325
embassies 365
emergencies 21
Estes Park 144-50, **146**
accommodations 147-8
activities 145-7
climate 136
drinking 149
food 148-9
nightlife 149
sights 145
tourist information 149
tours 145-7
travel seasons 136
travel to/within 149-50
events, see festivals & events
exchange rates 21, 368

F

Fairplay 199-200
farmers markets 243
festivals & events 354-5
5Point Film Festival 25
420 Rally 80-1
A Taste of Colorado 80
Aspen Music Festival 26
Boulder Creek Festival 25-6, 115
Brews & Blues Festival 264
Cherry Creek Arts Festival 80
Cinco de Mayo 80
Colorado Brewers' Festival 26
Crested Butte Arts Festival 290
Denver Cruiser Ride 80
Denver March Powwow 81
Emma Crawford Coffin Race 26

First Friday 80
Five Points Jazz Festival 80
Frozen Dead Guy Days 25
Great American Beer Festival 79
Great Fruitcake Toss 313
High Mountain Hay Fever Bluegrass Festival 342
Leadville Trail 100 26
MeadowGrass 313
Mountainfilm 264
National Western Stock Show 25
Ouray Ice Festival 271
Pikes Peak International Hill Climb 26
PrideFest 80
San Juan Brewfest 276
Snow Daze 26
Telluride Bluegrass Festival 26, 264
Telluride Film Festival 26, 264
Telluride Mushroom Festival 264
Territory Days 313
Westcliffe Stampede Rodeo 342
Winter X Games 25
films 346, 355
fishing
Aspen 227
Blanca Wetlands 336
Breckenridge 194
Conejos River Anglers 339
Dillon 184
Estes Park 147
Glenwood Springs 218
Gunnison River 293
Hot Sulphur Springs 162
Minturn 213
Redstone 237
Ridgway State Park & Recreation Area 268
Rio Grande 340
Salida 239
Steamboat Springs 166
Telluride Flyfishers 262
Toads Guide Shop 297
Vail 205
Flagstaff Trailhead 113
Florence 320
food 17, 52-5, **17**, **52**
festivals 207, 228
Ford, Barney 349, 351
Fort Collins 19, 150-6, **152**, **19**

accommodations 151
activities 151
drinking 153-6
food 151-3
nightlife 153-6
sights 150
tourist information 156
tours 151
travel to/within 156
Fort Garland 332
Four Corners 257-60
Fourteeners 16, 30, 34, 40, 43, 46, **16**
foxes 358
Frisco 185-8
Fruita 303-4

G

galleries
Aspen Art Museum 223
Baldwin Gallery 223
Boulder Museum of Contemporary Art 112
Breckenridge Arts District 191
CU Art Museum 113
Dairy Arts Center 109
David B Smith Gallery 73
Denver Art Museum 65
Denver Art Society 73
Kirkland Museum of Fine & Decorative Art 76
Museo de las Americas 76
Museum of Contemporary Art (Denver) 72
SPACe Gallery 328
gambling 96
Garden of the Gods 18, 31, 310, **18**
gardens, see parks & gardens
gay travelers 91, 116-17, 367-8
geography 356-7
geology 23-4, 356-7
Georgetown 178-9
Georgetown Loop Railroad 179, 374, **23**
Glen Haven 145
Glenwood Springs 216-20
Golden 102-5
Granby 161-2
Grand Junction 301-3
Grand Lake 159-61
Great Sand Dunes National Park 17, 332-5, **333**, **17**
Great Stupa of Dharmakaya 159

Gunnison 294-6
Gunnison National
Park 292-3

H
Hahns Peak 165
happy hour 55
health 365-6
hiking & backpacking 16,
22, 30-4, **16**
Aspen 224, 225-6
Barr Trail 322
Breckenridge 192, 193,
193-4
Buena Vista 241, 242
Cedar Mountain 170
East Bellows Trail 285
Estes Park 145
Fort Collins 151
Fourteeners 16
Frisco 186
Fruita Paleontological
Area 304
Grand Lake 160
Great Sand Dunes
National Park 334, 336
Incline Trail 322
Jud Wiebe Trail 262
Leadville 247, 247-8
Liberty Cap Trail 300
Loveland Pass 183
Minturn 213
Monument Canyon
Trail 300
Music Pass Trail 342
North Crestone Trail 344
North Vista Trail 293
Oak Flat Loop 293
Perimeter Trail 270
Petroglyph Loop Trail 253
Rainbow Trail 342
Rocky Mountain National
Park 139
Routt National Forest 170
Royal Arch Trail 113
Shrine Pass 206
South Colony Lakes
Trail 342
South Crestone Lake
Trail 344
Spanish Peaks
Wilderness 328
Spruce Canyon Loop
Trail 253
St Elmo 238
Steamboat Springs
163, 166
Sterling 157
Trail Through Time 304
Twin Lakes 245

Vail 204, 205
Venable-Comanche Loop
Trail 342
Winter Park 179, 180
Wonderland Lake
Trailhead 115
history 348-52
Native American 348, 351
hitching 374
holidays 368
Holliday, John Henry 'Doc'
216, 217
Hoosier Pass 198
horseback riding
Aspen 227
Bear Basin Ranch 342
Big Corral Riding
Stable 275
Buena Vista 242
Estes Park 145-7
Fairplay 199
Grand Lake 160
Idaho Springs 175
Meeker 173
Redstone 237
Ride with
Roudy 262
Vail 205-6, 206
Winter Park 179-80
hot springs 24, 358
Hot Sulphur Springs 162
Hovenweep National
Monument 258, **51**

I
Idaho Springs 175-8
Independence Pass 247
insurance 366
Interlaken 245
internet access 367
internet resources 21
itineraries 27-9, **27**, **28**, **29**

J
James Peak 83
Jones, Mary Harris
'Mother' 352

K
kayaking 77
Keystone Resort 188-9
King, Stephen 354
Kremmling 162-3

L
La Veta 328-9
Lake City 287-8
language 20

Leadville 246-9
legal matters 367
lesbian travelers 91, 116-17,
367-8
Lewis, Meriwether 349
literature 354

M
Mancos 256-7
Manitou Springs 321-5
marijuana 346-7
Maroon Bells 224, **5**
Meeker 173
Mesa Verde National Park
10, 251-6, 252, **254**,
2, **10**
accommodations 254-5
activities 253
food 255
history 251
sights 251-3
tourist information 255
tours 253-4
travel to/within 256
Mexican food 54-5
microbreweries 12, 22-3, **12**
Aspen Brewing Co 234
Animas Brewing 280
Beryl's Beer Co 90
Black Shirt Brewing
Co 89
Breckenridge
Brewery 198
Bristol Brewing Co 316
Broken Compass
Brewing 198
Carbondale Beer
Works 220
Cannonball Creek
Brewing Company 105
Coors Brewery 102-3
Dolores River
Brewery 261
Durango Brewing Co 280
Eldo Brewery 291
Glenwood Canyon
Brewing Company 219
Goed Zuur 90
Great Divide Brewery
Company 91
High Alpine Brewery 295
Kannah Creek Brewing
Company 302
Main Street Brewery &
Restaurant 259
Mountain Sun 125
New Belgium Brewery 151
Ouray Brewery 272
Palisade Brewing
Company 306

Periodic Brewing 249
Phantom Canyon
Brewing 316
Ratio Beerworks 91
Riff Raff Brewing Co 283
Rockslide Brewery 303
Sanitas Brewing 125
Ska Brewing Co 280
Steamworks Brewing 280
Telluride Brewing Co 266
Three Barrel Brewing
Co 341
Trinity Brewing Co 316
Vail Brewing 211
Wynkoop Brewing Co 92
Million Dollar Highway 15,
269-73, **15**
Minturn 212-14
mobile phones 20, 368
money 20, 21, 364-5, 368
Montrose 296-8
Morrison 105-6
motorcycle travel 371, 373
mountain biking 14, 37, 39,
14, see also bicycling
Alpineer 289
Aspen 226
Buena Vista 242
Fruita 303-4
Kokopelli Trail 304
Leadville 247, 248
Rocky Mountain National
Park 141
Salida 238-9, 239
San Juan Hut System 268
Shrine Pass 206
Southwest Colorado 14
Steamboat Springs 166
Winter Park 179
mountaineering, see rock
climbing
museums 24
Avery House Museum 150
American Mountaineering
Museum 102
Anasazi Heritage
Center 260
Barney Ford Museum 190
Bent's Old Fort National
Historic Site 325
Black American West
Museum & Heritage
Center 74
Blair-Caldwell African
American Museum 65
Boggsville Historic
Site 326
Buell Children's
Museum 325

museums *continued*
Buffalo Bill Museum & Grave 103-4
Camp Amache 326
CELL 76-7
Children's Museum 65
Colorado Railroad Museum 103
Colorado School of Mines' Geology Museum 102
Colorado Ski Museum 203
Colorado Sports Hall of Fame 76
Colorado Springs Pioneers Museum 312
Cortez Cultural Center 257
Creede Underground Mining Museum 285
CU Museum of Natural History 112
Denver Museum of Nature & Science 69, 58
Dinosaur Journey 304
Edwin Carter Discovery Center 191
El Pueblo History Museum 325
Enos Mills Cabin Museum & Gallery 138
Estes Park Museum 145
Fort Collins Museum & Discovery Science Center 150
Frisco Historic Park & Museum 185
Frontier Historical Museum 216
Golden History Center 102
Hamill House 178
History Colorado Center 69
Holzwarth Historic Site 138
Ice Age Discovery Center 223
Kauffman House Museum 159
Kirkland Museum of Fine & Decorative Art 76
Leadville Heritage Museum 246
MacGregor Ranch Museum 145

Marcia Car 170
Molly Brown House Museum 73
Money Museum 312
Moraine Park Museum 138
Morrison Natural History Museum 106
Museum of Boulder 109, 112
Museum of Colorado Prisons 318
Museum of Northwest Colorado 170
Museum of Western Colorado 301
National Center for Atmospheric Research 112
National Mining Hall of Fame 246
Nederland Mining Museum 133
Ouray County Museum 270
Pioneer Museum 294
Pioneer Village Museum 162
Ridgway Railroad Museum 268
Rio Grande County Museum & Cultural Center 341
Rocky Mountain Dinosaur Center 322
Rosemount Museum 326
Royal Gorge Dinosaur Experience 318
Salida Museum 238
San Luis Museum & Cultural Cente 337
Sterling Overland Trail Museum 157
Summit Ski Museum 191
Tracks and Trails Museum 170
Trinidad History Museum 329
Ute Indian Museum 296
White River Museum 173
World Figure Skating Museum & Hall of Fame 312
music 45
music festivals 264, 342

N
narrow-gauge railways, *see* train travel
national parks & wilderness areas 32
Black Canyon of the

Gunnison National Park 18, 292-3, 18
Colorado National Monument 11, 300-1, 11
Dinosaur National Monument 13, 171-3, 13
Eldorado Canyon State Park 113-14
Flat Tops Wilderness Area 173
Great Sand Dunes National Park 17, 332-5, 333, 17
Gunnison National Park 292-3
Holy Cross Wilderness Area 212-13
Hovenweep National Monument 258, 51
Indian Peaks Wilderness Area 134
Lory State Park 150
Mesa Verde National Park 10, 251-6, 252, 254, 2, 10
Mount Zirkel Wilderness 163-4
Pearl Lake State Park 163
Rocky Mountain National Park 9, 136-44, 137, 140, 8-9
Stagecoach State Park 165
State Forest State Park 158
Steamboat Lake State Park 164-5
Native American art 353
Native American history 348, 351
Nederland 132-5
northern Colorado 60, 136-73, 137

O
Oak Creek 169-70
Old West sites 13, 22, 13
opening hours 368
Ouray 269-73

P
paddling 40, *see also* rafting
Pagosa Springs 281-3
Palisade 304-6
Paonia 299-300
parks & gardens
Austin Bluffs Open Space 312
Betty Ford Alpine Gardens 203
Buena Vista

River Park 241
Butterfly Pavilion 109
Carpenter Park & Pool 113
Central Park 112
Chautauqua Park 109
Civic Center Park (Denver) 72-3
Coller State Wildlife Area 283-4
Colorado National Monument 300
Commons Park 72
Confluence Park 65
Denver Botanic Gardens 69-71
Eben G Fine Park 112
Garden of the Gods 310
Pawnee National Grassland 156-7
Red Rock Canyon Open Space 310
Rio Grande Park 223
Royal Gorge Bridge & Park 318
San Luis State Park 333
Washington Park 69
Western Colorado Botanic Gardens 301
Peak to Peak Hwy 150
Pearl Street Mall 109
Penitente Canyon 340
Pikes Peak 18
Pikes Peak Highway 46-7
Pikes Peak Cog Railway 322, 374
planetariums 112
planning 20-1
calendar of events 25-6
children, travel with 56-8
Colorado basics 20-1
Colorado's regions 59-60
internet resources 21
itineraries 27-9, 72
plants 357
politics 346-7
population 347
postal services 368
Powell, John Wesley 350
public holidays 368
Pueblo 325-8

R
rafting 14, 40, 14
Arkansas River 14, 244, 319
Beaver Creek 215
Breckenridge 194
Buena Vista 242

Dinosaur National
Monument 172
Durango Rivertrippers 276
Glenwood Springs 218
Idaho Springs 175
Kremmling 162-3
Mild to Wild Rafting 276
Mountain Man Rafting &
Tours 284
Pagosa Outside 282
Rio Grande 285
Salida 239
Scenic River Tours 295
Steamboat Springs 166
Three Rivers Resort 287
railways 23, 338
Rainbow Lakes 150
Rangely 171
Red Feather Lakes 159
Red Rocks Park &
Amphitheatre 103
Redstone 236-7
religion 347
Rico 261
Ridgway 268-9
road trips, see scenic trips
rock climbing 38-9
Boulder 114
Denver 78
Estes Park 145
Rocky Mountain National
Park 139-41, **137**,
140, 8-9
accommodations 136,
142-3
activities 138-42
climate 136, 143
drinking 143
food 136, 143
highlights 137
information 143-4
sights 138
travel seasons 136
travel to/within 144

S
safety 41, 182, 364
Salida 237-41
San Luis 337-8
San Luis Valley 332-41,
308-9
sandboarding 334
Sangre de Cristo
Mountains 341-4
San Juan Mountains 332, 2
Santa Fe Trail 324-32
scenic drives 41-51, **42**
Alpine Loop 289
Bachelor Loop 285

Collegiate Peaks 43-4
Cottonwood
Pass 41-2, 241
East Portal Road 293
Gold Belt Tour 46
Guanella Pass Scenic
Byway 178-9
Highway of Legends
49, 331
I-70 180
Imogene Pass 289
Independence Pass 43,
224-5, 247
Million Dollar Highway
15, 269-73, **15**
Old Fall River Road 138
Peak to Peak Hwy 47,
49, 150
Phantom Canyon 319
Pikes Peak Highway 46-7
Rollins Pass 180
San Juan Skyway 45-6
Santa Fe Trail 50-1
Shelf Road 319
South Platte River
Scenic Byway 157
South Rim Road 293
Top of the Rockies 42-3
Trail of the Ancients
49-50
Trail Ridge Road 44-5, 138
West Elk Loop 47
senior travelers 364-5
Shrine Pass 206
Silverton 13, 273-306, **13**
skiing & snowboarding
22, 34-7, **35**, see
also cross-country skiing
Arapahoe Basin Ski Area
189-90
Aspen 223-4, 226-7, 230
Beaver Creek 214, 215
Breckenridge 191-2, 194
Copper Mountain 200
Crested Butte Mountain
Resort 289
Crested Butte Nordic
Center 289
Eldora Mountain Resort
133
Frisco 185-6
Glenwood Springs 217
Granby 161
Keystone Resort 188
Leadville 247, 248
Loveland Pass 183
Minturn 213
Salida 239
Silverton Mountain Ski
Area 273

Steamboat
Springs 165, 166-7
Vail 203-5
Winter Park 179-80
Southeast Colorado 60,
307-44, **308**
accommodations 307
climate 307
food 307
highlights 308
South Fork 283-4
South Platte River Scenic
Byway 157
South San Juans 339-40
snowboarding, see skiing 7
snowboarding
Southwest Colorado 60,
250-306, **252**
accommodations
250-306
climate 250-306
food 250-306
highlights 252
travel seasons 250-306
St Elmo 238
Sterling 156-7
St Mary's Glacier 83, 175
steam trains, 14, **15**, see
also train travel
Steamboat Springs 163-9,
164, 19
Summit County 183-201
sustainability 359

T
tea 112
telephone services 20, 368
Telluride 18, 261-306,
263, 18
Thompson, Hunter S 354
time 20, 368-9
tipping 368
toilets 369
tourist information 369
Trail Ridge Road 44-5, 188,
141, 48
train travel 14, 23, 371-2,
374, **15**
travel to/within Colorado
370-4
Trinidad 329-32
tubing 40, 334, see
also rafting
Boulder 113, 115
Twin Lakes 245-6

U
Ute Mountain Tribal
Park 260

Ute people 211, 260, 296

V
vacations 368
Vail 13, 13, **202**, 13
accommodations 207-8
climate 174
drinking 210-11
entertainment 211-12
events 206-7
festivals 206-7
food 208-10
history 211
information 212
nightlife 210-11
sights 201-3
travel seasons 174
travel within 212
trave to/from 212
visas 20, 369
volunteering 369

W
Walden 159
walking tours
Boulder 126, **126**
Denver 75, **75**
weather 20
Westcliffe 341-4
wildlife 24, 357-60, **154-5**
wine 53-4
Winter Park 179-83
work 369

Y
yoga 77, 114

Z
ziplining 239
zoos & wildlife sanctuaries
Alamosa National Wild-
life Refuge 335
Arapaho National Wildlife
Refuge 161
Cheyenne Mountain
Zoo 312
Colorado Wolf & Wildlife
Center 322
Denver Zoo 73
Little Book Cliffs Wild
Horse Range 305
Love Meadow 241
Nature & Raptor Center
of Pueblo 325
The Farm at Lee
Martinez Park 150
Wild Animal
Sanctuary 158

Map Legend

Sights
- Beach
- Bird Sanctuary
- Buddhist
- Castle/Palace
- Christian
- Confucian
- Hindu
- Islamic
- Jain
- Jewish
- Monument
- Museum/Gallery/Historic Building
- Ruin
- Shinto
- Sikh
- Taoist
- Winery/Vineyard
- Zoo/Wildlife Sanctuary
- Other Sight

Activities, Courses & Tours
- Bodysurfing
- Diving
- Canoeing/Kayaking
- Course/Tour
- Sento Hot Baths/Onsen
- Skiing
- Snorkeling
- Surfing
- Swimming/Pool
- Walking
- Windsurfing
- Other Activity

Sleeping
- Sleeping
- Camping

Eating
- Eating

Drinking & Nightlife
- Drinking & Nightlife
- Cafe

Entertainment
- Entertainment

Shopping
- Shopping

Information
- Bank
- Embassy/Consulate
- Hospital/Medical
- Internet
- Police
- Post Office
- Telephone
- Toilet
- Tourist Information
- Other Information

Geographic
- Beach
- Gate
- Hut/Shelter
- Lighthouse
- Lookout
- Mountain/Volcano
- Oasis
- Park
- Pass
- Picnic Area
- Waterfall

Population
- Capital (National)
- Capital (State/Province)
- City/Large Town
- Town/Village

Transport
- Airport
- BART station
- Border crossing
- Boston T station
- Bus
- Cable car/Funicular
- Cycling
- Ferry
- Metro/Muni station
- Monorail
- Parking
- Petrol station
- Subway/SkyTrain station
- Taxi
- Train station/Railway
- Tram
- Underground station
- Other Transport

Note: Not all symbols displayed above appear on the maps in this book

Routes
- Tollway
- Freeway
- Primary
- Secondary
- Tertiary
- Lane
- Unsealed road
- Road under construction
- Plaza/Mall
- Steps
- Tunnel
- Pedestrian overpass
- Walking Tour
- Walking Tour detour
- Path/Walking Trail

Boundaries
- International
- State/Province
- Disputed
- Regional/Suburb
- Marine Park
- Cliff
- Wall

Hydrography
- River, Creek
- Intermittent River
- Canal
- Water
- Dry/Salt/Intermittent Lake
- Reef

Areas
- Airport/Runway
- Beach/Desert
- Cemetery (Christian)
- Cemetery (Other)
- Glacier
- Mudflat
- Park/Forest
- Sight (Building)
- Sportsground
- Swamp/Mangrove

Greg Benchwick

Rocky Mountain National Park & Northern Colorado

A longtime Lonely Planet travel writer, Greg has rumbled in the jungles of Bolivia, trekked across Spain on the Camino de Santiago, interviewed presidents and grammy-award winners, dodged flying salmon in Alaska and climbed mountains (big and small) in between. He has expertise in international development, food, wine, Latin America, sustainable travel, skiing and adventure sports, and has also contributed to such media outlets as *Newsweek*, the *Washington Post* and BBC radio. When he's not on the road for Lonely Planet, Greg writes speeches for the United Nations, hangs out with his baby girl and tries to have a new adventure every day. Follow Greg on Instagram at www.instagram.com/gregbenchwick. Greg also wrote the Transportation chapter.

Liza Prado

Denver & Around, Boulder & Around

Liza has been a travel writer since 2003, when she made a move from corporate lawyering to travel writing (and never looked back). She's written dozens of guidebooks and articles as well as apps and blogs to destinations throughout the Americas. She takes decent photos too. Liza is a graduate of Brown University and Stanford Law School. She lives very happily in Denver, Colorado, with her husband and fellow Lonely Planet writer, Gary Chandler, and their two kids. Liza also wrote the Directory chapter.

Contributing Writer

Loren Bell Rocky Mountains When Loren first backpacked through Europe, he was in the backpack. That memorable experience corrupted his six-month-old brain, ensuring he would never be happy sitting still. His penchant for peregrination has taken him from training dogsled teams in the Tetons to trailing gibbons in the jungles of Borneo – with only brief pauses for silly 'responsible' things like earning degrees. When he's not demystifying destinations for Lonely Planet, Loren writes about science and conservation news. He base-camps in the Rocky Mountains, where he probably spends too much time on his mountain bike and skis.

OUR STORY

A beat-up old car, a few dollars in the pocket and a sense of adventure. In 1972 that's all Tony and Maureen Wheeler needed for the trip of a lifetime – across Europe and Asia overland to Australia. It took several months, and at the end – broke but inspired – they sat at their kitchen table writing and stapling together their first travel guide, *Across Asia on the Cheap*. Within a week they'd sold 1500 copies. Lonely Planet was born.

Today, Lonely Planet has offices in Franklin, London, Melbourne, Oakland, Dublin, Beijing and Delhi, with more than 600 staff and writers. We share Tony's belief that 'a great guidebook should do three things: inform, educate and amuse'.

OUR WRITERS

Benedict Walker
Curator, Southeast Colorado & the San Luis Valley

Benedict was born in Newcastle, New South Wales, Australia, and grew up in the 'burbs spending weekends and long summers by the beach whenever possible. Although he is drawn magnetically to the kinds of mountains he encountered in the Canadian Rockies and the Japan and Swiss Alps, beach life is in his blood. Japan was Benedict's first gig for Lonely Planet, in 2008/9, and he has been blessed to have been asked back three more times. He has since worked on numerous Lonely Planet titles, including guides to Australia, Canada, Germany and the USA. He has also written and directed a play, toured Australia managing the travel logistics for major music festivals and played around with his original major of photography and film-making. Join him on his journeys on Instagram: @wordsandjourneys.

Carolyn McCarthy
Mesa Verde & Southwest Colorado

Carolyn specializes in travel, culture and adventure in the Americas. She has written for *National Geographic*, *Outside*, *BBC Magazine*, *Sierra Magazine*, *Boston Globe* and other publications. A former Fulbright fellow and Banff Mountain Grant recipient, she has documented life in the most remote corners of Latin America. Carolyn has contributed to 40 guidebooks and anthologies for Lonely Planet, including *Colorado*, *USA*, *Argentina*, *Chile*, *Trekking in the Patagonian Andes*, *Panama*, *Peru* and *USA National Parks* guides. For more information, visit www.carolynmccarthy.org or follow her Instagram travels @mccarthyoffmap.

Christopher Pitts
Vail, Aspen & Central Colorado

Chris was born in the year of the Tiger, and his first expedition in life ended in failure when he tried to dig from Pennsylvania to China at the age of six. Hardened by reality but still infinitely curious about the other side of the world, he went on to study Chinese in university, living for several years in Kunming, Taiwan and Shanghai. A chance encounter in an elevator led to a Paris relocation, where he lived with his wife and two children for over a decade before the lure of Colorado's sunny skies and outdoor adventure proved too great to resist.

OVER PAGE MORE WRITERS

Published by Lonely Planet Global Limited
CRN 554153
3rd edition – May 2018
ISBN 978 1 78657 344 5
© Lonely Planet 2018   Photographs © as indicated 2018
10 9 8 7 6 5 4 3 2 1
Printed in China